A History of England in Eight Volumes
Founder Editor, Sir Charles Oman

Volume II
ENGLAND UNDER THE NORMANS
AND ANGEVINS

A History of England in Eight Volumes

I

ENGLAND BEFORE THE NORMAN CONQUEST
by Sir Charles Oman

II

ENGLAND UNDER THE NORMANS AND ANGEVINS
by H. W. C. Davis

III

ENGLAND IN THE LATER MIDDLE AGES
by Kenneth H. Vickers

IV

ENGLAND UNDER THE TUDORS
by G. R. Elton

V

ENGLAND UNDER THE STUARTS
by G. M. Trevelyan

VI

ENGLAND UNDER THE HANOVERIANS
by Sir Charles Grant Robertson

VII

ENGLAND SINCE WATERLOO
by Sir J. A. R. Marriott

VIII

MODERN ENGLAND, 1885-1945
by Sir J. A. R. Marriott

ENGLAND UNDER THE NORMANS AND ANGEVINS

H. W. C. Davis

LONDON: METHUEN & CO LTD
NEW YORK: BARNES & NOBLE INC

First published November 11, 1905
Reprinted twelve times
Thirteenth edition, revised, 1949
Reprinted 1957 and 1961

13·3
CATALOGUE NO. 2/3372/10 (METHUEN)

PRINTED IN GREAT BRITAIN AT
THE UNIVERSITY PRESS, ABERDEEN

INTRODUCTORY NOTE

BY THE GENERAL EDITOR

IN England, as in France and Germany, the main characteristic of the last fifty years, from the point of view of the student of history, has been that new material has been accumulating much faster than it can be assimilated or absorbed. The standard works of the 19th-century historians need to be revised, or even to be put aside as obsolete, in the light of the new information that is coming in so rapidly and in such vast bulk.

The series of which this volume forms a part is intended to do something towards meeting the demand for information brought up to date. Individual historians will not sit down, as once they were wont, to write twenty-volume works in the style of Hume or Lingard, embracing a dozen centuries of annals. It is not to be desired that they should—the writer who is most satisfactory in dealing with Anglo-Saxon antiquities is not likely to be the one who will best discuss the antecedents of the Reformation, or the constitutional history of the Stuart period. But something can be done by judicious co-operation. In the thirty-four years since the first volume of this series appeared in 1904, it would seem that the idea has justified itself,

v

as the various sections have passed through many editions and revisions varying from six to sixteen.

Each is intended to give something more than a mere outline of one period of our national annals, but they have little space for controversy or the discussion of sources. There is, however, a bibliography annexed to most of the series, which will show the inquirer where information of the more special kind is to be sought. Moreover, a number of maps are to be found at the end of each volume which, as it is hoped, will make it unnecessary for the reader to be continually referring to large historical atlases—tomes which (as we must confess with regret) are not to be discovered in every private library.

The general editor and his collaborators have been touched lightly by the hand of time. All regret the too early decease of our colleague Henry Carless Davis, sometime Regius Professor of Modern History in this University, who wrote the second of the eight volumes of the series. He had several times revised his contribution. Most of us survivors continue to do the same from time to time, as the pen (or sometimes the spade) produces new sources of information. Naturally the spade is particularly active for the purveying of fresh material for the first of our volumes, and the pen (or the press) for the two last. Information must be kept up to date, whatever the epoch concerned, even though it is known that much undiscovered evidence may yet be forthcoming in the near future.

C. OMAN

OXFORD, 1st *April*, 1937

PREFACE

THE period of English history which is covered by the present volume possesses a distinctive character and unity. With the Norman Conquest the nation passes at one bound from the Dark into the Middle Age; the death of Henry III. marks the moment of transition from the first to the second stage of our medieval history, from the inventive and experimental era to that of consolidation and completion. The years 1066-1272 witnessed the beginning and the end of some remarkable developments; the creation of English Feudalism, the rejuvenation of the English Church, the decisive conflicts of Church and Feudalism with the State. They also witnessed the trial and failure of autocracy at home, and in foreign policy of a premature imperialism. The common law and the royal courts of justice were created; the principle of representative government gained general recognition. Behind all these developments we can trace the progress of another and a wider movement in which they are but episodes. It is not, as Thierry asks us to believe, a duel between two races. It is much rather a struggle of native against foreign ambitions and ideas; a struggle of which the influence

is apparent in every class and almost every individual.
The policy of the Crown is moulded at one time by
the dream of continental acquisitions, at another by
the ambition of realising that Empire of the British
Isles which the House of Cerdic had projected. The
Baronage are dubious whether, like their French cousins,
to pursue the path of individual aggrandisement, or,
in the manner of the West Saxon witan, to aim at a
collective control of the administration. The Church
vacillates between the national and œcumenical ideals,
in one breath admitting the Roman theory of the
Papal power, and in the next denying its logical
corollaries. The masses, finally, are divided between
their ancestral love of liberty and their gratitude for
the orderly despotism of their alien rulers. By the
year 1272 these doubts and difficulties have been
provisionally solved. The policy of the Church and
Baronage is stereotyped; De Montfort has given a
clear and consistent form to the aspirations of the
masses; the Crown has reluctantly accepted an insular
policy and the idea of a limited prerogative. And,
as the result, England has entered upon the truly
English phase of her development. We dwell particularly upon the political aspects of the change, for
politics are the main subject of this volume. But in
art, in literature, in social life, there are similar and
simultaneous revelations of the national genius; and of
these also some account will be found in the following
pages.

The period has been illuminated by the researches
of many considerable historians, and the specific references which are hereafter made to the writings of
Bishop Stubbs and Professor Freeman, of J. R. Green

and Miss Norgate, of Professor Maitland, Mr. J. H.
Round, and Sir James Ramsay, by no means acknow-
edge all the obligations of the writer to their labours.
But the book is based throughout upon the original
authorities. Although the great chronicles of the
period have been sifted over and over again by expert
critics, there remain many sources, both narrative and
documentary, which for one reason or another have
been imperfectly utilised in previous works. Of these
the writer has endeavoured to make some use.

In conclusion he would express his grateful thanks
to the Editor of this series and to Mr. A. L. Smith,
of Balliol College, for many valuable suggestions and
corrections; to Mr. Grant Robertson, of All Souls
College, for generous permission to reproduce two
coloured maps from his forthcoming *Atlas of the British
Empire;* and above all to the Master and Fellows of
Balliol College for the indulgence which has made it
possible that this book should be completed.

H. W. C. DAVIS.

BALLIOL, OXFORD, 1905.

PREFACE TO THE FOURTH EDITION

IN this edition I have introduced references to a
number of important works which have appeared
in the last ten years, and have sometimes modified my
original conclusions in deference to the results which
those works embody.

H. W. C. DAVIS.

BALLIOL, OXFORD, 1915.

PUBLISHER'S NOTE TO THE ELEVENTH EDITION

THE bibliography has been enlarged and brought up to date by Mr. H. A. Cronne of King's College, University of London. A note explaining the principle of revision will be found on page 541 at the beginning of the Bibliography.

1937.

PUBLISHER'S NOTE TO THE THIRTEENTH EDITION

SOME minor corrections in the text, additions to the bibliography, and new appendices LOCAL JUSTICE UNDER THE NORMAN KINGS, CRIMINOUS CLERKS, THE PROVISIONS OF OXFORD AND OF WESTMINSTER, have been made by Miss N. D. Hurnard of Lady Margaret Hall, Oxford.

1949.

CONTENTS

CHAPTER I

CHAPTER II

CHAPTER V

CHAPTER VI

CHAPTER VII

CHAPTER VIII

CHAPTER XVI

CHAPTER XVII

APPENDICES

TABLES

come. Without creating a new kingdom the Conqueror enrolled another name on the list of European powers; and the list was destined to remain what he had left it until the fifteenth century. But the inner significance of the Norman Conquest is the reverse of that which appears upon the surface. In one sense the Conquest ranks among the migrations; but in a truer sense it is the result of a reaction against the influence of the barbarians. It marks the defeat, in one corner of the West, of the new order by the old, of the Teutonic conqueror by Latin civilisation. The withdrawal of the legions from the shores of Britain marked the point at which the hold of the Roman Empire on the West began to be relaxed. When William landed at Pevensey the wheel had come full circle, and the spiritual heirs of the Empire held within their grasp so much of the imperial inheritance as the Teuton had succeeded in guarding from the attacks of other rivals. When Harold fell beneath the Dragon Standard, the last stronghold of Teutonic law and institutions, of a liberty which had degenerated into licence, of an aristocracy who had outlived their function and their virtues, was opened wide for the entry of the Italian priest and Gallic legislator.

The struggle thus decided had been long and desperate. In the course of it each side learned some lessons from the other, and each experienced a striking transformation. The Teuton became half Christian; the Roman provincial accepted a code of morals and a system of government which was more than half barbarian. The first Teutonic invaders had encountered and had crushed the solid mechanism of a despotic government; their descendants were subdued by the moral force of a tradition. The final victory of the Empire was won at a moment when it was difficult to speak of the Empire as existing at all, except in a figurative and transcendental way. The outward form of the old order had vanished irrecoverably; the sacred palace and the official hierarchy, the legions and the courts of law, the engineer, the architect, the tax-collector, with all their works and deeds were a memory and a name. Only the spirit of the Empire still survived; the craving for a visible and political union of all civilised peoples, the instinct for administration, the legal subtlety, the capacity for self-restraint and for concentrating the faculties upon the pursuit of a distant object. While these remained, Rome remained, and a civilisation

LIST OF MAPS

ABBREVIATIONS

S. C.   = Stubbs' Select Charters (9th edition, 1913).
S. C. H. = Stubbs' Constitutional History.
P. & M. = Pollock and Maitland, History of English Law.
R. S.   = Rolls Series.
N. C.   = Freeman's Norman Conquest.
W. R.   = Freeman's William Rufus.
E. H. R. = English Historical Review.
D. N. B. = Dictionary of National Biography.
F. E.   = Round's Feudal England.
G. de M. = Round's Geoffrey de Mandeville.
A. E.   = Ramsay's Angevin Empire.
Regesta = Davis' Regesta Willelmi Conquestoris et Willelmi Rufi.
C. D. F. = Round's Calendar of Documents.

xx

CHAPTER I

THE NORMAN CONQUEST (1066-1072)

THE Norman Conquest of England was the outcome
struggle, short and spasmodic in its character, betwe
handful of adventurers and a decadent nation lying on the
fringe of European politics; and although it nearly affected
interests of several powers it occasioned no general disturban
international relations.   In fact if the importance of an event
to be measured by the commotion which it makes among
temporaries the Norman Conquest might be regarded as of
moment for European history.   None the less it is one of t
events which stand as a boundary mark between two stage
civilisation; and there is something more than accident in
rapidity with which, after the victory of Senlac, Europe eme
from the Dark Age into that splendid twilight which a l
proportion of civilised humanity still prize more highly than
morning light of the Renaissance or the mingled storm and
shine of the Reformation.   Senlac was a symptom, to some ex
a cause, of changes affecting every field of European activity.
the first glance Duke William and his Normans fall into the s
category with the Goths of Alaric, the Franks of Clovis, the Vik
of Cnut and Harold Hardrada; the Conquest of England se
but another example of those predatory migrations which n
and unmade so many barbarous kingdoms between the clos
the fourth and the beginning of the twelfth century of our
And even from this point of view the year 1066 constitutes a t
ing point in history, since the Conquest of England settled
broad outlines of European political geography for some tim

1

Strug
of La
and
Teuto

not less complex nor less glorious than that which had been lost
was still within the bounds of possibility.

The Norman Conquest gave England a place in universal The
history; not only because it dragged her into continental politics Norman
and twisted more closely the ties which bound her Church to the People
Papal See, but also because it increased her sensibility to new ideas
and infused into her society and institutions a spirit and vigour
which they would never have developed from their own resources.
The Normans brought with them to England the experience and
the aspirations of an older and more intellectual stock than that
from which they and their new subjects were descended. It would
be easy to exaggerate the degree of Norman originality. Genius
of any kind was rare among them; in the higher kinds they were
totally deficient.[1] But there are two types of ability, each invaluable to a race of pioneers, with which we are familiarised by the
Norman chroniclers. On the one hand we have the great soldiers
of the invading host—the Bellêmes, the Bigods, the Grantmesnils,
the Mowbrays; men who are equally remarkable for foresight in
council and for headlong courage in the hour of action, whose wits
are sharpened by danger and whose resolution is only stimulated by
obstacles; incapable of peaceful industry, but willing to prepare
themselves for war and rapine by the most laborious apprenticeship; illiterate but shrewd; violent but cunning; afraid of nothing
and yet instinctively inclined to gain their point by diplomacy rather
than by force. On the other hand there are the politicians, men
such as William Fitzosbern, Henry I., and Robert of Meulan,
cautious, plausible deliberate; with an immense capacity for detail,
and an innate liking for routine; conscious in a manner of their
moral obligations, but mainly concerned with small economies and
gains; limited in their horizon, but quick to recognise superior
powers and to use them for their own objects; indifferent for their
own part to high ideals, and yet respectful to idealists; altogether
a hard-headed, heavy handed, laborious, and tenacious type of men
England suffered much at the hands of the one type and the other
But the soldiers gave her unity, the statesmen gave her peace, and

---

[1] Orderic (iii., 474), like most of his contemporaries, enlarges chiefly on the high
spirit and turbulence of the Norman race. "Indomita gens Normannorum est et
nisi rigido rectore coerceatur ad facinus promptissima est. In omnibus collegiis
ubicunque fuerint, dominari appetunt, et veritatis fideique tenorem praevaricantes
ambitionis aestu multoties affecti sunt."

both in a curt, high-handed, and ungracious way served a useful purpose as drill-sergeants. They raised the English to that level of culture which the continental peoples had already reached, and left it for the Plantagenets of Anjou to make England in her turn a leader among the nations. Henry II. and Edward I. were nation-builders in a higher sense than the Conqueror. But it was the Norman Duke who made their work a possibility. And the history of the Norman Conquest may be read with interest, if not for its own sake, at all events as a prelude to a more brilliant future.

Anglo-Saxon England Had the forces which engaged at Senlac corresponded more nearly to the full fighting strength of the English and the Normans, the battle would have been more impressive as a military episode, but far less valuable as an object lesson in the science of politics. On any field and in an engagement on any scale, nothing short of the most desperate odds could have prevented the superiority of Norman tactics and equipment from producing their natural effect. But if the battle had been one between great armies, and if William, after his victory, had been able to march on the capital in overwhelming force, we should not have realised how slight a blow was needed to shatter the political fabric which the Anglo-Saxon had painfully built up in the course of several centuries. As the case stands we see that the death of a king and the defeat of some hastily collected levies could reduce the most ancient state n Europe to a state of bewilderment and anarchy.

The old English kingdom had never been much more than a federation of tribal commonwealths for the purpose of mutual defence ; the importance of co-operating even for this purpose had been seldom realised except in the last extremity of danger. Provincial jealousies and the feuds of noble houses had often spoiled the fairest and most needful plans for common action ; and unity was preserved much more by the force of sentiment than from a conviction of expediency.

The West Saxon Monarchy The customs of the West Saxon state demanded that the descendants of Cerdic, even at their worst and weakest, should keep the royal title. Any representative of the House who possessed the capacity to rule as well as reign was expected by public opinion to make the most of his position for his own advantage and the common good. On the one or two occasions

when such a King had ruled in Wessex an English nation flashed
into existence; when he disappeared, so too did the brief consciousness of unity.   But the dynasty remained as the memorial of these
brilliant moments, as the promise and potency of others yet to
come.   Philosophers have mocked at hereditary monarchies as
though they were equally irrational and useless in every stage of
civilisation.   But so long as social duties are envisaged in the
form of personal obligations, monarchy is the one practicable form
of government, and it is better that the monarchy should be
hereditary. Symbols, while men are still at a loss to distinguish
between them and the realities for which they stand, ought to be
as indestructible as men can make them.   A family is, in such
an age, a better symbol of national unity than the most gifted
individual, simply because the family will last the longer, and by
the mere force of longevity will command more loyalty than the
genius of any self-made ruler.   When the line of Danish usurpers
was abruptly terminated by the death of Harthacnut, England
was able to seize the opportunity of freedom because the House
of Cerdic, though represented only by a feeble devotee, still commanded unquestioning respect.   The case was different at the Position of
death of Harold son of Godwin.   Excusably but rashly this Mayor Harold
of the Palace had chafed against conventions which his father had
respected.   He failed to see that the cause of national unity owed
much more to these conventions than to the ability which his
house had placed at the disposal of the lawful King.   In the vain
belief that energy, diplomatic skill, and the art of appealing to
common interests, were a sufficient title to the first dignity in the
state, he had induced the nation to disregard the principle of
heredity and to take himself as the successor of St. Edward.   His
error was apparent even before his death at Senlac; neither urgent
perils nor gratitude for his great services could keep the nation
true to him.   But the full consequences of the miscalculation were
felt when he was gone.   The English had been reasoned out of
their attachment to the House of Cerdic, and they had not learned
to follow the House of Godwin.   The truth that might is right
had been impressed on them with only too much effect; those who
could have done something to defend an established dynasty fell to
quarrelling over an elective crown which they were none of them to
wear; while those who had no hope of gaining the prize for them-

selves stood aloof, determined to make the best terms that they might with the victorious candidate. On the day after Senlac England was no nation but a geographical expression. Each province, each town, each family looked to its own interests. Government was at a standstill. There was no thought of concerted resistance.

William marches to Canterbury, Sept.-Oct., 1066

The day after the battle was spent by the Normans in collecting the spoils and burying their dead. Amongst the fallen, at the spot where the standards of the Dragon and the Fighting Man had been planted and where afterwards the high altar of the Abbey Church of Battle stood, the corpse of Harold was found, naked and mutilated almost beyond recognition. Whether from vulgar resentment or, as one would prefer to think, from a fear that Harold dead might be a more dangerous rival than Harold living, William refused his adversary the honour of a Christian burial. The last of the West Saxon Kings was dishonourably interred on the sea-shore; and the site of his grave is said to have been kept a secret.[1] On the second day William and his men returned to Hastings to wait for the expected submission of the English. But five days elapsed without the appearance of ambassadors; and it became plain that a further demonstration would be needed before the country would understand the full import of the fight of Senlac. Ignorant of what resistance might be taking shape behind the curtain of the Sussex Weald, William shaped his march to the north-east, that he might seize the Cinque Ports and secure his communications with Normandy before moving northward upon London. At Romney he took a stern revenge for the mishandling of some Norman ships which had steered to this port, mistaking it for Pevensey. The severity struck terror into the garrison which Harold had placed in his new castle on the cliff at Dover. Without waiting to test the boasted impregnability of the place they sent their messengers half way to Romney to arrange a capitulation. Accordingly the castle and the town passed without a struggle into Norman hands, but not before the common soldiers had fired the town for the sake of plundering and had reduced the greater part of it to ruin. But

---

[1] Another story is that he was honourably buried by the Canons of Waltham. See the tract De Inventione Sanctae Crucis (ed. Stubbs). The legend that Harold escaped and became a hermit first occurs in Ailred's tract De Vita et Miraculis Edwardi Confessoris (Michel, Chron. Anglo-Normandes, ii., p. xxix.), a composition of the next century.

the Duke, lest this outrage should discourage others of the English from a quiet submission, gave compensation to the victims.   After a stay of eight days in Dover, during which he received reinforcements from Normandy and strengthened and garrisoned the castle, he moved inland to Canterbury which he found as ready as Dover to receive him.   The way to London was now open, when an unexpected mischance checked his march.   Disease had appeared among his troops, as the result of the autumn season and their own excesses, even before they left Dover; and at a day's march beyond Canterbury William too fell ill.   For a month his main host remained motionless waiting for his recovery, and it was fortunate that he had no opponent bold enough to profit by this enforced idleness.

THE CAMPAIGN OF 1066

As it turned out the delay was not an utter waste of time. **Feeling** The men of south and eastern England began to realise that no **in the Country** leader of the national cause was forthcoming, and accordingly be- **and** thought them of making peace while there was yet time.   Win- **London** chester, the dower-town of the Confessor's widow and the ancient capital of Wessex, followed the lead of Canterbury and Dover, without waiting to learn the attitude of London and the Witan. Edith herself commended the decision of her citizens and joined with them in sending gifts to the author of her brother's fall. Other towns of less consequence took their cue from Winchester.

Their citizens, to use the graphic but uncomplimentary simile of a Norman poet, flocked to William's camp like flies to a running sore.[1] Only London made no sign, and this was soon discovered to be the result of divided councils. Three different parties had formed within the capital. The earls Edwin and Morcar had carefully refrained from compromising themselves by an appearance at Senlac. The fall of Harold was to them almost a matter for self-congratulation. Possibly they hoped that the crown might be conferred on one of themselves, more probably they anticipated an opportunity of converting their earldoms into independent principalities by selling their services to the highest bidder. Another party, headed by the most patriotic of the clergy, thought that the time had come to restore the House of Cerdic in the person of

Election of Edgar Atheling Edgar Atheling. Thanks to the persuasions of this party the Atheling was proclaimed as King; and Edwin and Morcar, while abstaining from all promises of allegiance, undertook to help him in the struggle with the Norman. But they confined themselves to promises; and all attempts to organise resistance broke down before the intrigues of a faction which had resolved, for one reason or another, to make terms with William. No doubt the foreign bishops belonged to it; but the leaders who are mentioned by name were native Englishmen. Esegar the sheriff of Middlesex had fought at Senlac. He had seen enough of Norman military methods to know the futility of resistance, and was now in secret correspondence with William; a promise that he should be left to rule London at his pleasure secured his complete devotion to the invader.[2] The Primate Stigand saw no hope of legitimising his more than dubious position except by making terms with the invader. The English had disowned the Primate as uncanonically appointed; and the place in their councils which should have been his now belonged to his rival, Aldred the Archbishop of York. Though Stigand's usurpation of the see of Robert of Jumièges was one among the pretexts which William had alleged for the invasion, the Archbishop might still curry favour by turning traitor

William moves on London, Nov.- Dec., 1066 before treachery ceased to be valuable. With such allies in London William could afford to act deliberately, and when, about the beginning of November, he resumed his march, instead of attempting to force the passage of the Thames at London he

---

[1] Guy of Amiens, 612 ff.   [2] Guy of Amiens, 660 ff.

moved up the stream and crossed at Wallingford; a move which cut the communications of London with the north and gave the hesitating full time for reflection. On the north bank of the river he was joined by Stigand to whom he gave a welcome as politic as it afterwards proved to be hypocritical. Then began a slow wheeling movement of the invading army towards London. Both before and after the crossing of the Thames the country was ruthlessly laid waste, and if the evidence of the chroniclers were wanting that of Domesday Book would still enable us to trace the line of march. The Londoners found themselves threatened London with starvation and blockade; they threw their last scruples to submits the wind, and resolved to make a virtue of necessity. On his arrival at Little Berkhampstead the Duke was greeted by an embassy of peace.[1] It included all the men of mark who had remained in London; the submission which they offered was unanimous and unconditional. Edwin and Morcar do not seem to have been present. They had drawn off to the northward with their forces while the way was still clear.[2] But the Atheling, Aldred of York, Wulfstan bishop of Worcester, Walter bishop of Hereford, and some unnamed representatives of London made their appearance and offered the crown to the invader. The offer was accepted after a show of hesitation which was perhaps demanded by the conventional morality of the age. The Duke encamped outside the city while his advance guard constructed a fortress within the city walls and made other needful preparations for his reception. On Christ- William's mas day he was crowned at Westminster by the Archbishop of Corona- York; and Stigand, whose highest function was thus transferred tion, Dec. 25, 1066 to another, received the first intimation that his treachery had been futile. The true character of the King's title, though obscured by the use of the ancient ritual, was impressed on the spectators by an untoward accident. The shouts of acclamation which greeted the new sovereign when the Archbishop presented him to the people were misinterpreted by the Norman guards who stood outside the minster. They supposed that the King's life was threatened and fired the surrounding houses to create a diversion. The congre-

[1] See Mr Baring's remarks in *E. H. R.*, xiii., p. 17 and Stenton, *William the Conqueror*, p. 222.
[2] The Chronicle (D. Text) and Florence says that Edwin and Morcar came to Berkhampstead. W. Malmesbury describes them, however, as flying to the north; which is indirectly confirmed by William of Poitou, who says that they met the Duke at Barking, *i.e.* after his coronation.

1*

gation, alarmed in their turn, rushed into the open air without waiting for the conclusion of the ceremony, and the King was left almost alone with the officiating bishops. The necessary forms were hastily fulfilled while the confusion was still at its height. Amidst a tumult sufficient to shake the strongest courage William took the royal oath, promised to treat the English with the same justice as his Norman subjects,[1] and issued the customary first injunction of an English king, that peace should be observed throughout his realm. Seldom has an English reign commenced with a more appropriate or inauspicious incident. The panic was a grim commentary on the difference between the facts and fictions of the situation. Hailed as the lawful heir of native kings, as the free choice of a free people, the new sovereign moved in a cloud of fears and suspicions, trusting for protection to the interested and lawless loyalty of a soldiery whom his subjects execrated.

Measures after the Coronation

To amend this state of things was the work which lay immediately before the King. For the present there had been enough of conquest and rapine. The west and north, which the invader's hand had not yet touched, might be left to themselves until the government of the south and east had been placed on a secure footing. Nothing was so likely to accelerate surrenders as the spectacle of order emerging from chaos in the conquered districts. Without delay William began to provide for the government of London, the maintenance of discipline among his followers, and the establishment of his authority in the open country. The new castle at London was pushed forward; a new sheriff was appointed in the place of Esegar;[2] but at the same time the citizens received a charter confirming to them and their children the privileges which they had enjoyed in Edward's day.[3] The Norman garrison received strict orders to refrain from violence and plunder, and military courts were established with a summary jurisdiction over all offenders. A pardon, though not a free one, was offered to all Englishmen who had not actually fought on Harold's side. Those who accepted the boon were allowed to ransom their estates by the payment of a fine to which in some cases was added the obligation of providing hostages. The fines, no doubt, were heavy and, however light, would still have remained unreasonable; since

---

[1] W. Malm., *Gesta Pontificum*, p. 252.
[2] See Round, *G. de M.*, Appendix P.   [3] *Select Charters*, p. 97.

passive obedience to a King who had been chosen by the nation and anointed by the Church was no crime in English or in Norman law. But such terms were moderate in that age of iron; and William felt no scruples about revising them when his power was more thoroughly established. Twenty years later the Domesday Book shows that few Englishmen remained amongst the tenants-in-chief of any shire. Even the most fortunate only kept, in the long run, a portion of the lands which had been theirs in Edward's day. The King himself was not rapacious; but he could not afford to disappoint his Normans, or to leave the land ungarrisoned. The slightest evidence, or a mere suspicion, proved fatal to an English landowner. The natural leaders of the conquered race were slowly eliminated by a proscription which was the more odious because cloaked with all the forms of law.

For the present, however, the situation made fair promises im- More sub-perative; and men of wealth were allowed to delude themselves missions with the hope that the change of rulers meant no change in the position of the native race. Many submissions were accordingly received at Barking, which the King had selected as a safer residence than London. The midlands and the north began to come in; and the appearance of Edwin and Morcar seemed to prove the wisdom of the King's moderate policy. They were met with no reproaches for their tardiness. William gave them fair words and restored all their possessions. The one condition which he attached to his pardon was that they should remain, as honoured guests, about his person. Captivity, so courteously disguised, lost half its sting, and it is said that the vanity of Edwin was soothed by the suggestion that he should marry one of William's daughters. Meanwhile those whose offences it was safe to punish had to pay a heavy ransom for the slightest act by which they had implied a preference for William's rivals. While Edgar Atheling was still in the position of a king, elected but uncrowned, the abbacy of Peterborough happened to fall vacant. The choice of the monks fell upon one Brand, their prior, who in his simplicity applied for confirmation to the Atheling. For fighting on that side, or any side at all, the good man had no mind, but it was his ill fortune to be, in unquiet times, no weather-prophet. His mistake of judgment cost the abbey forty marks of gold, and yet Peterborough came off lightly by comparison with lay offenders.[1]

---

[1] See the Conqueror's charter of confirmation to Abbot Brand, *Regesta* No. 8.

Total confiscation was the usual penalty. The chaplain William of Poitiers mentions a progress which the King made at this moment to receive submissions, and eulogises the compassion which his master showed to suppliants. The wholesale changes of ownership in the south-eastern counties, to which Domesday Book bears witness, are probably the outcome of this journey; in the beggarly portions sometimes left to the widows and children of fallen Englishmen we may discern the workings of that compassion which moved the biographer to eloquence.

The spoils of England

There was wisdom in praising a man who understood so well the advisability of rewarding his apologists. The lion's share of the spoil went, as was natural, to the barons who had helped the enterprise with their swords. But many of the movables seized in Harold's treasury, or received in the form of gifts and fines, found their way to the men who controlled the public conscience. Valuable presents, jewelled roods, books in costly bindings, precious stuffs, and vessels of silver, were distributed far and wide among the monasteries of France. Most lavish of all was the largesse offered to St. Peter's Church at Rome; and Harold's famous banner, the Fighting Man, was presented to Pope Alexander as a fitting recompense for that which he had sent to William before the expedition. Those critics, who even in the councils of the Pope had questioned the justice of the Norman cause, were now reduced to silence. Nearer home we hear of two Normans, the one a monk and the other a plain knight, who declined to share in the spoils of what they still regarded as an unrighteous undertaking. This honest couple obtained some celebrity by their refusal but found no imitators.[1] In the eyes of most contemporaries William was justified by his success and the use to which he turned it.

William returns to Normandy, 1067

Though several months had elapsed since William turned his back on Normandy, nothing had occurred in his absence to disturb the peace of the Duchy; and in fact an illness, so timely that rumour imputed it to poison, carried off Conan II. of Brittany, one of Normandy's most restless neighbours, while William's attention was absorbed in the affairs of England.[2] Yet the need of fresh supplies and reinforcements, and the reflection that Normandy, for some

---

[1] Freeman, *N. C.*, iv., pp. 444 f.
[2] Bouquet, *Recueil*, xi., pp. 30, 50, 413 *n*. The story of the poison comes from William of Jumièges.

years to come, must be lef' in the hands of vicegerents made William desirous to revisit the Duchy before entering upon the second and more toilsome stage of his English venture. He cannot have anticipated, nor was it to be the case, that the remo e north and west of England would accept the revolution which he had effected until personal contact had taught them to respect him. He was probably at a loss to know the precise form which resistance would assume. But Harold's sons and other members of the House of Godwin were at large in the south-west; and it was unlikely that the King of Denmark, Sweyn Estrithsson, who had already been once disappointed of the English crown, would let the present opportunity pass unheeded. Either of these rival interests was certain to command the aid of a considerable party. Accordingly the King had not left England without taking elaborate precautions to secure the lands already won. The country south of the Thames he placed in the charge of his half-brother, Odo, bishop of Bayeux, on whom at the same time he conferred the earldom of Kent and the custody of Dover castle. Odo's government extended, for practical purposes, no farther west than Winchester. All beyond was hostile country, and his duty was rather to guard communications with the continent than to prosecute further conquests. North of the Thames William Fitzosbern received a similar but more responsible position. His government included East Anglia, the Fen Country, and the earldoms of Edwin and Morcar. As warden of the newly constructed castle at Norwich he was to provide against possible invasions from Denmark.[1] As Earl of Hereford he was to watch the Welsh and to prevent them from concerting measures of resistance with the English patriots. Bernicia alone of all the northern districts was left outside the sphere of Fitzosbern's command. Osulf the native earl had up to this point disregarded the Normans altogether; the task of dealing with him was committed to a Northumbrian thegn, Copsige by name, whose local influence and former connection with Tostig created a presumption that he would be a useful and a pliant

---

[1] William of Poitiers gives the name of the castle as Guenta. Ramsay, *Foundations*, ii., p. 179, identifies Guenta with Winchester, a hypothesis also adopted by Lappenberg, ii., p. 69. But Norwich (*Venta Icenorum*) fits better with the details in William of Poitiers. Orderic subsequently mentions Fitzosbern as governor of the Isle of Wight, a statement which is confirmed by Mr. Round's investigations (V. C. H. Hants, vol. i., p. 408); but Hugh of Grantmesnil was the first governor of Hampshire (Orderic, vol. ii., pp. 167, 186, 218). Ralph Guader, afterwards earl of Norfolk, was a son-in-law of William Fitzosbern (Orderic, ii., 222).

instrument.   As a final precaution all those Englishmen who might serve as the figure-heads of a rebellion were taken to Normandy in the King's train.   Edgar Atheling, Stigand, Waltheof the Earl of Northampton and Huntingdon, Edwin, and Morcar are specially mentioned among the hostages who graced the Conqueror's triumphal entry into Rouen.   Their enforced journey afforded another proof, if proof were still needed, that their submission had failed to earn William's confidence and that, however honourably they might be treated at his court, they were an object of contemptuous curiosity to the meanest of his Norman subjects.

Discon-
tent of
England,
1067   In Normandy the King remained until the close of the year. We learn that he made careful dispositions for the government of the Duchy,[1] but are left to conjecture what other business claimed his attention.   It cannot however have been unimportant, since ominous events occurred to complicate the position of his lieutenants some time before he reappeared in England.   The luckless Copsige had scarcely set foot in his new earldom before he was attacked at a banquet by the partisans of Osulf who fired a church to which he fled for sanctuary, and slew him in the act of attempting to escape the flames.   On his death the Northumbrians put aside all care as to their future relations with the Norman; and five weeks later their chosen leader perished ignobly in a scuffle with a highway robber.   But the resistance of the southern shires took a less spasmodic shape.   William's regents quickly acquired an evil reputation.   They were charged with oppressive conduct towards all the noblest of the English, and with condoning the worst excesses of their soldiery.   The castles which they built far and wide, and the unpaid labour service which they exacted for this purpose, brought home the meaning of conquest to the minds of the English with a new and galling emphasis.   At Hereford the completion of the castle was followed by an obstinate revolt.   Eadric, surnamed the Wild, a thane of mark in northern Herefordshire, had never made submission to the Normans.   As often as the castle garrison attacked his lands they were beaten off, and sympathisers gathered round him so fast that in August he was able in his turn to begin aggressive operations.   The brothers Bleddyn and Rhiwallon, the princes of North Wales and Powis, came to his assistance ; the allies carried fire and sword to the walls of Hereford and even farther eastward,

[1] Orderic, ii., 177.

while the garrison waited idly for assistance which the regents could ill afford to give.

For in the east also there had been an alarm of danger from an unexpected quarter. The malcontents of Kent enlisted on their side no less a person than Eustace of Boulogne, who after figuring with more prominence than distinction in the fight at Senlac had failed to obtain the rewards to which he thought himself entitled by his relationship with the Confessor and the Conqueror. The exact form which his revenge was to have taken we do not know, and it is possible that he did not know himself. But he arranged with his English confederates to land by night at Dover and, as a first step, to surprise the castle. The moment of execution was not ill selected. Eustace and his knights made their appearance while Odo of Bayeux and his deputy De Montfort were on the other side of the Thames; and the Kentishmen lost no time in assembling to aid the Count's design. If the besiegers could have shown a creditable front for a day or two they would have been assisted by a more general rising. But Eustace drew off at the first repulse; an unexpected sally changed his retreat to a rout, and for the second time in his life he fled from Dover covered with disgrace. When the times became more settled William could afford to despise so pusillanimous a rival. Eustace was in the end restored to favour and received a share of William's later conquests. But the support which he had found in England caused no little anxiety to the regents; it boded ill for the Norman interest if the King of Denmark should seize the opportunity of William's absence.

But Sweyn, though urgently invited by the rebels, neither sent nor came. It may be that his natural irresolution was increased by the diplomacy of his rival, for there is a story, apparently relating to this juncture, about an English abbot who bore to the Danish court a flattering message from the Conqueror, and obtained a truce.[1] In the choice of such a messenger there is nothing to surprise us. The leaders of the English hierarchy were now convinced that in William's success lay the only hope of a return to settled government. Thanks to the efforts of such men as Aldred of York and Wulfstan of Worcester, the King, on his return to England (Dec. 6, 1067), found that a native party, recruited from all classes, had been formed in his favour. Their

Eustace of Boulogne

---

[1] *N. C.*, iv., p. 750.

loyalty was not even shaken by the confiscations and the heavy
Danegeld which signalised his return. The conquered districts
remained absolutely quiet while he proceeded to the reduction of
the west.

Revolt of
Exeter,
1067-8

The precipitation of Harold, rather than any want of good
will for his cause, had prevented the men of the south-western
shires from mustering to the English side at Senlac. The influence
and estates of the House of Godwin were nowhere greater than in
Devonshire and Cornwall; to Exeter Godwin's widow and the
remnants of her family naturally turned their steps when the
midlands and the east were lost. In wealth, in privileges and
in importance this city might challenge comparison with London,
York, or Winchester, and it was the natural metropolis of south-
western England. Supported by many of the local thegns, and
emboldened by their own want of military experience, the citizens
imagined that they could treat with William upon equal terms.
They spent the year 1067 in organising their resources. Their walls
were strengthened, forces were levied in the neighbouring shires;
the foreign traders living in the town were compelled to give
assistance, and embassies asking for co-operation were sent to other
towns. On receiving from William a demand that their chief men
should appear before him and swear fealty the citizens of Exeter
replied that they would neither take an oath nor admit the King
within their walls. They were prepared to pay him the accustomed
royal dues but would admit no other limitation of their independence. To this remarkable offer, which proved how completely the
idea of national unity was overshadowed in English minds by a
provincial patriotism, William made the short reply that it was
not his custom to rule upon conditions of such a character; early in
the year 1068 he marched on Exeter, leading an army in which
Englishmen appeared for the first time beside his mercenaries and
Norman vassals. The projected federation of the western boroughs
had come to nothing; those of Dorset submitted passively when
the Conqueror appeared before their gates[1]; and the news of his
unimpeded advance had a sobering effect upon the citizens of
Exeter. Before he reached that city he was met by ambassadors
offering hostages and absolute submission. Their offers were
accepted, but they only represented the party of common sense and

[1] Round, F. E., pp. 436 f.

moderation.   Another party, who held themselves too deeply com-
promised for pardon, insisted upon a prolongation of the struggle,
and the gates were closed in William's face.   It was to no purpose
that he led the hostages before the walls and put out the eyes of
one as an earnest of what the others might expect.   A siege of
eighteen days was necessary, the walls were already undermined,
before saner counsels regained ascendancy ; there were bitter complaints of treachery when the civic authorities concluded a surrender.
But the citizens found little cause to regret their humiliation.   They
were spared from pillage and escaped with no worse punishment
than the burden of constructing and maintaining a new castle.
This leniency, greater than was elsewhere shown to more deserving
cities, was justified by subsequent events ; when next we find the
citizens of Exeter in arms they are fighting in defence of the new
castle against their fellow-countrymen.

The occasion for this display of gratitude was not long in
coming.   An Indian fakir, we are told by Plutarch, once demonstrated to Alexander the difficulty of conquest by laying a dry Revolt of
ox-hide before him and inviting him to stamp i level with the Edwin and
ground ; whenever one edge was pressed down the others only rose 1068
the higher.   For a time it seemed as though William's efforts
would be frustrated in this way.   The submission of Devonshire
followed upon that of Exeter, and an uneventful march through
Cornwall satisfied the King that the remotest corners of the South
were cowed.   But Gytha had escaped from Exeter before the
surrender : the sons of Harold were collecting ships and men at the
court of Diarmaid of Dublin ; and in the north and midlands
rebellions suddenly broke out under the leadership of the Englishmen on whom William had most relied.   The details, as given in
our authorities, are fragmentary and hard to piece together.   This
much is clear that Edwin and Morcar escaped to Mercia and raised
their standard in alliance with the Welsh, while almost simultaneously the Northumbrians declared for Edgar Atheling, taking
as their leader the Englishman Gospatric, who had recently purchased from William the right of succeeding Copsige in Bernicia.
If there was a connection between the two outbreaks the commanders had no common plan ; and it is even doubtful whether
Edwin and Morcar fought for the Atheling or for their own hand.
They endeavoured to give their venture a national complexion.

Their envoys scoured England to enlist supporters, and prayers for their success were offered in many of the churches. But their personal popularity and great connections availed them little against the general awe of William. In the end they were compelled to make the most of Mercian levies and of assistance lent by the Welsh prince Bleddyn who, through his brother's death, had recently become sole ruler of Powis and North Wales. The earls may have counted for a moment on the sons of Harold who about this time set sail from Dublin; but these invaders failed in an attempt on Bristol; their expedition degenerated into a series of forays along the south-west coast; and at the mouth of the Avon they were so roughly handled by the men of Somerset that they returned in discomfiture to Dublin. Meanwhile the army of the earls melted into air at the news of William's coming. He allowed them to make their peace once more since, contemptible as they were, their names had still some weight among the English. But from this moment they were earls in name only and other means than their influence were rapidly prepared for holding down the midlands. The shire of Leicester, with the dignity of an earl, was given to Robert of Meulan; the county borough was colonised with Normans; and castles were erected both at Warwick and at Nottingham before the King moved off to deal with the rebellion of the north.

The Rising of the North, 1068

Here too his task was one of no great difficulty. Gospatric's plan had been formed in a moment of impulse; although the citizens of York, against the persuasions of Archbishop Aldred, insisted upon joining him, he found himself without an army and without allies. Indeed the King of Scots, to whom he should naturally have turned for help, was at this moment harrying Bernicia in revenge for a raid which Gospatric had committed upon Cumberland a few months previously, when rebellion was still undreamed of.[1] Caught between two fires Gospatric preferred to throw himself upon the mercy of the Scot. They met upon the banks of the Wear in the neighbourhood of Durham where Gospatric had formed a camp of refuge; and Malcolm, moved to pity by the forlorn plight of Gospatric and the Atheling, offered them

---

[1] The order of events at this point is extremely obscure. See *N. C.*, iv., App. R., and Ramsay, *Foundations*, ii., p. 80. The main fact, that Malcolm received the fugitives, is given in the D. and E. texts of the Chronicle. The meeting at Wearmouth is given, with the erroneous date of 1070, in Simeon of Durham, *H. R.*, p. 190.

an asylum in Scotland. But at the same time he opened negotiations with the Norman through the instrumentality of Ægelwine,
bishop of Durham.[1] Consequently William met no opposition
when he drew near to York. The citizens, submitting to the
inevitable, sent envoys to meet him with the keys of the city. He
made a quiet entrance, laid the foundations of a castle within the
walls, received the submission of some Northumbrian thegns who
had not followed Gospatric's flight, and accepted Malcolm's offers
of friendship.[2]

A successor to Gospatric was found in the person of the Flemish *Robert de Commines*
adventurer Robert de Commines, and William thought that for
the present he could afford to leave the north in the hands of this
subordinate. After quartering a garrison of 500 men at York the
King marched peacefully and by slow stages to the south, pausing
as he went to commence new castles at Lincoln, Huntingdon and
Cambridge. All resistance seemed at an end, and he now ventured
to dismiss the mercenaries by whom he had been hitherto supported.
He was not alone in his view of the situation; for at this very
moment Godwin's widow, Gytha, and her supporters, who had so
long continued to hope for a reaction, stole away from their hiding
place on the Isle of Steep Holm in the Bristol Channel and went,
like many an English refugee before them, to claim the protection
of Baldwin VI. of Flanders.

Suddenly Northumberland gave the signal for the outbreak of *Second Northern Rising, 1069*
new and worse commotions. Robert de Commines had descended
on that wild country with a retinue which spoiled and harried
without distinguishing too nicely between friends and enemies.
The first impulse of the wretched Northumbrians was to escape by
flight; but the hard winter made flight impossible. They turned
at bay; and on the night of January 28 when Robert and his
men, unconscious of the danger, were at Durham enjoying the
bishop's hospitality, an armed multitude broke through the gates
and rushed into the city. Many of the Normans were murdered
in their beds. The bishop's house was fired and Robert de Commines perished in the flames. Of the 700 men who had formed
his retinue barely one or two escaped to tell the story. Meanwhile

[1] Orderic, ii., 185.
[2] Orderic *u.s.* says that Malcolm did homage; but this may be a Norman invention.

at York an armed band of Englishmen attacked the new castle; and the Atheling returned from Scotland, at the head of a small force, to direct their enterprise. It was a premature outbreak William answered the urgent summons of the garrison by a forced march which brought him down on the besiegers long before he was expected. They scattered not without some loss of life. The Atheling fled to Scotland and William, after building a second castle, this time outside the city walls, retired to keep the Easter feast at Winchester. Two such rapid victories over York blinded him to the possibilities of mischief which still lay undeveloped in the north.

Coming of the Danes, Aug., 1069
Spring wore into summer and events still seemed to justify his confidence. Nothing occurred to disturb the peace except a second and last raid of Harold's sons upon the west which ended as ingloriously as the first. But then, in the latter half of August, the long-expected Danish fleet was sighted off the eastern coast. It did not bring King Sweyn himself, but his two elder s ns, Harold and Cnut, and his brother Osbiorn were on board; the ship crews were a motley horde of Danes, Frisians, Saxons, Poles, and Wends, some the subjects of Sweyn, others free volunteers attracted by the wealth of England. There were in all 240 vessels, carrying perhaps 10,000 men.[1] So far as numbers went it was a formidable expedition; when, after aimless attempts to effect a landing in Kent and Suffolk, the ships crept into the Humber it seemed that the cause of Sweyn would be supported by a considerable part of England. The Danes were met not only by the survivors of the former insurrection, by the Atheling, Gospatric, and their fellows; but also by men like Waltheof who had so far accepted the Norman rule; and with their chiefs there came an immense multitude of common men, "riding and marching gladly" as the Chronicler has it.[2] The people of Lincoln and Northumbria, who were not forgetful of their Danish ancestry, probably felt more enthusiasm for the nephew of Cnut than they had ever felt for Harold or the Atheling.

Fall of York, Sept. 1069
Slowly as the fleet had moved the Danes outpaced the preparations of the King. The garrisons at York sent word to their

[1] As to the crew which an average ship might carry see the *Miracula S Edmundi*, §§ 50, 67, in Liebermann's *Ungedruckte Geschichtsquellen*; in each case the number of passengers is about 60, and the ship is described as overladen.
[2] *A. S. C.*, D. text.

master that they could hold the castles for a year if need be, and accordingly William took his time. But the boast was ill-justified by the event. On September 21st, the Danes and English streamed into the city without encountering the least resistance. The Frenchmen fled to the castles and set fire to the adjacent houses. The flames spread until York was left a mass of blazing ruins. Even the minster was destroyed, and Archbishop Aldred, who had loyally supported the defenders, died of a broken heart. In ten days' time the castles were won, their defenders slain, the vaunting captain, William Malet, a prisoner on a Danish ship. For the last time on English soil the English axe and foot-soldier made good their ancient reputation. A hundred years after the storm of York the minstrels sang of the prowess shown by Waltheof,

> Stout of arm and broad of breast,
> Strong and long in every limb,
> Siward's son, the glorious Earl,

and of the havoc which he made among the enemy "hewing their heads off one and one, as they came out by the wicket". Even William could admire the feat of the faithless Englishman; but to the Norman fugitives who brought him the disastrous tidings his bearing was less magnanimous. The story goes that every man of them lost his nose and his right hand. And the story may well be true. The penalties of the age were ruthless, and William was never a lenient judge of his subordinates.

The rebels and their Danish allies were not long in learning Minor that he was a general of another stamp than William Malet. The Risings news of the victory at York was a spark which kindled many fires. The men of Somerset and Dorset mustered in force to the siege of Montacute; those of Devon and Cornwall marched on Exeter to expel the Norman garrison; the castle of Shrewsbury was threatened by Eadric the Wild and his Welshmen. A tiro might have doubted by what plan to meet so many dangers. William had no doubts. He left the minor risings to be quelled by his lieutenants, and the rejoicings for the fall of York were scarcely over before he appeared with a mounted force upon the shores of the Humber. There, between the mouths of the Ouse and Trent, the Danes had beached their ships and formed their winter-quarters. But at the news of the King's approach they fled, first to the coast of Lindsey, and then, as he still held to the pursuit, to Holderness on the other side of the estuary, where for want of ships he could not reach them.

William in the North Leaving a force in Lindsey to watch their further movements, William wheeled round to the west, and at Stafford crushed without difficulty an inchoate insurrection of the Mercians which threatened his communications. Then came the news that the Danes, weary of their bleak quarters in the Humber, were on the march to hold the Yule-tide feast in York. He pushed forward to the Aire ; although that river, swollen by the rains and guarded by rebels, caused him a delay of three weeks, an unwatched ford was at length discovered, and by a long circuit through the hills of the West Riding he descended upon York. Once more the main body of the Danes escaped him, though a few remained to aid the English in defending the city. Their resistance was stubborn, but the city was not provisioned for a siege ; when a Danish force had attempted and failed to break the blockade, surrender was inevitable.[1] Again the city received a garrison; again castles were commenced ; and the work of the rebels was utterly undone. It only remained to cut off their supplies and to make an example of the province which had harboured them. For the best part of two months William was engaged in harrying the cultivated lands between the Ouse and Tyne.

Harrying of the North, 1069 The district over which he passed is naturally less fertile than the south of England ; and the inhabitants had never been allowed to develop the resources of their land. What the raids of the Dane and Scot left untouched was often destroyed in the private wars of the Northumbrian aristocracy. Still in the upland dales and river valleys there were numerous villages and wealthy churches; on the coast a few ports like Whitby could boast a measure of prosperity ; there were substantial results to be shown for centuries of occupation. These William set himself to destroy with method and deliberation, sparing neither land nor men. It is true that beyond the Tees his march caused little loss of life, but this was merely because the inhabitants had time to escape across the Tyne. In Yorkshire, where there was less time to learn and to forestall his plans, every village through which he passed became a scene of massacre. A few miserable refugees lurked in the hills and supported existence on the flesh of horses, dogs, and cats. Others sold themselves into

---

[1] W. Malmesbury, *G. R.*, iii., § 269. The city surrendered " civibus longa inedia consumptis," which implies a siege.

slavery; "they bowed their heads for meat in the evil days," to quote the grim expression of a contemporary document.[1] The devastation was complete; from York to Durham there was not left a single inhabited village when the Conqueror stayed his hand; and in this state the land continued until, some years later, a few devoted monks ventured out into the wilderness to repair the ruined churches and to till the deserted fields.[2] The land between the Tees and Tyne recovered more quickly from the blow than Yorkshire; the tenants of St. Cuthbert had at least saved their lives, and some returned in time to their devastated farms. But even in this region there were places of importance, such as Jarrow and Wearmouth, which never regained their lost prosperity: and for Yorkshire we have the evidence of Domesday Book to prove the extent and lasting nature of the desolation. To take but one example: on the fief of Richmond, in 1086, were lying waste over 100 villages and hamlets containing land for upwards of 400 ploughs. There had been little or no discrimination between the innocent and guilty. The lands of churches suffered equally with those of rebels, and the submissiveness of Edwin and Morcar availed little to their Yorkshire tenants.

The leaders of the rebellion were treated more leniently than the rank and file. Gospatric, from his stronghold at Bamborough, sent to sue for pardon, and obtained it. Judging the good-faith of others by his own, he did not venture within William's reach; but Waltheof, who showed a more confiding disposition, was rewarded not only with the restoration of his earldom, but also with the hand of the Conqueror's niece. These defections and the flight of the Atheling to Scotland left the national party without a head, unless they could prevail on Sweyn to pursue his venture single-handed. But of this there was no hope. Sweyn had contented himself with acting through a lieutenant who was either despondent

Departure of the Danes, 1070

[1] *Codex Diplomaticus*, iv., 263.
[2] Besides Orderic, the following authorities give valuable details: Simeon of Durham, *H. R.*, pp. 188, 189, and *H. E. D.*, iii., § 22. W. Malmesbury, *G. R.*, iii., § 249. *G. P.*, pp. 208-10. Raine, *Historians of York*, ii., pp. 107, 361, 362. *Chronicle of Evesham*, p. 90 (R. S.). The state of the North about 1080-1100 is illustrated by a document in the *Whitby Cartulary*, p. xxxviii., recounting the tribulations of that place; by Ailred's account of Hexham (Raine, *Priory of Hexham*, i., p. 191); by Simeon, *H. R.*, p. 201, etc.

or corrupt. Bribed, as it was conjectured, by William, Jarl Osbiorn withdrew his fleet in the summer of 1070. Retreating as he had come, he paused at London to sign a treaty in his master's name, and then disappeared from English shores.

William in the West, 1070

Before the Danes had finally departed William completed his work by ravaging the shires of Stafford, Derby, and Chester, all more or less involved in recent risings. It was still the winter season and his mercenary troops rebelled at the prospect of a march through the wild Peak country. The king disdained to expostulate with those whom he had not the power of threatening, and coldly informed them that he at least would not turn back; others might do as they thought fit. The rebuke was effectual; the mutineers followed him patiently through swamps and streams, over pathless heights and moors, until at length, after many dangers braved and atrocities committed they drew rein beneath the peninsular rock of Chester. The citizens, already cowed by a repulse which they had suffered in Eadric's company at Shrewsbury, seem to have submitted without resistance; but they were not allowed to go scot-free, and we are told that 205 houses—almost one half of the entire number in the city—were destroyed. Even so Chester was more fortunate than the open country through which the King had come. A Worcestershire writer tells a piteous story of the starving country people who flocked southward to beg their bread at the doors of Evesham and other monasteries.[1] It is small wonder that the first Earl of Chester appointed by the King, his step-son the Fleming Gerbod, found the fief little to his liking and went home to fight in the domestic wars of Flanders, or that for some time after William's march no Norman priest dared show his face in those harried and resentful regions.

Still, the wars of independence seemed to have reached their end. The risings of Southern and Western England had collapsed before the energy of the King's lieutenants; and it was a hopeful sign for the future that, both at Exeter and at Montacute, the Norman cause had been supported by a number of the native English. Shortly after the submission of Chester Eadric the Wild. the last rebel of note who still remained in arms, came to the King and made his peace.

[1] *Chron. Evesham*, p. 90.

But there was one more centre of resistance left, and at the Outbreak at Peter-borough eleventh hour a new leader came forward to rouse the conquered nation for a last attempt at freedom. In the fen-country a warm welcome had been given to Jarl Osbiorn and the sons of Sweyn. The fact was duly noted by the Conqueror, and when the abbacy of Peterborough, lying on the outskirts of the disaffected region, was vacated by the death of Abbot Brand (November 27, 1069), his office was given to Turold of Fécamp, who had already shown, during a brief tenure of the abbacy of Malmesbury, that he possessed the qualities of a ruler and a warrior.[1] He set out for the scene of his new duties; and when he reached Stamford the news that a Norman had been appointed ran like wildfire through the fens. Certain of the Peterborough tenants sent to the Danish fleet, then lying at Ely, and offered their aid as guides to the famous Golden Borough, that the treasures which Saxon kings and magnates had bestowed might not become the prey of Frenchmen. The invitation was accepted with alacrity, and the Danes showed their affection for the monastery by stripping it bare and dispersing the community. When Turold, a few days later, rode into Peterborough with eight-score Norman knights behind him, he found a smoking heap of ruins and no man to greet him save one sick monk in the infirmary. From the minster everything of value had been taken; shrines and crosses and gospel-books and vestments, the abbot's crosier, the golden crown and foot-stool of the great Christ in the rood-loft, all were gone to swell the booty in the pirate camp at Ely. It was not to be expected that Turold or his master would pardon the Englishmen who had suggested such an outrage. The Peterborough tenants resolved that, with Danish help or without it, they would hold out to the last extremity; and after the departure of the fleet they fortified themselves in Ely. Their leader was one Hereward,[2] a man who had shown Hereward the Danes the way to Peterborough; of his antecedents we can say nothing with confidence except that he was a tenant of Peterborough, holding lands in the south-west of Lincolnshire, on the edge of the fen-country and not far from the manor of Bourne wi h which his name is linked in legends. To the same source we owe the information that he was a son of Leofric, Earl Godwin's rival, or otherwise connected with the House of Mercia to which

---

[1] W. Malmesb., *G. P.*, p. 420.   [2] See the Appendix.

the manor of Bourne originally belonged. The tradition comes to us through late and doubtful channels ; it may have been perverted to gratify the pride of families claiming descent from the last of Saxon leaders. There is an antecedent probability that one whose lead was accepted without question by men of the noblest English blood belonged to no mean stock. But in our most authentic sources of information Hereward appears, like Eadric, only after he has risen to a position of command. At an early date English poems were written in honour of the hero and sung throughout the fen-land. A part of one, professing to be founded on a work of Hereward's own chaplain, has been preserved in a Latin para- phrase.[1] It describes how he was outlawed at the petition of his own father, passed through marvellous adventures in Bernicia, Ire- land, and Cornwall, and then took service with the Count of Flanders; how the news of the Conquest brought him back to Eng- land, to avenge the murder of his brother by the Normans; and how he purged his home of alien intruders. Whatever may be the substratum of fact which underlies the story, truth and fable are so closely interwoven in it that one can hardly venture on the task of separating them. We are on somewhat firmer ground when we come to the stories which bear on the defence of Ely;[2] but even here we are baffled by the problem of arranging the anecdotes in their proper sequence and of extracting a continuous

The Here-narrative from them. Some of them appear to come from men
ward who had been present at Ely and were well acquainted with Here-
Cycle ward and his belongings. The hero himself is graphically described : a man short and stoutly made but wonderfully agile for his build, conspicuous for his long golden hair, with an oval face and eyes which were of a light colour but not exactly matched. His Flemish wife Torfrida is a more mysterious figure, whose very strangeness is perhaps a guarantee of the narrator's fidelity to fact ; a lady skilled in magic and given to the study of the liberal arts, who excelled all womankind in her luxury yet often displayed a man's sagacity in meeting every sort of danger ; so that when she separated from her husband many evils fell upon him for

[1] The *Gesta Herewardi*, printed in the second volume of Michel's *Chroniques Anglo-Normandes* and in the Rolls edition of Gaimar.
[2] See especially the *Historia Eliensis*, Bk. II., §§ 102 ff., which relates two sieges, the second apparently a duplicate of the first. The writer used good material, but with little skill ; his confusions are explained by his own statement (II., § 107) that he collected facts *de pluribus historiis*. Wendover, *s. a.*, 1071, gives some local traditions.

want of her advice, and he would often confess that things did
not go as well with him as in her day.[1]   Except for the personal
traits which they afford, these ballad fragments are valueless as
history.   But their existence is a fact which should not pass
unnoticed.   They are the material from which, under more favourable circumstances, an English epic of the Conquest might have
been constructed.   The Hereward whom they portray is the ideal
Englishman as conceived by the subjects of the Conqueror ; and it
is instructive to compare William, as he stands revealed in history
with the Hereward of legend.   The failure of the patriotic cause
becomes more intelligible when the typical patriot is contrasted
with the conqueror point by point; the one high-spirited,
resourceful, and adventurous, but inconsequent and devoid of
general ideas; the other solid, methodical, tenacious, a scientific
general and statesman, far sighted in his plans, immovable in
his purpose.

Hereward's rising first became important when the Earls
Edwin and Morcar proclaimed their sympathy with it by an abrupt The De-
departure from the court (1071).   Edwin indeed soon ceased to be fence of
                                                                Ely, 1071
a danger.   After six months of aimless wandering among the
Welsh, the Scots, and the English, he was treacherously slain by
his own men.   But Morcar reached the Isle of Ely; and his name
was sufficient to bring together all the northern leaders who were
still unreconciled with William.   Although the day of great rebellions was over there were men enough in the isle to make the
King uneasy, and he came in person " with ship-fyrd and with land-
fyrd " to conduct the siege.   He encountered an obstinate resistance
so long as the garrison of Ely kept faith with one another.   An attempt to reach the island by a causeway resulted in disaster.   Hereward and his men set fire to the rushes in the fen; the causeway,
built of trees and beams and hurdles, was totally consumed; and
the same fate befell a witch-wife whom, in deference to the super-
stitions of his soldiers, William had placed upon a wooden tower
to assist the forlorn hope with her incantations.   But treachery was
afterwards brought into play.   According to one version it was
Morcar who insisted on surrender because he put faith in the King's
false promises.   The local story said that the monks of Ely gave
the King admission, upon being threatened with the loss of all their

---

[1] See the *Gesta*, p. 337 (R. S.) and the pseudo-Ingulph in Fulman, p. 67.

lands outside the isle. By one means or another William made himself master of Ely before the year was ended. Hereward and his sworn companions effected their escape to the Bruneswald ; Morcar and the other leaders lost their liberty for good and all ; the men of humbler rank were mutilated and dismissed. The monks of Ely suffered treatment which clears them of treachery or convicts the King of faithlessness. William indeed made an offering of a mark of gold at the shrine of their patroness St. Æthelthryth ; but he exacted from her unworthy servants a fine which could only be paid by stripping her church of its most precious ornaments.

The End of Hereward

The later adventures of Hereward are narrated in some detail by the ballads, but possess no historical importance. Outlaws flocked to his standard in the Bruneswald. and for some time he remained a scourge to the Normans of the fen-land. The highest estimate of his forces puts them at a total of 700 men; his biographer says that he had no more than 100 mounted and 200 unmounted men with a few cross-bowmen and archers.[1] But the fyrds of nine counties were unable to dislodge him, and William was glad to grant him peace on honourable terms. Of his after-history there are two widely different accounts. One relates how he was slain by private enemies in 1073 when he was on the point of starting with the King for Maine ; but according to the *Gesta* he lived for many years and died a quiet death.[2] The question is insoluble and of no great moment. Hereward's career as a national leader ended with his flight from Ely. Thenceforward William was the undisputed King of England.

Settlement with Scotland, 1072

There was still some danger that Scotland would take up the cause of Edgar Atheling whose sister Margaret had been lately wedded to King Malcolm. The slight memorials of Margaret's career which we possess, the life by Turgot, the chapel in Edinburgh castle, the book of Devotions in the Bodleian library, have served to perpetuate the legend of her saintliness. But the love of power and family affection were deeply rooted in her nature ; and her marriage was followed by a revival of Malcolm's interest in her brother's fortunes. In 1072 William thought it necessary to overawe Scotland by an exhibition of armed force. Accompanied by a fleet he marched through Lothian to the Forth. The Scots retreated before him, and he found the country no better than

[1] *Gesta*, p. 393 (R. S.). Gaimar, 5554. [2] Gaimar. 5605. *Gesta, ad fin.*

a wilderness. But at Abernethy he was met by Malcolm. A treaty was arranged and among other hostages Malcolm gave his son. The exact terms of the treaty have been the subject of much controversy. It seems clear that Malcolm received a grant of lands in England and at the same time did homage to William. But the question still remains whether this homage was for Scotland or only for the English fief. The practical results of the treaty were threefold. It postponed for some years a renewal of hostilities between the two countries. It enabled William, for the first time, to deal freely with the lands between the Tyne and Tweed ; an opportunity of which he availed himself to degrade Gospatric from his earldom and confer it upon Waltheof, the most highly favoured of the loyal English. Finally the treaty secured the expulsion of the Atheling from Scotland. After a visit to Flanders, where he received hospitality but no encouragement, and an attempt to visit France which was frustrated by a storm, the luckless claimant took Malcolm's good advice and made his peace with William. The King of England readily granted favourable terms to one who, though contemptible as a leader, might be employed with effect by the unscrupulous kings of Edinburgh and Paris. Edgar received a pension and an estate in Hertfordshire ; he became a favourite at Court, and a bye-word for simplicity, although, for one brief period of three years, he showed, as a regent of Scotland, some statesmanlike ability (1097-1100). He found in William's eldest son a congenial spirit ; they travelled in company on the first Crusade ; and the last appearance of the Atheling in history is at the field of Tinchebrai, where he fought on Robert's side. More fortunate than his patron he received a full pardon from Henry I., and lived obscurely in a private station to extreme old age.[1]

---

[1] W. Malmesb., *G. R.*, iii., § 251. *A. S. C.* (E. text), *s.a.* 1085.

CHAPTER II

THE REORGANISATION OF ENGLAND

Char-
acter of
William's
Measures
WITH the year 1072 we enter upon the second stage of
William's reign. The next fifteen years were, for England, comparatively peaceful; the events which mark them are for
the most part events on a foreign soil, the results of a continental
policy which, although Norman in its origin and objects, depended
upon the resources of England for success and had the effect of
making England a member of the European system. These events,
small in themselves, but prophetic of the future and eloquent of
the change in England's relations with the surrounding world,
must be noticed in their place. But first it will be well to describe
the steps by which, in the course of these fifteen years, the State,
the Church, and the relations of the two, were transformed to suit
the ideas of William and his councillors; and to give some idea of
the new order of things which ensued from the grafting of Norman
ideals upon English traditions, of feudal upon Anglo-Saxon law.
William was no legislator. The law-book known as the *Lois de
Guillaume* is a late and unauthorised compilation of customs collected from all kinds of sources.[1] The authentic *Leges*, when
stripped of later accretions, are neither numerous nor important
except as indications of a larger policy. The most significant of
them was a statement of the King's conservative intentions in respect of private law: "I command that all men have and hold the
law of Eadward with those additions which I have ordained for the
advantage of the English people".[2] Beyond these we have only
an ordinance separating the spiritual from the secular law-courts,[3]

---

[1] Matzke. *Lois de Guillaume*, p. lii.

[2] *Select Charters*, p. 98. This version of the Leges, from the *Textus Roffensis*,
is more authentic than the longer version which is printed in the *Foedera* from the
Red Book of the Exchequer. See Stubbs' *Lectures on Early English History* (1906),
pp. 57-89, the best commentary.

[3] *Select Charters*, p. 99. Probably of the year 1076 (Böhmer. *Kirche und Staat*,
p. 92).

and some ecclesiastical canons which William approved and possibly assisted in framing.[1] He had little inclination and less aptitude for expressing his policy in general terms. It is only by analysing and comparing his administrative measures that we discover the general principles which undoubtedly underlay his government ; and it is often difficult to say whether he foresaw the full effects of his most celebrated measures. But for our present purpose it is more important to observe what he actually effected than to ask what he may have intended.

In the distribution of confiscated lands he followed a course which was suggested by the traditional policy of the Norman dukes and facilitated by the manner of the Conquest. England was reduced, as we have seen, piecemeal ; and every Norman of consequence who shared in each new enterprise clamoured for a portion of its spoils. Hence, when the conquest and the division were complete, many barons had been invested with enormous fiefs, but these were as a rule composed of manors scattered over the length and breadth of England ; and the settlers had no more prospect of establishing dependent principalities in England than formerly in Normandy. But in Normandy it had been the rule to bestow appanages of unusual size and compactness on the relations and connections of the ducal house ; and the fief of Bellême upon the border of Maine was an isolated but a striking precedent for the appointment of local viceroys with unusual powers to protect and extend a disputed frontier. Such appanages and viceroyalties made their appearance on a larger scale in England.[2] Of the Conqueror's half-brothers, Odo of Bayeux received the greater part of Kent, and Robert of Mortain the greater part of Cornwall, each with the title and powers of an earl in his own shire. William of Warenne, the husband of the Conqueror's step-daughter Gundrada, became Earl of Surrey [3]; while Odo of Champagne, who had married William's sister, is said to have received the Honour of Holderness although the grant, if actually made, was posterior to the compilation of the Domesday Book. Such grants as these were probably suggested by family feeling rather than by political considerations. But other positions of no less importance were conferred on men

---

[1] Eadmer, *Hist. Nov.*, i., p. 6. Wilkins, *Concilia*, i., p. 367. *Vita Lanfranci*, § 33 (ed. Giles).

[2] See the Appendix.

[3] Perhaps not till the next reign ; see Orderic, iii., 217 and note. On Gundrada, see Freeman's article in *E. H. R.*, ii., 680-701.

whose soldierly abilities formed their chief title to promotion. In the west, Hugh Lupus, who succeeded Gerbod the Fleming in the earldom of Chester, Roger of Montgomery the Earl of Shropshire, and William Fitzosbern Earl of Hereford, were either the sole or the greatest tenants-in-chief in their respective shires; they legislated, appointed sheriffs, did justice, and made war upon the Welsh with almost as much freedom as a Count of Maine or Anjou enjoyed in his own sphere. Similarly in the north the Honour of Richmond was conferred first on Brient of Penthièvre and, when he died, upon his brother Alain;[1] while the earldom of Bernicia passed from Gospatric to Waltheof, from Waltheof to Walcher bishop of Durham, then to a certain Alberic, and finally to Robert Mowbray. In districts less disturbed by national resistance and foreign invasion some analogous but less extensive grants were made. Thus Ralph the Staller acquired the earldom of Norfolk and the custody of Norwich Castle; while in other cases a powerful baron received one or more shrievalties which he contrived to make hereditary and the first step to an earldom. Of these successful aspirants Henry of Beaumont at Warwick is a good example. Such an increase of dignity did not always mean enlarged

The Earls under the Conqueror

authority. In fact nothing was further from William's thoughts than to allow any but the most favoured and indispensable of his lieutenants to enjoy the ancient powers of an earl.[2] It was not enough for him that, of the older and larger earldoms, Mercia and Northumbria (in the original sense) could be suppressed after the final ruin of Edwin and Morcar; or that Huntingdon and Northampton, on the fall of Waltheof, passed into the hands of a nonentity, Simon of St. Liz, who was probably recommended as much by his insignificance as by his marriage with Waltheof's daughter. The rights of the lesser earls were diminished whenever opportunities occurred, and had become comparatively slight at the end of William's reign. They may have led the military forces of their earldoms; they may have held demesne-lands in virtue of their office.[3] But the only right which they indubitably enjoyed was that of receiving the third-penny from the profits of the shire-

---

[1] De la Borderie, *Histoire de Bretagne*, iii., p. 25.

[2] See Appendix, "The Earls of the Norman Period".

[3] See the *Instit. Cnuti* in *Textus Roffensis*, p. 45, for a mention of the "comitales villae quae pertinent ad comitatum"; and Round, *F. E.*, p. 114, for an instance of such lands in Somerset.

court and in some cases the third-penny of a borough's revenues.
In matters of justice and finance, and for all the ordinary purposes
of local government, the King preferred to act either through extraordinary commissioners in whom we may see the descendants of
the Carolingian missi and the prototypes of the English Justices in
Eyre, or else through the sheriffs who, although usually of baronial
rank, were attached to the royal interests by the consciousness
that their offices might be taken from them at a moment's notice.
It was through the sheriff that the King in general, controlled not
only the earls but the whole body of the baronage, chastising the
least usurpation, and noting the least sign of discontent.

This constant surveillance produced a widespread irritation; The Ris-
and in the year 1075 a rebellion broke out which, although ulti- ing of the
mately joined by few, received in its early stages some countenance 1075
from a number of the most influential lords and prelates.	It began
with Roger, Earl of Hereford and Ralph Guader, Earl of East
Anglia, two barons of the younger generation.	The original griev-
ance was the prohibition of a marriage which had been arranged
between Ralph and the sister of his friend.	It was aggravated
by the conduct of royal sheriffs who asserted rights of jurisdiction over Ralph's estates;[1] and the aggrieved youths ransacked
the history of William's career for examples of ingratitude and
perfidy, with which to stir the sympathies of their equals and
inferiors.	In the absence of the King from England the forbidden
marriage was celebrated with publicity and splendour.	Under
cover of the bridal feast, a conspiracy took shape into which Earl
Waltheof was enticed.	His name was expected to be valuable
to the enterprise because the two prime movers counted more on
English than on Norman help.	They are said to have suggested
the division of England into three earldoms for themselves and
Waltheof, and to have dangled the prospect of the crown before
his eyes.[2]	The extravagance of these proposals was apparent, and
the sincerity of the proposers more than doubtful.	Waltheof soon
repented of engagements into which, if we could trust his own
excuses, he had only entered on compulsion.	He disclosed the plot
to Lanfranc, who in conjunction with the Chief Justiciars immedi-

---

[1] *Lanfranci Opera*, i., 64 (ed. Giles).	Letters xxxvii., xxxviii., xlvi., in this collec-
tion, are valuable for the history of the revolt.
[2] Orderic, ii., 261.	*Cf.* the *Vita et Passio Waldevi Comitis* (ed. Michel), pp. 112 ff.

2

ately undertook to deal with it.   The alarm of the government is
evinced by the conciliatory tone which was at first adopted towards
Earl Ralph.   But when his defiance precipitated war, the weakness of his party was at once exposed ; and Lanfranc could soon
assure the King that nothing in the situation called for his return.
Waltheof's defection left the earls without a claim on English

Suppres-
sion of the
Rising.
sympathy.   Roger, on attempting to leave Hereford and effect
a junction with his ally, found the passage of the Severn barred
against him by the fyrd of Worcestershire.   The loyalty of these
English troops was confirmed by the exhortations of two English
prelates, Wulfstan Bishop of Worcester and Æthelwig Abbot of
Evesham ;[1] Earl Roger was held at bay, while in the east the rising
of Earl Ralph collapsed before another force of the same character.   Ralph had collected mercenary troops and, for his mother's
sake, was supported by some of the Bretons who had shared in the
labours and the booty of the Conquest ; but he was defeated in his
first encounter with the Justiciars and their English followers, and
fled to Norwich Castle.   His last hopes depended on a fleet which
Sweyn of Denmark had promised, but delayed, to send him.   Leaving
Norwich Castle to be defended by his bride the earl sailed for
Denmark to plead his cause in person.   He obtained his wish
and a fleet of two hundred vessels shortly appeared on the East
Anglian coast.   But Norwich had already surrendered when the
fleet arrived.   The Danish captains consoled themselves by plundering York Minster; but with this exploit ended the last Danish
invasion of England, and the first rising of the new baronage
against the crown.

Fate of
Waltheof
The king's hand fell heavily upon the chief conspirators, although he was scrupulous to keep within the letter of the law.
The penalties for treason were milder in Normandy than in England ; and Earl Roger, in virtue of his Norman birth, escaped
with a sentence of perpetual imprisonment.   Waltheof, in whose
innocence the King had affected to believe so long as the rebellion
lasted and English sympathy was still of value, suffered the death-
penalty prescribed for treason by old English law.[2]   He was found

[1] Florence.
[2] S. C., p. 70 (Law of Alfred). W. Malm., *G. R.*, iii., § 255, apologises for William ;
Waltheof had concealed part of the truth from William.   Florence, however, takes
the side of Waltheof, and is in such a matter the preferable authority.   Orderic, ii.,
265, accuses Judith of informing against her husband.   So the pseudo-Ingulph,
p. 72, and the *Vita et Passio*, p. 100.

guilty at the same Council which condemned Earl Roger; but the final sentence was delayed in Waltheof's case; it was only after five months had elapsed that he was beheaded at Winchester, without publicity and at an early hour of the day, for fear lest a rescue might be attempted. Lanfranc, who heard his last confession, pronounced him guiltless of the offence for which he died. Although we have only the word of English sympathisers to support the theory that his death was demanded by his own wife and by Normans who coveted his lands, it may well have been true that William was moved by other considerations than those of abstract justice. He may have been alarmed by the casual offer of the conspirators to place Waltheof on the throne; he may have felt the temptation to sweep from his path the last of the old race of English earls. The third and principal offender, Ralph of Norfolk, *Later* was pursued by William's vengeance to the refuge which he had *history* *of Earl* found in Brittany. Unable to live at peace with superiors of any *Ralph* kind, Ralph plunged into a conspiracy against Duke Hoel and assisted Geoffrey, Count of Rennes, to hold the Castle of Dol against their common lord. In the autumn of 1076 William crossed the Channel to join with Hoel in the siege of Dol. Their enterprise failed of its immediate purpose since Philip of France shook off his habitual sloth, came up in haste, at the invitation of the rebels, and raised the siege.[1] But William, although humiliated for the moment by his suzerain, had gained the main object for which he undertook his expedition. While he lived, no baron dared to emulate the example of the fallen earls.

How little the King relaxed his jealous watch upon the baronage *Arrest of* in later years may be seen from the fate of Odo of Bayeux, who *Bishop* *Odo, 1082* had been one of his most trusted agents. A bishop more in sympathy with the knights whose garb he imitated than with the humble scholars whose eulogies he purchased by his patronage, magnificent in all his tastes, and possessed by an ambition which disdained the most honourable of subordinate positions, Odo was ill content with an English earldom. Early in the reign his encroachments upon the estates of Canterbury embroiled him with the Primate Lanfranc, and from that time Odo's influence at court

---

[1] Date in the *Chron. S. Albini* (Bouquet, xii., 479). *Cf.* also Bouquet, xii., 479 *n.*, and De la Borderie, *Histoire de Bretagne*, iii., p. 27. Freeman's account (iv., p. 636) is vitiated by his reliance on Orderic who confuses the two sieges of Dol, in 1076 and 108). Earl Ralph remained in Brittany till 1096, then joined the Norman contingent in the First Crusade. He died before the capture of Jerusalem.

had waned.   In popular estimation he was still the second man in England; but we know that he was excluded from one or two of the commissions of regency which the King appointed during his frequent visits to the Continent;[1] and even if this exclusion was not habitual it must have galled him.   He began to form wild projects for his own aggrandisement which clashed with William's wishes; and in 1082 he gathered his friends and vassals for a foreign expedition.   A current story made Rome his destination, and declared that he had fixed his hopes upon the reversion of the Papacy; but it is more likely that his purpose was to intervene in the wars of Emperor and Pope and procure from Gregory VII. a reward in the shape of spiritual or secular promotion.[2] Whatever the project it was great enough to allure the Earl of Chester; and the two were already preparing to leave England when the King, who had been absent in Normandy, was informed of their project and returned in time to prohibit their departure and arrest his half-brother.   The levying of troops within the kingdom was illegal and a menace to the peace.   Even if William believed that Odo's mysterious movements were in no way directed against himself he could not submit to see England depleted of her Norman settlers by the emigration of every magnate who nursed an imaginary grievance.   Odo's plea that, as a bishop, he was answerable only to the See of Rome availed him nothing.   By Lanfranc's advice the King evaded an answer to the abstract claim (based on the forgeries of the Pseudo-Isidore), and replied that in Odo he arrested not the Bishop of Bayeux but his steward and the Earl of Kent.   Odo remained in prison till the King's death.   No punishment fell upon the Earl of Chester; nor do we hear that any of Odo's less important allies suffered for his offence.   The single example was sufficient.

The Oath of Salisbury, 1086   Suspicions of the same character led William in 1086 to a more remarkable and sweeping measure.   The preceding year had been troubled by well founded rumours that Cnut of Denmark, the son and successor of Sweyn Estrithsson, was preparing a fleet of unexampled size for the purpose of recovering England; and William

---

[1] Stubbs, *C. H.*, i., p. 375.

[2] Orderic, iii., 188.   The *Roman de Rou*, 9208 ff., suggests that the real cause of Odo's disgrace was a design to secure the succession for himself.   This is to some extent confirmed by the Conqueror's death-bed speech as reported in Orderic, iii., 247.   But see Giesebrecht's *Deutsche Kaiserzeit*, iii., p. 53, and the letter of Gregory, *Register*, viii., 60.

had seen fit to import a mercenary army in the autumn and to keep a part of it on foot throughout the winter. The domestic difficulties of Cnut led to the postponement of his expedition; on July 10th, 1086, he was assassinated and his wild scheme went with him to the grave. But before this news was known in England the King had summoned an extraordinary meeting of his tenants and their vassals. It was held on the first of August, at Salisbury, and all who attended were required to take an oath that they would be King William's men against all enemies. The form of the oath may have been that which is given among his authentic laws. If so, the purport of the oath was not altogether what is commonly supposed. The recorded formula is evidently framed with an eye to the contingencies of invasion and usurpation. It implies the doctrine that allegiance overrides all other ties of fealty—a doctrine which was nothing new in England or in France.[1] But the doctrine is merely latent in the oath; and there are reasons for doubting whether the doctrine was universally recognised in England before the reign of Henry I. Too much importance has been attached to the meeting of 1086, which was a temporary expedient to meet a temporary danger. The meeting cannot possibly have included all landowners; and although it is possible that, after the meeting, the oath was taken by the suitors of every shire-court, such proceedings do not in any way denote the introduction of a new theory of sovereignty.

It is a remarkable testimony to the force of custom that William whose interest it was to loosen the bonds between lords and their dependants should, on the contrary, have furthered the introduction of feudal tenures and feudal incidents. It is plain from Domesday Book that he encouraged the process by which the allodial freeholder of the Anglo-Saxon period was degraded to the position of a mesne tenant. Nor was this all; the King allowed his tenants-in-chief to assume, over all who held of them, certain rights of jurisdiction which they had indeed enjoyed as a matter of course on their estates in Normandy, but which according to the principles of English law could only be claimed in virtue of a special grant from the Crown.[2] That the Conqueror was not entirely ignorant of this theory may be inferred from his charters to religious houses in which even the smallest rights of jurisdiction

Private franchises

---

[1] For the existence of the doctrine in France, see Adam, *Origin of the English Constitution*, p. 187.

[2] See on this subject Maitland, *Select Pleas in Manorial Courts*, Introd., *passim*.

that may be exercised by the recipients of his bounty are carefully enumerated. But in his grants to lay-lords, which were usually made by word of mouth, he would seem to have observed less caution. As in Normandy, so in England, he granted the right to "hold the pleas of the crown" with a sparing hand. But it seems to have been taken as a matter of course that a baron, besides instituting a feudal court for his military tenants, should **Manorial** also exercise through manor-courts the whole or part of the juris-**Juris-** diction of the hundred-court. The general rule which William **diction** laid down that the courts of hundreds, no less than those of shires, should preserve their ancient competence became, through his own grants, a dead letter; and the importance of the hundred-courts steadily diminished from the moment of the Conquest, although Henry I. and his successors made several efforts to revive them. The manorial court was in many cases older than the Conquest;[1] and, even where it had not existed, the rule that the lord was responsible for the good behaviour of his tenants must have invested him with a quasi-magisterial authority since, in early law, the functions of the surety, the constable, and the magistrate are seldom rigorously distinguished. The Norman Conquest encouraged the development of inchoate rights and took away their exceptional character from those which were already well established. Leaving untouched the old agricultural economy, and even preserving to some extent the Anglo-Saxon system of police[2] which had been based upon it, the new dynasty and baronage converted the estate which had been no more than a farm, an agricultural unit, into a liberty or jurisdiction. The process was incomplete when Domesday was compiled; in the minds of the compilers *manerium* was still synonymous with *terra*.[3] But the change by which the manor-court became an important feature in our judicial system had already begun in the year 1087; the documents of the next century show that once begun, it was rapidly completed.

[1] The theory that the manorial court is but the continuation of a primitive township-moot is rejected by Professor Maitland, *Domesday Book and Beyond*, p. 147, on the ground that no mention of a township-moot occurs in any of our texts. Professor Vinogradoff, *Growth of the Manor*, p. 273, adduces a passage from Domesday (i., 269, *b*) as implying the existence of a township-court; but the passage will bear another construction.

[2] Even if the frankpledge system was the invention of the Norman kings (see Morris, *The Frankpledge System* (1910) c. 1), a theory rejected by Maitland and Liebermann, it is only an elaboration of the Anglo-Saxon expedient of suretyship.

[3] See the article by Mr. Round in *E. H. R.*, xv., p. 293; a reply to the theory of Professor Maitland that *manerium* was already a word " charged with technical meaning ".

It is difficult to estimate the change which was thus produced The Villein-Class in the condition of the lower orders.   Their opportunities of combination were so slight that we cannot take their patience as a proof of their contentment.   We know that the class of petty freeholders decreased and that the Norman lawyer paid little heed to the nice gradations intermediate between servitude and freedom which the law of Edward recognised.   There was too a disposition to regard as serfs all who rendered agricultural services to a lord, although many who held by such services had been free men in the past.   We note with satisfaction that the class of slaves decreased and vanished under Norman rule, but our satisfaction is tempered by a doubt whether this was due so much to the elevation of the slave as to the depression of the villein.   Certain facts suggest that in old English law the civil rights of the villein were protected even against his lord, that the shire-court could intervene to save him from eviction or from the increase of his customary services.[1]   But the new jurisprudence recognised no limit to the demands which a lord might make upon the time and labour of his villeins, and counted all that they possessed as his.   Furthermore it was considered lawful to sell the villein with or without his holding.   In 1088, for instance, when William of St. Calais was proclaimed a rebel, the villeins on his Yorkshire manors were seized and sold or held to ransom by the sheriff.[2]   To this extent the villein was regarded as a slave.   On the other hand there were some rules of law and economic facts which ameliorated his condition.   If assailed by his master, and still more if assailed by a third party, in life or limb or honour, the villein was entitled, at the worst of times, to such protection as the shire-court could afford.   Among the numerous villeins of the royal demesne there were many who kept their old civil rights, the Crown being the first of landlords to recognise the expedience of a generous policy towards its tenants.   For the villeins of private owners flight, though neither an easy nor a pleasant course, was always a possible alternative to the endurance of excessive requisitions; in

---

[1] Vinogradoff, *Villeinage, passim.*

[2] Monasticon, i., 245.   Vinogradoff, *Growth of Manor*, p. 346.   But there was a strong feeling against the separation of the villein from his holding.   See *Lois de Guillaume*, § 25 (Schmid, 341), " Nec licet dominis removere colonos a terra dummodo debita servitia persolvant ".   The *Dial. de Scaccario*, i., § 11, calls the villein *adscripticium*.

growing towns or depopulated manors the fugitive was welcome
and no questions were asked about his antecedents.   Consequently
we find that the earliest manorial records (they date from the reign
of Henry I.) recognise the fixity of the labour services in which
the villein chiefly paid his rent.[1]   It might be the legal right, but
it was not the interest, of the lord to increase the services at his
pleasure or to maintain them at an intolerable level.

Mesne Tenants

We cannot suppose that prudential motives weighed less powerfully with the lords in their treatment of free tenants.   But
subsequent legislation proves the existence of serious abuses and
it is not difficult to see how these arose.   Frequently the lord
obtained the power of life and death over thieves and other classes
of offenders, if caught within his territory.   When they were the
tenants of another lord their trial was watched by a royal Justice;
but when the judge was also lord no such definite check existed.
The ordinary feudal court was but a shade less dangerous to liberty
in the cases, naturally frequent, where the vassals by whom the
judgments ought to have been framed were either insignificant or
timid.   A frivolous claim might lead, if the demandant's appeal
to the ordeal of battle were admitted by the court, to the
disgrace and dispossession of a rightful owner.   The law of forfeiture was more elastic than it should have been, and fines were
commonly out of all proportion to the infractions of feudal duty
which they punished.   An appeal to the shire-court was only possible when the technical formalities of justice had been neglected
in the private court.   Within a narrow sphere the shire-court still
possessed importance.   Quarrels between tenants-in-chief or the
mesne tenants of different lords might be adjusted there according
to the ancient laws and customs; and we hear of cases in which
Normans as powerful as Bishop Odo and the sheriff Picot were
constrained to give the redress which these laws demanded.   For
the rest, the shire-court was more occupied with criminal justice
and with fiscal business than with helping inferiors against their
lords.

Types of the New Baronage

Much depended on the character of the individual lord and
sheriff.   An Ivo de Taillebois or a Robert of Bellême knew neither
justice nor prudence in his dealings with inferiors; and the tenant's
plight cannot have been much bettered when he appealed from such

[1] See the extents in the *Liber Niger* of Peterborough (Camden Society).

judges to a Picot or an Urse of Abitôt. B it there were better types than these to be found in the new ruing class. Arnulf de Hesdin, not the least important of the Conqueror's barons, is highly praised by an English writer [1] who had some personal knowledge of him, as a man who was remarkable for the skill with which he farmed his lands and the liberality which he displayed towards his poorer neighbours. Roger of Montgomery was somewhat censured by his English burgesses at Shrewsbury for a fancied partiality to the Frenchmen who had settled side by side with them ; and Hugh Lupus of Chester was a gross and boisterous prodigal. But Orderic Vitalis, who had known their English subjects, and was himself a native of their marches, felt a sincere respect for them ; and the Earl of Chester is further recommended to posterity by his close friendship with the saintly Anselm. It may be that in these men we have rare exceptions, and that they were only praised by comparison with a prevailing ruffianism. But we have good reason for thinking that what had been the exception in the first, became the rule in the second, generation of the Anglo-Norman baronage. In the days of Rufus and of Henry I power passed from the hands of the Ivos and Urses to those of men like Richard of Rulos, the knight who is remembered in the traditions of Crowland for liberal benefactions, the draining of the Depedene fen, and the foundation of new villages where previously there had been wastes tenanted only by the water-fowl.[2]

On the towns the first effects of the Norman Conquest were The no doubt disastrous. There were few which escaped so lightly Towns as London, Exeter and Winchester. From Domesday we obtain an almost unvarying story of castles built, of royal dues increased, of houses destroyed or dismantled, wherever there had been, or might still be, resistance. The result was a temporary decrease in the numbers of the burgess population. But the houses of that age were easily rebuilt, and much rebuilding had in fact been done by the year 1086. Trade silently returned to the accustomed channels when " the good peace " of the Conqueror was

---

[1] Will. Malmesb., *G. P.*, p. 437 : " Mirus ad agriculturae sollertiam, mirus ad munifice sullevandam pauperum inopiam ".

[2] Pseudo-Ingulph, p. 78. Mr. Round (*F. E* , p. 166) attacks the tradition as " quaintly anachronistic ". No doubt the author's chronological indications are confused. But Richard of Rulos, who belongs to the generation after Arnulf de Hesdin, may well have imitated that baron's zeal for agriculture without committing an anachronism.

2*

established ; and the temporary losses due to war and pillage were more than compensated by the new maikets which union with Normandy opened to the English merchant.   Colonies of foreign traders had already commenced to settle in London and other ports of the east coast before the death of the Confessor.   They now increased in number and in importance ; while the immigration of Jews, the only capitalists in an age when usury of any kind was a forbidden trade for Christians, was a sign and perhaps a cause of increased commercial activity.

Town govern- ment

There were but few changes in the government of the towns. The charter which William gave to London is but a guarantee of ancient privileges.   The care with which Domesday records the customs of less important towns proves that towards these also William's policy was conservative.   Even where the outward appearance of a town was altered by the building of a castle or the introduction of a Norman garrison, life flowed on in the old channels ; the castellan was not allowed to assume a dictatorship.   The lords of the soil on which the town was built might cause trouble by pushing the jurisdiction of their courts to the furthest point and claiming this or that indignant burgess as a serf.   But the King's peace was over all, and the King saw his interest in upholding the good laws of the Confessor.   The Frenchmen who had come in since the Conquest may have enjoyed for a time the benefit of their native laws and customs ; they were certainly privileged in respect of tallages and other dues ; and sometimes they formed a separate quarter in their place of settlement, enjoying special favours and immunities. But the municipal customs of English burgesses remained unaltered. The lawmen of Lincoln and Stamford, the judges at York and Chester, the folk-moot and husting in London, assembled and did justice as of old by the forms of compurgation and ordeal, and in accordance with a law of immemorial antiquity.[1]   The Norman sheriff, or his deputy, exercised considerable powers in matters which concerned the Crown.   He enforced military service ; he collected the royal dues wherever the borough had failed as yet to secure the privilege of farming these for a lump sum ; he presided in the borough-court.   But in matters of domestic concern the folk-moot

[1] Lawman, *judex*, doomsman are synonymous terms ; *cf.* the *Memorials of South- well Minster*, p. 192 (ed. Leach).   The existence of borough-courts at this time is denied by Ballard, *D. B. Boroughs*, pp. 51-53.   But see Miss Bateson's remarks in *E. H. R.*, xx., p. 147.

of householders paying scot and lot was left to legislate for the community; and in the law-court the sheriff had no power to shape the judgments. These were delivered by the doomsmen, and it only lay with him to execute the doom. The boroughs were thus to a great extent autonomous. But corporate life and activity, if they were not destroyed, were on the other hand not directly stimulated by the conditions of the new era. The Conquest brought to urban centres an increase of wealth and luxury, a larger knowledge of the external world, its thoughts and doings. But the time had not yet arrived when foreign example was to produce municipal democracy. In northern France the communal movement had just begun, and in 1072 the province of Maine produced an urban republic of a revolutionary kind. But the commune of Le Mans withered in the iron grip of the Conqueror before it had time to cast seed either on Norman or on English soil.

The central government of England passed through some changes in this reign, but of the changes none were radical. What chiefly strikes the observer is the increased energy and method of the administration, the constant attention which the king in person devotes to all affairs of government; of new organs for the expression of the royal will we hear little or nothing. Thus the exchequer and its financial system remained substantially the same; the King's hoard was still kept at Winchester, the old West Saxon capital, and received the same sorts of dues as heretofore; one large item in William's revenue was still the rent of food and provender which came in from his demesnes.[1] But all dues from the Danegeld downwards were assessed and exacted with more care. We do not need the assurances of chroniclers to convince us that the compiler of Domesday was wealthier and more provident than any King before him. Again there was little outward distinction between the Great Councils in which the king met his chief vassals and the Witans of Anglo-Saxon sovereigns, except that the assemblies over which William presided were held with greater pomp, and every tenant-in-chief was expected to produce his full military quota, that the king might review the feudal host and his foreign guests convince themselves of his readiness for war.[2] The same men

Central Administration

---

[1] *Dialogus de Scaccario* (Oxford edition, 1902), pp. 89, 90.
[2] W. Malmesb., *G. R.*, iii., § 279. A writ of Rufus relating to the duty of attendance " in festis " is printed in the Ramsay Cartulary, vol. i., p. 235.

deliberated in the Council who would have deliberated in a Witan, and the same business, judicial and political, came under their consideration. But whereas the meetings of the Witan had become those of an oligarchy dictating to a titular king, the Great Council, in political matters, had rarely to do more than hear and approve the previous decisions of a vigorous master.[1] In the names and attributes of the great executive officials there is some change; but those of William, like those of the Confessor, are chiefly members of the royal household who have been charged with public duties, and although the household of a Norman Duke differed in details from that of a West-Saxon King there was a strong general resemblance, since both were copies of the Carolingian model.[2] Here again what strikes us as really new is the increase of activity, the constant use of the household as a means for putting into execution the resolves of one controlling mind. In time the change of spirit produced a change of form, and the increase of public business elevated inferior but more industrious officials at the expense of the great nobles who held the highest posts by hereditary right. And even in the reign of William we discern the beginnings of an office to which the new bureaucracy would in the future be subordinated. During his frequent visits to the Continent the duty of representing him for ordinary purposes devolved upon commissions of Justiciars, among whom the lead seems to have been taken by some trusted individual, a William Fitzosbern, an Odo, or a Lanfranc. From this practice arose the office of the Chief Justiciar.

Domesday Book, 1085-6

In no measure is the methodical character of the new government revealed more clearly than in the compilation of the Domesday survey. The practice of employing a sworn jury to ascertain the rights of the sovereign was no novelty in France; and geld-rolls of particular localities had been compiled, presumably on the evidence of such juries, at earlier dates in William's reign.[3] But

[1] The Ordinance separating the Spiritual and Temporal Courts is issued "communi concilio et consilio" (S. C., p. 99). The Domesday survey was ordered after "deep speech" with the Great Council (A. S. C., 1085). But we hear surprisingly little of the Great Council on other occasions. On the Great Council in Normandy, see Lappenberg, ii., p. 20, and Haskins in the *Amer. Hist. Review*, xiv., pp. 472-4.

[2] Lappenberg, ii., p. 21.

[3] See De Gray Birch, *Introduction to Domesday*, for these earlier rolls: the Northamptonshire Geld Roll is printed by Ellis in his Introduction to the Record Edition of Domesday; the Inquisitio Geldi (of 1084) in the same volume with the Exon Domesday, pp. 1-75.

the new survey surpassed all previous experiments in comprehensiveness and wealth of detail. It was ordered after a discussion in the Christmas Council of 1085, and carried out, in spite of many complaints and some rioting against the innovation, in the course of the year 1086.[1] Special commissioners went on circuit through the hundreds and addressed a string of questions to sworn juries comprising, besides Norman settlers, the priest, the reeve, and six villeins, from each township. A list of the questions has been preserved, and may be translated to show the minuteness of the survey:—

" What is the name of your manor? Who held it under King Edward? Who holds it now? how many hides does it contain? how many ploughs are there on the demesne, and how many belong to the tenants? how many villeins, cottiers, slaves, freemen, socmen, are there? how much woodland? how much meadow? how many pastures? how many mills? how many fishponds? how much land has been added or taken away? what used to be the value of the whole? what is the value now? how much did each freeman and socman hold? how much does he hold now?"

We still possess copies of the original returns relating to the estates of the religious house of Ely. The information which these and the rest contained was rearranged to form the Domesday Book; a register which was preserved in the treasury at Winchester and was, at least as late as the reign of Henry II., the decisive authority on all questions of taxation and royal dues. The country is taken shire by shire; in most cases the account of the shire begins with the chief borough or boroughs; then follows the survey of the royal demesne; and thirdly the tenants-in-chief are taken one by one. The survey, as we possess it, is incomplete, for it ignores the four northern shires, and a number of towns, amongst them Winchester and London. Omitting all facts which have no bearing on the fiscal interests of the Crown it often fails us where we are most in need of information; the scanty references which it makes to institutions have raised more questions than we can ever hope to solve. But it is a mine of information respecting local customs, the relative strength and distribution of social classes, the territorial possessions of great families, the manner and extent of Norman colonisation, the industries and resources of each several shire; in innumerable details it enables us to correct and supplement the narratives of the chroniclers.

[1] See the contemporary account, discovered and edited by W. H. Stevenson, in *E. H. R.*, xxii., pp. 72 ff.

Ecclesi-
astical
Appoint-
ments

Important as these measures were they are rivalled in importance by the reforms which William sanctioned in the English
Church.   Certain of his ecclesiastical measures have an obvious
political significance; it was one of the simplest devices for secur
ing his supremacy that he should take every opportunity of filling
English sees and abbacies with Normans chosen either from his
chapel or from religious foundations, such as that of St. Stephen
at Caen, which were intimately connected with his dynasty; and
we have good reason for supposing that in his frequent depositions
of obnoxious English prelates and in the selection of their successors
he paid more attention to expediency than to the requirements
of the canons.[1]   Still of his appointments some were conspicuously
good and hardly one can be denounced as scandalous.   Here and
there his nominees showed a deplorable want of tact, but even in
Thurstan of Glastonbury, the most notorious of them all in this
respect, his English detractors could not deny the existence of piety
and a certain fervour for the interests of religion.   The ordinary
Anglo-Norman prelate showed himself a good steward of his church,
a mighty builder, a zealot for order and decency.   The best of them
added to these the higher qualities of the reformer.

William
and the
Papacy

The Conquest of England was undertaken with the Pope's
approval; but Alexander's sanction had only been granted, after
considerable hesitation, at the urgent request of the future Gregory
VII.[2]   We are entitled to conjecture that the Conqueror was under
pledges to do much more than free the English Church from a
usurping and schismatic primate.   William was expected to justify
his enterprise by realising in England the programme of reform
associated with the names of Cluni and of Hildebrand; and he was
willing to fulfil the expectation.   Although the Norman Dukes had
always been tenacious of their right to appoint and remove bishops
and abbots at their pleasure, though William in particular had
been quick to resent any hint of Papal interference in this matter,
yet in other respects his predecessors and himself had welcomed
the Cluniac ideas; they had encouraged the foundation of new
monasteries and schools for clerks; they had invited foreigners
to assist them in the work of reform; and William had even
acknowledged the benefits to be obtained from following the advice

[1] So Eadmer, *H. N.*, p. 9.   Florence, *s.a.* 1070.   Orderic, ii., 225; iii., 240.
[2] See Gregory's letter to William in *Monumenta Gregoriana*, p. 414.

of the Holy See in purely spiritual matters.[1]   He desired to pursue
the same policy in England, and to execute any changes which
Rome desired, subject to the condition that the Pope should not
abuse his position as an authority on matters of discipline and
doctrine to intervene between the King and the clergy in their
temporal relations.

There was much need of reform in the English Church; it failed State
to reach, not only the Hildebrandine ideal, but even the moderate of the
English
level of efficiency and purity which two or three generations of Church
reform had secured in France and Burgundy.   From a modern
point of view it may seem a matter of indifference that Cluniac
monasticism, after producing a brief period of ferment in the
England of Edgar and Dunstan, had abandoned the hopeless task
of converting the stolid island clergy to the practice of a stricter
rule; that English monks except in their celibacy were hardly to
be distinguished from the secular clergy; and that the latter,
whether canons or parish priests, were usually married and copied
the layman both in his dress and in his mode of life.   But when it
is remembered that asceticism and strict discipline were essential
features of the ideal to which the English clergy tendered a lip-
homage, it cannot be considered a slight evil that asceticism and
discipline were nowhere to be found.   The sharpness of the contrast between practice and theory was fatal to the vigour and the
moral influence of the English Church.   Learning and piety alike
were at a low ebb in every grade of the hierarchy.   Even Godwin
and Harold, despite their antipathy to Norman churchmen, had to
admit that bishoprics might be more usefully conferred on aliens than
on native Englishmen; and of Wulfstan, who was in many ways a
brilliant exception to the general torpor of his profession, his apolo-
gist can only say that while despising the attainments which were
fashionable among the Norman clergy he was not altogether so
illiterate as had been commonly affirmed; and that if he countenanced the English practice of long drinking bouts, even in his own
household, this was from courtesy and not because he was himself
a heavy drinker.[2]   Much may be excused in the man whom even
Normans admired for his uncompromising attack upon the Bristol

---

[1] Orderic, ii., 48: " Dixit se quidem legatos Papae de fide et religione Christiana
ut communis Patris libenter suscepturum ".
[2] W. Malmesb., G. P., p. 281.   Vita Wulfstani, iii., § 2, etc.

slave trade. But his moral enthusiasm was not shared by his English colleagues. They had his weaknesses without his merits. Episcopal responsibilities must have sat very lightly on the episcopal conscience when a prelate so respectable as Aldred of York was not ashamed to hold four sees in plurality ; and the neglect of the Archbishops to hold Church Councils, at a time when these assemblies were the recognised means of exciting and maintaining zeal among the rulers of the church, is a proof that the English Church had fallen into that torpor which sooner or later overtakes a small corporation when freed from the pressure of public opinion and forced by isolation to depend upon its own innate resources. The English Church had never forgotten its partnership in the Catholic communion ; but it had underrated the advantages to be derived from intercourse with other churches ; it had been content to maintain the formal bond of unity by showing deference to the Pope as the visible head of Western Christendom ; and this deference, genuine though it was, led to no important consequences in an age when the centres of ecclesiastical reform were to be found anywhere except at Rome. But the traditional respect for Rome now at length proved useful : it facilitated the schemes of reform which the Conqueror set on foot. From the outset all of these, whether their object was political or religious, were laid before the English Church as either suggested or approved by the Holy See. In the year 1070 Papal legates were invited into England and permitted to hold synods. By their help William effected the deposition of Stigand and such other changes in the personnel of the episcopate as he considered immediately desirable. In particular he obtained their cordial approbation of Lanfranc as the new Primate and future organiser of reform. This step once taken, the purpose for which William had summoned them was fulfilled they left the country and Lanfranc took their place in English eyes as the representative of Roman ideas and the regular intermediary between the Pope and the national Church.

Archbishop Lanfranc

Lanfranc's official policy did not entirely correspond with his professions of obedience ; he deliberately abandoned some important articles in the Papal programme ; and the Concordat which he established between the English Church and State was of a kind more acceptable to William than to Hildebrand. A statesman rather than a logician the Archbishop followed, in matters of faith and discipline, the straightest path of orthodoxy; but in the sphere of politics he attenuated the theocratic principles of Cluni to suit the wishes of the King. Politics were Lanfranc's true vocation although his versatility, the lack of early opportunities for showing his true bent, and some conventional scruples which lingered in his mind when he at length emerged from the cloister to enter public life, left his contemporaries in doubt as to the exact nature of his greatness. In Normandy he was known as the finest teacher of his time, the master of Anselm and Ivo of Chartres; beyond the Alps as the dialectician who had convicted Berengar of heresy before two Papal councils; in England as a model bishop, a zealot for monasticism, and the most subtle lawyer in the Curia Regis. In all of these capacities he did good work, because he was incapable of failing in any business which he undertook; but the English estimate of his character, though incomplete, came nearest to the truth. His controversial writings throw little or no light upon the inner meaning of the beliefs which they defend, and are chiefly remarkable for the lawyer-like dexterity with which he marshals texts from his authorities to define the orthodox position. In fact he taught that it is the first duty of the theologian to define, and of the Christian to believe, the teaching of antiquity; that rational explanation is an intellectual luxury, innocent yet of no great advantage for the Christian life; and that metaphysics have their root in an arrogant desire to compress the laws of God within the limits of a finite understanding.[1] His remarks upon those ulterior problems which his age regarded as fair matter for discussion illustrate the fancies, sometimes noble, more often puerile, but always inchoate and unconnected, which floated through the minds of medieval men of action. In the *Elucidarium*, which is commonly attributed to him[2] and in any case expresses the teaching of his school, these fancies, culled from the most various sources, are passed in review with bewildering rapidity. At one moment we hear a faint echo from the schools of Greek philosophy; that nothing in the world is unconscious of the divinity, and that even things inanimate have a soul which perceives their Creator and keeps them steadfast to his law. Then follows a rude attempt at cosmography; there are three heavens, a material which is visible to man, a spiritual in which the angels dwell, an intel-

The School of Lanfranc

---

[1] See the dialogue against Berengar, *De Corpore et Sanguine Domini.*
[2] Now attributed to Honorius of Autun (see Hauck-Herzog's *Realencyclopädie* (3rd ed.), s. v. Honorius).

lectual in which the Trinity unfolds its nature to the blessed.   Sub-
joined is a mystical commentary upon the story of Creation: the
first man was called Adam because the four quarters of the earth
are in the Greek language, Anatole, Dysis, Arctos and Mesembria;
and the name formed from their initials denotes at once the nature
of man, as a microcosm, and his destiny which is to spread and
multiply through every land.   Then follow speculations, half
Rabbinical and half scholastic, concerning angels and their pro-
perties.   To every man and every nation a guardian angel is
assigned; in heaven there are nine legions of the angels, because
nine is the square of three and the most perfect symbol of the
Trinity; the fallen angels could not be redeemed, first because of
each of them is *sui generis* so that if Christ had taken upon Him
the nature of one fallen angel He would thereby have redeemed
that one alone, and secondly because the angelic nature is incapable of death, and without death there is no redemption.   The
work closes with some reflections upon practical morality in which
the legend of a golden age and the Stoic's praise of Nature are
blended with the ideas of St. Benedict.   Few knights, the author
says, are good for they are wont to live on plunder and clothe
themselves by rapine.   There is little hope for the merchant since
nearly all his wealth comes through deceit and perjury.   Of craftsmen but a few escape damnation since they too are deceitful and
the Scripture says that no darkness and no shadow of death may
conceal those who work iniquity.   But the tillers of the soil are
for the most part saved, inasmuch as they lead a simple life and by
the sweat of their brows provide the people of God with food; also
it is written "happy are those who eat the labour of their hands".

Such were the thoughts which occupied the minds of Lanfranc
and his pupils in the lecture room at Avranches and the cloister-
schools of Bec and Caen.   It is in his career as a diplomatist and
an administrator that we detect the master-mind; there is little
to connect his statesmanship with his philosophy.   But the weak,
as well as the strong, qualities of leading men leave their mark on
history, and the character of Lanfranc's thought was of some
moment for the future of the English Church.   It was not to be
expected that the followers of such a master should be as successful
in elevating its theology as they undoubtedly were in reforming its
daily life and institutions.

The main idea of Lanfranc's English policy was strictly practical. Church Councils
Following in the wake of the Cluniacs and Hildebrand he desired
to draw a sharp distinction between the hierarchy and the laity,
between the spheres of secular and spiritual government. Even
before Lanfranc's appointment one step had been taken towards
this end. The ecclesiastical changes of 1070 were effected in
assemblies composed entirely of ecclesiastics, and the principle of a
distinct legislature for the Church was thus revived. For the
future these synods of the clergy were held at the same place and
season as the feudal councils of the tenants-in-chief; and although
the prelates had their seats in both assemblies, the chief connecting
link was the King's personality. William maintained as King of
England the habit, which he had formed as a Norman Duke, of
taking part in the deliberations of his clergy; [1] and the extent of
his controlling power was considerable. He required that no
general synod should be called, and no resolutions introduced without his sanction. But this power was exercised with caution ; and
apart from the occasions when it was used to procure the degradation of prelates whose patriotism was their chief offence, the King's
ideas were felt more as a restraining than as a directing force. The
duty of framing a policy and expressing it in canons apparently
devolved on Lanfranc, and the Anglo-Norman Church was less
Erastian than it seemed.

The edict of 1076 by which William decreed the separation of Ecclesi-astical Courts
the lay and spiritual courts[2] can hardly be regarded as a departure
from his usual reserve, since its object was to free ecclesiastical
judges from an irksome and unprofitable control. The spiritual
jurisdiction of bishop and archdeacon had hitherto been exercised
in the public courts; and we gather from the terms of William's
ordinance that the doomsmen claimed the right of acting as
assessors in spiritual no less than in secular causes, with the result
that the canons of the Church were relaxed or corrupted by an
admixture of local custom. The change was one at which every
reformer would rejoice ; the advisability of a moral censorship being
once admitted no man of common sense could approve the idea of
placing this censorship under the control of the very class which it
was intended to correct. Some opposition might have been excited
if the measure had been logically complete, if the bishop and arch-

[1] See the preamble to the decrees of 1072 in Milo Crispin's *Vita Lanfranci*, § 33.
[2] Printed in S. C., p. 99. On the date see Böhmer, *Kirche und Staat*, p. 93.

deacon had been debarred from exercising any influence upon the course of secular justice. This does not seem to have been the case. Not only did the archdeacon retain his right of superintending the ordeal by fire and water, but the bishop also made his appearance in the shire-court and continued for some time to share the presidency with the sheriff,[1] presumably because an old and respectable tradition required the bishop to provide that earthly justice should be tempered with Christian mercy. Within a generation or so reformers took exception to this amiable anomaly, and the episcopate abandoned of its own free will a right which, if impugned by the lay power, would probably have been defended to the death.

TheHildebrandine Reforms   The two reforms for which the Hildebrandine party showed most eagerness were the enforcement of clerical celibacy and the prohibition of lay investitures; and it is remarkable that, on these questions, William's tenacity of purpose and Lanfranc's common sense should have triumphed over the imperious idealism of Gregory VII. The latter, on his election to the Holy See (1073), threw to the winds the caution which had marked the policy of Alexander II. In Papal Councils of 1073 and 1075 decrees of the most uncompromising kind were passed, forbidding clerical marriages, declaring those which had been contracted null and void, and launching the sentence of excommunication against all who conferred or received an ecclesiastical benefice by lay investiture. Simultaneously the Pope preferred a claim to feudal suzerainty over almost every crown in Europe, vainly supposing that by means of such pretensions he could exact for his new laws the respect which his position as head of a religious commonwealth had failed to secure. The grounds of the claim were different in each case, but in reference to England he maintained that the Conquest had been sanctioned by Alexander on condition that the conquered land should be held as a fief from Rome. To the triple attack the

---

[1] *Leges Edwardi, Leges Henrici VII.*, S. C., p. 104. Writs of Henry I. and Stephen addressed to bishop and sheriff jointly in the Gloucester Cartulary, i., 164, 239, 240; ii., 34, 45. But, towards the end of Henry's reign, the bishop probably appears in the shire-court only as a suitor. *Leges Edwardi, III.*: " Ubicumque regis justitia, vel cujuscumque sit, placita tenuerit, si ullus episcopus veniat illuc et aperuerit causam sanctae ecclesiae, ipsa prius terminetur ". This refers only to shire-courts held by justices. *Leges Henrici, VII.*, § 3 : " Agantur itaque primo debita verae christianitatis jura," refers to shire-courts in general and has been taken as proving that the bishop was a judge ; but this is extremely doubtful.

English King and Church returned three different replies. The Council of W nchester in 1076 adopted the decree concerning clerical marriages with the important reservation that, while forbidding the marriage of all priests and deacons for the future, it recognised the validity of existing marriages in the case of parish priests on whom the obligation of celibacy had not, for some time past, been regarded as even morally incumbent.[1] To the claim of homage the King replied in a firm but respectful letter, professing his perfect willingness to render such obedience as had been usual on the part of former Kings of England, but entirely repudiating the position of a vassal.[2] Neither in the decrees of the Council nor in the King's letter was there any reference to the question of investitures; but Lanfranc was despatched on a mission to the Roman court (1076), in the course of which he appears to have procured a friendly settlement. He conceded the principle that it lay within the province of the Pope to insist on free elections; but he also maintained the existence of a special privilege conceded to the English Crown by which it was allowed the full control of the higher ecclesiastical patronage. The Pope confirmed the privilege for William's life-time,[3] and the latter may have shared with Lanfranc the belief that in postponing they had really solved the controversy. This episode altered the feelings of William and Lanfranc towards the Papacy. Their relations with Alexander II. had been of the most cordial kind; and Lanfranc in particular deferred to his old pupil with a readiness which left nothing to be desired at Rome. Of Gregory VII. they were more suspicious, and his request for homage extinguished any personal regard which they may once have felt for him. It may be true, as a German chronicler asserts, that English ports were closed to the merchants of the Emperor's dominions at some period of his war with Gregory.[4] But William's sympathy with the Papal cause went no further, if it went so far; and when the war led to a schism, England assumed an attitude of neutrality, not to say indifference. We have a letter from Lanfranc to a legate of Clement the anti-Pope in which, while recommending his correspondent not to enter England without the King's permission, he remarks that England has not yet decided between the rivals, and expresses a doubt whether the

[1] Wilkins, *Concilia*, i., p. 367.
[2] The letter is in *Lanfranci Epistolae* (ed. Giles), i., 32. On the date see *Regesta*, No. 134.   [3] Orderic, ii., 304.
[4] *Chron. Bertold. Constant.* in Bouquet, *Recueil*, xi., 25.

Emperor's great success in capturing Rome (1083) does not prove that
Heaven is on the imperial side.[1]   But if the Pope of the moment
was unpopular in England, the Papacy as an institution commanded
deep respect; even when relations with Gregory VII. were most
strained Lanfranc acknowledged that the Pope possessed a canonical
authority over himself and the English Church ; and Gregory,
bitterly as he resented the refusal of homage at the moment,[2]
learned in later life to esteem William as a king who, with all
his faults, was more devoted than many others to the Roman See.[3]
It is true that Eadmer mentions, among the Conqueror's rules of
ecclesiastical policy, two which might have been so pressed as to
destroy the Pope's authority in England.   William would allow
no Pope to be recognised in England, and no papal letters to be
received by any of his subjects, without his consent.   We know,
moreover, that he disliked to let his clergy, whether Norman or
English, resort to Rome and Papal Councils.[4]   On the other hand
we know that the uncompromising Gregory found no cause for
serious complaint in William's conduct ; and there is every reason
for thinking that the King merely desired to prevent encroachments on the secular prerogative.   Lanfranc's correspondence and
career prove that he and his master conceded important powers to
the Pope, not only in matters of conscience and the faith, but also
in administrative questions.   They admitted for example the necessity of obtaining the pallium for an archbishop, and the Pope's
power to invalidate episcopal elections ; they were scrupulous in
obtaining the Pope's consent when the deposition or the resignation
of a bishop was in question ; and they submitted the time-honoured
quarrel of York and Canterbury to his decision.   These admissions
are sufficient to prove that the canonical obedience which Lanfranc
promised was not a matter of mere words.   Obedience may not
have been welcome to his master or himself, and its consequences
were mitigated when Lanfranc obtained for himself a legatine commission from Alexander II.   But the duty of obedience was never
in itself disputed.

Some minor consequences of Lanfranc's primacy, though inter-

(left margin) William, Lanfranc and Gregory VII.

---

[1] *Lanfranci Epistolae*, No. 65 (ed. Giles).

[2] See the letter quoted in Baronius, 1079, § 25 : " Pecunias sine honore tributas quanti pretii habeam tu ipse potuisti dudum perpendere ".

[3] *Monumenta Gregor.*, p. 478 : " Caeteris regibus se satis probabiliorem ac magis honorandam ostendit ".

[4] Stubbs detects a reference to the schism of 1080; *Lectures on Early English History* (1906), p. 100.

esting in ecclesiastical history, must be dismissed with a bare Minor Ecclesiastical Changes.
mention. In 1072, with the King's help, Lanfranc asserted the
supremacy of Canterbury over York, thus giving to the Church
of England a formal unity which it had not possessed before.[1]
The Council of London in 1075 decreed, in accordance with the
canons of Laodicea and Sardis, that every bishop should have
his seat in some important town. The change came too late to
give the bishops of England that influence on municipal development which was exercised by their continental brethren; but it
produced some changes in nomenclature and some new cathedrals.
The see of Sherborne was removed to Old Sarum, that of Selsey to
Chichester, that of Lichfield to Chester; Dorchester-on-Thames,
Elmham, and Wells were superseded by Lincoln, Thetford, and Bath.
In many cases where there was no such removal great churches
arose, of which we may still see traces in the crypts of Worcester
and York, the transepts of Winchester and Ely, the east end of
Gloucester, and the undefaced portions of St. Albans. Many
houses of secular canons were appropriated to the use of monks;
ruined and impoverished monasteries were rebuilt, repeopled, re-
endowed. Alike in secular and regular foundations the ancient
discipline was restored. Good or bad the new prelates were
a strenuous race and left their names in local, if not in national
history. Among abbots we may instance Serlo of Gloucester and Norman Prelates
Vital of Westminster as patterns of the Cluniac school; Paul of St.
Albans, who built the greatest abbey church in England with the
ruins of a Roman town, reviled his English predecessors as uncouth
and simple men, and hoped to destroy their memory at the same
time as their monuments; and Thurstan of Glastonbury, a still
more truculent reformer. He, when his English monks refused
to sing the new-fangled chants of William of Fécamp, hunted the
recalcitrants through their own church with knights and archers,
till some were slain and many wounded and the steps of the high
altar ran with blood. Such arguments were too forcible for his
master; Thurstan went back to his Norman monastery in deep disgrace. A fervent man and of some piety, so the English historian
of his abbey tells us; but his virtues were not generally recognised.
Of the new prelates the most remarkable for his attainments was
Thomas of York who, not content with a Norman schooling, had
gone as far afield as Germany and Spain in search of knowledge,
but wasted his later years in efforts to emancipate his see from the
control of Canterbury. Distinction of other kinds was achieved by

---

[1] W. Malmesb., G. R., § 298. Regesta, Nos. 64, 65. It seems clear that Lanfranc used spurious charters to establish his claim. See Böhmer, Die Fälschungen
Erzbischof Lanfrank (Leipzig, 1902)   [2] W. Malmesb., G. P., p. 66.

Walkelin of Winchester, the enemy of monks and friend of seculars;
by Gundulf of Rochester, " the most skilled of all men in the mason's
craft," the architect of Rochester Castle; by Walcher of Durham
who won the crown of martyrdom through the misbehaviour of
his foreign favourites; and by his successor William of St. Calais,
an adroit diplomatist and cunning lawyer whose career was but
commencing when the reign of the first William ended.   There
are many types of Norman churchmen, but a family resemblance
may be traced in all.   They lack the finer virtues; they are positive,
practical, astute, narrow-minded, intolerant of opposition.   But
the age had need of spiritual drill-sergeants; and to this rôle the
Norman prelate was perfectly adapted.

Foreign Relations, 1074-7   From this survey of William's reorganising work we may now
turn to the wars and foreign relations of his later years.   They are
of less moment than we might expect.   We are told that he felt
some jealousy of Robert Guiscard and used to say it would be
disgraceful in a Norman Duke to be eclipsed by one of his own
subjects.   None the less he was content to match the conquest of
the two Sicilies with that of England, and undertook no later enterprise which might compare in audacity with Guiscard's attack on
the Byzantine Empire; although there is a tale that, in the year
1074, he was almost induced by Hanno, the rebel Archbishop of
Cologne, to seize the old imperial capital of Aachen.[1]   Respect for
the legal rights of his equals and superiors was deeply engrained
in William's character, and there were prudential reasons for observing moderation.   Ruling over a discontented and alien nation,
and until 1086 never free from the fear of English or Danish
pretenders, he could ill afford to court new enemies by a course
of indiscriminate aggression.   In spite of serious provocations it
was his rule to stand on the defensive.

Scotland, Wales and Ireland   His forbearance towards the minor powers of the British Isles
is more remarkable than his abstention from foreign undertakings,
since in this case an aggressive policy would have been acceptable
to his new subjects.   He had every excuse for wars of conquest.
The Ostmen of Dublin gave shelter to the sons of Harold; the
North Welsh joined the rising of Edwin and Morcar in 1069;

---

[1] Lambert of Hersfeld (ed. Holder-Egger), p. 195. *Cf.* Freeman, *N. C.*, iv.,
p. 538, as to the probable reason; also Wissowa, *Politische Beziehungen zwischen
England u. Deutschland.* Bruno, the Saxon chronicler (§ 36, ed. Wattenbach),
represents Henry IV. as asking the help of William in this very year.

Malcolm of Scotland came on more than one occasion to the help
of Edgar Atheling, and, even after the Atheling gave up the contest, showed himself a bad neighbour to Northumbria.   In all these
cases there was good excuse for wars of conquest, and no doubt as
to the superiority of William's military resources.   For the defence
of the borders he had the fyrd at his disposal; if he wished for
mercenaries he possessed the right to levy Danegeld; and the introduction of the feudal system placed at his disposal an unpaid force
of about 5,000 knights and mounted men at arms.   But he showed
considerable reluctance to use his strength.   When in 1079 Malcolm
wasted all the country north of the Tyne, the only measure of retaliation was a counter-raid which went as far as Falkirk.   Northumberland, though entrusted to the keeping of an earl, seems to have
been lightly valued by the King; the building of Newcastle in 1080
showed a disposition to treat the Tyne as the real frontier on that
side; and the recovery of Westmoreland and Cumberland was left
to William Rufus.   On the side of Wales indeed there was a
distinct advance.   But this was due to the energy of individual
marchers.   On the north coast Robert of Rhyddlan, who held all
royal rights in North Wales at the trifling rent of £40, pushed
his frontier forward to Diganwy.   On the central march the Earls
of Shropshire planted their town and castle of Montgomery as an
outpost in the richest part of Powis; and the Earls of Hereford
carried their raids as far to the westward as the Usk.   Once only,
in the year 1081, William brought an army to the aid of his
lieutenants.   His march, though it led him to St. David's, resulted
merely in the release of certain English captives and a promise of
tribute from Rhys of Deheubarth.[1]   The difficulty of conquering
such a land as Wales is great; but the Welsh kingdoms of Gwynedd,
Powis and Deheubarth had seldom been more feeble or divided,
and the efforts of the marchers, if properly directed and assisted,
might have been far more productive than they actually were.
Concerning Ireland we are told in the English Chronicle that, if
William had lived two years longer, he would have won that land
by his wariness and without any weapons.   The boast may refer
to negotiations of which we have no other record.   But William's
hopes appear to have been based on Lanfranc's relations with
the See of Dublin and certain Irish princes.   The English Primate
received professions of obedience from two successive Archbishops

[1] See Lloyd's *History of Wales* (1911), pp. 393-5.

of Dublin,[1] and his exhortations to ecclesiastical reform were heard
with patience.[2]   It is rash to suppose that he was equally successful as a political propagandist, and in fact we have no proof that
he exposed his influence to such a test.

The truth is that feudal armies, both by the laxity of their
discipline and by the short term of their annual service, were
unsuited for offensive warfare; and the gelds which William raised
from time to time were spent on other purposes than conquest.
Even with the wealth of England at his disposal he had no easy
task to hold all that force or fraud had won for himself and his
ancestors in France.   He was surrounded on three sides by aggrieved
or envious princes, and new problems forced themselves in swift
succession on his mind.   Before he had been King of England
many years he lost the Flemish alliance which had been valuable
to him for more purposes than one.   His wife's father, the great
Baldwin V., died in the year 1067 leaving two sons, of whom the
elder took the whole succession according to the established custom
of the House of Flanders.   The younger, Robert, consoled himself
for a time with the county of Frisia which he had acquired by a
well-chosen marriage.   But the early death of Baldwin VI. and
the minority of his son Arnulf encouraged the Frison to defy a
rule of inheritance which was still repugnant to ordinary ideas of
equity.   Civil war ensued in which the sympathies of the Conqueror were undisguisedly ranged on the side of the legitimate
successor.   He permitted William Fitzosbern, the most valued
of his counsellors, to abandon the regency of Normandy for that
of Flanders; and the earl, although he took no more than ten
knights to share in his adventure, was the controlling mind in
Arnulf's councils until ward and guardian fell together on the
field of Cassel (1071).   Even after this conclusive victory it was in
vain that the Frison asked for William's recognition of his title;
and Arnulf's brother Baldwin, received constant aid from Normandy in his forays upon Flemish territory.   The result was a
feud which long menaced the peace of Normandy and culminated
in 1085 with the equipment of a Flemish fleet to aid Cnut of
Denmark in invading England.   Only the accident of Cnut's

---

[1] Patricius in 1074; Donatus in 1085.   See the profession of obedience made by
Patricius in *Opera Lanfranci*, i., 356.
[2] *Lanfranci Epistolae*, No. 43, No. 44.

assassination persuaded Robert to let his grievance slumber.[1] He
was the sole enemy whose hatred the Conqueror gratuitously drew Brittany
upon himself. The feuds with which he had to deal elsewhere had
been inherited from his forefathers. The timely death of Conan
II. by no means put an end to the old disputes with Brittany.
The Conqueror's relations with Duke Hoel and his successor Alain
were of a chequered kind; hollow reconciliations alternated with
inconclusive wars until, in the year 1086, a marriage between Alain
and the Conqueror's daughter Constance excited hopes of a more
lasting peace, which William did not live to see frustrated.[2]
Maine presented a more serious problem, and although the Maine
resources of England were brought to bear upon this discontented
province, William's success went no further than the destruction
of one among several dangerous enemies to the Norman overlordship. The story is involved and must be told in detail.[3]

In the year 1069 at a moment when William's hands were free
as they had not been for many years, the nobles of Maine and the
burghers of Le Mans came to the conclusion that he was no longer
to be feared, since he had ceased to live on their side of the
Channel. They united therefore, drove out the Norman garrison
from the castles of Le Mans, and sent to Italy for Azo of Liguria,
the son-in-law of their famous count, Herbert "Wake-dog". He
came but the situation did not please him. He was an old man
who desired a quiet life and doubted the ability of the Manceaux
to keep out the Conqueror. Moreover he suspected that they
liked his money better than himself, and was resolved to spend as
little as he could on a doubtful cause and doubtful friends. By
way of a compromise between his ambitions and his prudence he
left his wife and child to rule in Maine with the help of his chief
supporter Geoffrey of Mayenne; but returned for his own part to
Liguria. No sooner had he gone than the men of Le Mans, The Com-
deciding to be rid at once of the new dynasty and of the nobles mune of
upon whom it leaned, banded themselves together as a commune 1072-3
for the mutual defence of liberties. They drove out Azo's representative, laid siege to the castles of obnoxious barons, and hanged

[1] Varenbergh, pp. 52-60. Will. Malmesb., G. R., iii., §§ 257-8.
[2] For the marriage see the Breton Annals in Bouquet, xii., 559, 562, 563. Constance died without issue in 1090.
[3] The chief authorities are the Gesta Pontificum Cenomannensium (Bouquet, xii.,
539 ff.) and Orderic. The best modern account in Halphen's Comté d'Anjou au
xie Siecle, pp. 180-1.

or blinded those of their old oppressors on whom they could lay hands. The nobles however made so stout a resistance that the citizens were soon in urgent need of allies. They bethought them that Fulk of Anjou was in name their overlord, and invited him to their assistance. He granted it in the belief that sooner or later the commune could be brought beneath his sway; and in a short time the united forces of Anjou and Le Mans cleared the city of its enemies. But in the moment of success the joint forces of England and Normandy, with William at their head, appeared upon the frontier. Fulk and the family of Azo vanished from the scene. The nobles hurried back to their castles. The commune began to think of protecting itself from William's vengeance. But preparations had been delayed too long; one by one the castles fell; the spirits of the citizens sank as William, leaving a devastated country in his wake, approached Le Mans. They made their submission; their ancient privileges were restored; but the commune and the claim to self-government which it involved were utterly ignored by the victor. From Le Mans the King experienced no further trouble; the spirit of the citizens was broken. On his remaining enemies he produced less effect. The quarrel with Fulk was suspended by an arrangement which secured the overlordship to him and the title of Count to William's eldest son, and left excuses in abundance for reviving the claims of Anjou at the first opportunity. The nobles of Maine were cowed, but only for the moment. One of them, Herbert of St. Suzanne, subsequently contrived to make head against the King and the King's lieutenants for three years (1083-5) until his submission was purchased by a grant of the most liberal terms.[1] Maine was to cause much trouble in the future.

The Rebellion of Robert, 1074-9   Of all William's enemies the most feeble but also the most pertinacious was his overlord, the King of Paris. While the hostility of Anjou, Maine and Brittany threatened only the outlying parts of Normandy, the House of Capet regarded the very existence of a Duchy which separated Paris from the sea as an intolerable hardship. It was fortunate for William that the opportunity of seizing England came to him when France was ruled by a regent, and that regent his own father-in-law: but it was still more fortunate that Baldwin's ward, on attaining to the age

[1] Orderic, iii., 196.

of manhood, showed himself as ineffectual and petty in his designs
as he was implacable in his hostility. The two were usually on
bad terms, and Philip showed some ingenuity in devising methods
of annoyance. But, with the one exception of his march to raise
the siege of Dol in 1076, he carefully refrained from personal encounters, and the episode of Gerberoi is a sufficient proof of the
wholesome fear which the Conqueror inspired in him. About the
year 1074 Robert Curthose quarrelled with his father.[1] Invested
with the Duchy of Normandy in the year 1066, and with the county
of Maine in 1073, Robert had never been allowed the slightest share
in the government of either province. He clamoured for what he
termed his rights, sulked when they were refused him, took offence
at the gibes and horseplay of his brothers, and fled with his boon-
companions to the border stronghold of Raimalast.[2] He was
followed and expelled from the duchy; after aimless visits to his
father's enemies and his own relations in Flanders, Lorraine,
Suabia, and Aquitaine, he turned his steps to Paris and invoked
the help of Philip I. The French king allowed him to take up
quarters in the castle of Gerberoi in the Beauvoisis that he might
harry the adjacent parts of Normandy. But when William reproached his suzerain with this breach of treaties and of feudal
obligations, and demanded reparation, Philip not only disowned
connection with his guest but joined William in laying siege to
Gerberoi.[3] He may have salved his conscience by betraying the Siege of
father as he had betrayed the son. At all events his assistance Gerberoi
was too slight to save William from a humiliating failure. The ¹⁰⁷⁹
castle was not taken, and in one of the skirmishes outside the
walls Robert met and worsted his father in a single combat. The
old King was wounded in the hand; his horse fell beneath him
pierced by an arrow; his very life was in danger until an English
thane, Tokig of Wallingford, leaped from his saddle and forced
his master to mount in his place. William withdrew, and shortly
afterwards allowed his barons to end by mediation a conflict which
shocked their moral sense and left them no alternative, while it
continued, but to fight against the sovereign of the moment or
the sovereign of the future. It was a superficial reconciliation,

---

[1] Lappenberg, ii., p. 129.   [2] Orderic, ii., 294.
[3] See *Regesta*, No. 115a for a charter issued by Philip and attested by William I.
in obsidione . . . circa Gerborredum in 1079. Orderic (ii., 387) omits the single
combat of son and father but see the *A. S. C.* (D. text).

and soon destroyed by further quarrels. Robert again became a
fugitive, and was perhaps again assisted by his shifty overlord.
Quarrels For this or other reasons William was at the end of his life on
with the worst of terms with Philip. The latter tolerated, if he did
France,
1080-7 not encourage, the raids of the inhabitants of Mantes upon the
Norman border. William retaliated with a claim to the whole
district, known as the French Vexin, in which the offending city
stood. This claim, a fertile cause of discord in the future and
only to be settled by the expulsion of William's line from Normandy,
rested upon the assertion that Philip's father, Henry I., when
hard pressed by his brother and a fugitive from Paris (1031-4)
had bartered the French Vexin for the help of Robert the Devil,
but subsequently had taken advantage of the Conqueror's minority
to resume his grant. A grievance so long allowed to slumber
might not have borne the test of close examination. It served,
however, to excuse an expedition against Mantes (July, 1087);
the town was taken unawares, sacked, and reduced to ashes. But
the revenge was dearly purchased; in leaping a ditch, or through
a stumble on hot ashes, the King's horse threw his rider with
violence against the pommel of his saddle. A serious internal
lesion was the consequence. The expedition was perforce abandoned and William returned, a doomed man, to his Norman
capital.

Death-bed   His last words and dispositions are recorded with unusual
Disposi- fulness, and no doubt with the usual rhetorical embellishments,
tions of
William by two writers who apparently relied upon the information of eye
witnesses and are in harmony on all essential points. The King
was accurately informed as to his condition, but expressed no regret
for the nearness of his end, and occupied his mind with arrangements for the future welfare of his soul and his dominions. He
dictated to his notaries a list of the gifts which he bequeathed
from his treasures to the poor and the churches of Normandy and
England. At the persuasion of the bishops and abbots who stood
by his bedside he released from prison, Wulfnoth son of Godwin,
Wulf son of Harold, Alfgar, Morcar, Siward Barn, Roger of
Hereford, and Odo of Bayeux—all the men, in short, whether
English or Norman, whom he had incarcerated for reasons of
policy and state. Among these pardons that of Odo of Bayeux
was the only one which his heir eventually allowed to stand and

it was the only one which William had been loath to grant; not from any rancour which he felt against his half-brother, but from a well founded apprehension of the mischief which ambition so unbridled might produce.   It only remained to divide his sovereign rights among his sons.   Orderic Vitalis makes the dying man express remorse for the means by which he had gained England, and refuse to nominate a successor to a throne which he held by no just title.[1]   It is more likely that William entertained some slight respect for the elective character of the English monarch, perfunctorily recognised at his own coronation.   None the less he gave utterance to his private wishes and took some steps for their fulfilment.   He handed the regalia, the crown, the sceptre, and the jewelled sword, to William Rufus, the constant companion of his later years, his favourite and most obedient son, and sent him to England in the company of a royal chaplain who bore letters commending the interests of the king-designate to the Primate Lanfranc.[2]   Concerning Normandy and the absent Robert an ominous silence was preserved, until at length the Archbishop of Rouen ventured to remind the King of his duty to his eldest son, and of the legitimate expectations which had been excited by the previous investiture of Robert with the Duchy.   William was not easily persuaded.   He recapitulated with some heat the numerous instances of his son's ingratitude; but at last, with an effort, restrained himself and said, " God is my witness, and you who are here present, that I forgive Robert his offences against myself, and grant him the whole Duchy.   It must be your part to move him to repentance.   I have forgiven him, let him not forgive himself so easily, for bringing my old age with sorrow to the grave."[3] He added a prophecy that Normandy would be wretched under such a ruler.   His youngest son, Henry Beauclerk, then came forward to supplicate a blessing and a portion.   William replied by giving him the promise of five thousand pounds of silver and

The English Succession

The Norman Succession

---

[1] Orderic, iii., 242.

[2] See the account, from the Harleian MS. of William of Jumièges, quoted by Hardy, *Descriptive Catalogue*, ii., 14.   This version of the death-bed scene probably rests on the authority of Abbot Guntard of Jumièges whom Orderic mentions as having been present.   It is most valuable as corroborating Orderic, whose account would otherwise be suspect from the rhetorical form in which it is cast.   But the Jumièges version contradicts Orderic in so far as it implies a distinct nomination of Rufus to the English throne.   *Cf.* Orderic, iii., 242.   Hen. Hunt., 211.

[3] See the Jumièges narrator *u.s.*

a commendation to the good will of his elder brothers. Ill content, but eager to secure his modest legacy, Henry left the sick-room; and shortly afterwards the Conqueror breathed his last, in the sixty-first year of his life, the fifty-third of his ducal power, the twenty-first of his reign in England. He had outlived his wife Matilda, the one human being for whom he had ever felt a strong affection; and with the exception of Lanfranc, then far away in England, there were few who mourned his death for the sake of private friendship. His servants, following the custom of the age and the nature of their kind, stripped his corpse and went their ways. The dead King was conveyed to Caen at the charges of a country knight, to be buried in the church of St. Stephen which William and Matilda had founded as an act of expiation for the slight which they had offered by their marriage to the Church's rules of consanguinity. Owing to a conflagration in the city the funeral was scantily attended; the ceremony was interrupted by a knight named Ascelin, whom William had defrauded of the site on which St. Stephen's stood, and could not be resumed until due compensation had been paid; and finally the putrefying body burst asunder when it was forced into the stone sarcophagus which the masons in their haste had made too narrow. Meanwhile in the surrounding country the Norman aristocracy turned the occasion to their own account. The Duke was dead and the Duke's peace at an end. Robert of Bellême, riding soberly to court, was met on the way by the momentous news; he wheeled about and galloped back to his fiefs upon the southern march. First he expelled the ducal garrisons by which the castles on his land were held, then he betook himself to pillage far and wide. The example was contagious and soon every baron in Normandy did what seemed good in his own eyes.[1]

A week or two before this stormy ending to the Conqueror's chequered life one of the less noted victims of his great achievement died quietly and generally mourned at Bruges. The visitor to the Church of Saint Sauveur in that town is still shown the epitaph and other relics of Gunhilda the daughter of Earl Godwin, who, after the flight of her family from England, lived as a recluse in Flanders and died on August 24th, 1087; a woman who, as her

The Conqueror's death, Sept. 7, 1087

The English Exiles

[1] Orderic, iii., 261.

epitaph relates, was "cheerful and gentle to her servants, just and benevolent to strangers, parsimonious to herself, but bounteous to the poor". In Denmark, Norway, Scotland, Flanders, wherever in Europe there was hospitality and a kindly feeling for the English nation, such hapless exiles were to be found, attesting William's greatness by their forlorn condition. Of desperate adventurers also, who had staked their all in the cause of Harold or the Atheling, the courts and camps of East and West were full. Even to Byzantium a number made their way, enlisted under Alexius Comnenus in the Varanger guard, and showed in hard fought battles with Robert Guiscard and his Normans the same qualities and the same defects which had gone down before the Norman charge at Senlac. How tenaciously these exiles at Byzantium cherished the memory of England may be judged from the fact that in the fourteenth century their descendants still bore the weapons and spoke the language of a native land which they had never seen. It is not surprising if to all these outcasts, from the princess to the Varanger guardsman, the Norman should seem, as he seemed to the half-Norman William of Malmesbury, a very prince of robbers.

The average Norman soldier was not much more than this. The king, he says, was given to avarice and greedy of gain: That William stood above the average is proved by the exultation and relief with which his nobles learned of his decease, and by the deliberate judgment of Englishmen who remained at home and submitted to his rule. The Peterborough Chronicler, who had seen William and lived for some time at his court, is an outspoken critic. The king, he says, was given to avarice and greedy of gain : he took from his subjects many marks of gold and many hundred marks of silver with little need and small regard for justice. He made large forests for the deer; he loved the high deer as if he were their father. He was a very stern man and a wrathful so that none durst do anything against his will; he imprisoned earls and thanes and at the last he spared not his own brother; he deposed bishops and abbots; he built castles and oppressed the poor. The rich complained and the poor murmured, but he was so stark that he recked nought of them; if they would live or keep their lands they must will all that the king willed. And yet the chronicler is proud, for England's sake, of such a king. This William, he says, was a very wise and a great man, more honoured and more power-

The Character of William I

3

ful than any of his predecessors. " Amongst other things the good peace that he made in this land is not to be forgotten."

The mendacity with which he maintained his claim to England, his duplicity towards would-be traitors, the betrayal of Stigand, the execution of Waltheof, the harrying of the north have all been cited, with more or less of justice, as blots upon the English part of his career. But the offence for which his English subjects were least ready to forgive him was that of making the New Forest as an appendage to his royal seat at Winchester. On this subject the chroniclers are unanimous in indignation ; they talk of sixty villages destroyed and miles of fertile fields laid waste, of thousands of inhabitants expelled, of churches wantonly profaned and ruined. It is in the last clause of the indictment that we may see the secret of their heat. The soil of the New Forest can never have been generally productive; and the amount of arable which Domesday mentions as having been afforested is by no means large ; according to one calculation 140 hides, or 16,800 acres.[1] Spoliation and wilful destruction undoubtedly took place, but not on a gigantic scale. The introduction of the forest law, hitherto unknown in England, was in the end responsible for much more human suffering. For this too William must bear the blame ; it is a poor excuse that for breaches of the forest law as for other crimes he was content to exact no heavier penalty than mutilation, and left it for his successor to make the slaying of a deer a hanging matter ; a slightly better one that he inherited the tastes and would not forgo the most cherished privilege of Norman dukes, that in this matter as in so many more he simply transplanted to England the general custom of his native land. For good or evil he must be accepted by posterity as the pioneer of a rich and vigorous but defective social system, inheriting its prejudices with its virtues, heroic chiefly in his magnanimity, his strength of will, his love of order, his freedom from some among the grosser vices of his race and generation.

His forests

[1] But see the *Victoria County History of Hampshire*, vol. i., p. 411.

CHAPTER III

THE REIGN OF RUFUS

THE administrative system which the Conqueror imposed upon Character
his English subjects outlived him by rather less than fifty of the Period,
years (1087-1135); a term which, however short it may appear to 1087-1135
us who look back at it across so many intervening centuries, is
longer than that which has been vouchsafed to constitutions more
celebrated and more pretentious. Judged by the durability of his
work the Conqueror compares not unfavourably with most of the
statesmen who have framed the governments of half-civilised and
growing nations. But the visible monuments were less important
than the remote and unpremeditated consequences of his policy.
When his constitution went to the ground in the anarchy of
Stephen's reign, the fable of Cronos was repeated, and the parent
was deposed by his offspring. The forces which alternately de-
pressed and exalted King Stephen and his rivals were those to
which the Conqueror had given free scope for development. To
him the feudal aristocracy owed their lands and jurisdiction and
their military strength ; to him was due that reformation of the
English Church which made it once more the leader of opinion
and by divorcing it from the world gave it a title to command the
world.

In the period of unstable equilibrium, during which the growth
of feudal and ecclesiastical discontent was counterbalanced by the
growth of a despotic central government, there is no single statesman by whom the order of events is determined, though there is a
single issue with which all events of note are connected in one way
or another. Outside England the stage of politics was still adorned
by some commanding figures. In England itself the period produced no man of genius, although some English conflicts were
dignified by the accident which made the half-Lombard, half-

Burgundian Anselm their involuntary protagonist. The ability of English politicians, if it was not the slave of royal caprice, fought the battle of ideas inherited from the past or borrowed from abroad. Even Anselm was dragged into his greatest struggle with the temporal power by unreflecting deference to the will of the Universal Church as expressed through the mouth of Popes and Councils. Flambard the chief minister of Rufus, Robert of Meulan and Roger of Salisbury the confidants of his brother, were merely efficient and unscrupulous subordinates. As for their masters, it would be a gross exaggeration to credit Rufus with genius on account of his wild dreams of conquest or Henry on account of his capacity for taking pains. If we look at their work, rather than at their idiosyncrasies of method, it is plain that Henry continued what Rufus had begun, and that the improvements for which Henry is responsible are extremely modest in their scope; while Rufus in his saner moments aspired no higher than to reunite the lands which his father had ruled and to complete the plans which his father left unfinished. In the pursuit of this double object the two brothers sowed unconsciously the seeds of a new order. They made a practice of maintaining mercenaries; they met this and other expenses of their policy by enlarging the royal prerogative or by making inroads on ecclesiastical endowments; they developed a rudimentary form of bureaucratic government to facilitate their exactions; and when their power was challenged by the Church or aristocracy they appealed to the support of the conquered race. But they were driven from one of these expedients to another without prevision of the goal to which their changes led. They were conservative by temper and reformers by the accidents of their situation. There is a striking difference between their personalities. The one was impetuous, passionate, and changeable; the other prudent, slow, and obstinate. Rufus was so illiterate that he could not spell his way through an ordinary letter; Henry, without pretensions to finished scholarship or breadth of mind, had the instincts of an educated man and, himself impervious to the ideals of his age, understood that they must be treated with a semblance of respect. Rufus fought and squandered, leaving extortion to his clerks and judges; Henry, parsimonious and pacific, was his own chief minister. Rufus disdained the forms of justice and allowed to others the same licence which he exercised in his

Henry and Rufus compared

own person; Henry displayed so much of reverence for the letter of the law that he reserved to himself the sole right of exceeding it. But with all these differences the two men followed the same obvious and open path of policy, Rufus with an intermittent energy which cloaked his want of force, and Henry with a persistent cunning and ill-faith which gave him among his contemporaries an undeserved renown for wisdom.

The line taken by their policy is at once intelligible if we analyse the situation as it stood in the year 1087. The dominions of the Conqueror, though partitioned for the moment, were too closely knit together by the family and territorial connections of their aristocracies for any statesman to regard their permanent separation as desirable. The King of England and the Duke of Normandy had rival claims upon the allegiance of almost every important land-holder from the Tweed to the borders of Anjou and the Isle of France. The rebels of one brother were the loyal subjects of the other; and the barons on both sides of the Channel found their account in provoking and protracting quarrels of every kind between their rulers. This was a state of things which could only lead to one result. The acquisition of Normandy became the first object of English policy. It was so with Rufus; it was so with Henry I. But behind this problem lay others of hardly less importance. Surrounded on every side by envious or apprehensive powers the Norman dominions could only be secured against attack through further conquests. To subdue Wales and Maine, to humble Scotland, France, and Anjou, were imperative duties; and in these objects we have the key to the foreign wars and the diplomacy of the two brothers. Finally there was a danger to be apprehended from the Church. Though the Conqueror had maintained his "customs" to the end, and though Hildebrand had died in exile, the Papacy remained even to an English statesman the most formidable, as it was the newest, of European powers. The defeats which Hildebrand had sustained were eclipsed by the memory of his successes. Rome inspired the terror which is felt for an unfamiliar and incalculable force; and the power of Rome was steadily increasing as each new wave of religious zeal swept over Europe. The reformed Churches and the reforming Papacy were attracted to one another by an overpowering sympathy; and the shadowy allegiance which the Pope had received from time immemorial was

Policy of Rufus and Henry I.

rapidly acquiring form and content with the good will of all the best men in every country. How far the new sentiment of loyalty to Rome would carry men was doubtful; there was no doubt that it would clash at several points with the temporal allegiance demanded by an English king. And the danger from a rebel hierarchy was greater even than that from a rebel baronage; for while there was every probability that the English would side with the Crown against a Norman Lord or Duke, their fidelity was more problematical if it came to a conflict between their ghostly advisers and their earthly sovereign. Hence Rufus and Henry made the attempt, not indeed to break from Rome, which would have meant separation from the visible unity of the Church, but to make the connection a slight one, and liable to interruption at the royal pleasure.

Such being the ends which were pursued by the Crown throughout this period, it remains to see how far each of them was realised first by the Red King and then by his successor.

Accession of Rufus, 1087
The news of the Conqueror's death reached Rufus while he was still on Norman soil. He crossed the Channel in hot haste and made it his first concern to seize the royal hoard at Winchester. He brought with him Morcar and Wulfnoth son of Godwin, the two most considerable of his father's English prisoners, in case the barons of England should have already caught the infection of revolt from their Norman cousins. But, as it proved, there was no immediate need of an appeal to racial sentiment. The friends of the new King had acted with energy; the friends of Robert had not yet formulated their intentions; everything was quiet in England. Rufus only needed to present himself and his father's commendatory letter to Archbishop Lanfranc. If Lanfranc accepted him there was none to gainsay his coronation. It is said that Lanfranc hesitated to fulfil the Conqueror's request; he may well have done so, for the vices of Rufus were notorious. But the prince was importunate, and in the end he had his way. At Westminster, on September 26th, Lanfranc performed the ceremony of coronation. Rufus added to the customary clauses of the coronation oath a promise that he would be guided in all matters by the Archbishop's advice; and this satisfactory declaration decided the leaders of the baronage to tender their allegiance. That on a matter of national concern they should take their cue from the Archbishop

is a fact of much significance. Evidently it was thought that birth
and the wishes of a dying king should be allowed to settle the
question of the succession unless there were grave objections to the
candidate thus designated. But the right of granting or with-
holding the crown had passed away from the nation without coming
into the hands of the Great Council. It is the Church which holds
the balance between rival claimants, and the Archbishop is tacitly
accepted as the spokesman of the nation. No doubt Lanfranc
was an exceptional Archbishop ; but since the same deference was
shown to the opinion of the Church in 1100 and in 1135 we are
justified in assuming that on this occasion also the office counted
for more than the individual who held it.

The new king mounted the throne with little preparation and
less fitness for that high position. The Conqueror had steadily
declined to give his sons a share of power, and the youthful
Rufus was left to occupy himself with chivalric diversions, with warfare in a subordinate capacity, and in pursuing the more fashionable and flagrant vices of his class. At the time of his father's
death he can have been little more than twenty-seven years of age ;
but in the opinion of William of Malmesbury, his most lenient
critic, he had already sunk below the possibility of greatness or of
moral reformation. His appearance and demeanour were an index
to his character. He is described as of an ungainly build, square
and short and corpulent. His face was of a fiery hue, a circumstance to which he owed his nickname ; his eyes, grey and flecked
with spots of brown, were deeply set beneath a frowning forehead.
He was restless in his movements and impatient in conversation.
His habitual expression was a sneer, and he enjoyed the reputation of a witty talker. But he was no orator and stammered so
violently that when excited he became almost inarticulate. On
public occasions he endeavoured to imitate the reserved and stately
carriage of his father ; but he was liable to fits of passion during
which he threw decorum to the winds. In private life he showed
himself familiar and accessible, vaunted his contempt for the ordinary restraints of morality, and bragged of his most indefensible
designs with brutal naïveté. He was in fact the incarnation of a
spirit against which the better conscience of his age had already
risen in revolt ; of that gross and ferocious chivalry which the
régime of petty feudal states had produced all over Western

*Person-
ality of
Rufus*

Europe; a chivalry which, except in rare moments of exaltation or dejection, remained insensible to religion or romance; which respected no profession but that of war, obeyed no law but that of feudal honour, and admitted no rights except in equals or superiors. With the Crusades a new and gentler form of chivalry came into being; the accolade became a rite of mystical, and even of religious import; some elements of a higher moral code were infused into the law of " courtesy ". But the older school survived for a considerable time and in the days of Rufus it still kept the upper hand. The palm of knightly excellence, as that school understood the term, was equally divided between William of England and his confederate, the gay, unblushing, blasphemous Duke William IX. of Aquitaine. Contemptuous of priests and monks, oppressive towards the peaceful and industrious, merciless to those who sinned against the feudal contract, towards loyal knights, whether they were his friends or enemies, Rufus was courteous, lenient, and exact in the observance of his plighted word. He took delight in a bold feat of arms, even if performed at his expense ; he deemed no honour too great, no pay too high, for those who had earned distinction of this kind. He was a poor judge of ability, and the barons whom he promoted were in every way inferior to his father's favourites. But nowhere in Europe was there such another train of warriors as that which he enlisted in his service. His court became the Mecca of adventurers from both sides of the Alps. They took the wage of mercenaries, but lived with their paymaster on the footing of parasites and boon-companions. In peace or war they were always at his side; his ordinary retinue might easily have been mistaken for an army and was almost as destructive. Thieves and robbers of the vulgar kind trembled before the Red King's face. They found him no less vigilant than his father in the maintenance of the public peace, and for their benefit he reintroduced the death penalty which the Conqueror had abolished. But the knights of the household were privileged offenders. Wherever they accompanied the King they lived at free quarters on the country-side; on their departure from a homestead they staved the casks of ale and mead, and burned or sold the provisions, which they had not been able to consume. It was lucky if they did no worse ; for the law was powerless to protect life or limb or female honour against the favourites of the King. At the news

of the King's approach his subjects fled for shelter to the woods
and hills.[1] But Rufus cared nothing for the odium which his
followers brought upon him. He lived in dreams of conquest
which could only be realised with the help of mercenary knights;
while they were with him Rouen, Poitiers, Paris, and Rome itself
seemed to be within his grasp.[2] The proudest moments of his life
were those in which he marshalled all his chivalry, mercenaries and
barons together, at the three great festivals of Christmas, Easter,
Pentecost. That these gatherings might be celebrated with the
more magnificence he employed the men of London and the neighbouring shires for two years upon the building of a banquet-hall
in Westminster. No structure so magnificent had been reared in
France or England since the days of the old Roman empire; but
the Red King grumbled that it was too small by half. His designs
were nothing if not grandiose, and there is a certain plausibility in
the legend which represents him as standing on the shore of Wales
and swearing that he would bridge St. George's Channel with his
ships to conquer Ireland.[3] If statesmen were to be judged by
their ambitions and not by their achievements, the otherwise grotesque comparison which William of Malmesbury institutes between
Rufus and Julius Cæsar might be allowed to pass.[4]

In such a king there was little to attract either the native
English or the Church. Yet the first events of his reign brought
Rufus into a close alliance with both. However unpromising
might be the new king's antecedents the rule of one tyrant seemed
preferable to that of many, and a feudal rebellion of the year 1088
had the momentary effect of making the interests of the sovereign
identical with those of all the friends of peace and order. The plot
originated, strangely enough, with Odo of Bayeux whom Rufus
had released from prison and reinstated in his earldom.[5] Probably
the cause of the bishop's treachery is to be found in his old feud
with Lanfranc who held at the King's side the position to

Rebellion of Odo of Bayeux, 1088

[1] Eadmer, *H. N.*, p. 192. Hen. Hunt., vii., § 19.
[2] Suger, *Vita Lud.*, § 1: "Dicebatur equidem vulgo regem illum superbum et
impetuosum aspirare ad regnum Francorum". Gaimar speaks of designs on the
Empire: "S'il péust auques régner À Rome alast pur challenger L'ancien droit de
cel pais Que i avait Brenne et Belins". For Poitiers see W. Malmesb., *G. R.*, iv.,
§ 333.
[3] Giraldus, *De Institutione Principum*, p. 144 (ed. Anglia Christ. Soc.).
[4] W. Malmesb., *G. R.*, iv., § 320. For the character of Rufus see Orderic, iii.,
315; iv., 9. W. Malmesb., *G. R.*, iv., §§ 305, 312, 321. Suger, *Vita Ludovici;*
Roman de Rou, 9390.
[5] Odo is called *Justiciarius totius Angliae*, at this date, in the *Flores Historiarum*, vol. ii., p. 19 (R. S.).

3*

which Odo would naturally aspire, and on which he might reasonably count if his conspiracy succeeded in its object. This was nothing less than the substitution of Robert for his brother on the English throne. Specious excuses might be pleaded for the revolution. Robert was the eldest son; the partition of the Conqueror's dominions would mean a diminution in the consequence of the Norman race; and most of the barons had done homage to Robert in the life-time of his father long before they became the men of Rufus. But the conspiracy was not formed at the suggestion of Robert who, though disappointed at his brother's success— he had boasted that the English would wait for him if he were as far away as Alexandria—was disposed to take his disappointment in a philosophic spirit. His help apparently was not invoked until the train was laid; his interests were but the pretext through which Odo designed to make himself a Mayor of the Palace, and the bishop's accomplices to vindicate their independence of the royal authority. The character of the enterprise is betrayed by the names of those concerned. It is true that Robert of Mortain and William of Eu, both members of the ducal house, may conceivably have taken Robert's side in all good faith. But with them were banded others about whom there can be no doubt; Roger of Montgomery the astute Earl Palatine of Shropshire; Bernard of Neufmarché, the lord of Brecon, who had won by the sword every foot of land that he held beyond the Wye; Robert Mowbray, the sombre warden of Bamborough and Northumbria; his uncle the fighting bishop of Coutances, who had been taken from his Norman diocese to act as castellan of Bristol.

Outbreak of Hostilities   Their scheme was to paralyse the government by raising insurrections in half a dozen districts; in the midst of the general confusion thus produced a Norman army was to invade the south-eastern counties. Hostilities commenced at Easter, when the rebels with one accord absented themselves from the King's festival. At Norwich Roger Bigod, at Bristol Geoffrey of Coutances and Robert of Mowbray, garrisoned their castles and harried the surrounding country. William of Eu devastated the royal demesnes of Berkeley. Roger of Lacy captured Hereford and advanced with Bernard of Neufmarché to the attack on Worcester. In the south-east Roger Montgomery at Arundel, Robert of Mortain at Pevensey and Gilbert de Clare at Tunbridge prepared themselves

for war ; and Odo, occupying Rochester, admitted into this castle
a body of Norman troops which Robert had sent over as the
earnest of a larger force to come. It was a critical moment and
the hearts of the King's supporters failed them. William of St.
Calais, the bishop of Durham,[1] whom Rufus had taken for his chief
counsellor, deserted his master so early as the month of February
and retired to his see to watch the course of events. There could
be no better indication of the way the wind was blowing.

Fortunately for William the most formidable of the western
risings was defeated at an early stage. Wulfstan of Worcester
placed his knights and local influence at the service of the royal
garrison ; the fyrd responded to his summons ; the passage of the
Severn was successfully defended by the joint efforts of English
landowners and Norman mercenaries ; the greater part of the rebel
army was slain or captured. Somerset and Gloucestershire still
lay at the mercy of other malcontents. But the great danger lay
in the east and Rufus, with the true instinct of a general, refused
to let his attention be diverted from Kent and Sussex. Even for
these two shires the forces at his disposal were insufficient, with so
many ports to guard and so many castles to attack. He took the
bold step of appealing to the English. The fyrds of all the nearest Rufus
shires were summoned by peremptory writs to London, where the and the
King supported by Lanfranc and the bishops appealed to the English
loyalty of the assembled multitude. He promised them better
laws than there had ever been in England ; he promised the remission of all novel dues and taxes ; he promised to annul the
hated forest-laws so far as they infringed the rights of property.[2]
No attempt was ever made to fulfil these undertakings and it is
improbable that they were seriously meant. But they produced
the desired effect. The people applauded William, promised to
die, if need be, in his cause, and bade him play the man. A great
host, accompanied and encouraged by the old Archbishop, marched
with the King to Tunbridge ; and in two days the garrison was
cowed into surrender. The siege of Pevensey, in which Odo had
taken shelter with Robert of Mortain, was a more serious matter.
For six weeks the main body of the royal troops were engaged in
vain attempts to breach the defences of the Castle. In their rear

---

[1] For his antecedents, Simeon of Durham, *H. E. D.*, iv., 1.
[2] Florence of Worcester. *A. S. C.* Orderic, iii., 271.

the garrison of Rochester harried the environs of Canterbury and London; and Robert had ample time and opportunity to appear in England with the full force of his Duchy. He went the length of sending an expedition to the relief of Pevensey. But the coast was well guarded by the fyrd; and Rufus had taken timely measures to secure the ships of Hastings and the Cinque Ports. Attempting to disembark at Hastings the Normans were completely beaten; Robert renounced the cause of the rebels; and Pevensey, face to face with the prospect of starvation, surrendered on conditions. Odo promised that he would induce his allies at Rochester to submit and would then leave the kingdom. He was accordingly sent forward with an escort to fulfil the first of these conditions. But when he appeared before the gates of Rochester and issued his commands the garrison made a sally, captured the escort, and carried off the bishop as their not unwilling prisoner. They had not yet lost hope of Norman help and they prepared to stand a siege.

Siege of Rochester — Once more Rufus appealed to his English subjects; but this time with more confidence in his power to command. His writs went out through town and country calling on all men, French and English, to join his army if they would be "unnithing," that is, escape the name of traitor and its consequences.[1] An immense host, from town and country alike, responded to the call. In May the siege of Rochester began; Duke Robert showed no further sign of interest in the rebellion; close quarters, the summer heats, and a pestilence of flies prostrated the defenders; and in June the bishop negotiated for surrender. Rufus at first refused to grant conditions and his threats of condign punishment found a sympathetic echo in the ranks of his English followers. But there were other supporters whose wishes had to be consulted. Of the loyal barons some, like Roger of Montgomery, who had only returned to their allegiance at the eleventh hour and whose sons or kinsmen were in the beleaguered castle, insisted upon leniency, all were reluctant to sanction the infliction of corporal pains and penalties on men of their own rank. It was finally arranged that the besieged, even those who were the men of William, should have their lives and liberty; but their English lands were to be forfeit and they must depart from England. On these terms

[1] W. Malmesb., G. R., iv., 306. A. S. C., 1088. For the use of the word "nithing" compare A. S. C., 1049, in the story of Swegen's outlawry, "se cing tha and eall here cwædon Swegen for nithing". The word is Scandinavian.

the gates were opened and Odo and his friends marched out in shame and confusion. They begged that the king's trumpets should not sound the usual peal of triumph at their departure; but the King swore that not for a thousand marks of gold would he forgo the pleasure of insulting traitors. Shouts of execration passed along the English lines as Odo rode between them. "Halters, bring halters! Gallows for the Bishop!" was the universal cry. But the King's word was pledged and Odo departed scathless to live for some years longer as the evil genius of the Duke, his nephew.[1]

With the fall of Rochester the rebellion collapsed. The insurgents of the west and north threw up the game. Some were pardoned, chiefly the older men and those who had been on good terms with the Conqueror ; for attachment to his father's memory was one of the few amiable traits in the Red King's character. But the examples of William of Eu and Robert Mowbray were to show that clemency was wasted on a Norman. Many men of less consideration forfeited their lands and were exiled from the kingdom ; it would have been well for Rufus if he had made no exceptions. Among those whom he refused to pardon was the shifty William of St. Calais, who, though he had sailed perilously near the wind in his desertion of the King and subsequent neutrality, ventured to appear before the Great Council under a safe conduct and defend his cause. The trial, which ended with a sentence of exile, is remarkable because the bishop in his pleadings sounded the first note of discord between Church and State. He claimed the right to be tried by judges drawn exclusively from his own order; but perceiving that Lanfranc and his fellow-bishops were not inclined to interpret the feudal principle of judgment by peers in this new sense, he appealed against the King's court to the Holy See and produced a copy of the False Decretals to vindicate his privilege and the papal jurisdiction. The question of principle was one which Lanfranc at least had no inclination to discuss. He contented himself with advising the King that in respect of his temporalties the Bishop of Durham was a lay-baron and liable to forfeiture by the judgment of a feudal court. A judgment was passed to this effect; the Bishop was allowed to leave the country and please himself about the appeal to Rome.

Trial of William of St. Calais

---

[1] Orderic, iii., 276.

It was not prosecuted, since there was no likelihood that a Papal judgment would make Rufus relax his hold upon the Durham temporalties; a see without its revenues had no attraction for William of St. Calais. He remained in Normandy until an opportunity arose of regaining the lost favour of the King and abjuring pretensions by which so little had been gained.[1]

Ranulf Flambard

This trial is the last occasion which brings Lanfranc before us as the principal adviser of the king. They were soon estranged from one another by William's impudent repudiation of the pledges which he had given at his coronation and in the middle of the baronial rising. "Who can fulfil all that he promises?" was William's only answer to expostulations. Death soon relieved him of his inconvenient monitor (May 24th, 1089), and he was now at liberty to choose his advisers as he would. The chief rank among them still belonged to Robert Bloet, who bore the office of Chancellor. But it is probable that Ranulf Flambard who, at least as early as the year 1093, was the recognised head of the administration had already won the King's ear. Flambard[2] was the son of a parish-priest in the diocese of Bayeux. Having entered orders he came to England in the Conqueror's reign and took service under the bishop of London (at what date we cannot say); but when his hopes of ecclesiastical preferment were frustrated he wormed his way into the royal court and, although illiterate, established a certain reputation by means of a ready wit and a malicious tongue. He appears in Domesday as a landowner on a modest scale who had suffered by the enclosure of the New Forest; but it would be dangerous to infer that he was of no consequence in the year 1086. Indeed it is possible that he played an important part in the compilation of the great Survey; such is the meaning which has been attached to Orderic's story that Flambard remeasured the whole of England for the benefit of the Exchequer. But, since Orderic puts the remeasurement in the reign of William Rufus, his statement that Flambard was the moving spirit must be regarded with suspicion. It is safer to accept the ordinary view that Flambard's pre-eminence at the Exchequer only began with the death of the old King; and Orderic's tale may possibly relate to

[1] See the *Libellus de Injusta Vexatione Willelmi Episcopi* (Monasticon, i., 244) and Freeman's comments, *W. R.*, ii., p. 469.

[2] For the following account see Orderic, iii., 310 ff., and the *Continuatio prima* of Simeon's *H. E. D*

the process of editing by which the original returns for Domesday
purposes were digested in their present form.[1] This work may
have been executed by Flambard either before or after the accession of the second William; and as it was impossible to utilise the
returns until they had been codified the editor would naturally,
though unjustly, be regarded as responsible for the increased
taxation which ensued upon his work. Be this as it may, Rufus
was not long in discovering the financial abilities of Flambard.
The estates of the vacant see of Canterbury were handed over to
the upstart to be farmed for the royal benefit; he was promoted
to the rank of Treasurer;[2] and we may trace his hand in the
"unlawful gelds" by which, according to the English Chronicle, Flam-
the nation was oppressed in the year 1090. Flambard is credited bard's
finance
with having trebled the yield of ordinary taxation, and this may
well have been the case if the Danegeld was collected in the same
spirit as the feudal aids and incidents. All the customary limits
to the rights of wardship and marriage, all the rules as to reliefs,
were swept aside, and Rufus carried to extremes the Conqueror's
custom of exacting enormous fines for the least offence. The obsolete doctrine that a fief was a precarious estate, and granted only
for a life-time, was rigorously applied in all cases where the Crown
was not restrained by fear. Thus, a few years later than this time,
when Hugh of Shrewsbury fell in battle against the King's enemies,
his brother Robert of Bellême paid the enormous relief of £3,000
for the privilege of succeeding to the earldom. Vacant sees and
abbacies were still more hardly treated than lay fiefs. The new
custom was that, when a prelate died, his lands, instead of being
committed to a steward in trust for the successor, were seized into
the King's hand. A relief was demanded from every tenant of the
see; the revenues were paid into the Exchequer; and at the King's

---

[1] Orderic mentions the original Domesday survey in vol. iii., 201; the supposed
revision by Flambard in iii., 311. In a charter of William II., not earlier than 1093,
certain land is said to be enrolled "in meis brevibus quae sunt in thesauro meo
Wyntoniae," that is in the original Domesday returns (*Regesta*, No. 468).

[2] See the charter in *Hist. Dunelm. Scriptores Tres.* (Surtees Soc.), App. xxiii.
The Continuator of Simeon says, "propter quandam apud regem excellentiam
singulariter nominabatur *Capellanus* regis" (p. 135, R. S.). So the *A. S. C., s.a.* 1099,
"Ranulf his *capellane*". Certainly he had no other title in 1087-8; see the charter
in Monasticon, i., 261, which he attests as Capellanus. That he was custodian of the
king's seal appears from the story of his capture by kidnappers, in the Continuator.
Mr. Archer, *E. H. R.*, ii., p. 107, argued from this story that Ranulf held the rank
of Chancellor. But Treasurer and Chaplain are the only titles for which we have
documentary evidence.

pleasure lands were sold or granted on easy terms to favourites.
The vacancy might be prolonged for years, particularly in the case
of abbeys which were not rich enough to tempt one of the royal
chaplains; and when at length an appointment had been made the
King's nominee was expected to buy back the temporalties by the
payment of a large relief.[1]

Robert
in Nor-
mandy

Through such extortions Rufus was soon in a position to punish
his brother Robert for the assistance given to Odo of Bayeux. But
even if there had been no previous quarrel the state of Normandy
was in itself sufficient to invite attack. While England suffered
under an incipient despotism, in Normandy the far worse evils of
an anarchy prevailed. Duke Robert could display upon occasion
the qualities of a good general, and in the exile Odo he had at
least one able counsellor to guide him. But on the rare occasions
when he listened to advice the Duke's plans were frustrated by his
incapacity for sustained effort. Ordinarily he lived at Rouen,
surrounded by a swarm of worthless favourites, and left his subjects
to defend themselves. Maine slipped from his grasp within a year
or so of his accession; and he sold or mortgaged to his younger
brother Henry, for 3,000 marks of silver, the province of the
Cotentin from which not less than one-third of the ducal revenue
had been derived.[2] In the lands which nominally remained beneath
his sway every lord acted as an independent sovereign. Private
wars were waged without let or hindrance; new castles were built
without the licence of the duke; and every castle, new or old, became a nest of robbers whose occupation was to burn the villages,
drive the cattle, and hold to ransom the serfs or burgesses, of their
masters' enemies. In such a condition of affairs the only men interested in perpetuating Robert's rule were the barons who had
power to oppress their neighbours; and even these were not in
every case far-sighted enough to resist the overtures of Rufus.[3]

[1] These abuses are implied by the Charter of Henry I., S. C., p. 100. See also W.
Malm., *G. R.*, iv., § 314. Orderic, iii., 312. Florence, *s.a.* 1100. *Cf.* Round, *F. E.*,
p. 309, for a relief demanded from the tenants of the see of Worcester.

[2] Orderic, iii., 267, says that Henry *bought* the Cotentin. Wace, 9408, 14505, says
that it was *pawned* to him. Robert of Torigni (Cont. Will. Gemmetic.), viii., § 2,
mentions both stories without deciding between them. W. Malmesb., v., § 392, says
that the sum in question was the Conqueror's legacy to Henry, who remitted the
debt to Robert in exchange for the Cotentin. *Cf.* Palgrave, iv., p. 229.

[3] Orderic, iii., 290. *Cf.* also iv., 105. Ralph of Caen (ap. *Hist. des Croisades
Occidentaux*, iii., 616) says of Robert: "Misericordiam ejus immisericordem sensit
Normannia, dum eo consule per impunitatem rapinarum nec homini parceret nec
Deo licentia raptorum".

Treason was, or was believed to be, on foot in Normandy as Robert early as 1088. Shortly after the fall of Rochester the Atheling and Henry Henry came to England to claim his mother's lands, bringing with him Robert of Bellême, a younger son of Roger Earl of Shrewsbury and one of the captains whom Robert had deputed to assist the conspiracy of Odo. They were well received at court, and Henry obtained a promise of his inheritance; he became the man of Rufus, and so did his companion. On their return to Normandy they were, not unnaturally, arrested as traitors and imprisoned. But the Earl of Shrewsbury obtained the permission of the King to cross to Normandy and protect his son. All the vassals of the House of Talvas rose at the bidding of their chief, and after a brief campaign, in which the balance of successes was distinctly with the Duke, Robert, too indolent to follow up his victories, made peace by liberating both his prisoners. They were far from grateful for this favour. Henry, retiring to the Cotentin, prepared for war; Robert earned an evil reputation by plundering the lands of friend and foe and inflicting hideous tortures on his captives. Rufus would have been the natural ally of both rebels. But with more than ordinary want of foresight he broke his word to Henry, and gave their mother's English lands to Robert son of Hamon. This perfidy lost Rufus the opportunity of acquiring Normandy without a war. But war with Robert involved no serious risk, and in the early summer of 1090 the Red King declared his intention of taking vengeance for his brother's share in the rebellion of two years before. He invaded eastern Normandy with a large force mainly recruited from among his English vassals; the border castles were partly The Nor-taken, partly bought with English gold; and Philip of France, who man War had come to Robert's aid from a well grounded conviction that the 1090-1 King of England would be a more dangerous neighbour, was in-duced by a substantial bribe to desert the side which it was his interest to support. In the autumn the Norman capital itself was nearly captured by the treachery of the citizens. Anxious to keep their English trade and smarting under the misgovernment of Robert the men of Rouen opened negotiations with the King of England. There was no commune yet in Rouen; but the dis-affected had taken as their leader a certain Conan, who was the richest of their number and had used his wealth to enlist a retinue of mercenary soldiers. The plot was hatched under the very eyes of Robert who had taken up his quarters in the castle of Rouen, leaving the management of the campaign to his subordinates. Conan promised to admit the troops of Rufus to the city; the Duke, aware of the treason but unable to protect himself against it, could only send an appeal for help to Henry and Robert of Bellême. They had little cause to love the Duke; but they loved Rufus even less, and rebellious burgesses were the common enemy of all their class. They came accordingly to Rouen, and slipped in at the south gate unperceived by Conan and his friends, who, at that very moment, were admitting through the western gate 200 horsemen of the English army. The two forces met in the streets, and a desperate struggle ensued in which the burgesses took part on one side or the other as loyalty or interest suggested. In the end the troops of Rufus fled, and Robert, who had watched the contest from the shelter of a church outside the walls, rewarded his allies by making over to them the richest of the rebel citizens. It is recorded that one of these, the richest after Conan, gave a ransom of 3,000 marks to his unconscionable gaoler. Others paid according to their wealth; to Conan alone all mercy was denied. Henry claimed him as the spoil of war and refused to hear his abject prayers for mercy; the demagogue was hurled from the castle tower as a warning to all base-born traitors; his body was dragged through Rouen at a horse's tail and thrown into the Seine.[1]

The men of Rouen made no further move in favour of the English King. But in February, 1091, the long-expected arrival of Rufus with new forces and a new supply of gold left Robert no option but to sue for peace. It was concluded partly at his expense and partly at that of Henry, who was not admitted to the negotiations. Rufus kept his conquests and received in addition the ducal seat of Fécamp.[2] In return he promised aid against the Manceaux and the Norman rebels, and undertook to reinvest the Duke's supporters with their English lands. The second of these engagements was partially fulfilled. William of St. Calais and other rebels of less note received their pardon, although Rufus with politic bad faith persisted in excluding Odo of Bayeux from the benefits of the amnesty. The clause relating to rebels was ingeniously made the excuse for an attack upon the Cotentin. Robert had repented of

---

[1] Orderic, iii., 351. W. Malmesb., v., § 392. The spot where Conan fell was long known as Conan's Leap (R. de Monte, p. 106).

[2] The King and the Duke held, in July, 1091, an important enquiry into the rights of the Duke of Normandy, which is one of our chief sources of knowledge respecting Norman constitutional law. It was first adequately edited by Professor Haskins in *E. H. R.*, xxiii., pp. 506-8.

the bargain with his youngest brother; and Rufus needed no pressing to accept the bribe of Mont St. Michel and Cherbourg, the two
keys of the Cotentin, which Robert offered for the help of English
troops.   Henry made a gallant but ineffectual attempt to hold the
Mont St. Michel against the united forces of the Duke and King.
After a fortnight he was compelled, by want of food and water, to
capitulate.[1] He kept his liberty, but was stripped of all his lands.
For some years to come he was a penniless adventurer often dependent for the bare means of subsistence upon the enemies of Normandy
and England.

Before leaving the Duchy Rufus insisted upon the expulsion of Malcolm
the harmless Edgar Atheling who had lived, since the Conqueror's and
death, at the Norman court as the guest and boon-companion of Rufus,
Duke Robert.   The Atheling, in his distress, sought a refuge in 1091
Scotland with his sister's husband; and Margaret's influence was at
once exerted to raise a war with England.   In May, 1191, Malcolm
crossed the border at the head of a considerable force.   He advanced no farther than the Wear, and hearing that the fyrd and
feudal levies of the northern shires were on the march, he beat a
precipitate retreat.   But Rufus lost no time in avenging the affront.
He returned to England, bringing with him his two brothers that
the settlement of Normandy might not be undone by their intrigues
while he was employed elsewhere; and early in the autumn marched
into the Lothians.   His army suffered from inclement weather;
and the fleet which carried his supplies was dashed in pieces by the
equinoctial gales.   This check was enough to change his purpose;
for Rufus with all his energy was the reverse of a tenacious general.
He invited Robert to take the part of mediator; and with his
brother's help obtained a peace, under which the Atheling was restored to the estates which he had lost in Normandy.   In return
for this concession, for the restoration of twelve English manors
which Edgar the Peaceful had granted to the Crown of Scotland,
and for a pension of twelve marks of gold, Malcolm promised to
Rufus the same obedience which he had rendered to the Conqueror.

Thus peace was restored on both sides of the sea.   But it was
not to be expected that Rufus would keep faith with those in whom
he did not stand in awe.   Robert pressed in vain for the fulfilment

---

[1] Orderic, iii., 379.   Wace, 9600, says that Robert allowed the garrison to fetch
water and sent his brother a barrel of wine.

84 ENGLAND UNDER NORMANS AND ANGEVINS [1087-

of the promises made at the beginning of the year, and returned to Normandy in dudgeon shortly before the Christmas feast. In the following year (1092) Malcolm learned what he might expect from Rufus. Since the year 945 the kings of Scotland, in virtue of a grant from Edmund the Glorious, had claimed, though they had not always succeeded in holding, the stronghold of Carlisle and a strip of country further south which comprised the western halves of the modern Cumberland and Westmoreland.[1] This district, which at one time had served as an appanage for princes of the Scottish line, was now an earldom held of Malcolm by the Northumbrian Dolfin. In the summer of 1092 Rufus marched northward, drove out Dolfin, and laid the foundations of a castle and a new walled city at Carlisle. A garrison and many villeins with their families were settled there to form the nucleus of an English colony. The complaints of Malcolm at this breach of common justice were met with counter-accusations. He ventured to the King's court at Gloucester in 1093, hoping that with the influence of friendly English barons he might obtain some satisfaction. But Rufus refused to meet him as an equal and demanded that Malcolm should answer before the Great Council for some unspecified offences. Malcolm denied that his submission had been meant to make him a vassal in this sense. He offered to do right to Rufus, but only on the borders of the two kingdoms and before a court formed from the baronage of both; on the rejection of this offer he went home to prepare a new invasion. He raised the northern counties late in the year 1093; but he met his match in Robert Mowbray. The earl and his men laid an ambush for the Scots on the banks of the Alne, at a place which to this day is known as Malcolm's Cross. Malcolm was slain by the earl's steward Morel of Bamborough; the fact that Morel was the king's "gossip" made even English chroniclers regard the deed as one of the blackest treachery; but for the later story, which has found its way into some texts of Turgot, that the king was killed at a peaceful conference, in the act of receiving the keys of the castle of Alnwick (which did not then exist) from the ancestor of the Percy family, there is no foundation.[2] With Malcolm fell Edward, his eldest son by Margaret. The King left six other sons. Duncan, the eldest, the child of an earlier and

The English annexation of Carlisle, 1092

Death of Malcolm, 1093

---

[1] See Appendix, "Cumberland and Scotland".
[2] Palgrave, *England and Normandy*, iv., p. 358.

irregular union, would have been the natural successor if he had been in Scotland to assert his title. But he was a hostage at the English court, and even the imperious will of Margaret would have been insufficient to force one of his half-brothers upon the Scots. There was a national party which had long chafed against the foreign fashions, the foreign favourites, and the foreign ideas of centralisation, which Margaret was responsible for introducing. Their discontent, suppressed with difficulty while Malcolm lived, flamed out when the news of his disaster was received. Margaret, already stricken with mortal disease, outlived her husband and her eldest son long enough to see the downfall of her aspirations. Aided by the Norwegians of the Isles the national party elected Malcolm's brother Donaldbane. He entered Edinburgh in triumph on the Accession day when Margaret's body was carried out for burial to Dunferm-of Donald line. The sons of Margaret fled. The Englishmen whom the bane dead King and Queen had brought into the country were expelled; the old Celtic monarchy, hostile to England and every kind of English influence, was revived; and the alliance between Donaldbane and Magnus King of Norway brought the Scandinavian peril, which had troubled the Conqueror's early days, to the doors of England in a new and formidable shape. We need not credit Magnus with any deliberate scheme for the recovery of Cnut's Empire; but it is evident that the Norsemen, notwithstanding the rise of the Anglo-Norman power, still looked with hungry eyes towards England.

Rufus was not the man to remain inactive while Celt and Duncan Norseman were cementing a hostile coalition. He left the sons of and Margaret to shift for themselves. It was not his policy to perpetu-bane ate a West-Saxon dynasty. But between himself and the hostage Duncan there was no hereditary feud; and this prince, on condition of rendering homage and fealty for the kingdom which he had still to win, was allowed to invade Scotland with a mixed host of Englishmen and Normans. The usurper had no forces capable of standing against southern knights and men at arms. He fled to his allies in the Isles, while the population of the Lowlands passively acknowledged Malcolm's son. But the new sovereign's reign was brief and troubled. Riots arose against his foreign following. Some were slain; the rest he was compelled to dismiss and being thus left defenceless he fell an easy prey to a coalition which had been formed between the friends of Donaldbane and those of Edmund the second son of Malcolm and Margaret. In the year 1094 Duncan was slain at Monachedin, on the banks of the river Bervie in Kincardine.   Donaldbane began a second reign; we are not told how the claims of Edmund were satisfied, but there had been an agreement between himself and Donaldbane for the division of the kingdom and since they remained on friendly terms this arrangement may have been fulfilled.   The plans of Rufus were thus thwarted; and it was well for him that the alliance of Donaldbane and Magnus did not lead to the result which might naturally have been expected.   Three years elapsed before the King of England could turn his attention to the affairs of Scotland.   From 1094 to 1097 he was fully occupied with a Norman war, with a dangerous rebellion among the English baronage, and with an ecclesiastical controversy which weakened his already slender hold upon the allegiance of his English subjects.   Few kings have been more favoured by fortune than William Rufus, and it was not the least part of his good luck that the accident which led to the overthrow of Malcolm's power did not leave Scotland an even more dangerous neighbour than it had been when a queen of the House of Cerdic swayed its policy.

Ecclesiastical Difficulties, 1092-3

At the very outset of the Scottish difficulty, between the campaign of Carlisle and the breach with Malcolm, the first step was taken towards that conflict between Church and State which, after raging intermittently for the best part of a century, was to be suspended rather than settled by the murder of an Archbishop and the public self-abasement of the most powerful sovereign who had ever occupied the English throne.   In a sense the conflict was inevitable; for it was waged between two inconsistent theories of society both of which were firmly rooted in the characteristic institutions of the Middle Ages; it would have been an incredible good fortune for England to have escaped from a strife which in one form or another disturbed every other realm of Western Christendom.   But the form which the duel of Church and State assumed on English soil was a peculiar one and the result of special causes.   In the year 1092 there was no particular reason for supposing that the system devised by Rufus and Flambard for the spoliation of the national church would be challenged, much less overthrown, for a considerable period of time.   Among the English

prelates there were some who felt sincere misgivings at the degradation of their office.   They resented, and not from wholly
interested motives, the attempt to saddle them with all the obligations of a feudal tenant.   Odo, the abbot of Chertsey, expressed
a general feeling when he resigned his dignity on the ground that
he would not hold it of the king in the manner of a layman
(1092).   A bishop or an abbot was a trustee holding property for **Lay In-**
the benefit of his ecclesiastical inferiors and the poor ; was he tamely **vestitures**
to submit when required to furnish knights and money in the same
proportion as a baron who held his lands to his own singular profit
and advantage ?   And how was it possible that one who had taken
on himself all the obligations of lay vassalage should preserve at
the same time the independence and outspoken frankness of a
Christian teacher ?   The feeling grew that it was nothing short
of simony to accept an ecclesiastical preferment on the terms
for which alone the Red King would confer them ; those who
stooped to make a bargain with him were harassed by their own
self-reproaches and the pitying contempt of others.   Herbert
Losinga, a man of excellent character, famous for his learning, and
honourably distinguished for his charity, paid a relief of £1,000
upon his admission to the see of Thetford.   The story ran that
when, following the usual custom, he opened the gospel-book at his
consecration to seek for a prognostic verse, his eye was met by
the salutation with which Christ welcomed Judas on the night of
the betrayal : "Friend, wherefore art thou come ?"   The bishop
groaned in spirit, for he felt that he also had sold his Lord for
silver.[1]   He kept the see, indeed ; but his conscience gave him no
rest until, at a later time, he had visited Rome, confessed his fault,
and received forgiveness and re-investiture from the Vicar of St.
Peter.   His remorse finds expression in the charter which he gave
to the Cathedral at Norwich.   He speaks in the preamble to this
document as one who is a penitent for sins committed against
knowledge.[2]   Such was the general attitude towards the new
system of patronage.   But from men like Herbert Losinga no
vigorous remonstrances were to be expected.   It is difficult for
those who have benefited by abuses to advocate reform.   The

---

[1] W. Malmesb., *G. P.*, p. 154.
[2] See the charter in the edition of Losinga's letters by Goulburn and Symonds,
i., 146.

bishops moreover had an excuse which they deemed sufficient for their inactivity. Without a primate to convene them they could not assemble in a synod or make a collective protest to the King. In leaving the see of Canterbury vacant Rufus and Flambard had destroyed for the time being the corporate unity of the English Church. There was no accredited spokesman of the bishops, no one who had a special obligation to initiate resistance. The bishops hoped that some day they would be vouchsafed a leader, and that the king's malpractices would then come naturally and quietly to an end. They went so far as to ask the sanction of Rufus for a form of prayer that Heaven would be pleased to soften his heart and accelerate the choice of a new primate. They entered into a harmless and transparent conspiracy with the Earl of Chester and the monks of Bec, as the result of which Abbot Anselm of Bec, the pupil and friend of Lanfranc, was brought to England and to the King's notice. In and out of season they sang the praises of their candidate, with no other result than that of rousing the Red King's ire. " Pray as you please ; I will do as I please," he stammered when they laid their form of prayer before him ; [1] at another time he swore by the Holy Face of Lucca that neither Anselm nor any other man but himself should have the see of Canterbury. If Gregory VII. had been living this outrageous declaration would not have passed without a rebuke at which even Rufus might have trembled. But that great-hearted lover of justice and hater of iniquity had passed away in the same year as the Conqueror ; the rivals between whom the chair of Hildebrand was in dispute were, with all their virtues, very far from possessing his dauntless temperament. Neither Urban the representative of the reforming school nor Guibert the Imperialist anti-Pope was disposed to court a quarrel with a King who so far stood committed to neither party and, in the evenly divided state of European opinion, might well be able to turn the scale whichever way he pleased. The Church of England was thus left without an advocate, and might have remained for years in this condition, but for the trifling accident of an illness which seized on Rufus at the beginning of Lent, 1093.

There may have been men so steeled against common beliefs

[1] W. Malmesb. *G. P.*, p. 79.

and common fears of the unseen that in health and in sickness alike they have made a law of their own baser impulses without con- templating the possibility of retribution in this world or another. Rufus was a sinner of a more ordinary kind. He had become the slave of his passions ; his daily actions gave the lie to every pre- cept of the Christian code ; and nothing so delighted him as to shock the worst of his companions by some daring blasphemy. But in the hour of danger he believed and trembled. The bishops ventured to his bedside with somewhat tardy exhortations to re- pentance and restitution. He heard them out, and humbly took the advice of Anselm on the question whether the penance which they had proposed was adequate. From Anselm he received the same counsel as from the bishops. His government had been harsh beyond all reason ; therefore the debts which were due to him must be forgiven, and the captives who lay in his prisons must be released. The laws of the Confessor had been set at nought ; they must be solemnly confirmed and executed for the future in good faith. His ministers had oppressed the people ; they must be called upon to render a strict and terrible account. Lastly the wrongs of the Church must be redressed. The King promised all that was required of him, and sent the bishops to lay his vow upon God's altar in the neighbouring minster-church. As an earnest of his repentance he issued a writ for the release of all prisoners, and disposed of the two great ecclesiastical dignities which lay vacant in his custody. The broad diocese of Lincoln, including no less than nine shires between the Thames and Humber, he conferred upon his faithful chaplain Robert Bloet. The appointment showed that, even in the face of death, Rufus thought no shame of driving a hard bargain with his Maker. It is perhaps the voice of personal or professional spite which describes the chaplain as a reckless sinner, abandoned to every form of lust. Robert Bloet had a son, and he was no friend to the regular clergy ; these facts are enough to account for the worst charges brought against him. But, at the best, he was simply a favourable specimen of that discreet and courtly class of officials, whose public services were more conspicuous than their private virtues, and who were habitually paid or pensioned off with bishoprics. In this case at least Rufus made the minimum of sacrifice. With the primacy however he could not venture to juggle so transparently. The appointment of Anselm was demanded by the unanimous voice of the bishops and the nation. Rufus submitted with the best grace that he might; and Anselm, vainly protesting against an honour of which he alone thought himself unworthy, was literally dragged to the King's bedside for investiture. The ring was forced upon his finger, the pastoral staff pressed into his reluctant hand, and the bishops sang *Te Deum* in the royal presence, with the comfortable conviction that all the difficulties of the Church were solved by the election of a saint to rule her.

They judged the man more justly than the situation. Anselm is better known to us than any other leading figure of the Middle Ages. His letters and the writings of his faithful friend Eadmer enable us to follow the workings of his mind in every phase and relation of his varied life; they explain the apparent paradox that one who had been so long absorbed by questions the most remote from practical life that we can well imagine, should in old age have taken on himself a foremost part in the great political controversy of his generation; and they justify in full the estimate which contemporaries formed of Anselm's character. He had been a wanderer in youth; in later life he was thrust, by the exigencies of his time and the admiration of those who knew him, into the position of a spiritual director and a party leader. But throughout his career he was at heart a saint, a man to whom action appeared a feverish dream, the visible world a transitory shadow, and contemplation the true end and function of the soul; not self-centred, since he made it his mission to assist others in realising the ideal which he had set before himself; but a profound individualist who saw in the whole universe nothing real or valuable except God and His law on the one side, and on the other the individual with his consciousness of God and his knowledge of the scriptures and traditions which explained the will of God. Very characteristic is the story of his early life as he unfolded it to his companions.[1] Details of time and place are either forgotten or ignored; nothing is remembered except the vicissitudes of the ascent to spiritual humility and peace; how as a boy he dreamed of Paradise at Aosta in the shadow of the Alps; how as a youth he threw himself into his studies and sought the key to the world-

---

[1] See besides Eadmer's biography the anecdotes of the monk Alexander (from MS. CCC., 457), quoted by Mr. Rule in his preface to the *Historia Novorum*.

riddle in the learning of the schools; how he left the schools, when he had learned the hollowness of all their wisdom, and plunged into the secular pursuits which were natural to his youth and station; how again he repented and fled northward over the Alps on the quest for another and a better path to happiness; how he was lured to the school of Bec by Lanfranc's teaching and was fired with the passing ambition to emulate his master and become the teacher of the Latin world; how finally he found contentment as a cloistered monk in the complete forgetfulness of self and all ambitious dreams. As he had begun so he continued; with a fixed conviction that for every man the first duty is that of bringing himself into harmony with the divine law. Critics have shown some reason for believing that Anselm belonged by descent to the old royal line of Burgundy. There is something royal in the serenity with which he carried his convictions into practice; in the unshaken confidence with which he exhorted all who asked his guidance to adopt the same course as himself; in his sympathy for the weak-kneed, in his large toleration for ignorance and harmless superstition. His intellectual greatness is attested by the influence which his idealism has exercised on the most various types of thinker since his day.[1] Yet there is perhaps more greatness in his immovable conviction as to the possibility, on the one hand of reconciling faith with reason and grounding Christianity on the firm rock of deductive argument;[2] on the other of taking the law of Christ and His Church as the sole guide to action in every part of human life. The latter belief, indeed, is easy and natural to one who conceives himself as entrusted with a mission to defend his convictions with the sword and even, it may be, to convert the world by force. But Anselm was no fanatic of this description. Like St. Paul he advocated a course of non-resistance and non-interference. The duty of the Christian was to obey while he could do so with a good conscience, to protest when he could not obey, and to suffer in patience when his remonstrances were disregarded.

It was this attitude which made him, in the eyes of the English bishops, the obvious successor to the primacy. There was no man

---

[1] Cf. as to Anselm's intellectual importance Rashdall, *Universities*, i., p. 41. Church, *St. Anselm*, and the studies by Franck, Hasse, and J. M. Rigg.

[2] Cf. Anselmi Epistolae, II., xli. (ed. Migne): "Nam Christianus per fidem debet ad intellectum proficere, non per intellectum ad fidem accedere, aut si intelligere non valet a fide recedere".

Conditions
of An-
selm's ac-
ceptance living whose remonstrances were more likely to have weight with Rufus; and at the same time there was no man less likely to involve the Church in an unnecessary and unequal conflict with the lay authority. But they had failed to realise the complexity of the situation and the rigidity of Anselm's logic. The abuses of the existing régime went further than they understood; and revolutionary principles were involved even in the less conspicuously oppressive demands of the King. Anselm had gauged the future more correctly. So long as Rufus lived—and from the hour of his repentance the King's health began to mend—there would be no change of system. Rufus lost no time in repudiating the promises which he had made with reference to secular administration; was it to be expected that he would be more scrupulous about his engagements to the Church? The answer to this doubt was given by the King himself. He told the aged Bishop Gundulf of Rochester that he had received nothing but evil at the hands of God, and God should get no good of him. As Archbishop it was certain that Anselm would be drawn into conflicts which he had neither the strength nor the experience to wage with any prospect of success; the previous conduct of the bishops was enough to show how little he could count on them to support his individual efforts. He at first declined to consider his appointment valid, on the ground that he had been invested against his will and without the leave of the Duke of Normandy, his natural lord, or of the community of Bec, his ecclesiastical superiors. The more technical of these objections having been removed by the consent of Robert and the monks of Bec to forgo their claims upon his services, he told the King that he could only accept consecration upon definite conditions. They were threefold: that he should receive all the lands and possessions which had belonged to the see of Canterbury at the time of Lanfranc's death, and that all leases or enfeoffments which the King had made in the time of the vacancy should be accounted null and void; that he should not be expected to retract the profession of obedience which, in common with the other prelates of the Norman Church, he had already tendered to Pope Urban; and that he should be accorded the position of the King's chief counsellor in all matters, according to the ancient privilege of his office. The first of these demands was one which Rufus could not for very shame refuse; after some haggling, which entirely

failed to shake the Archbishop's resolution, a royal writ enjoining
the completest restitution was drawn up and promulgated.[1]   As to
the second and third demands Rufus was less conciliatory.   There can
be no doubt he made some general promises; but it is equally certain
that he gave no formal guarantees, and Anselm added considerably
to his later difficulties by the readiness with which he accepted
half-assurances.   He allowed himself to be consecrated without
more delay ; and, when the moment came for making his profession
of obedience to the Holy See, he departed from the ordinary custom
as far as to refrain from specifying the name of the Pope to whom
he pledged his faith.   No doubt the object was to give Rufus the
opportunity of acknowledging Urban without the semblance of
compulsion.   But the King, as might easily have been guessed,
still cherished the policy of standing neutral between the rival
Popes ; and the form of Anselm's profession made it possible to
assert that he had withdrawn his adhesion from Pope Urban.[2]

The King's recovery was followed by the resumption of his Norman
designs on Normandy.   The richest half of the Duchy was in his Campaign,
possession but he grudged the other half to Robert; and in the 1094
course of 1093 he indicated his intentions by accepting the allegiance of the Count of Eu, one of the most powerful and discontented
of the Norman barons.   The Duke retaliated at the Nativity by
sending ambassadors who, after taxing Rufus with this and other
breaches of the treaty of 1091, called on him to give compensation
or else prepare for war.   Rufus accepted the challenge as it was
intended and the result was a desultory war (1094).   Rufus fixed
upon Eu as his base of operations ; Robert and Philip of France
joined their forces to resist him ; on both sides castles were besieged
and taken, the open fields were harried, and the villages were
burned.   At length the King of France was detached by bribes
from his ally, while Henry the Atheling (who had been living for
the last two years the life of Ishmael at the border castle of
Domfront) was approached by Rufus, induced to condone past
wrongs, and put into the field against his eldest brother (1095).
The advantage rested on the whole with Rufus ; but in his plans
there was one fatal flaw.   No kingdom of that age was capable of
providing the funds required for a continuous series of campaigns.

[1] Monasticon, i., 105. Anselmi Epistolae, III., xxiv. (ed. Migne). *Foedera*, I., 5.
[2] Anselmi Epistolae, III., xxxvi. (ed. Migne).

The resources of England had been strained to the utmost for the operations of 1094. Aids had been demanded, in addition to military service, from the feudal tenants of the King; the burden of the Danegeld had been increased; and the money with which to bribe the King of France had only been procured by a unique device. Twenty thousand men of the fyrd were summoned to appear at Hastings and each of them received instructions to bring ten shillings for the expenses of his journey. They came expecting to be shipped to Normandy, and it must have been with very mingled feelings that they received the command of Ranulf Flambard to give up their journey-money and go home. The fraud was too gross to be repeated even by a Flambard. No more specious source of income could be found, and in December Rufus returned to England smarting under the consciousness that his prey had escaped him at the moment when success seemed certain. An unsuccessful Welsh expedition embittered him still further and left him eager for an object on which to vent his irritation. In Anselm he found the victim whom his injured pride required.

Quarrel of Rufus with Anselm, 1095
The King and the Archbishop had already come into collision It was the secular struggle of Pope and Emperor reproduced in miniature on English soil; the question at issue was that of the relations between the spiritual and temporal powers. To Rufus the appointment of a Primate meant chiefly the enfeoffment of a new vassal with a lucrative estate. By accepting investiture Anselm had become his liege man liable to all the incidents of vassalage; and William asserted this view of their relations with his usual brutal frankness.[1] Anselm, though by no means eager to wrangle over abstract definitions, did not shrink from objecting to the practical consequences of the Red King's theory. On being asked to give an aid for the Norman war the Archbishop at first refused. He was no ordinary vassal; his estates had been so impoverished during the vacancy that he could only make a contribution by oppressing his own tenants; he would not give his detractors a handle for the charge of simony. Finally, as a token of good will, he offered from his ordinary revenues the modest present of 500 marks. It was refused with scorn, and Anselm distributed the sum among the poor. Then came word that the King had repented and would

---

[1] Monasticon, vi., 1271: " Hoc donum factum est die crastina qua Anselmus Archiepiscopus meus ligeus homo factus est ". Cf. Regesta, No. 336.

take the money for his pressing needs ; but the bishops who brought the message had to return with empty hands and explain that the money was already spent. "Tell the Archbishop," said Rufus in a fury, "that I hated him yesterday, and hate him more to-day, and shall hate him even more to-morrow." Nor was this the only collision between the two. Anselm had not forgotten the right, conferred upon him by his office, of acting as the King's adviser. When the host was marshalling at Hastings for the spring campaign of 1094 he came to the King with suggestions for ecclesiastical reform. He wished in the first place for a general synod of the bishops, such as had not met for many years, to rebuke the vices of the nation. "What vices?" said the King in discomposure. Anselm looked him in the eyes and mentioned one in particular with which the King and all his court stood charged by common fame. The subject dropped, and the Archbishop pressed for appointments to the vacant abbeys which the King was still farming without regard to his promises of twelve months ago. At this the King boiled over; his purse was a more tender subject with him than his character. "What is that to you?" he said. "The abbeys are my abbeys. You do what you please with your own manors," he continued, with a pointed allusion to the dispute about the recent aid, "and I will do the same with my abbeys."

In spite of these outbreaks there had been no serious rupture in The Papal the year 1094. It was difficult to quarrel with a man so patient Question and courteous as Anselm showed himself. But the quarrel came at length in February, 1095. The question of the Papal obedience was still unsettled, and the time was drawing near when Anselm must either go to Rome to fetch his pallium or else forfeit his see for the omission of this customary observance. He asked the King's leave for a journey to the Pope. "Which Pope?" was the reply. To this there could only be one answer. Rufus seized the opportunity. No Pope should be acknowledged in his dominions without his consent. If Anselm declared for Urban he was a traitor to the King; and it was in vain that the Archbishop recapitulated the conditions upon which he had been consecrated. The utmost which the King would concede was that the question should be laid before the Great Council, on which he thought that he could rely for a decision favourable to his claim. But there were subjects on which Anselm would not accept even the verdict of the Council.

The canon law could not be set aside by any secular assembly. If the Council decided for him, well and good. If not he would leave the kingdom.

Council of
Rocking-
ham, 1095 The Council met on February 25th at Rockingham.[1]   Eadmer has given us a vivid narrative of the proceedings as they appeared to one who stood with the Archbishop in the antechamber while the King and his Council debated in secret as to Anselm's fate. It is much to be regretted that we have no report of these discussions, which would throw considerable light on the vexed question of the customs of the Conqueror, their exact intention, and the nature of the relations with Rome which they permitted. At an early stage in the debate Anselm was asked to acknowledge the jurisdiction of the Council; and his answer raised a difficulty which at once diverted attention from the original articles of accusation. "In the things that are God's I will render obedience to the Vicar of St. Peter's; in things touching the earthly dignity of my Lord the King I will to the best of my ability give him faithful counsel and help." The words are more emphatic than precise. But the position taken up by Anselm was apparently as follows. Without discussing the general question of a bishop's duty in a time of schism, he maintained that for himself there was no possibility of departing from the obedience of Pope Urban; and that the King had known this from the first. In settling the limits of his obedience to the Pope the Archbishop must be guided by the canon law alone; no pretended custom, no verdict of the Curia Regis could overrule the will of the Universal Church as expressed by the mouth of Popes and Councils. There were thus two separate points at issue; and a third was introduced when Anselm announced that in the event of condemnation he would appeal to Urban. All three seem however to have been persistently confused in the discussion; and the parties which arrayed themselves against and for the Archbishop paid little attention to his abstract propositions. The bishops were annoyed that the Church should be embroiled with Rufus over a question in which they felt very little interest; and they accused their chief of a design to impair the "imperial" dignity of the Crown; a charge which lost much of its sting when raised by the versatile William of St. Calais, who, only a few years before, had defended against the King and Council the

[1] For the date see Rule's preface to Eadmer, *H. N.*, p. lxii.

very principle with which he now reproached the Primate. The
barons on the other hand gravitated to the side of Anselm. The
King might have had their sympathy if the question at issue had
been simply one of defending his prerogative. But he had made
the mistake of attempting to influence their verdict by the plainest
threats; and prudence no less than pride of class impelled them to
vindicate the independence of a court before which any one of
them might at any moment be arraigned. Moreover the most
hardened courtiers felt some respect for the courage of the accused
Archbishop. Robert of Meulan, who on all ordinary occasions was
the staunch supporter of the Crown, expressed the general opinion
when he said that it was impossible to condemn a man who went
to sleep while his adversaries were arguing and, when they had
finished, tore their arguments in pieces with a word or two. The
upshot was that neither party would vote for the Archbishop's
condemnation. The bishops, who based their decision on the
technical ground that they were incompetent to judge their superior,
atoned for this fit of independence by telling Anselm that they
renounced all faith and friendship with him. The barons however
refused to follow this example, though pressed to do so by the
King. "We find no fault in the man," was their blunt reply to all
persuasions.

Anselm's position at the close of the Council was anomalous Rufus ap
and difficult. He had been acquitted by his peers, but he was proaches
the Pope
disowned by his fellow-bishops and treated by his sovereign as an
enemy. He felt that he could do no further good in England and
asked for leave to quit the country. But in reality it was the
King who had suffered a defeat at Rockingham, and Rufus was
not a little embarrassed by the situation. He would have been
glad to see the last of Anselm; but an English Primate in
the hands of a hostile Pope would be a serious danger to the
monarchy. Gregory VII. had shown the world that even an
Emperor could not hold his own against a Papal sentence when
its justice was acknowledged by his subjects. And, even though
Anselm were detained in England a prisoner in all but name, he
would not want for popular support. There were more laymen on
the Archbishop's side than those who had spoken for him in the
Council. The people had suffered in silence under the burden of
oppressive fines and gelds and forest courts; but their patience

4

would be exhausted if religion were attacked in a man whom they revered as a saint and in an office to which they looked as the chief bulwark against royal tyranny. At Rockingham the silent masses found a voice. While Anselm waited at the doors of the Council to hear the issue of the debate from which he had been excluded, the multitude which had forced its way into the hall swayed and murmured like an angry sea; and an unknown knight came forward in the name of all to express their sympathy and to bid the Archbishop go forward on his chosen course with a good heart. A feudal government without a police, without a standing army, and without the means of raising either, was only strong in the disunion of its subjects. Let the long-suffering commons once resolve on common action and the whole fabric of oppression would come crashing down. The one chance for Rufus was to find a Pope through whose complaisance Anselm might be met with his own weapons. Anselm had appealed to a Pope; the King might do the same; and a Papal sentence of deposition would be the ruin of the Archbishop's popularity. Acting on this idea the King persuaded Anselm to remain in England under a truce. Meanwhile two clerks of the royal chapel were despatched to Italy to investigate the situation and approach in the King's name whichever Pope appeared to be in the ascendant. These envoys were William Warelwast and Gerard, afterwards Archbishop of York; both were diplomatists of mark, and with commendable sagacity they fixed on Urban as the man of destiny. But when it came to bargaining they and their master were no match for the Italian with his inherited traditions of finesse. Urban intimated that he could not sit in judgment on an English prelate until his jurisdiction was acknowledged by all parties. The bait was taken and the Red King awaited with confidence the arrival of the Papal legate who was charged to receive the English profession of obedience and to hear the charges against Anselm. The legate was the Cardinal-bishop of Albano. He listened to the King's case without a sign of doubt or disapproval; and carefully avoided any communications with the friends of the accused, until the King had made his public and formal declaration in favour of Pope Urban. Then at once the case of Anselm was decided; the King learned to his chagrin, the nation to its delight, that the Pope would never consent to Anselm's degradation. There was no alternative but

to accept the defeat and to go through a form of reconciliation
with the Archbishop.

We have dwelled upon this celebrated episode at some length The
because there is none in English history which illustrates more Theory of
clearly the hold of the Papal theory on the medieval conscience. Power
Rufus, who had no personal scruples to restrain him and the
strongest motives for attenuating the theory to the furthest point
which the public conscience would allow, is constrained to admit
that a sovereign cannot renounce a Pope who has falsified the
expectations formed of him ; that a profession of obedience, instead
of being a free contract, is harder to cancel than the oath of a vassal
to his lord. The King's supporters maintain his right to delay the
act of choosing between rival Popes; but they assume that in the
end he must decide; a Church without a Pope would be a body
without a head. The customs of the Conqueror are cited as
limiting the powers of the Pope in England ; that is to say the
Crown, though subject to the Holy See, is in a position of privileged subjection ; but the powers which the Pope retains are very
large. Though it is possible to prevent an Archbishop from
carrying an appeal to Rome it is out of the question to remove
him without Rome's concurrence, or to insist that his allegiance to
the Holy See shall be rendered mediately through the King. The
fact is that, in England as everywhere in medieval Europe, there
was a fixed and justifiable conviction that the Church could not
safely place herself in the power of the lay authority. Otherwise the hierarchy and the Pope would never have made good the
Papal claim to interfere in judicial and administrative matters.
The immense importance which the Middle Ages attached to
the visible framework of the Church made every breach in that
framework assume the character of an attack upon the welfare of
the individual soul, of an injury which the Christian could not
afford to accept with patient resignation. Later experience raised
the question whether the interests of the faith were served by
calling in the Papacy to supervise the national churches. But it
must be admitted that the Papal power of Anselm's time, imbued
with the lofty Hildebrandine spirit and wielded by such a commanding personality as Urban, was better qualified than Rufus
and Flambard and their creatures to guide the English Church ;
nor was it altogether chimerical to expect that, even when the

memory of Hildebrand grew fainter and his claims devolved on successors of ordinary ambitions and abilities, the sense of a supernatural mission and of world-wide responsibilities would steady the judgment of the Curia and produce in it a higher level of statesmanship than could be found in the governing class of any single nation.

The Council of Clermont, Nov., 1095 How well the Papacy already realised the extent of its influence, and how ambitious were the schemes with which the consciousness of power had inspired it, may be seen from the proceedings of the Council of Clermont, held a few months after the submission of Rufus was made public. No sovereigns appeared at this momentous gathering; no national churches were represented in their corporate capacity. It was a gathering of prelates and lay nobles from Italy, France, and the Low Countries; even in Italy there still existed a considerable party which denied the legitimacy of Urban's title, and Germany as a whole was committed to the support of Guibert the Imperialist anti-Pope. Yet the Council of Clermont, speaking in the name of Latin Christendom, framed two resolutions of universal application and the most far-reaching consequences; of which one, if strictly carried out would have revolutionised the fabric of every national society; while the other aimed at making Christendom a militant republic commanded by the Pope.

Measures: (1) The Investitures Decree The first was a decree forbidding lay investitures. Gregory VII. had struggled long and earnestly against this practice which he found, at his accession, prevailing in every Church of Europe. He had opposed it on the general ground that it offered opportunities for simoniacal bargaining which were certain in the long run to prove too much for the lay lord. The power which could withhold the insignia of spiritual office from a lawfully elected prelate was obviously in a position to make the ceremony of election a mere form and to reserve all vacant benefices for those who were prepared to buy promotion. But the zeal of Gregory was tempered with common sense. In spite of the uncompromising language which he used in such manifestoes as the well-known decree of 1075,[1] he showed in his practice that he knew how to distinguish between the fair and the unfair use of lay-investiture. Where, as in Germany, the result of the Crown's right had been the steady demoralisation of the hierarchy, Gregory would not

---

[1] The text is not preserved. The substance is given in Arnulf's *Gesta Archiepiscoporum Mediolaniensium. M. G. H. Scriptores*, viii., 27.

entertain the idea of compromise. But he acknowledged that
William the Conqueror could be trusted to make creditable
nominations and to demand from the nominees no more than a
reasonable measure of submissiveness; he decided that for the
present it was wisest not to affront the less scrupulous Philip I.;
and consequently he had tolerated both in France and England
the continuance of the ancient usage. Since his death the attitude
assumed by the French and English Crowns toward the hierarchy
had been such as to cast grave doubts upon the policy of compromise in any form. It was plain that the fitness of a candidate
was the last circumstance to be considered in making an appointment; and that the homage which formed an integral part of the
ceremony of investiture was interpreted in both countries as a
promise of unconditional obedience. Apart from this the extreme
reformers felt that a priest, the steward of the mysteries of God
and the mediator between heaven and earth, was degraded by the
mere formality of submission to a godless layman. They denied the
right of the Crown to exercise even a negative voice in ecclesiastical
elections, or to demand fealty even in respect of the lands belonging
to the Church conferred. Their argument carried the day at the
Council of Clermont; and although their decree was so concisely
worded as to leave some room for doubt, it seems to be correctly
paraphrased by a synod which, meeting shortly afterwards at
Rouen, decided that the only case in which a priest might render
fealty to a lay lord was when the fief in question pertained to no
ecclesiastical position.[1]

The consequences of this decree will come before us presently. Effect of
At the moment it aroused little interest, and in England it seems the Decree
to have passed wholly unregarded. This is singular, since we can- land
not suppose that English churchmen were ignorant of the decisions
framed at Clermont, or that Anselm would have neglected to insist on the observance of the decree if he had considered it as binding. It was adopted, as we have seen, by the Church of Normandy;
and the Council of Rouen by which it was promulgated met just
before the time when Normandy passed into the hands of Rufus.
Yet in 1096 two English bishops were invested in the traditional manner without a protest from Anselm, who consecrated

----

[1] The decree of Clermont in W. Malmesb., *G. R.*, iv., § 345, who gives the best
account of the Council.   The decree of Rouen in Orderic, iii., 473.

them, or from any other prelate; and it was not until the decree had been reaffirmed by the councils of Bari and the Lateran, at which Anselm was personally present, that the Archbishop made any objection to lay investiture. We may choose between two explanations. Either the decrees of the Council were not regarded as applying to England; but in that case it is hard to see why the later councils of Bari and the Lateran should be regarded as of superior validity. Or else, which is more probable, Anselm may have held that he was not bound to enforce the decrees until he was formally apprised of them. From the modern point of view this passive attitude would have been highly incorrect; but, in the eleventh century, general councils were still a novel phenomenon; and the nature of the obedience due to them may well have been a matter of dispute even in reforming circles. That Urban should have neglected to urge the immediate execution of this decree is

(2) Decree for a Crusade

not surprising when we consider that he had upon his hands the second project endorsed by his Council, that of the Crusade.

Whoever may have been behind the scenes urging this project upon Urban's attention and suggesting ways and means—there were those who affirmed that the whole scheme originated in the crafty brain of Bohemond of Otranto,[1] the portionless younger son of Roger Guiscard—still upon Urban fell the responsibility for exciting and directing the popular enthusiasm. None but a Pope could have brought so many jealous and aspiring princes into line; and without the Pope's countenance the preaching of Peter the Hermit and his fellows would have met with a lukewarm reception. No precedents existed to guide Urban in his task; for a patient examination of the evidence has shown that neither Sylvester nor Sergius IV. nor even Gregory VII. deserve the credit, which is sometimes given them, of having preached a Holy War; and Urban was probably the first responsible statesman to whom the idea of a Crusade had been more than the fancy of a moment.[2] In a sense the events of the last hundred years had been leading up to the Crusade. The growth of Papal influence, the spread of the reforming movement, the advance of the Almor-

[1] This is twice affirmed by W. Malmesb., *G. R.*, iv., §§ 344, 387. His view is accepted and developed by Palgrave, *England and Normandy*, iv., p. 590.
[2] See Havet's edition of Gerbert's letters, Introd. For Sergius IV., Riant, *Arch. de l'Or. Latin*, vol. i., p. 40, and *E. H. R.*, xvi., p. 367. For Gregory VII., Luchaire, *Premiers Capétiens*, p. 228.

avids in Spain, the interference of the Seljukid Turks with pilgrims, but above all the growing numbers of the feudal aristocracy, the consequent impoverishment of the young branches of royal and princely houses, and the immense success of previous robber expeditions such as those of the Normans to Italy and England—all these were causes which predisposed Europe at large, but in particular the Latin nations, to look with favour on the suggestion of Pope Urban. He appealed to many other motives besides that of the religious sentiment; and the Crusading movement continued, for almost two centuries after his death, with very little encouragement from Rome. None the less the first access of enthusiasm, which seemed as though it would sweep away the whole lay population of France and Italy to the Levant, was the result of carefully devised appeals, and remains the most striking evidence on record to attest the influence of the medieval Papacy.

Whether the Crusades as a whole were good or bad in their effects is a question for the historian of Europe. So far as England was concerned they exercised an influence of so slight and negative a kind that we are prevented by the dearth of evidence from deciding the question in one way or the other. In 1096 the excitement aroused in the Latin countries by the Pope's appeal was communicated in some degree to England;[1] but it lost much of its intensity in crossing the Channel. In France it had penetrated to the lowest strata of society; Guibert of Nogent tells us that it was a common thing to meet serfs with their wives and children driving eastward in ox-carts on the highroad to Jerusalem; the fields lay deserted and whole towns stood empty in those provinces where the Crusade had been most vehemently preached. Our one estimate of the numbers of those who left the British Isles to join the first and greatest enterprise is 20,000; and this is probably as much exaggerated as most other medieval estimates of numbers; it ought to be divided by four or five at least.[2] Subsequent expeditions, and the standing garrison of the Latin Kingdom of Jerusalem, were recruited by a small but fairly constant flow of English pilgrims, which was occasionally augmented by an unsuccessful rebellion or a civil war. But even to the Crusade of Richard I. the

England and the Crusades

---

[1] *A. S. C., s.a.* 1096.
[2] Orderic, iv., 70, says that 20,000 pilgrims sailed " de Anglia et aliis insulis Oceani ". *Cf.* iii., 483, 555.

English people contributed their money more freely than their services. It might be argued that an impulse which continued to be felt, however fitfully and sporadically, from the end of the eleventh to the end of the fourteenth century, must have modified the national character in a perceptible degree. But the men whom the crusading ideal influenced most powerfully were, in nine cases out of ten, those who left England never to return. The majority who, like Edgar Atheling, returned with more or less credit after one or two campaigns, seem to have resumed their former occupations, like men recovered from a long delirium. *Caelum non animum mutant qui trans mare currunt.* The Crusades may have been a wholesome outlet for religious emotion and superfluous energy; our evidence hardly entitles us to regard them as a school of character.

Nor were the effects of a more material kind so considerable as they have been supposed. The Crusades produced a literature of travels, and gave a slight impetus to the study of Arabian science. But it is doubtful whether the travellers did much to widen the horizon of national thought; the most curious of their memoirs, that of Saewulf[1] for example, or that of Ambroise the clerk of Coeur de Lion, were simply another form of entertaining romance; and science, in England as in the rest of Europe, benefited far more by the peaceful intercourse of savants like Adelard of Bath and Michael Scott with the Greeks and Arabs who were to be found comparatively near at hand in Spain and Southern Italy, than by all the adventures of Crusaders. The greatest advantage which the Crusades conferred on England was that of carrying off a certain proportion of the non-industrial classes; and except in a few rare cases like that of Coeur de Lion's Crusade, it was the most violent, most needy, and least capable portion of the baronage who took the cross. Against this advantage must be set a serious drawback. The Crusades, which were a source of wealth to the peoples of the Mediterranean sea-board, meant for England and other countries of the outer Ocean a constant and unproductive drain of capital. It is possible to exaggerate the exactions of intending Crusaders; for villeins and burgesses, though unable to leave one fief for another without discomfort and material loss, were protected by custom to an extent which we can hardly conceive in this era of free competition. A Crusade might mean a heavy tallage in the days when the Crown had not yet intervened

---

[1] The author of a tract *De Situ Hierusalem*, printed in D'Avezac's *Recueil de Voyages* (Paris, 1839), iv., pp. 817-54. Saewulf visited Jerusalem in 1102-3.

to put a check upon the right of private taxation. But the Crusader's usual course was to sell or pawn his land; in the latter case the creditor, in lieu of interest, took the rents of the land until repayment or for a fixed term of years. Where this course was adopted the chief hardship suffered by the tenant was that he fell into the hands of a man of business, that his dues were more strictly collected, and that, as the loan was spent elsewhere, he was the poorer by the loss of an open-handed customer. It may be remarked that there is very little evidence to show that English towns or villeins purchased liberties on any considerable scale from the Crusaders either of the eleventh or of succeeding centuries.

The eventful year 1095 was one in which the internal affairs of England left Rufus little leisure for watching the progress of affairs upon the Continent. Even the war in Normandy was left entirely to Henry Beauclerk, while his brother dealt in turn with the ecclesiastical problem, with an English rebellion, and with a Welsh invasion.

The rebellion was almost entirely the work of those whom Rufus The Re-had pardoned for their share in Odo's conspiracy of 1089; Hugh bellion of Montgomery of Shrewsbury, his neighbour Roger Lacy, Gilbert 1095 of Tunbridge, Odo of Champagne the lord of Holderness, all showed that leniency had been misspent upon them. Blackest of all was the treachery of William of Eu, who had but lately made his peace by deserting Robert of Normandy, as he had previously deserted Rufus; but Robert Mowbray, the Earl of Northumberland was scarcely more excusable. Freely pardoned for his first rebellion, the earl had been allowed but two years previously to inherit the vast English estates of his uncle and accomplice, the Bishop of Coutances; yet he now assumed the lead among the malcontents. They complained in general terms of the King's strict government; and the nature of their grievances may be gathered from the case of Robert about which we have unusually full information. He had come reasonably near attaining that degree of independence which was the ideal of his caste, and was realised only in a few fiefs such as that of Chester. There was a sheriff in Northumberland, but the office was held by the earl's own henchman, Morel, the castellan of Bamborough;[1] and thus the royal

---

[1] See the Durham charter in the Monasticon, i., 241, attested by "Morealis vice-comes".

4*

prerogatives in Northumberland practically belonged to Mowbray. But the boundaries of the earldom, and still more the old opportunities for extending it, had been seriously curtailed in recent years by the growth of rival jurisdictions. On the south he was shut in by the great franchise of St. Cuthbert; to the north again the bishop possessed the churches of Lindisfarne and Hexham with the lands pertaining to them and all the royal prerogatives over the tenants; [1] while on the west was the newly organised shire of Carlisle. Thus hemmed in the earl was driven to amuse himself with piracy; Norwegians whom he had plundered appealed to the King for redress; and Rufus, after compensating them from his own treasury, summoned the earl to appear at the Easter Court of 1095 and stand his trial. The summons was disregarded, except that it brought the nascent conspiracy to a head; a second and more imperative summons was answered with a declaration that the earl would not appear unless he received hostages and a safe-conduct.[2] William's reply was to collect an army and march northward. He suspected the existence of a plot but seems to have been in the dark as to its object and the names of the ringleaders, since he appointed Anselm to discharge the unaccustomed duty of holding the Kentish ports against a possible invasion from Normandy.[3] The fact was that the conspirators, well aware how little they could trust to Robert's aid, had selected another candidate for the throne. Odo of Champagne had married Adelaide the niece of the Conqueror; and it was their son Stephen of Aumâle in whose behalf William Rufus was to be deposed. Some information was obtained by Rufus on his way to the north; for Gilbert of Tunbridge, in real or assumed remorse, disclosed a plan for waylaying him in an ambush and divulged the names of those concerned. The snare was avoided; the conspirators, cowed or forestalled by the rapidity of the King's movements, left Robert Mowbray to fight his battle single-handed. He had thrown garrisons and supplies into his castles of Tynemouth and Bamborough and both places made a stout resistance. Tynemouth, the first to be attacked, held out for two months. Bamborough, where the earl himself was in command, held out still longer, thanks to its impregnable position. Half-way through the siege the King

Robert Mowbray defeated

---

[1] For Robert's feud with Durham *cf.* Simeon, *H. E. D.*, iv., 4. It was patched up in the year 1094. See *Regesta*, No. 349 and notes.

[2] Orderic, iii., 406.   [3] *Cf. Anselmi Epistolae*, III., xxxv.

was called away to the south by the news of Welsh incursions on
the Middle Marches; and he did not return until he had led an
expedition into the heart of the Snowdon country as a warning
that the English frontier was no longer to be violated with impunity.[1]
But meanwhile his lieutenants had captured Robert Mowbray in
the sortie; and when the King reappeared at Bamborough the
earl's heroic wife was constrained to surrender by a threat that
otherwise her husband's eyes would be put out. Though saved
from this penalty the earl was consigned to a prison from which
he emerged only to take the cowl in the monastery of St. Albans.
Even so he was more fortunate than some of his confederates.
The sheriff Morel saved himself, on the fall of Bamborough, by
supplementing the revelations of Gilbert of Tunbridge; and at
the Epiphany of 1096 the Great Council met to do justice on the
accused. Hugh of Shrewsbury and some others, whose connections
stood them in good stead, escaped with the payment of enormous
fines. Roger of Lacy and Odo of Champagne lost their English
lands; but a number of uninfluential men were hanged or blinded.
A worse fate than death fell upon William of Eu; arraigned as a
traitor, and defeated in the trial by battle which was the privilege
of Norman blood, he suffered the loss of his eyes and a yet fouler
mutilation. It was the punishment which the mercy of the Conqueror had substituted for death;[2] but rumour said that the
Count of Eu might have escaped more lightly if the kinsmen of
his injured wife had not pressed for the most vigorous sentence
which the law permitted. The example, although its barbarity
must be condemned, was one which taught the baronage a wholesome lesson; it was high time that some worse penalty than
imprisonment should be inflicted for repeated and gratuitous
rebellions.

Punish-
ment of
the Rebels
1096

During these events Robert of Normandy had formed the
design of going on crusade. The enterprise was of a kind which
appealed to his facile and emotional temperament, and he must
have welcomed with relief an excuse for leaving Normandy where,
since the beginning of his rule, he had been defied by his vassals, plundered by his favourites, and impoverished by his extravagance to such an extent that, as gossip had it, he was often
unable to leave his bed for want of clothes. Still his descent and

Normandy
pledged to
Rufus,
1096

---

[1] For details see Lloyd, *History of Wales*, pp. 405-6.
[2] See the law in S. C., p. 99.

title made him a valuable recruit. The Pope sent an embassy to England for the special purpose of reconciling the Duke and his royal brother; and Rufus allowed himself to be appeased the more readily because Robert offered him Normandy in pawn for the sum of 10,000 marks, to be repaid at the end of three years.[1] Small as this sum appears to us, it could only be raised with difficulty from a land which in the last few years had been drained by every method of extortion which the craft of Flambard could devise. An aid was demanded from tenants-in-chief; a Danegeld of four shillings on the hide, that is at double the ordinary rate, was extorted not only from laymen but also from the demesnes of churches.[2] The rule of later times was that those who contributed to the one impost should be exempted from the other; but there is reason for thinking that some men and churches paid twice over.[3] At all events the burden fell with especial heaviness upon ecclesiastics. Some of them ventured to expostulate with the King, saying that they could only pay the sums demanded by grinding their villeins to the dust. The reply was characteristic: " Have you not gold and silver boxes full of dead men's bones ? "[4] Many churches had no option but to follow this hint, and reliquaries, crosses, gospel-books, and vestments were stripped of their precious ornaments to pay the price of Normandy.

Robert and the English Crusaders The adventures of Robert in the East do not call for detailed notice. He was the leader of a host recruited from Normandy, Maine, Anjou, Brittany, and England, which, after many losses, is said to have numbered 15,000 at the siege of Antioch.[5] The nobles who accompanied him were, with a few exceptions, the younger sons of Norman houses; and so far his expedition bore a likeness to those by which Apulia, Calabria, and Sicily had been conquered earlier in the century. He took with him his trusted counsellor, Odo of Bayeux, who died however at Palermo on the

---

[1] The Pope's mediation is described by Hugh of Flavigny (Pertz, *Scriptores*, viii., pp. 474, 475). As to the sum lent by Rufus the main authorities are agreed. Robert of Torigni (Cont. Will. Gemmet., viii., 7) says that Normandy was to be restored whenever Robert should return and repay the loan. Eadmer and Hugh of Flavigny say that the loan was for three years ; Orderic, iv., 78, says five years, probably because this was the term for which Robert was actually absent.

[2] See the narrative in *Leges Edwardi*, § xi.

[3] Florence, *s.a.* 1096, speaks of a benevolence which was paid by prelates as well as lay lords. This is distinct from the Danegeld. *Cf.* Eadmer, *H. N.*, p. 74 ; " Pecunia per Angliam partim data, partim exacta ".

[4] W. Malmesb., *G. R.*, iv., § 318.   [5] Orderic, iii., 555.

outward journey.[1] Edgar Atheling, although no warrior, sailed
afterwards to join the Duke whose brother-in-arms he had always
been.[2] Of the other Englishmen who took service under Robert's
banner we find the names of William de Percy,[3] the great benefactor
of Whitby Priory ; of Arnulf of Hesdin, who had narrowly escaped
condemnation on a charge of complicity with Robert de Mowbray,
and may have taken the cross in gratitude for the providence which
brought him safely through the ordeal of battle ;[4] and of Baldwin
son of Godwin, a man of the true English stock, who remained in
Palestine after the Duke's return, and, falling into the hands of
the infidel, suffered martyrdom for the faith in 1102.[5] The greater
barons of England preferred to remain at home in imitation of their
King. They may be excused for their reluctance to take service
under such a general as Robert. Yet the Crusade is the most
creditable episode in the Duke's otherwise inglorious career. He
proved himself on more than one occasion worthy of the high
position among its leaders to which his birth and dignity had
raised him ; he was one of the leaders of the vanguard in the
assaults on Antioch and Jerusalem ; and the Crown of Jerusalem
was offered to him before it was conferred on Godfrey of Bouillon.[6]

For England the chief result of this Crusade was a union with Later
the Norman Duchy which lasted till the Red King's death. It is plans of
upon the doings of these years that the fame of Rufus chiefly Rufus, 1096-1100
rests. Relieved from the fear of dynastic plots he was able to push
to a conclusion his struggle with the Church, to follow up his plans
of conquering Scotland and Wales, and to embark upon a policy of
continental conquests. The details of his activity, except in ecclesiastical affairs, are meagrely related by the chroniclers ; and for that
reason his record must be judged with caution. But the general
impression to be formed from the facts at our disposal is one not
altogether favourable to his ability.

For his treatment of Anselm in these latter years there is Final
considerable justification. They quarrelled, and Anselm left the Quarrel
kingdom in the year 1097, because the Archbishop positively with Anselm,
refused to recognise the "ancestral customs" by which the Con- 1097
queror had sought to regulate the relations of his bishops with

[1] Orderic, iii., 266.   [2] Ibid., iv., 70.
[3] Monasticon, i., 410.   [4] Liber de Hyda, p. 301.
[5] W. Malmesb., G. R., iii., § 251 ; iv., § 384.
[6] W. Malmesb., G. R., iv., § 389. So too Henry of Huntingdon.

the Papacy. Unless we are prepared to blame the Conqueror's policy we cannot find fault with Rufus, whose offence in the eyes of his opponent was chiefly that of continuing his predecessor's course; and it is to the King's credit that he not only allowed the Archbishop to depart from the kingdom, but also refrained from attempting to replace him. On the other hand Rufus showed an utter want of statesmanship and generosity in dealing with the minor points at issue. The Archbishop was subjected to a petty and half-hearted persecution in the forms of law, threatened with ruinous amercement for an alleged default of feudal service, and exposed to various small indignities on his departure from the kingdom; nor could Rufus resist the temptation of appropriating and exploiting the lands of the see of Canterbury as soon as Anselm's back was turned. The old system of prolonging vacancies was carried to extremes. At the time of the King's death the sees of Winchester and Salisbury, and eleven abbacies of consequence, were in his hand. Their spoils had formed for some years no inconsiderable item in the royal revenues; and the King never disguised his intention of keeping them vacant as long as it was possible to do so. Hence the main dispute fell into the background; and public opinion, which on the question of abstract principle, might well have leaned to the King's side became almost entirely favourable to Anselm. The King appeared, through his own fault, less moderate than was actually the case, and for the sake of small advantages incurred suspicions which were fatal to his popularity. Apart from the side-issues his position was a strong one; and there is no need to accept the insinuation of Anselm's biographer that Pope Urban's reluctance to proceed to extremities with the King was solely due to the gold of William's envoys. Anselm had precipitated a question with which the Papacy did not yet feel strong enough to deal, and the weight of precedent was in the royal scale. But Rufus had managed his case with so little prudence that, although successful in keeping the Archbishop at arm's-length for the remainder of his reign, he left his successor no alternative but to conciliate the English Church by hushing up the quarrel without a definite decision of the points at issue.

Rufus and
Scotland
    In his dealings with Scotland Rufus showed to greater advantage, since in this case at least he condescended to learn a

lesson of prudence from an early failure. He obtained less than
he had hoped but as much as any previous King of England.
In 1097 he espoused the cause of Edgar, a son of Margaret and
Malcolm. The prince was allowed to collect a force of volunteers
in England and, aided by the counsels of his uncle the Atheling,
had little difficulty in deposing Donaldbane who was blinded and
relegated to a prison for the remainder of his life. Ascending the
throne as the declared vassal of the English King,[1] Edgar contrived
to maintain himself even after the departure of the Atheling to
join Duke Robert in the Holy Land. The most dangerous enemy
of Scotland was at that time the King of Norway, whose interest
in the politics of the Western Isles has been already mentioned;
but a treaty, more prudent than glorious, secured Edgar from
attack at the expense of whatever rights his ancestors had claimed
over the Isles. This difficulty settled, the reign of Edgar was
unmarked by further troubles. He outlived his patron, Rufus,
and till his death (1107) faithfully acknowledged his dependence
upon England.

The submission of Scotland was easily obtained because the
consequences of submission were unimportant to the weaker nation.
In the case of Wales, where conquest would infallibly be followed
by a Norman occupation, there was a resistance, more sporadic it
is true, but at the same time more obstinate and difficult to overcome.[2] The forays of the Conqueror and his marchers had borne
their fruit; we have already noticed the extent to which, in north
and central Wales, the borderland had been colonised and fortified
with castles before the year 1087. In the early years of Rufus'
reign the tide of invasion was chiefly concentrated on the southern
march. Undermined by treachery and rebellion the kingdom of
South Wales fell an easy prey to adventurers, who pushed their
way to the west without assistance from the King of England, and
without any intention of placing their conquests at his disposition.
On the field of Brecknock, in 1093, Rhys-ap-Tewdwr the last
King of South Wales fell in battle against a coalition of his own
vassals with certain unnamed "Frenchmen". With his death the

The Welsh Marches

---

[1] *Cf.* Monasticon, i., 238 : " Edgarus, filius Malcolmi regis Scottorum, totam
terram de Lodoneis et regnum Scotiae dono domini mei Willelmi Anglorum regis
et paterna haereditate possidens," etc. But the authenticity of this charter has
been disputed (see *Regesta*, No. 363).

[2] For the following events see *Annales Cambriae, Brut y Tyw.*, Florence, and
Orderic. Their evidence is summarised in Lloyd, *History of Wales*, pp. 396-411.

curtain falls and we are left in ignorance of the steps by which
the invaders turned their victory to account. But when it rises
again there are Norman settlements in Brecknock under Bernard
of Neufmarché,[1] in Radnor under Philip de Braose,[2] and in
Glamorgan under Robert Fitz Hamon; while in the far south-
west a third marcher, Arnulf of Montgomery, is building in
Pembroke a fort of earthworks crowned with a rough palisade,
to serve as a base for conquest and marauding expeditions.[3]
The three chief lordships of South Wales have thus come into
being; English churches are already receiving endowments in the
conquered territory; the diocese of St. David has been incorporated with the province of the English primate; and the Welsh
have been driven to the hills. In the meanwhile the marchers of the
north, though less brilliantly successful, had not been altogether
idle. When Rufus came to the throne, the Norman boundary
on the north-west was fixed at the river Conway where Robert
of Rhuddlan had pitched his castle of Deganwy; and it was in
defending this boundary against the men of Gwynedd that the
heavy-handed Marquis met his death (1088). But within a year
or two the Earl of Chester had pushed his way across the Menai
into Anglesea and the eastern coast of the island was dominated
by a castle built at Aberlleiniog. The Welsh were thus hemmed
in by advance posts both on the north and south. But the hold
established by the pioneers was insecure. The Red King had no
mind to help the marchers by exempting them from service in
Normandy and England; and every occasion on which their forces
were divided owing to royal requisitions was eagerly seized by the
Welsh princes. During the Norman campaign of 1094, Cadwgan
the leading chief of central Wales, carried fire and sword through
the marches of Chester, Shrewsbury, and Hereford; and Mowbray's
rebellion in 1095 enabled a band of patriots to storm the castle of
Montgomery. Again in the year 1096, when the King was called
across the Channel to take possession of the Norman Duchy, there
was another outbreak; all the castles, with the exception of Pembroke, which had been built in South Wales since the commencement
of the reign were taken and destroyed. The audacity of the Welsh
did not pass unnoticed; in each of these three years a punitive

---

[1] See a charter of Bernard, c. 1088, in *Cart. Glouc.*, i., 315: " Bernardus de Novo
Mercato omnibus hominus ministris et fidelibus suis de honore de Breuheynauc,"
etc. *Cf.* also Giraldus, *Opera*, vi., 28, and Orderic, iii., pp. 43-4.

[2] Round, C. D. F., No. 1120 (grant by Philip, temp. William II, made at Radnor).

[3] Giraldus, *Itin. Cambrense*, i., 12.

force, headed by the king in person, took the field and penetrated the mountain valleys of the Snowdon district; but the first two expeditions were undertaken in haste and after the campaigning season of the year; while the third, in which an elaborate and leisurely attempt was made on Gwynedd with three converging columns, only proved that heavy Norman cavalry were useless for a war conducted among hills and forests. Rufus, who had sworn to exterminate the entire male population, was so far from realising his threat that he withdrew after heavy losses and without a single victory. In regard to Wales his record is one of ignominious failure; it was left for his successor, the pacific Henry I., to show that the successes of the English Harold might be rivalled by men of Norman training.

Still the reign of Rufus left indelible marks of its influence on the face of Wales. The marchers were more successful than their sovereign in the struggle to recover the lost settlements; and in the south, where there was no longer a royal house to act as the rallying point of resistance, Anglo-Norman influence appears to have been restored and even extended by the year 1100. It is only in the north that the outbreaks of 1094-6 resulted in a permanent loss of territory. When, in the year 1098, the Earls of Shrewsbury and Chester swept through North Wales, crossed the Menai Strait, and rebuilt Aberlleiniog, it seemed for the moment as if all resistance was at an end. But the invaders, while engaged in the congenial work of torturing captives and desecrating churches,[1] were attacked by an altogether unexpected enemy. Magnus Barefoot of Norway, fresh from a campaign against his turbulent vassals in the Isle of Man,[2] was induced to help the fugitive Welsh princes in their desperate situation. His fleet came to land in Anglesea near Aberlleiniog and the Earl of Shrewsbury, when engaged in repelling the attempted disembarkation of the vikings, was mortally wounded in the eye by an arrow from the bow of Magnus. Although the Norse fleet disappeared as suddenly as it had come the Normans, thoroughly alarmed, evacuated Anglesea; and a treaty was shortly afterwards concluded with the princes Gruffudd of Gwynedd and Cadwgan of Mid-Wales which recognised their independence and left them in possession of Anglesea, Powis, and Ceredigion, besides

The Loss of Anglesea, 1098

[1] Florence. Giraldus, *Itin. Cambrense*, ii., 7.
[2] So the *Chronicon Regum Manniæ*. *Cf*. Freeman, *W. R.*, ii., p. 146.

those portions of the north-west in which no Norman had hitherto
ventured to settle.

Robert of
Bellême
inherits
Shrews-
bury

With the death of Hugh of Shrewsbury the affairs of the
Welsh march acquired a new importance in the history of
England. Hitherto the policy of allowing the marchers a free
hand had produced no serious inconveniences; in extending their
palatinates they had fought the battle of the Crown. But the
vacant earldom passed into the hands of a man who had both
the ability and the inclination to assert himself at the expense
of the royal authority. For the sum of £3,000 Rufus sold
Shrewsbury to the dead earl's brother Robert of Bellême. Robert
had inherited through his mother, the infamous Mabel Talvas, the
march-fief of Bellême which his maternal ancestors, ruling under
the title of prince, had kept to all intents and purposes independent
of ducal control;[1] he now began to imitate in England the policy
which they and he had so successfully pursued in Normandy. He
persuaded Rufus to increase his earldom by a grant of the great
fief of Blyth. At Bridgnorth, at Tickhill, and at Carreghofa on the
line of Offa's dyke, he raised castles which proved his consummate
skill as an architect and engineer. By cultivating the favour of
his master he obtained the fullest licence to work his will upon his
weaker neighbours; and now at length, in the words of Orderic, the
Welsh and English were forced by their own experience to credit
the wild tales which they had heard of his evil deeds in Normandy.
His cruelty was all the more terrible because he seemed to be devoid
of passion; the more courteous his speech, the more serene his aspect, the more he was feared by those who knew him. He delighted
in the spectacle of suffering. The cruel mutilations which were
sanctioned by the laws of Normandy and England were too insipid
for his taste. He invented new forms of torture; and was in the
habit of laughing and jesting with his parasites while some unhappy
wretch was being roasted at a slow fire in their presence.[2] It is related that he put out the eyes of his godson with his own hands

---

[1] See the charter of William of Bellême to Lonlay in *Neustria Pia*, p. 424. The
donor describes himself as "Willelmus princeps" and "provinciae principatum
gerens". For a further discussion see *E. H. R.*, xxiii., p. 121. For the early
character of the family see Orderic, iii., 294: "Malefica est prosapia eorum, alit
nefas et machinatur, quasi jus hereditarium. Hoc nimirum horrenda mors eorum
attestatur, quorum nullus communi et usitato fine, ut caeteri homines, defecisse
invenitur." For Mabel Talvas see Orderic, ii., 411.

[2] For the character of Robert see Orderic, iii., 294 ff., 422; iv., 32. W. Malm.,
G. R., v., § 398.

because the child's father had irritated him by the breach of an agreement. The story is well attested, and we may infer from it the treatment which he meted out to his inferiors when they were so unfortunate as to cross his path. There was work to be done on the Welsh March which was perhaps best left in the hands of men emancipated from all scruples. But Rufus was ill advised to bring into his kingdom and to place at the head of his baronage a man in whom absolute faithlessness was coupled with abilities of a high order. An accomplished general and diplomat, wary in counsel, eloquent in speech, and bravest of the brave in action, Earl Robert was of all the Anglo-Norman baronage the fittest to fill the place left vacant by the successive failures of Bishop Odo and Robert Mowbray, to become the leader of the feudal opposition.

From the foregoing account it will easily be gathered that the statesmanship of the Red King, in its most creditable period, was not so brilliant as his contemporaries believed. During the years when his hands were comparatively free we find that a nominal victory over Scotland is balanced by failure in Wales and a short-sighted policy in England. It must be added that he entered upon a course of foreign policy which the resources of his oppressed and exhausted kingdom were totally unable to sustain, and which was further rendered ridiculous by the fitfulness with which he pursued it. The flatterers who compared him to Julius Cæsar had in their minds the scheme for the conquest of France with which he amused himself in the last year or two of his life. The ways and means are left to conjecture; it is in fact unlikely that he had given serious thought to them. He talked of acquiring France, much as he talked of going to Rome and emulating the doughty deed of Brennus and the Gauls, until in 1097 a quarrel concerning the Vexin precipitated him into war with the House of Capet. Then honour demanded that he should do something to justify his boast. For the best part of a year (Nov., 1097—Sept., 1098) he waged continuous war on France with the help of French vassals, and notably of William of Poitou.[1] But the result was by no means in proportion to the efforts which he had made. Although the title of King of France was still borne by the feeble and incompetent Philip the supreme power was actually vested in his son Louis, a ruler whose statesmanship has perhaps been overestimated,

Continental Policy of Rufus, 1096-1100

---

[1] Orderic, iv., 2? ff. Suger, *Vita Ludovici*.

but whose achievements as a general deserve all the praise which they receive from his biographer. Inexperienced as he was, threatened on the side of Normandy by armies superior in numbers to his own, and on every other side by vassals of more than doubtful faith, Louis fairly held his own; he lost a few castles, but held the more important points of the French Vexin. It was fortunate for him, and it is some excuse for Rufus, that the war in the Vexin was waged simultaneously with another in Maine, where Hèlias de la Flèche, the successor of Hugo of Liguria, made a bold stand for independence and, though robbed of his capital by Rufus, kept the war alive until the king's death enabled him to reach the goal of his ambition.[1] But for this war, which twice demanded the personal presence of the King in Maine, the success of Louis might have been less brilliant. On the other hand it was no accident that Rufus was saddled with both wars at one and the same time. In each case he was the aggressor, and his ill-success is a proof that he presumed upon his own strength and the apparent weakness of his enemies. Early in the year 1100 chance threw into his hands a tempting opportunity. William of Poitou, fired with a sudden whim to follow better men than himself in undertaking the adventure of the Holy Land, assumed the cross and offered to mortgage Poitou with the Duchy of Aquitaine to his ally of England. The offer was accepted without hesitation, and Rufus was on the point of leaving England for Aquitaine when all his schemes were cut short by an untimely death.[2] One is tempted to speculate on the prospects of success which this accession of territory opened up to Rufus. It is just possible that France might have succumbed if simultaneously attacked by English armies from the north and west. But to raise armies capable of holding the field for a longer term than the forty days of feudal service would have been no easy matter, considering the impoverished state of England; and Rufus could only have advanced to the conquest of France after disposing of Maine and Anjou, not to mention other principalities such as Flanders, the interests of which were less directly involved in the fortunes of the House of Capet.

The plan was great, but whether the servile William of Mal-

---

[1] Orderic, iv., 40-60, and the *Gesta Pontif. Cenomannensium, u.s.* Freeman, *N. C.,* v., p. 106.

[2] Orderic, iv., 80. W. Malmesb., *G. R.,* iv., § 333.

mesbury was justified in holding that the execution would have
been worthy of the plan is more than doubtful.   How many
combinations superficially more promising have wrecked the reputation of their contrivers when brought to the touchstone of
experience!

CHAPTER IV

THE REIGN OF HENRY I

ON the second of August, 1100, Rufus fell in the New Forest mortally wounded by an arrow which rumour persistently asserted to have been shot from the bow of his attendant Walter Tyrrell. The truth was never ascertained. Tyrrell, it is true, fled the country; but we know that in later years, when he had nothing to fear from a confession of the truth, he solemnly denied that he had been present when the King was slain;[1] and that his lands in England were not confiscated, though they would scarcely have escaped this fate if responsibility for the accident had been brought home to him.[2] That the King's death was the result of accident does not appear to have been questioned; and this may be regarded as conclusive against any hypothesis of foul play. The man who benefited by the King's death was his brother Henry; and Henry's opponents, who were entirely unscrupulous, would not have hesitated to tax him with assassination if there had been the faintest possibility of making out a case.

Accession of Henry I Henry was one of the King's hunting party, and though not a witness of the accident, was the first to be informed of it.[3] He left his brother's body where it lay, and riding at full speed to Winchester, the seat of government, seized the keys of the royal treasure. He was not a moment too soon. Hard on his heels came the treasurer William of Breteuil, a supporter of Duke Robert's claim to the succession, who demanded the restoration of the keys, and reminded Henry that special respect was due

---

[1] Suger, *Vita Ludovici*. Orderic, iv., 83, gives the fullest account of the King's death. The *Roman de Rou* and Eadmer exculpate Tyrrell and make Rufus the author of his own fate. Giraldus, *De Institutione Principum*, 176, gives Radulfus de Aquis as the assassin.

[2] Lappenberg, ii., p. 207 *n.*

[3] *Roman de Rou*, 10105, gives a vivid account of this.

to the claims of his elder brother, a Crusader and the liege-lord of them both. The prince retorted that Robert was an alien ; and, drawing his sword, protested that the sceptre of the Conqueror should never pass to such a man. The argument was plausible ; according to the ideas of the age a younger son born in the purple had a better claim to inherit the throne than an elder born while the father was still of private station. The barons who were present advised the treasurer to yield, and the sinews of war remained in Henry's hands.[1] Most of the great men who had been at court when the death of Rufus was announced had already dispersed, and were preparing for the carnival of anarchy which was to be expected in an interregnum ; those who remained were easily induced to abandon the cause of the absent heir. On the following day, when the obsequies of the Red King had been unceremoniously and hastily performed, Henry was elected King by a handful of supporters who arrogated to themselves the rights of a national assembly ;[2] and on August 5th he was crowned at Westminster. The Archbishop of Canterbury, who should have performed the rite, was still in exile ; Thomas of York, on whom in the absence of the primate the duty properly devolved, was old and in failing health ; and, since the return of Robert to Normandy might be expected at any moment, the new king was consecrated, in defiance of all precedent, by the bishop of London.[3] But this irregularity was more than covered, in the eyes of the nation, by the solemn charter which Henry issued within a day or two of the coronation and ordered to be read to the people in every shire-court of the Kingdom.[4] In this document he promised redress of grievances to the Church, the barons, and his subjects at large ; the evil customs which his brother had introduced were to be absolutely abolished. No longer should vacant benefices be exploited for the benefit of the royal treasury, or sold to the highest bidder. No longer should

Charter of Henry I

[1] Orderic, iv., 87.

[2] See the list of witnesses to Henry's Charter, as given by Liebermann, *Transactions R. Hist. Soc.* (N.S.), viii., p. 21.

[3] W. Malmesb., *G. R.*, § 393 : " Haec eo studiosius celebrabantur ne mentes procerum electionis quassarentur poenitudine, quod ferebatur rumor Robertum Normanniae comitem ex Apulia adventantem jam jamque affore ".

[4] Eadmer, *H.N.*, iii., 55. The different copies of this charter contain many variants. The text is critically discussed by Liebermann, *u.s.* That the charter was to be read in the shire-court appears from the preamble to the copy in Wendover. A useful commentary in Stubbs' *Lectures on Early English History* (1906), pp. 107-122.

feudal aids and dues be assessed on an arbitrary scale, or exacted in unprecedented cases. The fines imposed in the King's feudal court should be proportionate to the offence. Firm peace should be established throughout the kingdom. The "law of Edward," as amended and expanded by the Conqueror's legislation, should be religiously observed. Rufus in his day of repentance, had made promises not much dissimilar to these; and it must be owned that Henry, when once he was firmly seated on the throne, violated the letter of almost every article in this celebrated charter. But it produced the desired effect upon public opinion. Henry was acclaimed as a King truly English in descent and spirit; and even we, who smile at the facility with which his subjects allowed themselves to be deluded, must admit that the government which he gave them, though not precisely what they might have chosen for themselves, was in its legality and moderation not altogether unworthy of the manifesto with which it was inaugurated.

Settlement with the Church

The first acts of the King gave every reason for confidence in his good intentions. Ranulf Flambard, the prime instrument of William's extortions, was thrown into prison; and the government was placed partly in the hands of the least obnoxious of the old officials, partly in those of "strenuous and sagacious" men like Robert of Meulan, who had won Henry's favour in the days of his adversity and were now advanced to share in his good fortune. Immediately after the coronation Henry wrote in deferential terms to Anselm, apologising on the score of necessity for having presumed to accept the crown from the hands of another prelate, and promising that if the primate would return he should have the position to which his rank entitled him. "I commit myself and the people of the whole realm of England to the guidance of yourself and of those who have the right to share with you in guiding me."[1] Whatever doubts Anselm may have felt as to the sincerity of the invitation were overruled by the authority of the Pope. Paschal ordered him to return without delay, and thus at the very outset of the reign the first step was taken to heal the breach between the Church and the English Crown. A final settlement proved to be more difficult than Henry had hoped; for Anselm returned with the fixed intention of enforcing the recent decrees of the Lateran Council against lay investiture, and thus brought

[1] See the letter in S C., p. 120.

into the foreground a doctrine of which nothing had hitherto been heard in England. His first acts on his return were to refuse homage for the temporalties of his see and to intimate that he could not recognise the new bishops whom Henry had invested since the coronation. It was in vain for the King to represent that the Crown's right had never been disputed in the reigns of his father and his brother, and that Anselm himself had received investiture from Rufus. The Primate had returned not to discuss, but to execute, the recent legislation of the Church and he was prepared to fight to the last against a practice which had never troubled his own conscience. But this resolution, though pregnant with trouble for the future, was tempered by a wise reluctance to endanger the King's title by an immediate quarrel. Anselm accepted the King's proposal that the dispute about investiture should be referred to Rome ; and in the meantime lent the weight of his authority to a marriage which did more than any other of Henry's early measures to establish the King in the affections of his English subjects. The bride was the princess Edith, a daughter of Malcolm Canmore and St. Margaret, who had been educated in England under the care of her mother's sister, the abbess Christina. Through her mother Edith was related to the Confessor and "of the right King kin of England". No more suitable Queen could have been found; but there was a doubt whether she had not made her profession as a nun. This she earnestly denied. According to her own statement she had occasionally worn the religious habit, but solely as a protection against importunate suitors, and with no idea of entering religion. This subterfuge had been so usual among Englishwomen of rank in the early days of Norman rule that Lanfranc had framed a special canon for their benefit, to exempt them from the obligations which the assumption of the veil was usually taken to imply ; and we can well believe that even a Princess may have found the veil her only safeguard against the feudal right of marriage as understood and exercised by Rufus. Still, in an age when forms and habits were with difficulty distinguished from intentions, the obstacle might have been insuperable but for Anselm's intervention. He decided that there was no impediment to the marriage; and it was duly celebrated, not without some covert sneers on the part of the Norman courtiers, among whom Henry and Edith were long known by the nicknames of

Godric and Godgifu, but to the great rejoicing of the native English. The marriage can hardly be said to have influenced Henry's policy. His Queen, of whom the most courtly panegyrist can only say that she was not altogether despicable in appearance,[1] remained a cipher at her husband's court, and devoted herself to charitable works while he amused himself with mistresses. Once only, in the great Investitures controversy, we catch a glimpse of fluttering efforts on her part to mediate between Archbishop Anselm and the King. Her whole character was insignificant and of her letters to Anselm there is none which gives a clearer picture of her mind than one in which she begs the saintly man to moderate the rigour of self-discipline, and to remember how the apostle Paul exhorted Timothy to use wine for his stomach's sake.[2] It was the good lady's fortune to be taken as a symbol of the union and concord of two nationalities; on her wedding day she passes from the view of history and we shall have no further occasion to notice her domestic virtues and unhappinesses. We return to the fortunes of her husband.

Return of Duke Robert, Sept., 1100

Apart from the suspended question of investitures, the outlook at the end of the year 1100 was favourable to Henry. Robert, it is true, had returned to Normandy in September, to the joy of a considerable portion of his Norman subjects with whom legitimacy went for more than merit. But experience had failed to teach him wisdom; the rich dower which he acquired on his homeward journey, by a marriage with an heiress of the house of Hauteville,[3] was squandered before he touched Norman soil; and he made no haste to assert the title of King of England which he had assumed while still in Italy.[4] Those of his barons who held lands in England slipped across the Channel to do homage at his rival's court; and Philip of France sent his son and heir, Louis le Gros, with a message of congratulation to King Henry whose position in the circle of reigning princes now seemed to be beyond dispute. Un-

[1] " Haud usquequaque despicabilis formae " (W. Malmesb., *G. R.*, § 393).
[2] *Anselmi Epistolae*, III., 55: " Nolite igitur, bone Pater et sancte, nolite tam intempestive corporis viribus inedia destitui, ne orator esse desistatis. Quia ut Tullius ait in libro quem de senectute composuit: oratoris munus non ingenii est solum, sed laterum etiam et virium. . . . Audi Paulum Timotheum propter dolorem stomachi vinum bibere suadentem."
[3] Sibylla of Conversana, a great-niece of Robert Guiscard (Orderic, iv., 78).
[4] Rashdall, *Universities*, i., p. 82, quoting from the dedication of the *Regimen Sanitatis Salerni*.

fortunately for Robert he had friends in England who could not be content to leave him in his natural indolence.   There was hardly one of the great English barons who did not think that the Duke would be preferable to Henry as an overlord; and Robert was soon involved in schemes for an invasion of England, under the impression that he had only to show himself and the whole baronage would rally to his side.   His efforts were stimulated by the counsels of Ranulf Flambard.   Early in 1101 the ex-treasurer escaped from his prison, thanks to friends who supplied him with a cask of wine to intoxicate his jailors and a smuggled rope by which to lower himself from the window of his cell;[1] he made his way to Normandy and at once became the Duke's chief favourite and minister.   Under his management the intended expedition was soon in train.

Henry was not caught unprepared.   Long before the Norman fleet appeared the English fyrd had been called out to Pevensey to guard the coast; and rustic levies were drilled into some semblance of discipline under the personal direction of the King. Anselm and the Church were on his side, and the Archbishop did not hesitate to take the field in person.   There was no fear that the loyalty of the native English would be shaken.   With the baronage it was different.   Of all their number the King could only trust a few personal friends; and his one hope lay in the conviction that the rest would not declare themselves until they saw on which side the victory would lie.   The situation was threatening when, on the first of August, Robert landed at Portsmouth through the treacherous aid of certain English pilots (*butse-carles*), and began his march on London.   Some of the wavering barons declared for him; others used the opportunity to require extravagant concessions from his brother.   Henry paid them in their own coin, with promises which he had no intention of observing when the need was past.[2]   But service thus purchased was of dubious value; and when the armies met at Alton, on the road from Portsmouth to London, it was fortunate for Henry that the Duke consented to treat instead of fighting.   Robert threw away the prize within his grasp in return for a pension of 3,000 marks and a promise of assistance in recovering his rebellious dependency of Maine.   In-

Robert invades England, 1101

---

[1] Orderic, iv., 107.   W. Malmesb., *G. R.*, v., § 394.   *Anselmi Epistolae*, IV., ii.
[2] Orderic, iv., 112.

adequate as they were these solatia for the loss of a throne were never actually received. The Treaty of Alton was the most ill-considered step in the whole of Robert's long career of folly.[1]

Rebellion of the Mont-gomeries, 1102

The agreement between the brothers included a stipulation that each should help the other in the punishment of traitors ; and Robert had no sooner returned to Normandy than Henry began his preparations for revenge on those who had covertly or openly betrayed his cause. The method of attack was characteristic of the man. One by one the guilty or suspected barons were summoned to stand their trial before the Curia Regis, on charges which carefully avoided reference to the King's main grievance.[2] Ostensibly there was an amnesty for those who had supported Robert ; but they were brought to trial for minor breaches of the law, exorbitantly fined, and in some cases disinherited, before they realised the need for common action. The three Montgomeries, Robert of Bellême, Arnulf of Pembroke, and Roger of Poitou the lord of the land between the Mersey and the Ribble, were however more far-sighted than the rest. With feverish haste they began to strengthen their castles ; Arnulf enlisted the aid of his father-in-law Murchertach, King of Dublin, and Robert bought the help of the Welsh princes, of whom several had become his vassals, by lavish grants of horses and arms, lands and lordships. When at length the King's writ went forth summoning Robert to stand his trial on five and forty separate counts, it found the earl prepared, and the whole force of the kingdom was needed to deal with the rebellion of the great house of Montgomery (1102). But the three brothers stood alone. The barons whom Henry's judicial proscription had not yet touched were cowed into loyalty ; the English fyrd mustered with no less zeal than in the previous year. Without loss of time the Montgomery castles were attacked ; when Arundel in Sussex and Tickhill in Yorkshire had been invested the royal forces converged upon the earldom of Shrewsbury, and Bridgnorth speedily surrendered. The chief of Robert's Welsh supporters, the prince Jorwerth ap Bleddyn, was seduced by a promise of the principality of S. Wales.[3] The rebel brothers, cut off from their allies and

[1] Orderic, iv., 113. W. Malmesb., G. R., v., § 395. Roman de Rou, 10399. Florence and the A. S. C. mention a stipulation that if either brother died without legitimate issue he should be succeeded by the survivor.
[2] Orderic, iv., 161 : " Nec simul, sed separatim variisque temporibus et multimodis violatae fidei reatibus implacitavit " ; iv.. 167 : " Infidis erat impacabilis inimicus ".
[3] Brut y Tyw., p. 70.

driven back on Shrewsbury, had no course open to them but
surrender. The barons in the King's host wished them well and
endeavoured to negotiate a favourable peace. But Henry could
now afford to show himself unbending; and the clamorous demand
of his English troops for vengeance on the traitors was not without
effect upon his mind. The brothers were sentenced to lose all the
lands and honours which they held in England. Robert migrated
to Normandy, where he spent the next few years in harrying the
adherents of the Duke to whom he attributed his ruin; Arnulf
betook himself to the court of Dublin, and divided the remainder
of a stormy existence between Normandy and Ireland. Except as
allies of their abler brother Robert neither he nor Roger of Poitou
had ever merited consideration; and of the three only Robert was
destined to play an important part in the history of the future.

The fall of the Montgomeries left Henry without a serious New dif-
rival. Orderic quotes a contemporary song in which the situation ficulties
is clearly stated : "Rejoice King Henry ! and give thanks to God ! Church
for thou hast begun to rule freely now that Robert of Bellême is
conquered and driven out of thy kingdom ".[1] It was now possible
to bestow some attention on the claims which the Church, in the
person of Anselm, had advanced in the preceding year. The King's
intention was, from the first, to yield none of the rights which had
been exercised by his father; the fact that they had been abused
by Rufus, the probability that they might be abused by future
rulers, were nothing to him. Like Anselm he was averse from any
discussion of principle; but while the Archbishop appealed to the
legislation of the Church, Henry took his stand on the customs of
the kingdom. Early in 1101, when an invasion from Normandy
was imminent and his position one of considerable uncertainty and
danger, Henry wrote to the Pope intimating that he could make no
concessions. "The dignities and customs of the realm of England
shall not be diminished in my life-time. And even if I should
subject myself to this humiliation, which may God forbid ! my
barons and the people of England would not permit it." [2] It is a
remarkable proof of Henry's statesmanship that he should have
resisted the temptation, which proved too strong for the Imperialists

---

[1] Orderic, iv., 177, who gives a rhyming translation in Latin.
[2] This letter is given in the *Quadripartitus*, ii., § 5. It is dated 1103 in *Foedera*,
i., 8, but can hardly be later than 1101.

of Italy and Germany, of entangling himself in abstract and irritat
ing controversies as to the right relations of the Church and State

Arch-
bishop
Gerard's
Anti-
papalism

The temptation was the greater in his case because he had by his
side an acute and daring controversialist, who had already broken
a lance with the advocates of Papal claims. Gerard of York [1] was
prepared to prove by history and natural reason that the Papacy
was an institution of merely human ordinance; that the title
"Mother of the Churches" belonged more properly to Jerusalem
than to Rome; that the Pope's claim to be "the oracle of faith"
was unwarrantable; and that the powers which the Roman court
had exercised in recent years were greater even than those of Christ
and the Apostles. There is no need, says Gerard, in a passage
which the Protestants of the sixteenth century might well have
copied, there is no need that the Pope should expound to us the
will of God. Have we not the Scriptures to instruct us? Let him
go and preach to the Gentiles who have not yet received the faith![2]
There was one feature in Gerard's speculations which may have
recommended itself to the King, and was certainly approved by
some of his supporters. The Archbishop of York, following the
lead of foreign imperialists, maintained that Kings were ordained
by God to rule the Church no less than the State. But even this
claim, which left its mark upon the policy of Henry's reign, was
not supported by him in so many words. In common with his
bishops he confined himself to protests against recent extensions
of the Pope's prerogative; he frankly admitted that, in some
degree, the Pope was entitled to regulate the English Church.
It was dependent on the See of Rome; but the terms of the dependency were fixed by the concordat between the Conqueror and
Gregory VII.

The
Negotia-
tions with
Anselm

The negotiations with Anselm and the Pope dragged on for
several years. Paschal, although he must have been sorely tempted
to temporise after the manner of Gregory VII., finally decided to
stand firm; and Anselm, as on all other occasions, held fast to the
line of conduct prescribed for him by Rome.[3] But the personal

---

[1] The facts relating to his life are collected by H. Boehmer in *Libelli de litis Sacerdotii et Imperii*, iii., 642 (M. H. G., 4°). In his later work, *Kirche und Staat*, pp. 261-3, Boehmer decides that the author was not Gerard but one of his confidants. But the argument which induces Boehmer to abandon his original view does not seem conclusive.

[2] These doctrines are propounded at length in the six *Tractatus* which Boehmer published from the unique manuscript (No. 415, C. C. C., Cambridge).

[3] Anselm's indifference to the principle involved in the Investitures controversy is clear from *Epistolæ*, III., No. lxxiii.

relations of the King and Archbishop remained not unfriendly ; and Henry showed a marked anxiety to meet the wishes of Anselm in any matter where the royal prerogative was not endangered. Pending the final declaration of the Pope, Anselm was allowed to hold a council (Sept. 29, 1102) with the object of enforcing the reforms of discipline already indicated by Lanfranc. New canons were passed to enforce celibacy upon the clergy ; and a number of abbots, among them three whom Henry had promoted, were deprived of their croziers on the charge of simony. The obduracy of Paschal led (April, 1103) to a suggestion from the King that Anselm should go to Rome in person, and use his personal influence to secure a favourable settlement. This mission, which Anselm Anselm's cheerfully accepted in the interests of peace but without any Second expectation of success, merely served to show that Paschal, though (1103-5 not prepared to go to extremities against the King of England, would make no compromise upon the central question in dispute ; and the Archbishop, judging it useless to return to England while he was unable to satisfy the King's demands, took up his residence at Lyons. In this position the controversy remained until the year 1105. During the time of suspense Anselm showed a spirit of forbearance which is entirely inconsistent with the hypothesis that he had been the prime mover in the quarrel between England and the Holy See.[1] He maintained a friendly correspondence with the King; he resisted the overtures of the French court, which would not have been sorry to use his misfortunes for the purpose of damaging a powerful neighbour ;[2] and he intimated to his English supporters that they were under no sort of obligation to decline intercourse with any bishop, whom the King had invested, until they received, as Anselm himself had received, a personal command from the Pope to that effect.[3] The behaviour of Henry was not so creditable as that of his adversary and went far to justify the fears with which the reforming party contemplated the prospect of a lay supremacy. He appropriated the revenues of the Archbishopric to his own use, and encroached upon the sphere of the ecclesiastical tribunals. Anselm's canon against the marriages of the clergy having proved ineffectual, the King took the matter into

---

[1] A hypothesis adopted by Sir James Ramsay, *Foundations*, ii., p. 248, etc.
[2] See the letters of Philip and his son to Anselm, *Anselmi Epistolae*, IV., l., li.
[3] *Anselmi Epistolae*, III., xc.

his own hands ; and under the pretext of a zeal for reform, extorted heavy fines from those who still retained their wives.[1] No long time elapsed before the bishops, even the anti-Papal Gerard of York, were fain to confess that Anselm and Paschal had been wiser than they, and to beg that Anselm would return to give them his protection.

Disputes with Robert (1103-4) For some time, however, the question of Normandy left the King with little time or interest to bestow on the affairs of the Church. The treaty of Alton raised as many difficulties as it settled, since each of the brothers made it the pretext for interfering with the other's government ; and Henry in particular twisted its terms to suit his purposes with complete unscrupulousness. He complained that the Duke had come to terms with Robert of Bellême, and took no account of his brother's truthful, if humiliating, apology that it had been impossible to crush the outlaw. The Duke in his turn ventured to express dissatisfaction that Henry's promise of an amnesty to William of Warenne, Earl of Surrey, had never been fulfilled, and paid a visit to England in 1103 that he might urge Warenne's cause in person. As soon as he disembarked the Duke was met by Robert of Meulan, the Achitophel of the English court, who informed him that the King regarded his visit as an insidious attempt to stir up fresh disorders in England, and would infallibly detain him as a captive. Robert would willingly have taken ship for Normandy without delay. But, the winds proving contrary, he was glad to purchase his safety by surrendering, at Mellent's suggestion, his pension as a gift to the Queen Matilda.[2] In the end William of Warenne recovered his earldom ; but Henry on his side insisted that the Norman fief of Breteuil should be given to the husband of his illegitimate daughter Juliana. In 1104 the King paid a visit to Domfront and his other Norman possessions ; he took the opportunity of administering to his senior a sharp lecture on the art of government, which was none the less stinging because thoroughly deserved. To pacify Henry the Duke presented him with the county of Evreux. But Robert was powerless to redress the one legitimate complaint which Henry had against him. Normandy had become the gathering ground of those barons who had left England under compulsion, or because their demands were not conceded. Under the ægis of Robert of

---

[1] *Anselmi Epistolae*, III., cix.   [2] *Roman de Rou*, 10600 ff.   Orderic, iv., 162.

Bellême they could plot against England as they pleased ; and the Duke, however willing, was utterly unable to repress them. Well-wishers of the King were forcibly expelled from Normandy ; to their complaints were added those of the entire Norman church, the property of which was as little respected by the party of disorder as that of the Duke or Henry's friends.

This situation explains and justifies the deliberate resolve of Henry to dispossess his brother. It proved an easy matter to isolate Robert from his natural allies, the Count of Flanders and the King of France. The former was bought over to Henry's side by a renewal, on an increased scale, of the pension which William I. had granted to Count Baldwin V. for his assistance in the Conquest.[1] The reigning Count, Robert of Jerusalem, was engrossed in petty wars against his vassals, and blind to the danger in which the reunion of England and Normandy would place his struggling kingdom. The Duke's own resources were exhausted ; his brother lavished the wealth of England in collecting mercenaries from Anjou, Maine, and Brittany ; for his own part he could only rely upon the unpaid service of militia from the Norman towns and upon a few barons, such as Robert of Bellême, who doubted the possibility of obtaining terms from Henry. There could be no doubt as to the issue ; our only ground for surprise is that Henry, after opening the war in the spring of 1105 by the capture of Bayeux and Caen,[2] allowed more than twelve months to elapse in futile negotiations before he put the finishing touches to his work. At length, on September 28th, 1106, the decisive moment came ; the armies of the brothers met beneath the walls of Tinchebrai, and an hour's fighting concluded the unequal struggle. At the first onslaught the Duke's knights held their own ; but his infantry were routed by a flank attack of Henry's mounted men ; and Robert of Bellême fled from the field at the first symptom of defeat. His desertion was fatal to his cause. The Duke surrendered with 400 knights ; 10,000 of the Norman burgesses were captured, and no man concerned himself to count the multitude of their fellows who fell in the flight. They were the chief sufferers, as was usual in such battles ; for of Robert's knights not more than 60 were killed, and

Marginal notes: Conquest of Normandy (1105-6) · Battle of Tinchebrai

---

[1] Pirenne, *Histoire de Flandre*, i., pp. 98 ff., and the treaty of 1103 in *Foedera*, i., p. 6 (where it is incorrectly dated). The pension formerly 300, now 400 marks.
[2] See Serlo's *Versus de capta Bajocensium civitate* (Bouquet, xix., p. xci.).

of Henry's few or none.[1] Normandy lay at the feet of the victor, a not unwilling spoil; and the English could boast that Hastings was avenged; for although mercenaries and Norman rebels formed the larger half of the victorious cavalry, the King's foot-soldiers were chiefly drawn from England.[2]

Treatment of Duke Robert and his allies

The captured Duke received the respect due to a prince of the royal blood and to a crusader. He was kept in confinement, first at Devizes and afterwards at Cardiff, until his death in 1134. The King turned a deaf ear to the requests for his brother's release which Rome, as in duty bound, advanced from time to time; but there is every reason for rejecting the idle stories, told by some of our authorities, of indignities and cruelties inflicted on the captive.[3] Though unscrupulous the King was not malignant. Of his other captives William of Mortain, his own cousin, was treated the most severely. Henry, not content with inflicting a sentence of perpetual imprisonment, the heaviest penalty which Norman law allowed against a treacherous vassal, ordered William's eyes to be put out.[4] But William's treachery had been more than usually gratuitous. He had deserted Henry's cause because he was not allowed to hold the Earldom of Kent in addition to that of Cornwall which he had inherited from his father. And Rufus had already set the example of dealing with all traitors according to the English law as amended by the Conqueror; there was no longer any reason for treating the crimes of Normans more leniently than those of Englishmen. It is surprising to find that Robert of Bellême escaped with his liberty, and was allowed to retain a part, though only a small part, of his lands and offices in Normandy. The forbearance of the King lends colour to the allegation that

[1] See *E. H. R.*, xxv., p. 296, for a contemporary letter describing the battle. The description of Orderic (iv., 224) is fuller and differs in many details. Eadmer, *H. N.*, 184, gives a letter from Henry I. to Anselm, announcing the victory. The numbers of Robert's army, as given above, are taken from this letter.

[2] Orderic, iv., 229. W. Malmesb., *G. R.*, v., § 365, suggests that the victory was ordained by providence: "ut eo die subderetur Angliae Normannia quo ad eam subjugandam olim venerat Normannorum copia". William I. had landed on Sept. 28.

[3] Date of his death February 3, 1134 (Orderic, v., 18, and the *Historia Monasterii S. Petri Gloucest.*). He was buried at Gloucester where his tomb remains. The story that he was blinded, in *Annales Winton, s.a.* 1133. But see Orderic, iv., 402, and W. Malmesb., *G. R.*, v., § 389, who agree that he was well-treated. Disbursements for his benefit are mentioned in the Pipe Roll of 1130-1. Henry gave Gloucester the manor of Rodele for the health of his brother's soul (*Cart. Mon. S. Petri Gloucest.*, i., p. 110).

[4] Hen. Hunt., p. 255. He was set free in 1118, and became a monk in 1140 (*Bermondsey Annals*).

Bellême's flight from Tinchebrai was not the outcome of mere cowardice. But his treachery, if treachery it was, did not avail him long. Six years later, on a variety of charges, he was condemned to imprisonment for life, and the sentence was rigidly enforced; although his imprisonment does not appear to have been aggravated by privations.[1] Henry's retribution might be leaden footed but it was marvellously sure.

The battle of Tinchebrai opened a new era in the history of the Duchy. It was the first care of the victor to infuse into the administration of his new province something of the order, economy, and respect for private rights, which were the good features of his English government. Measures were taken to protect the public peace; religious houses and individuals were reinstated in the lands of which they had been deprived by an unbridled baronage; all the grants which had been made from the ducal demesnes since the death of William I. were cancelled; and all officials were held to a strict account by the Ducal Court of the Exchequer. The unlicensed castles, which during Robert's reign had sprung up in every corner of the duchy, were overthrown; the greatest of the Norman nobles were made to understand that even they were not above the law; the privileges of the great city of Rouen were confirmed.[2] Unhappily the King committed one mistake, of a kind to which he was by no means prone, and left his enemies with an opportunity, which they were quick to seize, of disturbing the new settlement. After Tinchebrai the infant son of Robert, William surnamed the Clito, had fallen into Henry's hands; but he handed over the boy to the charge of the Heliede St. Saens, who had married Robert's natural daughter. The King was afraid, we are told, that if any accident befell the boy while in his hands, he would incur suspicion. But the result of his generous imprudence was worse than any reproach against which it guarded him. A party soon arose in Normandy which favoured the Clito's title to the Duchy; and for more than twenty years the continental policy of Henry was determined by the rebellions and the diplomatic intrigues which were hatched in the interest of this youth.

Settlement of Normandy, 1106-7

---

[1] Orderic, iv., 234, 305. Pipe Roll, p. 12. In 1130-1 the sheriff of Wilts accounts for the sum of £20 spent on the food and clothing of Robert of Bellême. *Cf.* W. Malmesb., *G. R.*, v., § 398: " Ad mortem perpetuo inclusus ergastulo ".

[2] Orderic, iv., 232, 233, 237, 269.

Of the Clito we shall have more to say.   Some little time elapsed before he became a serious danger.   In the meanwhile the long-drawn quarrel with the Church was settled by a compromise. This was due to the vigorous action which Paschal took in the year 1105, when it became evident that mere arguments were thrown away on Henry.   The Pope excommunicated Henry's bishops and also Robert of Meulan, who rightly or wrongly was supposed to be responsible for the King's obstinacy.   Henry was informed that he too would fall under the ban unless he showed himself submissive. Negotiations between Anselm and the King were accordingly re- sumed ; and in 1106 a treaty was drawn up which satisfied the reforming party without doing violence to the King's suscepti- bilities.   It was agreed that Henry should renounce the right of investing prelates with the ring and staff ; but that he should receive their homage [1] for the temporalties attaching to their dignity.   The terms of this agreement have been highly praised, and it certainly dealt with the question of forms and ceremonies in a spirit of plain common sense.[2]   On the other hand it did practically nothing to secure the substantial object with which the reformers had started their crusade.   They had hoped to secure the independence of the episcopate.   This boasted concordat, and that of Worms between the Pope and Emperor, which was sub- sequently framed on the same model, left to the temporal sovereign all the power of influencing ecclesiastical elections which he had hitherto possessed ; and without free elections there could not be a free episcopate ; whereas, given a free system of election, it mattered nothing by whom, and with what forms, a bishop was put into his office.   Even among the contemporaries of Anselm and Paschal there was at least one man, Ivo of Chartres, who saw this truth ; [3]

---

[1] Eadmer, *H. N.*, 186.   Mr. Rule, p. xlvii., contends that this is inaccurate ; and that the bishops from this time forward rendered fealty but not homage.   Such a distinction is found later ; and in 1116 the bishops refused to do homage to the king's son.   On the other hand they promised that when William should become king " se hominia fideli mente facturos " (*H. N.*, p. 237).   See Glanvill, ix., § 1.

[2] Paschal is generally credited with the suggestion of the compromise.   But from some of Anselm's letters (*Epistolae*, IV., lxxiv.-lxxvii.) it would seem that Henry made the offer to give up investitures if he were allowed homage.   He did so " renitentibus multis ".

[3] Ivo, *Epistolae*, No. lx. ; *cf.* also No. ccxxxvi. (ed. 1610).   His opinions on this subject obtained the approval of moderate ecclesiastics in England (see *Hugh the Chanter*, p. 110, ed. Raine).   Eadmer, *Vita Anselmi*, p. 414, says that Henry conceded the right of free election ; *cf. H. N.*, p. 191.   But W. Malmesb., *G. R.*, v., § 417, is more accurate : " Investituram annuli et baculi concessit in perpetuum ; retento tamen electionis et regalium privilegio ".

and although it is unlikely that a Pope of the twelfth century could have effected a reform which proved to be beyond the power of a Hildebrand and an Innocent III., we should have felt more sympathy for Paschal if he had recognised and pursued the unattainable ideal than we can feel for the barren victory which he actually secured. The whole episode of the Investitures controversy is an illustration of the law that, in protracted quarrels, the original causes of dispute slip out of sight.

The fortunes of Henry had now reached their zenith. He had surmounted the initial difficulties of his position; accounts were settled with his more formidable opponents. Anselm, whose devotion to the Church made him, in spite of their personal friendship, an inconvenient counsellor to his master, was removed by death in 1109. His see remained vacant for four years until the King had found, in Ralph of Séez, bishop of Rochester, a successor on whose pliancy he could rely. Robert of Bellême, who took the first opportunity to embrace the cause of the Clito, was thrown into prison, as already related, before his projects had matured (1112). Ranulf Flambard, although by a timely desertion of Duke Robert and by the intercession of the Papacy he procured the restitution of his see of Durham,[1] was too unpopular with every class to be a danger; the remainder of his life was divided between futile efforts to win Henry's confidence, and projects for the embellishment of his city and cathedral. The few members of the English baronage who might have been formidable were subject to strict supervision ; and the most important of the fiefs which had been confiscated were retained in the King's hand. The feudal rights of the Crown were judiciously exercised to prevent the growth of great baronial honours. Following his father's rule Henry divided the inheritances of tenants-in-chief among their sons according to his pleasure ; the English fiefs, which were usually the most important, he gave to that son in whom he had most confidence.[2] When the Honour of Gloucester devolved upon an heiress it was given with her hand to the King's natural son, Robert ; and Ralph le Meschin was only allowed to

The Baronage (1106-12)

---

[1] See the writ in Monasticon, i., 241.

[2] Cf. Leges Henrici, lxx., § 21: " Primo patris feodum primogenitus filius habeat; emptiones vero vel deinceps acquisitiones suas det cui magis velit ". This rule, repeated in Glanvill, does not correspond to the general practice. But the passage is interesting as a proof that the conflict between the old idea of partition and the new idea of primogeniture was already a problem to English lawyers.

inherit the palatine earldom of Chester on condition of renouncing the Honour of Carlisle, which had previously come to him by marriage. Sterner measures were seldom necessary, although in 1110 three barons at once were summarily sentenced to forfeiture and exile. Their names were Philip de Braose, William Malet, and William Bainard; all three were politically obscure and the nature of their offence is unknown. It was the last case in which the King did summary justice upon English barons.

The Lion of Justice

The use which Henry made of his commanding position was characteristic of the period and the man, but came as a surprise to his English subjects. They hoped little from him although they preferred him to his brother and Robert of Bellême. An Englishman in the eyes of his nobles, Henry was a Norman to the people; and his first measures, involving as they did a large expenditure and regular taxation, are related in the English Chronicle with a running commentary of complaints. "It is not easy to describe," so runs one entry, "the misery of this land which it suffered at this time through the various and manifold oppressions and taxes that never ceased nor slackened;" and under the year 1107 we find the significant remark "that was the one and fortieth year since the French began to rule this land". Another twenty years elapse before we hear the last of such complaints and Henry is recognised by his subjects as the "Lion of Justice". But, early in his reign, he had taken on himself the task which was being performed in a smaller sphere by the contemporary counts of Flanders and Anjou. He had the Norman love of thrift and order, without the old Norman lust of conquest. He delighted to foster the resources of his realm in the spirit of a careful landlord. He exacted the utmost farthing of his rights, and enforced prerogatives which he had expressly abandoned by his charter; but he might have said, with Tiberius, that he preferred to shear his subjects rather than to flay them. A conservative in every fibre of his being, he rejected the Red King's ideal of an arbitrary despotism; while he rarely deferred to the opinion of his prelates and great men, he showed a certain respect for their privileges. The law-book, which bears his name and was in fact compiled by a clerk of his Curia Regis,[1]

---

[1] Liebermann, *Ueber die Leges Henrici*, and *E. H. R.*, vol. xvii., p. 147. The text is given in Liebermann's *Gesetze der Angel-Sachsen*, I., pp. 547 ff. See Stubbs' *Lectures on Early English History*, pp. 143-165, for a good commentary.

seems to reflect the spirit of his government in the large concessions which it makes to feudalism. To judge from this book The *Leges*
we should say that the Curia was inclined to tolerate all feudal *Henrici*
rights, however indirectly dangerous to the prerogative, unless
they had been expressly abolished by the royal authority. The
author states, for example, that archbishops, bishops, earls and
other officials have *la haute justice* over the lands pertaining to
their dignity; [1] and although the generalisation is too sweeping we
know from Henry's charters to the sees of Bath and York [2] that he
did not hesitate to confer the widest powers of jurisdiction on some
favoured vassals. All the rights which the Crown had ever possessed
in the city of Bath were bestowed upon the bishop. The King was
satisfied with such restrictions as would make rebellion hopeless.
He forbade the custom of private war; no castle might be built,
no dwelling fortified, without his licence [3] and he insisted that every
under-tenant should regard the King as his chief lord. [4] In his
dealings with the Church he became rather less than more autocratic in the course of time. Of his later appointments to
bishoprics none was so scandalous as that of his larderer to Hereford in 1102; William of Corbeil, his third Archbishop, was freely
elected by the monks and suffragans of Canterbury whereas Ralph of
Séez, Anselm's successor, had been openly nominated. But Henry's
bishops were by no means servile. They stood upon their rights,
and their rights were generally respected. Chance has preserved
a record of an interesting incident which happened shortly before
the death of William Atheling. One of the prince's friends accused
the bishop of Bath of unjustly refusing to enfeoff him with an
estate which he had purchased from a tenant of the bishop; and
William, as his father's deputy, issued a writ directing the bishop
to give seisin to the claimant. The bishop took counsel with his
tenants, decided that neither the King's son nor the King himself
had a right to ask for more than what was just, and refused to
obey the writ on the ground that the alleged claim was invalid by

[1] *Leges*, xx., § 2.
[2] Monasticon, ii., 267.   Raine, *Historians of York*, iii., p. 22.
[3] *Leges*, x., xiii., § 1.
[4] See the charter to Miles of Gloucester in Round, *Ancient Charters*, p. 8 : " Volo
et praecipio quod omnes tenentes de praedicto Maritagio faciant ei hominagium
ligium, in mea salva fidelitate, sicut domino suo." For the doctrine of Liege
Homage see *Leges*, xliii., lv.

the custom of his court.[1] The tragedy of the White Ship prevented matters from going further; but the bishop's protest shows
that the idea of appealing to the law against the Crown was already
The Curia a familiar one on English soil. The rule of law is the key-note to
Regis the inner history of the reign. Henry's Curia Regis was a different
tribunal from that of Rufus, of which Eadmer said, with as much
justice as severity, that all its judgments depended on the King's
nod and nothing was considered by the judges save the royal
pleasure. In his law-courts, as in all other departments of the
administration, Henry relied on men whom he had selected from
the ranks of the inferior baronage. "He raised them from the
dust to do his service" is the remark of the admiring Orderic
Vitalis. But the King asked of his judges no more than a strict
adherence to law and precedent. It was their boast that in their
keeping the law remained unalterable *semper et ubique;* and the
boast was true so far as it signified that the law was declared
without respect of persons.[2] The law of the King's court was a
strange medley of scraps from the code of Saxon Kings, of feudal
custom borrowed from the practice of the Norman courts, of
maxims from the civil law and the decretals. But it gained
steadily in bulk and consistency through the accumulation of new
precedents. The judgments of the court were carefully enrolled,
and from the law as laid down in that record there was no appeal.[3]
The severity of the court was excessive. At the beginning of
his reign Henry reintroduced the penalty of death for offences
against property. We hear of one session held by a justiciar,
at Hundehoge (Huncote) in Leicestershire, in which forty-four
thieves were hanged. In 1124 there was a great inquest on the
moneyers of all the mints in England, with the result that more
than ninety were foully mutilated for debasing the King's coin.
Traitors were blinded with hot irons, and the author of the
Leges knew of precedents for flaying such offenders; we hear of no
case in which the justices imposed this sentence; but the hideous
practice of quartering the half-hanged criminal probably dates
from the period of Henry I. It is little wonder that the ec-

---

[1] Monasticon, ii., 268.
[2] "Supersunt regis placita curiae, quae usus et consuetudines suas una semper
immobilitate servat ubique" (*Leges*, ix., § 10).
[3] "Recordationem Curiae Regis nulli negare licet" (*Leges*, xxxi., § 4).

clesiastical privilege of sanctuary was strenuously maintained in favour even of confessed malefactors.[1] The conscience of laymen no less than of churchmen revolted against these punishments. But the law had at least the merit of impartiality. The severity of its penalties affected great and small alike; and there was no class too humble to be protected by the Curia Regis. The *Leges Henrici* deny, for instance, that the lord may do what he pleases with his villein. " If a lord slay his villein blameless let him pay the were to the kindred ; for the man was a serf to serve and not to be slain." [2]

Wergilds, compurgation, the ordeal, and many such relics of archaic procedure were perforce tolerated by the Curia Regis.[3] But the inclination of the judges was towards more enlightened forms of proof and more drastic penalties. The law which they administered diverged widely from the law of the Confessor which the King had sworn to maintain. It could not well be otherwise. When Henry came to the throne there was one law for the West Saxon, another for the Mercian, a third for the man of the Danelaw; in addition every shire had local and unwritten customs; and, to complete the confusion, the Norman settler still claimed to be worthy of the law under which he had lived in the duchy.[4] These differences the Curia Regis declined to recognise. The rule was that the law of the King's court stood above all other law and was the same for all. It would have been an important rule enough if it had been applied merely to those cases which were called up to the central and supreme court. It acquired additional importance when the King's justices began to visit the shire-courts and do justice there. *The King's Law*

Even under the first two Norman Kings it had been a common practice to send royal commissioners to the shire-courts, either for the purpose of collecting necessary information from local juries, or to try offences against the royal peace. The returns for Domesday Book were collected by such commissioners; and both before and after this great inquest we hear of justices making circuits for *Itinerant Justices*

---

[1] *Cf.* the decree of Clermont (W. Malmesb., *G. R.*, iv., § 345): "Qui ad ecclesiam vel crucem confugerint, *data membrorum impunitate*, justitiae tradantur ".

[2] *Leges*, lxxv., § 3.

[3] *Leges*, lxvi., lxviii., lxix. Rufus threatened to abolish the ordeal. " Per hoc et hoc meo judicio amodo respondebitur, non Dei, quod pro voto cujusque hinc inde plicatur " (Eadmer, *H. N.*, 102), but he did not keep his word.

[4] *Leges*, vi., § 2.

5*

judicial purposes.[1]   These visitations limited the power of the
sheriff, since the justices reserved to themselves the more important
cases of which the shire-court had cognisance.   Sometimes the
experiment was tried of appointing a local justiciar with a permanent commission, to relieve the sheriff of the duty of trying
"royal pleas"; and again there were cases in which the offices of
sheriff and justiciar were combined in the person of a single court
official.   But, if it is safe to generalise from the evidence of the
Pipe Roll, the itinerant commissioners were already, in the year
1130, recognised as the most serviceable agents of royal justice in
the shires.   They may not have been sent annually to every shire ;
but we may safely assume that their visits were frequent.   The
result was to plane away the more salient anomalies of provincial
law and custom.   Uniform rules of public and of private law were
enforced throughout the land.   No doubt there was a hard battle
between the old law and the new on many points of secondary importance ; and local custom won the battle in some cases, for example
in the law of inheritance to non-military land.   But before Henry's
death the most distinctive of the old provincial differences was practically destroyed.   Provincial jealousies died hard ; their influence
can still be traced for three or four centuries after 1135.   Provincial
peculiarities of speech and manners and tradition are still with us.
In the twelfth century they were so strong that a native of Yorkshire was unintelligible, and only not a foreigner, to a man of
southern extraction.[2]   But the common respect of north and
south for the King's writ, their submission and increasing attachment to the same principles of law, their interest in the monarchy
as a bulwark against robbery and oppression, had made them
one people.   In the Conqueror's lifetime it was still possible
for an English or Norman rebel to scheme for the partition of
England into several kingdoms.   After 1135 the monarchy one
and indivisible was accepted as inevitable by the most daring of
feudal conspirators.   For this great advance towards national unity
we have to thank the Curia Regis and the Lion of Justice.

It is difficult to trim the balance between centralisation and
local autonomy.   The weak point of Henry's judicial system was

---

[1] See the Appendix " Local Justice under the Norman Kings ".
[2] W. Malmesb., *G. P.*, p. 209 : " Sane tota lingua Nordanimbrorum, sed maxime
in Eboraco, ita inconditum stridet, ut nichil nos australes intelligere possimus ".

his neglect to secure the active co-operation of the middle and lower class of freemen. At his accession the courts of shire and hundred were in a moribund condition. On the one hand they had lost the greater part of their police duties and civil jurisdiction through the rise of private law-courts. According to the *Leges Henrici* all great lords have criminal jurisdiction, all landholders have ordinary sac and soc. The public courts may not judge an offence committed on the land of a lord with competent jurisdiction, even though the complaint be made to them in the first instance. A suit can only be removed from a private to a public court if the lord refuses, or unwarrantably delays, to give his judgment; no appeal from the lord's judgment is recognised by the ordinary law.[1] On the other hand the increasing activity of the Curia Regis and of itinerant commissioners withdrew from the sheriff and the suitors of the shire-court many of the powers and duties which feudalism had not dared to seize. The courts of shire and hundred were meeting at infrequent intervals according to the caprice of the sheriffs; attendance was sparse, and small pains were taken to enforce the regular appearance of those on whom devolved the duty of representing the several townships; the work to be done was unimportant. There was a real danger that the development of feudalism would be fatal to the stated assemblies in which the King, by the mouth of his sheriff, communicated with the people and enforced his will; that royal justice would be represented in the shires only by periodical sessions of royal judges; and that the whole inferior judicial business of the country would slip into the hands of landowners. This danger Henry met to some extent by the ordinance of 1109-11 [2] which enacted that the courts of shire and hundred should meet at the same times and places as of old; and that suits arising between the free tenants of different lords should be heard in the shire-court. He thus set aside the feudal principle that every lord was entitled to try a case in which his free tenant was the defendant.[3] He forced his barons to be content with settling cases which affected no one outside the boundaries of their fiefs. The shire-court is thus provided with important work. But the hundred-court, though ordered to meet,

Marginal notes: Private Jurisdictions

Ordinance concerning Shire-court and Hundred-court

---

[1] *Leges*, xx., xxvii., xxxiii., xli.   [2] S. C., 122.
[3] Approved in *Leges*, xxv., although the author elsewhere quotes the ordinance of 1109.

has no precise functions allotted to it; and it was left for Henry's grandson to give the suitors of shire and hundred a definite share in the administration of the law. The local courts were kept alive; but they served little purpose beyond that of registering the judgments of a sheriff whose obligation to be guided by the verdict of the suitors sat lightly on his shoulders. Except to register royal decrees or requisitions [1] the shire-courts no longer acted as local parliaments. Their activity, such as it was, depended on the maintenance of pressure from above.

Fiscal
System

But it would be captious to expect the democratic theories of the nineteenth century in a statesman of the twelfth; the importance of promoting corporate life in the smaller communities of which a nation consists is a discovery of modern times. The government of Henry I. must be judged by the success with which it fulfilled his primary objects of keeping the peace and filling his Exchequer. That he achieved the first of these two objects we are assured by the English Chronicler, a critic by no means easily propitiated, " Good man he was, and there was great awe of him. In his day no man dared to harm another." And the elaborate machinery of his Exchequer proves that no pains or skill were spared to extract from the administration all the profit that was possible. It is unfortunate that we have only one of the great rolls on which the receipts of Henry's Exchequer were entered, and that a roll so late in date as the year 1131. We are prevented by the paucity of our materials from tracing the chronological development of the system, or even from realising the state in which Flambard left and Henry found the Exchequer. We know that the main sources of revenue were unchanged; and that in the new system as in the old the sheriff was the principal agent through whom they were collected. The great Justiciar, Roger of Salisbury, to whom the official tradition of the Angevin period ascribes the credit of reorganising the Exchequer, seems to have been conservative in his reforms, and to have borrowed little or nothing from foreign models. For the rest we must be content to describe the system as it stood, when practically complete, about the year 1130.[2]

---

[1] The " dominica necessaria " mentioned in the ordinance of 1109-11. On the paucity of the suitors in later times, see Maitland, E. H. R., iii., p. 417. The local administration of Henry I. is reviewed by W. A. Morris in E. H. R., xxxvii., pp. 161-172.

[2] See Mr. Round in Commune, c. iv.; E. H. R., xiv., p. 417; and the preface to the Dialogus de Scaccario (ed. Hughes, Crump, and Johnson). The Pipe Roll of Henry I. is printed by Mr. Hunter in the Record Commission Series. On the Anglo-Saxon fiscal system, see Round in V. C. H., Hants, i., p. 415.

The head-quarters of the Exchequer, from 1066 to the death of The Henry II., were at Winchester which in spite of the growing import- Exchequer ance of London preserved its position as the seat of national government. Twice every year, at Easter and at Michaelmas, the sheriffs visited Winchester to render their accounts. They paid a fixed sum, the *firma comitatus*, for the privilege of farming the more ancient of the royal dues and rents; but for the proceeds of taxation and the law-courts, for feudal dues and other sources of revenue, they accounted according to the sum which was actually to be collected. At the beginning of the reign a part of the sheriff's receipts still came to the Exchequer in the form of agricultural produce, hawks and hounds and horses. Later the King decreed that all such miscellaneous renders should be commuted at a fixed rate for money payments; a measure of no small advantage to the royal tenants who, under the old system, had paid more heavily for their land in bad seasons, when prices ruled high, than in years of plenty when prices were low.[1] Owing to the frauds of local moneyers a further change was necessary. The coins tendered by the sheriff were assayed and he was only credited with the amount of silver which they actually contained. This expedient was not altogether new; the practice of demanding certain payments "in blanch" went back to the pre-Conquest period; but its universal application dates from this reign.

In the Exchequer itself there were two chambers; that of Receipt in which the coin tendered by the sheriff was counted, assayed, and stored; that of Account in which he made his statement of expenses and receipts before the barons of the Exchequer. To this board belonged all the great officers of state and the judges of the Curia Regis. The Justiciar, Treasurer, and Chancellor took the lead in the proceedings; and the accounts as finally passed by the board were duly entered on the Great Roll of the Pipe from the evidence of which there could be no subsequent appeal. The business of the Exchequer was primarily of a fiscal character, but in practice was often indistinguishable from that of the Curia Regis. The same men sat in both. The Exchequer collected the fines which the Curia imposed, and the Curia called to account those through whom the Exchequer had suffered loss. There was no purpose to be served by insisting on the separateness of the two boards since their functions were so closely connected.

[1] See further Stubbs' *Lectures on Early English History*, p. 140.

The
Towns

From this impressive and orderly system of administration we turn with pleasure to watch the irregular and sporadic development of self-governing communities in the chief towns of the period. Here alone the Curia Regis and the Exchequer were not averse from leaving some scope for individual effort. The borough-courts, though under the presidency of a nominated reeve or bailiff, kept something of the democratic spirit which underlay old English institutions. At Hereford we find the suitors of the borough-court assembling annually at the call of the common bell to receive from the bailiff an account of his stewardship;[1] and the *Leges Anglorum* assert that in all boroughs the "folk-moot" is the supreme governing body.[2] Many boroughs had now the right of farming all the royal dues to be collected within their limits. By 1130 both London and Lincoln had secured the still higher privilege of rendering their account at the Exchequer instead of through a sheriff nominated by the Crown. And to London belonged the unique right of farming the shire in which it stood. In 1130 the duties of a sheriff throughout Middlesex were discharged by four elected citizens. A little later the King, by a new charter, conferred on the citizens the right of electing their own sheriff and justiciar.[3]

In part, no doubt, the towns owed their favourable treatment to their insignificance. Few of them were populous; the majority were still agricultural communities. Even in London it was the custom to suspend the sessions of the hustings-court during the harvest-season;[4] and at Winchester, the second city in the kingdom, the trading class appears to have been composed of retail dealers who catered for the King's court and the household of the bishop.[5] Of foreign trade there was little. Wine and other luxuries came to a few eastern seaports from Normandy and the Rhine[6]; Chester and Bristol exported corn and luxuries to Ireland in exchange for furs and hides and cattle; Flemish merchants

[1] Johnson, *Ancient Customs of the City of Hereford*, p. 10.
[2] *Leges Anglorum* in Liebermann's *Gesetze*, I., p. 655.
[3] On the date of Henry's Charter to London see Mr. Round in *Geoffrey de Mandeville*, Appendix P.
[4] *Liber de Antiquis Legibus*, p. 206.
[5] See the survey made early in the reign of Henry I. and known as the Winton Domesday. It is printed in the Record Commission edition of Domesday; translated and annotated in the *Victoria County History of Hampshire*, i., pp. 527 ff.
[6] See the privileges of the merchants of Lorraine trading with London, *E. H. R.*, xvii., p. 495. The date of this document is about 1130.

travelled from fair to fair and monastery to monastery in quest of the wool which they needed for their looms. It would be unsafe to argue too confidently from outward appearances; but London, as it is described by foreigners in the first half of the twelfth century, a city of wooden houses and thatched roofs, whose narrow streets were intersected by unsavoury kennels, and at night infested by troops of savage dogs, must have compared unfavourably in wealth and amenity with the great communes of Northern France and Flanders.[1] Henry I. seems to have felt no fear of London, and with London no other town in England could compare.

It was the King's policy to conciliate the towns even at the expense of his own pocket. We find him for instance remitting, in the case of Norwich, Oxford, Colchester and Wallingford, all or part of the *auxilium* which they paid in lieu of Danegeld. His charter to London reduced the ferm of the city from £600 to £300.[2] It was therefore natural that he should prove accommodating when his interests and theirs appeared to be identical. The merchant-class believed that the best way of ensuring prosperity was to purchase a monopoly from the King; the King on his side was always prepared to sell the merchants of any town the right of incorporating as a gild, with the power of making bye-laws for the regulation of their own body, and a local monopoly of the trade in particular commodities. Gilds for mutual protection, for charitable, religious, and convivial purposes were common enough in England before the Conquest, and it is possible that here and there gilds-merchant had been formed by the year 1066.[3] But the idea of vesting such monopolies in corporate fraternities was borrowed from abroad, was not generally diffused until England came into close connection with Normandy, and did not become a cardinal feature of the English economic system before the reign of Henry I.[4] From the economic point of view the effects of the new principle were pernicious. The gild-merchant was the first step towards the establishment of that cumbrous protective system which proved the ruin of so many medieval towns. But it was not without utility

[1] See *Hugonis Flavin. Chronicon* in Pertz, S. S., viii., 496.
[2] See Mr. Round's remarks in *E. H. R.*, xviii., p. 309.
[3] Stubbs, *C. H.*, i., pp. 449 ff. Gross, *The Gild Merchant*, i., p. 5, denies this.
[4] Convivial gilds are mentioned as existing after the Conquest at Battle (*Historia Fundationis*, p. 20) and elsewhere. Anselm, *Epistolae*, II., vii., treats them as pretexts for drunkenness. *Cf.* Map, *De Nugis*, ii., § 12, " domus bibitorias, ghildhus Anglice dictas ".

as a school in which an important class of the community learned
the art of self-government and the advantages of union.   There
is a further interest attaching to the history of gilds-merchant.
They sometimes acquired by grant or usurpation the government
of the boroughs in which they arose and formed the root from
which municipal corporations grew.   But the theory which made
this the universal mode of municipal evolution is now set aside.
There are boroughs, such as London, in which the gild-merchant
develops late or not at all, and which yet take the lead in the
advance towards self-government.[1]

The charter of Henry I. to London[2] is worth a careful study,
both for the reason that the privileges of London formed the ideal
of every other English borough, and because they illustrate the
general ideas of the King's policy.   Most of the rights enumerated
in the charter are rights to be exercised by the individual citizens.
They shall not be called upon to plead in any court outside the
walls for any plea.   They are exempted from the Danegeld and
the murdrum-fine ; the maximum amount in which any one of them
may be amerced is fixed at 100 shillings ; none of them shall be
liable to the judicial duel; and they shall hold their lands according to the custom of the city.   It is assumed that the government
of the city will be conducted as before by the sheriffs, justiciar,
aldermen and hustings-court ; the King makes no attempt to innovate or interfere in details.   To form a picture of the hustings-
court, in which the citizens sat on four benches in a hollow square
to hear the dooms pronounced by alderman and sheriff, or of the
folk-moot to which all were convoked by the great bell of Paul's
and the summons of the beadle—for these and similar glimpses of
civic life we must betake ourselves to private records of the London
customs.[3]   The King is chiefly interested in the revenue which
London yields to the Exchequer.   He does not fear revolutionary
movements among the citizens ; nor does he consider it his business
to improve their institutions.   His policy is one of *laissez-faire*, and

---

[1] Mr. Crump, *E. H. R.*, xviii., p. 315, prints a charter of 1252, granting a
merchant of Florence and his heirs the privileges of a London citizen, " quod sint in
gilda mercatoria," etc.   But see the editor's remarks.

[2] S. C., p. 129.   Round, *G. de M.*, pp. 347 ff.

[3] See the texts quoted by Miss Bateson, *E. H. R.*, xvii., pp. 480 ff., " A London
Municipal Collection of the Reign of John ".   Also the document " Libertas
Londoniensis " in Liebermann, *Gesetze der A.-S.*, I., p. 673, a memorandum of the
first half of the twelfth century, relating to the liberties of London.

much more lax than seemed advisable to his Angevin successors. Under Henry II. and Richard I. the privileges of the Londoners were considerably curtailed. But the robust confidence in the loyalty of the Londoners which Henry I. displayed was justified by the events of his life-time; and although the city took an energetic part in the civil strife of the next reign, its influence was steadily thrown upon the side which seemed to be that of law and order.

The struggles of the Church for independence found less favour with the King. There were no economic advantages to be gained by full submission to the Pope, or by abstention from the good old practice of controlling canonical election for the benefit of royal nominees; and the freedom claimed by the reforming party in the Church was perhaps irreconcilable with the freedom of the state. Rightly or wrongly the King omitted no precaution to shield the Church from Papal supervision; and his relations with Rome were, consequently, strained. Already in the year 1115 Paschal II. wrote him a reproachful letter, expressing sorrow that the Holy See was deprived of its just rights over England; that his legates and epistles could not enter the kingdom without special licence; and that no appeals were allowed to come to Rome.[1] The Norman Church was similarly shielded from the interference of the Curia. In both countries the customs of the Conqueror were applied with a rigour which Gregory VII. had never anticipated when he acquiesced in them. The Pope's complaints fell on deaf ears. Thurstan of York who ventured, against the King's command, to invoke Papal assistance in his efforts to shake off the yoke of Canterbury, incurred a sentence of exile, which was only remitted (1121) when Calixtus II. threatened to lay the whole of England under interdict. More cautious, if not more devout, than his Angevin descendants, Henry yielded at once before the prospect of this penalty; and Thurstan was excused, on his return, from making any profession of obedience to the Primate.[2] It was impossible to ignore the Pope. In 1119, when the English bishops were summoned by Calixtus to the Council of Rheims, the King reluctantly permitted them to go, merely warning them that he

Ecclesiastical Policy, 1106-30

---

[1] Eadmer, *H. N.*, p. 228.
[2] Eadmer, *H. N.*, pp. 244, 291. W. Malmesb., *G. P.*, pp. 262 ff. Simeon, *G. R.*, p. 262.

would have no "superfluous inventions," no innovations in the canon law, imported into his dominions.[1] It was a warning which the bishops disregarded ; and appeals without the royal permission became frequent in Henry's later years.   In 1128 a bishop of Llandaff, emboldened no doubt by the success of Thurstan, appealed against his rival of St. David's, obtained a favourable judgment, and induced the Pope to put such pressure on the King that the judgment was executed under royal authority.[2]   In other directions too the interference of Rome became a matter for alarm. The King found it desirable, in 1125, to let the Cardinal John of Crema enter England and hold a council of the English Church at Westminster, at which the Archbishops appeared as the inferiors of the Papal legate. The excuse for such visitations was afterwards removed by procuring a legatine commission for the Primate, William of Corbeil ; but the advancement of a subject to this high position can hardly have been welcome to Henry except as the smaller of two evils.   It became more difficult to interpose his veto when the legislation of the English church offended against the rights of Crown or subject ; and he was compelled to use undignified expedients.   In 1127 the Archbishop-legate and his suffragans demanded the royal sanction for a Canon under which the wives of priests, if they obstinately refused to separate from their husbands, should be reduced to slavery. In appearance Henry yielded and the decree received his seal. But the royal judges found ways and means of evading the new law. "So all went home, and the decrees stood for naught ; all held their wives, *by the King's leave*, as they had done before."[3]   The incident is not to be forgotten in our final estimate of Henry's ecclesiastical policy. With all his faults he stood between the nation and a threatened tyranny, which was none the less to be dreaded because it was claimed by single-minded zealots.   We may wish that his opposition to the extreme ecclesiastical party had been franker and founded on more generous principles ; but in that case his policy might have been less fortunate in its results. Greater rulers than he had tried the plan of open defiance to the Church ; but their boldness had redounded more to their own honour than to the welfare of their subjects.

Enough has been said of Henry's domestic policy to explain

[1] Orderic, iv., 373.   [2] Cont. Florence, *s. a.* 1128.
[3] *A. S. C. ;* Florence.   Henry's confirmation of the decrees in *Foedera*, i.,8.

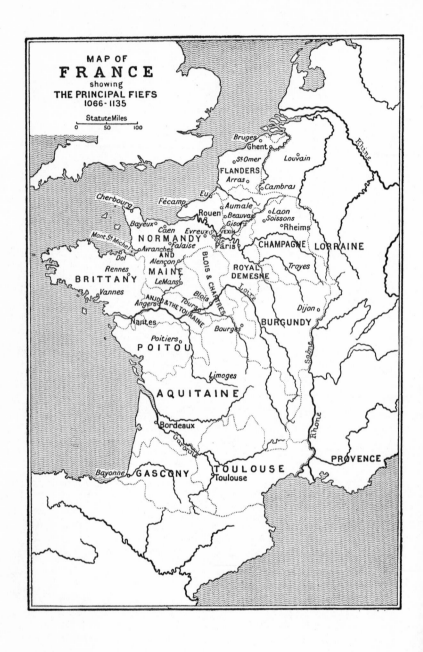

MAP OF
FRANCE
showing
THE PRINCIPAL FIEFS
1066-1135

Statute Miles
0   50   100

Bruges
Ghent
Louvain
St.Omer
FLANDERS
Arras
Cambrai
Eu
Fécamp
Cherbourg
Aumale
Rouen
Beauvais
Laon
Bayeux
Caen
Evreux
Gisors
Soissons
Rheims
Mont-St-Michel
NORMANDY
Falaise
VEXIN
Avranches
Paris
Dol
AND
CHAMPAGNE
LORRAINE
Rennes
MAINE
ROYAL
BRITTANY
LeMans
BLOIS & CHARTRES
DEMESNE
Troyes
Vannes
Blois
Anjou & THE TOURAINE
Tours
Dijon
Angers
Nantes
BURGUNDY
Bourges
Poitiers
POITOU
Limoges
AQUITAINE
Bordeaux
Garonne
Rhone
Saône
GASCONY
TOULOUSE
PROVENCE
Bayonne
Toulouse
Rhone

the admiration which he excited among contemporaries, and his significance in the process of national development. It is now necessary to pass in brief review the difficulties, partly with foreign powers and partly with his own subjects, which arose from his efforts to settle the succession on his own descendants. From the battle of Tinchebrai to the day of his death this problem weighed upon his mind; and he left no stone unturned to defeat the elective principle from which his own right was derived. Accident and the bad faith of others made wild work with his best-laid schemes; but since a part of his purpose was achieved, and since his policy led to a sharpening of the old jealousy between Rouen and Paris, the story must be told as a preface to the events of after years. The Problem of the Succession

In 1108 the downward progress of the French monarchy came to an end, and a more brilliant epoch in the history of the Capets was inaugurated by the accession of Louis VI. (*le Gros*). More of a soldier than a statesman, but judicious in his choice of counsellors, Louis set himself the double task of recovering the demesnes which had slipped from the fingers of his predecessors, and of knitting more firmly to the Crown the towns and vassals of the Isle of France. It was a policy of narrow aims and petty undertakings, but pursued with indefatigable energy; and before long the King was enough a master in his own house to look with impatience on the great fiefs which hemmed him in and mocked his feebleness with their nominal professions of fidelity. The dream of sweeping them away and of reuniting France beneath one sceptre came to him comparatively late in life. He complained in his old age of human fortune. " How wretched is our lot, never to possess experience and strength at the same time! Had I been wise when I was young, or had I the strength now that I am old, I should have conquered empires." But from the commencement of his reign he aspired, if not to incorporate Flanders and Normandy with his own dominions, at least to weaken them and put them in the hands of satellites who would allow his subjects of the Isle of France free access to the sea. It was his good fortune to find, in William Clito, a pretender to Normandy who commanded no mean following in the Duchy. In 1111 the Count of Arques, fearing with some reason that Henry already repented of having spared the Clito, carried his ward to the court of France; an excuse for embracing the boy's cause was easily discovered by Louis in a promise, to dismantle the Louis VI. and William Clito

border castle of Gisors, which his rival had made long ago and
never kept.   Count Robert of Flanders, in spite of treaty obligations and his English pension, declared for the candidate of France.

War with
France
(1111-3)

On both sides the war was conducted in a dilatory fashion and
two years passed without a decisive battle.   The feudatories of
Northern France, whom jealousy of Henry had brought into the
field against him, grew weary of the struggle ; and early in 1113 he
secured a formidable ally in the person of Count Fulk V. of Anjou.
The Count had married the daughter of Helias the deliverer of
Maine ; he gladly espoused the cause of Henry in return for a
recognition of his right to succeed his father-in-law, who had died
in 1109.   The treaty was cemented by the betrothal of Fulk's
daughter to the only lawful son of Henry, the young William
Atheling ;[1] and as soon as this arrangement was announced the
French King came to terms.   The treaty of Gisors (March-April,
1113) amply compensated Henry for the vexations of the war.   He
was recognised as overlord, not only of Maine, but also of Brittany ;[2]
and, though these concessions gave him no rights which he did not
already exercise, it was something gained that France should have
renounced the design of confining his power within the Norman
frontier.   The foundations of his grandson's continental empire
were laid by these two treaties of the year 1113.

Resump-
tion of
the War
(1116-9)

But some time passed before the incipient union of Normandy
with Anjou was completed, or Louis definitely abandoned the cause
of William Clito.   A new war opened in the year 1116 for which
each side laid the blame upon the other.   Henry revenged himself
for his suzerain's support of the Clito by abetting the aggressions
of Theobald IV. of Blois and Chartres.[3]   The alliance with Blois
entailed a temporary rupture of that with Anjou; and Fulk
appeared in arms against Henry at the side of King Louis and
the Count of Flanders.[4]   The allies carried fire and sword into
Normandy in 1117 and 1118; treachery spread through the ranks
of the Norman nobility and Henry could trust no one.   It would
have gone hardly with him but for the feuds which divided the
great baronial houses.   Thanks to their mutual jealousy the

[1] Orderic, iv., 306.
[2] *Ibid.*, iv., 307.   *Cf.* Luchaire, *Premiers Capétiens*, p. 300.   Ramsay, *Foundations*, ii., p. 271, doubts the cession of Brittany.
[3] Orderic, iv., 307.   Suger, 85 (ed. Molinier).
[4] Henry Hunt., p. 239.   Orderic, iv., 310.   *A. S. C.*, *s.a.* 1117, 1118.

Norman lords were evenly divided between the French and English sides; and the towns of Rouen, Bayeux, Caen, Coutances, and Avranches, followed the fortunes of their lawful lord with unwavering loyalty. For three years Henry stood at bay; but in 1118 the withdrawal of Baldwin VII., who was mortally wounded in a raid on Normandy, weakened the forces of the King's enemies; the next year saw them divided by his diplomacy and defeated in the field. The Count of Anjou threw over his suzerain, and gave his daughter in marriage to the Atheling,[1] according to the promise which he had made six years before; a few weeks later at Brémule[2] in the Vexin, Louis and his following were signally defeated by the King of England (Aug. 20, 1119). This battle, the most decisive since Tinchebrai, was the outcome of an accidental meeting and the opposing forces were small in number; on the English side there were about 500 knights, on the French a hundred less. In spite of the importance which Henry's panegyrists attach to it, we can only regard the fact that it virtually ended the war as a proof of the French King's distaste for the continuance of a long and exhausting struggle. Louis turned from arms to diplomacy; at the Council of Rheims he endeavoured to enlist the sympathies of the Pope and Europe on behalf of William Clito. Calixtus undertook to intercede with Henry in the pretender's interest. But the Pope's appeal merely elicited from Henry a laboured vindication of his past behaviour, and an offer to the Clito of three English earldoms in satisfaction of his Norman claim. The offer was refused and the Clito remained at the court of France. His allies rapidly melted from his side. The Norman rebels were conciliated by the offer of generous terms; the new Count of Flanders, Charles the Good, returned to a sounder policy by making peace with Henry; and finally Louis himself was content to accept the homage of William Atheling as the heir of Normandy. The second phase of the succession wars had ended even more favourably for Henry than the first.

But in 1120 an unforeseen catastrophe wrecked the King's plans, and left the future of his dominions once more in uncertainty. On November 25th the Atheling and his company, returning from

Death of William Atheling

---

[1] *A. S. C., s.a.* 1119. Orderic, iv., 347. Suger, 91.
[2] Or, according to Lappenberg, ii., p. 264, Brenneville. But see Luchaire, *Premiers Capétiens,* p. 323.

Normandy in a vessel called the *White Ship*, were wrecked and drowned through the folly of a drunken pilot; Henry, a widower since the death of Queen Matilda (1118), was left without a son to succeed him. His only daughter, Matilda, had been married to the Emperor Henry V. in the year 1114,[1] and it was out of the question that her husband should be allowed to inherit England in her right. Within three months of his son's death the King contracted a second marriage, taking for his bride Adelaide the daughter of Godfrey of Louvain, the Duke of Lower Lorraine. It is noteworthy that this is one of the few recorded instances in which he asked and followed the advice of the Great Council respecting an important question of policy. The marriage was popular in England and had the advantage of strengthening Henry's connection with the Empire; but it stimulated the supporters of the Clito to more vigorous action. The Norman rebels who had been pardoned in 1119 furbished up again their well-worn complaints of injustice and oppression. Fulk of Anjou, determined that in spite of the Atheling's death his own descendants should sit upon the throne of England, gave his second daughter Sibylla in marriage

Last Norman Rebellion, 1123-5

to the Clito; for two years a rebellion against Henry, supported by the gold of Anjou, raged through the length and breadth of Normandy. Now, however, were reaped the fruits of the alliance with the Empire; Henry V. massed his forces on the Rhine and diverted the attention of Louis from the affairs of Normandy until the crisis of the struggle was past;[2] and the Pope seconded the efforts of the Emperor by declaring the marriage of the Clito with Sibylla of Anjou null and void. Thus supported the King of England could deal with the rebels at his leisure. One by one their castles fell; and, though the greater men were treated with the usual leniency, their aiders and abettors felt the full weight of the King's wrath. We hear of three in particular who were sentenced to perpetual imprisonment and to lose their eyes. It was in vain that the King's chief ally, Count Charles of Flanders, interceded for the trouvère Luc de Barre, whose lampoons were his chief offence; the unhappy poet only escaped the blinding-

---

[1] She was the twin-sister of William Atheling. She was sent to Germany for her betrothal in 1110; but the marriage, owing to her youth, was not celebrated till the Epiphany feast of 1114 (Rössler, *Kaiserin Mathilde*, pp. 13 ff.).

[2] Giesebrecht, *D. K. Z.*, iii., pp. 944 ff., who dwells chiefly on the German aspect of the campaign. It was a failure if the Emperor had serious intentions of invading France; but from the English point of view it proved useful.

irons by dashing out his brains against the walls of his cell.[1]
These severities had the desired effect, and Normandy, after fourteen years of civil war, returned to a state of peace. Accident
came to the King's aid; his second marriage proved unfruitful, but Matilda's
the death of the Emperor Henry V. (May 23, 1125) made it pos- claim
sible to designate Matilda as her father's successor. The Great recognised
Council of England did homage to her on Christmas Day, 1126, in
the presence of Henry and her uncle David of Scotland. The latter
took the oath in the character of an English earl; and the next to
swear was Stephen, Count of Mortain and Boulogne, the Conqueror's
grandson, himself a possible claimant to the Anglo-Norman heritage.
There were many, no doubt, who preferred Stephen to Matilda; for
no woman had yet ruled in Normandy or England. But the Council
were overawed and accepted Henry's scheme without discussion.

The proclamation of Matilda as the future Queen of England
was followed by the marriage of the Clito to the French Queen's
sister (Jan., 1127), and by the revival of his claim on Normandy.
The pretender was invested with Flanders as soon as that county
fell vacant through the murder of Charles the Good (March 2).
Henry retorted by betrothing his daughter to Geoffrey, the son Matilda's
and heir of Fulk of Anjou. It was an arrangement gratifying to second
the King's dynastic ambition, and guaranteed the Duchy against marriage,
invasion on one side. But it was viewed with dislike in England, 1127
and Roger of Salisbury, the King's most faithful servant, declared
that he would not have done homage to the Empress if he had anticipated that she would be given in marriage to a foreigner.[2] The
Normans resented the prospect of subjection to their hereditary
foes of Anjou, and a number of them quitted the Duchy to follow
the fortunes of the Clito. But the marriage was celebrated in
spite of all protests (1129);[3] in August, 1128, the Clito died of
a wound received at the siege of Alost; in 1131 the English
baronage renewed their oath to Matilda;[4] and in 1133 the birth

---

[1] Orderic, iv., 461.

[2] W. Malmesb., H. N., § 3. Cf. A. S. C., 1127, "All the French and English
thought ill of it". The Clito's marriage, in Orderic, iv., 474.

[3] The marriage was delayed owing to the youth of Geoffrey, who in 1127 was
only fifteen years of age. The Empress was ten years older than her second husband (Rössler, p. 100).

[4] W. Malmesb., H. N., § 6. This renewal of homage deserves to be noticed; the
opponents of Matilda's claim afterwards maintained that they had not foreseen the
Angevin marriage when they swore allegiance to her, and were therefore no longer
bound by their oath. This argument is destroyed by the ceremony of 1131.

of the future Henry II. appeared to place the succession beyond all dispute.

It does not appear that Henry devoted much attention to his relations with other powers, except when the intrigues of the Clito forced his hand. The first marriage of his daughter, with whatever intentions it may have been arranged, was not allowed to involve him in the vortex of Imperial questions. He asserted the old claims of his house to suzerainty over Maine and Brittany, but studiously refrained from utilising opportunities of continental aggrandisement such as were opened to him by the disordered state of Flanders between 1125 and 1128. In his dealings with Wales and Scotland he showed equal moderation.

Henry's policy towards Wales

Apart from one indecisive invasion of Wales, in the year 1114, he was content to play upon the mutual jealousies of the Welsh princes, to encourage the aggressions of marcher-barons and his own castellans, to strengthen the ties which bound the Welsh sees of Bangor, Llandaff, and St. David's to Canterbury, and to fortify the conquests of the two previous reigns. In the southern marches he relied upon the House of Clare, which he established in Ceredigion, and upon his own son Robert, to whom he gave in marriage Mabel the heiress of the Earldom of Gloucester and the Honour of Glamorgan.[1] Respecting the Flemish colonies which he planted in Pembroke and Ceredigion we have little information. But the colonies were industrial, and the breeding of sheep formed their chief occupation; the settlers were partly, if not entirely, Flemings who had originally quartered themselves in the north of England.[2] The over-population of Flanders, and the suffering to which that country was from time to time exposed by bad seasons and the inroads of the sea, may account for the migration; England, so long the ally of the Counts of Flanders, would naturally suggest itself as a suitable place of refuge. That Henry's colonies struck root and flourished is proved by frequent references in the Welsh annals; it is said that they have left their mark upon the dialect and customs of Pembrokeshire; but they were not intended, nor did they serve, to promote a policy of conquest.

[1] Round, *G. de M.*, p. 433.
[2] Florence, *s.a.* 1111. W. Malmesb., *H. N.*, § 34. Flanders was at this time suffering from over-population (Pirenne, *Histoire de Flandre*, i., 136). *Cf. Cart. Gloucest.*, i., p. 265. The Bishop of St. David's is sending missionaries to the Flemings (1113-5) to convert them "ad pascua vitae de pascuis ovium realium quibus intendunt".

Relations with Scotland were materially smoothed by a marriage between Alexander I. and Sibylla a natural daughter of Henry I. The English party at the court of Scotland gathered strength; Turgot, the confessor of St. Margaret, was appointed in 1107 to the see of St. Andrews; Alexander served with a body of Scottish knights in the English army which Henry took into Wales in 1114. But matters changed for the worse on the accession of David I., the youngest of the sons of Malcolm Canmore (1124). In his domestic government David distinguished himself by a preference for English favourites and institutions; William of Malmesbury remarks that an English education had made him more courtly than his brothers and had wiped away from his character the rust of Scottish incivility; and he had received in marriage Waltheof's daughter who brought him the earldom of Huntingdon as a marriage portion (1114). None the less he made it his first object to shake off the English supremacy and to extend his sovereignty over the northern shires of England; indeed his marriage provided him with a claim, in his wife's right, upon the earldom of Northumberland. The troubles which followed the death of Henry gave him an unlooked-for opportunity of making this claim good.

CHAPTER V

STEPHEN

Stephen
and his
Rivals

ON the death of Henry I. there was hardly a man in his dominions who desired the accession of the Empress. Her sex, the arrogance of her temper, above all her Angevin marriage, were objections which in most minds overrode all scruples as to oaths and pledges.[1] Henry, her eldest son, might have been more favourably regarded if his youth had not made it certain that the regency would remain for many years to come in the hands of his mother. But Henry's hereditary claim was hardly stronger than that of Theobald of Blois and Stephen of Boulogne, the grandsons of the Conqueror in the female line; the minds of Englishmen and Normans instinctively turned towards these brothers. As between Theobald and Stephen the choice was more difficult; and deliberations were impeded by the accident that, while the leaders of the territorial aristocracy were in Normandy with Henry at the moment of his death, the leaders of the Church and the Curia Regis had been left in England to represent their master in his absence. The interests of these two parties differed widely; the members of each hastened to settle the succession in the manner which appeared most suitable to themselves. Hence two sovereigns were simultaneously elected on the two sides of the Channel. While the leading men in Normandy were inviting Theobald to come and rule them, Stephen sailed hastily to England; while they were providing for the defence of the frontier against an Angevin army, which appeared as soon as the King's death was known, Stephen was negotiating with the Londoners, with Roger of Salisbury the Justiciar, and with William of Corbeil the Archbishop of Canter-

[1] Rössler's defence of Matilda's character (*Kaiserin Mathilde*, p. 28) rests upon the flimsiest arguments; and he admits that her conduct after 1141 is open to the charge of arrogance (*ibid.*, p. 281).

bury. Immediately before Christmas Theobald and his supporters met at Neubourg under the impression that the fate of the Anglo-Norman inheritance lay in their hands; their deliberations were interrupted by the arrival of a monk from England, who announced that Stephen was already recognised and crowned as king. Those who were the lords of English fiefs could not but recognise that Stephen was master of the situation, and hastily withdrew the pledges which they had given to Theobald. The Count, a timid politician, with a taste for small undertakings and safe profits, renounced his claims without more ado. He espoused the cause of Stephen, negotiated in his brother's name a six months' truce with the Count of Anjou, and offered his influence at Rome to procure the recognition of Stephen's title from the Pope.[1]

This recognition was speedily obtained, in spite of energetic Precarious protests from the envoys of the Empress. All the weight of position of Stephen French influence was used in favour of the House of Blois and against that of Anjou; Stephen could plead that he had accepted the crown to save England from the anarchy of an interregnum; the oaths by which he and his supporters had bound themselves to uphold Matilda's claim were said to have been sworn under compulsion · his envoy boldly affirmed that the Empress was the daughter of a nun and illegitimate.[2] The Pope's decision removed the most obvious objection to Stephen's title; for there were few so bold as to affirm that the Holy See could not remit the consequences of a perjury. But the manner of his accession was not the least of the causes which made his reign humiliating to himself, and disastrous to the nation. He was the nominee of a small clique;[3] every supporter whom he gained was purchased by concessions injurious to the royal power; the favours which he conferred were accepted without thanks; his chief supporters never scrupled to renounce their allegiance as soon as he showed hesitation in satisfying their exorbitant demands.

The various bargains by which he bought adherents supply the clue to nearly all the troubles of his reign. At his first landing he

---

[1] See the letter of Innocent, recognising Stephen's claim, in Rich. of Hexham, p. 147 (R. S.).
[2] See the account of the proceedings at Rome in *Historia Pontificalis* (Pertz, S. S., xx., p. 543) and *Foliot Epist.*, i., pp. 100 ff. (ed. Giles).
[3] For the small number of magnates and bishops present at his coronation see Round, *G. de M.*, p. 11 (signatures of witnesses to his first grant); also Malmesbury and the *Gesta Stephani*.

secured the allegiance of London by extensive grants of privileges, which speedily bore fruit in the formation of a commune, modelled on the foreign pattern and as dangerous to the royal power as any of those in France or Flanders.   The scruples of the Primate and the bishops were overcome by promises, not only to restore the liberties of the Church as they had existed before the aggressions of Rufus and Henry I., but also to permit free election, free legislation in church synods, and the exclusive jurisdiction of church courts over ecclesiastical property and persons.   Nor were the compacts with individuals less perilous.   The King of Scotland obtained the cession of Carlisle and Cumberland, with a half-promise of Northumberland as an earldom for his son.   Robert of Gloucester, the step-brother of the Empress and the greatest of the English earls, would only tender a conditional allegiance. He consented to be the king's man for so long a time as the king should maintain him in his lawful state and dignity.[1]

State of Normandy, 1135-7   For the moment, however, Stephen's situation was rendered somewhat less precarious by the errors of his rival.   Geoffrey the Handsome failed to rise above the provincial ambitions of his ancestors.   His policy was purely Angevin.   To him the inheritance of Henry I. meant chiefly the union of Normandy and Anjou ; it was therefore upon Norman soil that he chose to match himself with Stephen.   The mistake was grave.   No offers or arguments could reconcile Louis VI. to an Angevin occupation of Normandy ; and it would have needed prudence far greater than Geoffrey possessed to heal the secular feud of Angevin and Norman.   Normandy might be won and held with the resources of the English crown ; to reverse the natural order of proceedings, to treat Normandy as the stepping-stone to England, was irrational, indeed preposterous. Yet this was the course which Geoffrey obstinately pursued until the year 1139.   His raids upon the Duchy need not detain us here. They were occasional and unsystematic.   The truce arranged with Theobald ran out, and three months more elapsed before Geoffrey reappeared in Normandy.   He retreated at the end of thirteen days, baffled by the implacable animosity of the Norman population ; and was content, when Stephen paid a flying visit to the Duchy in 1137, to conclude another truce for a period of two years. This was Stephen's opportunity ; but he failed to use it.   Within

[1] W. Malm., *H. N.* i., § 14.   Gervase, i., 94.   *Gesta*, p. 8.

a short space of time he had rendered himself as unpopular as the Angevins. He refused to be guided by the Norman magnates, and openly expressed his preference for the services of Flemish mercenaries. A few months later Geoffrey was able to resume the war in Normandy with better prospects than before ; experience of Stephen had made the Normans less critical of the rival candidate.

Meanwhile, in England, fortune favoured the Angevin cause. Beginning The energy and valour of Stephen availed him little ; he had neither of Trouble the foresight nor the decision of character which might have turned in England these qualities to good account. Nervously alive to the difficulties of his position he stood on the defensive, and even for purposes of defence rarely ventured far afield ; when the princes of South Wales, according to their usual practice, inaugurated the new reign with fire and sword, he scarcely attempted to assist his English subjects and allowed the marches west of the Wye to relapse into a state of anarchy. Yet with all his caution he rarely detected a conspiracy until it culminated in rebellion. The treacherous matured their preparations undisturbed, and chose their own time to defy him. When it came to open war he carried himself in knightly fashion. But his knightliness was that of the reckless jouster. He attacked the nearest enemy as though it were a point of honour to answer the first challenge ; he never paused to reflect in what quarter he should strike to inflict a paralysing blow.

These defects were fatal in a time when success depended upon meeting craft with craft, and upon crushing the one or two arch-traitors round whom all plots and intrigues centred. In 1136 Hugh Bigod Earl of Norfolk, one of his first supporters, seized the castle of Norwich ; simultaneously in Devonshire a certain Robert, the lord of Bampton, declared war on the government and Baldwin de Redvers captured the castle of Exeter by surprise. With more or less difficulty all three rebels were reduced. But the war with Baldwin de Redvers showed the weakness of the government. Exeter Castle sustained a three months' siege and only surrendered when the wells within the walls ran dry ; the King, sorely against his will, was compelled by the barons in his army to let the garrison go free. While Exeter held out, Baldwin de Redvers raised in the Isle of Wight a pirate-fleet which preyed without let or hindrance on the commerce of Portsmouth and Southampton ; when forced to abjure the realm he repaired to the court of Geoffrey of

Anjou, in whose interest it was plain from the first that the whole plot had been formed. The head and front of the Angevin conspiracy was Robert Earl of Gloucester, who had broken his faith to Stephen as soon as it was pledged. The Earl pretended that his life was a mark for the plots of royal favourites; his enemies attributed his change of front to resentment that his influence with the King was overshadowed by that of William of Yprés, the leader of Stephen's Flemish mercenaries; his friends alleged that he had only feigned submission to promote the interests of his sister the more effectually.[1]   Whatever the motive, Robert remained in Normandy plotting with the Angevins from the spring of 1137 and his English adherents were tranquilly proceeding with the fortification of their castles. " When the traitors perceived," says the English chronicler, " that the King was a mild man and soft and good and did no justice, then did they all wonder. They had done homage to him and sworn oaths, but they held no faith." The ablest ministers of Henry I. still remained in Stephen's service; the machinery by which the Lion of Justice had detected and paralysed incipient rebellion was still intact; but no government is so inert as a bureaucracy which lacks a master spirit; and the kingdom was allowed to drift unchecked towards anarchy.

Outbreak of the Dynastic War, 1138   The crisis came in the year 1138. The treachery of Gloucester was immediately followed by a breach of faith on the part of the King of Scotland, who now demanded as the price of his support that the earldom of Northumberland should be immediately granted to his son Henry. The Scots threatened the north late in 1137 and actually crossed the border early in the following year; a counter-raid on Stephen's part (February, 1138) merely furnished David with an excuse for organising a third and more systematic invasion. Encouraged by this diversion the barons of the western and southern shires, where Gloucester's influence was strongest, raised the standard of revolt. The lead was taken by Geoffrey Talbot who held out in Hereford. This fortress, attacked by the king in person, fell after a siege of four or five weeks. But in the course of the siege Stephen received a formal defiance from the Earl, and the news that fifteen or sixteen of the strongest castles in the kingdom were held by friends of Robert and the Empress. Dover and Canterbury in the east; Bristol in the west; Exeter in Devonshire; Dorchester, Ware-

---

[1] W. Malm., *H. N.*, i., §§ 14, 17.   Orderic, v., 108.

ham, and Corfe in Dorset; Castle Cary and Dunster in Somerset;
Ludlow and Shrewsbury on the Welsh marches, were the chief of
the rebel strongholds; but there were others of less importance.
The danger was hydra-headed, and the capture of a castle more or
less made little difference to the issue of the war. But there could
be no doubt where the head-quarters and main forces of the
Angevin party lay. If the great earldom of Gloucester, with the
dependent shire of Glamorgan,[1] could be seized for the King, then
Earl Robert would lose the larger half of his resources, and minor
strongholds could be easily reduced. Stephen missed his opportunity.
He failed to secure the friendship of Miles the sheriff and justiciar
of Gloucestershire, who next to Earl Robert was the most powerful
subject in the West and had been a faithful servant to King Henry.
Nor was an attack made on Bristol castle, the southern outpost of
the Earl and the key of Gloucestershire. The King indeed recon-
noitred Bristol in the course of the summer; but concluded that
the place was impregnable and turned away to pursue his favourite
plan of attacking scattered fortresses without plan or method.

As yet his opponents were compelled to stand on the defensive; Battle
their forces were too small and scattered to allow of offering battle of the Standard
in the open. For the necessary reinforcements they looked to Aug. 22,
Scotland; and in August King David, encouraged by the result of 1138
earlier forays, invaded Yorkshire with a considerable army. So
disorganised was Stephen's administration, so little had he considered the probable movements of the Scot that, after six months
of border warfare, the northern counties were still unprepared
against attack. In dismay and perplexity the barons of the north
assembled at York to discuss the situation; they were half-disposed
to take whatever terms they could obtain from David. Fortunately
Archbishop Thurstan, though an old man and in broken health,
showed a bolder spirit than the laymen. He appealed to the
patriotism of the barons, promised that every parish-priest in
Yorkshire would bring his flock to join their army, and offered
to accompany them in a litter since he could no longer ride.
While the debate was still in progress the confidence of the barons
was restored by the arrival of Bernard de Balliol bringing the
King's commission to act as their commander. They set out to

---

[1] For Earl Robert's sheriffs and shire-court in Glamorgan see *Cart. Gloucest.*, ii.,
pp. 10, 135, 139.

6

repel the invader, taking with them the banners of the patron saints of York, Beverley, and Ripon which they hung from a mast set upright on a car and surmounted by the Host in a silver shrine. In a level plain two miles beyond Northallerton they found the Scottish host prepared for battle. After a brief halt for deliberation they took an oath to stand by one another to the death; Ralph Nowel, the bishop of Orkney, who had come with them in Thurstan's stead, bade them remember the valour of their Norman ancestors and acquit themselves like men. They drew up their array with care and skill. The Standard was placed at the centre of the host; round it were grouped the elder knights on horseback; the parochial levies were marshalled on the flanks and in the rear. The younger knights, forsaking the usual Norman tactics, dismounted and took up their position on foot before the Standard; their line was interspersed with clumps of archers. It was the desire of King David to adopt a similar formation, placing his archers and best knights in the forefront of the battle. But the men of Galloway, the most unruly element in his motley host, claimed the vanguard as their privilege, and boasted that they would go further with bare breasts than any of the King's French minions in their armour. Fearing to revive the old feud of Celt and Norman, the King let the Galwegians have their way; the knights, under the command of himself and his son, marched to the attack in the second line and rearguard; a mob of bare-legged Highlanders hovered on the flanks to right and left. The Galwegians charged furiously shouting "Alban! Alban!"; but they were unprepared for the volleys of English arrows which, in the words of an English narrator, "buzzed like bees and flew like rain"; nor could their light spears and swords make any impression on the mail of the opposing knights. Prince Henry, by a flank attack, did some execution among the parochial levies on the English side, but this diversion came too late. The Galwegians, having lost their chief, fled as precipitately as they had advanced, sweeping away the King and his "battle" with them. David made a desperate effort to stay the rout, but could only rally a sufficient force to ensure himself an unmolested and deliberate retreat.[1] Little as the King of England had done to help his

---

[1] The Battle of the Standard is most fully described by Ailred of Rievaux, *De Bello Standardi* (ed. Howlett), Richard of Hexham (ed. Howlett) and Henry of Huntingdon. See also Oman, *Art of War*, ii., p. 387.

supporters the victory was for the moment of great service to his cause. It had deprived the rebels of their chief ally. In the following year, after his kingdom had been raided, David was glad to sign a peace (April 9, 1139). But the terms which he obtained from Stephen were almost as favourable as if the English had been the defeated party. Stephen conferred upon Prince Henry the whole of Northumberland except the castles of Bamborough and Newcastle; the only equivalent which the English King demanded was a contingent from Scotland to help him in his warfare with the English rebels.[1]

Scarcely had the danger from Scotland been averted before Stephen provoked a contest with more formidable enemies. His power hung upon the favour of the Church. To his brother, the Bishop of Winchester, he owed the general recognition of his claim; to the Pope he was indebted for a verdict which had deprived Matilda of her strongest plea. In matters of administration he relied entirely upon the clerical servants of Henry I. The most important of these belonged to one and the same family, to that of Roger Bishop of Salisbury, who had been the late King's Treasurer and chief minister. The bishop had declined to accept a definite office in the Curia of Stephen; but he was still a valued counsellor; Stephen had been heard to say that if Roger demanded half of the kingdom he should have it as long as the times remained unsettled.[2] A son and namesake of the bishop, Roger le Poer, was in possession of the Chancellorship; one nephew, Nigel Bishop of Ely, controlled the Treasury; a second, Alexander of Lincoln, though not mentioned as holding any office, enjoyed high influence at court. Nothing could exceed the arrogance of the kinsmen. Bishop Roger issued writs "on the king's part and my own," as though considering himself a coadjutor, not a servant of the King; his pretensions were bitterly resented by the Beaumonts and other lay barons who aspired to a share of Stephen's favour. The ministers, aware of the jealousies to which they were exposed, began

The Quarrel of Stephen with the Bishops, 1139

---

[1] Bromton (Twysden, 975) says that Henry received Northumberland in exchange for Northampton and Huntingdon. The authority is a poor one but it would make the treaty more intelligible; and the latest charter showing a connection between Henry and Northampton is dated 1136 (Lawrie, *Early Scottish Charters*, p. 88). On the other hand Henry issues a charter at Huntingdon in 1145 (*ibid.*, p. 138), which suggests that he had still a connection with that Honour.

[2] For the position of Bishop Roger under Stephen see Round, *Ancient Charters*, p. 38. *Sarum Charters*, p. 7. W. Malm., *H. N.*, §§ 24-5, 32.

to fortify their castles, to increase the numbers of their retinues, and otherwise to pursue a line of conduct which their friends termed common prudence and their enemies conspiracy. The King saw fit to take the unfavourable point of view.[1] A Great Council, held on June 24th, 1139, at Oxford, supplied him with a sufficient pretext for disarming them. The proceedings were opportunely disturbed by a brawl which broke out between the trains of Bishop Roger and the Earl of Richmond. Stephen assumed without investigation that the bishop was to blame; and proceeded to demand that every member of the offending family should surrender the castles which he held. The demand was in conformity with the laws both of Normandy and England. The Crown had a right to garrison all castles in a time of public danger. But the fallen ministers refused to surrender their only safeguards against private animosity and public justice. Their arrest was instantly commanded, and only Alexander of Lincoln forestalled the execution of the decree by flight. He escaped to Devizes, the strongest of his uncle's castles, and made his preparations for an obstinate defence. But the King retaliated with vigorous measures. He brought his captives before the walls of Devizes, and threatened to hang Roger le Poer unless the garrison capitulated; the old bishop only induced his master to postpone the execution of this threat by taking an oath that he would abstain from food and drink until the castle was surrendered.[2] For three days the garrison remained obdurate and the starving bishop kept his oath. At length his mistress, Maud of Ramsbury, who was in the castle, insisted on surrender. The other castles of the family were given up without more ado, and the owners were allowed to depart in peace and ignominy. But Alexander of Lincoln, as having made open war upon his sovereign, forfeited the temporalties of his see.

The Council of Winchester, Aug. 1139   The King's precautions had been taken by means of proceedings which, though more than a little grotesque, were wholly justifiable, and even warranted by the letter of law. He had grounds for suspecting the bishops' loyalty; he demanded the securities to which he was legally entitled; he used force when those securities were withheld, but after he had obtained them stayed his hand.

---

[1] On the causes of the quarrel see Hen. Hunt., p. 265. *Gesta*, p. 46. Cont. Flor. Wig., *s.a.* 1138. W. Malm., *H. N.*, §§ 19, 20. Orderic. v., 119.
[2] So the Cont. Flor. Wig.

The case looked otherwise to his contemporaries. He had offered
violence to ecclesiastical persons, whom he should have been content with citing before a church-court. He had threatened to
hang one man, he had half-starved another, who, even if guilty of
the blackest treason, should have been subjected to none but spiritual penalties. Stephen's warmest friends were perplexed to find excuses for his conduct. The scripture, "Touch not mine anointed!"
was freely quoted and as freely interpreted to prove the King a
criminal. The original offence was aggravated by his treatment
of the see of Lincoln ; he could not resist the temptation of making
grants from the lands of which Alexander had been deprived ; [1] but
it was an admitted principle of justice that the see ought not to
suffer for the offences of the individual bishop. It was unfortunate for Stephen that his own choice had placed him, in such
questions, at the mercy of a rigorous judge. After conferring
the see of Canterbury on Theobald of Bec (1138), he had consoled
the disappointed ambition of Henry of Winchester by allowing
aim to receive the legatine commission which would more properly
have gone to the new Archbishop. Thus the Bishop of Winchester
became, for practical purposes, the head of the English Church
while he was still smarting from the disappointment of his fruitless
candidature. Always zealous for the honour of his order he was
now stimulated by resentment. He determined to deal strictly
with his erring brother; and, shortly after the fall of the bishops,
Stephen was cited before a legatine Council to explain his violation
of church privilege. The assembly met at Winchester on August
29th ; the legate presided, and the Primate, whose promotion was
the secret cause of the proceedings, lent them the sanction of
his presence. It is interesting to conjecture how the Conqueror
or Henry Beauclerk would have treated such a summons. Stephen
was too weak, the support of the Church was too sorely needed
by his cause, for a denial of the Council's jurisdiction to be possible.
He refused to stand in person at the bar; but he came to Winchester and allowed his case to be argued by attorney. The
legate, speaking in the name of Rome, opened the Council with
an uncompromising indictment of his brother's conduct. Stephen
had sinned against the rights and liberties of the Church, to whose

[1] See the grant from Stephen to the Earl of Lincoln in Round, *Ancient Charters*,
p. 39.

favour and support he owed the royal dignity; and if there were no other way of procuring reparation for the bishops he should be excommunicated. Stephen's representatives put in the plea, which had already done good service on similar occasions, that their master had arrested not a bishop but a treacherous minister. But the clergy were now for the first time at liberty to express their opinion of this ingenious argument. Under no circumstances, the King was told, could a bishop be tried except by a tribunal of ecclesiastics and the canon law. To this Stephen replied with perfect justice that he had not put the bishops on their trial; he had merely required the keys of their castles to which he was entitled whether they were innocent or guilty. With a momentary flash of spirit he sent word to the Council that he appealed to Rome against any sentence which they might pass upon him, and that any of their number who left the kingdom without licence would find it easier to go than to return. The ground was cut from under the feet of the clergy. Any further proceedings on their part were useless in face of the appeal; and the King was plainly resolved to prevent them from stating their side of the case at Rome. They were obliged to content themselves with some vague promises of reparation, which Stephen had no intention of fulfilling.

Matilda appears in England, Sept., 1139   But Stephen's victory was dearly purchased. No time could have been less suitable for a quarrel with the clergy; it was the very moment when the plans of the Empress and Earl Robert became ripe for execution. Soon after the separation of the Council the King was informed that the exiled Baldwin de Redvers had landed at Wareham and had seized Corfe Castle; and that William de Mohun had fortified Dunster, the strongest place in North Somerset, on the Empress's behalf. By a rapid march and assault the King succeeded in terrifying Mohun; but he was called away from the siege of Corfe by the news that Matilda was expected in the east. He began to secure the ports and coasts against an invasion but left this work also half-completed upon learning that the castellan of Marlborough had begun to burn and pillage in Matilda's name. While Stephen was still at Marlborough the Empress landed in the south, accompanied by her brother Robert and 140 knights.[1]

---

[1] The date at which the Empress landed is given in W. of Malm. as September 30. The Continuator of Florence (ed. Thorpe) gives two distinct dates: "mense

The earl with a handful of followers rode off to assume the command of Bristol and the western rebels; the Empress took up her abode at Arundel Castle, with the Queen-dowager Adelaide, whose husband William of Albini was favourable to the cause of Anjou.

Civil war was imminent, but not yet unavoidable. The rebels actually in the field were few; the intending rebels were widely dispersed and imperfectly prepared. The majority of the barons had still to choose a side; and their attitude for the future depended upon the impression which Stephen created in the present. That he was brave all men knew; that his resources were superior to those of the Empress seemed more than probable. But the real doubt was whether he had the ability to strike shrewd blows and to press the advantages which offered. Stephen hastened from Marlborough to Arundel; he found the Queen-dowager alarmed at her own temerity and inclined to sacrifice her guest; there can be little doubt that if he had accepted the opportunity of securing Matilda's person, his cause both in England and in Normandy might have been retrieved. He threw away his advantage by allowing the Empress a safe-conduct to rejoin her brother. It was a concession thoroughly in accord with the new fashioned code of chivalry, and Stephen was always more of a knight than a statesman. But we are told that he followed on this occasion the advice of Bishop Henry, who represented to him that it was best to let his opponents concentrate and then crush them at one blow. If the bishop really gave this counsel he can hardly be acquitted of bad faith; and later events suggest that he was not unwilling to accelerate his brother's fall.[1] For the present he gave Stephen his nominal support, and was the only English bishop to do so.[2] The rest either declared openly for Matilda or waited for a convenient opportunity of defection from her rival.

Meanwhile the west was secured for the Angevin side. Miles of Gloucester threw off the mask, received the Empress in his city,

Octobri " and " ante festum S. Petri ad Vincula, Kal. Aug." Of these the latter is an interpolation in an inferior MS.; the former comes the nearer of the two to Malmesbury's date, and also more consistent with the course of events. Mr. Round retains the second date, Aug. 1, and rejects that of Malmesbury. But *cf.* Rössler, p. 242; and Weaver's edition of *John of Worcester*, p. 55 *note*. Orderic (v., 121) says that the Empress landed in the *autumn*.
    [1] Gervase, i., 109.   [2] *Gesta*, p. 57.   W. Malmesb., *H. N.*, § 37.

and placed at her disposal the shires which he controlled.[1] Earl
Robert sacked the city of Worcester and burned it to the ground;
Hereford was captured and became the northern outpost of Angevin
influence; the revolt of Brian of Wallingford gave the Empress an
advanced position in the heart of Stephen's country, and served as a
base for raids which left broad tracts of the Thames valley waste
and ruined. Dorset, Wilts, and the south-western shires, formed a
debatable land in which castle warred on castle, and now one party
now the other gained the upper hand. Those parts of England
were the most fortunate which held aloof under independent rulers.
Westmoreland and Cumberland formed a part of David's kingdom;
his son Henry ruled Northumberland under the title of an English
earl but with no intention of fulfilling his feudal obligations.[2] On
the marches of North Wales the Earl of Chester maintained a
neutral attitude, intriguing with both parties, but allowing neither
to meddle in his sphere of influence. There remained to Stephen
the nominal possession of the midlands, the east and the south-east.
Here he maintained his sheriffs and attempted to do justice under
the accustomed forms. But in the country north of the Thames
and in East Anglia the peace depended on the good will or self-
interest of local magnates, who protected their tenantry with the
strong hand, but with incomplete success. Both claimants found
themselves obliged to make any grant of privilege which was
demanded by a wavering supporter. Lands and titles, rights of
justice, rights of coinage, rights of castle-building, the offices of
sheriff and justiciar, were granted without stint or limitation. The
more unscrupulous and far-sighted barons passed from one court
to the other, inviting Stephen to outbid the Empress, and carrying
back the offers of Stephen to be confirmed and extended by his
rival. Others usurped as much of jurisdiction and of royal demesne
as they thought that they could hold with the strong hand, and
founded local tyrannies with no better title than that conferred by
an impregnable keep and a mercenary retinue.

The state to which less-favoured districts were reduced is
described by more than one contemporary; and, when all allow-

---

[1] The Cont. Flor. Wig. (ed. Thorpe) gives two accounts of Miles' defection,
one in 1138, the other in 1139. But Miles was on the side of Stephen as late as
August, 1138 (Round, G. de M., p. 285). The first account is an interpolation; see
Weaver, John of Worcester, p. 55.

[2] Lawrie, Early Scottish Charters, Nos. cxxiii.-cxl. and the editor's notes. No.
cxxxviii. shows that the power of David extended to the Ribble.

ance has been made for the natural exaggeration by which each The
writer attributed to the whole country the evils that he saw in beginning
his immediate neighbourhood, there remains a terrible picture of Anarchy
rapine, cruelty, and wanton insolence. They forced the folk to
build them castles, says the last of the writers of the English
Chronicle; and when the castles were finished they filled them with
devils and evil men. They took those whom they suspected to
have any goods, both men and women, by night and day, and put
them in prison for their gold and silver, and tortured them with
pains unspeakable. Some they hung up by the feet and smoked
them with foul smoke; some by their thumbs or by the head, and
they hung burning things on their feet. About the heads of some
they put a knotted string which they twisted till it went into the
brain. Others they put in a chest that was short and narrow and
not deep, and they put sharp stones in it and crushed the man
therein. They were continually levying an exaction from the
townships that was called *Tenserie,* and when the wretched folk
had no more to give, then plundered they and burned the townships. " Well mightest thou walk a whole day's faring nor ever find
a man inhabiting a township or tilled lands." Such was the state
of the fen-lands in which for many months Geoffrey de Mandeville, the worst of the King's adherents, maintained a rebel army by
ferocious ravages. The state of the west country is described by a
clerk of Winchester, the biographer of Stephen. Some men, he
says, left their homes and fled to distant regions. Others built
themselves a hut of wattle-work in the shadow of a church and
passed their days in fear and anguish. They ate the flesh of dogs
and horses; they ate raw herbs and roots. In some places they
died in herds of famine; in others the harvest rotted in the fields
because the farmers had perished or were fled. Some of the
miscreants to whom this state of things was due are mentioned by
name; in Durham the Scotsman William Comyn, whom David had
thrust into the see; in Yorkshire William of Aumâle; in the fens
Geoffrey de Mandeville; at Devizes Robert FitzHubert; at Cricklade William of Dover and Philip of Gloucester; at Bristol Philip
Gay; and respecting each there is the same tale of tenseries, kid-
napping, tortures, devastation. The evidence of the chroniclers is
confirmed by the earliest Pipe Roll of the succeeding reign. In
1156, four years after the conclusion of peace and eight years after

the close of serious campaigning, the Exchequer was still remitting Danegeld on account of waste; and even in shires which are not known to have been exceptionally harried we find that the remissions bear a substantial proportion to the total due. The waste was rapidly restored to prosperity; by the eighth year of Henry II. it had practically ceased to figure in the accounts of the Exchequer. From this we may conclude that in 1148 the desolation of the west, the Thames valley, and certain midland shires, was quite sufficient to justify the highly-wrought descriptions of our witnesses.[1] Surrey, Middlesex, Kent and Sussex, escaped more lightly than the other shires, although even in the south-east the Flemish mercenaries of Stephen earned themselves an evil name. But everywhere there was the same paralysing and hopeless sense of insecurity, worse in its effects upon national welfare than physical pain, the loss of wealth, or the passionate resentment of the despoiled worker against the predatory drone.

The Battle of Lincoln, 1141

Early in 1141 events were brought to a head by an unexpected outbreak in the eastern midlands. The Earl of Chester had long cherished the hope of recovering the Honour of Carlisle, which his father had been forced by Henry I. to surrender upon succeeding to Chester; and which Stephen had granted in 1136 to Prince Henry of Scotland. Having failed, first in a plot to assassinate the Prince, and afterwards in overtures to Stephen for help to conquer Carlisle by force of arms, the earl threw in his lot with his half-brother William of Roumare, who, though recently created Earl of Lincoln by the King, was aggrieved that he had not also obtained the custody of Lincoln castle, which he claimed as of hereditary right. The two conspirators kept up the mask of friendship till the last. Stephen was their guest at Lincoln shortly before the mid-winter of 1140; as soon as he turned southward to keep his Christmas court at London, they inaugurated their revolt by seizing the castle. It is an instructive comment on the current ideas of political obligation that their guilt was held to lie, not so much in their defection from the lawful King, as in their omission to send him a message of defiance. Rebellion had ceased to be a crime, and all the earls of the northern counties, even those who owed their dignity to Stephen, began to waver in their allegiance. The King

[1] See the *E. H. R.*, xviii., p. 630, " The anarchy of Stephen's reign ". Mr. Round, *Geoffrey de Mandeville*, takes a different view.

returned without delay and laid siege to Lincoln castle; but the
feudal contingents which gathered at his summons were lamentably
small; even with the help of the Breton and Fleming mercenaries
whom he brought, he had no hope of succeeding except by a
blockade. Meanwhile the Earl of Chester had gone to the west
in search of help; and, on February 2, a great host led by the
Earl of Gloucester appeared under the walls of Lincoln. Stephen's
advisers urged him to remain within the city until reinforcements
should arrive; but he insisted on delivering a pitched battle with
his inferior forces. Defeat was a foregone conclusion. His feudal
levies broke at the first charge; the foreign mercenaries forsook
him when they saw his fortunes trembling in the balance. Deserted
and surrounded the King would neither fly nor yield. A citizen of
Lincoln handed him a Danish axe; with this he kept his enemies
at bay until it was shattered in his hand. Then, as he still fought
on with his two-handed sword, a stone hurled from behind felled
him, and he was overpowered. With his capture the battle, and
to all appearance his reign, were at an end. The loss of life on
either side was small. Not more than a hundred knights were
killed. The citizens of Lincoln, who had espoused the cause of
Stephen, were the chief sufferers; many of them were drowned in
the Witham as they attempted to regain the walls; the rest were
hunted down and massacred "like sheep" by the mounted men-
at-arms.[1]

Stephen was taken from Lincoln to Bristol castle where he was
not only kept under the strictest guard, but even loaded with
chains, either as an additional humiliation or to increase the difficulty of escape. His cause collapsed without a further effort; his
supporters submitted to the Empress with an alacrity which suggests that they had for some time been weary of a losing cause ;
David of Scotland set the example, well content to hold the
northern shires from a sovereign who was his kinswoman. The
Normans, abandoning all hope of Stephen's restoration, offered the
Duchy for the second time to his brother ; and Theobald, although
no longer to be tempted by the bait, thought he could not help
Stephen better than by asking that the King should be released
in exchange for the surrender of the Duchy. No doubt the offer

Matilda elected Queen by the Clergy

---

[1] The best accounts are in W. Malmesb., *H. N.*, §§ 38 ff. John of Hexham,
§ 12. Hen. Hunt., pp. 268 ff. Orderic, v., 127. *Gesta*, 70 ff.

would have been accepted by Geoffrey of Anjou if it had not been coupled with a stipulation that Theobald should have Touraine as a compensation for his claims; but this condition was enough to prevent the negotiations from going further. Normandy had still to be conquered by the House of Anjou; but in England Kent was the only district which held out for Stephen. Here his Queen, Matilda of Boulogne and William of Yprès, the captain of his mercenaries, were endeavouring to collect a new army; but their efforts were frustrated by the defection of the legate and the Church. Henry of Winchester, within a few weeks of his brother's capture, allowed Matilda to enter the ancient capital of Wessex in triumph, and placed all his influence at her disposal on condition that he should have the first place in her counsels and the control of all ecclesiastical patronage.[1] Five weeks later he summoned a council of the clergy to ratify his promises. The assembly met at Winchester and, on the first day of the proceedings (April 7), debated with closed doors; on the morrow the legate in a public oration signified their decision to the people. The clergy, he said, had been justified in crowning Stephen, for Matilda had delayed unreasonably before coming to assert her title. But Stephen had broken the promises on which he was elected. He had imprisoned bishops, he had otherwise oppressed the church; he had not given to the realm the good peace which he promised at his coronation. Therefore the clergy, to whom it specially appertained to elect and consecrate a sovereign, had transferred their allegiance to the Empress.[2] In vain a deputation of the Londoners protested against this resolution and demanded the release of Stephen. They were told that their trust in Stephen was misplaced and dismissed

[1] Gesta, 75. W. Malm., H. N., § 42. Matilda's charter to Glastonbury, Monasticon, i., 44. Round, G. de M., p. 57.
[2] Nothing in the shape of a popular election can be proved from the authorities. Matilda was proclaimed Lady of England at Winchester by the Bishop on March 3 (W. Malm.). This was a personal transaction: the Bishop spoke for himself and his personal adherents. The election of April 7-8 was made by a purely clerical assembly, as described above. The significance of the title Dominus, Domina, is discussed by Round, G. de M., pp. 67-73, and by Rössler, p. 424. It appears to have been borne by the lawful successor before coronation. It was so used by Richard and by John. There is no ground for supposing that it was only assumed after election and denoted an elective title. Still less reason is there for supposing that it means "Regent". The instance which Dr. Rössler quotes for this theory is conclusive against it. Henry FitzEmpress was recognised by Stephen as "Dominus" in 1152; but Henry was in no sense Regent; this is proved by his convention with Stephen, Foedera, i., p. 18.

without further ceremony. In two months time the Londoners repented of their loyalty and Matilda was able to take up her residence at Westminster (*c.* June 20).

But already her own faults of character had undermined the foundations of her power. We are assured by the panegyrist of Henry of Winchester that the bishop's submission to Matilda was a feigned one, made in the interests of his brother. It seems more likely that he was estranged by the harshness with which the Empress proceeded against the friends of the fallen king. Those who had offered their submission met with a cold reception at her court. The grants of Stephen whether to laymen or religious houses, were indiscriminately cancelled; in vain the legate, the King of Scots, and the Earl of Gloucester, pleaded for some show of clemency. Matilda scarcely deigned to honour the remonstrances of these, her principal supporters, with a hearing. She showed herself no less autocratic than her father, but infinitely less discreet. The Londoners were the first to show their resentment. Since the accession of Stephen their corporate spirit had developed; and they had recently taken the step, completely novel in England, of forming a commune, on the French pattern, administered by elective magistrates. The Empress, on her entry to the city, demanded a tallage from them, in spite of their representations that they had been taxed beyond endurance by the King; and refused to allow them any greater privileges of self-government than they had enjoyed in Henry's time. The offended citizens rang their bells, flocked to arms, and sallied forth to attack Matilda in her palace; the Empress and her suite, who heard the tumult as they were sitting down to dinner, had barely time to procure horses and to fly before the mob arrived at Westminster. Matilda fled to Oxford, deserted on the way by most of her following and in particular by the legate; while William of Yprès and the Queen took possession of London in the name of Stephen.[1]

Immediately after leaving the Empress the legate opened a correspondence with Stephen's partisans in London. The Empress retaliated by a sudden march on Winchester. She brought with her the King of Scots, the Earl of Gloucester, and the whole of

Matilda's Unpopularity

The Siege of Winchester

---

[1] *Gesta*, 75. Cont. Flor. Wig. W. Malm., *H. N.*, § 48. Hen. Hunt., 275. Matilda's policy, judging from her acts, was to conciliate by the most extravagant grants those who could give military assistance, and to neglect all other supporters.

her military strength; the legate was obliged to shut himself up in Wolvesey castle, on the south side of the city, and abandon all else to her mercy. On July 31st the Imperialists entered Winchester, and laid siege to Wolvesey; the garrison offered a stout resistance, firing those parts of the city which lay in dangerous proximity to the castle, and the legate fled to entreat the royalists for help. They made a prompt response with the result that the army of the Empress found themselves, within a few weeks, cut off from all supplies and as much in the position of besieged as besiegers. On September 14th Matilda began a retreat which the pressure of the enemy upon her rearguard soon converted into a headlong flight. The Empress herself never paused until, strapped in a horse litter and almost dead with fatigue, she entered the friendly walls of Gloucester. Her brother was taken prisoner in covering her train from pursuit, and David of Scotland narrowly escaped the same fate.

The royalists were not without hopes of inducing the captive earl to forswear his sister's cause. He received the most tempting offers while he lay in prison, but refused them with a steadfastness which was all the more remarkable by contrast with the shifts and changes of his fellow-barons. Since he could not be seduced from his loyalty he was exchanged for the King. The Empress had no choice in the matter, for the earl was the one hope of her cause. But the King's release was followed by a rapid increase in the number of his partisans; and the clergy consented to lay aside their former quarrel with him. The versatile legate held a synod at Westminster, on December 7th, in which he contrived to vindicate himself from the imputation of treachery, and the King from the old charge of infringing the church's privilege. Letters in favour of Stephen from Pope Innocent were produced and read before the synod. Stephen was once more recognised as King, and the supporters of the Empress were threatened with excommunication. This was the severest check which her cause had yet received; in despair she appealed for help to her husband Geoffrey of Anjou. The request was carried by the Earl of Gloucester. He found Geoffrey engaged in the more congenial work of annexing Normandy piecemeal; the Count was by no means inclined to sacrifice his own objects for the sake of his wife's crown. The utmost to which he would consent was that their eldest son, the young Henry of Anjou, should join

his mother; and Gloucester returned bringing the boy with him.
The presence of the prince in England made little difference to the
popularity of his mother's cause; but it is worthy of notice that
his stay was prolonged for four years and that he thus received
a considerable part of his education from English teachers and on
English soil.

In Gloucester's absence his party had suffered a severe loss. The
Oxford, which the Empress had taken for her headquarters, was of Parties
surprised by Stephen in September, 1142; and Matilda, after after 1142
standing a siege of some weeks in the castle was forced to make
a night-escape leaving the garrison to effect a surrender as best
they could. The loss of this important stronghold left the Angevin
party without a chance of maintaining themselves in the Thames
valley and the eastern counties. They fell back upon the West.
For the future their efforts were chiefly directed towards securing the
Welsh marches and the shires between the English and the Bristol
Channels; while Stephen divided his attention between raids into
their country and efforts, sometimes more and sometimes less
successful, to repress treachery and insubordination among his
followers.

The contempt in which he was held by his own side is illus- Geoffrey
trated by an incident which passes almost unnoticed by the de Man-
chroniclers. Stephen had recently procured for his son Eustace deville
the hand of the princess Constance, the sister of Louis VII. The
bride was brought to England about this time by Matilda of
Boulogne.[1] On their way through London they were apprehended
by one of Stephen's chief supporters, Geoffrey de Mandeville, the
custodian of the Tower. He allowed the Queen to depart, but kept
the princess, with the intention of demanding a ransom, and was
with difficulty compelled to give up his prey. It was the crowning
act of audacity in a career which has justly been used as a typical
illustration of feudal ambitions and methods in this, the golden age
of feudalism. Mandeville had inherited considerable territorial influence in the eastern counties, and for that reason had been purchased by Stephen, in 1140, with the bribe of the Earldom of Essex.

---

[1] Mr. Round infers from the narrative of Newburgh (Bk. I., § 11) that the date of
this outrage is to be fixed in March or April, 1140. But the language of Newburgh
really gives no clue to the date. It must have been later than the betrothal which
took place early in 1140; how much later we cannot say.

On the defeat and capture of his patron he had joined the Empress in return for a confirmation of his earldom and the grant of additional privileges.   Matilda made him custodian of the Tower of London, and gave him the offices of sheriff and justiciar, for himself and his heirs, in the shire of Essex.   After the flight of the Empress from Winchester the earl returned to Stephen, who besides confirming Matilda's grant, added to it the offices of sheriff and justiciar in London, Middlesex, and Hertfordshire.   As the result of these transactions Geoffrey became the sole representative of the Crown, for fiscal and judicial purposes, in three counties and in the city which was already beginning to be regarded as the capital.   But, still unsatisfied, he sold himself a second time to the Empress, during her stay at Oxford.   This last act of treachery was probably detected when Oxford and the papers of Matilda fell into the hands of Stephen.   Detected it was; and the King for once proceeded to make an example.   At a Great Council held at St. Albans in the autumn of 1143 Mandeville, who had appeared without any suspicion of the evidence against him, was suddenly arrested as a traitor; he was only released after he had surrendered the Tower and all his castles.   That he should be released at all is surprising; but the same strange code of honour which permitted a vassal to rebel after due notice given, forbade a lord to seize the intending traitor by surprise.   Stephen was obliged to consult the real or feigned scruples of his supporters, although the mischief consequent upon indulgence to so dangerous a conspirator might easily have been foreseen.   Mandeville was no sooner released than he flew to arms and defied the king.   The earl had at his command a small army of mercenaries and desperadoes; with their aid he seized Ramsey Abbey and, evicting the monks, converted it into a stronghold from which he carried his depredations far and wide.   He sacked the towns of Cambridge and St. Ives, and the open country for miles round Ramsey was converted into a desert.   No manor was safe from his tenseries; his men moved from village to village in disguise to mark down for imprisonment and torture all who had the means of paying a ransom.   It was in vain that Stephen took the field against the robbers.   Moving from fort to fort among the fens, they continually eluded his pursuit; Mandeville continued to be the pest of the eastern midlands until a chance arrow cut short his career in the summer of 1144.   His cruelties have been immortalised in one of the best known passages of the English Chronicle. Yet to such a degree had feudalism debased the moral standard of the age that Mandeville found admirers, even among men of religion;[1] he was a good knight according to the standard of the day, and some pity was felt for him when he died under the ban of excommunication.

The forces of feudalism were by no means crushed with the fall of Mandeville. The area subject to the Empress diminished slowly and steadily under the stress of Stephen's energetic operations against outlying castles such as Farringdon. But his subjects suffered less from the raids of the Angevins than from the depredations and the private wars of bandits who professed his cause or simply fought for their own hand. It was impossible, in the face of such treacherous supporters, to succour Normandy. Rouen fell to Count Geoffrey in January, 1144; the Count of Flanders and the King of France came to his aid; and Arques, the last Norman castle to fly Stephen's banner, surrendered in the summer of 1145. The acquisition of the Duchy, though purchased by the cession of the Norman Vexin to King Louis, was more than an equivalent to the Empress for her English losses; and Stephen, none the wiser for his former experiences, chose this moment to begin a new and dangerous conflict with the Church. Formerly he had quarrelled with the legate and the party who made the immunities of the clergy their watchword; now it was Theobald and the party of monastic reform whom he estranged. And behind these new opponents stood not only the official head of Christendom, but also St. Bernard, who from his cell at Clairvaux made and unmade Popes, branded the greatest teachers of the age as heretics, and was able, by the mere force of eloquence, to set the flower of French and German feudalism in motion against the assailants of the Holy Land.

Stephen's Losses, 1142-5

Stephen quarrels with the Church

The wave of religious enthusiasm which swept over Europe in the first half of the twelfth century had long since crossed the Channel and invaded England. Years before Stephen's accession its effects had been seen in the growth of new religious houses, the rising arrogance of ecclesiastical courts, the general inclination to make the court of Rome a supreme tribunal for all cases which

---

[1] See the extract from the Chronicle of the Holy Cross of Waltham, quoted by Round, *G. de M.*, p. 323.

could by any stretch of logic be classified as spiritual. St. Bernard
had long watched the English movement, in which his order took
so prominent a part, with a solicitous eye. He craved to see men
of his own school in the high places of the English church; and
it was a sore blow to him when, upon the death of Archbishop
Thurstan, a connection of the King, by name William FitzHerbert,
was thrust into the see of York, for which the reformers had found
a worthier candidate in Henry Murdac, the abbot of the new house
of Fountains (1141). Theobald refused to take any part in the
consecration of the royal nominee. St. Bernard more than once
pressed the Papacy to cancel the election and nominate Henry
Murdac.[1] In 1147 the reformers got their way; a council, held
at Paris by Eugenius III., a pupil and devoted follower of St.
Bernard, declared in favour of the Abbot of Fountains. The
King refused to accept this decision, and it soon came to an open
quarrel between himself and the reformers.

The
Second
Crusade
1147

St. Bernard's power was at its height. This was the year of
the departure of the Second Crusade when Europe was astounded
at the spectacle of a King of France and an Emperor marching as
allies to the Holy Land, and had not yet learned from their failure
to doubt the infallibility of the monitor whom they obeyed. In
England not less than on the Continent the appeal of St. Bernard
found a responsive echo. A fleet of 160 vessels, recruited in part
from Flanders and the Rhineland, but mainly from the south and
east of England, gathered at Dartmouth to sail for Portugal and
aid Alfonso I. of Portugal in the siege of Lisbon. Some of the
English pilgrims were hardy buccaneers from Southampton, Hastings, and the Cinque Ports, who had already served in similar
enterprises from the love of adventure or the hope of booty, and
were ready, at the slightest provocation to forsake the Crusade for
piracy. But the greater part were zealots, who had joined the
crusade from sheer conviction, and who cheerfully subjected themselves to the severest military and moral discipline in the interests
of a holy cause.[2] Such was the spirit of the third estate. It was
shared, to some extent, even by the baronage; of whom not a

[1] See Bernard's letter protesting against Celestine's resolve to give FitzHerbert
a hearing (*Opp.*, i., c. 229).
[2] See Osbern, *De Expugnatione Lyxbonensi* (printed in the Roll Series, Memor.
of Richard I., p. cxliv.). *Gesta Stephani*, pp. 119, 120.

few, formerly notorious for their depredations in the civil war, quitted England to march with the main crusading armies. It need not then surprise us that the Papacy and Bernard felt secure in taking up the glove which the King of England had thrown down to them. The English clergy were summoned to a Council held at Rheims (March, 1148) that they might assist in censuring Stephen's conduct. He was able to prevent them from attending; but he would have been excommunicated in their absence if he had not been saved, in spite of himself, by the intercessions of Archbishop Theobald. The Primate eluded the vigilance of Stephen's coast-guards and, crossing the Channel in a crazy fishing smack, arrived at Rheims in time to obtain a respite from the Pope. The reward was a sentence of banishment, as a result of which Theobald remained in exile on the Continent for some months after the council. But the King found that Theobald's cause was one with which all English parties sympathised; before the end of the year it was necessary to let the Archbishop return in peace, and resume his lawful place as the first adviser of the Crown. Theobald's victory was the more striking because he had been opposed by the bishops; and it bred in Stephen's mind a deep-rooted suspicion of the Papacy. In 1150 when Cardinal Paparone appeared, bringing palls for the archbishops of Ireland, he was refused a safe-conduct through England, and thought it advisable to make his journey by way of Scotland.[1]

Council of Rheims, 1148

A few years earlier Stephen could not have afforded to show this independence. But the Angevin cause was losing ground apace. Earl Robert of Gloucester died in 1147, leaving no one to take his place as the leader of the Empress's English supporters. Matilda lost hope and returned to Normandy within a few months of her brother's death. The task of rallying her friends for a new struggle was left in the hands of the young Henry of Anjou, who had left England in December, 1146, but returned as his mother's representative in 1149.[2] The prince's prospects of success were small.

Position of the Angevin Party, 1147-50

---

[1] For the Council and for Stephen's relations with Rome at this time see the *Historia Pontificalis* in Pertz, S.S. xx., pp. 515-539, and the *Vita Malachiae* in St. Bernard's works, i., c. 688. Theobald had long been on bad terms with the King and a protégé of the Holy See. Bernard, *Opp.*, i., c. 197. Theobald's letter to Adrian IV. in John of Salisbury's *Epistolae*, i., p. 38 (ed. Giles). His journey to Rheims in Gervase, i., 133.

[2] For the supposed visit of Henry to England in 1147 see Mr. Howlett's preface to the *Gesta*. Mr. Round (*E. H. R.*, v., p. 747) thinks that the author of the *Gesta* is

Though Stephen had by no means succeeded in restoring the fiscal machinery of Henry I., even in those shires which had been consistently loyal, his sheriffs and his law-courts were recognised by the law-abiding.[1]   Except on the shores of the Bristol Channel and in the Welsh marches the men of the Empress were reduced to the defensive and blockaded in castles far apart.   The King's friends were disloyal; the peace was insecure; but both sides were equally exhausted, and popular sympathy was on the side of Stephen, as being the candidate in possession.   Supported by a mere handful of English barons Henry had no other course but to make large sacrifices for the friendship of the King of Scotland.   He pledged himself to confirm Stephen's grant of Cumberland and Northumberland; he salved over the feud which still subsisted between David and Ranulf of Chester by promising to the earl the enormous Honour of Lancaster as a solatium for Carlisle.   But even these grants could not secure an army for the Prince; Stephen outbid him with the Earl of Chester, who held the key of the situation; and Henry returned to France to administer the Duchy of Normandy, which had been conquered by his father in his name.[2]   The death of Count Geoffrey, in 1151, threw upon Henry's shoulders the whole burden of the Angevin inheritance; and immediately afterwards came the marriage of the young ruler to Eleanor, the heiress of Aquitaine and divorced wife of Louis VII., which entailed a feud with France.[3]   All things worked together to make Stephen's position more secure, and he entertained hopes of bequeathing the kingship to his son, Eustace.

Stephen and Henry of Anjou reconciled, 1153   But in the execution of this plan he had to reckon with the Church.   The only way of giving Eustace a valid title seemed to be that of procuring his coronation in his father's life-time.   But the power of crowning him lay with the Primate, a firm supporter of Rome and mortally offended by Stephen's attitude in the matter of the see of York.   Stephen sacrificed his candidate to dynastic considerations, and recognised Henry Murdac as the Archbishop

mistaken in the date and is really speaking of the visit of 1149.   Sir James Ramsay refers to 1147 the visit which is put under 1151 by the Continuator of the *Historia Regum* (p. 324).

[1] See Mr. Howlett's preface to *Chronicles and Memorials*, etc., vol. ii.   But, as to the confused state of the central government, see G. L. Turner in *Transactions of the R. Hist. Soc.*, xii., p. 117 (New Series).

[2] On the negotiations of Ranulf with Henry and with Stephen see Mr. Round's paper in *E. H. R.*, x., p. 87.   I have accepted Mr. Round's chronology.

[3] Hen. Hunt., p. 283.   Gervase, i., 149.   R. de Monte, p. 165.   W. Neubrig, i., § 31.

of the northern province. It was a useless concession. The Papacy
remained inexorable and forbade the English bishops to hallow
Eustace on any terms whatever. The Papal injunction was loyally
obeyed. In fact it was issued at the instigation of Archbishop
Theobald, and Theobald carried with him the national clergy,
who after many waverings had at length decided in favour of the
Angevin cause. For the fourth time in eighteen years ecclesiastical
feeling had settled the fate of the Crown. In spite of the danger
which menaced his continental dominions, Henry of Anjou was
emboldened to make a fresh attempt on England (1153). He
could bring with him only a small force, 140 knights and 3,000
foot-soldiers. But no more were necessary. As soon as the prince
had shown, by the capture of Malmesbury and the relief of Wallingford, that he was a leader of ability, the midlands, so long loyal
to Stephen's cause, began to waver; the great barons hastened to
pay their court to the rising sun. The death of Eustace (Aug.,
1153) deprived Stephen of all desire to prolong the hopeless struggle.
He allowed Theobald to open negotiations on his behalf; in Treaty of
the autumn definite terms were arranged between the parties. Winchester, Nov. 6
The most important were that Henry should be recognised as
the heir to the Crown, Stephen's private estates being reserved
to his surviving son, William, Earl of Surrey; that Henry should
do homage to Stephen and cause his adherents to do the
same; that Stephen's followers should do homage to Henry, re-
serving that which they owed to the King; and that the King
would consult with Henry in all the business of the realm. It was
furthermore agreed that the mercenaries of both sides should be
dismissed, and that the unlicensed castles, of which there are said
to have been 1,115, should be destroyed; so at least the chroniclers
assert, though nothing is said upon these subjects in the official
text of the treaty; and the chroniclers are borne out by the acts
of Stephen's last few months of government.[1] As at the treaty of

---

[1] Rössler is of opinion that the *Carta Conventionum* which is given in the *Foedera*,
i., p. 18, does not contain the whole of the terms arranged at Winchester. This is
probable enough; for the *Carta Conventionum* relates entirely to the future relations
between Stephen and Henry; and there were other questions to be settled. It is
however unlikely that, if the Prince was to govern as Regent in place of Stephen,
this would not have been mentioned in the Carta. Diceto ascribes this position to
Henry but wrote after the event; and we have no proof that he does more than
express roughly the situation which he conceived to follow upon the conclusion of
the treaty. John of Hexham is our best authority for the statement that the prince
became regent; but even John is habitually inaccurate. Robert de Monte and
Gervase say nothing of a regency created in Henry's favour. Rössler's theory is
due to his anxiety to show that the title *Dominus*, assumed by Henry in 1152, meant
"Regent" (Rössler, pp. 403, 431).

Alton in 1101, so now, the contending claimants for the crown had
recognised in feudalism their common enemy. The credit for im-
pressing this view upon the Count and the King belongs to the
national clergy; but the praise due to the clergy would be greater
if they had played the part of mediators some ten or fifteen years
earlier in the struggle. Apart from Theobald the leaders of the
Church were either timorous or too narrow-minded to look at the
struggle in its bearing upon national welfare; and Theobald was
long in shaking himself free from the ties of gratitude to Stephen,
and in rising to the responsibilities of his position. Perhaps even
Theobald would not have been moved to mediate unless his resentment had been stirred against Stephen by the King's violence to the
bishops and his defiance of the authority of Rome. The Church
had acquired in the course of the last half-century an influence
which its ablest representatives were incapable of managing for
the best interests of the nation. There is little cause for accusing
Henry II. of ingratitude towards the clergy.

Death of
Stephen,
1154

Scarcely a year after the settlement of the succession Stephen
met his end (Oct., 1154). In the last months of his life he had done
something to scotch the many headed monster of feudalism and to
atone for twenty years of wasted energies. But he had shown himself unable to work on friendly terms with the supplanter of his
son; and Count Henry had retired to Normandy to wait until the
old King's death should give him a free hand in England. Stephen
did not die too soon. Admirable as a knight, respectable as the
lord of a small fief, he had been pushed by ambition into a position
which would have tasked the ablest statesmen of the age. Too
simple to anticipate intrigues, too scrupulous to destroy the root
from which they sprang, too vacillating to crush them when they
began to take effect, he failed alike in peace and war. Among all
our medieval sovereigns none owed his title in so real a sense to the
election of the nation; few showed themselves more incapable; none
was a greater curse to the nation. One purpose, and that ignoble,
he effectually served. His reign furnished a warning, never to be
forgotten, against the evils of an uncurbed feudalism, and prepared
public opinion to accept the drastic centralisation of Henry II.

CHAPTER VI

THE OLD ORDER AND THE NEW

THE favourite art of any age is the best clue to the spirit of the age; it is significant that architecture engrossed the artists of the Anglo-Norman period. Painting and sculpture, essentially imitative in their nature, depend for success upon a fine perception of nuance in colour, contour, and proportion. In this faculty the age was wanting; it was pleased with simple hues and the indefinite repetition of a simple pattern; it had not studied nature; it was more concerned with the soul than with the body. But in architecture the best minds found a satisfaction for some of their profoundest feelings; for their love of the mysterious and the massive; for their inveterate tendency to denote unseen realities by a concrete symbol; for the sense of brotherhood in an imperishable society; for the desire to testify their faith by some material contribution to the resources of the Church. So churches sprang up broadcast; cathedrals for the dioceses, minsters for conventual communities, chapels and parish churches for the poorest country manors. The architects expressed in stone and mortar what they conceived to be eternal truths. Incidentally and unconsciously they revealed the peculiarities of their own age and nationality. These buildings remain like the fossil skeletons from which geologists divine the features of an otherwise forgotten stage of life. From the churches alone we might infer the presence of a conquering race. Ground-plan and ornament alike carry the thoughts of the spectator beyond the Channel and across the Alps; the foreign influences are palpable; the breach with the past of English art is violent and sudden; the absence of a transitional stage denotes that we are dealing with an importation, not with a natural development. At the same time the new architects, though im-

Anglo-Norman Architecture

migrants, are obviously at their ease. They build slowly, solidly, for unborn generations. They show the interest of a settler in the conditions of the land which they have overrun. They form a school, with developing traditions; they are not ashamed to go their own way; they make a style which is not purely Norman any more than it is Saxon. The founders of the school work in the spirit of military engineers. Their churches are like fortresses, plain, severe, with walls of rubble or roughly jointed ashlar; with narrow windows, heavy portals, and a keep-like tower at the extremity or centre of the fabric. The second and third generations show a progressive tendency to innovate upon the ancient ground-plan, and to conceal brute mass beneath a veil of chiselled ornament. From the colossal austerity of Winchester and St. Albans the style advances till we reach the sumptuous decoration of Peterborough and the Bristol Chapter-house; and in becoming more splendid it unbends. It falls into harmony with the English atmosphere and landscape; it is adorned with frescoes, bas-reliefs, mouldings, the work of English craftsmen who co-operate, we feel, as much for the honour of the native saints and for the pleasure of a native congregation as to earn the wages of an alien lord or prelate. From the parish churches alone, with their quaint and homely ornaments, we might infer the gradual reconciliation of the rulers who built with the ruled who worshipped in the building.

Fusion of Races   Four reigns, covering less than a hundred years, all but obliterated the distinction between the Norman conqueror and his English subjects. Here and there a noble might be found, even in the days of Henry I., who openly avowed his contempt for English ways and English lineage; here and there a complaint of " French " tyranny is raised by the sons of the men who fought on Harold's side at Senlac. But the ordinary Norman, whether knight or burgess, quickly accommodated himself to the prejudices of his adopted country; and, when the disgrace of Senlac had been cancelled by the triumph of Tinchebrai, the ordinary Englishman was resigned to the new order; or even contended that it was not new, and that the Norman dynasty were the rightful heirs of Alfred, Athelstan and Edgar. In all classes, except the highest, mixed marriages became an every-day occurrence;[1] nor was it easy to distinguish at a glance between a Norman and an English household. The saintly

[1] Orderic, ii., 214, 224. W. Malmesb., *G. R.*, iii., §§ 245-6.

bishop Wulfstan was accounted English of the English. Yet Wulfstan maintained a train of knights and was served at table, in the Norman fashion, by pages who had entered his service to learn the usages of chivalry. The one feature that stamped his housekeeping as English was a conviviality which his foreign brethren thought immoderate and insular. Though temperate in his own potations the Bishop prolonged his entertainments from high noon to sunset; and he remained at table to keep his guests in countenance, passing the cup himself but watching to see that others were not stinted.[1] In this as in more important matters Wulfstan showed himself exceptionally conservative. Even the vices of the English were soon laughed out of good society. Now and then the pride of race revives in a moment of excitement, or is suggested by a legal formula. The Yorkshire barons, at the battle of the Standard, are invoked by their leader as " unconquerable Normans " and bidden to remember Senlac ; the writs of Henry I. and Stephen are frequently addressed to their subjects " French and English ". But the work of Henry I. had made the distinction almost meaningless; between those whom the law regarded as equal there could not be any profound inequalities of social status. Yet the assimilation of the two races proceeded otherwise than might have been expected from the past history of the Normans. They had been the pupils of the Frank; but they became the teachers of the Anglo-Saxon. For two centuries after Senlac the social usages, the dress, the language, of the English upper classes were entirely French. Henry I., who knew the English tongue well enough to dispute about sac and soc and infangthief, talked nothing else but French. He, no doubt, was educated on the Continent. But Henry II. also was unable to talk English ; and he was educated by an Englishman on English soil. English was admitted in the law-courts, but only upon sufferance for those who could not plead in French or Latin ; for social purposes the tongue of Caedmon and of Alfred was altogether inadmissible. It could hardly be otherwise since the English tongue had differentiated into dialects so various that the Yorkshireman was unintelligible to a native of the western shires. The north and south communicated perforce through the medium of a foreign language. English was sometimes heard in the pulpit. In the days of Henry II. the great

French Complection of English Society

---

[1] W. Malmesb., *G. P.*, p. 281. *Vita Wulfstani*, iii., §§ 2, 8, 16.

Abbot Samson of St. Edmunds endeared himself to country con-
gregations by his Norfolk brogue. But preachers who aspired to
the fame of eloquence talked French or Latin. English was supposed to be incapable of expressing any but the simplest ideas.[1]

The
Division
of Classes:
(a) The
Villein

The influx of French ways and fashions led to a considerable
simplification of the social hierarchy. The English-speaking peasant
was separated from his French-speaking landlord by a gulf which
made the differences of status between the slave and villein, the cottier
and freeman and socman, scarcely worth consideration. The free
and unfree peasants were popularly labelled with the common name
of villeins ; and the law more often than not attempted to treat the
various degrees of men thus catalogued as though they stood on the
same level and were all destitute of civil rights. Polite society
despised the villein too much to be curious about his rights or want
of them. " *Odit anima mea servos,*" says Walter Map, the satirist
of court-circles and the mouthpiece of fashionable prejudice.[2] His
spirit was shared even by the citizens of the free towns who had retained far more of English sympathies and customs than the feudal
classes. Many towns claimed as their privilege that residence within
their walls for a year and a day conferred freedom on the serf of
any lord. But this privilege was chiefly used to protect the original
burgesses against antiquated claims on their persons and property.
The villein met with a cold reception if he endeavoured to settle
in a chartered town. He ran the risk of being surrendered to his
lord before he had succeeded in prescribing for his freedom. Even
when freedom was gained he would, if possible, be refused the
burgess franchise. The Church, as was natural for a landowning
corporation, showed no great desire to promote the custom of
manumission. It is to the honour of Lanfranc and Anselm that
they destroyed the institution of slavery by prohibiting the slave-
trade ;[3] nor need we doubt the statement of Roger of Wendover,
late authority though he is, that the Church in Stephen's reign
claimed for English villeins the same immunity from the horrors of
civil war which their continental brethren already enjoyed under
the *Treuga Dei.*[4] On the other hand the Church admitted that
no son of villein parents might enter orders without his lord's

[1] Joceline de Brakelond, pp. 30, 95. W. Malmesb., *G. P.*, p. 201.
[2] Map, *De Nugis*, v., § 4.   [3] Eadmer, *H. N.*, pp. 141-4.
[4] Wendover, *s.a.* 1142.

consent. This rule was one of the *avitae consuetudines* which were embodied in the Constitutions of Clarendon, and it passed without a challenge from the Archbishop or the Pope. The attitude of the upper classes towards the villein was more humane in 1154 than it had been in 1088. The villein was now generally admitted to deserve protection of life and limb. But he was tied to the soil, and liable to be bought and sold like any chattel; in respect of civil rights he was left helpless as against his lord, nor was he allowed to rank as a free doomsman in the courts of shire and hundred; while in the intercourse of daily life he was treated with chill contempt as a being hardly human.[1]

On the other hand the distinctions between different classes of free men were less absolute in England than abroad. To a French or Flemish knight the citizens of the proudest communes were simply serfs who had usurped a lawless liberty. In England we find a Gilbert Becket, a Norman of knightly rank, settling in London to make a livelihood by trade; and FitzStephen describes the Londoners and the youth of the King's household as tilting amicably together on a feast-day.[2] It is true that the chivalric ideal was beginning to influence the upper classes of English society. Already the severe probation of the aspirant to knighthood, the elaborate ritual which accompanied the ceremony of investiture, the duty of quixotic generosity to equals and superiors, the passion for tournaments and pageantry, were combining to make the daily life and interests of the military class something wholly different from those of meaner men.[3] But the first effects of chivalry were beneficial. It counteracted the brutal spirit which pervaded early feudalism; and, while exalting the knight at the expense of men of peace, the code of honour insisted on the obligations of the knight to his inferiors. It is an exceptional case, in Stephen's reign, to find an adventurer like Geoffrey de Mandeville extolled as the mirror of knightly excellence; a couple of generations earlier such an estimate of the man would have been unhesitatingly accepted. The new spirit is accurately reflected by John of Salisbury who, in enumerating the duties of a knight, gives the first place to

(b) Gentle and Simple

---

[1] *Leges Henrici*, 29 § 1; 43 § 2; 75 § 3. Gift of a villein about 1148 in *Cart. Gloucest.*, ii., p. 4. Writ to apprehend fugitive villeins, *Chron. de Rameseia*, p. 212.
[2] FitzStephen, *Materials*, iii., p. 9.
[3] See the *Polycraticus* of John of Salisbury, vi., §§ 7, 8, 10. Will. Neubrig, v., § 4. John of Hexham, § 14.

those of defending the Church and the poor. Every knight was to
be, with regard to the defenceless, what only Emperors and Kings
had been in a ruder social state. Thanks to these features, the
earliest chivalric ideal did not impair the harmony of classes to
such a degree as the degenerate chivalry of the fourteenth century.
The special privileges of the knight were as yet admitted without
discontent as being the reward for special services.[1]

Absence of Social Discontent In spite of civil wars and the feuds of Church, Crown, and
Baronage, the general framework of society in the twelfth century
was stable and unshaken. Crown and Church and Baronage were
recognised as necessary elements in the constitution ; while each
encroached upon the others there was no thought of a war of ex-
termination. Still less did the lower classes rebel against the complex
hierarchy in the shadow of which they made their precarious gains
and exercised their modest privileges. To whatever rank of society
we look we form the idea of a life which was free, careless and
boisterously mirthful ; of men who were quick to pity and relieve
misfortune, but equally quick to put unpleasant memories behind
them. The gaiety of the medieval Englishman was as notorious
as the fact that nature had endowed him with a tail. His foreign
critics reproached him with a frivolity (*levitas*) which in their
opinion contrasted unfavourably with the gravity of Frenchmen.[2]
The English were proud of this trait and of their country's reputation as a " merry " land. " Nowhere," says a monk of St. Albans
in a metrical description of England, " nowhere are faces more joyous
at the board, or hosts more eager to please, or entertainments more
sumptuous. By nature the Englishman is liberal ; his hand is
always extended to the aged and bent ; he is never weary of giving."
This genial buoyancy and good-fellowship were the product of
medieval Christianity working upon kindly natures. Men whose
belief in eternity was vivid and unshaken could afford to make
light of temporal misfortunes ; the conviction that good and bad
fortune were in no way due to human causes, but the working
of an inscrutable providence, made them at once less solicitous

---

[1] A theory which survives, with so many others equally obsolete, in *The Vision of Piers Plowman*.

[2] *Opera Bernardi*, i., p. 715 (ed. Mabillon), where a remark of Petrus Cel-
ensis is quoted by the editor " *Nec indignetur Anglica levitas si ea solidior sit
Gallica maturitas. . . . Certe expertus sum somniatores plus esse Anglos quam
Gallos.*"

for their own earthly ambitions, and more compassionate to those
who had dropped out of the race. The annals of medieval England supply many instances of men who turned their backs upon
the woes and joys of a transitory world, to find their peace
in quiet meditation. But the masses went another road, rejoicing "Merry
like children in their share of the goods of this life, and refusing to England"
be permanently saddened by misfortune. To judge from the
stray remarks of writers who are primarily concerned with graver
subjects the daily life of common men was eminently mirthful. To
William FitzStephen, the lawyer and politician, with his keen eye
for the realities of the world in which he lived, London is above
all things a city of festivals and recreations. He glows with pleasure
in describing the sports of the Londoners ; the cock fights and the
football matches of the school-boys; the archery matches, the
foot-races and the water tournaments of the young men; the
skating for which the whole city turned out in hard weather. All
these things are to him and to the Londoners, as he knows them,
far more important and interesting than the knotty questions
of politics. Ecclesiastics, whose natural tendency was to treat
as vanity everything that was not business or religion, have the
same tale to tell, though they deplore, as in duty bound, the follies
which they chronicle. The polite society which they admonish
or denounce is composed of men who give their whole minds to
festivals and shows and sports; whom no decrees of Popes and
Councils can wean from their passion for the mimic warfare of the
tournament; who delight in all the ritual of venery, and cannot
brisk a stag without flourishes from an orchestra of horns and
trumpets ; who will spend hours in laughing at the tricks of jugglers
and the tales of minstrels, or failing human entertainers will divert
themselves with apes and parrots ; who exult and quarrel and
gesticulate over a game of chess or dice as though a kingdom were
at stake. Dress is a passion and manners are a fine art with the
man of fashion as described by Neckam and John of Salisbury.
He carries a fortune on his back ; he is gay in all the colours of
the rainbow ; even his horse is decked with curiously broidered trap-
pings, with gold and silver harness. In conversation he claps his
hands, waves his arms, gesticulates, or for variety talks upon his
fingers. At one moment he struts like a peacock, at another he
blusters like a game-cock. The description reads like that of a

Neapolitan rather than an English gentleman.[1]   And as it is in
courts and castles so is it in the villages of the remotest shires.
A pilgrimage to the shrine of the local saint is the occasion for
boundless jollity; the crowd which prostrates itself before a relic
carried in procession has hardly risen from the ground before it
is roaring with laughter at the scurrilities of a buffoon.[2]   No figure
is more common or more welcome on the country-side than the
jongleur with his harp and his performing animals.   Every saint's
day is a holiday; every holiday is celebrated with a banquet in the
guild-house which even the smallest of upland parishes maintains.[3]
Among both high and low we hear of ennui; we hear of asceticism
which is repelled by this loud and never-ending jollity; and now and
then, in some unexpected corner, there is a flash of the faith which
removes mountains, an outburst of that zeal which may found
a monastery or create a sect of heretics, or drive children and
illiterate hinds to take the cross and start out for Jerusalem.   But
over and under gloom and zeal, discontent and aspiration, there
runs the perennial current of mirth which is mundane, unrefined,
sometimes even brutal.   Even in monasteries there was cheerful
living.   On a certain Sunday the archdeacon Gerald Barri came to
Canterbury and was invited to dine with the monks in their refectory.   He found the hall in a clatter with the passing of servants
and rich viands to and fro; at the tables there was a babel of conversation, and the brothers gesticulated to each other when the
noise was too great for articulate speech.   It was as good, or as
bad, thought Gerald, as a stage-play.   There were no less than
sixteen courses to the dinner; which set him thinking of St.
Swithin's house at Winchester, where the monks rebelled when the
dinner was cut down to ten courses from thirteen.   Good liquor
ran like water at the feast; there was claret and cider; there was
mead, and pigment, and mulberry wine; beer was of no account at
Canterbury on a festal day.   So nature, expelled with a fork,
returned and asserted herself, even in the strictest of medieval
communities.

[1] *Polycraticus*, i., § 4 and *passim*.   Neckam, *De Rerum Natura*, pp. 323, 351.
[2] W. Malmesb., *G. P.*, p. 438.
[3] Map, *De N gis*, ii., § 12 : "Ad domum in ora nemoris magnam delatus est,
quales Anglici in singulis singulas habebant diocesibus bibitorias, ghildhus Anglice
dictas".   Cf. *Anselmi Epistolae*, II., vii. ; and the *Historia Fundationis Monasterii
de Bello*, p. 20.

Examine it where we will at the beginning of this period, Eng- Intellectual and Religious Revival
lish society was marked by a general want of earnestness or in-
tellectual life; the tide of the twelfth century renaissance had risen
high upon the Continent before it forced a way into these islands.
But even in England the approach of a new age in thought and
morals could be augured from the beginning of the century. Side
by side, but for the most part independently of one another, the
pioneers of the intellectual and the religious movements made their
appearance from abroad ; Englishmen, who had been trained in
France and Italy, returning with the harvest which they had
gleaned in exile; Frenchmen submitting to expatriation for the
sake of preferment or of an ideal; most of them individually
insignificant but in the gross a portentous army of invasion.

The less picturesque of the two bands, but from our modern English Scientists
point of view the more significant is that of the scientists, literati,
and logicians, who brought with them a new interest in nature, a
more discriminating admiration for the literature of antiquity, a
more sceptical and analytic school of speculation. At the court of
Henry I. might occasionally be seen the figure of Adelard of Bath,
the "English philosopher" who had travelled to Italy, Sicily and
Asia Minor, in quest of scientific information. As the author
of a dialogue, *De rerum causis*, and as the translator of Euclid
into Latin, he holds a definite though humble place among those
who restored the intellectual contact of the west with the east,
of medieval learning with ancient science.[1] The spirit which he
kindled is seen in Robert of Cricklade's laborious abridgment of
Pliny's *Natural History ;* times had changed indeed when learned
theologians placed their knowledge of humanities at the service of
the scientist. Unfortunately these allies were by no means content
to serve science in a scientific spirit. Even natural history was perverted in their hands to serve as a vehicle for the illustration of
moral precepts, such as Polonius lavished on Laertes. The pelican,
the camel, and the crocodile were treated as types or allegories ·
the wildest legends about natural phenomena passed unquestioned
if they tended to edification. Truth is a mistress who disdains to
accept a divided allegiance ; and the sciences languished in proportion as they were studied for an ulterior object. Medicine found a
more favourable reception than the others ; to a certain extent it
had been studied in monasteries before it was raised to the dignity

---

[1] For a further account of his scientific work see A. & C. Jourdain, *Récherches
Critiques sur l'age et l'origine des traductions latines d'Aristotle* (Paris, 1843),
p. 277. R. L. Poole, *Exchequer in the Twelfth Century*, pp. 56-7, argues that
Adelard was an Exchequer official under Henry I. C. H. Haskins has established
the chronology of his writings and his life (*E. H. R.*, xxvi., 491-8; *ibid.*, xxviii.,
515-6).   7

of a science. Salerno, the home of doctors trained in the Greek tradition, was one of the places visited by Adelard of Bath; thither or to Montpellier, which enjoyed a scarcely inferior reputation, many Englishmen resorted in this century for the study of medicine. But the technical jargon and the extravagant pretensions with which they returned made them an inviting mark for satire.[1] The boundary line between science and quackery was a faint one, and the genuine student suffered for the sins of the impostor. This was particularly the case with the study of the stars. In the popular mind astronomy and astrology were persistently confounded; and while the orthodox allowed that the influence of the stars on human character and fortunes was capable of demonstration [2] they accused all astronomers of dabbling in the black art. Two successive bishops of Hereford, Robert of Lorraine (1079) and Gerard after-wards Archbishop of York, earned a doubtful reputation by observing the stars. Gerard was popularly reputed to have sold himself to the devil for the sake of forbidden knowledge. Exposed to such charges it is not wonderful that early English scientists adopted an apologetic attitude, and claimed the merit of utility for their researches on grounds which would scarcely bear examination. " The exercises of the liberal arts are useful for a more certain com-prehension of the subjects which belong to theological speculation."[3] Such is the general tenor of the defence; though now and then we hear the plea that " science is useful in this vale of misery because it teaches us how to live rightly in the midst of this perverse and wicked generation ".[4]

English
Scholars
Although it lay with these investigators to begin that criticism of received ideas which culminated in the fifteenth-century Renais-sance, their circle of auditors was to be for a long time very limited; and a greater impetus was given at this time to the development of learned studies by humanists who had been merely trained to ex-pound the Latin classics. At the end of the eleventh century Laon was the favourite resort of Englishmen with a taste for such learning;[5] but later the palm of scholarship was disputed between Paris and Chartres. Of Anglo-Norman scholars none are more attractive

---

[1] *Metalogicus*, i., § 4. St. Bernard, quoted by Manriquez, *Ann. Cisterc.*, i., 393.
[2] Neckam, *De Rerum Natura*, p. 41. John of Salisbury also (*Polyc.*, ii., § 19) be-lieves that there is something in astrology.
[3] Neckam, p. 294. [4] *Ibid.*, p. 42.
[5] *Liber De Miraculis S. Mariae Laudunensis*, ii., § 6 (Migne, *P. L.*, clvi.).

than Herbert Losinga, whose correspondence with his favourite pupils throws a flood of light on the range and methods of classical teaching in his day.   Losinga was filled with admiration for the classics; but he found it necessary to apologise for studies which were thought hardly compatible with his profession and rank.   He compares himself to the cock in the fable who had found a pearl upon a dunghill; even in the classics there were thoughts which deserved the attention of a serious mind.[1]   But humanism did not long remain upon the defensive.   Under the great teachers of the school of Chartres it became at once more scientific and more self-confident.   John of Salisbury, the most learned scholar of his day, does not hesitate to claim for classical learning a superiority over the science of the lawyer or the dialectician.[2]   The classics are to him, no less than to the scholars of the Renaissance, a fount of wisdom and a school of morals.   He would gladly have seen the classical curriculum of Chartres, in which he had himself been trained, adopted by all English schools.[3]   Unfortunately his hope was not to be fulfilled.   At the time when he was completing his studies the enthusiasm for law and logic thrust back all other studies into the background.   The translation of Aristotle's Organon by James of Venice in the year 1128, and the publication of Gratian's " Concordantia Discordantium Canonum " about 1141, were two events which heralded an intellectual revolution.   They indicate the triumph of the new studies.   Henceforth philology was relegated to the grammar-school; those who desired wealth and position took up the study of the Code and the Canons ; while the lover of knowledge for its own sake threw himself heart and soul on the lore of Universals and Particulars, and enlisted under the Realist or Nominalist flag.   Of the students of civil and canon law it is un- Lawyers necessary to say much.   They were practical men whose studies were chiefly important in connection with political disputes of which we have spoken and shall speak again.   The type of them is Thomas Becket, the busy official and diplomatist, who qualifies for higher stations by a year spent in the study of law at Bologna and Auxerre.   One serious attempt was made in Stephen's reign to found an English school of law; it was for this purpose that Archbishop Theobald summoned the Mantuan jurist Vacarius to Eng-

[1] *Epp.*, xxviii., xxx. (ed. Anstruther).
[2] *Polycraticus*, vii., § 9, etc.   [3] *Metalogicus*, i., § 24.

land. But even Vacarius taught with an eye to the controversies
of the moment; to defend ecclesiastical liberties against the unjust customs of the Crown, and to prove that these liberties were
founded upon natural right and reason. Vacarius was silenced,
and the books of the civil and canon law were proscribed. Though
his text-book, the *Liber Pauperum*, was afterwards popular in
Oxford, it was not until the reign of Henry II. that this famous
professor founded an English school.[1] We may therefore leave the
study of law, and turn rather to that of logic which came into
England from the schools of Paris. The French capital, with its
nascent university, was at this time the recognised mistress of the
west in theology and the liberal arts, and produced in Abelard
the greatest of medieval teachers in both subjects. There were

Schol-
astics

Englishmen among the pupils whom Abelard gathered round
himself at the Mont St. Geneviève.[2] Even John of Salisbury
came for a time beneath that potent spell, and though he lived
to witness and endorse the condemnation of his master's heresies,
could never speak of Abelard otherwise than with respectful admiration.[3] John of Salisbury transferred his attention in after life
to other fields of study; but some of Abelard's English pupils
became, in their turn, professors of no mean reputation. Of these
the most distinguished was Master Robert, who set up a school
at Melun and counted among his pupils both Thomas Becket and
John of Salisbury; one of the first acts of Becket, when elevated
to the primacy was to obtain the see of Hereford for his sometime teacher. Less orthodox, but far renowned for subtlety, was
Master Adam, surnamed "the English Peripatetic," who taught
in the school of Petit Pont at Paris.[4] Of the paradoxes in which
he delighted some examples have been preserved by one of his English pupils. He had syllogisms to prove that whatever is known
is unknown; that the greater number is smaller than the less;
that the same statement may be both false and true; and many
other such curious conclusions.[5] These riddles have ceased to
interest; they lost their charm even in the life-time of their author.
But the importance of the new logic is not to be measured by the

---

[1] Liebermann, *Magister Vacarius* (*E. H. R.*, xi., pp. 305, 514). *Polycraticus*, viii.,
§ 22.   The teaching of Vacarius, in its political bearings, seems to be summarised in
Polycraticus, vii., § 20.   *Cf.* also Robert de Monte, *s.a.* 1149, and Gervase, ii., 384·
[2] Rashdall, i., p. 59.   [3] *Metalogicus*, i., §§ 10, 17.
[4] *Metalogicus*, iii., § 3; iv., § 3.   [5] Neckam, p. 302·

eccentricities of its teachers.   It was not entirely nor mainly concerned with quibbles; it gave a valuable training in the habits of
analysis and definition ; and if, when applied to the sciences, it led
men to as many errors as true conclusions, the fault lay in the
premises rather than the arguments.   For acuteness of reasoning
within narrow limits the medieval logicians have never been surpassed.   Their lives and their books are now a subject for the
antiquary much more than for the historian ; but the broad
results of their teaching are written large on every page of political
and social history.

It was inevitable that the new intellectual spirit should lead to
the organisation of intellectual training.   But in England new
schools were founded by slow degrees.   Those of which we hear
were connected with cathedrals, monasteries, and parish churches ;
in an important town there were usually one or two *magistri*
secured by authority in the possession of an exclusive privilege
which they jealously preserved.   The range of subjects which they
professed to teach was limited ; the schools were usually maintained
with the purpose of training clerks.   Buildings for the school were
supplied by the see or religious foundation with which it was
connected ; but the master was usually paid by the fees of the
scholars, and if a boy received his education gratis, it was at the
master's expense.[1]   For the ordinary layman education was regarded
as superfluous.   Gilbert of Sempringham took a different view and
founded a school for all the boys of the parish which he served.[2]
But the purpose of his school was quite as much to impose a quasi-
monastic discipline as to form the minds of his pupils by instruction.
Orthodoxy was not altogether hostile to education, but was always
on the alert to quarrel with " science falsely so-called ".   St.
Bernard went so far as to reprove an English Abbot for minute
studies in the Old Testament.   " Believe one who has tried," the
saint warns his misguided friend, " you will find more wisdom in woods
than in books.   Trees and stones will teach you what you cannot

English
Centres of
Learning

---

[1] Rashdall, i., 28 ; ii., 600.   Grant of Stephen to the cathedral school at Salisbury,
Sarum Charters, p. 8.   School at Winchester, John of Salisbury, *Epp.*, p. 21.
Schools of London mentioned in a writ of Henry of Winchester, Round, *Commune*,
p. 117 ; described by FitzStephen, p. 4.   For the schools of Huntingdon, Lincoln
and Canterbury see Miss Bateson's article in *E. H. R.*, xviii., p. 712.   The school
of Thetford in Herbert Losinga's *Epp.*, No. xxxvii.   Map, *De Nugis*, i., § 10, speaks
of the eagerness of villeins to obtain an education for their sons.
[2] See the *Life* by Miss R. Graham, p. 4.

learn from any master." [1] In Shakespeare's mouth the sentiment is profoundly true ; coming from a theologian who was unusually indifferent to nature it is simply a plea for intellectual inertia. The Church as a whole was of Bernard's way of thinking ; but the cross-fire of rival philosophic schools made it necessary that the Oxford armoury of apologetics should be overhauled. So arose at Oxford a school of commentators on the sacred texts. In the years 1117-1121 we find a Norman theologian, Theobald of Etampes, lecturing in Oxford, probably under the patronage of the canons of St. Frideswide, to classes of sixty or a hundred students. Shortly before the death of Henry I. we find that Theobald's work has been taken up and continued by two English teachers, Robert of Cricklade and Robert Pullein. Both were pillars of orthodoxy. The former became prior of St. Frideswide's. The latter was highly praised by St. Bernard and rose to be a Cardinal and Chancellor of the Curia. The mention of these distinguished teachers in a town, which had neither wealth nor political importance to commend it as a place of residence, suggests the existence of an organised academy ; and it is certain that Oxford became, in the course of the next fifty years, the chief seat of clerical education, and the centre of an intellectual activity which overstepped in all directions the limits imposed on the curriculum of the place by the earliest teachers.[2] Elsewhere than at Oxford there was higher teaching, of a more or less systematic kind, in the reign of Stephen. At Canterbury, under the aegis of Archbishop Theobald, we even find the germ of a University ;[3] and in London wandering teachers of note found a welcome which proves that the four existing grammar-schools were insufficient for the requirements of the students congregated in the capital.[4]

The   While the pioneers of the intellectual movement made their way
Monastic into the heart of English life without attracting general attention,
Movement the monastic movement was a subject for universal remark and almost universal admiration. The new orders which originated at the end of the eleventh and commencement of the twelfth century, as a protest against the commonplace virtues and comfortable

[1] *Bernardi Opera*, i., 110 (ed. Mabillon).
[2] See Prof. T. E. Holland in *E. H. R.*, vi., pp. 241 ff. A. G. Little, *ibid.*, vi., p. 565. Rashdall, ii., p. 334.
[3] Liebermann in *E. H. R.*, xi., p. 308.   [4] FitzStephen, p. 4.

MAP OF
ENGLAND & WALES
showing
THE MONASTIC REVIVAL
1124 - 1154

Statute Miles
0   20   40   60   80

Monasteries of Order   + LINCOLN
of Sempringham
Monasteries of Order   + Furness
of Savigni
Monasteries of Order   + Rievaulx
of Citeaux
Other Orders   + CARLISLE

Tweed

Melrose

Newminster+

CARLISLE+
+Holme
Cultram

Calder +

Rushen   Furness+

IRISH SEA

Jervaux+   Rievaulx
        Byland+
    Fountains+   +MALTON
                    WATTON+
        Sawley+   Meaux+
        Kirkstall+

Basingwerk   +Roche   BULLINGTON
                MATTERSEY+ SIXHILLS ALVINGHAM
                WELBECK+   +Louth Park
                 Rufford+ LINCOLN. Kirkstead
                NEWSTEAD+   +Revesby
                        HAVERHOLME+ CATTLEY
            Combermere   SEMPRINGHAM +Swineshead
                        +Vaudey
            Buildwas +Garendon
        Bordesley+ +Merevale   Sawtrey+
        +Cwmhir   +Combe +Pipewell
                    +Stoneleigh   Sibton+
            Dore+ Biddlesdon+
        Flaxley+   +Warden
    Whitland   CHICKSAND
                +Bruern +Woburn Coggeshall COLCHESTER
        Neath Tintern   DUNSTAPLE
            +Margam +Kingswood Thame Stratford
                        ST.BARTHOL. Langthorne
                +Stanley SMITHF+
                        ST.SAVIOURS
                        SOUTHWARK
                                +Boxley
                    Waverley+

        +Ford
    Buckfastleigh   Quarr
                CHRISTCHURCH

ENGLISH CHANNEL

routine of the Benedictines and the Cluniacs, entered England in the reign of Henry I. First came the missionaries of the Norman order of Savigny, founded by St. Vital of Mortain (1112). Their earliest English house was that of Furness (1124-7); fourteen others had been founded by the year 1147 when the Savigniacs merged themselves in the Cistercian order.[1] The Cistercians, whose second abbot, Stephen Harding (+ 1133), was an Englishman from Sherborne, were naturally quick to follow the example of their Norman brethren. Their pioneers were a band of monks from l'Aumône, in the diocese of Chartres, who founded an English house of the Cistercian rule at Waverley in 1129. A second mission, independent of the first and despatched by St. Bernard from Clairvaux, founded Rievaux abbey in 1131-2, with the assistance of Walter of Espec, a devout and wealthy Yorkshire baron. In 1132 a secession, from St. Mary's house at York, of Benedictine monks who desired to live under the strict Cistercian rule, led to the establishment of Fountains. From these three houses, and from those of Tintern (1131) and of Whitland (1140), which owed their rise to the bounty of the Welsh marchers, the Cistercian movement diffused itself through the British isles.[2] It was most popular in the north of England where religious houses of an older date were sparsely distributed, small, and insignificant. But sooner or later it affected every district; for it was the outcome of one of those mysterious and universal tides of enthusiasm which are the most salient feature of medieval history. The monastic ideal touched a sympathetic chord in the hearts of men whose daily life was one prolonged negation of the principles on which monasticism was based. William of Malmesbury scarcely exaggerates when he says that there was no wealthy man in England but thought shame of himself if he had not contributed to the building of a monastery. The Cistercians became rich through the gifts of the men who made and maintained the anarchy of Stephen's reign. They were countenanced and encouraged by Henry I., the most unromantic and calculating sovereign of his age.

To the extent of English sympathy with the monastic revival the history of the Order of Sempringham is a striking testimony.[3] In origin it was purely English, founded by the son of a Lincoln-

The Order of Sempringham

---

[1] For the Order of Savigni see *E. H. R.*, viii., pp. 668 ff.
[2] *E. H. R.*, viii., pp. 625 ff.   [3] Miss R. Graham, *Gilbert of Sempringham, passim.*

shire knight; its benefactors were drawn from the English baronage; and all its houses were established on English soil. The founder received a part of his education in French schools and was assisted by St. Bernard in the composition of his rule. But his work was spontaneously undertaken, and with the object of satisfying a real need of English society. Gilbert of Sempringham founded his first houses for the benefit of pious women who desired to turn their backs upon the world and yet were, for one reason or another, unable to enter nunneries of the older rules. To the female communities he added others of canons who were to act as chaplains and teachers; and the manual work connected with the estates was entrusted to lay brethren of menial station who embraced the celibate life, sometimes from genuine enthusiasm, more often as an escape from villeinage or poverty. The first house of the new rule was built about 1131, and by the time of Stephen's death no less than eleven had been called into existence. The rule, revised by St. Bernard, was sanctioned by Eugenius III. in 1147, and within the next half century the Gilbertines acquired an honourable reputation for the strictness of their discipline and the purity of their lives. When the founder died (1189) in extreme old age the order contained 700 canons and 1,500 sisters.

Tendencies of the Monastic Movement The order of Sempringham absorbed the merest fraction of the endowments which piety, or deference to the fashion of the hour, lavished upon the monasticism of twelfth century England. More than one hundred new foundations date from Stephen's reign, and about the same number from that of Henry II.[1] It was the century of the ascetic. Yet in the meridian of success the shadow of reaction is discernible; prosperity begot abuses which became the mark of stinging criticism. The seculars, with their jealousy of pretensions to superior holiness, the lawyers, with their chilling common sense and keen eye for the material motive, detected in the Cistercians some faults, less gross perhaps than those of the old-fashioned orders, but not less odious or less corrosive of the inner life. Avarice was a common charge. Ranulf Glanvill, the Chief Justiciar, said that never in the course of long experience had he seen more shameless forgeries than those by which the White Monks were accustomed to strengthen a defective title;[2] nor were they

[1] Howlett, *Chronicles of Stephen*, etc., i., p. xiii.
[2] Giraldus, *Opera*, iv., 244.

much more scrupulous in their pursuit of legacies.   They thought
it no crime to remove a neighbour's boundary in the interests of a
saint; they depopulated thriving townships to enlarge their sheep-
walks; they appropriated the tithes of parish churches and had
been known to use the sacred building for a sheep-fold or a fuller's
shop.   Not less circumstantial are the complaints of spiritual pride.
"They are proud of their pale faces," says one writer, "and sighing
is with them a fine art; at any moment they are prepared to shed
a flood of tears.   They walk about with downcast heads and half-
closed eyes.   They move at a snail's pace muttering prayers the
while.   They cultivate a ragged and dirty appearance, humbling
themselves that they may be exalted." [1]   There were in fact, within
the medieval church, differences of ideal and practice as striking as
any which can be drawn between the Laudian and the Puritan, the
Anglican and Methodist.   The new orders were the Puritans and
Methodists of the twelfth century.

Modern criticism, regarding the movement from a social point
of view, has detected other evils in monasticism.   The religious
revival transferred no inconsiderable portion of the national wealth
to corporations which claimed the privilege of special law courts and
of a special law.   To some extent it diminished the productive power
of society, although it is true that the new orders were chiefly
recruited from the leisured classes.[2]   It weakened the discipline
of the national church, since the new monasteries were frequently
exempted from episcopal control and subject only to the Pope.
It entangled English churchmen in the ever narrower and more
material conflicts of the Papacy and Empire.   The Cistercians and
kindred orders, it is true, rendered some services to economic progress.   They reclaimed waste lands, although their critics say that
they only took the waste when nothing better was forthcoming.
They improved a number of useful arts and trades; they did
something for the preservation of the best books and the highest
studies then accessible to Europe.   But on the whole their activity
was prejudicial to material welfare and their spirit hostile to the

---

[1] John of Salisbury, *Polycraticus*, vii., § 21.   *Cf.* Giraldus, *Speculum Ecclesiae*,
and Map, *De Nugis, passim.*   The testimony of Giraldus is the more remarkable
because elsewhere he admits the virtues of the Cistercians (vi., 43).
[2] But the lay-brothers of the Gilbertine Order were largely drawn from the lower
classes.   Graham, *Gilbert of Sempringham*, pp. 12, 20.

free play of the intellect.[1] While encouraging by precept and example a profuse and indiscriminate charity they did more than any body of men before or since to sap the sense of social obligation, and the confidence in the possibilities of human societies, which are the cardinal virtues of the modern world and the only motive-springs of progress.

The Monastic Ideal
There was however a bright side to monasticism. The glorious ruins, by which alone the great foundations of the twelfth century are remembered, bear the stamp of a noble serenity and soaring hope which we can admire even though its essence is to us a riddle. Let it be granted that the position of the founders was paradoxical and inconsistent; that they started from a position of extreme individualism and ended by merging themselves in an institution more narrow and cramping than any of those composing the social life from which they turned away; that they postulated indifference to the goods of life as a fundamental principle for the guidance of the individual, and at the same time expected him to higgle, to canvass, to defraud, for the benefit of his fraternity. The inconsistency was gross, but failed to paralyse the inner life, because it was unconscious. The belief that the solitary walk with God is possible for man; the determination that no material obstacles should be allowed to stand between the weakest soul and God; the admission on the part of worldly men that there was a higher life beyond their ken, which they should promote in others even though they despaired of attaining it in their own persons; these are the feelings which dignify the movement; and realising these we can admire without a shade of pity the violent and almost theatrical scenes which they produced in the life of that day. The multitudes of weeping, praying, chanting, volunteers who drew the carts and shaped the stones and dug the foundations for a new monastery,[2] were too often enlisted in the service of an unknown God. Yet it was well that they should feel however remotely the existence of the divine, and believe, with however little personal experience, in the accessibility of God to man.

[1] " There is no evidence that the Cistercians in the twelfth century made any provision for secular education, nor would this have been consistent with their general policy " (Graham, " Intellectual Influence of Eng. Monasticism " in *Trans. R. Hist. Soc.*, xvii., pp. 42 ff. (new series) ; a most learned and valuable study).
[2] For the religious exaltation of the penitents of this time *v.* R. de Monte, p. 151, and the letter of a French abbot in Migne, *Patrol. Lat.*, clxxxi., col. 1707 ; also another letter, by the Abp. of Rouen in 1145, printed in Migne, *P. L.*, cxcii., col. 1127.

CHAPTER VII

THE BECKET CONTROVERSY

HENRY of Anjou ascended the throne with a fixed determina- Becket as
tion to ignore the predecessor upon whom, with some in- Chan-
justice, he laid the sole responsibility for nineteen years of anarchy. cellor
If he ever mentioned Stephen it was to call him a usurper; the
arrogant and unforgiving temper of Matilda, to whom the youth
owed his earliest lessons in the art of government, can be traced in
this and in some other features of his early policy.   He never extended his favour to those who had supported the dead king, but
crushed them if he could, and, if he could not, let them understand
that they were fortunate to keep their lands and titles.   Henry of
Blois, relegated, for the first time in his life to a position of obscurity, left England in profound chagrin; the earls of Stephen
nursed their offended dignity at a safe distance from the court.
But the old partisans of the Empress did not fare much better.
Nigel of Ely, it is true, was invited to reorganise the Exchequer
which his uncle, Bishop Roger, had virtually created; the advice of
the Primate received the respectful attention which was due to his
invaluable services.   But the King's private ear was monopolised
by new and unknown men; and he was an enigma to those by
whose exertions he had been elevated to the throne.   The little
that they knew of him suggested gloomy apprehensions.   They
saw for themselves that he was rash and riotous and unconventional.
They expected, from his record in Normandy and Anjou, to find
him the slave of passion and intolerant of all restraining influences.
He gave the impression of volcanic energy.   There was little doubt
that he would make his mark, but much doubt whether his reign
would be for the good of Church or State.   Rumour said that he
disliked ecclesiastical pretensions, and the language of his friends
gave countenance to the report.

The Archbishop could not but feel that the Church had played, in the last reign, a part too prominent for her own safety. To provide her with an intercessor in the royal councils was his first anxiety. He obtained his wish. A few months after the coronation his sometime servant Thomas Becket was raised, through his influence, to the Chancellorship.[1] The Chancellor's position was a great one. He ranked as the first subject in the kingdom. He controlled the ecclesiastical patronage of the Crown, and influenced, in the interests of the King, the canonical elections to bishoprics and abbacies. He also administered all vacant or escheated baronies and the wardships of the Crown. He was the custodian of the Great Seal, and no official document of importance could pass without his approbation. He had the privilege of appearing, with or without a summons, at every sitting of the royal council.[2] The office gave Becket unrivalled opportunities of moulding the impressionable mind of his young master. Henry's senior by some years, he was not too old or staid to share the king's diversions. The two became inseparable. They hawked and hunted together; they bandied jests and romped like schoolboys in the public streets, to the no small astonishment and scandal of grave courtiers. Few detected under this outward mask of levity the subtle intellect of the jurist and reformer, or the iron determination of the future martyr. Henry had so far lived in the shadow of his mother and of too-

Becket's Early Life

powerful supporters; the youth of Becket had been spent in subordinate capacities. The Chancellor came of a respectable but undistinguished stock. His father, a small Norman landowner, had settled in London to become a trader; and, though at one time prosperous enough to hold the sheriffdom of Middlesex, had fallen upon reverses and ended his life in straitened circumstances.[3] The young Thomas began life with no equipment but the education received in a city grammar-school and in the schools of Paris. For a time he served a wealthy kinsman as a clerk and keeper of accounts. Later he entered the employment of Archbishop Theobald, who came from the same Norman village as his father; and it was thus that the youth obtained his opportunity. More than

---

[1] *Materials*, ii., 304. The date of Becket's appointment is 1155 ; see the charters cited in Eyton's Itinerary.

[2] FitzStephen, pp. 20 ff.

[3] FitzStephen, p. 14. *Materials*, v., 515. Grim, p. 359.

once in Stephen's reign he went, for the Archbishop, on confidential missions to the Curia. Here he won golden opinions, and did good service to the Angevins by persuading Eugenius not to recognise Eustace as the heir of Stephen.[1] Subsequently he qualified by a year spent in legal studies at Bologna and Auxerre, for the office of Archdeacon of Canterbury (1154). From this obscure though responsible position he was called in 1155 to the highest office in the kingdom. He rose to the level of his new situation; and whatever might be said as to their want of personal decorum, the efficiency with which he and his master conducted the administration cannot be disputed. The demesne lands which had passed into private hands, by the inconsiderate grants of Stephen or through the usurpations of the lawless, were resumed. The last of the unlicensed castles were destroyed. The Flemish mercenaries were paid off and dismissed from the country, or allowed to settle in the Pembroke colony. Those of Stephen's party who assumed a defiant attitude towards his successor were threatened with war and soon realised the need of buying pardon by the surrender of their castles and a considerable portion of their lands. Order was re-established in every corner of the country; the lands which had fallen out of cultivation were again brought under the plough, and the prosperity of the boroughs rapidly revived.[2] The Chancellor in private converse with his clerical friends assured them that work of this kind filled him with weariness and disgust.[3] But his instincts were sounder than the theories of duty with which the conventions of the age and his profession had saddled him. Though pressed by Theobald to return to his archdeaconry he easily allowed himself to be dissuaded from this course by the King.

Reorganisation of the Government

Side by side with the work of restoring settled order other projects of a less urgent kind, some useful, others the natural but mischievous outcome of the King's antecedents, were raised in swift succession. Young though he was, Henry could not rest until he had settled the succession to the crown. In April, 1155, a Great Council held at Wallingford promised fidelity to the king's eldest son William, or, should he predecease his father, to his brother, the infant Henry. Later in the year another assembly met to

Early Projects of the King

[1] FitzStephen, p. 16. Gervase.   [2] Gervase, i., 160. R. de Monte.
[3] See his correspondence with Theobald in *Joan. Sarisb. Epp.*, i., 95, etc. Also *Mat.*, ii., 305.

discuss a plan for conquering Ireland and giving it to the King's youngest brother, William of Anjou. Adrian IV., the only Englishman who has ever occupied the Papal chair, was persuaded to sanction Henry's plan, for which a double justification was forthcoming in the heterodoxy of the Irish nation and in the claim, which the Pope founded upon the Donation of the Emperor Constantine, to lordship over all the islands of the western seas.[1] But it was found advisable to postpone the attack on Ireland, partly owing to the opposition of the Empress-mother, who perhaps realised more clearly than her son the difficulties which would have to be surmounted ; partly because of disputes which arose between Henry and his second brother Geoffrey. The latter, under the terms of their father's will, was entitled to receive Anjou and Touraine whenever Henry should succeed in making good his claim upon the English throne. Geoffrey stood upon his rights; but Henry took refuge in the plea that he had never given his consent to this part of the will. In the summer of 1156 the aggrieved Geoffrey endeavoured to raise the Angevins against his brother; but the war was over almost as soon as begun. Geoffrey, beaten at every point, was considered fortunate to receive, in discharge of his claims, a single castle and a pension of £1,000 ; as a further solatium he was allowed to accept the vacant county off Nantes which the Bretons offered him in the next year. The next thought of the King was to conciliate the injured Louis VII., whose friendship would be an ample security against Angevin or Norman rebellions. A marriage was suggested between Prince Henry, who by the death of his brother William (1156) had already become the heir to the English crown, and the infant daughter whom his second wife had lately borne to Louis. Strange as the plan must seem when we remember that the bridegroom's mother was the divorced wife of the bride's father, it was accepted by the easy-going Louis, who promised to restore the Norman Vexin on the consummation of the marriage. Outwardly all was friendship and good will between the rivals. But one small incident proved how hollow was the reconciliation. Henry in his character of Count of Anjou, demanded recognition as the hereditary seneschal of France. It was

---

[1] R. de Monte, *s.a.* 1155. M. H. G., vi., 403. For the Bull *Laudabiliter* see the Appendix. We have the best of evidence to prove that some such privilege was granted. *Metalog.,* iv., § 42.

a great office, the most important which Louis had it in his power
to bestow; the holder might well aspire to some such position as
that which the Mayor of the Palace had occupied in Merovingian
times.   Louis admitted the justice of the claim.   But he also took
care to destroy the importance of the office.   He recognised in the
Angevin an ambition which it was dangerous to gratify and dangerous to rebuke; but he trusted for safety to that cunning with which
nature usually endows the weaker party.

The extent of Henry's ambitions was a problem to his own age   Ambitions
and has remained a problem to posterity.   He was the ruler of a   of Henry
hybrid Empire; nothing could be more artificial than the tie which   II.
bound England to Normandy, unless it were that which Henry had
himself created between Normandy and Aquitaine; and he was
drawn in different directions by the discrepant interests of the three
mutually suspicious nationalities over which he ruled.   As Duke
of Normandy he inherited unsettled claims and running feuds
in northern France; as Duke of Aquitaine he had principally to
consider questions affecting the Pyrenees and Languedoc and the
upper basin of the Loire.   In both capacities he was divided
between his natural cupidity and the respect for feudal law which
common prudence inculcated.   He coveted the lands of the French
Crown; but he dared not set the example of unprovoked attack
upon a suzerain.   His instinct led him in the direction of boundless
conquest; prudence restricted him to the prosecution of colourable
claims, to a policy of rounding off and knitting up his territories by
furtive annexations of a county here, a city there.   But these petty
claims he pursued with the ferocious legalism of a Shylock, to whom
his pound of flesh is chiefly valuable because it is torn from the
body of a rival.   He hated the kingdom which he did not dare to
crush.   He was prepared to go as far with the dismemberment of
France as his own safety would allow.   How far this was he did
not live to show.   For he was an English king as well as a French
feudatory, and the problems of England grew upon him as his mind
matured.   At first he regarded his island kingdom chiefly as a mine
of treasure from which to draw the revenues for continental wars.
But it was not for nothing that he had been born the grandson of
Henry I., the Lion of Justice.   From the first he understood that a
kingdom is lucrative only when it is well administered; from the first
his standard of administration was a high one.   Hence he attacked

at the first opportunity a number of problems which his predecessors had left untouched or incompletely settled; the question of
Scotland, the question of Wales, the frauds of fiscal officers, the
defects of royal justice, the encroachments of clerical and feudal
courts. These were to be preliminary labours; their completion
would leave him free to pursue the continental schemes which he
inherited from Norman and Aquitanian predecessors. But time
passed without bringing him to the end of the preliminaries; they
became more difficult than he had originally expected; they also
became more interesting. The slumbering love of justice was
aroused in him. He did not abandon the dreams of his youth;
but he resigned himself to their postponement. Come what might
he would see the land of his adoption rightly ordered before he
entered on a wider sphere of action. There was in fact no mechani-
cal consistency about his plans. They grew and changed; the
means became an end; what had been the end became a distant
dream; and at the last the stress of circumstances made it impossible to pick and choose his course. He did not as he would, but as
he could; he fought blindly and for bare existence.

Wales,
Scotland,
Toulouse
But at the time of which we speak the ball was at his feet. He
could take his own path; and he was Angevin enough, as yet, to
turn his back on England. He did what seemed enough for the
reform of English administration. He also settled, for the time
being, with the Welsh and Scots. Early in his reign he seized the
opportunity of King David's death to repudiate the concessions
which he had made to Scotland while still at feud with Stephen;
the boy-king Malcolm was compelled to surrender Northumberland
and Cumberland as the price of friendship with his powerful
southern neighbour. The North-Welsh were about the same time
attacked in their mountains by an army which Henry led in person; [1]
the English fortresses west of the Conway were repaired, and Owain
prince of North Wales was forced to make a profession of homage.
But as soon as these necessary precautions had been taken the
King threw himself with zest into plans for extending his foreign
possessions, and squandered for this purpose sums which could
ill be spared from English needs. His wife had a shadowy claim
to the county of Toulouse,[2] and against Toulouse war was ac-

[1] R. de Monte. Giraldus, vi., 137.
[2] R. de Monte, p. 201, states the claim.

cordingly declared. The Chancellor, who already in the quarrel with Geoffrey had shown himself a war-minister of resource, left nothing to be desired in the energy of his preparations and the fertility of his devices. Already in the reign of Henry I. it had become a general practice to let ecclesiastics compound at a fixed rate for the knight-service due from their estates, and the same privilege had been sometimes allowed to mesne tenants. This system of *scutage* (shield-money) was now extended. Only the lay barons were called upon to render personal service against Toulouse; all churches and all mesne tenants compounded at the rate of two marks on the knight's fee; and the money so raised was employed in hiring mercenaries. It proved insufficient and with the Chancellor's assent, if not at his suggestion, the deficiency was made good in part by the ordinary expedients of tallaging the towns and Jews, and partly by an arbitrary tax or *donum* levied on ecclesiastical lands.[1] The complaints of the clergy were bitter. But the impost was paid; and early in the summer of 1159 Henry marched southward from Normandy at the head of a great host. Cahors was taken without difficulty; but Louis of France came to the rescue of Toulouse. The count was the husband of the French King's sister and the only southern vassal of consequence on whom Louis could depend. When Henry arrived before Toulouse it was to learn that Louis was already within the walls. Becket pressed his master to assault; it was never the Chancellor's habit to respect the obligations of conventional morality when they stood between him and his object. But Henry shrank from the idea of an open attack upon the person of his feudal suzerain. He contented himself with investing the town and plundering the adjacent country, a course which served no other purpose than that of masking his retreat. He soon withdrew from personal share in the operations, leaving them to the Chancellor and the Constable. Towards the end of the year a truce was concluded with Toulouse which ripened into lasting peace; and Henry began to lay his plans for vengeance upon Louis. It was not hard to find treacherous vassals and subjects of dispute along the extended frontier which separated the territory of Louis from the Angevin possessions; in

---

[1] *Becket Materials*, v., 378. Stubbs, *Benedictus*, ii., p. xcv. Round, *F. E.*, p. 225, and *Antiquity of Scutage*, pp. 4-7. P. and M., *H. E. L.*, i., pp. 245 ff., gives (mainly from Madox) the most accurate account of scutage.

1160-1 there were discursive operations on both sides and two considerable forces manœuvred in the Vexin without coming to close quarters. In these alarms and excursions the Chancellor was again a leading figure. He brought to the English host 700 knights of his own household, 1,200 others whom he had hired for the campaign, and 4,000 sergeants. His knights dined at his own table and received 3s. per diem for the charges of their squires and horses. They formed the *corps d'elite* of the army and the Chancellor rode in full panoply at their head. He distinguished himself by meeting in single combat and unhorsing a French knight, which was perhaps the most remarkable incident of the campaign.

Becket made Archbishop, 1162

In the middle of these events occurred the death of the Primate Theobald. His last petition to the King was for a successor who should be worthy of the see of Canterbury.[1] The King, after some months of deliberation, decided that no fitter person could be found than Becket. With some difficulty the electors were persuaded to accept his nominee. Alone among the bishops the austere Gilbert Foliot of Hereford protested [2] against the choice, for such a position, of a man who was not a monk, nor in priest's orders, and whose antecedents gave every reason to anticipate that he would gladly sacrifice the Church to the interests of the King. No doubt these objections were echoed in secret by many who publicly assented to the King's demand. But in the end Becket was elected by the almost unanimous voice of those who had any claim to be consulted.

The Church-Courts

There can be little doubt that Henry was influenced, in his selection of a primate, by the anticipation of conflicts with the Church. Events had been leading to that issue for some time past, in spite of the personal friendship between the King and Theobald.[3] The growing claims of the church-courts and their notorious abuses were a standing challenge to the secular authority. When the Conqueror separated the lay-courts and courts-Christian he restricted the latter to those cases which touched the cure of souls. This definition proved more elastic than he had anticipated. The courts of the Church showed the aggressive tendency which is

[1] *Joan. Sarisb. Epp.*, i., 57.
[2] FitzStephen, p. 36. Foliot (*Materials*, v., 524) afterwards alleged that the election caused general dissatisfaction.
[3] *Materials*, iii., 43.

common to all legal tribunals, and showed it in an altogether
exceptional degree.   To some extent their encroachments were
encouraged by the laity.   The canon law was more scientific, more
comprehensive, not infrequently more equitable, than the uncouth
tangle of precedent and custom by which the royal courts were
governed.   Suitors, desirous of benefiting by the wisdom of
Justinian or the Roman Curia, readily admitted that the breach
of an ordinary contract might be considered as a form of perjury
and therefore within the cognisance of an archdeacon's court.   But
there were other cases in which the pretensions of the courts-
Christian were more objectionable and dangerous.   The Church
claimed the exclusive cognisance of all disputes affecting the
property of a religious house or see or benefice.   She also claimed
all crimes committed by clerks or against them.

In this criminal jurisdiction lay the gravest evil.   The category Criminous
of clerks included many who neither exercised nor aspired to the Clerks
functions of a priest.   It included the learned professions ; it
included the servants and minor officials of all ecclesiastical institutions.   Nothing was easier than to obtain consecration as a
clerk in minor orders.   Little or no education was required ; there
was no real attempt to examine the moral character of the postu-
lant ; and the obligations which orders entailed were not sufficiently onerous to outweigh the obvious advantages.   A clerk
could not marry ; that was the only serious disability to which he
was subjected.   On the other hand a crime however heinous, if
committed by a clerk, could only be judged by the courts-Christian ;
and the worst penalties which such a court could inflict were degradation and imprisonment.   The clerk once degraded from his
orders lay at the mercy of the Curia Regis for any future crime ;
but degradation was a penalty rarely inflicted, since the Church was
reluctant to admit that the sacred office, once conferred, could be
taken away for any offence short of heresy ; and the bishops avoided
sentences of imprisonment because they would then be at the
expense of making prisons and maintaining the prisoners.[1]   Generally
speaking any culprit could make his peace, upon conviction, by a
penance and the payment of a fine.   And it was suspected that
the forms of ecclesiastical procedure made it unreasonably difficult
to procure conviction.   There were two stages in the trial of a

---

[1] *Materials*, v., 150.   W. Neubrig., ii., § 16.

criminal charge before a spiritual judge. In the first the evidence brought by the accuser was marshalled and sifted; secondly, if the evidence was regarded as inconclusive, the accused had the right of clearing himself by the oath of compurgators. The law of evidence, as understood by the Church, was comparatively scientific, and many accusations which the untutored common sense of a lay judge would have regarded as completely proven were rejected as baseless in the courts-Christian. As for compurgation, it was not the mere farce which we sometimes imagine; it did not enable a defendant to escape the consequences of proven guilt; men against whom there had been insufficient evidence sometimes failed to obtain the needful number of witnesses to character.[1] In point of procedure the Church-courts were more efficient than their enemies allowed. But their justice not infrequently miscarried. And the great grievance, that the guilty even if convicted were insufficiently punished, was undeniably true.

Appeals to Rome

The encroachments upon civil jurisdiction though less obviously dangerous were such as no far-sighted statesman could view without alarm. For a civil case which had once been drawn into the ecclesiastical forum could always be carried to Rome or to a court of special commissioners nominated by Rome. It was not merely that appeals were possible. The pope had the right of stopping a case at any stage of its hearing in an inferior court, and calling it up to his own. Such at least had become the customary rule in Stephen's time, and the correspondence of Archbishop Theobald points to the conclusion that litigants caught at every opening for an appeal or evocation.[2] The rule of the Conqueror that no case ought to go to Rome without the royal licence was simply disregarded; and great was the indignation in orthodox circles in the year 1159 when Henry, announcing that such unlicensed appeals were an offence against the royal dignity, proceeded to make an example of Theobald's official, John of Salisbury, for permitting litigants to raise them. The unfortunate John protested, with much truth, that the practice was not of his invention; that he had merely done what was expected of him by the Primate and the bishops. It was

[1] The limits within which compurgation was allowed may be gathered from cases which are reported in *Materials*, ii., 374; iii., 264, and in *Joan. Sarisb. Epp.*, i., 171.
[2] See the early part of John of Salisbury's correspondence. He was Theobald's official. The evil was causing protests as early as 1156. See Jaffé-Loëwenfeld, *Regesta Pontificum*, Nos. 10, 128; 10, 139.

to no purpose. He became the scapegoat of his superiors and went into exile. He deserves our pity for he had been unjustly punished. But we cannot wonder that the King should be indignant at an innovation which taxed England for the benefit of Roman tribunals, and brought many cases touching the royal prerogative or profit under the cognisance of a distant, and it might be, an unfriendly power.

Various complaints and scandals had recently attracted Henry's attention to the abuses of ecclesiastical tribunals. Complaints of extortion and corruption on the part of clerical judges were frequent and probably well founded, since the average archdeacon was a man of no position and indifferent character, who farmed his court at a fixed rent, and made a profit by exacting enormous fees and fines. In 1158 a citizen of Scarborough petitioned for the royal assistance against a certain archdeacon, who had blackmailed him by repeated threats of prosecuting his wife on charges of adultery, although there was in fact no evidence against her. The King referred the matter to the Archbishop of the northern province expecting that the archdeacon, if found guilty, would be handed over to the royal officers for punishment. To his astonishment he found that the Archbishop's court denied the right of the lay power to punish the archdeacon. The king appealed to Theobald, but foreign affairs diverted his attention before he received his Primate's answer and for the time the matter was allowed to drop; though not without an angry remark on the King's part that the archdeacons of England extorted annually from his subjects more than the sum total of his revenue.[1] The question of criminous clerks had come before him even earlier. At the commencement of his reign he had wished to try an archdeacon of York who was charged with having poisoned William FitzHerbert, the Archbishop of York ; and he had been much aggrieved when the Church claimed the jurisdiction and acquitted the accused. In this case the verdict was probably a just one. Charges of poisoning were recklessly advanced upon the slighest evidence ; the reasons for the acquittal of the archdeacon are on record and appear to be conclusive.[2] But other cases were constantly occurring in which

Begin-nings of the Dis-pute

---

[1] *Materials*, iii., 44. On December 25, 1159, the King issued a decree " ut nullus decanus aliquam personam accusaret sine testimonio vicinorum " (R. de Monte).
[2] John of Salisbury was the judge, and reports the case in *Epp.*, i., 171.

flagrant guilt escaped without punishment or with insufficient punishment; and it is probable that the king's plans for enforcing stricter justice had already begun to assume a settled shape.

Becket sides with his Order

If however he counted on Becket's assistance he had miscalculated. The new Archbishop was no timeserver. He warned the King that in future their views and interests were likely to diverge; he took the first opportunity of severing his connection with the State by the resignation of the Chancellorship.[1] It is difficult to pronounce on a character about which con emporaries disagreed so sharply; but we may fairly conjecture that Becket was one of those men whose thirst for approbation makes them self-deceivers; who see what is expected of them in any position to which they attain, and instinctively set themselves to realise that ideal without endeavouring to test it by their private judgments. Such men are far from being vulgar hypocrites; they pursue the course which they believe to be right; but they pursue it at first from interested motives, afterwards from habit or the passion for consistency. They may be compared to an artist whose skill in producing an admirable effect is greater than his power of appreciating the same effect in the work of other men. They know how to excite admiration without altogether realising the value and the limitations of the qualities by which that admiration is secured.

Becket became an exemplary Archbishop according to the standard of the age. In his charities, in his penances, in his attention to the offices and ceremonies of the Church, he erred, if anything, in the direction of excess. He who had been a man of the world and of affairs became at one stroke an ascetic and a student. In one respect he did not change. He showed all his old aptitude for business, and attended to the estates of his see with the same care which he had formerly shown in administering the resources of the nation. His household, to the scandal of old-fashioned piety, was filled with lawyers, whose days were spent in discovering and substantiating claims which had long been suffered to lie dormant. Collisions with the most powerful and favoured of the barons were the natural consequence. But the Archbishop had no respect for persons. From small and great alike he demanded restitution, enforcing the demand with the threat of spiritual censures. In vain the King appealed to the

[1] Bosham, 181. Gervase, i., 174.

customs of the Conqueror, by which no baron might be excommunicated without the royal licence; in vain the Archbishop's
intimates pressed for greater moderation.   From compromise of any
kind Becket was constitutionally averse; nor would he admit for a
moment that any custom could limit the power of the Church to
loose and bind.   With the question of the ecclesiastical courts he
dealt in an equally unflinching spirit.   In 1163 a canon of Lincoln
was acquitted, in the teeth of the evidence, on a charge of homicide.   An itinerant justice, dissatisfied with the bishop's finding,
endeavoured to re-open the case in his own court.   But the canon,
in the language of Becket's biographer, "being a man of high
birth, overwhelmed with grief and indignation attacked the judge
with abuse ".[1]   The sheriff complained to the King, and the King
to the Archbishop; Henry demanded that the canon should be
made to answer in the King's court first for the homicide and
secondly for his insults to the King's representative.   Becket opposed both demands.   He would not allow the question of the
homicide to be re-opened in any way; as for the contempt of
court, he insisted that the Church should be the judge.   The
canon was sentenced to pay a heavy sum in alms to the poor, and
to give an ample apology to the sheriff.   But neither the manner
of the trial nor the verdict suited Henry's wishes.   He had intended that the canon should be hanged, and he openly accused
the Archbishop of perverting justice.   Becket riposted with homilies
upon the duties of a King and the rights of an ecclesiastic; the
quarrel rose to such a pitch that he and Henry no longer met in
person, but exchanged their recriminations through intermediaries.
In a council held at Woodstock they came to an open quarrel on The
a trifling fiscal question.   The King proposed to appropriate to Debate
the treasury a land-tax called the sheriff's aid [2] which that officer stock
had hitherto received as his fee for holding the courts of shire and
hundred.   Becket constituted himself the champion of the sheriffs
and declared that Church lands should not pay a penny of the aid,

---

[1] The judge in question was Simon FitzPeter, a justice in eyre for Bedfordshire
(FitzStephen, p. 45).   *Cf.* Grim, p. 374.   Other cases of protection afforded to criminous clerks in Bosham, 264, and FitzStephen, *l.c.*

[2] Not the Danegeld, as Mr. Round has shown, *F. E.*, p. 497.   The *auxilium
vicecomitis* is mentioned in the Red Book of the Exchequer, pp. 768, 774-7, as a
sum for which the sheriffs account to the Exchequer.   It is mentioned from time
to time in the manorial extents of the thirteenth and fourteenth centuries.   *Cf.*
Monasticon, i., 308; and Ramsay, *Angevin Empire*, p. 38.

except to those who were lawfully entitled to receive it. He carried the assembly with him, and the King with a bad grace withdrew the proposition. It was a new experience for Henry to be brow-beaten in debate; and it may be that irritation had its share in determining the King's next step. A few months later he held another Council at Westminster and proposed to amend the law respecting clerks accused of crime. He did not ask that they should be tried before a lay tribunal; but that the bishops should try them in the presence of a royal officer; and that the accused, if convicted, should be first degraded from his orders, and then surrendered to the secular arm for further punishment. The canon law furnished some slight grounds for supposing that this had been the custom of the church in earlier times, and it was to the canons that the King appealed in justification. Becket however at once produced a rule prohibiting the infliction of two punish-ments for one offence. Degradation was, he argued, a sufficient penalty for any crime; the lay power might punish the second

The Con-
stitutions
of Claren-
don, 1164

offence if it pleased; but of the first the Church alone ought to have cognisance.[1] The King fell back on another argument. He asked for no more than the rights which had belonged to his pre-decessors. Were the bishops willing to recognise the "ancestral customs of the kingdom"? Unprepared to discuss the question of historic fact, but in perfect agreement with the attitude of their ecclesiastical superior, they returned the evasive answer that they would respect the customs "saving their order". The King quitted the assembly in a rage. Instead of arguing further with the bishops he began to besiege the Pope with requests for a confirmation of the customs. Alexander III., true to the cautious principles of Roman diplomacy, avoided a direct answer. The moment was not one at which he could afford a breach with Henry. The strife between Papacy and Empire had lately revived in an acute form. Frederic Barbarossa had committed himself to the support of an anti-pope; Alexander was an exile in France; and all his hopes of restoration depended on the support of the French and English Kings. Ac-cordingly he sent the Abbot of l'Aumône to mediate between the Archbishop and the King. Becket received from the envoy an

[1] The King's proposal is given most clearly in Diceto, i., 313; his appeal to the canon law in *Materials*, iii., 266. Compare Maitland in *E. H. R.*, vii., p. 225. Becket's arguments will be found in *Materials*, iii., 268 ff.; v., 271.

assurance that nothing was required of him beyond a formal assent
to the ancient customs; that the King, though mortified by his
rebuff at Westminster, was prepared to acquiesce in defeat if he
could do so without loss of dignity; and that the law relating to
criminous clerks should not be changed.[1]   On this understanding
Becket yielded.   He was then informed that his acceptance of the
customs must be as public as his previous repudiation; and a
Council was summoned to Clarendon to witness his submission
(Jan. 25, 1164).   But when the Council met and the King's
conditions were unfolded, Becket discovered that his promise was
to be construed more strictly than he had been led to expect.
The King opened the proceedings by producing a list of the
customs relating to the church which he regarded as ancient and
necessary to be observed.   These Constitutions, as they were
afterwards to be called, embodied, not only the recent proposals
touching criminous clerks, but also many other articles which
were equally offensive to the defenders of ecclesiastical liberties.
Disputes respecting advowsons were henceforth to be tried in the
King's court.   Bishops and beneficed clergy might not leave the
kingdom without a royal licence.   Except when the King directed
otherwise, no ecclesiastical case should go beyond the court of the
Archbishop to any higher tribunal.   No suits relating to ordinary
contracts might be heard in the courts-Christian.   Of these rules
some were really old, and had been admitted by the Church in
the days of William I.; but the proposed method of dealing with
criminous clerks was a daring innovation.   It is true that for
treason and for breaches of the forest law the clergy had long
been liable to the King's court;[2] and in Normandy the Duke
had sometimes intervened when the sentence of a bishop or archdeacon seemed grossly inadequate to the offender's guilt.   But
for the regular punishment of criminous clerks by the secular arm
the King could find no precedent.   He relied, as it would seem,
entirely upon an ambiguous text in the *Decretum*, which had hitherto
received an interpretation very different from that which he proposed.   Becket, however, was not disposed to rest his case on
custom or the letter of the law.   He took a higher ground.   Rules,
he said, however ancient are of no validity when they conflict with

[1] Grim, p. 378.
[2] See the decrees of the synod of Lillebonne in 1080 (Orderic, ii., 318).

natural rights and the divine order of the universe. The privileges
of the clergy were inalienable, and their persons sacrosanct. No
law, no agreement, could justify the secular authority in punishing
with death or mutilation those who had been consecrated to God's
service, whose hands had performed the eucharistic miracle, whose
lips had pronounced the words of life and death. " Touch not
mine anointed " was his final argument ; nor were the bishops who
listened to his argument unwilling to count themselves and him
as prophets. The King and the laity, though worsted in the war
of words, were unconvinced; and the bishops found that their
pretensions would be roughly controverted. On the third day of
the Council, as they were debating in a separate chamber, the
lay-barons entered and intimated that those who withstood the
wishes of the King would do so at their peril. Foliot, bishop of
London, was for standing firm against this lawless intimidation;
some of the bolder spirits took his side. But, to their consternation,
Becket the Archbishop yielded. " It is the King's will," he is reported to
gives way have said, " that I should perjure myself. I will commit the crime
which he requires and do penance for it in the future as best I may." [1]
At this remarkable change of front the opposition collapsed, and the
bishops in a body agreed to accept the Constitutions. If any of them
did so with the mental reservations of the Primate, the fact had no
influence on their future conduct. Fear, if not honesty, kept them
true to their word. There is something to be said for Becket.
We can hardly suppose that the threats of the barons were made
without the approbation of the King ; and duplicity is a legitimate,
if not particularly admirable, weapon with which to meet superior
force. A man of the true martyr's temperament would have held
firm : and probably this course, besides being more honourable,
would have better served the cause which Becket had at heart.
When all was over Becket felt heartily ashamed of his own conduct.
He refused to seal the Constitutions, and the King refrained from
forcing this last humiliation either upon him or upon the other
bishops. As he rode away from Clarendon the Archbishop was
sharply reproved by zealous followers, who could afford to despise dangers against which they were protected by their obscurity.
He admitted his fault and, by way of a public penance, suspended
himself from the service of the altar, until the Pope commanded

[1] *Materials*, v., 527.

him to resume his priestly functions for fear of causing scandal. It was probably at the same time that Becket received Alexander's dispensation [1] authorising him to disregard any promise which he might have made in derogation of ecclesiastical liberties or the rights of the Roman See. He had never intended to do otherwise, but he could now repudiate his oath in the comfortable assurance that Rome was on his side.

A breach of faith, in one form or another, the King had prob-ably expected from the first; he had known Becket long enough to be aware that the Archbishop never admitted a defeat. When he learned that Alexander, notwithstanding the forlorn position of the Holy See, refused to approve the Constitutions, it was only natural to suspect the secret influence of the Archbishop. Suspicion be-came certainty when Becket was discovered in the act of taking flight for France. The sailors of the ship in which the Archbishop was embarking detected his identity and refused to take so dangerous a passenger on board. A little later the Archbishop came to court with apologies for his fruitless escapade. The King asked with a sneer if the kingdom was not large enough to hold them both. He spoke calmly, but it was evident that his irritation was profound. Becket retired from court with indefinable forebodings. For these he had only too much reason, although the attack, when it came, took an unexpected form. A certain John the Marshal, a tenant of the see of Canterbury, who had been non-suited in Becket's court, seized the opportunity of the Archbishop's disgrace to impugn the judgment in the Curia Regis. Becket received a summons to appear and answer the charge of denying justice to his tenant. He replied by sending proxies to answer in his place, but offered no explanation of his own failure to appear. Henry assumed that the Archbishop disdained to appear before a secular tribunal, and summoned him to answer for the contempt of the royal court. A Great Council, held at Northampton, tried the case between the King and Becket. But Becket, to the King's chagrin, escaped with no worse penalty than a moderate amercement. For once Henry allowed himself to outstep, not only the limits of fair-dealing, but the letter of the law. On the spur of the moment,

The Council of Nor-thampton, Oct., 1164

---

[1] *Materials*, v., 84. Becket also maintained that his promise, being given " in bona fide, sine dolo malo, et legitime," could not be construed as a surrender of Church privileges (*Mat.*, iii., 66).

without the slightest warning of his purpose, he called the Archbishop to account for the sums, amounting to more than £20,000,
which had passed through his hands in his capacity of Chancellor.
Becket protested, probably with truth, that he had been freed from
all outstanding claims of this description at the time of his election
to the primacy. It was plain that nothing short of his complete
ruin was intended. The bishops pressed him to save the Church
by sacrificing himself. Let him resign if need be, and throw himself
on the King's mercy. This Becket would not do. He was prepared,
if time were given him, to produce his accounts and clear himself of
the imputation on his honesty. Or he would compound at once
with the King, for all claims against him, by the payment of 2,000
marks. The composition was rejected; and Becket as his position
grew desperate reverted to an attitude of absolute defiance. He
forbade the bishops to sit in judgment upon him and entered an
appeal to Rome in stay of any sentence which might be passed
against him with their co-operation. They were overawed and
refused to attend the Council further; but the victory over them
was gained by means which exposed the Archbishop to a last and
worst attack. By appealing to Rome he had openly defied the
Constitutions. On this ground he was condemned by the lay-
barons. It may be pointed out that, as no bishops concurred in
this sentence, it had no ground whatever to be considered as the
sentence of an ecclesiastical court; and Becket, granting him to be
a criminous clerk guilty of perjury and treason, was still entitled to
be tried by his own order. Henry no less than his opponent was
breaking the Constitutions; but the King would perhaps have
answered that Becket was tried by a lay-court because he had, by
his own appeal, prevented the bishops from judging him. Things
however had come to a pass when there was little thought of law
on either side; it was a trial of strength between two unbending
wills, each prepared to use every available weapon of attack. The
barons came from the Council-chamber, with the Justiciar at their
head, to inform the Archbishop of the sentence which had been
passed on him in his absence. They found him sitting in the great
hall of the castle, his cross in his hand. At the first words of the
judgment he started to his feet. "What is this you would do?
You are come to judge me? It is not your right. This is no
sentence. I have not been heard. It was not for this cause I was

Becket's
Condem-
nation and
Flight

summoned. You cannot judge me. Let my guilt be what it may, I am your father; you are barons of the palace, lay powers, secular persons. I will not hear your judgment." He swept from the hall still carrying his cross. The Justiciar's amazement prevented him from completing the recital of the sentence and its nature was never known. As Becket departed some called him "traitor". He turned furiously on them and said that if he had not been a priest he would have proved upon their bodies that they lied. Some of the King's household followed him with gibes and taunts; they gathered up the rushes from the floor and threw them in handfuls after his retreating figure. But he was allowed to regain his lodgings without worse molestation (Oct. 13).[1]

That night Becket sent to ask the King for a safe-conduct and for leave to go abroad. He was bidden to wait till the next day; but when the morning broke he was gone. From Northampton he made his way to Lincoln and thence in disguise to the coast. On November 2nd he was safely at Gravelines. Subsequently, when apologising for his flight, he said that his life had been threatened; and no doubt there were men about the Court who would not have hesitated to kill him at the least hint from the King. But Henry, with all his faults, was no assassin. Imprisonment was the worst danger to which the Archbishop would have been exposed, and im-prisonment would certainly have produced a reaction in his favour. The advantages of seeking a refuge in France were obvious. The Pope was there; and from Louis VII., who realised the desirability of embroiling his Angevin rival with the Church, the Archbishop had received assurances of cordial sympathy. On the other hand the flight of Becket alienated from his cause the chief of his former partisans. The most respectable of the bishops, men like Foliot and Robert of Hereford, whose independence of judgment and honesty of purpose cannot be called in question, rallied to the side of the King. The barons resented the Archbishop's refusal to admit the jurisdiction of the Council; and among the inferior laity there was little sympathy for Thomas, though much was felt for his followers who were visited with confiscation and exile.[2] His

---

[1] See *Materials*, iii., 49, 296, for the two fullest accounts of the proceedings at Northampton.

[2] For the state of English feeling see the letter of Arnulf of Lisieux (*Materials*, v., 308). The Bishops of Worcester and Winchester supported Becket; so did several abbots (*ibid.*, iii., 86, 106). Will. Neubrig., ii., § 16, and John of Salisbury

flight subjected the English government to some inconveniences. No one knew who was to fulfil the necessary duties of the Primate; those whose duty it was to enforce the Constitutions were uneasy at the thought that the King might eventually be compelled to disown their action. But it soon became apparent that, so far as England was concerned, Henry had no cause for serious anxiety. In England there would be no agitation for the recall of the Archbishop, so long as he refused to make a compromise and fought the battle singlehanded. From France Henry had only to apprehend the pinpricks of a malicious but timid diplomat. Louis was ready to give Becket protection and hospitality, to make offers of intercession, and to reproach Henry with his want of moderation. Further than this Louis would not commit himself, at least while the Pope remained inactive. Everything depended on the action of the Curia. No one could calculate the effect which might be produced on English opinion by a papal interdict, or a papal sentence of excommunication against the King. To prevent these sentences from being launched became Henry's first anxiety.

Becket and Alexander

The Pope was an exile; and he was confronted by a rival whose claim had some grounds of plausibility. It was supposed that the risk of losing his most valuable ally would prevent him from taking Becket's part with energy. But Alexander soon discovered that his position was stronger than it looked. He had been recognised by the English Church, and there were limits to the obedience which Henry could expect from the bishops and the clergy. The Pope, after a personal interview with Becket, condemned the Constitutions and quashed the sentence passed at Northampton. He insisted upon negotiating for a peaceful settlement; but he promised that, if the King remained obdurate till the Easter of 1166, Becket should be free to launch the severest censures. At first the King showed an inclination to let the Pope and Becket do their worst. At the imperial diet of Würzburg an English embassy promised that their master would henceforth support the anti-pope. But it was found that English opinion would not tolerate a breach with Alexander. When the envoys of the Emperor visited England the King's own servants treated them as heretics; and Henry was

(*Materials*, v., 164) seem to express the views of moderate men. They are friendly to Becket, but consider that his claims and his manner of defending them were both open to censure.

compelled to disavow the step of his ambassadors as soon as it became a matter of common knowledge. The Pope gained courage when he saw this sign of weakness. In April, 1166, Becket received the legatine commission which would give his censures full effect; a few weeks later, at Vézelay, he began to excommunicate his enemies with bell and book and candle. For the present he spared the King; but he intimated that, even for Henry, the time of grace was drawing to a close.

Grave was the perplexity of the English bishops when the sentences of Vézelay were transmitted to them. They informed the King that it was their bounden duty to obey the Pope's vice-gerent, since his sentences were in no wise repugnant to the ancient customs.[1] Henry wept for rage when he received this warning; the Archbishop, he said, had resolved to ruin him both soul and body.[2] As a last resort the King appealed to Alexander, and exhausted his ingenuity to prove that the Constitutions contained nothing of which the Holy See could legitimately complain. By a fortunate coincidence the later months of 1166 were a critical period in Alexander's fortunes. The Pope, who had now returned to Rome, was menaced with a new imperial invasion. He had no army capable of resisting Frederic Barbarossa's southward march. The one hope was to conciliate the moral support of all the other European powers. Alexander therefore hastened to make peace between Becket and the King of England. The sentences of the Archbishop were suspended,[3] and he was forbidden to issue others while negotiations were in progress. Papal legates, aided by the King of France, endeavoured to devise a concordat which Henry might construe as a promise of complete submission, and Becket as an unmeaning form of words. But it was no easy matter to hoodwink two able and determined men. The King would not abandon the Constitutions; the Archbishop would neither approve them nor condone them. They might be ancient; they might be allowed by the Curia; but they were impious, and he would have none of them.[4]

The Sentences of Vézelay, 1166

---

[1] Foliot in *Materials*, v., 258, 417.   [2] *Materials*, v., 381.   [3] *Ibid.*, vi., 85.
[4] See the report of the conference of Gisors (Nov., 1167) in *Materials*, vi., 245. Less is said about the Constitutions in the later conferences; but this apparently is due to Becket's consciousness that the Pope felt less strongly than he did about the Constitutions. His objections to later proposals appear to be pretexts rather than substantial reasons.

8

The deadlock appeared to be complete when an error of impatience on Henry's part placed him at a fatal disadvantage. His mother's history had taught him how difficult it was to entail the English crown; he had decided that the only certain means of securing the succession was to procure the coronation of the heir in his own life-time. Such ceremonies, although without a precedent in English law, were warranted by the examples of France and of the Empire. The Great Council offered no objection to the innovation; and only one impediment had hitherto prevented Henry from carrying his scheme into effect. The right of crowning the King belonged exclusively to the Archbishop-Primate; the coronation had been postponed again and again in the hope of a settlement with Becket. More than once Henry attempted to obtain the Pope's permission for the Archbishop of York to perform the ceremony; but Alexander, naturally reluctant to deprive Becket of any hold which he possessed upon the King, had resisted the request. Once the Pope had given way when Henry's help was more than usually important to him, but he had cancelled his concession before it could be utilised. In 1170 the King's patience was exhausted; and the young King's coronation was hurriedly celebrated at Westminster before the bishops selected to officiate could be served with papal inhibitions. Alexander had already been patient under such heavy provocations that it was natural to expect his indulgence for this crowning act of disobedience. But for once Henry had gone too far. Becket's complaints were promptly taken up by the Curia. The offending bishops were threatened with suspension and Henry's Continental dominions with an interdict; it seemed likely that the validity of the coronation would be called in question.[1] Henry resolved to avert this supreme danger by a precipitate submission. At Fréteval, in July, 1170, he met the Archbishop for the last time and went through a form of reconciliation. It was a mere form; for nothing was said on either side about the original cause of quarrel. But Becket received permission to return in peace to Canterbury; and the King certainly

---

[1] Licence to the Archbishop of York to celebrate the coronation in *Materials*, vi., 206; probably of the year 1167. The King seems to have believed in 1170 that the Pope had confirmed the previous licence by word of mouth; this was stated by the envoys whom he had despatched to Rome (*Materials*, vii., 226 ff.). The agreement of Fréteval in *Materials*, vii., 332. The King's alarm at Alexander's threats in Bosham, 462.

understood that, in return, the informality of the coronation would
be allowed to pass. He could not obtain a definite promise to this
effect; but rather than risk a struggle to the death, he left the
question to his opponent's magnanimity.

But the Archbishop was resolved to celebrate his restoration by The
condign punishment of the suffragans who, after opposing him for Bad Faith
six years on the question of the Constitutions, had publicly usurped of Becket
his highest functions. At Fréteval he positively refused to let
them make their peace with him. Immediately after leaving the
King he persuaded Alexander to send him letters, to be published
at his discretion, by which the delinquents were suspended from
their functions. When the letters arrived he found that they contained expressions condemnatory of the Constitutions, which
Alexander perhaps imagined that the King had given up. The
impolicy of reviving this well-worn quarrel at such a moment was
obvious; and Becket wrote to the Pope for amended copies of the
letters, which should omit all reference to the Constitutions. He
meant to remain on the Continent until his request had been
satisfied. But the purpose of his delay was suspected and Henry
pressed impatiently for his immediate return to England, where
Papal letters might be prevented from reaching him.[1] Becket
reluctantly obeyed. But he could not endure the thought of temporising with the bishops. In every way it seemed best to throw
down the glove before he met them face to face. The original
letters, with their hostile references to the Constitutions, preceded
him to England. The ports were closely watched to intercept
such literature; but Becket's envoy evaded suspicion and the
letters were duly served on those whom they concerned before
Becket arrived in person at Dover. Great was the wrath and
consternation of the King's party to learn how they had been
outwitted. The King was not in England; but the regency with
the young Henry at its head ostentatiously declined to hold any intercourse with Becket. The Primate's audacity increased with his danger. On Christmas day he excommunicated the bishops who had taken
part in the coronation. It was the last straw. Henry received the
news while he was keeping the Christmas festival at Bures near
Bayeux. "My subjects are sluggards, men of no spirit," he ex-

---

[1] The affair of the Papal letters in Bosham, 471, and *Materials*, vii., 370-413.
Henry's letter demanding Becket's return in *Materials*, vii., 400.

claimed; "they keep no faith with their lord; they allow me to be

made the laughing-stock of a low-born clerk." Four knights who
heard these words, slipped away to the coast without being noticed,
and crossed the straits in the first ship they found. On landing
they made their way to the Archbishop's house at Canterbury.
Admitted without a suspicion of their purpose they bluntly accused
Becket of having plotted the downfall of the young King. He
retorted with defiance though he read murder in their faces. They
retired to put on their armour in the courtyard; and the terrified
chaplains of the Archbishop dragged him almost by force into the
cathedral where the service of vespers was beginning. The knights
pressed hard upon his footsteps. He would not allow the doors to
be barred behind him and turned at bay as they drew near.
"Absolve the bishops!" they cried, and as he remained obdurate
one of them seized him by the arm to drag him from the consecrated building. It was Reginald FitzUrse, who had once been
Becket's man, and at the touch of the traitor the pride of the
Archbishop flamed out for the last time. "Off, pander!" he cried.
"Touch me not! thou owest me faith and service." The knight
slashed furiously at the Archbishop's head; a monk caught the
blow on his arm, but the Archbishop was wounded in the face and
fell into the arms of his defender. A few more blows ended the
tragedy; Hugh of Horsea, surnamed the Evil Deacon, planting
one foot on the neck of the dead man drove his sword-point
through the skull, and the brains gushed out upon the floor. Their
vengeance sated, the murderers left the church to sack the Archbishop's palace; and in the twilight the monks returned to perform
the last offices for their patron. Of his title to be a saint no doubt
was felt when they discovered beneath his robes the hair shirt of
the penitent and the scars of self-inflicted scourging. Whatever
criticisms had been suggested by his trickery and broken promises
were silenced before these proofs of holiness. Henry was soon to
learn that Becket was more formidable in death than he had ever
been in life.

CHAPTER VIII

THE CONQUEST OF IRELAND

THERE is a striking contrast between the fortunes of the Early Celtic and Teutonic races. The latter climb, slowly and Irish History painfully it is true, but with a steady and continued progress, from stage to stage of civilisation. The former, after soaring at the first flight to a comparatively elevated point, are inclined to be content with their achievement, and are not only overtaken but even passed by their more deliberate competitors before they have realised that their superiority is challenged. It is the old story of the hare and tortoise. The apologists of the Celtic genius have explained this precocity and incompleteness of development as if it were entirely due to the accidents of geographical position; and in the case of Ireland the influence of geography upon national destiny is more than usually apparent; here more than elsewhere the Celt has both gained and suffered by his banishment to the outer verge of Europe. Their remoteness from the main theatres of conflict between the Roman and barbarian gave the Irish an advantage over other peoples during the transition from the ancient to the modern world, when the antithesis of old and new was mainly one of brute force and intelligence, when culture and conservatism were synonymous. Secure against invasion in their island fortress the latest converts to Roman Christianity were able to meditate and study while their teachers were struggling for existence; when the death-throes of the Western Empire were at an end the Irish issued forth, with a vigour unimpaired by conflicts and a faith unweakened by defeats, to share in the conversion of the victorious barbarians. Nor were the illiterate heathen their only pupils. Even for the older centres of intellectual and religious life, for the great cities and religious houses which had survived the general cataclysm, Ireland had a message; she who had been a pupil now became a mistress, in profane and sacred lore alike. From the sixth to the ninth century the Irish scholar and the Irish missionary are ubiquitous. They are equally at home in the storm-swept isles of Western Scotland or on the bleak moors of Northumbria or in the rich dales of the Rhineland. At the courts of Frankish kings, in the cloisters of Italian monasteries, among nations of strange tongues and sanguinary cults, they make a momentary appearance, deliver their message with a seeming indifference to the manner in which it is received, and resume their wanderings, unspoiled by admiration, undaunted by the persecutor. They are such teachers as we should expect from a race which has always lived in the past or future, enchanted by tradition or intoxicated with ideal hopes. They were imbued with a vague and mystical philosophy; they had renounced all the cares and joys of common men to live a life of rigorous asceticism. Their preaching was, like their lives, a riddle; a source of wonder to their pagan auditors, often a block of stumbling to the orthodox; but still the sympathetic could trace in act and word the charm which comes

Decay of the Irish Church

from high ideals and self-renunciation. Too soon, however, the Irish seminaries lost the glow of their first inspiration. The seclusion which had originally fostered spiritual development then became their bane. No teachers from the outer world arrived to fill the place of those who had gone forth; no new ideas came in to take the place of those which had degenerated into commonplace; a decay of spiritual energy set in among the Irish clergy, until they became such as they are described for us by St. Bernard, in his life of Malachi, and by Giraldus in his Topographia; diligent in the performance of their ordinary duties, conspicuous examples of the more elementary virtues, but unlearned, guiltless of enthusiasm for their sacred calling, without much influence for good or evil.

We may well believe that some fate of this kind would have fallen to the lot of any Church confined within a remote and narrow island. But as geographical conditions fail to explain the finer qualities of Irish culture in its prime, so they fail to account for the torpor by which we find the Irish people overcome in the age of Abe'ard and Bernard, of Henry II. and Frederic Barbarossa. The striking triumphs of the Irish Church in the field of missionary labour, and its failure to ameliorate the condition of the lay society in the bosom of which it was planted, are both to be explained by reference to the same characteristic, to that proud and impatient individualism which is deeply engrained in the Celtic character. The Irish clergy formed an aristocracy of a peculiarly exclusive kind. They spurned the world with all its cares and pleasures as something unworthy of attention, as a clog and check upon the spiritual activities. This habit of mind is common to monasticism in every age and climate; but in Ireland more than elsewhere the monastic ideal of self-concentrated preparation for a future life held sway to the exclusion of all others. The monastery was the typical and almost the only institution of the Irish Church; and the Irish monk approximated the more nearly to the recognised pattern of perfection in proportion as he withdrew from intercourse even with those of his own calling. The saint of native legends is a hermit by profession, a teacher either by accident or under a divine compulsion which he obeys with pious resignation; and it is no uncommon thing to find him regarded as a mysterious thaumaturge who is quick to visit with his vengeance those who by chance or design intrude upon his meditations. The ordinary monk, as he encounters us in early Irish history, does not aspire to this degree of solitude and sanctity; but the only social duty which he recognises is that of defending, if need be with the sword, the foundation through which he is enabled to emancipate himself from the responsibilities of a secular existence. A Church so constituted could not flourish long; it gradually sank to the level of the rude laity whose reformation it had refused to take in hand. Such is the law of nature; there can be no truce between the higher and the lower rule of life; and, of the two, that which stands on the defensive will surely disappear.

The nation suffered from the same defect as the Church. There is no doubt much exaggeration in the anecdotes of Irish manners to which the malice or credulity of Giraldus has given currency. Steeped in the prejudices of the conquerors, his kinsmen, he palliates their most discreditable deeds by reckless accusations aimed at the whole conquered people. Had faith been broken with the Irish? If so, his excuse is that they are a race who do not know the meaning of good faith. Had there been wars of vengeance and retaliation, prosecuted to the last extremity? At all events the Irish had not been treated worse than they were in the habit of treating their own kith and kin. To Giraldus no superstition is

Irish Civilisation

too barbarous and no vice too loathsome to be attributed even to
those tribes who fell within the range of his personal observation;
it is, therefore, not surprising if he describes the inhabitants of remoter districts as beings hardly human. In the west of Connaught,
he assures us, the natives had never learned to make bread or
cheese, had never seen a boat or ship of wood, and were totally
unacquainted with the calendar, the festivals of the Church, and
the rudiments of Christianity. But these wild tales and others of
the same kind deserve as little credence as that of the barnacle-
geese whom he had seen " with his own eyes " growing like limpets
on the rocks along the Irish coasts. The Irish were not uncivilised
but semi-civilised; and those who branded them as savages were
guided by criteria of which the force will hardly be admitted at
the present day. To the mind of Giraldus or St. Bernard the
last word had been said when it was admitted that the Irish paid
no tithes, and were apt to marry within degrees prohibited by
the over-refining spirit of the canon law. The real defect, which
the early observers do not notice, is impatience of restraint. The
Irish chafed against the elementary rules of justice and of established government. Under any polity the island could hardly
have been prosperous. Intersected by vast extents of barren hills
and bogs and forests, it offered little encouragement to the agri-
culturist and naturally suggested the half-nomadic existence of a
hunter or a herdsman. Cattle, furs, and skins formed the Irishman's sole source of wealth; even for a supply of corn he depended
largely upon the Ostmen and the nearest English ports. There
were no mines in Ireland, and few natural advantages to stimulate
the growth of peaceful industry. But even had these advantages
existed they would have been worthless under the wretched political
system which long use and wont had consecrated.

Political
Organisa-
tion

The idea of national unity had still a certain influence, but
many generations had elapsed since it had been embodied in the
person of such rulers as Brian, the hero of Clontarf. The title
of the High King survived, nor was there wanting a succession of
adventurers to claim and hold at the sword's point the nominal
supremacy which it conveyed. Erin was however a kingdom
without a capital or revenue or government. Tara lay desolate,
a shattered and forsaken ruin; Meath, the royal demesne, was
partitioned among petty chiefs. The power of the High King

depended on the lands which he inherited or won by conquest; his title gave him, at the best of times, no advantage beyond a precarious tribute of cattle and uncertain rights of jurisdiction. Still, it was the highest honour open to an Irishman, and furnished the pretext of never-ending feuds between the four monarchies of Ulster, Leinster, Munster, and Connaught. These also, like the higher dignity, passed from hand to hand and family to family in accordance with the vicissitudes of endless civil wars. The competitors were found among the chiefs and princes who divided and disputed within each province the immediate lordship of the soil. It would be impossible to state with accuracy the number of such rulers at any given time in early Irish history ; but, in the period of the English Conquest, there were in Leinster between thirty and forty of them, and in Meath alone, the smallest of all the provinces, not less than thirty.[1] The native annals are little more than a catalogue of the raids and feuds and wars of vengeance in which these petty despots courted immortality. In those rare intervals when a reigning chief neglected to occupy the thoughts of his retainers by a foreign war, there was seldom wanting a pretender to impugn the legitimacy of his title. The universal custom of tanistry, under which the nearest agnate of full age was designated as the heir apparent, to the exclusion of the monarch's children, provided a never failing source of civil strife within the pettiest principalities.

The Celts were not the only inhabitants of Ireland although The Ostmen they formed by far the greater portion of the population. Since the ninth century there had been Scandinavian colonies in occupation of Dublin, Waterford, Wexford, Limerick and possibly some smaller coast-towns. Their founders belonged to the first generation which had left the shores of Norway and Denmark to seek a fortune in the civilised and wealthy south; in their constitutions and in their relations with the native race these settlements are analogous to those established at the same period in the English Danelaw ; like the colonists of England, the Irish Ostmen accepted Christianity, forsook buccaneering for more peaceful occupations, and came to terms with the native princes on whose territory they had settled. A Danish seaport was a godsend to the neighbouring septs. It gave them a market for the hides and

[1] Orpen, *Song of Dermot*, p. 322.

8*

marten-skins which were their chief articles of export; and the ships of the Ostmen, plying regularly to Bristol, Chester, Rouen, La Rochelle and Bordeaux, brought back to the island the corn and wine, the slaves and trinkets, which the Celt desired but was incapable of procuring for himself.[1]   Nominally dependent upon the leading dynasties of the east and south the Ostmen remained in fact autonomous, governed by jarls and hereditary patriciates of lawmen.   These municipal republics were of the smallest size. Wexford, even in the twelfth century and after a long period of prosperity, could only put into the field an army of 3,000 men.[2] The power of the Ostmen crumbled at the first touch of a Norman Marcher, and it is surprising that they should have held their own against the greatest kings of Ireland for 300 years.   The truth is that they held in the Atlantic the same position as the Venetians in the Mediterranean.   The Norse trader was useful for many purposes to many powers, and he played upon the mutual jealousies of those who might have crushed his liberty.   He kept in touch with the Vikings of the Western Isles, and even with the rulers of distant Scandinavia.   He courted the West-Saxon dynasty; he paid oc- casional tribute to a prince of Meath or Leinster.   If attacked by one set of his patrons he invoked the assistance of the rest.   When victorious he showed a politic forbearance, when beaten saved him- self by temporary submission; and allowed neither promises nor gratitude to bind him to his disadvantage.

Such was the state of Ireland at the accession of Henry II.; divided, disturbed, an easy prey for any resolute adventurer who cared to attack a country so poor and so remote.   The later Vikings, if they ever landed to spy out the land, soon turned contemptuously away.   Political exiles such as Harold, the sons of Harold, Arnulf of Montgomery, used Ireland as a temporary asylum or recruiting ground.   To Rufus a tradition attributes the boast that he would bridge the sea with ships and conquer Ireland; but the purpose, no less than the suggested means of execution, seemed to contemporaries but another proof of his insensate greed.   Henry II., when young and rash and at a loss for an appanage with which to pension off a brother, had discussed the feasibility of an Irish expedition; but on consideration he

---

[1] Giraldus, v., 187, 228, 232.
[2] *Song*, l. 543.   Giraldus. v., 248 ff.

gave up the scheme.[1] It was left for broken men, the wildest spirits from the wildest part of his dominions, to undertake the adventure which so many wiser heads had rejected as chimerical.

To explain the opportunity which was offered to Strongbow and the Geraldines in 1166 we must retrace our steps to the latter part of Stephen's reign. At this time the most restless of the chiefs in Eastern Ireland was a certain Diarmait mac Murchadha.[2] He was hereditary prince of the Hui Cinnsellaigh, a tribe whose territories, corresponding to the modern diocese of Ferns, embraced the greater part of Leinster between the river Barrow and the sea; by fighting and diplomacy he had risen to supremacy over all the princes of the province and was recognised as King of Leinster. On Meath also he cast a longing eye; but here he found himself opposed by Tighernan O Ruairc, the lord of Breifne, a province corresponding to the shires of Leitrim and Cavan. From rivalry the two princes passed by natural stages to a bitter feud; and in 1152 Diarmait carried off his enemy's wife not so much from love of her as from the desire to inflict disgrace upon her husband. The princess returned to Breifne in the following year; she was none the less esteemed by Tighernan and his people for the abduction, to which, it is said, she had been a not unwilling party. But the conduct of Diarmait was neither forgotten nor forgiven; for fourteen years, at every critical point of his fortunes, he found the power of Breifne thrown into the scale of his opponents; and in the year 1166 Tighernan at length succeeded in bringing to his aid Ruadhri, the King of Connaught and High King of Ireland. The army of Leinster was defeated; the province fell into the hands of Ruadhri and Tighernan; and Diarmait was driven over seas, a homeless exile, whose only hope of a return depended upon foreign help. It was to the King of England that he addressed himself in the first instance. He came to Henry's court in Normandy and proffered his allegiance as the price of restitution to his kingdom. It was an unpropitious moment for the application. Engrossed with the Becket controversy and the affairs of France, the King of England had no desire to revive the Irish scheme. All

(marginal note: Diarmait of Leinster)

---

[1] *Ante*, p. 202.

[2] The names of Irish chiefs, tribes, etc., are spelled in accordance with the forms given in the Irish abridgment of the *Expugnatio Hibernica* (ed. Whitley Stokes), *E. H. R.*, xx., pp. 77 ff. The biography of Dermot is given by Orpen, *Ireland under the Normans*, pp. 39 ff.

that Diarmait could obtain was a licence authorising him to raise
recruits from among Henry's Welsh and English subjects.[1]

But the results of this permission exceeded the wildest expectations. Among the marchers of South Wales Diarmait had the
good or evil fortune to discover allies of the same metal as the
Normans who had subjugated southern Italy, bearded the Cæsars
of Byzantium, and exploited the enthusiasm of the first crusaders.
Among these adventurers the most prominent was Richard of
Clare, the earl of Pembroke, and the lord of Striguil, a man whose
abilities as a soldier, general, and politician, would long since have
raised him to the first rank in the English baronage, but for the
extravagance with which he had squandered his patrimony and the
constancy which he had displayed in supporting to the last the
ruined cause of Stephen. Embarrassed in his circumstances and
aware that he could never hope for Henry's favour, the earl asked
nothing better than a new field in which to repair his tattered
fortunes. His eagerness for the enterprise did not prevent him
from driving a hard bargain with the Irish prince. In his knack
of blending knight-errantry with business the earl was a true
Norman. He stipulated for the hand of Diarmait's daughter and
the reversion of Leinster; he also insisted that he should not be
required to fulfil his part of the contract until he had obtained
King Henry's licence for his venture.[2] Diarmait was accordingly
obliged to enlist less important but more accommodating helpers
for the projects which he had immediately in view. As he had
tempted Earl Richard with the hope of Leinster in which he had
no hereditary right, so to the inferior recruits he offered the city and
lands of the Wexford Ostmen. The offer was accepted by the
half-brothers Robert FitzStephen and Maurice FitzGerald, two
minor barons of the marches, half-Norman and half-Welsh in
parentage; they were the sons by different fathers of Nesta, the
daughter of a South-Welsh prince, who had lived for some time at
the court of Henry I., as a hostage for her father's good behaviour
and a mistress of the English King. They promised to appear
in Ireland with a sufficient force by the commencement of the
summer, and Diarmait returned forthwith to Leinster to prepare
for their reception (Aug., 1167).[3] He found his dominions
still in the possession of his enemies; but after experiencing a

[1] Giraldus, v., 227. [2] Song, p. 355.
[3] For the date, Orpen, op. cit., pp. 100, 141.

defeat he worked upon their clemency so far as to procure
for himself a regrant of a part of his ancestral principality.[1]
He settled for the present in Hui Cinnsellaigh to await the allies
whose imminent appearance was unsuspected by any man in Ireland
save himself.   He waited more than a year; but in May, 1169,
the sons of Nesta, accompanied by Maurice de Prendergast, a The sons
kindred spirit whom they had taken into partnership, landed at of Nesta
in Ireland
Bannow with a force of between 400 and 500 men.   One-fourth
of this diminutive host were mounted knights.   The rest were
archers armed with the longbow, a weapon not yet so famous as
it afterwards became, but one of which the possibilities had been
already tested in many a skirmish of the South-Welsh border.
If the current stories are to be believed the Welsh archer of this
period might stand comparison with the English yeomen who fought
at Crecy and at Agincourt.   We are told that he could send his
shaft through an oak-door of a palm's breadth in thickness, or
through the toughest coat of mail.   The most ingenious of tac-
ticians could not have devised a force more perfectly equipped for
the peculiar difficulties of Irish warfare.   The Irish kerne wore no
defensive armour, and at close quarters fought on foot armed with
a battle-axe of the pattern which the Vikings had made popular.
When forced to await a charge an Irish army relied upon the
protection afforded by woods, morasses, and abatis constructed of
felled tree-trunks; the enemy who succeeded in finding a passage
through these obstacles had only to disperse a rabble which was
entirely undisciplined and susceptible to sudden panics.   Against
mailed knights and on an open field no odds could give the Irish
any prospect of success; destitute of any better missiles than stones
and javelins they were unable to employ their favourite skirmishing
tactics against a force accompanied by archers; and they could
always be driven from a strong position, or goaded to a hopeless
charge, by a sustained and well-directed fire of arrows.   The
"Flemings" whose arrival passed almost without notice on the
part of Diarmait's enemies, soon carried all before them.   Wexford
fell at the first attack, and from this stronghold, which Diarmait,
according to his promise, bestowed on the sons of Nesta, the
adventurers swept through the length and breadth of Leinster,
scattering every force which could be put into the field against

[1] See the *Four Masters, s.a.* 1167.

them.[1] So overwhelming was their superiority that even defection from their ranks could not bring them to a standstill. Maurice de Prendergast, dissatisfied with his share of the booty, deserted to the prince of Ossraighe (co. Kilkenny); but his former companions continued their triumphant course until the High King, Tighernan of Breifne, and all their allies, were driven to negotiation. They endeavoured for a time to sow dissension and mistrust between Diarmait and the newcomers; but being foiled in this design they withdrew and agreed to recognise Diarmait as the rightful lord of Leinster.

The Summons to Strongbow

But the time for compromise had passed. The High King and his supporters were to learn that they had provoked an enemy who never forgave an injury or missed an opportunity of taking vengeance. The King of Leinster saw already in imagination the whole of Ireland at his feet. Late in 1169 he sent an urgent message of reminder to the Earl of Pembroke. " We have watched the stork and the swallow; the birds of summer have come and gone; but neither the east wind nor the west has brought the man whom we desire to see. All Leinster has returned to us. Come with speed and with a strong hand; then shall the four provinces bow down before the fifth." [2] Either the King's clerks had read their Ovid to good purpose or else Giraldus, to whom we owe the letter, has embellished it with the flowers of his own vaunted scholarship. But the tone is dramatically appropriate to the characters of the sender and the recipient; rapacity and romance were inseparably intertwined in the conquerors of Ireland.

Expedition of Raymond le Gros, May, 1170

The promises, if not the rhetoric, of Diarmait's letter produced their due effect upon the earl; he at length applied to Henry for a sanction of the contemplated enterprise. The end in view and the reward which had been promised to the earl appear to have been carefully concealed. He preferred his request in the tone of a disappointed man embarking on a desperate venture; what he most desired, he said, was to be reinvested with the lands of which he had been deprived since the late King's death; if this boon were denied him, he should at least be granted leave to seek his consolation elsewhere. Henry made light of the petition; the arch-dissimulator was for once deceived; he gave the earl a careless permission to repair his fortunes where and as he pleased. No

[1] Giraldus, v., 233.   [2] Ibid., 247.

opportunity of reconsidering the matter was given to the King. The earl returned to the marches and began to organise his expedition without loss of time. Towards the end of April the first corps of the adventurers was in readiness. Raymond le Gios, a trusted vassal of the earl, was put in charge of them and despatched in advance to reassure the King of Leinster. He landed near Waterford on May 1st, 1170, with a following of ten knights and seventy archers ; a cliff adjacent to the sea was occupied and strengthened with extemporary fortifications ; and in these incommodious quarters the pioneers settled to await the arrival of Diarmait or their master. The Ostmen of Waterford had learned by this time the danger of despising the smallest expedition from England ; they sallied from their walls to attack the castle and drive the invader into the sea. But they were repulsed with heavy slaughter and retired, leaving seventy of their number as captives in the power of Raymond. All were beheaded, with the general's leave, by a female camp-follower whose lover had fallen fighting on the English side.[1]   It is the first and not the least of the atrocities which stain the annals of the Conquest, but it inspired the Ostmen and the Irish with a salutary fear of English prowess; Raymond held his eyrie without further molestation until, in August, he was joined by his master and a force, the like of which had never before appeared on Irish soil. Strongbow brought with him 200 knights and upwards of 1,000 foot-soldiers. He had, we know, some credit in the ghettoes of the Western shires.[2]   But, even so, it is impossible that with his ruined fortunes he should have paid so great a multitude in any coin but promises. The readiness with which the marchers volunteered to serve him is the best proof that we could ask of his military reputation.

Strongbow appears, Aug., 1170

He was in fact a leader to inspire no ordinary degree of confidence and hope in all who served him. A chance observer, judging from his presence and physique, might have committed the mistake of regarding him as insignificant. His face was of a delicacy almost feminine, his bearing modest and reserved, his voice weak and thin, his conversation unassuming.[3]   But beneath this unpromising exterior there lurked an iron resolution. Good fortune could not intoxicate him; no failures could turn him from a purpose once conceived. Farseeing in council, fiery in action, he had a persuasive

---

[1] *Song*, ll. 1404 ff. Giraldus, v., 248 ff.
[2] Jacobs, *Jews of Angevin England*, p. 64.   [3] Giraldus, v., 272.

eloquence which made any plan however desperate seem plausible.
The fate of the Irish was sealed from the moment that he set foot
on their shores. The Geraldines had shown how easily an Irish
host could be defeated. The example of Richard Clare proved that
lasting conquests were no more difficult than plundering expeditions. Others completed the work which he began, but to him
more than to any other single man belongs the praise or blame for
the foundation of the English Pale.

**Fall of
Dublin**
The cities of the Ostmen were the keys of Ireland, and upon the
task of reducing Waterford and Dublin he concentrated all the
forces which he had brought or which King Diarmait could command. The walls of Waterford, which had so many times defied
the naked kernes of Irish armies, could not save the city now. It
fell at the first attack. The besiegers remarked a house built into
the wall, of which the upper stories projected forward and were
supported upon wooden posts. They cut away the posts; the house
fell dragging with it no small part of the wall; and through the
breach thus opened the earl and his men poured into the city.
The attempt on Dublin was only delayed until the earl assured
his hold on Leinster by celebrating his marriage with the princess
Aife, the daughter of Diarmait. In the interval the Ostmen of
Dublin enlisted the High King on their side; and the earl, on
drawing near the city, discovered that an army, collected from all
parts of Ireland, was at Clondalkin, lying across the roads by which
Dublin was usually approached from the south. But a detour
through the mountains brought the invaders to the walls of Dublin
before their approach had been detected by the enemy.[1] Cut off
from their base of operations the army of Ruadhri fled without
a blow; and the earl's men entered Dublin, by a stroke of well
calculated perfidy, during an armistice for which the defenders had
asked as a preliminary to a capitulation upon terms. Hasculf, the
Jarl of Dublin, took to his ships and was followed by the greater
number of his subjects. They embarked while the Normans were
plundering the town and sailed northward to find assistance or a
refuge in the Western Isles. The victors let him go in peace, and
proceeded to make Dublin their head-quarters for the winter season;
but, before the winter set in, they raided Meath as though to warn

[1] *Song*, l. 1570.

the Irish that nothing less than the conquest of the whole island was in contemplation.

Dublin was in fact the key of Ireland, and the fall of the city spread dismay among the enemies of Diarmait. A synod of the Irish church gathered hastily at Armagh to discuss the situation, but could make no practical suggestions to the laity. The assembled fathers came to the conclusion that the Flemings were a judgment, provoked by the iniquities of the Bristol slave-trade; and suggested that all the slaves in Ireland should be set at liberty. Henry II. regarded the situation with hardly less concern, though from a different point of view. He had authorised a freebooting expedition and it had become a war of conquest. He had hoped to rid himself of disaffected subjects, and it now appeared that he had helped them to acquire a kingdom. He saw no advantage in taking Ireland for himself; but he also saw the danger of allowing Ireland to become the property of others. His first precaution was to cut off the supplies of the adventurers by forbidding any ship to leave an English harbour for the voyage to Ireland. His second was to threaten the adventurers with forfeiture and exile unless they returned by the ensuing Easter. These measures had the effect which he desired. An Irish kingdom might be better than an English earldom; but the conquerors had not yet succeeded in supporting war by war. Cut off from England they were helpless, and it was necessary to conciliate the King at any cost. The lesson was driven home by the death of Diarmait in the spring of 1171. The tribesmen of Hui Cinnsellaigh had never ratified the bond which made them the marriage-portion of a woman and the chattels of an alien. They turned their backs on Strongbow, elected a nephew of Diarmait as their ruler, and attacked the Geraldines in Wexford.[1] The contagion of their patriotism spread and for the second time the High King, at the head of a national levy, came into the field against Earl Richard. For two months Dublin was rigorously invested and cut off from communication with the garrisons of Waterford and Wexford, which were equally hard pressed by hostile neighbours. The earl humbled himself to sue for peace and offered to hold Leinster as the vassal of Ruadhri. The High King tried to beat him down, offering to cede the towns of the Ostmen and no more; only at the eleventh hour,

[1] *Song,* l. 1735.

Marginal notes: Strongbow in difficulties, 1171

when his provisions were exhausted, did the earl succeed in proving by a desperate sally that he was still an enemy to be respected.[1] The besieging army melted as rapidly as it had come together. A hurried march upon Hui Cinnsellaigh brought the Irish claimant to his knees, and he became the vassal of Aife's husband for her father's hereditary dominions. Leinster was saved; but the earl had come too late to rescue the garrison of Wexford, nor could another storm like the last be weathered without new reinforcements. If these were to be obtained from England Strongbow had no alternative but to appease the suspicions of Henry by any degree of submission which the King might choose to demand. Leaving Dublin in charge of a lieutenant, and appointing Domhnall Kavanagh a son of Diarmait as his justiciar "to hold the pleas" in Leinster, the earl sailed for England late in the summer of 1171.[2]

Henry prepares an Expedition

He found his suzerain at Newnham in Gloucestershire; for Henry had resolved upon an Irish expedition and was already on the road to Milford Haven. Eight months had elapsed since the tragedy of Canterbury cathedral; and the suspense in which Henry had been left as to the consequences of the deed was already yielding to a conviction that Alexander would not commit the folly of a decisive breach with a supporter so valuable as the King of England. Until the end of March Henry had lived in fear of a personal sentence of excommunication which would have received the approval of no inconsiderable minority among the most law-abiding and disinterested of his subjects, and would have precipitated the outbreak of those civil commotions towards which the merits and defects of his government, his own impartiality and the corruption of his officials, his repression of evil-doers and his own extortions in the forms of law, his ill-judged favours to his sons and his politic severity towards his barons, were dragging his dominions on both sides of the English Channel. Now, when the arrival of legates bearing terms of peace was hourly expected, the only doubt which remained was the extent to which he would be humiliated before his absolution was pronounced. The King preferred the slight risk of a rebellion in his absence to the tedium of expectant inactivity, and to the shame of awaiting sentence under the eyes of alienated friends and of malicious critics whom he dared not punish. In July, at Argentan, he had obtained the approval of the Great

[1] The negotiations in the *Song*, ll. 1840 ff. [2] *Song*, l. 2181.

Council for the project of invading Ireland. In September, when Strongbow met him, he was on the road through Gloucestershire to Milford Haven, the port at which his fleet and army were assembling.

The results of the interview were more satisfactory to the earl than they might have been if his successes had been gained in quieter times. The moment was not one at which Henry could afford to risk a further loss of reputation by opening a war against the picked warriors of the Welsh marches and on a soil where the hand of every man would be against the cause of law and government. The earl obtained his pardon on condition of surrendering the seaports which were the most valuable of his conquests; for Leinster he was permitted to do homage, on the ordinary feudal terms. He crossed to Waterford in the King's company and then, departing from the royal host, retired to live in the quiet enjoyment of his curtailed but still considerable conquests, no longer a King but a mere palatine.[1] His later appearances in the field of history are few and far between. During the baronial rebellion of 1173 he proved a loyal supporter of a master who had small claims upon his gratitude; and he was rewarded about 1174 with the office of Justiciar in Ireland, which he only lived to enjoy until June 1176. Of his marriage with Aife the only offspring was a daughter by whose marriage to the famous William Marshall the line of the Clares of Pembroke was merged in another, equally short-lived and almost equally distinguished. The sole memorial of Strongbow, in the country which he opened to the English, is his reputed effigy upon his tomb in Dublin, but in a sense all Ireland is his monument.[2]

The few months for which Henry II. remained in Ireland were almost entirely spent at Dublin. His first object, like that of Strongbow, was to make good the English occupation of the seaports. He planted garrisons in Dublin, Waterford, and Wexford, and entrusted the three commands to lieutenants of whom he had personal experience. In Dublin, which he intended to be the seat of government, he founded a colony of English traders amongst whom the men of Bristol, tempted by the concession of exceptional privileges, were largely represented. At the head of the administration

(margin notes: Strongbow falls out of Sight)

(margin notes: Henry in Ireland, Oct., 1171-April, 1172)

---

[1] Giraldus, v., 273. *Song*, ll. 2617 ff. R. de Monte, 252, says that Henry had promised to make Strongbow the Constable or Seneschal of Ireland.

[2] It seems clear that the original effigy was destroyed in 1562, by the fall of the roof of Christ Church (Orpen, *Ireland under the Normans*, I., pp. 359-60).

he placed a Justiciar of Ireland. The first holder of the office was Hugh de Lacy, the commander of the Dublin garrison, who received with it the enormous fief of Meath to be held with privileges similar to those enjoyed by Richard Strongbow in Leinster.[1] The danger of forming these enormous honours was too obvious to escape a King who in other parts of his dominions neglected no opportunity of pruning feudal principalities and jurisdictions. But common prudence demanded the creation of a counterpoise to Leinster; and if the subjugation of the island was to be completed by the privite enterprise of the settlers it seemed essential to group them under a small number of superiors. Henry had no intention of spending his resources upon Ireland. He contented himself with receiving the facile homage of the Irish chieftains; and, although disappointed that Ruadhri sulked defiantly behind the barrier of the Shannon, he declined to cross the river and call the High King to account.[2]

The Council of Cashel, 1172

If the fidelity of the princes was dubious, that of the clergy seemed to be sincere. The latter had substantial reasons for acquiescing in the English Conquest. Those who desired to see ecclesiastical reform despaired of effecting it unless they invoked external aid against the forces of tradition and established interests. St. Bernard had assisted them with missionaries; in 1150 Eugenius III. had despatched a cardinal-legate to the island, with instructions to organise the Irish Church upon the model which England and every other Western nation had long since adopted. But the decrees of Irish Councils remained inoperative; the endowments of the Irish church were in the hands of lay impropriators; the inferior clergy were frequently married men, differing in little save the tonsure from the laity; and the payment of tithes had never been enforced. The price with which Henry purchased the adhesion of the reformers was an engagement to assist their cherished projects; and the Council of Cashel, which met with his approval early in the year 1172 served the double purpose of announcing the alliance of the Church with the invader. and of inaugurating effectual reform.[3] The Irish clergy have been sharply criticised for their

---

[1] Hoveden, ii., 34. Benedictus, i., 30. *Song*, l. 2725.
[2] Giraldus, v., 275. Benedictus, i., 25.
[3] Benedictus, i., 28. The letters of Alexander III. in *Liber Niger Scaccarii*, i., 42-8, prove that he admitted Henry's title to Ireland. The attitude of Rome may have weighed with the Irish clergy.

submission as though they had sold the national freedom for a mess of pottage. But the charge is based upon a complete misapprehension of the previous state of Ireland. The Church cannot be blamed for welcoming a ruler of any nationality who had the power to end once and for all the secular conflicts of lawless and rapacious chieftains. National unity was a tradition of the distant past; national liberty had been synonymous with anarchy.

It was a misfortune that the approach of Papal legates and the rumour of impending rebellion took Henry back to England before his plans for the administration of Ireland had been fully framed. From this time to the sixteenth century no statesman of the first rank had an opportunity of dealing with Irish difficulties face to face. The relations of the immigrants to the native population were left to be adjusted at haphazard; the work of annexation and settlement was pursued by individuals acting as their private interests dictated. The English colonies lay far apart and in the midst of hostile septs; there was no attempt to protect them by well planned military roads or lines of forts; the points of strategic importance were neglected in favour of indefensible positions which promised well as pasturage or corn-land.[1] When the Irish discovered that they were not to be assailed continuously or by an overwhelming force they recovered heart, adopted the weapons and tactics of their enemies, and raised themselves to a level of comparative equality in military skill.[2] The design of maintaining royal garrisons, even in the coast-towns, was abandoned as early as 1173; and Henry found himself compelled to depend upon the good will of the adventurers. Loyal as they proved themselves he regarded their conquests with suspicion; even before the death of Earl Richard the King had entered upon a new policy, that of balancing the natives against the Anglo-Irish. At the very moment when Strongbow's henchman, Raymond le Gros, extended the borders of the English Pale to the Shannon and laid hold of Limerick,[3] the King of England was concluding a treaty with Ruadhri (Oct. 6, 1175). Under this agreement the High King was allowed to retain Connaught and his hereditary rights in all other parts of the island except Meath, Dublin, Waterford and Wexford; the only conditions were that he should take the oath of fealty to Henry and his successors, should assume the responsibility for collecting a tribute

Ireland after Henry's Departure

---

[1] A map showing the distribution of the *motes* (primitive castles) erected by the Norman settlers is given in Orpen, *Ireland under the Normans*, vol. II.
[2] Giraldus, v., 383.   [3] *Song*, l. 3430. Giraldus, v., 322.

of the tenth hide of all cattle throughout Ireland, and should respect all the other rights and services to which the King of England was entitled.[1] Suspicion of the Clares and Geraldines was the motive which induced Henry to propose this treaty. They were indeed too strong for his officials, and would have continued the war with Ruadhri but for the untimely death of Richard Strongbow. This loss paralysed their energies. Limerick was evacuated in the spring of 1176;[2] the historian of the conquest is loud in his complaints of the slights and injuries which the pioneers henceforth experienced at the hands of the King's Justiciars.

Ulster

To this policy of mistrust and furtive counterchecks we may attribute the desultory character of the English advance in south and western Ireland. In the north-east conquest progressed more rapidly under the management of a leader who was fortunate in possessing the entire confidence of Henry II. John de Courcy received in 1176 a licence to keep as much of Ulster as he could conquer for himself. In the following year he proceeded to use his permission; he acted with such energy that, before the end of 1177, he had fought five pitched battles, gained three decisive victories, and brought under his control the best part of the province. What he had won he held with the strong hand, building castles at all the vulnerable points of his miniature principality, and maintaining good peace for all his subjects without distinction of race.[3] It would have been well if the King's Justiciars had shown equal skill and resolution in their wider sphere of action. But they were usually inefficient. The best of them was Hugh de Lacy, whose second period of office (1177-1185) was marked by some useful measures; he built a number of new castles in Meath and Leinster, and pursued a policy of conciliation towards the natives, persuading them to settle on their old possessions under English rule, with a guarantee of all their former rights. But the ever ready suspicions of the King were excited by the marriage of De Lacy with a daughter of the King of Connaught. The equitable conduct of the Justiciar in his dealing with the natives was taken as evidence of designs to found an independent Anglo-Irish kingdom, and he was twice recalled to England to explain his conduct.[4]

[1] Benedictus, i., 102.
[2] Giraldus, v., 332.
[3] Ibid., 339 ff.; Orpen, Normans, c. xii.
[4] Ibid., 352-3. Benedictus, i., 270.

The King's own plans with regard to Ireland were not less chimerical than those which he imputed to De Lacy. Henry intended that it should form an appanage for John the youngest, the favourite, and the most worthless of his sons. As early as 1177 John was designated Lord of Ireland and received the homage of the leading English colonists.[1]   In 1185, at the age of nineteen, the prince was despatched with an ample retinue and a considerable force of mercenaries to take up the government, and complete the conquest of the island. The result of the experiment was what any one but the blindest of indulgent fathers might have predicted from the first. The prince and his favourites diverted themselves with gibes and horseplay at the expense of the uncouth chiefs, long-locked and saffron-shirted, who came to render homage at the court of Dublin; the pride of native loyalists took fire; the two greatest of the Irish princes, the Kings of Limerick and Connaught, refused to expose themselves to the like treatment and withheld their homage. The funds entrusted to the prince for the payment of his troops were squandered on his pleasures; the soldiers either deserted to take service under Irish chiefs or consoled themselves by living at free quarters in the coast-towns; their commanders, men for the most part as worthless as their ruler, chose to enrich themselves by oppressing the colonists and evicting the loyal Irish rather than to risk the hazards of the war for which they were engaged.[2] Even the King's devotion to his son could not blind him to the miserable failure of the prince in this, his first position of responsibility. Within a few months John received orders of recall. He left the island and the reins of government were entrusted to De Courcy.

Here for the present we may leave the subject of Ireland. In subsequent chapters it will sometimes be necessary to notice facts of Irish history which bear upon the development of the sister-country. But the Anglo-Irish colony, for many years to come, remained self-centred. All that appeared to have been effected for England by Strongbow and his master was that a new province, which rarely defrayed the expenses of its own administration, had been added to the royal demesne, and that a new group of necessitous and turbulent marcher-lords had been called into existence.

[1] Benedictus, i., 162.
[2] Giraldus, v., 389-93.   Orpen, *Normans*, c. xvi.

In Ireland itself there had been sown the seeds of racial hatred
which were to strike their roots deeper and deeper in proportion as
the differences of language, blood, and civilisation, which had originally separated the two populations melted into insignificance; and
in the emphatic words of the Four Masters the treachery of Diarmait
mac Murchadha had made the whole country "as it were a shaking
sod ".[1]

---

[1] For a description of the manner of the Norman settlement, see Orpen,
Ireland under the Normans, c. xxiii.

CHAPTER IX

THE SONS OF HENRY II

H ENRY'S reconciliation with the Papacy followed immediately The upon his return from Ireland. The terms of peace were Confer-arranged at a meeting with the legates on May 21st, 1172, at ranches, Avranches, and ratified in the following September by a full and [1172] public absolution of the King from all the censures launched against the enemies of Becket. Henry's surrender had been far from unconditional. When the original draft of the concordat was laid before him he demurred to it threatening that, unless the legates abated their demands, he would break off all negotiations. The final agreement accordingly omitted all reference to the Constitutions of Clarendon. The King, it is true, promised that he would not prevent ecclesiastical appeals to the Pope's court, providing he was allowed to exact from all appellants an oath that they meditated no infringement of royal rights or of the liberties of the English church he restored the lands of the see of Canterbury in their integrity; he granted an amnesty and restitution to all the supporters of the late Archbishop. But for the rest Alexander could only obtain a pledge that the King would abandon all customs prejudicial to the Church which had been introduced in his own time.[1] Strictly interpreted this concession would have justified the King in enforcing all the most disputed articles of the Constitution; since he had invariably contended that the Constitutions were from first to last a statement of ancient and well-established usage. But it was privately agreed that he would claim no jurisdiction over clerks in criminal cases. In this respect Effect of the cause of ecclesiastical liberty reaped a lasting triumph. From the New the time of the conference of Avranches until the reign of Henry Concordat VII. no attempt to limit the benefit of clergy was successful, and

[1] *Materials*, vii., 514. Benedictus, i., 32, 33.

the number of those who benefited by the privilege increased till it became an intolerable nuisance which no abstract theories could palliate. For a while Henry II. entertained some hopes that indirect pressure might be used to make the clergy resign of their own free will the immunity which he no longer dared to dispute. His judges were instructed to leave offences committed against the clergy to the cognisance of the courts-Christian; and Richard of Dover, whom the King had nominated to the primacy, scandalised the friends of privilege by pointing out that if, as was only logical, the Church were to be protected from malefactors by no other penalties than those to which the ministers of the Church were liable, the victory gained at Avranches amounted in its consequences to defeat.[1] But the Papacy allowed no logic to defeat the interests of the hierarchy. In 1176 Henry was compelled to promise that offences against the persons and property of the clergy should be punished by the lay courts and with greater severity than if they had been committed against laymen.[2]

But on other points the King obtained substantial concessions. He was allowed to keep his jurisdiction over the forest offences of the clergy.[3] The courts-Christian were no longer allowed to adjudicate upon suits relating to lay freeholds; and it was settled that the right of presentation to a benefice fell within this category.[4] Ecclesiastical elections continued to be held in the forms which the Constitutions had prescribed; and the King, while scrupulous in avoiding simoniacal transactions of the vulgar kind, usually contrived to exercise a decisive influence on the result.[5] In the list of names which the electors were required to place before him there was seldom wanting one, at least, which he had contrived to suggest; the elections of 1186 to York and Lincoln showed that such suggestions were not to be lightly disregarded. In each case he overrode the opposition of the chapter, appointing the Carthusian Hugh of Avalon to Lincoln, and prolonging the vacancy of York that he might confer it in due course upon Geoffrey, the most favoured of his illegitimate offspring.[6] In the choice of Primates it was only natural that an especial degree of influence should be claimed; Richard of Dover and Baldwin of

---

[1] Richard's letter occurs in the works of Peter of Blois, *Epp.* lxxiii.
[2] Diceto, i., 410.   [3] *Ibid., l.c.*   [4] Glanvill, x., § 12.
[5] Peter of Blois, *Epp.* lxvi. Giraldus, i., 141.   [6] Benedictus, i., 345, 352.

Worcester, who succeeded in turn to the seat of Becket, were royal nominees, and not accepted without considerable reluctance by the constitutional electors. It must however be admitted that the King steered a just mean between his own interests and those of the Church. The men whom he promoted were usually well qualified for their spiritual functions; and chosen rather for their inoffensiveness than in the expectation that they would be culpably complaisant.

In the matter of appeals the King resigned himself to a qualified submission. A custom which, before the reign of Stephen, had been almost unknown in England thus became part and parcel of the Church's constitution; and it was left for the national parliament of the fourteenth century to resume the resistance to papal jurisdiction. In this as in other matters Henry was content to claim that existing usages should be respected by the Papacy as well as by the Crown. When, in 1184, a claim of the right to tax the English clergy was tentatively advanced by Lucius III. the King stood firm, and induced a national synod to endorse his protest. The incident supplies the clue to the whole ecclesiastical policy of his later life. To undo all the evil results of his predecessor's reign was a hopeless aspiration; the Church must be allowed to keep a part of what she had gained in the period of anarchy; but there should be no further aggressions on her part.

This policy was one which enabled Henry to avoid any further controversy with the Church. For the future his worst enemies were to be those of his own house. Quarrels with his sons, due to an impolitic mixture of indulgence and suspicion, are the chief feature of the years from 1172 to 1189. They gave the occasion which had long been coveted by his enemies at home and abroad; and, if they failed to break down the administration which he had built up in England, they had at least the effect of weakening the already fragile ties by which the continental provinces were retained in his allegiance. *The Family of Henry II.*

No useful purpose would be served by following out the course of these disputes. Their causes and effects are however worth attention; the former as throwing light upon the personality of the King, who found in them a painful retribution for his worst defects; the latter, because they were momentous for the future of the Angevin dominions and for English constitutional development.

Of Queen Eleanor we have hitherto heard little. By bestowing her hand on Henry she had doubled the extent of his continental possessions ; and at one time it had seemed probable that she would be the cause of mortal feud between Anjou and France. Fortunately for himself and for his vassal, the King of France, her repudiated husband, had too much magnanimity or too little spirit to cherish a lasting resentment against those who had injured him so deeply both in his public and his private character. Already in 1158 the two kings had concluded an alliance on the basis of a betrothal between Henry's eldest son by Eleanor and the infant daughter of the marriage between Louis and his second wife, Constance of Castile. This agreement may be regarded as a proof that on both sides there was a real desire to separate political from personal considerations. The disputes which had arisen since 1158 were such as had always disturbed the relations of the Court of Paris and the great French feudatories. The aggressive had usually been taken by Henry rather than by his suzerain who, though not entirely wanting in foresight or the capacity of pursuing a design once formed, was chiefly remarkable for a placid and contented temperament. The master of a weak and ill-compacted kingdom, the heir of claims which he could not honourably abandon or safely press, exposed on all sides to the ambition of unscrupulous and restless neighbours, Louis threw himself upon that popular respect for legal rights which no ambition, however reckless, could then afford to disregard. He paraded rather than concealed the insignificance of his resources; and his frankness was repaid with a mixture of contempt and forbearance which he had the philosophy to endure with patience, and the shrewdness to turn to good account. "The Emperor," he said on one occasion to Walter Map, the English scholar, "the Emperor has knights and men at arms; your lord, the King of England has gold and silk and jewels and all good things in abundance. We of France have only bread and wine and gaiety;" [1] and with this portion he at least would be content. In such self-revelations there is always more or less of insincerity. The words of Louis indicate what he wished to seem rather than what he actually was. He would have been less than human if he had not observed with satisfaction, and occasionally

[1] Map, *De Nugis*, v., § 5.

turned to profit, the embarrassments which Eleanor, her children
and her heritage entailed upon his upstart rival of Anjou.

These embarrassments were neither few nor, for a man of Henry's nature, susceptible of an easy solution. If Eleanor had remained in the back-ground for twenty years she had not been unimportant. Her position resembled that of a piece upon the chess-board which though it is not moved forms the pivot of elaborate combinations and supplies the key to the whole game. Henry's hold of Aquitaine depended on her personal popularity. Barely tolerated as her consort and the guardian of her children, he was detested as a foreign interloper and a would-be autocrat. This the Queen knew; nor did she scruple to use her advantage when she was provoked. Whatever love she may once have cherished for her husband was soured into hatred by his frequent and unveiled infidelities. The story of Rosamond Clifford, the maze, and the poisoned bowl, must be relegated, for chronological reasons, to the realm of fable. But the impression which it gives of the Queen's character is true to life. Hot southern blood, a masculine audacity, and untiring perseverance in the prosecution of revenge, made her an opponent not to be despised. The revenge which she actually chose was more subtle and unnatural than that attributed to her by the legend. Her own children were the weapons that she used, and in Aquitaine she found the means of making them a menace to the stability of Henry's throne.

Eleanor of Aquitaine

Her sons, to do them justice, were apt pupils of their mother. "From the devil we came, to the devil we return," said Richard the most brilliant and the least abandoned of the four. Count Geoffrey went yet further when he boasted that it had ever been the way with Plantagenets for brother to hate brother and for the son to turn against the father.[1] It would have been well for Henry's peace of mind if he had recognised his sons in their true light. Instead of doing so he had placed them in positions which were eminently fitted to develop the worst failings of their natures. Anxiety for the future of his composite dominions, the desire that his death might not be the signal for a fratricidal strife, possessed him to the exclusion of all other considerations. He wished to prescribe the partition of the vast inheritance which he would leave them, and not only so, but to confer on them a legal claim to

The Princes

---

[1] Giraldus, *De Institutione Principum*, 155.

the allegiance of their future subjects; yet at the same time he had resolved that not a shred of real power should leave his hands while he had still the strength to rule. Impatience at the contrast between their nominal dignity and actual impotence, the determination of each to make himself the equal of all the rest, the fear that a portion once assigned might be curtailed in favour of another —such were the feelings which Henry's policy had prepared in the minds of his four sons. Only a spark was needed to produce a conflagration. It was Eleanor who lit the train; Henry and Geoffrey, the two elder brothers, were the first to open war. Both possessed in an unusual measure the power of exercising a personal fascination upon those who had the strongest grounds for doubting their sincerity. Such was the friendship between Geoffrey and the cold-natured Philip Augustus that at the funeral of the former, in 1186, the King of France could scarcely be restrained from leaping alive into the vault where the remains of his brother in arms had just been laid.[1] Still greater was the magic of Prince Henry's personality. "A restless youth and born for many men's undoing" is the judgment of the soberest historian of that day; who is nevertheless obliged to add that, in the words of Scripture, "the number of the fools is infinite" and that the Prince was not only influential in his life but even accounted as a hero after his unhappy death.[2] Less grudging is the tribute of the Prince's household servant. So generous was the young prince, we are told, that he would give his last coin to any comrade of the moment; in arms as furious as a wild boar, in peace forgiving, mild, and easy of access. The equals of his knights, who followed him for mere love and without the hope of gain, were nowhere to be found.[3] And Walter Map, though ready to admit the enormity of his repeated treasons against the most lenient of fathers, still maintains that chivalry, which had almost perished from the world before the Prince's time, was revived and elevated to a higher level of perfection by the example that he set.[4]

Their Grievances

Honours had been heaped upon Prince Henry from the beginning of the reign. In 1158 he had been designated as the heir to Normandy and betrothed to the daughter of his future suzerain. In 1169 he was allowed to do homage to Louis for Anjou and

---

[1] Giraldus, *D. I. P.*, p. 34.   [2] William of Newburgh, iii., § 7.
[3] Giraldus, *D. I. P.*, p. 32.   [4] *De Nugis*, iv., § 1.

Brittany, and we have already had occasion to notice his coronation
as King of England in 1170. But he was not allowed to rule a
single one of the provinces which had received him as their lord.
In the same way Geoffrey, whose marriage with Constance of Brittany
gave him, in 1171, the succession to her father's duchy, remained
a mere pensioner upon his father's bounty. In respect of money
neither he nor his elder brother were generously treated; although
there were good reasons why their father's resources should be
studiously husbanded, it was only to be expected that the contrast
between their future prospects and their present poverty should
fill them with impatience.

Scarcely was the reconciliation with the Papacy complete before
the young King fled to the court of his father-in-law and, on being
ordered to return, demanded that he should be put in possession of
either Normandy or England. For the moment the breach was
healed by vague promises from the old King. But it was soon
reopened in another form by one of his most adventurous de-
partures in the field of foreign policy. Several times in the course
of the long struggle between Frederic Barbarossa and the Papacy
the idea of offering the imperial crown to the King of England was
discussed among the Italian supporters of the Pope, and we are
told that on one at least of these occasions Henry II. was actually
sounded.[1] Acceptance of the offer would have meant a violent
breach with the traditions of his house and his own settled plans.
But he was attracted by the dazzling prospect and wished at least
to place himself in a position from which he might with safety
make a bid for the Empire should a favourable opportunity be
presented to him. To this end it was essential that he should
secure a free passage through the lands of the Count of Maurienne
whose straggling Alpine principality[2] had by chance or calculation
expanded in such a manner as to control all the highways between
Italy and France. Negotiations were accordingly commenced for a
marriage between the heiress of Humbert III., the reigning Count,
and John the youngest of the Angevin princes. The marriage
contract (1173) was wholly favourable to Henry's plans. It provided
that at the Count's death the young couple should take the greater

The First
Quarrel,
1172-3

---

[1] Giraldus, *D. I. P.*, p. 13. Peter of Blois, *Epp.*, No. cxiii. The first of these
authorities refers to the negotiations with Maurienne as a consequence of the Italian
invitation. But see *E. H. R.*, xxi., pp. 363-7.
[2] It comprised Chablais, Savoy, Maurienne, Aosta, Piedmont.

part of his inheritance. An unexpected accident, the death of the bride within a few months of the betrothal, brought the scheme to nothing. But in those few months it had produced unforeseen complications. Humbert stipulated that John should receive from his father a fief befitting his future dignity, and three castles of Anjou were consequently conferred upon the prince. The young Henry protested against a grant which he regarded as prejudicial to his own vested rights. He had been designated heir of Anjou, and without his consent no part of Anjou might be alienated.[1] For the second time he fled to the French court where, at his mother's instigation, he was quickly joined by Geoffrey and Richard. A formidable coalition of their father's enemies soon gathered round the princes. Louis VII., William the Lion of Scotland, the Counts of Boulogne and Flanders, all bound themselves to support the rights of the sons against the father. From every part of the old King's continental dominions came promises of support for the conspiracy; but nowhere was it so welcome as in England. Those who had suffered by the resumption of the royal demesnes, those whose castles had been occupied by royal garrisons, those who had been injured by the curtailment of private jurisdiction, or by the strict administration of the forest law, hastened to enrol themselves upon the prince's side.

The Rebellion of 1173   In the spring of 1173 war broke out on both sides of the Channel. Abroad there was a Breton rising headed by Count Geoffrey; but the chief operations fell in Normandy, which was repeatedly invaded from the side of France by the princes and their allies. In England the eastern counties furnished the main theatre of operations. The Earls of Leicester and Norfolk, with other barons of less note, enlisted mercenaries, fortified their own castles, and attacked others which held out for the crown. An offer of the earldom of Huntingdon brought to their assistance David the brother of the King of Scots; and William the Lion, to whom the younger Henry had promised that part of northern England formerly conferred on David I. by Stephen,[2] fulfilled his side of the contract by forays in full force across the border. On neither side in the conflict was there anything like scientific strategy; sieges

[1] Benedictus, i., 41.
[2] Jordan Fantosme says that William was promised Cumberland and Westmoreland; Benedictus, i., 45, only mentions Northumberland. Probably each gives a part of the truth.

and petty skirmishes, varied on the side of the rebels by indiscriminate pillage, were the only operations. The princes expected that
the first check to their father's cause would give the signal for
universal insurrection; and Henry II. thought this danger so
serious that he offered at an early stage of the war to invest
Richard with half of Aquitaine, and the young Henry with half of
England or Ireland, as the price of peace.[1] But the event proved
that his government rested on broad and firm foundations. The
unprivileged classes both in England and Normandy saw no reason
why they should exchange the rule of one strong man for that of
inexperienced youths and a feudal oligarchy. In Normandy they
stood neutral; in England the shire-levies made a loyal response to
the summons of the King's justiciars. The English rising melted
ignominiously before Henry could give it his personal attention;
at Fornham (co. Suffolk) the Flemish mercenaries of the Earl of
Leicester were routed by a royalist force ; the earl was taken; his
men were exterminated by a patriotic peasantry, armed with flails
and pitchforks. The attempt on Normandy was equally abortive.
In 1174 the King left his continental dominions to defend themselves, and visited England in order to conciliate the masses by a
public penance at the tomb of Becket. But, in the King's absence,
Rouen defied the united forces of Louis and the princes; it was
their supreme effort and it proved abortive. Their failure, the submission of the earls, the fortuitous capture of the King of Scotland
in a fog near Alnwick, enabled Henry II. to make peace on favourable terms in the autumn of 1174. He had learned from experience to recognise one at least of his mistakes; and he now promised
a competent revenue to each of the three rebel princes. But he
refused, as firmly as before, to give them any share of sovereign
power; and he insisted upon his right to make provision for Prince
John, who was endowed with castles and demesne lands in England,
in Normandy, and in Anjou, at the moment when his brothers were
received back into favour.[2]

From this first rebellion the old King emerged with unabated
power and credit. In some respects he was even a gainer by the
contest. The conduct of the English barons gave him an excuse
for the wholesale sequestration and destruction of important castles.
William the Lion only obtained his release by signing a treaty at

The Treaty of Falaise (Aug. 10, 1175)

---

[1] Benedictus, i., 59.   [2] *Ibid.*, 77, 78.

9

Falaise, of which the effect was to make him an ordinary tenant-in-chief of the English crown. He did homage to Henry "as the other men of my Lord the King are wont". He promised that the prelates and barons of Scotland should do homage to the King of England against all other men. He engaged the Church of Scotland to remain in such subjection to that of England "as it ought and is accustomed". In pledge of his sincerity he handed over to English garrisons the castles of Roxburgh, Berwick, Jedburgh, Edinburgh, and Stirling.[1] No King of England before Henry's time had ever gained so tight a hold on Scotland. And he was by no means content to let his rights remain unexercised. On more than one occasion in the next fifteen years William appeared at the Great Council; once at least he accepted Henry's dictation as to the internal affairs of Galloway and allowed the rights of a Scotch tenant-in-chief to be vindicated in the English Curia Regis. There were limits to his obedience, it is true. In 1188 he refused to let the Bishop of Durham enter Scotland to collect the tithe for the Crusade in Henry's name; and he persuaded Clement III. to declare that the Church of Scotland was independent of the see of York and immediately subject to the Papacy.[2] But William's ordinary relations with England were amicable; the Honour of Huntingdon which he received in 1185, and his subsequent marriage to a wealthy English heiress, reconciled him somewhat to the loss of independence.[3]

Later Relations with France

With France, finally, a peace was made which lasted till the death of Louis VII. (1180). It was agreed to celebrate, at the first fitting opportunity, a marriage between the French king's daughter Alais and Prince Richard, which had been first arranged as early as 1168. The chief outstanding frontier dispute, that relating to the suzerainty of Berri and Auvergne, was to be referred to arbitrators. Under the influence of the Papacy, now at length reconciled to Frederic Barbarossa by the Treaty of Venice (1177), the two kings swore that they would join in a crusade for the relief of the tottering Kingdom of Jerusalem. This last engagement was soon commuted; and the allies merely sent a force to assist the Count of Toulouse in the pious work of suppressing the Albigensian heresy. The other terms were not fulfilled at all.[4] Every cause of friction

[1] Benedictus, i., 96.   [2] Ibid., ii., 234.   [3] Ibid., i., 337, 347.   [4] Ibid., i., 198 ff.

which had previously existed still remained; the failure of the
health of Louis was the sole guarantee of peace.

Philip Augustus was a man of different mettle from his father. Philip Augustus
The position which he holds in the twelfth century is not unlike
that of Louis XI. in the fifteenth; by nature a Thersites, by destiny
called to be the foster father of a nation. Wary and suspicious,
less a soldier than a diplomat, and with no chivalrous accomplishments to gild his vices, incapable of lasting devotion to any idea
but that of personal aggrandisement, with an inveterate distaste
for the romantic, and an equally inveterate preference for crooked
courses, he found himself from the outset of his career the object
of a romantic devotion, as one set apart and consecrated by heaven
to deliver France from foreigners and anarchy. On the night that
Philip was born the Welshman, Gerald de Barri, then a student at
the University of Paris, was startled from his sleep by the clashing
of bells and universal tumult. Looking from his window he saw
the city all ablaze with lamps and candles, and in the solitary street
below him two withered crones capering for joy with lighted tapers
in their hands. He asked what they did there. " We have a king
now," was the answer, "a good stout boy who will put your king
to shame and loss, you Englishman! "[1] To the same author we owe
a tale of Philip's early years which paints him as the man of fate.
One day when his barons had met for a council in a grassy glade
the young King sat apart, biting a hazel twig with an abstracted
air. " I would give a good horse," said a bystander, "to know of
what the King is thinking." The Court-fool took up the challenge
and put his question to the King. " I was thinking," said Philip,
" whether God will ever grant to me or another king of France to
make this kingdom what it was in the days of Charlemagne."[2]
Many years had yet to pass before this ideal could be even partially
fulfilled, and the new reign opened inauspiciously. The two great
houses of Flanders and Blois contended furiously for the first place
in the boy-king's counsels. He wavered between them and at
length ran some danger of succumbing before the coalition into
which his caprices drove them. It was the mediation of the King
of England which gave Philip the necessary breathing-space.
Policy, and perhaps a lingering respect for conventional ideas of
loyalty, prevented Henry from lending himself to any project for

[1] Giraldus, *D. I. P.*, p. 146.   [2] *Ibid.*, p. 147.

the destruction or dismemberment of the Crown of France. He preferred to leave it in the hands of one upon whose gratitude he thought that he could count.

Philip and the Sons of Henry — He had reckoned without his sons and in ignorance of Philip's character. In 1181 the Princes Henry and Richard came to open war with one another. The latter had been designated Duke of Aquitaine in 1169, and in 1175 at the age of seventeen was sent to administer the duchy. That he alone should be so favoured was gall and wormwood to his brothers; the more so because he falsified their envious predictions of disaster, beating down rebellion and harrying disturbers of the peace with a tempestuous audacity which nothing could resist. They did their best to trip him by intriguing with his vassals; and he, in revenge, rode roughshod over their friends and vested interests. The feud came to a head in 1182, through an encroachment which Richard committed on his eldest brother's fief of Anjou. The heir-apparent fled for the second time to the French court announcing that he would no longer be kept in leading strings or brow-beaten by his junior. Unless he were allowed to rule in Normandy as Richard ruled in Aquitaine, and unless Richard gave him reparation for the trespass on Anjou, he would go to seek his fortune in the Holy Land. Between Richard whom he trusted and Henry whom he loved the old King stood irresolute. At length he offered, as a compromise, that Richard and Geoffrey should do homage to their elder brother. Father and sons met for this ceremony in Caen at the Christmas festivities of 1182. But Henry II. had undertaken a task too hard for him. Richard bluntly refused to become his brother's man; with infinite difficulty he was persuaded to give way; but now it was the turn of Henry FitzHenry to draw back from a transaction which would strengthen Richard's position without any corresponding advantage to himself. The insulted Duke of Aquitaine left the court heaping threats and contumelies on his father and his brother; and was accordingly treated as a rebel. The Aquitanian barons improved the occasion in their usual manner by inviting the young Henry to deliver them from the tyranny of Richard, whom they accused of nameless outrages upon the honour of their families. Richard's worst offence was to have ended the golden age of anarchy in Aquitaine. But his father chose to believe the charges and to approve the project of a fratricidal war.

Without delay the troops of Henry FitzHenry were launched on Aquitaine; and Bertrand de Born, the prince of mischief-makers, sounded in stirring verses the tocsin of rebellion. In the person of this meteoric and malignant troubadour all the worst and the best qualities of southern chivalry were blended. The lord of Hautefort and of near a thousand men-at-arms, he kept alive the good old Aquitanian custom, defending his own rights or invading those of others with the strong hand and utter fearlessness. He flew at no ignoble game; the Count of Périgord, the Viscount of Limoges, Prince Richard himself, had cause to remember Bertrand's prowess and rapacity. For his own aggrandisement and that of his order he was always ready to blow up the smouldering embers of rebellion, and he meddled fearlessly in high politics to perpetuate the chaos out of which he made renown and profit. A power of personal fascination gave him friendships which he could never have acquired by solid worth. The old *Life* [1] says that " he was lord when he would of King Henry of England and his sons "; and he abused his influence to sow discord. " At all times he wished that father and son should be at war together, and brother at war with brother ; and always he would that the Kings of France and England should be enemies. If they had peace or truce he set to work to unmake it with his *sirventes* and to show how each was dishonoured by that peace." Among the troubadours of the time he held a leading place, but he had no skill or liking for their common theme of love. His poems were lampoons and fiery calls to battle. " I am never happy," says one of them, " unless the rich barons are at feud " [2] and this feeling, thinly disguised or nakedly averred, runs through all his verse. Even when he takes the spring for his subject he has only a passing word of appreciation for the fresh leaves and the flowers and the musical tumult of the birds in the green woods; he is glad of spring's coming because it is the season when knights go out to war, when the meadows are white with pavilions, when hinds and their flocks scurry over the plain before the advance-guards of armies ; when the earth trembles beneath the hooves of chargers marching in the ranks, when castles are beleaguered, and walls and towers crumble down in ruin. " Go, jongleur," ends the song " go to Richard Yea and Nay, and tell him

Bertrand de Born

---

[1] Raynouard, *Poesies des Troubadours*, v., pp. 76 f.
[2] Raynouard, iv., p. 151.

they are too much at peace." [1]   Of such an admonition there was
little need in 1182. Strife was already kindled; but the poet's
verses served the purpose of envenoming the conflict.

The War of 1182-3   For six months the brothers were at open war. Aided by
Count Geoffrey the elder prince took possession of the castles
which were offered to him by the rebels of Poitou, and ravaged
the lands of those who adhered to the Duke's cause. The old King
at first watched the war impassively, with what intentions it is hard
to say. A partisan of the princes does not hesitate to say that
their discords were deliberately fomented by their father, lest they
should unite against himself.[2] The more charitable explanation
is that Henry, regarding Richard as the author of the quarrel, desired to let him suffer some degree of chastisement. But it was
impossible to license civil war, even for a few weeks, without en-
dangering the peace of the whole Empire. The rebels of Aquitaine
were inciting the baronage of Normandy and England to follow
their example. Late in February the old King entered Aquitaine
and called upon the brothers to lay down their arms. But he found
that the rising had now become without disguise a war against his
own power. The heir-apparent and Count Geoffrey did not
scruple to attack their father when his army met theirs at Limoges.
His efforts to reason with them and arrange a peace were met by
treachery or open ridicule. Sorely against his will he was obliged
to treat them as enemies; and hostilities dragged on their dilatory
course, until Prince Henry sickened of a dysentery. He died on
June 11, 1183, lamented by friend and foe, not least by the father
whom he had so often wronged. Affecting stories are told of his
repentance; but none more significant than that his request for a
last interview with the old King was refused, for fear lest even on
his death-bed he might be meditating treachery. His father could
forgive, but dared not visit him.[3]

Richard's Rebellion of 1184   The last embers of revolt in Aquitaine were now extinguished
without difficulty. Geoffrey of Brittany sued for peace; Richard
was reinstated; the castles which the rebels had fortified were taken
into the King's own hands, and peace appeared at length secure.
But family discord had yet to pass through a last phase, the most

[1] Raynouard, ii., p. 210.   [2] Giraldus, *D. I. P.*, p. 33.
[3] See the contemporary account of Thomas Agnellus, *De Morte et Sepultura Henrici* (ed. Stevenson in Coggeshall, R. S.).

dangerous of all. Richard was now destined to hold the place
which his elder brother had formerly occupied, and the old King
desired that John should succeed Richard without delay in Aquitaine. The proposal seemed but reasonable, and would have been
so if the position of heir-apparent had carried with it any lands or
power to be held in the old King's lifetime. But, since it was in
the last degree improbable that Henry would be more liberal to
another than he had shown himself to his first-born, Richard refused to give up Aquitaine. His father retaliated by declaring
war and commissioning John and Geoffrey to chastise their brothers'
insolence. They obeyed Henry by harrying Poitou, but found
themselves no match for Coeur de Lion, and were soon put to the
defensive. The King not venturing to appear a second time in
the field against the heir-apparent, Richard had his way ; the design
of providing for John in Aquitaine was abandoned for that of
sending him to Ireland; and the death of Count Geoffrey in the
year 1186 lessened the prospect of future strife.

But the time had come when the hands of Philip Augustus Designs
were free for a policy of his own choosing. For the last few years of Philip
his attention had been concentrated on a feud with Philip Count 1186-9
of Flanders. Upon his marriage with the niece of the Count, in
1180, the King had received a promise that Vermandois and Flanders
south of the Lys should eventually be added to her marriage
portion. The Count, however, neglected to fulfil his promise;
disputes broke out in 1182, and culminated in an open war; it
was not until 1186 that peace was restored on the basis of a
compromise, Philip receiving a portion of the Vermandois. For
this fortunate result he was in some degree indebted to the benevolent mediation of King Henry, and it is clear that the quarrel
with Flanders might have been disastrous to France if the support
of England had been given to the Count. None the less the peace
of 1186 was welcomed by Philip chiefly as affording the opportunity of settling old scores with the Angevins. The grounds of a
quarrel were ready to his hand. He claimed that, in consequence
of Prince Henry's death, he was entitled to the retrocession of
Gisors in the French Vexin, the Princess Margaret's marriage
portion ; he complained that the marriage between Richard and
Alais was unreasonably delayed; disputes of the usual kind had
broken out between the French and English garrisons along the

Norman frontier; Henry refused to recognise Philip's pretensions to the guardianship of Arthur, the infant heir of Brittany. There was not one of these questions but might be amicably arranged; with regard to the most important of them Henry made a suggestion not unfavourable to France, that since Richard for one reason or another refused to marry Alais,[1] she should be contracted to John, and Aquitaine should be settled upon them and their children. The use to which Philip converted the proposal was characteristic. He disclosed it to Richard, with whom, if his complaints were sincere, his chief quarrel should have lain; and he induced the Prince to join him in a war for the overthrow of the old King.

The Fall of Jerusalem, 1187

The train was laid and everything prepared for the explosion when a catastrophe, long expected by the well informed, but to the popular mind portentous and the result of a divine visitation, turned every eye for the moment to the East. The Latin kingdom had at length succumbed to its assailants; the flower of the crusading families had fallen on the battle-field of Tiberias, and King Guy with the remnant of his army had been captured. Of all the great strongholds of Syria, Tyre and Antioch alone remained in Christian hands; even the Holy City had capitulated. The cross had been dragged through Jerusalem at the horse's tail, and the religion of the Koran proclaimed from the four corners of the Temple.[2] At the receipt of the news men of religion put on sackcloth; the laity all over Europe went into mourning; the Pope issued promises of plenary indulgences to all who would go to the succour of the Sepulchre.[3] The old Emperor Frederic Barbarossa assumed the Cross and called on Germany to follow him; Henry II., Richard, Philip Augustus followed his example.

Henry II. and the Holy Land

That Philip and Richard were sincere in their vow is attested by later events. Whether Henry, if he had lived, might have gone with them must remain an open question. The idea of a Crusade was nothing new to him. In 1185 he had been pressed by the Patriarch Heraclius to accept the crown of Jerusalem for himself

---

[1] Giraldus, *D. I. P.*, p. 91, asserts that Richard refused to marry Alais because she had been his father's mistress. Perhaps for once this authority should be preferred to the official chronicler (Benedictus, ii., 66) who says that Henry would not permit the marriage.

[2] For a good narrative of the war see Röhricht, *Geschichte des Königreichs Jerusalem*, pp. 422 ff. The main authority for the siege and capture of Jerusalem is the *Chronicon Terrae Sanctae*, pp. 245-50 (ed. Stevenson, in Coggeshall, R. S.).

[3] Ambroise, 35. Joceline de Brakelond, p. 29.

or for one of his sons. The Great Council, when consulted as to this offer, had begged that, for his own part, he would remain at home. He had acted on the advice and had refused to send one of his sons in his stead, although assured by the Patriarch that without such help Jerusalem must fall within two years. These clerks, the King said, had no conscience in their demands. But it is possible that the disaster when it came moved him more than the mere warning of its imminence. He went to the length of asking free passage for his army from the King of Hungary and Isaac Angelus of Constantinople.[1] Possibly he intended that John or Richard should represent him in the East. But, whoever were to be the leaders, the preparations for a Crusade were steadily pushed forward in England as in France. In both countries a tax upon movables, for the expenses of the Crusade, was imposed by the State at the suggestion of the Pope. The Saladin Tithe, as it was called, received the sanction of the English Great Council. It is interesting not only as the first instance in our history of the taxation of personal property, but also because in the assessment of individual contributions the jury of inquest was turned to a new purpose. The individual contributor was allowed to assess himself upon oath in the first instance, but if his oath were doubted, a jury of his own parish was empanelled to assess him. There could be no better illustration of the ingenuity with which Henry solved small questions of administrative detail, and pressed the ordinary citizen to co-operate in the work of government. But while the old King lingered in England, superintending these and other preparations, the broken threads of the conspiracy against him were gathered up afresh in Philip's hands. It is difficult to trace the steps by which the latter moved, and best on the whole to confine ourselves to the facts which are generally admitted. First came a rebellion against Richard in Aquitaine, stirred up as some alleged, by the old King himself to give a plausible excuse for holding back his son from the Crusade. Then followed a quarrel, whether real or feigned one cannot say, between Richard and Philip. While Richard was raiding Toulouse to punish Count Raymond V. for injuries inflicted upon merchants of Poitou, the King of France entered Berri to create a diversion in favour of his vassal. Richard marched in pursuit of the French army ; and the old King found himself, against his will and inclina-

The last Rebellion of Richard, 1187

---

[1] Diceto, ii., 33, 51. Giraldus, v., 362, and *D. I. P.*, 64.

tions, committed to a war with France by the action of his son.
Next, Richard, as though anxious above all things to be rid of the
war which he had made, induced his father to come to a conference
with Philip at Bonmoulins for the purpose of a reconciliation
(Nov. 18, 1188). Lastly, when the day of the conference came,
the late enemies appeared together in the old King's presence
and submitted a joint ultimatum. They demanded that the
marriage of Richard with Alais should be immediately celebrated ;
that the Count should be acknowledged as his father's heir ; and
that he should receive immediate possession of Poitou, Maine,
Touraine, and Anjou.[1] The second of these demands perhaps admits us to the secret thoughts of the Count. He may have feared
that the succession would be transferred from himself to John, the
old King's favourite ; he may have wished to acquire a position
from which he could maintain his title by force of arms if necessary.[2]
The first demand is a sufficient proof that Richard at least had no
expectation of the old King's submission. The proposed marriage
with Alais was, for the best of reasons, abhorrent to the Count ;
he had believed that she was or had been the mistress of his
father. And the terms were, in fact, at once refused. The result
was a dramatic rupture between the son and father. On hearing
the old King's answer Richard knelt before his ally and became the
man of France for all the Angevin possessions on that side of the
Channel.[3] The French King and the Count then rode away
together to Amboise and gave the word to their men for a campaign. Richard did nothing by halves ; before he went to rest that
night he had despatched two hundred letters of summons.[4]

Richard
and Philip
in Alli-
ance, 1189
    A few months however elapsed before the commencement of
actual hostilities. This delay was chiefly secured by the efforts of
the Pope to prevent the Crusade from being ruined by the outbreak
of a war which would keep the whole chivalry of France at home.
But the Church was powerless to keep such enemies apart for
long. In June, 1189, Richard and Philip entered Maine to hunt
the old King from his quarters at Le Mans. Approaching from
the west they found that the bridges of the river Huisne had been

[1] The last demand is only mentioned in the French biography of *Guillaume le
Maréchal*, 8146 ff.
[2] Cartellieri, *Philipp August*, p. 291, takes this view.
[3] So Benedictus, ii., 50. The incident is not mentioned in *G. le Maréchal*.
[4] *G. le Maréchal*, 18230 ff.

destroyed and that the fords were studded with calthrops to prevent their passage. But they sounded the stream with their lances till an unsuspected shallow was found, then, crossing, precipitated themselves upon the city. The old King fled, covering his retreat by setting fire to Le Mans, the place of his birth and the city which he loved best of all in his dominions. "God!" he cried as he looked back at the charred and smoking ruins, "I will requite thee for this as best I can; thou hast taken from me what I prized the most, and I will take from thee what thou prizest most in me, my soul."[1] Labour, disease and disappointment had aged him prematurely; he was a broken man and found no heart to continue the campaign. Instead of falling back on Normandy, where he would have found a safe refuge and reinforcements, he crept forward to Angers, like a wounded animal instinctively making for its lair. Richard pressed him hard on the retreat, riding furiously without his armour through the heat of the midsummer noon. He would have overtaken the King, had not the road been barred by William Marshal, one of the few knights for whom the onslaught of the Coeur de Lion had no terrors. "Slay me not, Marshal," cried the Duke with a fearful oath. "See you not that I am all unarmed?" "I will not slay you, but I hope the Devil may," was the Marshal's retort; and with the skill of a professional jouster he unhorsed, without harming, his future sovereign. The pursuit was checked, but no deeds of arms could redress the King's position. Arrived Henry at Angers he could only sue for peace. His enemies insisted on a Submits personal interview, although he was now so weak that he could hardly drag himself into the saddle. On July 4, he met his son and Philip at a conference between Tours and Azay. He gave them the kiss of peace, but as he did so muttered a curse in Richard's ear. "May God not let me die till I am worthily avenged on thee."[2] For the moment he had no choice but to grant whatever they required; the cession of Auvergne and the payment of an indemnity to Philip; the recognition of Richard as his heir, the immediate celebration of Richard's marriage with Alais; an amnesty to all who had conspired against him. He dragged himself from the conference, a dying man, but had still the strength Death of to ask for the list of those whom he was required to pardon. At Henry, 1189

---

[1] Giraldus, *D. I. P.*, p. 137. *G. le Maréchal*, i., pp. 301 ff.
[2] Giraldus, *D. I. P.*, p. 150.

the head of it he found the name of John, one of the few human beings in whom he still reposed some confidence. "Let the rest go as it will," he cried, and turned his face to the wall, refusing consolation. When pressed to make his last confession he at first refused. "Why should I reverence Christ?" he said. "Why should I do him honour who has taken all my honour from me?" At length he was persuaded; but to his confessor behaved more like a casuist than a penitent, extenuating every fault to which he owned, and denying others which on former occasions he had acknowledged.[1] Shriven however and absolved he was; and immediately afterwards his stormy spirit passed away. He died on July 6, 1189, at the age of fifty-six, having been a ruler since his boyhood, and King of England from his twenty-first year. Never in the course of a strenuous and chequered career had his star been so clouded as at the moment of his death. But the final catastrophe did nothing to impair what was valuable in his work, and apart from its dramatic interest is hardly worth consideration. The alliance of Richard and Philip lost all significance with Henry's death; the relations of France and England returned at once to the old footing.

Character of Henry II

There are few medieval statesmen who made so vivid an impression as Henry on their contemporaries; and we have the materials for a full picture of the King's appearance and demeanour. He was of a fair complexion with grey eyes; his hair, which he wore closely cut, was of a reddish hue. In stature he was not above the middle height; but he was broad-chested and powerfully built; he would have been corpulent in later life but for his feverish energy. Every minute of the day which he could spare from business was devoted to the chase; when darkness came he paced restlessly up and down his audience chamber; if ever he sat down his hands must still be busy with pen and paper or his hunting gear. His mind was always on the alert for useful knowledge; he made himself a linguist in the midst of state affairs, and knew something of most tongues that were spoken from Paris to Jerusalem; he never forgot a face which he had once seen, or a fact which had struck his attention. In conversation his features and his manner showed

[1] Giraldus, *D. I. P.*, p. 113. The biographer of the Marshal agrees with Giraldus about the list of traitors; but in other respects gives a less picturesque account of the King's death.

a feverish animation; his eyes seemed to flash fire when he was
excited; he expressed himself with vivacity and even with eloquence.
On ordinary occasions he was good-humoured and easy of access.
He submitted patiently to the importunities of the petitioners who
beset him whenever he appeared in public; no word of complaint
escaped him even when he was pushed and jostled, this way and
that, by the competitors for audience. But, like all his family, he
was liable to paroxysms of rage when his will was crossed; on such
occasions he threw dignity to the winds weeping, gesticulating,
cursing, even rolling on the ground, in the impotence of his fury.
At the same time he showed unusual forbearance to his intimates,
and took in good part the frankness of such monitors as St. Hugh
of Lincoln. He was stubborn in his friendships and in his enmities,
but more ready to be mollified towards a beaten foe than to acknowledge that he had been deceived in his choice of a favourite or
ally; and nothing except successful opposition to his will made him
vindictive.[1] The acts of cruelty with which he is charged are few.
Duplicity was his besetting sin but to do him justice it was usually
employed against men who had little sense of honour in public or
private relations.

Such then was Henry the man. Of Henry the statesman we
can form no fair estimate till we have considered certain aspects of
his domestic policy, which will be discussed in the following chapter:
it was in the field of legislation and administrative reform that he
achieved the most signal and durable successes. Hitherto we have
had occasion chiefly to speak of failures. He failed in the main point
on which he joined issue with the Church. In Ireland he entered
upon the work of others and advanced very little beyond the point
which they had reached. In his foreign policy he showed caution
and sagacity, but achieved no definite result; it pleased him, and
dazzled the imagination of his subjects, that he should mediate between brother sovereigns, support the Papacy against the Empire,
and play with offers of the imperial crown or the Kingdom of
Jerusalem. But glory, unless accompanied by substantial gains
had little or no attraction for him; and in practice he stood on
the defensive or made elaborate plans for rounding off his vast
territories by small acquisitions. It is the greatest blot on his

[1] Giraldus, v., 301; vi., 143.   W. Neubrig., iii., § 26.   Map, *De Nugis*, i., § 6;
v., § 6.   Peter of Blois, *Epp.*, lxvi.

career that he intensified the dissensions of his continental subjects by his ill-judged plans for a family partition. The mutual hatreds of Norman and Breton, Angevin and Aquitanian, were dangerous enough in themselves without being accentuated by fratricidal feuds in the reigning house. But when the balance is struck between failure and success we must allow that, for solid achievement, few rulers of the Middle Ages can be compared with him It was his work which gave England the most efficient and at the same time the freest government of which any medieval State could boast.

CHAPTER X

THE REFORMS OF HENRY II

IT was a modest programme of reform which Henry announced Purpose
at his accession.   He proposed to uphold the public peace as and Methods
it had been upheld by his grandfather, to re-assert the prerogatives of Henry
which Stephen had allowed to fall into abeyance, and to resume the
demesnes which had passed, through usurpation or ill-considered
grants, into the hands of private individuals.   But restoration, it
has been well said, is always revolution.   The King's purpose, harmless as it seemed, threatened privileges and possessions to which
the feudal classes and the hierarchy considered themselves entitled
by the clearest right; and the patient labour of a life-time was
needed before Henry found himself fully secured in the position
which, as a youth, he had hoped to attain by the simple expedient
of deleting Stephen's name from the list of his predecessors.
Gradually, as he became familiar with the needs of his adopted
country, he realised how vast and how complicated was the task to
which he had addressed himself; how many vague and uncertain
rights must be defined; how many principles which Henry I. had
applied but tentatively and partially must be pushed to their
logical conclusion; how much of new machinery must be created
to defend old rights.   The story of the Becket quarrel has already
shown us one part of the process of enlightenment; and the Constitutions of Clarendon are the most striking, though by no means
the only, instance which the reign affords of innovations masquerad-
ing in the garb of ancient custom.   The Concordat of Avranches
may be taken as a fair illustration of the King's attitude on those
occasions when he was forced to own that he had misinterpreted
the past, and misconstrued his own prerogative.   On some things
he gives way, on others he stands firm, taking more than is his
legal due on the plea that he accepts less than he had originally

claimed.   His opponents complained of his hypocrisy ; it is however possible, as it is more charitable, to suppose that he deceived
himself before he attempted to deceive them.   He had usually a
precedent to vouch for the most extensive of his claims.   His favourite course was to deduce a new rule of universal application from
isolated and arbitrary acts in which his predecessors had followed
the whim or the advantage of the moment.   No doubt his reading
of the past was coloured by his hopes for the future.   But he
appears to have made his claims in all good faith ; and it must be
owned that in the controversies to which they gave rise he had
seldom the worst of the argument.

The Great
Council
How far in his reforms he behaved as an autocrat, to what extent
he allowed himself to be guided by the opinion of the Great Council,
are questions as obscure as they are interesting.   If we took in their
literal sense the ordinances which embody his more important
measures of reconstruction we should form an exaggerated idea
of the Council's influence upon his policy.   The magnates were,
perhaps, allowed to criticise ; we have no reason for supposing that
any great act of legislation originated with their body, or received
substantial alteration at their hands.   In the case of the Constitutions of Clarendon it seems that the magnates were simply required
to accept, without amendment or qualification, a list of rules which
they had not discussed or helped to frame.[1].   Yet the preamble to the
Constitutions makes the express statement that they are the result
of an inquiry by the Council.   Judging from this instance we may
well believe that to all intents and purposes Henry was, beneath
the mask of constitutional formulæ, as despotic as the Anglo-
Norman kings.   It is true that he rarely announced a decision of
importance, even upon matters which later Kings of England regarded as the Crown's exclusive province, without hearing what the
Council had to say.   He took the barons into his confidence at
more than one stage in the Becket controversy ; and their dis-
approbation furnished him with his most cogent excuse for rejecting
the Crown of Jerusalem, when that unprofitable heritage was offered
to him.   But on these and similar occasions he probably foresaw
that the answer which he desired would be forthcoming.   As for

[1] So Becket asserted, naming Richard de Lucy and Jocelyn de Bailleul as the
real authors (*Materials*, v., 390.   Stubbs, *C. H.*, i., § 139).   Bosham, 279, states that
the Constitutions were produced on the first day of the meeting.

his legislation we have only to observe its tenor to be certain that it would never have been ratified by a feudal assembly without pressure of the strongest kind. The privileged orders had no option but to yield before his will. They knew that their inferiors were on the royal side. They remembered too that they had to deal with a ruler to whom England was but a single province of his Empire. They shrank from open resistance to the Lord of Normandy, Anjou, and Aquitaine. The evils which the continental possessions entailed upon medieval England have been often pointed out. It is well to remember the compensating advantages which the English people gained from the French connection. A merely English King could hardly have succeeded in bridling English feudalism with an administrative system so efficient, so impartial, so rigorous, as that of Henry II.

Foreign blood and a foreign training contributed at least as much as foreign possessions to Henry's success in the reforming of English institutions. The years which he had spent in England during his boyhood left him an Angevin in speech and in his ways of thought. He was able to approach English problems with the detached and impartial spirit of an alien; and although the institutions of Anjou and Normandy were too far inferior to those of his new kingdom to be serviceable as models for imitation, his familiarity with several types of government gave him a breadth of view and a power of analysis which he could not have acquired in the course of an insular experience, however long. Nor was this the only way in which his position as a lord of French fiefs was turned to good account for England. We can point to several cases of a notable reform effected on this side of the Channel as a result of similar experiments which he had tried with good success in Normandy. Measures suggested by the needs of one land were thus turned to account for another. But it is even more important to remember that, as the master of Rouen and Angers, Henry stood nearer to the central hearths of European civilisation than if he had been a purely English King of England. It cost him no effort to assimilate the most valuable ideas of that legal renaissance which in the course of his reign was spreading over France as it had previously spread over Italy. To appreciate his position in English history we must think of him as a pioneer of the new jurisprudence, which Stephen had with some success attempted to exclude from

England. Not that Henry owed much to the Civil law, so far as the substance of his measures was concerned. The law-book which goes by the name of Ranulf Glanvill, the Chief Justiciar, and undoubtedly describes the practice of the Curia Regis in the last years of the reign, is evidence enough that neither the King nor his advisers were prepared to treat the texts of continental jurisprudence as verbally inspired. A few aphorisms and such elementary antitheses as that between criminal and civil suits are the sum-total of the so-called Glanvill's indebtedness to Roman law.[1] We cannot imagine this writer or his royal patron attempting, as Alfonso the Wise attempted in the next century, to foist Justinian upon a community which had been formed in an atmosphere of feudal and Teutonic custom. But in the respect of Henry and his ministers for the conception of law, in their desire for precise, uniform, consistent rules, in their hostility to privilege, in their desire to make the Crown supreme over all causes and persons, we may trace not obscurely the spirit of the Glossators.

Classifi-
cation of
Henry's
measures

The measures of Henry II. cannot conveniently be discussed in their chronological sequence. For one thing the dates at which some of them came into operation have not been satisfactorily determined; and, besides this, it was the King's habit to pursue two or three distinct plans simultaneously. His ideas matured by slow degrees, and were put into practice piecemeal, as occasion served him. It will therefore be best to group his measures, according to their subject-matter, under the three heads of finance, the Curia Regis, and the local administration of justice.

(1) Finan-
cial

(1) The Exchequer, the key-stone of the fiscal system, altered little in this reign. Nigel of Ely, the first treasurer of Henry II., was content to restore the organisation which his uncle, Roger of Salisbury, had elaborated. Richard son of Nigel who succeeded to the office in 1168, and to whom we are indebted for an excellent account of the Exchequer system, showed his filial piety by a staunch conservatism, during the thirty years for which he held his office. The chambers of receipt and audit, which were the most important of the financial departments, continued to migrate from one royal residence to another; only the treasure remained stationary at Winchester, where it had always lain.[2] London, from

---

[1] Pollock and Maitland, i., p. 144.
[2] See the preface to the Oxford edition of the *Dialogus*, p. 45. Round, *Commune of London*, pp. 62 ff.

the commencement of the reign, was regarded as the natural metropolis [1] and the Exchequer was now more often to be found at Westminster than in any other place, though the treasure was not transferred thither till the reign of Richard I. But if the machinery of the Exchequer changed little, the same cannot be said of the revenue which it collected. When Henry ascended the throne the customary revenue derived from the shires amounted approximately to £8,000, and other sources of supply had to be found for about one-half of the ordinary expenditure. The only recognised tax was the Danegeld which, if collected in full, might have produced about £4,500.[2] But exemptions granted by previous kings had reduced the yield to half that sum. We have already seen to what unscrupulous expedients the King was driven in his early years by the pressure of an annual deficit. Arbitrary taxation of Church lands, arbitrary tallages upon towns and boroughs and demesne lands, the confiscation of old-standing perquisites of officials, might stave off the moment when new and general taxes must be imposed; but in 1159, if not earlier, it was necessary to impose a more comprehensive and more lucrative war-tax in the place of the Danegeld. This tax went by different names according to the class on which it fell. It was called a *donum* when levied from the shires, an *auxilium* in the case of the towns, a *scutage* so far as paid by the clergy or feudal mesne tenants. It touched every class save that of the military tenants-in-chief, who discharged their liability by personal service; the amount was arbitrarily fixed by the government in every case, although the Great Council claimed a voice in determining the rate of scutage, and shires and boroughs haggled with the Exchequer through their elected representatives. The general obligation to aid the King's wars with arms or money had not yet been called into dispute; and the fear of a rebellion constituted the only effective guarantee for moderation in the royal demands. The new tax was punctually paid, and immediately relieved the wants of the Exchequer. The amount which it realised was nearly £8,000, three times that of the old Danegeld.[3]

[1] See Henry the Second's letter to Foliot (*Materials*, v., 25) urging him to accept the see of London " Ibi quotiens in regno meo de magnis aliquid agendum occurrit, concilia celebranda sunt et consilia sumenda ". *Cf. Materials*, v., 42, " in ea civitate quae quasi caput regni est ".
[2] Ramsay, *Angevin England*, p. 252.
[3] *Ibid., op. cit.*, p. 21. Auxilium and Donum had been exacted in 1155-56; and at the same time a scutage was paid by the clergy. But these imposts were

But the tax could only be levied when a war was actually on foot or in prospect. At other times the King was compelled to rely on a stricter collection of his customary revenue and a more scientific management of his demesnes. The early Pipe Rolls of the reign show his government spending considerable sums to re-stock royal manors which had suffered from the anarchy; and similar measures were taken in Normandy and Anjou. In 1169 the King built dykes, thirty miles in length, along the course of the Loire to protect the farmers of Anjou against the ruinous inundations from which they had suffered in the past. Some no doubt were his own tenants; all were tax-payers and his feat of engineering redounded to the advantage of the treasury.[1] In 1163 there was a searching investigation of the ducal rights throughout all Normandy, and in 1171 a Domesday of the Norman demesnes was compiled.[2] But the King expected more advantage from checking the oppressions of feudal lords and the embezzlements of his own officials. In 1162 he held at Lillebonne an inquiry as to

Inquest of the way in which his Norman bishops treated their tenants, and as
Sheriffs, to the conduct of the Norman sheriffs. Eight years later he took
1170 a similar course in England, sending commissioners through all the shires to discover in the first place what "prises" had been taken by private lords from their tenants since 1166, and secondly what complaints there were against the sheriffs.[3] We are not informed what had been the result of the Norman inquiries. But the English *Inquest of Sheriffs* resulted in the dismissal of nearly all those whom the commissioners found in office. Their places were taken by men whose fidelity had been already tested by service in the Exchequer and the Curia Regis. The change was no doubt more profitable to the Crown than to the subject. No less was collected by the new than by the old sheriffs, but more came into the treasury. In one respect however the change redounded to the advantage of the masses. Without local ties and comparatively incorruptible, the new sheriffs had no need to connive from fear or

supplementary to the Danegeld, which was then collected for the last time; and were probably levied on those alone who were not liable to Danegeld; for the revenue set down for the year 1155-56 in the Pipe Roll is less by £7,000 than that for 1158-59, when the "Great Scutage" was taken.
[1] R. de Monte, p. 242.   [2] *Ibid.*, pp. 217, 251.
[3] *Ibid.*, 212. S. C., p. 174. Some of the answers to the English inquiries are printed in Mr. Hall's edition of the *Red Book*, App. A. and by Dr. Tait in *E. H. R.*, xxxix., 82-3; see Round's *Commune*, p. 125.

favour at the illegal extortions of private lords, which their predecessors had not ventured to check. The King might be a despot, but his despotism tolerated no rivals; and, in defiance of feudal tradition, he strove to secure for himself the monopoly of taxation.

The Inquest of Sheriffs closes the list of Henry's fiscal reforms. The Taxation of Movables It should, however, be mentioned that his rather fitful interest in the Crusades created precedents for a new form of taxation, which in his own time was not utilised for purposes of state but, in the hands of his successors, proved a valuable and an expanding source of revenue. The needs of the hard pressed Latin principalities in the Holy Land had turned the thoughts of churchmen to projects of taxing the West for the maintenance of crusading armies; and lay princes, though reluctant to allow the taxation of land for the benefit of any cause except their own, did not offer the same opposition to taxes upon movables. Both in England and in France the government enjoined, in the year 1166, that every man should contribute to the fund for the relief of the Holy Land, and fixed the contribution at the rate of a penny in the pound on movable property. Every man was required to assess himself upon oath for the purposes of this tax; and alms-chests were placed in every parish church to receive the sums collected.[1] On the same principle, but with more elaborate precautions against fraud, the Saladin Tithe was levied throughout England and France in the year 1188.[2] It may cause some surprise that taxes of the same kind were not immediately imposed for secular purposes. But the ill-success of a tax on movables which was subsequently levied for the ransom of Richard I. proves that the movable wealth of the community was not yet considerable enough to make it worth the while of government to face the odium which a novel tax infallibly produced. The Saladin Tithe, although levied for a purpose of which no one ventured to deny the worthiness, was bitterly resented. As the King was embarking for Normandy in July 1188, a lady of rank told him to his face that, on account of the tithe, he would be followed by the curses of his subjects.[3]

We have spoken of fiscal reform; it remains to speak of fiscal abuses. There were three irregular sources of revenue which the

[1] R. de Monte, *s.a.* 1166. Diceto, i., 329 (who makes the rate of the tax a groat on every mark).   [2] See the Ordinance for the Saladin Tithe in S.C., p. 189.
[3] Giraldus, *D. I. P.*, p. 288. The lady's name was Margaret Bohun.

King exploited with much profit to himself and much injury to
national interests. These were the towns, the forests, and the
Jews.

The Jews   Whether Jews had settled in England to any considerable
extent before the coming of the Normans is an open question.
But almost from the moment of the Conquest they had been a
source of profit to the Crown. The Conqueror encouraged Jews
of Rouen to take up their abode in London; and Rufus showed
to this colony a degree of favour which incensed the more orthodox
among his subjects.[1]   Henry I. granted to a Jewish family a charter
of privileges which all Jews residing in England with the royal
licence were soon allowed to share.[2]   In Stephen's reign they had
already commenced to settle in provincial centres, although the
London Jewry was still regarded as their head-quarters and possessed the only burying place which English Jews might use.
The English ghettos throve by their usury and drew upon themselves a share of the odium which the preachers of the Second
Crusade excited against the Jewish race in general.   The first
recorded accusation of a ritual murder was preferred against the
Jews of Oxford in the year 1144.[3]   Stephen intervened with a
strong hand to protect the maligned money-lenders, which may
be taken as a proof that the Crown already found them lucrative.
Under Henry II. the Jewries of the provincial towns obtained
royal recognition and the right to cemeteries of their own,[4] and
various facts attest the rising importance of the Jew capitalist.
A certain Josce of Gloucester financed the conquerors of Ireland.[5]
At York the great stone houses of another Josce and his com-
patriot Benedict were a cause of admiration to the simple, and of
indignation to the thriftless landowners whom it was the profession
of the usurers to fleece.[6]   But of all the Jews in Henry's time
there was none to compare with the famous Aaron of Lincoln
who is found, as early as 1166, doing business under royal protection

[1] W. Malm., *G. R.*, i., § 317.
[2] Rigg, *Exchequer of the Jews*, p. xi., and the reference in John's charter, *ibid.*,
p. 1.
[3] James and Jessopp, *Thomas of Monmouth*.   Perhaps there is a reference to a
still earlier charge in the Pipe Roll of Henry I., p. 146, where the London Jews pay
a fine "for the sick man whom they murdered".   The evidence in the case of 1144
is ably criticised in the introduction to *Thomas of Monmouth*, pp. x. ff.
[4] Benedictus, i., 182. Tovey, p. 8.   [5] Pipe Roll, 16 H. II., *sub.* Glocestre.
[6] Will. Neubrig., iv., § 9.

in nine shires.	When, upon Aaron's death, his fortune escheated
to the Crown it was necessary to organise a special department of
the Exchequer, the *Scaccarium Aaronis,* for the purpose of winding
up his affairs.[1]

The prosperity of the Jew depended entirely upon the protec- The Church and Jews
tion of the Crown.	His creed and his profession put him outside
the pale of citizenship.	The Church, indeed, admitted that the
Jew had certain rights; that he ought not to be condemned without
a legal process ; that Christians must refrain from disturbing his
services and profaning his cemeteries ; that the spoliation of a Jew
should be accounted simple robbery.	The value of these concessions
was, however, reduced almost to nothing by the rule that no Jew
might bring a charge against a Christian, and that Jewish testimony
ought never to prevail against that of true believers.[2]	The canons
furthermore denied that the usurer had any claim to rights of
property, and encouraged the lay power to confiscate his ill-gotten
wealth.	The extortions of the English Crown from the Jews were
therefore sanctioned, in a sense, by the law of the Church and the
conscience of the age.	But the object of the canonist was to
abolish usury.	The object of Henry II. and his successors was
to encourage it while profiting by the general detestation of the
usurer.	The Jew who became a Christian, or abandoned usury
for a less profitable trade, was amerced as though he had been
guilty of a crime.	But so long as he remained faithful to his
hereditary business the influence of the Curia Regis was always
at his disposal.	His debts, like those of the King, took precedence
of those due to ordinary creditors.	No bond, however preposter-
ously severe, would be cancelled or modified to the Jew's detriment
by the royal judges.	Thanks to his monopoly and royal favour
the Jew could count upon obtaining interest at the rate of twenty
per cent. from debtors of assured credit, and at considerably more
than cent per cent from the broken spendthrifts, and half-ruined
speculators, who formed the majority of his clientele.[3]	Jewish
usury was in fact the most expensive form of indirect taxation

---

[1] Jacobs, p. 91. Rigby, p. xxxvi.	[2] Jacobs, pp. 15, 185.	Benedictus, i., 230.
[3] The lowest rate on record is $13\frac{1}{2}$ p.c. (Round, *Ancient Charters,* p. 82); but in
this case the debtor seems to have received less than the nominal amount of the
loan.	*Dialogus,* ii., § 10, mentions 2d. in the £ per week as the customary rate;
cf. Jacobs, p. 67.	Jacobs, p. 87, quotes a case where a courtier borrows at half this
rate ; but he was probably treated with exceptional favour.

which has ever been applied to England. The Jews brought into the Exchequer about £3,000 a year, no inconsiderable fraction of the royal revenue ;[1] but this was a flea-bite compared to the sums which royal favour enabled them to squeeze out of their debtors. The Chronicle of Jocelyn of Brakelond affords some interesting illustrations of the usurer's methods at this date. St. Edmund's was a rich abbey but improvidently, not to say fraudulently, administered by the abbot and his underlings. Loans contracted without the knowledge of the community were allowed to run unpaid until the accumulated interest far exceeded the principal. Thus a sum of forty marks borrowed for the repair of the refectory entailed in a few years a liability of £100; the money-lender obtained a royal writ ordering full and instant payment; the abbot staved off the evil day of settlement by borrowing another £100 and covenanting to pay £400 at the end of four years. The second bond matured like the first; and a third had to be signed. This last was for £800, more than sixfold the sum which the abbot had actually fingered. Yet the abbey was solvent as the next abbot, Carlyle's Abbot Samson, was to prove. We need not be surprised that Abbot Samson asked the royal permission to expel all Jews from his town of Bury St. Edmunds, or that popular feeling against the race became intense in the latter years of Henry's reign.[2]

The
Forests

The forest-laws were almost as profitable and at least as odious as the privileges of the Jews. The lawyers of the Crown appealed to immemorial custom in justification of the forest prerogative and did not hesitate to prove, by the help of a forged code,[3] that the forest-law dated from the days of King Canute. It was in vain that they did so. Common sense and humanity protested against the system. "They are not afraid" says John of Salisbury, "for the sake of a brute beast to destroy a human being whom the Son of God redeemed with His own blood! They dare, in God's sight, to claim as their own property the wild creatures which are by natural law the property of the first comer! And it is often held a

[1] Jacobs, pp. xix., 327. Ramsay, *Angevin Empire*, p. 254, calculates Henry II.'s average revenue at about £20,000.
[2] Joceline de Brakelond, *Chron.*, pp. 2, 33.
[3] *Constitutiones Canuti Regis de Foresta* in Liebermann, *Gesetze* I., pp. 620-6. Liebermann, *Ueber Pseudo-Cnut's Const. de Foresta* (Halle, 1894). The Norman origin of the forest-system has been demonstrated by Petit-Dutaillis, in *Mélanges Bémont* (Paris, 1913), pp. 59-76, and in an appendix to the second volume of the French translation of Stubbs' *Constitutional History* (Paris, 1913).

crime to snare a bird!"[1]   But the forests were too profitable to be given up, even if the King had not been, like his predecessors, an enthusiastic hunter.   The area of the forests in the twelfth century is unknown, but we are told of sixty-nine belonging to Henry II., and the accepted statement that the forest jurisdictions covered one-third of England may not be far wide of the mark.[2]   Within the boundaries of a forest the ordinary law of the land did not prevail. All who resided in it, all who were arrested for offences committed in it, came under a law which a contemporary official describes, with unconscious humour, as being not absolutely, but only relatively just.   The freeholder who lived in the forest could not do what he pleased with his own.   He might not cut down trees or undergrowth upon his property.   He might not practise any trade which implied the consumption of fuel on an extensive scale.   He might not disturb the beasts of the chase, even though they broke his fences and fed upon his crops.   An army of foresters, agistors, reguardors, and verderers patrolled every forest to see that the King's rights of vert and venison were respected.   The least trespass on the rights of vert was punished with a heavy fine; but a severer fate remained for those who had disturbed the peace of the King's game.   The first clause of the Forest Assize of 1184 announces that from such offenders the King will no longer be content to take their chattels; but for the future he will exact "full justice," the penalties of blinding and shameful mutilation.[3]   The elaborate system of forest-courts which we find in the later middle ages had not yet come into existence.   But Attachment Courts, for dealing with petty offences, were convened by the local foresters at intervals of six weeks; special courts of inquest dealt with graver offences against the venison whenever these occurred; and at irregular intervals the Forest Justices came their rounds to hold a court analogous in composition to the full session of the shire-court, though far more arbitrary in its procedure.[4]   In comparison with these Justices, said Walter Map the satirist, Minos was merciful, Rhadamanthus reasonable, and Æacus long suffering.[5]

[1] *Polycraticus*, i., § iv.
[2] Inderwick, *King's Peace*, p. 137, attempts a map of the forests at this time; but see Turner, *Select Pleas*, p. cvii.
[3] Assisa de Foresta, Benedictus, ii., clxi.   S. C., p. 186.
[4] Turner, *Select Pleas*. p. xxxvii.   Assisa, § 11.
[5] Map, *De Nugis*, i., § 6.

Map knew the men of whom he spoke, for he had been an itinerant justice in his day. But the advantages which the Exchequer derived from the Eyres of the Forest were not to be despised; and the King who, even after the dangerous rebellion of 1173, had not shrunk from a general prosecution and amercement of all the tenants-in-chief who had trespassed on his forests,[1] was not likely to resign this odious source of gain when quieter times returned. Philosophers, satirists, and saints might remonstrate as they pleased. When Henry died the forest-law was both more rigorous and more actively enforced than it had been at his accession.

The Towns

It only remains to speak of the towns; and Henry's attitude towards them cannot be better illustrated than by a description of his dealings with the Londoners. He found them at his accession enjoying the privileges conceded by his grandfather; of these he at once abolished the most important; and he modified the rest in such a way as to limit the jurisdiction of the hustings court. By his charter of 1154-6 London lost the right of electing the sheriff and justiciar of Middlesex; also that of farming the shire at a fixed rent of £300. Henceforth the sheriff was a royal nominee; the pleas of the Crown came before the ordinary justices; and for the firm the city made an annual bargain with the Exchequer paying, it would seem, a sum which never fell below £500. These arrangements are in harmony with the King's general policy. They show his determination to restrict the growth of special privilege. On the other hand they show that he drove a harder bargain with London than with the baronage; for he admitted the hereditary right of the latter to many dangerous privileges, but regarded those of the capital as subject to limitation at the pleasure of the Crown. And while he insisted upon uniformity and fixed principles when it was his interest to do so, he declined to let his own prerogatives be limited by law. He kept the right of arbitrary tallage; and in respect of taxation the Londoners remained as much at his mercy as the smallest manor of the royal demesne. They were allowed to negotiate with the Exchequer on the subject of their tallages; but the last word remained with the Crown.[2]

[1] These trespasses, we are told, had been sanctioned by the King himself. Details of the fines exacted will be found in the Pipe Roll, 22 H. II. (ed. Pipe Roll Soc.), *passim*, and Introd., p. xxiv. Benedictus i., 91. Diceto, i., 402.

[2] See the charters of Henry I. and Henry II. compared in Round, *G. de M.*: pp. 367 ff.

In essence, then, the new government is autocratic. Yet the The Assize of Arms, 1181 Crown is popular.   Like the Tudors Henry II. kept no standing army; although for foreign service he had usually mercenaries at command.   But he was not afraid to arm his subjects.   In fact the Assize of Arms (1181) extended the obligations of military equipment and service to classes which had been previously exempt. Under the ancient fyrd-law only the free landholders were liable; and customary exemptions or commutations had made their burden light. The new ordinance summoned to the view of arms all burgesses, all free-holders however poor or privileged, all artisans or traders enjoying a yearly revenue of ten marks and upwards; the rich man was to find himself with sword and lance, with helmet and shirt of mail; the poor man with a leather jerkin, lance, and skull-cap; and woe to those who, on false pleas of poverty, appeared at the muster in the good old fashion armed with fork or flail.   No doubt the new militia would have moved the laughter of a modern general; but weaker forces had shaken feudal sovereignties to their foundations. A suspicious king would not have made this ordinance; a tyrannical king would not have long survived the innovation.

(2) To explain the popularity of Henry's government we need (2) The Curia Regis only remark the judicial reforms for which he is chiefly to be remembered.   He showed a never-failing interest in the proceedings of the royal court; and although his personal attendance at ordinary sessions became less frequent as his cares increased, he was always ready to consider any case which presented unusual difficulties.   He showed a laudable anxiety to secure a staff of justices who should be prompt and impartial in dealing with the complaints of the poorest suitors.   Walter Map tells a story of a conversation between himself and Glanvill the Chief Justice, which began with a eulogy from Map upon the incorruptibility of the Barons of the Exchequer.   The Chief Justice slyly answered that the King's court did indeed compare favourably with those of the Church.   "Yes" retorted the archdeacon "but if our King were as far away from you as the Pope is from the bishops, I expect you would be as dilatory as they are."   The Chief Justice laughed and admitted that he was fairly answered.[1]   In fact the King's judges had not enjoyed so honourable a reputation at the commencement of the reign, when the King was still inexperienced

---

[1] Map, *De Nugis*, v., § 7.

and uncertain of his position. John of Salisbury could then affirm that justice was never to be had without a bribe, and that the judges made no scruple about asking a suitor what he was prepared to pay for a judgment.[1]

Reorgani-
sation of
Curia
Regis
Much more however was needed than honesty and energy, if the King's court was not to be overwhelmed by the enormous and growing load of business with which it had to deal. If Henry's plan for endowing his sons with dependent principalities had taken effect, then it might have been possible to administer royal justice in the rough and ready manner of Henry I. But after the rebellion of 1173 this plan died a natural death. The King could not trust his sons sufficiently to make them viceroys with sovereign powers. He had therefore to organise his own court of justice in such a way that it might be equal to the work of declaring the law for all his subjects from the Tweed to the Pyrenees. Some of the changes which he made are described by an official chronicle under the year 1178.[2] About that date he made a separation between the judicial and the administrative departments of the Curia Regis. He selected a certain number of his more experienced and trusty servants to act as his Council in affairs of state; and he appointed a staff of five justices to deal with the judicial matters which came up for the royal hearing. These five were only to bring before the King such cases as appeared too hard for them to settle on their own responsibility. Their tribunal soon came to be known as the *Curia Regis in Banco*; it may be best described as containing within itself in embryonic form the function of the later Court of King's Bench and Court of Common Pleas.[3] It is to be distinguished from the Exchequer, which still continued to settle all cases touching the financial rights of the Crown. The appointment, in 1180, of Ranulf Glanvill to the office of Justiciar provided the *Curia Regis in Banco* with an efficient and trustworthy president, in whose hands all but the most exceptional and difficult cases could be safely left. From the treatise which bears his name we are able to form an idea of the remedies which the new court provided, and the legal principles which it enforced; for the *Tractatus de Legibus* takes as its special subject the law and procedure of the King's court, to the exclusion of inferior tribunals.

[1] *Polycraticus*, i., §§ 10, 16, 17.
[2] Benedictus, i., 207.
[3] Adam's *Origin of English Constitution*, p. 136, argues that the five had merely jurisdiction over Common Pleas.

The Curia Regis had still one great defect. It was migratory, as in the days when the King's presence at the sittings had been normal and expected. The suitor who desired royal justice must follow the King in his wanderings from town to town and province to province. Accident has preserved the petition of a certain Richard d'Anesty who had travelled in the King's wake for no less than five years in order to get judgment on his claim to an estate. When at length the estate was awarded to him he found that its value was almost swallowed up by the expenses of himself and his witnesses, by the fees of lawyers, by the customary gifts to the King, the Queen, and a whole swarm of courtiers. The court itself might be honest; but access to the court was only to be obtained by a ruinous expenditure of time and money. How was it possible for the countryman, oppressed by a powerful neighbour or an official, and unable to get the assistance of the shire-court, to raise a complaint in the King's court when, for all he knew, his suit might come up for trial in Normandy or Poitou?

    (3) The solution of this difficulty was found in a great extension of the system of Itinerant Justices.[1] It had survived the death of Henry I.; and the earliest Pipe Rolls of this reign mention certain Justices who had been recently perambulating through certain groups of shires. But, until the year 1166, the Eyres were even less general and less regular than they had been in the time of the King's grandfather. The Assize of Clarendon,[2] which was issued in that year, is the first intimation of a design to make the Justices in Eyre a permanent check upon the sheriffs, a permanent link between the shire-courts and the Curia Regis. The Assize claims for the Justices the exclusive cognisance of certain offences against the public peace, of robbery, homicide, theft, and the harbouring of thieves. It throws upon the sheriff and the hundreds the work of detecting and apprehending all who are guilty of such crimes; but it reserves the criminal for the sentence of the King's representatives. The duty of information against suspected persons is entrusted to juries of the hundreds, who are selected by the sheriff. The presentment of the jury is taken as a prima-facie proof of guilt, and the Justices are not required to examine the evidence *de novo*. Their business is to offer the prisoner the chance of

The Curia Migratory

(3) Local Justice. Itinerant Justices

---

[1] This is the object of the system as stated by Diceto i., 434.
[2] S. C., p. 170.

escape by means of the ordeal. If the ordeal turns in favour of the prisoner he goes free, unless he is a man notoriously defamed by the voice of the whole neighbourhood; in that case he escapes only by abjuring the realm and quitting England with the first favourable wind. If the ordeal confirms the finding of the jury, death or mutilation awaits the prisoner. The accounts of the Exchequer for the year of the Assize show that the new procedure led to a plentiful crop of presentations and of ordeals.[1] The Justices and the juries between them gave short shrift to criminals; the system was assuredly not worked with the less zeal because it brought a harvest of confiscated chattels into the Exchequer. The King claimed the goods of the convicted felon, and his right was rigorously enforced. But the result was to create a panic among the criminal classes, and a wholesome respect for the King's peace among great men whom the shire-courts were afraid to touch.

The Assizes of Freehold But there were more insidious enemies to the peace of the poor and the middle-classes than those who committed crimes of violence. There were feudal courts and manor courts in which the small freeholder might be deprived of his land by an arbitrary sentence, and many a feudal Ahab in the past had annexed the vineyard of a Naboth by means of a flagitious compact with a sheriff. The protection of titles to land was one of the crying needs of the age; and for this purpose also the Itinerant Justices were turned to good account. The changes which Henry II. effected in the law of land need not be here discussed in any detail. But he established three general principles of the first importance. In any suit relating to the title or the possession of land the suitor was to be allowed an appeal to the Itinerant Justices or the Curia Regis. The possessor of land was to be protected in his possession until a better title had been proved against him. All suits relating to real property, when brought before royal judges, were to be determined by the verdict of a jury instead of by the archaic and unjust ordeal of battle. These principles were elaborated, and the method of applying them was prescribed by a series of Assizes among which the more important were, the Grand Assize of 1179 relating to

---

[1] Quoted by Eyton, p. 98: " Pro polis parandis ad Juisium latronum 5s. Et Presbiteris pro benedicendis eisdem polis 20s. For what purpose these poles were required is not clear: perhaps they were used for lowering the accused into the pit of water. See for the procedure Liebermann, *Gesetze*, i., pp. 417-8.

the trial of proprietary actions;[1] the Assize of Novel Disseisin of 1166 for the protection of the possessor against unwarranted eviction; the Assize of Mort D'Ancestor for the protection of heirs against the claims of overlords; and the Assize of Darrein Present-ment for settling disputes as to advowsons. "A royal benefit" the first of these measures is called by Glanvill, and the same descrip-tion might be applied to all. They gave the new judicial system a popularity which its frequent perversion, both in this and in later reigns, to the advantage of a needy Exchequer might diminish but could not destroy. While the Eyres for criminal justice often shocked the susceptibilities of the King's subjects, they could not have too many Eyres for "taking the assizes". Magna Charta demands that each shire shall be visited by the Justices once in every quarter for this purpose.

Henry II. is to be regarded as the founder of the jury-system; Juries of for while it had been frequently used before his time in cases which Inquest touched the rights of the Crown, and in extra-judicial inquiries and Pre-instituted by the government, its use in suits between private in-sentment dividuals had only been occasional, a special privilege granted to favoured persons or at a heavy price.[2] After 1166 the jury was regularly employed for the detection of crime, and for the settle-ment of the most important class of civil cases. But the jury of Henry II. differs in many respects from the juries with which we are familiar at the present day. His jury of presentment, instituted by the Assize of Clarendon, combined the functions of the grand jury, the petty jury, the witnesses, and the judge, in a modern criminal trial. It heard no evidence, for it was composed of men who were assumed to know the criminal and the circumstances of the crime. It received no instruction as to the law; it was assumed to be familiar with the definitions of murder, theft, robbery, and similar offences. Similarly the jury empanelled to hear suits under the assizes of freehold decided of its own knowledge, without hearing witnesses, not merely as to questions of fact but also as to questions of law; the royal justices had nothing to do with the case except to enforce the finding of the jury and collect the fees. The new system exposed criminals and litigants to fewer risks of unjust treatment than the ordeal and the trial by battle. But as a method of

[1] For the date see Mr. Round's note in the *Athenæum*, Jan. 28, 1899.
[2] Pollock and Maitland, i., pp. 140 ff., and Brunner, *Schwurgerichte, passim.*

sifting evidence and declaring law it left much to be desired. The
retention of the ordeal for the benefit of indicted felons shows how
little the nature of evidence was understood. The King and his
advisers would, no doubt, have liked to make a clean sweep of
" God's justice"; but this salutary reform could not be carried out
until the Church had officially condemned the ordeal through the
Lateran decrees of 1215.

Feudal
Jurisdic-
tions
That the increased activity of the judicature should excite
alarm and jealousy amongst all feudal lords was only to be expected. The baronial revolt of 1173 was the protest of feudalism
against the new system, although the promoters did not venture
to state their aims with the frankness which Becket and the clergy
had shown nine years before. But the cause of feudalism was
weaker than that of the Church. Unlike the canonist, the feudal
lawyer could not appeal to the consciences of those whom he desired
to judge; and privileges which rested upon the foundation of Crown
grants to individuals were more easily to be undermined than those
which were the common property of an entire profession. We
may add that the resistance to the Constitutions taught the King
a valuable lesson. He attacked feudal courts by more insidious
means, and with less unbending impartiality, than he had shown
to those of bishops and archdeacons. With the more powerful
of his tenants-in-chief he condescended to negotiation and compromise. The Bishop of Durham, in 1166, was allowed to keep
in his own hands the execution of the Assize of Clarendon through
the palatinate; the King, it is true, sent a justice to see that his
measure was duly carried: but he took this step with profuse
apologies, and gave the bishop an assurance that it should not be
regarded as a precedent.[1] The Assize affirmed the right of sheriffs
to enter any liberty or honour whatsoever in search of criminals
indicted by the juries of the hundreds. But, in 1176, we find the
King conceding to the monks of St. Albans that no public official
shall be allowed to disturb their tenants upon any pretext.[2]
Henry II. confirmed old grants of jurisdiction, and made others
both to laymen and to ecclesiastical foundations. While he was
always ready to avail himself of any pretext for resuming such a
grant he allowed those lords of whose fidelity he was assured to

[1] See Henry's letter in Round, *G. de M.*, p. 112.
[2] Monasticon, ii., 228. Date from Eyton.

vindicate their rights of jurisdiction with energy, not to say with violence. Thus we are told of a dispute between Abbot Samson of St. Edmunds and the monks of Canterbury in which the abbot claimed, as the owner of a private hundred-court, to try certain tenants of the monks for homicide and, being denied his right, apprehended the accused persons by force of arms in their own houses. The King, instead of punishing this audacious act of self-help, merely offered to mediate between Samson and the monks; and, on finding that his offer was not received with a good grace, left the disputants to settle the quarrel in their own way.[1] He had, in fact, a wholesome respect for vested interests when they were not used against himself. The abbot of St. Edmunds was a useful agent in the administration of the eastern counties, and probably administered justice, in the eight hundreds and a half which belonged to his house, far better than any royal official who could be put into his place. For the sake of a principle it was certainly not worth the King's while to quarrel with such a man. And Abbot Samson was not uniquely favoured. The indulgence shown by Glanvill to the lords of private-courts is much greater than we should expect from a servant of Henry II. Glanvill asserts that a lawful judgment of a private court will be enforced by the King's court if it cannot be enforced by ordinary means; and that the King's justices are in the habit of advising feudal lords on knotty points of law.[2] We should have expected him to hold that feudal courts ought to be left unaided and un-counselled until their inefficiency and want of legal knowledge should afford a pretext for their abolition. But no doubt the lawyer took his cue from the King. The power of the Crown still rested on a feudal basis. Without feudal service the King would have been at a loss to provide the armies which his foreign policy required. Without baronial influence to back him in the shires his new autocracy would have been impossible. If the demands which he made upon the services of his tenants-in-chief were heavy, there was all the more need to keep their class in good humour by concession upon minor points, and to refrain from obviously unwarrantable invasions of their established rights.

The baronage were not grossly oppressed. But in many ways their duties were increased and their privileges limited. Early in

[1] Joceline de Brakelond, p. 20.   [2] *Tractatus*, viii., § 10; ix., § 8.

the reign the King attempted to increase the military obligations
of the barons, both of England and of Normandy, by compelling
them to produce for his service the number of knights which they
had actually enfeoffed upon their lands, instead of the number
with which those lands had been debited under Norman rule.[1] He
neglected no occasion for asserting his right to garrison private
castles with his own men.   He cut down the powers of his earls,
endeavouring to reduce them in all save the title to the position
of ordinary barons.   The militia of the shires, which he reorganised
and turned to account for purposes of police by his Assize of Arms,
was no longer left under the command of the earls but entrusted
to the care of the sheriffs and the Justices in Eyre.[2]   And he imitated the policy of Henry I. in promoting new families to baronial
rank and endowing them by marriages with the richest heiresses of
the kingdom; it was the officials of the Exchequer and the Curia
Regis whom he most delighted to honour in this way, and by the
end of the reign the greater part of the northern shires was controlled by barons whom he had created; men sufficiently important
to act as a check upon the older families, but not important enough
to be a menace to the Crown.

The
Rising
of 1173
leads to
greater
Severity   Such was in outline the policy which provoked the rising of
1173. It found supporters not only among inveterate enemies of
the public peace, who chafed at the new checks imposed upon their
violence, but also among barons of a more law-abiding disposition
who felt that their old dignity and influence were being undermined
by a subtle and slow-moving policy. The loyalty of the unprivileged
classes enabled the King not only to repress the malcontents, but
also to pursue his former policy with greater thoroughness. The
destruction and the confiscation of private castles went on more
rapidly than ever.   Royal castles were placed under the care
of the Justices; the office of castellan was seldom bestowed on
men of great position or allowed to remain in the same hands for
any length of time.   Except upon the marches the old rule against
private wars was strictly enforced; and the King even attempted
for a while to prohibit his subjects from carrying arms in time of
peace.[3]   This measure proved to be impracticable.   But even

---

[1] The Norman inquest in R. de Monte, Appendix, p. 349; the English inquest,
S. C., p. 146. *Cf.* Mr. Round's comments on the latter document in *F. E.*, pp. 236 ff.
[2] Pike, *House of Lords*, p. 62.   S. C., p. 183.
[3] Benedictus, i., 93, " Ne aliquis arma gestaret per Angliam citra Sabrinam ".

without it the power of the barons to do mischief was temporarily destroyed.   When the princes rebelled in 1183 and looked to English feudalism for support, it only needed the seizure of a few castles and the arrest of a few suspected earls to prevent the peace of the kingdom from being in the slightest degree disturbed. Feudalism, it is true, was hydra-headed, and was only to receive the death-blow a full century after the death of Henry II.   But his methods of control were perfectly successful in his own hands and in the hands of those ministers who received their training in his school.   For the negligence, the incapacity, the weakness, of the three kings who succeeded him and allowed the old danger to revive, it would be unjust to blame Henry II.   He often treated his barons with injustice; but he taught them to respect his will and, in doing so, made England a state in which the poor and the defenceless enjoyed a greater measure of security, and class-distinctions assumed a less noxious shape, than in any other part of medieval Europe.

CHAPTER XI

THE CRUSADE OF RICHARD I

Character of Richard

WITH Richard's coronation a knight-errant succeeded to a statesman. At heart the new King much resembled those adventurers who had clustered round his elder brother, following their landless lord for the sheer love of a predatory and nomad life, and repairing tattered fortunes by the spoils and the ransoms of those whom they unhorsed in tournaments. Richard's open hand and reckless daring, his indifference to prudential considerations and the duties of common life, his contempt for the ordinary rules of morals and his fidelity to the fantastic code of chivalry, stamped him as the type of a class of which England hitherto had seen little, but with which the Continent had been only too familiar for a century and more. Rufus had prefigured Richard; but in the Lion-Heart there was an emotional susceptibility to high ideals which made him a greater man than Rufus, though it made him at least as bad a ruler. There would be much to say in Richard's favour, even as a king, if he had succeeded in imparting to his island subjects a spark of the fiery ardour which drove him to a hopeless struggle in the East. For the self-centred, plodding, material Englishman it would have been a moral education to realise the inner meaning of the aspiration which had consumed so many noble minds from the time of Godfrey de Bouillon. In the wretchedness of Stephen's reign a certain number had risen to the height of renouncing self for the common good of Christendom. But returning prosperity had brought with it a more complacent and more selfish temper; and lofty purposes had withered in the atmosphere of order and security. To recall the better impulses of the forgotten past would have been, on Richard's part, a benefit of a nobler kind than the adroitest continuation of his father's administrative labours. The heaviest charge against him is that he made no serious effort to win the sympathy or the co-operation of his subjects in the Crusade which filled his thoughts and dreams. He treated England as a mine from which to draw the resources necessary for the realisation of a private scheme; and, to further the fulfilment of his own vow, was not ashamed of encouraging others to purchase absolution from vows of the same nature. Some Englishmen accompanied him upon his quest; and those who stayed behind felt a certain pride in the greatness of the part which their ruler played in the Crusade. But on the nation as a whole the Crusade produced a slight impression, except in so far as the domestic disturbances and heavy taxes of the reign were set down to this cause.

In 1189 France was ringing with the summons to the rescue of The Third the Sepulchre, and the troubadour added his exhortations to those Crusade of Holy Church. "The baron," sang Pons de Capdueil, "who will not wear the Cross shall never count among the brave; now is the time when war and chivalry, the pursuits that are most pleasant in this world, can make us free of the happier world to come. What more can kings desire than the right to save themselves from Hell-flames by puissant deeds of arms? King of France, King of England, make your peace with one another, and he who first consents to this shall have the higher honour in the eyes of the Eternal." [1] In Richard at least the appeal touched a responsive chord, and Philip for very shame could not lag behind his ally. Before Richard made his first appearance as a king in England the two had met in conference, and pledged themselves to start for Palestine in the ensuing spring. That no discord might remain to impede the enterprise the King of England undertook to marry at the first opportunity the ill-fated Alais, whom he had so often rejected.

Richard came to England in the month of August, and was The Pre-received with the rejoicings which his earliest acts went far to parations justify. The hot-head friends of his rebellious youth found that of Richard they had nothing to expect from him. Traitors, he coldly informed them, must not look for the rewards of honest men. The friends of his father on the contrary were pardoned and promoted;

---

[1] From two songs by Pons de Capdueil in Raynouard, iv., pp. 87, 90. Of similar excitement in England there is no evidence. But for Wales see the account, given by Giraldus, of the tour which he and Archbishop Baldwin made, in 1188, for the purpose of preaching the Crusade (*Itinerarium Cambrense, Opera,* vi., pp. 153 ff.).

his generosity extended even to William Marshal by whom he had
been unhorsed in the last pursuit of the old King. A more general
act of amnesty, published before his arrival, had already liberated
those who were in prison on account of breaches of the forest-law
and offences against the royal peace. Though he issued no charter
Richard's coronation was hailed as the opening of a brighter age.
The first Great Council which he held furnished a corrective to
these anticipations, by proving that the new knight-errantry was
compatible with extortion and venality. Of the old officials of the
court and household some were forced to pay for leave to resign,
and others for leave to continue in their stations. Sheriffdoms,
and crown demesnes, offices, honours of every kind, were publicly
exposed for sale; and the King made a merit of appointing as his
Chancellor a man who, though a high bidder, was not the highest
in the market. This favoured individual, of whom in the future
much more was to be heard, was William of Longchamp, a Norman
of low birth, whose ancestors were commonly alleged to have been
runaway serfs of the bishop of Beauvais.[1] Richard, when only
Duke of Aquitaine, had found Longchamp a useful Chancellor;
and there can be little doubt that the upstart clerk was already
regarded by his master as the fittest person to be Regent. There
were however difficulties in the way of preferring such a man
to those more nobly born and higher placed; for the present
Longchamp was left to make what he could of his powers as
Chancellor. The Regency with the title of "Chief Justiciar" was
given or sold to the king's cousin Hugh Puiset, bishop of Durham,
and to William Mandeville Earl of Essex, the most trusted counsellor of Henry's later years. The insatiable ambition of Puiset
was further gratified with the earldom and sheriffdom of Northumberland which, when added to his episcopal palatinate, left him
virtually absolute in the country north of the Tees.[2] Such a
bargain recalled the worst days of Stephen and Matilda. But it
attracted less attention than that which Richard struck with his
father's vassal, William the Lion. For 15,000 marks the King
restored the castles of Roxburgh and Berwick, renounced the bene-

---

[1] See the letter of Hugh of Nonant, Hoveden, iii., 142.

[2] The character of Puiset is given by W. Newburgh, v., § 10: "*Homo in terrenis
disponendis prudentissimus, et sine multis litteris eloquentissimus; pecuniarum
sitientissimus; earumque scientissimus exquirendarum*," etc. On his descent see
Stubbs, Hoveden, III., xxxiii.

fit of all the special conditions which his father had imposed on
William by the Treaty of Falaise, abandoned the claim to the
direct allegiance of the Scottish barons, and declared himself
content with that degree of submission from William which had
been rendered by Malcolm and earlier kings of Scotland. The
wording of the treaty left it an open question whether the homage
claimed was due merely for the English estates of the Scottish
Crown, or for the realm of Scotland. The best informed of the
English chroniclers read the transaction as involving the restoration
of Scotland's independence, and criticise it on that assumption.[1]
Whatever may have been the English King's intention, of all the
arrangements which he made in view of the Crusade this must be
considered the most justifiable on the grounds of policy. He
sacrificed unprofitable rights to secure a valuable friendship; and
he reaped his reward in the immunity from Scottish invasion which
the English marches enjoyed while he was absent on his enterprise.

Far less satisfactory were the precautions which he took against   Bribes to
other possible disturbers of the peace. From his brother John   John and
Geoffrey
and his half-brother Geoffrey he exacted an oath that they would
not enter England in his absence. Such promises were broken as
easily as made; and the influence of the Queen-mother Eleanor
procured for John an absolution from his vow before many months
had passed. Richard placed more reliance, but with no better
reason, on the ties of gratitude. He allowed John's lordship over
Ireland to become a reality, which it had not been since 1185. He
gave his brother the hand of Isabelle,[2] the heiress to the Gloucester
earldom; the castles and honours of Marlborough, Eye, the Peak
and Ludgershall; the honours of Lancaster, Wallingford, and
Tickhill; the shires of Derby, Devon, Cornwall, Somerset, and
Dorset; and other grants of smaller value. The shires which
John received were entirely under his control; he took their profits
and rendered no account of them at the Exchequer; their sheriffs
were his servants; their judicial business was transacted by his
justiciars; and all the writs which ran within their boundaries were

---

[1] Text of the treaty in *Foedera*, i., 50. Comments in Benedictus, ii., 98, 102.
Hoveden, iii., 25. That Richard did not regard the treaty as destroying the English overlordship is clear from his agreement of 1194 with William (Hoveden, iv.,
144).
[2] Commonly, but erroneously, called Hadwisa. She is called Isabel in official
documents, *e.g.*, *Rot. Claus.*, i., 162.

issued from his chancery and in his name.[1] Geoffrey's price was comparatively moderate, for he could not be regarded as a possible claimant to the throne. But the King procured his election to the see of York, and so raised him from the obscurity of minor orders to the second position in the English Church.

How ill these arrangements were calculated to secure the peace of the kingdom appeared in the course of a few months. Richard had pushed on the equipment of his expedition with furious haste, spending even faster than he sold. In December he was able to leave England, and the date of departure for the Holy Land was fixed for April 1. Before this date arrived riot and discord had already broken out in England.

The Regency, 1189-90

The trouble which touched the King most nearly arose from the mutual jealousies of the representatives whom he had left behind. One of the co-regents, William Mandeville, had not long survived his elevation. His death, in October, 1189, left Hugh Puiset the sole head of the administration ; and the imperious prince-prelate looked to rule England as completely after his own liking as he had long ruled the liberty of Durham. But in the Chancellor he found his match ; on attempting to interfere in the business of the Exchequer he experienced a public rebuff, which was aggravated by an intimation that he must consider the sheriffdom of Northumberland as forfeit to the Crown. In a fury the bishop appealed to Richard ; but Longchamp, who had probably acted on a hint from his master, forestalled the appeal by a personal visit to the King in Normandy. With the approval of a Great Council, Longchamp was instantly appointed as the bishop's colleague in the Regency ; and the Humber was fixed as the dividing line between their jurisdictions.[2] Even this elevation failed to satisfy the Chancellor. Shortly after his return he took advantage of a dispute with his colleague as to their respective spheres, entrapped him in a royal castle, and kept him in confinement until the bishop was glad to purchase a release by resigning his justiciarship, his earldom, and his castles. Again the King

[1] Richard's grants to John in Benedictus, ii., 72, 73, 78, 99. *Cf.* the possessions of John as enumerated in his agreement with Longchamp, of July, 1191 (Hoveden, iii., 136). The palatine powers allowed to John appear in two of his writs given in the *Gloucester Cartulary*, i., 173 ; ii., 25. The first refers to him as issuing writs of right ; the second is addressed to his sheriffs and justiciars.

[2] Richard of Devizes, §§ 14, 15. Benedictus, ii., 106-9.

endorsed the action of the Chancellor; a patent issued on June 6th, at Bayonne (so late had accidents delayed the King's departure) nominated Longchamp as the King's chief representative in England. The Pope had already been induced to grant Longchamp, now Bishop of Ely, a legatine commission; and the upshot of his turbulent behaviour was to leave him supreme both in spiritual and in secular affairs.[1]   No doubt his rise corresponded to Richard's secret wishes; but the manner of it supplied the pretext for a long train of disorders and disputes, which began as soon as Richard sailed.

The other disturbances of these months are of a character more striking though comparatively barren in results.   A Crusade usually gave the signal for riots directed against the Jews, and this Crusade formed no exception to the general rule.   The storm had in fact been gathering for some years past and not in England only. Philip expelled the Jews from his dominions in 1182 and we are told of a pious knight of Lincolnshire who crossed the Channel expressly for the purpose of exhorting Henry II. to imitate so edifying an example.[2]   The spirit of the age is accurately mirrored in the tract " Against the Perfidy of the Jews," which was composed a few years later (1194-8) by Peter of Blois, one of the more literary and more graceless of the late king's flatterers.   Unlike earlier controversialists Peter expresses the conviction that the Jews are past reclaiming from their errors.   He writes to warn the orthodox against pernicious doctrine; his arguments are tinctured with vituperation of the bitterest kind.   The separation of the races was increasing year by year; and the more desperate sort of debtors began to see a chance of obtaining their release by the extirpation of the defenceless and unbelieving usurers. At Richard's coronation-feast some leading Jews, who had come with gifts from their community, were rudely ejected by a door-keeper.   The rumour spread that the King had ordered a general massacre of Jews, and an eager mob, encouraged by certain of the courtiers, went to work with a good will.   The unfortunate Jewish deputation were beaten and left for dead outside the hall.[3]   There

The Massacres of the Jews

London, 1189

---

[1] Richard's injunction is given by Diceto, ii., 83, where the legatine commission is also mentioned.

[2] Giraldus, *De Institutione Principum*, p. 40 (R. S.).

[3] W. Newburgh, i., p. 294 (R. S.); Benedictus, ii., 83; Hoveden, iii., 12; Diceto, ii., 69, are the main authorities.   Their discrepancies are discussed by Goldschmidt, *Gesch. der Juden in England*, p. 37.

10*

was a rush to the Jewry, where finding that all doors were barred and bolted the rioters began to fire the houses. Some of the inhabitants perished in the flames and others by the sword as they attempted to escape. Ranulf Glanvill the Justiciar made an ineffectual attempt to reason with the mob; but the authorities shrank from using force upon the coronation day, and the massacre continued while the supply of victims and the fury of the Londoners held out. The number of those implicated was so large

that Richard did not venture to inflict the punishment which they deserved. He contented himself with a proclamation announcing that the Jews were in his special peace, and there the matter rested until after his departure.

But this misplaced indulgence produced the natural effect. With the New Year the provinces began to emulate the crimes of London. One of the great fairs at Lynn, in January or February, ended with a general attack upon the Jews and the destruction of their ghetto. At Norwich, at Bury St. Edmunds, and at Lincoln, similar

outbreaks, though on a smaller scale, occurred. But the best
concerted and the bloodiest of all was that to which the Jews of York, 1190
York succumbed. The plot was laid by some crusaders[1] and
several knights of noble houses who had fallen into the clutches of
these, the princeliest usurers in northern England. A premature
attempt, though favoured by a fire in York which distracted the
attention of the citizens, ended with the plundering of one house,
and the massacre of one family, that of the great Benedict[2] who
had perished in the London riot. The remainder of the Jews
benefited by the warning and took refuge in the castle. But their
panic made them suspicious of the castellan who had befriended
them. They locked him out of the tower in which they had been
lodged; he appealed to the sheriff for assistance; the fyrd was
called to arms, and the conspirators found themselves, to their
gratification, acting under the mantle of the law. Their leader,
a knight named Richard Malebysse, took the direction of the siege
out of the hands of the officials; and his commands were reinforced
by the preaching of a hermit, who called upon the militia to exterminate the enemies of Christ. The attack was pressed day after
day; machines were brought up to effect a breach; and the Jews
at length realised the hopelessness of their position. On the last
night (March 16) they met in council; the famous poet, Rabbi
Yom-Tob, arose and gave them desperate advice. "We have the
choice," he said, "between apostasy and death. To desert our
faith is worse than any form of death. Let us then choose the
death which is most honourable. Shall we fall alive into the hands
of our foes, to perish amid scoffs and jeers? Let us rather do as
our fathers in the days of old; let us with our own hands yield up
our lives to the Creator." Life was still sweet to some who heard
the Rabbi's speech; but ninety of the hundred and fifty men who
were in the tower said that he spoke well. They made a pyre of
all the wealth that they had hoped to save; when it was kindled
each man cut the throats of his wife and children; and finally the
men slew one another. Soon the flames of the pyre laid hold upon
the tower; the wretched survivors appeared on the battlements
crying to the besiegers for mercy, telling the tale of their brethren's
fate, and throwing down corpses to attest the truth of what they

[1] On the share of Crusaders in the anti-Jewish riots see Diceto, ii., 78; W.
Newburgh, i., 308 (R. S.).   [2] *Ante*, p. 272.

said. The Christian mob was stirred to pity for a moment and
promised them their lives. But when the gates were opened the
fiercer counsels of the conspirators prevailed, and not a human
being of the garrison came out alive. After completing the pious
work of butchery the victors went to the Minster where the Jews
had stored their bonds and ledgers. The evidences of debt were
consigned to the flames ; the crusaders then started on their pilgrimage, and the rest of the gang dispersed to their several abodes.[1]
They were never adequately punished. Hugh Puiset protected
them as long as it lay in his power to do so ; Longchamp, who
showed a truer appreciation of his duties as Justiciar, found that
it would be difficult or dangerous to go beyond pecuniary penalties.
He sequestered the lands of Richard Malebysse ; but Richard afterwards redeemed them at an easy rate and won his way into the
royal favour ; his punishment was indirect and appropriate to his
crime ; he ended his career more deeply indebted to the Jews thar
ever. The chief blame was allowed, by common consent of all concerned, to rest on those who had left the country to follow the
Crusade. The storm of fanaticism subsided as suddenly as it had
risen. Right-thinking men remembered, though too late to help
the Jews, that the great doctors of the faith prohibited such persecutions ; and frankly condemned the late excesses as un-Christian.[2]
But, even after the conscience of society had made this tardy protest, there were some ecclesiastics who ventured to justify their
co-religionists. Richard of Devizes says of the London massacre
that the citizens had sacrificed the Jews to their father the Devil,
and regrets that Winchester, his own abode, "had spared her
vermin ". Ralph of Coggeshall asserts that the Jews had brought
their fate upon themselves by insults to the Christian faith and by
reducing many noble men to poverty.[3] To acquit of all blame for
the murders a Church whose ministers could use such language with

State of
feeling
towards
the Jews

---

[1] The most vivid narrative is that of W. Newburgh, i., pp. 312-22 (R. S.). Jacobs,
Jews of Angevin England, p. 131, quotes an interesting notice by Ephraim of Bonn.
On Rabbi Yom-Tob, the number of victims, the punishment of the rioters, etc., see
the appendix to Jacobs' collection, p. 385. The date of the massacre fixed by
Goldschmidt, p. 49.

[2] So Diceto, ii., 76: "Necem Judaeorum tam funestam, tam exitialem, viris
prudentibus placuisse credendum non est, cum Daviticum illud auribus nostris
frequenter occurrat *Ne occidas eos* ". St. Bernard had written against those who
persecuted the Jews (Bouquet, xv., p. 606).

[3] Richard of Devizes, p. 383 (R. S.). Coggeshall, p. 28.

impunity is out of the question. There was a dark side to medieval Christianity which it would be disingenuous to ignore.

Meanwhile the protracted preparations of the Kings of France and England had been completed. By mutual consent they had altered the day of their departure to June 24. On that day Richard at last received at Tours the pilgrim's scrip and staff from the archbishop of the city. On July 3 he met his ally at Vézelay. They cemented their friendship by arranging to divide equally between them whatever spoils might be acquired by either in the course of the Crusade. From Vézelay they marched by easy stages southward, and parted at Lyons to seek their respective ports of embarkation, Philip going to Genoa and Richard to Marseilles.

Richard's Start, June, 1191

The force which Richard had collected can only be estimated from the numbers of his fleet as given in the accounts of the Exchequer and the chroniclers.[1] He had taken into his service all the vessels which the Cinque Ports could produce, to the number of thirty-three. Six more had been obtained from Shoreham and Southampton, and four by gift or hire from private persons; the King commissioned for his own use a vessel called the *Esnecca* which was much larger than the rest and carried a crew of sixty-one men. In addition to this squadron he had requisitioned all the largest vessels which were to be found in the ports of Normandy and Poitou, and the total number of his ships is given in round figures at one hundred. We are told that on an average each would carry, besides the sailors, forty men at arms with their horses and forty foot-soldiers. Admitting the accuracy of this calculation we conclude that the King had provided for the transport of about 8,000 troops. Among this number were included some great ecclesiastics and officials; the Archbishop Baldwin, the ex-Justiciar Ranulf Glanvill who had resigned with the express object of going on Crusade; Hubert Walter Bishop of Salisbury, and the Bishop of Norwich. Many of the more important of the barons stayed at home; the Crusade, outside court circles, made little or no appeal to the natural leaders of the laity.

Strength of his Expedition

[1] See the extracts from the Pipe Roll, 2 Rich. I., in Archer, *Crusade of Richard I.*, p. 11; Hoveden, iii., 8; Richard of Devizes, § 20. The owners of the ships received a payment amounting to two-thirds of the value of each ship. The crews were paid by the King and received a year's wages in advance.

Richard at
Messina,
Sept.,
1190-
April, 1191

The beginning of the enterprise was not of a character to stimulate enthusiasm. The Kings coasted by easy stages along the Italian sea-board, and only reached Messina in September. Richard's dilatory progress excited so much impatience among his followers that a contingent led by the Primate and Ranulf Glanvill left him at Naples, and pushed forward in the hopes of reaching Acre before the close of the year.[1] The King had some excuse in the fact that his fleet had not yet joined him; he was sailing in hired vessels and lingering that his own might overtake him. At Messina, however, he found the fleet awaiting him. Private interests formed his only plea for wasting the remainder of the sailing season. Between England and the King of Sicily there was a quarrel of some importance to be settled; the opportunity of doing so was one which Richard felt no inclination to let slip.

Quarrels
with Tan-
cred and
Philip

William II. of Sicily, the husband of Richard's sister Joanna, had lately died, bequeathing to King Henry an enormous legacy. But Tancred of Lecce, a grandson of Roger I., who had seized the throne to the exclusion of his aunt, the Empress Constance and her husband, Henry VI., suspected England of favouring his rivals. He declined to pay the legacy or the dower of Joanna; and he kept the widowed queen in close confinement at Palermo.[2] Her release, demanded by Richard on his landing, was at once conceded; and Tancred sent with her to Messina a considerable sum of money. This, however, was far from satisfying Richard, who imperiously summoned Tancred to disgorge both the dower and the legacy. Pending the reply of Tancred the English King went over to Calabria, seized the castle of La Bagnara which belonged to Tancred, and gave it to Joanna as a dower-house. The citizens of Messina took their sovereign's side. They set upon English soldiers in the streets and markets, and jeered at the King's remonstrances; when, from his camp in the suburbs, he advanced in full force to chastise their insolence he found the gates closed, the walls manned, and the harbour patrolled by the fleet of the French King whose friendship with Richard had for some time past been strained to breaking point. But the defenders had underestimated their adversary's daring. Under a rain of missiles Richard and his men forced their way through a

[1] Diceto, ii., 87. Benedictus, ii., 115, 141. *Epp. Cantuar.*, p. 328.
[2] Benedictus, ii., 127. Rich. of Devizes, § 21.

postern gate; "they took Messina more quickly than a priest can
say his matins". The English sacked the city, although the King
in his clemency allowed the citizens their lives.[1] He announced
that he would keep Messina as a pledge for the fulfilment of
Tancred's obligations; and began to build a wooden fortress, which
he called Mate-griffon, on a height commanding the city. This
conduct furnished the King of France with the excuse for an open
rupture. Philip's suspicion that Richard intended to repudiate
the marriage contract with Alais had now darkened into certitude.
Another bride, Berengaria of Navarre, had been found for the
King of England and was even now on her way to join him. Dis-
guising the real cause of quarrel Philip complained of not receiving
an equal share in the captured city. The two Kings ceased to meet
in public; for days their counsellors rode distractedly backwards
and forwards from the lodgings of the one to the castle of the
other, vainly endeavouring to effect a reconciliation.

Gold in the end healed all these paralysing disputes. Tancred
paid the King of England 20,000 ounces of pure gold; Tancred's
daughter was betrothed to the young Arthur of Brittany, Richard's
nephew and now acknowledged as his heir, with a portion of
20,000 ounces more.[2] On these terms Richard surrendered so
much of the spoils of Messina as could be extracted from his
soldiers, and renounced all claims upon the city. He recovered
the goodwill of Philip by sharing with him the gold of Tancred,
according to the agreement made at Vézelay;[3] and, some months
later promised his ally a further sum of 10,000 marks to be
freed from the pre-contract with Alais. Affairs thus smoothed,
the winter season slipped pleasantly away. On Christmas Day
Richard gave a banquet to Philip and the French barons at Mate-
griffon. "I was there," says Richard's minstrel, Ambroise, "and I
did not see one dirty napkin nor one wooden cup or porringer, but
rich plate with carving and figures, and adorned with precious
stones; there was nothing cheap or common, and the feast was so

Later events in Sicily

---

[1] Ambroise, ll. 630-830 (ed. Gaston Paris). From this writer the author of the
Itinerarium merely translates with a few additions.

[2] Benedictus, ii., 132. Ambroise, ll. 951 ff. In the treaty as given in Benedictus,
Richard calls Arthur "carissimum nepotem nostrum et *haeredem*".

[3] Ambroise, l. 1051. Rigord, p. 31 (Bouquet). *Itinerarium*, p. 169, enlarges on
Richard's generosity. Rigord maintains that Philip received less than his lawful
share. Hoveden, iii., 58, gives the terms of settlement.

nobly served that every one was satisfied."[1] At another time the King of England paid a visit to a Calabrian seer, Joachim the abbot of Corazzo, who had lately startled the world by a prophecy that the sixth and last of the great persecutions foretold in the Apocalypse would commence in the year 1199, and would be shortly followed by the overthrow of Antichrist and the millennium. The abbot foretold to Richard the death of Saladin, and a destruction of the unbelievers such as there had not been since the beginning of the world. "Thou art the appointed instrument" he told the King.[2]

Richard in Cyprus

Such exhortations were much needed in the crusading host, not least of all by Richard. The King of France set sail for the Holy Land on March 30, 1191. Richard, however, delayed some days to await the coming of the princess Berengaria, who was to sail with him in Queen Joanna's company; and his voyage was interrupted in mid-course that he might achieve a conquest which served little purpose beyond that of satisfying wounded honour. A tempest drove some of his ships ashore upon the coast of Cyprus. The ruler of the island, a certain Isaac of the house of the Comneni, who had cast off his allegiance to the rulers of Constantinople and had arrogated the Imperial title, plundered the wrecks, enslaved their crews, and aggravated these offences by refusing the shelter of the port of Limasol to the ship which carried Berengaria and Joanna. On being informed of these occurrences the King landed a considerable force at Limasol, hunted the usurper from one stronghold to another and at length, having obtained possession of his daughter, compelled him to save her life by a surrender. The Emperor stipulated that he should not be put in irons; the promise was observed by loading him with chains of silver. Thus was Cyprus conquered; Richard placed the island in the charge of two English governors, confirming the inhabitants by a royal charter in the liberties of which they had been deprived by Isaac.[3] The Emperor's fate calls for no compassion. He had been one of the worst among the petty tyrants who established themselves upon the ruins of the Eastern Empire: observing an

---

[1] Ambroise, ll. 1055 ff.

[2] For Joachim see Tocco, *L'Eresia nel medio evo* (Florence, 1884). His interview with Richard in Benedictus, ii., 151. Hoveden follows Benedictus, but modifies the predictions of Joachim to reconcile them with later events.

[3] Benedictus, ii., 167. Richard of Devizes, § 61.

Oriental state, demanding divine honours from his subjects, treating his nobles as menials, and reducing all classes to a common level of poverty by his exactions.[1] And Richard's apologists affect to treat the conquest as a well-considered act of policy. Isaac was a traitor to the common cause, they tell us, in league with Saladin, a pirate who lived by plundering Christians; Cyprus moreover proved a useful possession when the King, was at Acre, and the Christian army was provisioned thence.[2] But the charge against Isaac is of the kind with which a fallen enemy is usually assailed; and Richard's own estimate of the value of his conquest may be inferred from the facility with which he afterwards abandoned it to the Knights Templar. In his dealing with Isaac he acted as a freebooter; it was the weakness of his character that any casual prospect of advantage served to divert him from his highest aims.

Never had the Holy Land called more pressingly for help than at the moment when Richard sighted Acre. The power of the Christian principalities was broken; the old spirit of self-confidence which carried the Franks of an earlier generation to victory had evaporated. At the siege of Jerusalem the patriarch and the generals had offered 100 besants a night to any foot-soldier who would help to man the breach, but few or no volunteers responded to the call; the Saracens were reputed invincible.[3] The military orders, it is true, fought bravely for their faith and lands; but the numbers of the Temple and the Hospital had been terribly reduced by the massacre which followed the defeat of Tiberias. Of the important strongholds only Tyre remained in Christian hands. Acre, the best harbour of Palestine and the indispensable base for the recovery of Jerusalem, was strongly garrisoned by the troops of Saladin. The first arrivals of the Crusade had bent their energies to the recovery of Acre; but the Sultan himself had brought up an army of relief, and the besiegers had been for time past as hardly pressed as the besieged. Master of Egypt and supreme from the Levant to the Euphrates, Saladin commanded a

The Siege of Acre

---

[1] See the accounts of Isaac in Benedictus, i., 254 ff., 261; and in Neophytus (extracts in Stubbs' *Itinerarium*, p. clxxxvi.).

[2] Ambroise, ll. 1387, 2065.

[3] *Chron. Terrae Sanctae*, 245. It is only fair to say that there were few knights in Jerusalem on this occasion. The burden of the defence fell upon the citizens. But the Saracens after 1187 had a low opinion of the Christians and looked for an easy victory over the remaining garrisons. See the letter of Saladin translated in Röhricht, *Königreichs Jerusalem*, p. 491.

practically unlimited supply of men and necessaries. His light
cavalry and archers enabled him to harass with impunity the bands
of heavily mailed horsemen who formed the main strength of the
Franks; the climate of Palestine had no terrors for his soldiers.
And to those advantages must be added others which he gained
from the demoralisation of his enemies. The misery and the vices
of the Christian camp at Acre beggared all description. "There
is no sobriety," wrote Baldwin's chaplain to a correspondent, "no
faith, no charity; a state of things which as God is my witness I
could not have believed had I not seen it." [1] Pestilence was
rife; it carried off the Duke of Suabia who, on the death of Barbarossa, had taken up the command of the imperial army; Baldwin
of Canterbury, Ranulf Glanvill, the patriarch Heraclius, the Count
of Flanders, were among the other victims. During the winter a
succession of storms prevented the fleet from bringing up supplies.
Prices rose to famine point, and there came a day when the richest
had to starve equally with the poorest. The exhausted crusaders
loitered in their tents allowing the Turks to challenge and insult
them with impunity. [2] With the spring the situation improved so
far that food became comparatively plentiful; the arrival of the
French King and the news that Richard was on his way revived
the hopes of the despondent, and induced them to resume the
Discords attack on Acre. But among the leaders discord raged. They
of the were wrangling over the Crown of Jerusalem which at the moment
Crusaders did not confer the undisputed possession of a foot of land. King
Guy who led the army of Jerusalem to annihilation at Tiberias had
survived the battle, falling into Moslem hands as a prisoner; and he
had since obtained his release in exchange for a promise, which he
entirely disregarded, to bear no further part in the war. [3] But his
title, which was based upon his marriage with Sibylla, the mother
of his predecessor, had always been disputed by the baronage of
Palestine. Many affected to regard his shameful defeat and
captivity as an excuse for withdrawing their allegiance; and the

[1] The English crusaders maintained the national reputation for gluttony and
drunkenness, Richard of Devizes, § 86; who also mentions that the English drank
their toasts *memorabili more servato perenniter* to the sound of trumpet peals; and
that a week of spare diet incapacitated them for seven weeks afterwards.
[2] *Epistolae Cantuarienses*, 328. For the famine see Benedictus, ii., 144. Hoveden,
iii., 69. *Monachus Florentinus*, ap. Hoveden (R. S.), vol. iii., cxxi. *Chron. Terrae
Sanctae*, 256. Ambroise, ll. 4397 ff.
[3] Bohâdin, 123.

death of Queen Sibylla, which occurred in the autumn of 1190,
still further weakened his position. His chief rival was Conrad of
Montferrat, the lord of Tyre, the husband of Sibylla's sister Isabelle.
The claim of Isabelle was strong and would have been still stronger,
but for the cynical disregard which she and her husband had treated
the canon law of marriage.   In order to link her fortunes with
those of Conrad, Isabelle had put away a husband whose worst
fault was his incapability of ministering to his wife's ambition.
But the kingdom required a strong and crafty ruler; and the
princes were disposed to overlook the flaw in Conrad's title. Accordingly Guy of Lusignan, after a vain effort to enlist the
sympathies of Philip Augustus, made his way to Cyprus and
entreated Richard's help.   The fugitive left dissension behind him
in the camp; for the rank and file of the Crusaders detested the
marquis on whom they laid, unjustly it would seem, the responsibility for the famine of the winter.[1] Such was the situation at
Richard's landing.   It seemed impossible that any leader should
restore unity or discipline.

Richard received a royal welcome.   "I do not believe," says Richard's
Ambroise, "that there has ever been seen or can be described such arrival,
joy as there was at the coming of the King.   The bells pealed, the 1191
trumpets blared, they sang for joy; each man made merry in his
own fashion."[2]   But his coming added fuel to the existing strife of
parties.   He had taken Guy of Lusignan under his protection.   He
encouraged the discrowned king to accuse Conrad of perjury and
treason; Guy's brother, Geoffrey of Lusignan, offered to prove the
charge upon the body of the marquis.   Conrad declined the test,
which his enemies refrained from pressing for fear that a tumult
might arise among the people.[3]   But the King of France began
another quarrel by calling upon Richard to give him, in accordance
with their bond, a half of Cyprus.   Richard retorted that he would
do so, if Philip would on his side give the half of Flanders which,
owing to the death of Count Philip in the pestilence, had escheated
to the Crown of France.   The princes had some difficulty in persuading the two kings to sink their differences.[4]

---

[1] Guy's voyage to Cyprus in Ambroise, ll. 1701 ff. For the dispute as to the crown
see *Epp. Cantuarienses*, No. cccxlvi.   Benedictus, ii., 141.   W. Newburgh, **iv.,**
§ 19.   Stubbs' preface to the *Itinerarium*, pp. cxxiv. ff.
[2] Ambroise, ll. 2355 ff.   [3] Benedictus, ii., 170.   [4] *Ibid.*, ii., 171.

For the time being, however, outward concord was restored. Sickness attacked both Richard and his rival; but their engineers pushed forward with the mines, and great catapults battered the city night and day with heavy stones. The King of England dragged himself from his sick-bed to direct the operations and to cheer the soldiers. His arrogance might provoke murmurs, but he stepped into the position of commander-in-chief by the right of skill and valour. Enemies and friends alike acknowledged his pre-eminence. "He was brave," says an Arab writer, "experienced in war, and fearless of death; if he had been alone among millions of enemies he would not have declined battle; when he attacked there was no resisting." [1] Saladin recognised a kindred spirit in the Englishman; he sent fruit and snow to Richard when the King was fever-stricken, and they exchanged complimentary messages. But in spite of these courtesies Richard carried on the war with the same iron rigour as his adversaries. On July 12, the garrison of Acre surrendered, having obtained a promise that their lives should be spared and their freedom granted, if Saladin would give up the true Cross and an appointed number of his Christian captives. These conditions were not fulfilled by the appointed date. According to the English writers Saladin repudiated them as having been accepted without his knowledge or consent. The Mohammedan sources affirm with greater probability that Saladin delayed to fulfil his share of the compact until the Christians, whose honour he had good reason to suspect, should give a guarantee of their good faith. However caused, his delay was fatal to the captives. Richard ordered a general massacre and the command was executed to the letter. On one day and at one place the Crusaders slew their prisoners in cold blood to the number of 2,600, only a few of nobler rank being reserved with a view to future exchanges (Aug. 19). It would have been difficult to keep so many under bolts and bars; [2] Richard may also have salved his conscience by

---

[1] Michaud, *Bibl. des Croisades*, iv., 304. For Richard's conduct during the siege see Benedictus, ii., 173 ff.; and Ambroise, ll. 4736 ff.

[2] The Crusading army at Acre was a large one; Saladin estimates it at 5,000 knights and 100,000 foot (Röhricht *op. cit.*, 554). But every available man would be required for the march on Jerusalem. As to the various explanations of Richard's conduct see Benedictus and Hoveden on the one side, Ibn al Athir, Bohâdin and Imad-ed-din on the other. The facts are collected in Röhricht, p. 576. Bohâdin, 242, says that the captives had been promised their lives, even if the ransom should not be forthcoming. Benedictus. ii., 188, 189, says that Saladin had previously

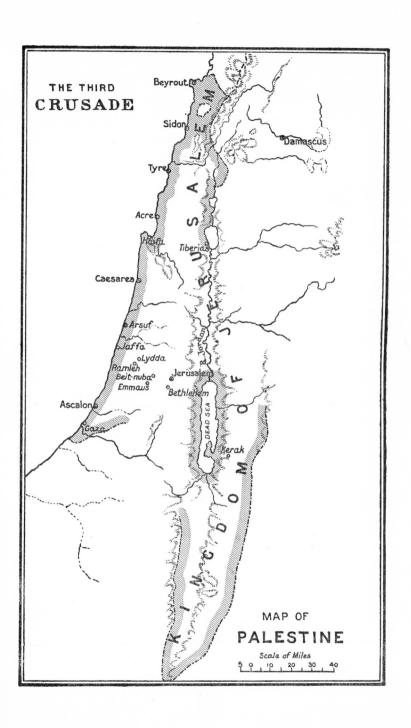

THE THIRD
CRUSADE

Beyrout

Sidon

Damascus

Tyre

Acre

Haifa
Tiberias

Caesarea

Arsuf
Jaffa
Lydda
Ramleh
Beit-nuba
Emmaus
Jerusalem
Bethlehem

Ascalon

Gaza

Kerak

DEAD SEA

R. Jordan

JERUSALEM

KINGDOM OF

MAP OF
PALESTINE

Scale of Miles
5 0   10   20   30   40

the reflection that the knights of the military orders had obtained no better treatment after the battle of Tiberias. But, even in the Crusades, the logic of prudence and revenge was seldom followed out so literally.

The fall of Acre by improving the position of the Christian army weakened the prudential motives which had checked their feuds, and supplied the occasion for others not less bitter. An English knight quarrelled with a follower of Leopold of Austria, who had hoisted the ducal standard on a house within the city over which the Englishman professed to have a prior claim. There was already bad blood between Richard and the Duke; for the latter, as a connection of the Comneni was interested in the fortunes of the Emperor Isaac. Richard took the part of his knight and ordered that the banner of the Duke should be thrown into the common sewer.[1] Unable to punish the affront, the Duke withdrew to make his plans for a return to Austria. He was not the only prince to do so. Philip's self-esteem had been wounded by the discovery that he, the suzerain of Richard, was of comparatively small account in Sicily or Acre. He refrained from an open rupture, mollified in some degree by the punctuality with which Richard resigned to him one-half of the captured city; in the dispute respecting the Crown of Jerusalem he helped to arrange a compromise under which Guy of Lusignan kept the dignity for his life-time, while the revenues were to be equally divided.[2] But the King of France soon resigned his share of Acre to Conrad of Montferrat, and on July 29th obtained from Richard a grudging consent to his departure. Philip had been seriously ill since the fall of the city, " so that every nail came off his fingers and the hair off his brow"; the succession to Flanders was, no doubt, a matter which could not be settled in his absence from France. But it was suspected that his premature return foreboded ill to the Angevin inheritance. And the suspicion was well-founded. At every point in the Crusade he had been eclipsed. All who served in the Crusade for pay, all who held themselves free to enlist under the banner where

(margin note: Richard, Duke Leopold and Philip Augustus)

(margin note: Philip goes home, Aug., 1191)

massacred his Christian prisoners; but this is probably an untruth, intended to justify Richard's conduct.

[1] Ansbertus in Hoveden, iii., p. cxxxviii. (R. S.). Ric. Divis., § 67. *Annales Maximi Colonienses.* Pauli, i., 234, places the scene of the quarrel at Ascalon in the following winter; but relies on late authorities.

[2] Benedictus, ii., 183.

the greatest glory was to be obtained, threw in their lot with
Richard, who had the reputation of being at once the bravest
leader and the most liberal of pay-masters.[1] Philip was young, ambitious and impatient of a rival. He felt himself the intellectual
superior of Coeur de Lion; he was resolved to prove his superiority,
if not in Palestine, then on the fields of France and Normandy.
The story ran that, on the homeward journey, Philip stopped at
Rome to ask that the Pope would absolve him from his vow to
respect the peace of the English dominions during the continuance
of the Crusade. This may be an invention but there is better
authority for an interview between the French King and the Emperor Henry VI., who chose to consider Richard's peace with
Tancred as a gratuitous attack upon his own Sicilian claims.[2]

The
March
to Jaffa,
Aug.-
Sept.,1191

Had Richard desired excuses for returning he could have produced a stronger case than Philip. In England the complications
which might reasonably have been predicted from the King's
arrangements had been aggravated by some accidental causes.
Longchamp had shown the arrogance natural to an upstart; and
his subordinates had committed blunders which gave his rivals the
opportunity of posing as the friends of liberty and of the King's
interests. The recognition of Arthur of Brittany as Richard's
heir had caused Count John to throw in his lot with the malcontents. While Richard was settling accounts with his allies in Acre,
England was trembling on the brink of revolution. The worst
news was yet to come, but enough had already arrived to raise
grave apprehensions. These troubles, which must hereafter be
noticed in more detail, failed to shake the King's purpose. On
August 22nd he broke up his camp at Acre. The Crusading army
had now agreed to place itself beneath his sole command. His intention was to capture Jaffa and then march in full force upon
Jerusalem. Success he regarded as certain, and he expected that
a few months would suffice to restore the Kingdom of Jerusalem.
His letters to the Justiciar spoke of the following Lent as the
season at which his return might be expected. But he had underrated the difficulties of the country and the strength of the enemy.
The road which his army took led them through the long and barren

---

[1] Benedictus, ii., 169. *Annales Maximi Colonienses.*
[2] Benedictus, ii., 228-30, 235. Hoveden, iii., 166. Luchaire in Lavisse, *H. G. de
la France*, iii., i., p. 110.

strip of land which fringes the sea-coast to the south of Acre. The heat and dust were excessive; little or no fodder could be found for the horses; for food the troops depended on their heavy baggage train and on the fleet which kept pace with their marches. Saladin's army, pursuing a course parallel with that of the Christians but further inland, cut them off from communications with Acre and access to the interior, waylaid them wherever they had to pass a defile or broken ground, and harassed them incessantly with clouds of skirmishers. Thus impeded the Christian army could seldom cover more than three or four miles in a day. They advanced in a column of which the nucleus was formed by three battles or divisions of mounted knights; the standard, floating from a car shaped like a tower, accompanied the middle division, and formed the rallying point when an attack was pressed. One-half of the infantry marched along the shore as a baggage guard; the other half covered the left flank of the knights, who only exposed themselves to the enemy on the rare occasions when it seemed advisable to repel the attacks of skirmishing parties by a counter-charge.[1] The object of the leaders was to avoid a battle, since no success could compensate for the loss of knights whom there were no means of replacing; the forces were to be husbanded for the final attack upon Jerusalem. Wise though it was, this studiously defensive attitude told upon the spirits of the army. Their courage, their discipline, their endurance, caused astonishment to the Moslems; but there were many who openly wished themselves back again in comfortable quarters at Acre. The dearth of supplies increased the general despondency; the foot-soldiers and servants wrangled and fought over the flesh of the horses that dropped upon the march. But throughout the long journey the King of England never showed discouragement. When help was needed at any point of the column he was foremost to the rescue "like a quarrel shot from an arbalest," and his war-cry, "Help us, Holy Sepulchre," turned the issue of many a hard-contested skirmish. At evening when the host encamped his herald raised and thrice repeated the invocation, "Save us, Holy Sepulchre"; the camp caught up the cry and it gave comfort to the most despondent. At length a Battle of pitched battle in the plain near Arsuf rewarded the Christians for Arsuf

---

[1] The Christian order of march is described by Bohâdin, 251; details of the march in Ambroise, ll. 6050 ff. Richard's hopes in *Epp. Cantuar.*, 347.

their long sufferings. Saladin attempted to take them in flank ; they were attacked in force and greatly outnumbered. But the knights, breaking loose from all restraint, charged furiously against the wing which menaced the Christian rear-guard. Richard, unable to check them, took the lead, and the Saracens were driven in confusion to the shelter of the hills and woods; on both sides of the line of charge the dead lay piled " like corn in swathes " for a distance of half a mile. For a moment the fate of Saladin's host seemed to tremble in the balance, but the exhaustion of the Christians checked the pursuit.[1] They had opened the way to Jaffa, and with this they were perforce content. They reached Jaffa on September 9th, nearly three weeks after leaving Acre which lay no more than sixty miles behind them. The first stage of the undertaking had proved toilsome beyond all their fears; the second and more diffi- cult yet remained to be attempted.

Attempt on Jer- usalem, Autumn, 1191

In the latter part of the year the army struck inland towards Jerusalem. They came to Ramleh by slow stages, while Saladin retreated steadily before them. At Ramleh they went into winter- quarters, but in the last days of December moved forward to Beit- nuba where they were within two days' march of the Holy City. Their hopes rose feverishly. Richard, by a personal visit to Acre, had brought back into the ranks the sluggards who had retired to spend the winter at their ease. His force was as strong as he could ever hope to make it; and he urged the princes to advance with him and invest the city. But there were obvious military objec- tions. The position of Jerusalem, surrounded by deep valleys on three sides, put difficulties in the way of a blockade. It was pointed out that Saladin could easily cut the communications of a besieging army; and that, even if the city were taken, it could not be held for want of troops prepared to act as a standing garrison. The military orders, who formed the most efficient part of the host, pressed these arguments with all the weight of their long experience. There were, however, some who alleged that the orders had private reasons of their own ; that they did not wish to see the Sepulchre recovered for fear lest the crusaders of the West would then regard their

[1] The main authorities are Bohâdin and Ambroise. Plans and descriptions will be found in Professor Oman's *Art of War in the Middle Ages*, p. 310, and Sir James Ramsay's *Angevin Empire*, p. 302. They differ slightly as to the formation of the Christian army which is not clearly described in the authorities ; but Ramsay's plan has the merit of corresponding most closely to the account of Ambroise and Bohâdin.

pilgrimage as ended, and would go home leaving Saladin at liberty to reconquer not only Jerusalem but Acre and Tyre as well. There was clamorous disapproval in the host when Richard yielded to his advisers and gave the signal for a retreat on Ascalon[1].

Yet there can be no doubt that he decided rightly. While Saladin remained unbeaten in the field Jerusalem could not be held, and Saladin was not likely to be lured into a battle at close quarters. The only hope of recovering the Latin Kingdom lay in the possibility that he might be willing to secure a lasting peace by withdrawing to the east of Jordan; for it was notorious that in the valley of the Euphrates he had difficulties which called for his undivided attention. But Saladin was not prepared to make the sacrifice demanded of him. He felt that peace with the Franks could never be secure so long as they retained a foot of land in Syria. At one time he assented to a strange proposal which came from Richard's side, that El Malec el A'del, the sultan's brother, should marry a sister of the English King, and that the Holy Land should be settled on the pair. But the proposal, as Saladin knew well, was not seriously meant.[2] If he consented to enter on negotiations he did so merely from the well-founded expectation that every month's delay would increase the difficulties and the discords of the Christians. Conrad of Montferrat had already made clandestine overtures for a separate alliance with the Sultan.[3] The Duke of Burgundy, upon whom the command of the French had devolved when Philip set sail, announced that his want of funds would compel him to depart at no distant date unless the King of England would come to his assistance;[4] other leaders were in the same plight. But Richard, although the immense price which he received for Cyprus from the Order of the Temple had put him in a better financial position than his colleagues, was neither able nor willing to comply with their demands. The main expense of rebuilding Ascalon had fallen on his purse; he was beginning to

Hopelessness of the Christian cause

[1] Ambroise, ll. 7050 ff. Hoveden, iii., 179. Stubbs, *Itinerarium*, p. cxxix., maintains that Jerusalem could easily have been taken, and that the military orders resisted the enterprise for fear that the Crusaders would return home when Jerusalem was taken. But Bohâdin and Ibn al Athir describe the city as impregnably fortified. Stubbs relies too exclusively on Hoveden.

[2] Bohâdin, 278.

[3] For Conrad's treachery see Bohâdin, 270, 283. Ibn al Athir. *Itinerarium*, v., § xi. For Richard's negotiations, Ambroise, ll. 7367 f. Bohâdin, 265-275. Ibn al Athir, ii., 53; the terms which Richard offered were continually changing.

[4] Ambroise, l. 8157.

complain that he alone had borne the burden and heat of the campaign. His health had suffered from his toils and privations; and the news from England grew more disquieting than ever. Shortly after Easter (1192) he learned that his Chancellor had been expelled from England by the party of Count John; and he announced that he could remain no longer, though he was prepared to leave behind him a force of 300 knights and 2,000 men-at-arms. He recommended the Franks to elect a new King of Jerusalem whom they might follow henceforth as their general.

The Murder of Conrad of Montferrat, April 20, 1192   The new election was of a kind to confirm him in his resolve. The choice of the electors fell upon his enemy, the Marquis Conrad, whose wealth and connections atoned in the eyes of the majority for incompetence and suspected treachery. But within a few days Conrad was assassinated at Tyre by two fanatics belonging to the Moslem sect of the Assassins.[1] Suspicion pointed to Richard as the instigator of the crime and affirmed that his apparent acquiescence in the choice of Conrad had been prompted by the knowledge that the new King's reign would be a short one. An Arab writer lays the blame on Saladin, affirming that he had offered the chief of the Assassins, the Old Man of the Mountain, a heavy bribe to murder not only Conrad but also Richard.[2] A third account, and the best supported, says that the murder was committed by the order of the chief of the Assassins, the Old Man of the Mountain, and as an act of revenge for the pillage of a Moslem merchantship. The King of England subsequently cleared himself before a Diet of the Empire which was by no means friendly to him; and Conrad's brother, Boniface of Montferrat, appears in the year 1197 in Richard's service.[3] These are weighty reasons for believing that the truth of the charge was never plausibly established. In any case the subjects of the Latin Kingdom took no notice of the current rumours; and, while still refusing to accept Richard's candidate, Guy of Lusignan, they elected Count Henry of Champagne, a descendant of the Conqueror's daughter Adela, and therefore of

---

[1] Hoveden, iii., 181. Ambroise, l. 8747.

[2] Letters, professedly from the chief of the Assassins, exculpating Richard, are given in Diceto, ii., 128, W. Newburgh, v., § 16. Hammer, *Hist. des Assassins*, pp. 204 ff., gives conclusive arguments for rejecting these as Christian forgeries; though Röhricht, p. 615, would leave the question open. Ibn al Athir, ii., 58, says that Saladin had offered the Old Man 10,000 pieces of gold to assassinate Conrad. On the sect of the Assassins see Archer, p. 377. Hammer, *op. cit.*

[3] Stubbs, *Itinerarium*, p. xxiii.

kin to the English royal house. Flattered by this mask of deference, moved also by the reproaches of his own subjects, who
declared that with him or without him they would fulfil their vow
of recovering the Holy City, Richard placed himself at the head Second
of a last advance in the direction of Jerusalem. The army march on Jeru-
reached Beit-nuba; the King himself advanced to Emmaus whence salem
the fortifications of Jerusalem could be plainly seen. But the
difficulties in the way of a siege remained as great as ever; the
reinforcements which Henry of Champagne had promised to bring
up from Acre did not appear; and the King reluctantly turned
away from the goal which he had so long coveted to reach. Tradition says that, when at Emmaus, he held his shield before his
eyes declaring himself unworthy to look on the city since he was
powerless to help it. An English chronicler throws the responsibility for the retreat upon the Duke of Burgundy.[1] But we have
a more trustworthy narrative from Richard's household servant,
who says that the King declined the responsibility of leading the
army to destruction, but professed himself willing to follow any
other leader who would take over the command; the Duke of
Burgundy refused the offer, but none the less composed a biting
satire on the cowardice of Richard.[2]

In both hosts there was now a desire for peace. Richard, as Negotia-
his envoys confessed to Saladin, asked nothing better than a treaty tions with Saladin
which should allow him to depart without a total loss of reputation.
The emirs pressed their master to give the Englishman every
encouragement in his intention of retiring; they were weary of
the war; the supplies of the army were failing, the religious ardour
of the men had long since evaporated.[3] Saladin was the chief
obstacle to peace. At the beginning of the war he had told his
counsellors that life was short and fate uncertain, and that such an
army as they had got together should not be disbanded without
securing some great advantage for the faith.[4] To this opinion he
still clung, and he pointed out the folly of allowing the Franks to
keep any base from which they might renew the war. Compelled
by the pressure of the emirs to enter upon negotiations, he admitted the necessity of leaving Acre in Christian hands; but he insisted that Ascalon, which Richard had commenced to fortify, should

[1] Hoveden, iii., 182. *Cf.* Coggeshall, 39. Joinville, c. 108.
[2] Ambroise, l. 10137.   [3] Bohâdin, 344.   [4] Ibn al Athir, i., 681.

be dismantled.[1]   Two months elapsed before the King could bring himself to sacrifice this cherished acquisition.   During this period hostilities were continued, though in a desultory fashion.   The Saracens besieged Jaffa; and when the garrison were on the point of surrendering Richard relieved them by a feat of reckless valour, which earned him the admiration of friends and foes alike.   Running his galleys aground on the beach beneath the city, he disembarked in the face of an overwhelming force, through which he afterwards cut his way with a handful of men.   Having entered the citadel he immediately sallied out at the head of the garrison, and drove the besiegers from the town of which they had already taken possession.   "Never even at Roncevaux did any man, young or old, paynim or Christian, so bear himself as the King upon that day."[2]   But a fever, the natural penalty for such exertions, prostrated the King after the relief of Jaffa, and increased his anxiety to depart.   At length his envoys agreed, in return for a three years' truce, to surrender Ascalon, provided that the Christians kept Jaffa, Cæsarea, Haifa, Tyre, Acre, Lydda, and Ramleh.[3]   Such terms were little to the liking of the Sultan;[4] and on both sides there was every intention of resuming the struggle at the first opportunity.   Richard felt the disgrace of making terms with infidels; he refused to ratify the treaty with the usual oaths,[5] and talked among his friends of returning at no distant time with a more efficient army.   But for the moment there was nothing to be gained and much to be lost by prolonging his residence in Palestine.   On October 9 he set sail from Acre, which he was never destined to behold again.

Peace concluded, Oct., 1192

Death of Saladin, 1193

The health of his great adversary was already failing; otherwise the truce, though favourable to the Saracens and humiliating to the Christians, would not have lasted long.   When Saladin signed the truce he said to his secretary: "Now you will see each one of these Frank lords established on the top of his strong tower.   May I not die while the Moslems are exposed to this peril!"   The holy war had become the passion of his life; he thought and talked of nothing else.   "I will not lay down my arms," he said, in a moment of bravado, but still with a vein of serious meaning, "I will not lay

[1] Bohâdin, 323-6.   [2] Ambroise, l. 11180.   Bohâdin, 332.
[3] Bohâdin, 342-5.   Diceto, ii., 105.
[4] Bohâdin, 348.   [5] Abou'l Feda, 66.

down my arms while there is a single unbeliever remaining in the world, unless I am stopped by death ".[1]   To his followers the aspiration seemed natural and just; the Sultan's biographer cannot mention Constantinople without adding the prayer "God help us to conquer it!";[2] an advance from the new Rome to "Rome the Great" seemed a light matter to men who had carried victory from Egypt to the Euphrates and beyond.   Where Saladin led the way he was sure of willing followers.   Seldom has a ruler been more popular than this democratic despot whose door stood open to all suppliants, who treated holy men with the deference of a son and scarred campaigners with the familiarity of a brother, who scattered his largesse with such royal prodigality that he had not fifty pieces remaining in his treasury at the hour of his death.[3] The West breathed more freely at his death, and he was indeed far from being the least dangerous of those Oriental despots who have bent their steps towards Europe.

Saladin died in 1193, at the age of fifty-seven, having reigned End of the twenty-four years in Egypt and nineteen in Syria.   His last days Crusades were clouded by misgivings; but the Moslem triumph was assured when Richard turned his back on Palestine.   Eighty years were to elapse before the close of the crusading epoch; the task which had baffled Coeur de Lion was yet to be attempted by a King of France and an heir-apparent to the English throne. Throughout these eighty years an intermittent stream of penitents and knights-errant flowed eastward on the business of the Holy Land.   Of these recruits the British Isles furnished no inconsiderable proportion.   But the crusading ideal showed, with each successive decade, a declining power of attraction.   It became the monopoly of the upper classes and the Church.   Poor men assumed the Cross as an atonement for misdoing; but they were allowed, or even encouraged, to commute their vows for money at an easy rate. The attempt to raise expeditions on the old scale was a total failure.   A Lincoln document of 1197 records the names of men who had responded to an urgent appeal from Celestine III., and had failed to perform their undertaking.   The names are those of paupers, old men, invalids, day-labourers and small tradesmen; of men whose service was worthless or only offered as a form.[4]   Yet

---

[1] Bohâdin, 25.   [2] Ibid., 172.   [3] Ibid., 8, 15.
[4] Hist. MSS. Comm., Various Collections (1901), i., p. 235.

of such men, of criminals or peccant monks and friars, and of bankrupt desperadoes the latest Crusades were in great part composed.[1]
There are few sights more pitiable than the last manifestations of
an enthusiasm which has lost its hold upon the respect of the
community.

[1] Prutz, *Kulturgeschichte der Kreuzzüge*, pp. 116 ff.

CHAPTER XII

ENGLAND DURING RICHARD'S REIGN

THE domestic history of England in the years 1190-1193 may Signifi-
appear, by comparison with the Crusade a dull and trivial cance of
the Eng-
subject.   Lofty aims, such as dignified the pettiest skirmish and lish events
lent a tragic significance to the most sordid squabble in the Holy of the
reign
Land, are wholly wanting here.   In the strife between the friends
of John and Richard we only find a wooden loyalty to the absent
on the one side, and on the other the vacillating ambition of a
clumsy traitor.   But historical events often possess an interest
independent of the personal motives in which they have their
source ; the plots of John and his supporters are not without significance in the story of constitutional development.   In the confusion
which these plots produced the iron bands of Angevin despotism
began to crack and part.   The Great Council, forced to act upon
its own responsibility, conceived a novel sense of independence.
The first city of the kingdom seized the opportunity to claim the
right of self-government, and acquired, with the free institutions,
the free spirit of the continental communes.   Finally the Church
revived the old and often defeated demand for free and canonical
elections.   Of these movements the last completely failed while the
others turned out to be premature anticipations of the future.
But the movements are still a sign of life.   The spirit of liberty
was growing up again in every class of English society.

The rule of the Chancellor was universally unpopular.   He Long-
kept a finer household than beseemed the grandson of a villein, champ's
Unpopu-
and religious houses complained that a visit of one night from him larity
crippled their revenues for the next three years.   The commons
jeered at his dwarfish frame, his halting gait, his ape-like countenance; and bitterly resented the contempt for all things English
which found expression in his favourite saying that, rather than

11

do this or that, he would become an Englishman. The barons could not forgive him for enriching his family with lands and offices which they coveted for themselves; he was detested by John because he had acknowledged Arthur of Brittany as the heir-apparent and had pressed the King of Scots to do the same. Even before he left Messina, Richard was assailed with petitions for the removal of the Chancellor. He replied by giving the Archbishop of Rouen two commissions of which the first, for immediate use, made that prelate the colleague of Longchamp in the regency; while the second, to be produced only if the first were disregarded by the Chancellor, ordered the latter's removal and gave sole power to the Archbishop.[1] But the Archbishop's appearance in England failed to compose existing differences. Gerard de Camville, the sheriff and castellan of Lincoln, had harboured robbers in his castle and, on being called to account before the justiciars, proclaimed himself the man of John, justiciable by no courts except those of the Count. The Chancellor laid siege to Lincoln; John seized the excuse for appropriating some royal castles which he regarded as a menace to his appanage. At this point the Archbishop interposed to arrange a compromise between the Chancellor and the prince (July 28).[2] But Longchamp, who regarded the Archbishop as a possible rival for the vacant primacy, repaid his mediation with a contempt which drove the object of it into opposition.[3] A trifling incident in the autumn of 1191 led to a second and more general attack upon the Chancellor. He had given orders that Geoffrey of York should not be allowed to land at any English port, except upon condition of swearing fealty to Richard.[4] When Geoffrey made his appearance at Dover, the Chancellor's sister who was in charge of the castle ordered his arrest. Geoffrey took refuge in the Priory Church, and returned an angry negative to a message demanding the oath of fealty. His enemies, after four days of

He quarrels with John, 1191

[1] Stubbs, *Diceto*, ii., 90 and note; which supersedes the earlier theory of the same critic in his note on Hoveden, iii., 96.

[2] Following Mr. Round, *Commune*, pp. 207 ff., we depart from the ordinary theory which supposes two distinct quarrels and campaigns, one in the spring, the other in the summer.

[3] For the question of the Primacy, *Epp. Cantuar.*, 330, 346. Diceto, ii., 92. Giraldus, *De Vita Galfridi*, ii., § 6.

[4] See Longchamp's letter of explanation, *Epp. Cantuar.*, 344. Giraldus, *Vita Galfr.*, p. 389, treats the order for arrest as absolute, but is unreliable, as being a hot partisan.

hesitation, haled him out by main force and led him away to prison in the castle. Longchamp, when informed of this outrage on the privilege of sanctuary and the person of an Archbishop, ordered that Geoffrey should be set at liberty and apologised, in all sincerity, for the feminine excess of zeal by which a legal order had been construed in an illegal sense. But John took up the cause of his half-brother, and invited the barons to confer with him at Marlborough on the scandalous behaviour of the Chancellor. The summons was accepted in good faith; the barons assembled under the conviction that the King's chief minister was also his chief enemy; the presence of the Archbishop of Rouen and of the justiciars, whom Longchamp had deeply wounded by his autocratic bearing, gave an official semblance to the gathering. They summoned Longchamp to meet them and justify his conduct between Windsor and Reading at the bridge of Lodden. After some bluster he was cowed, and promised to attend them on October the 5th. But when the appointed day arrived he broke his promise, fearing treachery. The Archbishop of Rouen thereupon produced the second of his two commissions and demanded the deposition of the Chancellor. The barons sent again to Longchamp requiring his attendance; but after some hesitation he replied by hurrying to London and calling on the citizens to assist him against Count John, whom he stigmatised with some justice as a traitor and conspirator. The citizens assembled in the Guildhall to hear the Chancellor, but declined to help him. They had no reason to suspect the Count, and every reason to believe that he would bid more heavily than Longchamp for their favour. Such indeed proved to be the case. John and the barons, arriving almost on the Chancellor's heels, were told that they might have the support of London if they would sanction the formation of a commune, a project which had floated before the minds of the citizens ever since their abortive attempt to realise it in the days of Stephen. The Prince at once assented to the bargain. No charter recording the precise terms of the grant has yet been discovered, and it may be that the grant was not reduced to writing. We know little of the constitution of the new commune, except that a mayor was appointed who henceforth acts as the representative of the city for all public purposes, and in the internal administration is assisted by échevins and "good men" (*probi homines*) whose special functions

The Barons join John

The Commune of London

are a subject for conjecture.[1] It is possible that Rouen supplied the model followed by the Londoners ; since the commune of Rouen was the earliest to be sanctioned by the Angevins and was widely imitated in their continental provinces. If this were so the foreign constitution soon suffered a metamorphosis ; and nothing French survived except the title and dignity of the mayor. The communal government, though the monopoly of a patriciate and tyrannical in its dealings with the poorer citizens, enabled London to assume a more independent attitude in all dealings with the Crown. King Henry, we are told by an indignant contemporary, would not have made such a grant for a thousand times a thousand marks. But to John, who never looked beyond the present, the result of the compact with the citizens was all that he could wish. In a meeting at St. Paul's (Oct. 8) the Londoners and barons with one voice declared that the Chancellor had forfeited his office ; and that the Archbishop of Rouen should succeed him as Richard's commission had directed. The proceedings ended with a protestation of fealty to John, only saving that which was due to Richard. The Count was therefore recognised as the next in succession to the throne, and the object for which he had stirred up the agitation was achieved.

Submis-
sion of
Long-
champ

To Longchamp, who meanwhile had taken refuge in the Tower, no other course but submission was now open. He emerged from his stronghold with a protest that he yielded to superior force, and a denial of the right, which the Great Council had assumed, to try and to deprive him. The proceedings against him were indeed of an unprecedented character, and from the merely legal point of view might be severely criticised. The fact remains that he had been repudiated by every class, and by the one assembly which could claim to represent the nation. On promising to surrender his castles he was allowed to retire from London. Attempting to leave the kingdom in the disguise of a woman, he incurred the rough

---

[1] See the *Sacramentum Commune* of 1193, printed by Round, *Commune of London*, p. 235. The *Probi Homines* may be the suitors of the husting-court, who are called *prudomes* in a text printed by Miss Bateson (*E. H. R.*, xvii., p. 493). There is also extant the official oath taken by a body called the Twenty-Four (Round, *u.s.*, p. 237) ; Mr. Round identifies them with the Common Council. But there is no proof that the office of the Common Council was judicial ; while the Twenty-Four swear to do justice without taking bribes. Miss Bateson conjectures that the *échevins* are identical with the Twenty-Four, and these with the Aldermen, of whose existence at this time there is ample evidence (*E. H. R.*, xvii., pp. 493, 494, 511). She argues, as against Round, that foreign examples had only a superficial influence on London. To the same effect, but with no further evidence, Corbet in *E. H. R.*, xvi., p. 766.

caresses of a Dover fisherman and universal ridicule; but there was no cause for his detention and he was soon allowed to go in peace.[1]

The position of John after his rival's fall is not easy to deter-mine. One authority asserts that the Council held at St. Paul's elected him Regent of the Kingdom.[2] It is more probable that this position devolved upon the Archbishop of Rouen who, like the Chancellor before him, now took the title of "Chief Justiciar".[3] The Count, in any case, soon realised that he had gained less than he supposed. The nation as a whole were faithful to their absent sovereign; and, if Richard returned from the Crusade, it was unlikely that he would reverse his original decision to treat Arthur as the heir-apparent. The return of Philip Augustus naturally led to an alliance between himself and John. The agreement was that the Count should marry the unfortunate Alais and receive French assistance in supplanting his brother. On Philip's side there were active preparations for invading Normandy in the spring of 1192; and it was the news of their design which finally led to Richard's abandonment of the Crusade. But the suspicions of the Justiciar and the Queen-mother were aroused; they forbade the Count to leave England, an order which he had not the spirit to disregard; and the barons of France declined to help their King in invading the lands of a Crusader.[4] Hence, in the year 1192, nothing serious was done to injure Richard, though in England John was busily intriguing for support. He found many barons who acknowledged his claim to the succession, few except his personal friends who preferred him to his brother.

But early in 1193 came news which gave a new stimulus to his treason.[5] Before leaving the Holy Land Richard had despatched his main fleet in advance, intending to effect his own return by an overland journey from Marseilles. But when he had come within three days' voyage of that port he learned that Raymond V. of Toulouse, the cousin and ally of Philip, was on the watch to

[margin note: John and Philip]

[margin note: Richard's Capture by Leopold]

---

[1] See the narrative of an enemy, Hugh of Nonant, in Benedictus, ii., 219.

[2] Richard of Devizes, § 50. To a certain extent this is supported by *Epp. Cantuar.*, 356, 357, where the monks of Canterbury say of John "superior, immo caput est justiciariorum". But they had a motive for the allegation.

[3] *Epp. Cantuar.*, 360.

[4] Benedictus, ii., 236. Ric. Divis., § 75.

[5] Main authorities for the following narrative are Coggeshall, 53 ff., who had the facts from Richard's chaplain; Ansbertus in Hoveden, iii., p. cxl.; and a letter of the Emperor Henry, *ibid.*, iii., 195.

arrest him. Doubling upon his course the King sailed up the
Adriatic to Corfu, where he chartered for himself and his retinue
a pair of pirate ships, in the hope that he might land unrecognised
on imperial territory and make his way through Germany in the
disguise of a merchant. But the Emperor Henry VI. was no less
hostile than Count Raymond and the ports of the Empire were
carefully watched for the arrival of suspicious strangers. No sooner
had Richard landed in the Friuli than he found himself a hunted
man. Most of his followers were captured at once; his own escape
was due to the devotion of an attendant who personated him and
drew off the pursuit on a cross trail. But the King chose to take
Vienna on his road, though it was the capital of his worst enemy,
the Duke of Austria ; and while lodging in an inn outside the walls
he was detected through the imprudent conduct of a page. He
was at once arrested by Leopold's command, and imprisoned in the
castle of Durrenstein. Early in 1193 he was surrendered to the
Emperor on the condition that Leopold should receive a moiety
of his ransom. For this outrage upon a Crusader, whose person
was protected by the censures of the church, there were various
excuses; the insult to Leopold, the charge of complicity in the
murder of Conrad, the hospitality which Richard had extended to
his brother-in-law Henry the Lion, the head of the Guelf party,
and lastly the alliance with the Sicilian usurper Tancred. Of these
pretexts the first and last may have had some real weight ; but the
behaviour of the captors suggests that the hope of a rich ransom
was the chief consideration in their minds.[1]

Intrigues
of Philip
and John

The Emperor informed Philip of the capture before the close
of 1192 ; it became known in England somewhat later. The Chief
Justiciar at once despatched ambassadors to search for Richard, and
to discover how his release could be obtained. They returned with
the information that the King's life and honour were secure; that
he had learned to amuse his leisure by intoxicating his gaolers and

[1] See Kindt, *Gründe der Gefangenschaft Richards I.* (Halle, 1892). This author
regards Henry VI. as intervening in his imperial capacity, claiming jurisdiction over
Richard no less than over Leopold, and considering his tribunal as competent to
hear the charges against Richard. This may have been the pretext. But the
desire of punishing Richard for the alliance with Tancred, and of using him as an
ally for the conquest of Sicily, is clearly the predominant motive in the Emperor's
mind. Bloch, *Forschungen zur Politik Kaisers Heinrich VI.*, lays more stress upon
the relations of Richard with the Guelfs. Luchaire, *H. G. de la France*, iii., i.,
p. 110, holds that Henry claimed Richard at Philip's instigation.

playing practical jokes upon them; and that the price of his release was to be the sum of 100,000 marks. On March 23rd Richard appeared before the Diet of the Empire at Speyer, cleared himself from the worst charges of his enemies, and received the Emperor's kiss of peace. But his release was to be postponed until a substantial instalment of the ransom was paid, or perhaps till an even remoter date. Philip and John were already at work plying the Emperor with inducements, both pecuniary and of other kinds, to hold his captive fast. The Emperor was needy and avaricious; he had promised to protect Richard against the designs of France, but when temptation came he hesitated. Fortunately for Richard there were powerful allies on his side. The Pope and the Guelf princes pressed hard for his release,[1] and the Emperor was finally bribed into an honourable frame of mind by the promise of an additional 50,000 marks, as a contribution to the war with Tancred, and by Richard's homage for England and all his other lands. On the humiliating transaction by which England became an imperial fief Richard preserved a discreet silence in writing to his subjects. But he assured them that the friendship which he had cemented with the Emperor was well worth the ransom money, and pressed them to be prompt in payment.[2]

An aid for the king's ransom was one of the three which, by feudal law, might be exacted without any form of national consultation and assent. The Justiciars and the Queen-mother determined on their own responsibility [3] how the burden should be distributed between the several classes of the nation, and began the work of collection in April, 1193. They demanded a scutage of twenty shillings from the knight's fee; a fourth part of the revenues and chattels of all laymen; the same proportion of the temporalties of the clergy, and a tithe of spiritualties. They also took the plate and the treasure of the churches; while the Cistercian, Gilbertine and Premonstratensian orders which possessed, or were supposed to possess, no gold and silver plate, were called

Richard's Ransom

[1] Hoveden, iii., 195, 199, 208, 214, etc.
[2] The surrender of England to be held as fief of the Empire has been sometimes regarded as a myth. But see Bloch, *Forschungen*, Appendix IV., for a refutation of these doubts. The transaction is described in Hoveden, iii., 202, 203. Terms of Richard's release, *ibid.*, iii., 215.
[3] Unless the contrary is implied in Diceto's words (ii., 110), "statutum est communi assensu persolvere," etc.; but this may merely mean a general acquiescence.

upon to surrender their wool-crop for that year.[1] Normandy was
similarly taxed, and both countries groaned beneath the burden.
But the sum which was realised fell ridiculously short of the
expectations which the government had formed. The collectors
filled their pockets; the tax-payers abused the privilege of assessing their own chattels; Count John, though he collected the taxes
in his shires, kept the proceeds for himself. Apart from these
contributory causes it is plain that the Justiciars had grossly
over-estimated the taxable resources of the country. They had
gone upon mere guess-work; it is doubtful whether any tax or
taxes could have extracted £100,000 from the country in one
year. Enough however was raised to satisfy the Emperor for
the moment. Richard was set at liberty in February, 1194, upon
giving hostages for the unpaid balance of the ransom.

John and
Philip
frustrated
Philip and John had not been idle in the past twelve months,
but their activity had chiefly served to prove the stability of
Richard's power. At the first announcement of his brother's
capture the Count joined his ally, and performed homage for
Normandy and the other French possessions, if not for England
also; while Philip began to negotiate with Cnut VI. of Denmark
for the hand of his sister and the support of the Danish navy.
The Count however showed himself a clumsy conspirator. The
Norman nobles refused to do him homage. The Justiciars of
England, from whom he demanded the crown as though Richard
were already dead, treated him with contempt. The Prince endeavoured to raise his vassals, but found himself, for want of
English support,[2] obliged to rely on foreign mercenaries. The
Justiciars laid siege to his castles and he hastily concluded a truce
to last until November; it would have gone still worse with him
but for their reluctance to take extreme measures against the
heir-apparent. Meanwhile Philip was disappointed of the Danish
fleet; the idea of invading England melted from his mind when
the Justiciars called out both the feudal levies and the militia to
patrol the coast; and an attack on Normandy met with indifferent
success. The King of France took Gisors and some other border-
castles, but was forced to retreat ignominiously from the walls of

---

[1] Diceto, ii., 110. Hoveden, iii., 210, 225. Maitland, *Three Rolls*, etc., p. xxiii.
Stubbs, Hoveden, iv., pref. W. Newburgh, iv., § 38.
[2] As to the general sympathy with Richard see Joceline de Brakelond, p. 39.

Rouen. The citizens were encouraged by the presence of the Earl of Leicester, the Justiciar of Normandy; a summons to surrender only elicited from them the retort that the gates were open if Philip chose to enter, and the challenge was declined.[1] When Richard's release became a certainty the Prince returned to France; for a time he and Philip amused themselves with discussing, and affecting to accept, the extravagant terms which Richard, through the faithful Longchamp, offered as a means of gaining delay. But early in 1194 they made their last effort. John promised his ally so much of Normandy as lay to the east of the rivers Seine and Iton, and also the eastern part of the Touraine, including Tours and Loches;[2] after which he wrote to his English followers urging them to rebel, while Philip invaded Normandy in force for the third time. But Hubert Walter, whom Richard had lately nominated Primate and Chief Justiciar, made short work of the English rising. The Great Council declared that John had forfeited his lands; his castles were besieged; and, when Richard arrived in England (March, 1194), it only remained for him to receive the ready submission of the garrisons of Nottingham and Tickhill. Whatever difficulties might await him in France, the King's authority in England was undisputed. The splendour and the enthusiasm with which he was received by the citizens of London made a profound impression on the German nobles who had come as guests in his train. They had expected to find themselves in a bankrupt and rebellious land.

But Richard had no mind to repay the loyalty of England by making English needs the first object of his attention. The perils of the Angevin inheritance engrossed his mind to the exclusion of all other subjects; and the last sparks of rebellion were barely extinct in England before he was at work on preparations for the wars in France. The most natural expedient for one whose sense of justice had never been sensitive was to sell again the lands and offices which had been already sold to provide the funds of the Crusade. The renunciation of old bargains presented no difficulty in cases where charges of overt or secret treason could be plausibly sustained. Other grantees, such as the unfortunate Bishop of Durham whose state had been already

Richard raises more money, 1194

[1] Hoveden, iii., 207.   W. Neubrig., iv., § 34.
[2] Teulet, *Layettes du Trésor des Chartes*, i., 175.

11*

pruned to some extent by the rapacity of Longchamp, were told
that by this time they must have amply reimbursed themselves
for the sums which the King had received from them.[1] So, on
one pretext or another, sheriffdoms and castles came into the
market for a second time in the space of five years; and the King,
in his reckless haste to close with the highest bidder, was only
prevented from selling Hugh Puiset's earldom of Northumbria to
the King of Scots because William the Lion refused to buy the
land without the castles which controlled it.[2] It is only surprising that the appanage of John was partly spared; the entreaties
of the Queen-mother were the principal cause of Richard's forbearance, but the King had no doubt learned by the events of
the last few months that John, contemptible when unsupported,
would be a formidable instrument in the hands of Philip. Whatever the motive, pardon was granted to the arch-conspirator,
though his abettors were stripped bare. "You are but a child,"
said Richard when the Prince crawled to his feet and sued for
pardon. "You have been ill-counselled and your advisers shall
pay for this." He ordered that the repentant prodigal should be
served with a good dinner;[3] nothing more was said as to their
quarrel; John was soon reinvested with Ireland and a large part
of his English fiefs. Other means were found to fill the depleted
Exchequer. A Great Council was called at Nottingham to hear
the tale of the royal necessities. The demand for taxation came
with a bad grace after the aids which had been paid for the King's
ransom; but the barons could not deny that the royal credit was
still heavily pledged to the Emperor, and that no honourable
peace with Philip was possible until an armed demonstration had
been made in France. They conceded a scutage of £1 on the
knight's fee, and a hidage at the rate of two shillings on lands of
non-military tenure.[4] His demands thus satisfied the King only
delayed in England long enough to be crowned anew at Winchester,
as a proof that his detention by the Emperor had not impaired his
dignity. In May, 1194, he left England never to return. The
task of governing the kingdom devolved upon the Justiciar Hubert
Walter; for the next six years the English were only kept in mind

---

[1] W. Neubrig., v., § 1.   [2] Hoveden, iii., 249.   [3] *G. le Maréchal*, 10366 ff.
[4] Ramsay, *A. E.*, p. 336, from the Pipe Roll.   Maitland, *Three Rolls*, p. xxiv.
Hoveden, iii., 242.

of the King's existence by demands for money, which increased both in number and in urgency with each successive phase of the interminable French war.

Hubert Walter[1] was not a statesman of the highest rank, but he is the first royal minister in English history who ruled with a free hand for any considerable period of time. His ideas of government can therefore be clearly distinguished from those of his master; and they are not undeserving of attention. For they show an originality of mind which neither the personal qualities nor the antecedents of the Justiciar would have led us to expect. The Primacy, to which he was elected, in 1194, at the King's express desire, has rarely been held by one so guiltless of all culture. Hubert was incapable of expressing himself with tolerable accuracy in Latin, at a time when Latin was still the official language of the Church and the royal Chancery. He had other and more serious defects. His boundless profusion and the magnificence of his household, which was thought excessive even for the first subject in the realm, fostered in him a spirit of avarice to which no source of gain came amiss.[2] He abused his position to acquire lucrative rights of marriage and wardship upon easy terms; and appears at one time to have been suspected of robbing the Exchequer in other and more flagrant ways. We know at least that Richard, in the year 1196, sent to England the Abbot of Caen, the ablest of Norman financiers, to investigate the accounts of the Exchequer; and the sudden death of the Abbot, after a banquet at which he had been entertained by the Justiciar, was regarded as more than a mere accident.[3] But as a minister Hubert showed some qualities which were useful to the King and the nation. He accepted without a murmur the thankless duty of raising money for the Norman war; and he showed a marvellous ingenuity in conciliating the classes which suffered most heavily from taxation. His political apprenticeship had been served in

The Character of Hubert Walter

[1] See the life of Hubert Walter in Gervase, ii., 406. Giraldus, iii., 23, 29. Coggeshall, 160. Stubbs, Hoveden, iv., pref.

[2] Gervase attempts an apology for this trait. The Archbishop gained his reputation for avarice by the zeal with which he reclaimed the possessions of his see from usurpers (ii., 411). But the apology only covers a part of Hubert's doubtful acts. The *Histoire des ducs* praises his generosity, " Moult vaillans clers et moult lrages et moult courtois " (p. 101), but tells a story to prove his extravagance and ostentation (p. 106).

[3] Hoveden, iv., 5.

a cramping school. Under Henry II. he had been the right hand of the Justiciar Ranulf Glanvill. Possibly he was the author of the law-book which commonly goes under Glanvill's name. However this may be, Hubert was steeped to the lips in the tedious formulæ, the labyrinthine rules of procedure, to know which was the whole duty of a royal judge. It is surprising, almost paradoxical, that such a man should have the courage to appease the middle classes by relaxing in their favour the autocratic system in which he had been trained; that he should spontaneously admit the smaller landowners to a share in the administration of their shires, and should bestow self-government upon the more important towns. Such however was his policy; he was the first statesman who attempted to satisfy in some measure that democratic spirit of which the beginnings are visible in the regency of Longchamp. It may reasonably be contended that our national liberties owe as much to him as to the authors of Magna Charta.

Policy of Hubert Walter, 1194-8

The measures through which he gave effect to his policy are chiefly contained in his instructions to the Itinerant Justices of 1194 and 1198, in his ordinance of 1195 for the conservation of the peace, and in his scheme of 1198 for the assessment of the carucage.[1] The Justices of 1194 were directed to provide in each shire for the election of four Coroners. Chosen by the suitors of the shire-court from their own number, these officers were to decide what matters arising in their shire should be regarded as Pleas of the Crown and reserved for the hearing of the Justices. The creation of the office took from the sheriffs an opportunity of levying blackmail, and gave the suitors an increased share in the administration of criminal justice.[2] The Articles for the Eyres of 1194 and 1198 introduced the representative principle into the spheres of fiscal business and of private law. They directed that juries, both for answering the inquiries of the Judges respecting royal dues and for trying cases under the Grand Assize, should be

[1] All printed in the *Select Charters*, pp. 249-58.

[2] Gross, *Select Pleas from Coroners' Rolls*, pp. xxv.-xxvii., still defends the theory which he advanced in an earlier work (*The Early History and Influence of the Office of Coroner*) that the coroner is to be found at Colchester and elsewhere before 1194. If correct this theory would weaken Hubert Walter's claim to be regarded as the creator of the office. But the objections which are brought against the theory by F. W. Maitland (*E. H. R.*, viii., p. 758) are conclusive. In 1194 Hubert Walter differentiated the duties of the justiciar from those of the coroner. Between 1194 and 1215 they were sometimes re-united (*M. C.*, § 24); but this was a temporary abuse.

chosen by a committee of four knights elected in the shire-court for that purpose. Hitherto such juries had been selected by the sheriff, who presumably had packed them in his own interest and in that of suitors by whom he had been bribed.

The importance of these changes is due to the fact that they entrusted local power and responsibility, not to great barons whose interest in local administration was at the best perfunctory, nor to the small freeholders who by this time had practically ceased to attend the shire-court except as witnesses or parties to a suit, but to the knights of the shire, a middle class of landowners whose wealth, tenure, and breeding, gave them a social position little inferior to that of the barons.[1] Many of these knights were tenants-in-chief, and therefore theoretically entitled to appear at the Great Council to which they were collectively summoned by the mouth of the sheriff.[2] But they were neither expected nor disposed to thrust themselves forward in an assembly where their voices carried no weight. They sought an outlet for their energies in local politics. In this sphere their interests were identical not only with those of their poorer neighbours but also with those of the Crown. No class had more to lose by the prevalence of crime, the lawlessness of the great, the frauds or oppressions of officials. The strength of the Tudors in the sixteenth century was largely due to their skilful use of these natural allies. But the Tudors merely completed and perfected a policy which had been taking shape for three centuries before their time. It originated with Hubert Walter. His confidence in the country knights appears in all the ordinances which we have mentioned, but in none more clearly than in that of 1195, which prescribes the appointment, in every hundred, of knights to act as custodians of the peace. Their office foreshadows that of the Justice of the Peace, into whose hands the whole work of county government was to pass in the course of the fifteenth and sixteenth centuries. The custodians of the peace, as appointed in 1195 and for a long time afterwards, were not invested with judicial powers. Their chief duty was to control the Hue and Cry, that rough machinery for the apprehension of criminals which had descended almost unchanged from the

(margin: Importance of his administrative changes)

[1] Maitland in *E. H. R.*, iii., p. 417. P. and M., i., 541 (1st ed.). *Select Pleas of the Crown for the County of Gloucester*, pref.
[2] *Becket Materials*, iii., 49-51; ii., 390, 391; iv., 41.

days of the heptarchic kingdoms and was still the only form of police in rural districts. But when the office had been once created new powers were rapidly conferred upon it. It was important, though not of a judicial character, before the accession of Edward I., and as its importance increased so did the readiness of the country knights to accept the obligations which it entailed.[1]

New forms of Taxation

Taxation was the last purpose for which the representative principle was utilised by Hubert Walter. The demands of the King grew more pressing with each successive year. It was in vain that the Justiciar strove to augment the customary revenue by encouraging trade and commerce. His Assize of Weights and Measures,[2] introducing one uniform standard for the whole country, was one of those reforms of which the effects, though far reaching, are slowly felt, and the same remark applies to his legislation against the frauds of cloth-workers and cloth-merchants. Nor were exceptional devices such as that of selling licences for tournaments, hitherto prohibited in England, much more successful.[3] New taxes had to be raised, and it was difficult to devise any form of impost which would be at once profitable and tolerable to the people. In 1197 the Justiciar vainly entreated the Great Council to equip a force of 300 knights to serve the King for one year in Normandy. He urged that the barons would in this way obtain a release on easy terms from the personal service which the King might otherwise demand. Bishop Hugh of Lincoln replied that the lands of his see were bound to no foreign service, and his plea found an immediate echo among the lay members of the Council.[4] Legally it was indefensible; feudal law bound the vassal to defend his lord's dominions wherever they might be. But the unanimous repudiation of a plain duty showed that discontent was too widespread to be met with high-handed measures of coercion. Richard and Hubert Walter thought it prudent to leave the baronage untaxed; and even Hugh of Lincoln received a grudging forgiveness when he crossed the Channel to explain his conduct to the King. Permission to tax the non-military landholders was obtained

[1] See "The Justice of the Peace" by C. A. Beard in Harvard Studies, vol. xx., pt. I.

[2] Hoveden, iii., 33.   [3] *Foedera*, i., 65.

[4] *Magna Vita*, p. 248. Date of the Council in Gervase, i., 549 (see Ramsay, *A. E.*, p. 355). See Mr. Round's remarks in *F. E.*, p. 528, which however fail to take notice of the all-important point that the other members of the Council claimed the same exemption as Hugh.

without difficulty; but the carucage of 1198 disappointed the
expectations with which it was imposed. It was a tax of five
shillings upon every plough-land (carucate) actually under cultivation, the number being calculated by the simple device of counting
plough-teams; the tax was thus far heavier than the old Danegeld,
which had been levied at the rate of two shillings and upon the
Domesday assessment of area, an assessment very favourable to the
owner.[1] But the sum realised by the carucage was small. The
tax-payers evaded their liability, obtained exemption by means of
bribery, or openly defied the Exchequer. The clergy in particular
refused to pay until a sentence of outlawry had been issued against
them. To meet this state of feeling the Justiciar allowed the
assessment to be made in every hundred by a sworn jury of the
neighbourhood, and there can be little doubt that these jurors, like
those of 1194, were chosen by popular election. His recourse to
this device at such a juncture throws a retrospective light upon
his former policy, and at the same time suggests that the intervention of representative committees in the work of government was
beginning to be popularly regarded as a panacea for every abuse.

In his dealings with the towns the Justiciar showed an even
greater disposition to rely upon elected officials. One of the first extant charters conceding to a town the privilege of electing its own
magistrate is that which he granted to Lincoln in the year 1194;
that this was no accidental concession is proved by the large
numbers of similar charters which were issued in the early years
of the next reign, when his influence was again in the ascendant.
His treatment of London stands, indeed, in striking contrast to his
general policy. No formal ordinance abolished the commune which
John had sanctioned in his brother's name. But John's grant,
which was of dubious validity, was not confirmed; and the commune, if it continued to exist, existed upon sufferance. It is not
mentioned in Richard's charter of 1194, or in John's of 1199—
both issued when the Archbishop was omnipotent. The Londoners
appear to have kept their mayor and the rights of self-government
which that magistracy symbolised.[2] But the still more valuable

Hubert
Walter
and
London

---

[1] See Mr. Round's article in *E. H. R.*, iii., p. 502. Stevenson, *ib.*, iv., p. 108.
The difficulty is to explain Hoveden's explanation of the tax (Hoveden, iv., 46).
[2] See the *Chronica Majorum*, etc., *ad init.* John's charter of 1215 *confirms* the
right of electing the mayor; otherwise we might have supposed, from the long
tenure of FitzAlwyn that he was a crown nominee.

privilege, that of rendering fixed aids and services in lieu of tallage, they did not keep, although in France this privilege was usually carried by a grant of communal self-government.[1] No doubt the tallages of London could ill be spared by the Exchequer. But perhaps there was another reason for refusing to ratify the commune. It was well to remind the turbulent populace of the capital that they owed to the special favour of the government whatever measure of liberty they enjoyed. That Hubert Walter feared the Londoners is proved by what the historians tell us of a civic

Fitz-
Osbert's
Protest,
1196

tumult in 1196. In that year a London lawyer William Fitz-Osbert, surnamed Longbeard, who had been elected to an office, probably that of alderman, aroused bitter feeling in the city by his attacks upon his colleagues. He alleged that in assessing the citizens for the purpose of tallages they favoured themselves and their wealthy friends at the expense of the poorer citizens. His agitation took a form which lent colour to the charge of treasonable designs; he convened mass-meetings of the poor at St. Paul's and elsewhere, and inflamed their minds by violent harangues against their oppressors. These meetings resulted in no more serious consequence than a petition to the King which was presented by FitzOsbert himself. But the other magistrates complained to the Justiciar that there was a conspiracy on foot to sack the houses of the rich, and that FitzOsbert was daily preaching violence and sedition. Hubert despatched a force of soldiers to arrest the demagogue; the sanctuary of Bow Church, in which FitzOsbert had taken refuge, was fired over his head ; and, half-dead from the wounds which he received in a last attempt to escape, he was tied to a horse's tail and dragged to the Tyburn gallows. There was the pretence of a trial at the Tower; but whether as a conspirator or as the poor man's advocate, FitzOsbert was condemned with indecent haste and upon unsatisfactory evidence.[2] The action of the Justiciar was however generally approved, and Richard, who had lately lent a favourable ear to the petition of FitzOsbert, now wrote to thank his minister for dealing so promptly with the disturber of the peace of London. Retribution came from an

[1] Giry, *Etablissements de Rouen*, c. xiv., and Prof. G. B. Adams in *E. H. R.*, xix., p. 702.
[2] W. Neubrig., v., § 20. Diceto, ii., 143. Hoveden, iv., 5. The first two of these authorities are unfavourable to FitzOsbert; but according to Hoveden he was a man " *zelo justitiae et aequitatis succensus . . . pauperum advocatus* ".

unexpected quarter. The monks of Canterbury, to whom Bow
Church belonged, had an old-standing feud with the Archbishop. Fall of
They complained to the Pope of the sacrilege; and Innocent III. Walter,
was moved in 1198 to demand of the King that the Archbishop 1198
should be released from the secular duties which had involved him
in the guilt of such a crime. Richard might have replied that the
combination of spiritual and secular power in the same hands was
abundantly justified by precedent. But the Pope's letter came
after the successful resistance of the Great Council and the failure
of the carucage. We may well believe that the King welcomed
this excuse for dismissing a minister who had disappointed his
unreasonable expectations. In July, 1198, a new and less scrupulous
Justiciar, in the person of Geoffrey FitzPeter, took up the reins of
power. The Archbishop retired with reluctance; but his disgrace
was not to be final; and it saved him from being associated with
the last extortions of the King who had latterly descended to the
most desperate expedients, such as that of breaking his Great Seal
and cancelling all the grants which had been issued under it.[1] It
would seem moreover that the Archbishop had reached the limits
of his capacity as a constructive statesman. When he returns to
power at John's accession his influence can only be traced in the
detail of administration. He helps his successor to pursue the old
paths, but suggests no new departure.

At this point it becomes necessary that we should retrace our
steps to notice briefly the course of the French war. The campaigns
of Richard's later years are of little intrinsic interest; but they form
the prelude to the disastrous struggles of the next reign, in which
Normandy was lost and the King, stripped of external resources,
was left at the mercy of a people exasperated by the taxation and
oppression which a continental policy had necessitated.

[1] Round, F. E., p. 545, proves that this took place in 1198, not, as stated by
Hoveden (iii., 267), in 1194.

CHAPTER XIII

THE LOSS OF NORMANDY

The
French
War, 1194
THE reappearance of Richard in Normandy (May, 1194) evoked the wildest enthusiasm among the lower classes, to whom a Frenchman was still a natural enemy. As he rode through the duchy the King was followed by crowds of people who danced for joy and sang ballads in his honour. The refrain of one of these songs has been preserved. It ran :—

> Dieu est venu avec sa puissance ;
> Bientôt s'en ira le roi de France.[1]

But the Normans expected more than Richard could perform. South of the Loire, indeed, he achieved some brilliant feats of arms ; within a few months he recovered Loches and Tours, and reduced the Aquitanian rebels to submission. He also proved his superiority in an equal field by compelling Philip to beat an undignified retreat from Fréteval. But money and men alike were wanting for more substantial enterprises ; as Bertrand de Born had said of him on an earlier occasion, he was hunting the eagle with a sparrow-hawk. Before the end of the year he found it expedient to conclude a twelve months' truce, leaving Philip in possession of almost all the territories which John had ceded [2] (Nov. 1, 1194).

Resumption of
the War,
1195-6
A settlement so irksome was only accepted by Richard to be broken at the first convenient opportunity ; in the summer of 1195 he lent a willing ear to the temptations of his Imperial suzerain. Henry VI., who had never disguised his hopes of extending the Empire to the left bank of the Rhine and of making France a vassal kingdom,[3] sent Richard a golden crown and an intimation that, if he invaded France, support would be forthcoming from the side of Germany. The King of England replied by inquiring

[1] *G. le Maréchal*, 10419 ff.   [2] Hoveden, iii., 257.   [3] *Ibid.*, 301.

what form the promised help would take. The negotiations transpired, and Philip indignantly renounced the truce. A conference at Vaudreuil, arranged by the advisers of the two kings in the hope of restoring their friendship, only completed the breach. Philip taunted his rival with bad faith; the King of England, worsted in the war of words, called his retinue to arms and hunted the Frenchmen headlong from the meeting-place. But the Emperor's fair promises came to nothing; and Richard found himself once more committed to an interminable and exhausting struggle. It was fortunate for him that a Mohammedan invasion of Castile moved Celestine III. to come forward as a mediator. The matrimonial troubles of the French King and his interest in Imperial affairs made it doubly important that he should not offend the Pope. He consented to make peace on the basis of a compromise. The settlement was delayed by the reluctance of Richard to accept any terms which the Emperor had not ratified, and of the Emperor to sanction a treaty which would leave the King of France at liberty to meddle in the politics of Germany. But in the first days of 1196 a treaty was signed under which the King of England resigned his claims on Gisors, the Norman Vexin, and Auvergne, but was allowed to retain Eu, Aumâle, Arques, and Driencourt in Normandy, and in Berri the castles of Issoudun, Graçay and La Châtre.[1]

The terms were more favourable to England than those of 1194. But, if the King of France obtained less than he had hoped, the treaty conceded to him all that he could claim with any legal justification. He was disposed to be content with his winnings; when Richard, in open defiance of the terms of the treaty, began to build at Les Andelys the famous stronghold of Chateau Gaillard, his rival contented himself with a formal protest that the peace was no longer binding upon France. Richard asked nothing better than an opportunity for re-opening the war and in 1197 there were desultory operations in Auvergne and on the Norman border. But his only hope of recouping his losses rested on a project which he now formed for a coalition between all the princes with whom Philip was embroiled. The first steps were taken in 1197 by the conclusion of an agreement with the Count of Flanders and Hain-

Richard averse from a compromise

[1] Text in Teulet, *Layettes du Trèsor des Chartes*, ii., pp. 182-4.

ault.[1] The death of the Emperor, which occurred in the same year, opened the prospect of obtaining a still more considerable ally. Richard's nephew Otto of Saxony came forward as a candidate; and the whole weight of English influence was thrown into his scale. As a vassal of the Empire Richard received a summons to take part in the election; and though he declined to appear in person his envoys pressed the cause of Otto both at Rome and in the Imperial diet at Cologne. A majority of the electors accepted Otto in preference to Philip of Suabia the brother, and Frederic the infant son, of the late Emperor. But the minority elected Philip of Suabia; Otto's energies were soon absorbed in a civil war, and consequently Richard gained but little by the elevation of his nephew. Still there was every probability that the Saxon candidate would in the end obtain the upper hand; meanwhile new recruits flowed rapidly into Richard's coalition. The Duke of Brabant, the Counts of Brienne, Guisnes, and Perche, Raymond VI. of Toulouse and Arthur of Brittany were allies who could not be expected to move until the success of Richard seemed assured. But their desertion threw Philip into grave anxiety and encouraged the King of England to accelerate his preparations. In 1198 a border-war broke out which, on both sides, was disgraced by wild and purposeless atrocities. Richard placed his trust in the routiers or mercenaries, of whom a large number had been enlisted for his service under the famous captain Mercadier of Perigord. These ruffians maintained themselves by pillaging friend and foe, churches and laymen, without distinction or pity. Their ranks were swollen by the outlaws, the renegade monks, and the lowest class of adventurers, from every land; and it is merely by a popular mistake that they received the title of Brabançons.[2] The Low Countries, with their over-developed feudalism, were one of the best recruiting grounds for mercenaries; but every band was cosmopolitan in composition. The routiers were no novelty to the Angevin dominions, but Henry II. had kept a tight hand over those whom he employed. Richard's frequent inability to pay them made it necessary that he should allow them greater licence; the result was that Mercadier and his men became almost as formidable to the King's subjects as to the French.

The Imperial Election, 1198

The War of 1198

[1] Diceto, ii., 152.   [2] Map, *De Nugis*, i., § 29.

The expense of warfare conducted with such instruments in- creased the natural avarice of the King; and it was in a quarrel with one of his vassals concerning an insignificant case of treasure-trove that he perished, at the moment when his projected coalition appeared to have become a formidable reality.　A peasant plough-ing on the lands of the Viscount of Limoges turned up with his ploughshare a golden ornament which is described as a representa-tion of an emperor and his family sitting at a table.[1]　Richard demanded the surrender of the whole; the Viscount insisted on retaining a portion for himself.　Over this question a war broke out in the course of which, while besieging the castle of Chaluz in the Limousin, the King was wounded by a cross-bow bolt in the shoulder.　Unskilful treatment of the wound caused it to mortify and he died in his tent before Chaluz (April 6, 1199).　The castle surrendered in his last moments, and the archer who had aimed the fatal shot was brought to his bedside.　Questioned by the King he boasted of his deed.　"It is thou," said the archer, "who didst slay my father and my brothers; now slay me also.　I do not fear thy tortures."　Richard ordered that the man should be released; but Mercadier sent him to the King's sister Joanna of Toulouse, by whose orders he was mutilated, flayed and torn asunder by wild horses.[2]

The character of Richard deteriorated after his return from Palestine.　The strain of an unsuccessful war sharpened his natur- ally irritable temper; the slightest check or contradiction excited him to madness.　His greed for money increased till it became a mania.　Yet to the last he kept some of the traits which had made him popular as a young man; the love of song and music, the skill in ordering a pageant or a festival, the appreciation of knightly deeds, the high spirits and the witty tongue.[3]　At his worst he respected moral courage and could take a rebuke with a good grace, when it came from a good man.　In the last year of his life a famous preacher, Fulk de Neuilly, came before him and bade him, in the hearing of the court, "give in marriage his three evil daughters".　"Thou liest," said Richard, "for I have no daughters."　"In sooth," returned the preacher, "thou hast three

---

[1] Rigord.　Possibly a Roman votive offering.
[2] *Annales Winton, s.a.* 1199.　Joanna was married to Raymond VI. in 1196.
[3] Coggeshall, 92.

evil daughters, pride and avarice and luxury." "Then," said
Richard, amused and not a whit offended, "I will give my pride to
the Templars, my avarice to the Cistercians, and my luxury to the
bishops."[1] From a very different accuser comes the charge of
treachery ; but it was perhaps a fit of spite which led Bertrand de
Born to give his brother in arms the nickname Yea and Nay.
Sincerity was a virtue for which the Plantagenets were never distinguished. But Richard kept faith or broke it in accordance with
the current standards of political morality ; the reputation which
he held for chivalry is attested by the elegy of Geoffrey Faidit on
his death. The heaviest charge lies against the king rather than the
man. Richard neglected English interests to pursue his schemes
of continental policy. But even in this he was justified by the
opinions of his age. No one disputed his obligation to defend his
lawful rights against unscrupulous encroachments. Honour demanded that he should transmit an unimpaired inheritance to
his successor. The question whether Normandy, Anjou and Aquitaine were worth the expenditure which they entailed was held to
be beside the mark.

The Re-
sources of
Normandy
In fact, however, the continental provinces were not to be despised, even from the commercial point of view. They had little or
no value for the English nation ; subsequent experience proved
that English trade with Normandy could prosper and increase even
when the duchy had become a French possession. But the Plantagenets derived large revenues from Normandy and Aquitaine.
Normandy, indeed, as may be seen from extant fiscal documents,
yielded profits not much, if at all, inferior to those of England.
Under the iron rule of Henry I. a more law-abiding spirit had been
impressed on Norman feudalism ; under his grandson the administration of the duchy assumed an ordered form. By the death of
Henry II. the Duke had recovered the most important rights of
sovereignty over the whole land, with the exception of a few fiefs,
such as that of Évreux, in which a private lord still held a palatine
position. Normandy was now mapped out in bailiwicks[2] of moderate extent and administered by royal nominees, who at stated

[1] Hoveden, iv., 76.
[2] The *vicecomitatus* are rarely mentioned after 1150. A list of the bailiwicks is
given by F. M. Powicke, *The Loss of Normandy*, pp. 103-19, who corrects the
earlier lists of Delisle and Valin ; the same author describes the older system of
viscounties (pp. 61-7).

intervals rendered an account to the Seneschal of the duchy in the Exchequer Court at Caen. The Exchequer was also the highest tribunal of justice ; and the assessors of the Seneschal, professional lawyers and administrators like the English Justices, made periodical eyres through every bailiwick. In spite of constant war upon the borders, law reigned supreme in the interior of the country. Commerce flourished ; the towns equalled or exceeded in wealth the most prosperous of English boroughs. The men of Rouen farmed their commune at a rent of £3,000 which, even if paid in the light coinage of Anjou, was larger than the firm of London. Even Caen, which had not yet acquired a commune, contributed more heavily than London to the ransom of Richard I.[1] In Richard's later years it is true that the defence of the duchy necessitated anticipation of the Norman, and heavy drafts upon the English, revenue. But, if the frontier could be made impregnable, or if Philip should be succeeded by an heir less able or less tenacious than himself, Normandy might once more become a source of profit to the Duke.

Fortune however was on the side of France. Philip outlived Henry II. who was the ablest, and Richard who was the most warlike, of the Plantagenets. At Richard's death the defence of Normandy devolved upon John Lackland, in whom short fits of energy alternated with long intervals of sloth, whose best-laid plans were usually stultified by lapses of folly and caprice. Six years of invasions, alarms, and exceptional taxation threw a heavy strain on Norman loyalty. Though still proud of their independence the Normans began to count the cost at which it was maintained. The towns were more friendly than the feudal classes to the English dynasty. For the House of Capet was notoriously hostile to communes, except when founded on the lands of the great vassals ; whereas the Plantagenets, both in Normandy and in Aquitaine, had shown considerable readiness to sanction communes of a moderate type. Rouen acquired a commune under Henry II., Évreux in the period of Richard's captivity ; and John, from the first, showed a disposition to be more liberal of charters than his predecessors. But even the towns might well begin to ask whether the harsher rule of Philip would not bring with it lighter taxation and less troubled times.

Change of feeling in Normandy

---

[1] For the Exchequer see Powicke, *op. cit.*, pp. 84-91 ; for the financial resources of the Duchy, *ibid.*, pp. 343-55.

John and Arthur

The death of Richard raised a knotty point of feudal law. He had designated John as his successor ; but it was an open question whether the younger brother should succeed as against Arthur, the son of Geoffrey. On both sides of the Channel there was a disposition to consider Arthur's claim ; but more in Normandy than England, since feudal principles were more congenial to the Norman mind. The biographer of William Marshal records a curious conversation between his hero and the Archbishop of Rouen. The latter raised the point of law and asked the opinion of the Marshal, who argued strongly in John's favour. The Archbishop deferred to the superior knowledge of his friend, but with marked reluctance. " Marshal," he said, " it shall be as you wish; but never will you have cause to repent of anything so much as of this choice." [1] A better known, but less trustworthy, story represents Hubert Walter as moved by similar misgivings. The Primate, we are told, addressed a solemn warning to the new King in the course of the coronation service, reminding him that allegiance was conditional upon good government.[2] Probably the story was suggested by the customary and formal admonitions embodied in the coronation service.[3] It comes from a writer who had seen the later years of John, and remembered the arguments which John's opponents subsequently based upon the elective nature of the crown. In official documents of John's first years there is nothing to suggest a coldness between the King and Hubert Walter. The King expressed in emphatic language his satisfaction with the Primate,[4] and conferred upon him the Chancellorship, an inferior office to that of the Justiciar but the highest which Hubert could accept without infringing the commands of Innocent III. But there is other evidence to show that John's accession was coldly received in England. A number of the earls, emboldened by the existence of a rival claimant, demanded their "rights" as the price of their allegiance, and were with difficulty induced to accept a temporising answer.[5]

Arthur and Philip

In striking contrast to the passive acquiescence of Normandy and England was the overt opposition of Brittany and Anjou. Twelve days after Richard's death a Breton army, led by the Duchess Constance, entered Angers and proclaimed her son as the

---

[1] G. le M., 11836 ff. [2] Matt. Paris, Chron. Maj., ii., 455.
[3] These are paraphrased in Wendover, iii., 140.
[4] Rot. Chart., i., 23. [5] Hoveden, iv., 88.

lord of Anjou, Brittany, and Maine.　Philip Augustus hastened to avow himself the supporter of a movement which, though in spirit equally hostile to himself and John, offered him an opportunity of a kind which none could turn to more account than he.　After seizing Évreux and harrying south-east Normandy he came to a conference with Arthur at Le Mans ; the young Count did homage for Anjou and Maine, and was surrendered by his friends to be educated under Philip's care.[1]

One of our best authorities for the period asserts that Philip subsequently invested Arthur with Aquitaine and Normandy.[2] This statement appears to be erroneous.　The ambitions of the French King were expanding as new opportunities presented themselves ; and he doubtless intended to make his guardianship of Arthur a pretext for the virtual annexation of Anjou and Maine. But he had not yet decided to annex Normandy or Aquitaine. He protested against John's conduct in assuming the ducal sword of Normandy without the consent of his suzerain ; but he offered to overlook the offence if John would confirm the cession of the Norman Vexin, made by Richard in 1196, and would recognise Arthur's title to Anjou and Maine.　So far as concerned Aquitaine he precluded himself from raising any claims by accepting the homage of the Queen-mother Eleanor.　He might have protested against the arrangement by which Eleanor subsequently resigned Aquitaine to her son, retaining only a usufruct for her life-time ;[3] but it does not appear that any such protest was made.　For the time being Philip contented himself with the indirect control over Anjou, Maine, and Brittany.　He was prepared to make peace if John would submit to the loss of these three provinces.

John however saw no reason for a tame submission.　The death of his brother had not dissolved the coalition of England, Flanders, and the Empire.　The position of Otto had recently been strengthened by an agreement with Innocent III. ; but the Emperor's poverty served as a guarantee that he would not lightly desert the wealthiest of his allies.　For greater security John delayed as long as possible the payment of the substantial legacy which Richard had bequeathed to Otto.　The course of events soon justified the confidence with which Philip's overtures had been rejected.　Before the end of September, 1199, the supporters of Arthur began to doubt the

Designs of Philip

Breach between Arthur and Philip

---

[1] Rigord, p. 50.　　[2] Hoveden, iv., 94.　　[3] *Foedera*, i., 77.

good faith of his guardian. Their leaders, William des Roches and the Viscount of Thouars, came to a secret understanding with John, in consequence of which the young Arthur fled from Paris and came to the court of his uncle. Their reconciliation lasted only for a few weeks. Arthur left John as he had previously left Philip, but the alliance of the Bretons with France was not renewed; and early in 1200 Philip agreed to the Peace of Le Goulet, of which the most important conditions were, that he admitted John's right to Maine, Anjou and the overlordship of Brittany, abandoned his own claims to the Norman Vexin in return for the cession of the Évrecin, and in fact recognised John as the heir to Richard's French fiefs with some trivial exceptions. For these concessions he received the sum of 20,000 marks under the name of a relief. The treaty was cemented by a marriage between Louis, the heir of France, and John's niece the princess Blanche of Castile.[1]

Thanks to his alliances, and to the increasing difficulties between Philip and the Papacy, John had emerged victoriously from the first stage of his duel with the French King. The most skilful states-man could hardly have been more successful; but the advantage which good fortune had given was soon thrown away. A foolish marriage and an ill-considered crime now blew up into flame the latent sparks of rebellion in every part of John's continental heritage.

John's second Marriage, 1200

At the end of 1199 he had divorced his wife, Isabelle, the heiress of the Gloucester earldom, on the plea of consanguinity. Their union had lasted for ten years; although Baldwin of Canterbury had protested against the marriage, a Papal legate had decided that there was no reason for treating it as void, unless an appeal should be successfully maintained at Rome; and it is probable that Isabelle's childlessness was the true motive for her husband's tardy access of conscientious scruples. Not venturing to entrust his case to the decision of the Pope, he persuaded a commission of Norman and Aquitanian bishops to pronounce the union null and void. The wrongs of Isabelle excited the indignation of the English baronage; the King's choice of a new wife set half Aquitaine against him. His original intention had been to sue for the hand of a Portuguese princess.[2] But after an embassy had

[1] Terms in Teulet, *Layettes du Trésor*, i., p. 217.
[2] Miss Norgate, *John Lackland*, p. 77, treats the Portuguese embassy as a blind to cover the plan of marrying Isabel of Angoulême. But this view is contradicted

actually been despatched to Portugal his eye was caught by another
Isabelle, the daughter of the Count of Angoulême, a girl of twelve
or thirteen years of age. She was already betrothed to Hugo of
Lusignan, son and heir of her father's neighbour, the Count of La
Marche. But the precontract did not prevent the King from
pressing his suit, or Isabelle's father from accepting the offer of
the highest bidder. The marriage took place in August, 1200,
at Angoulême.[1] Some critics have detected a deep-laid policy
beneath the apparent caprice of the King's fancy; and it is true
that the House of Angoulême had long been a thorn in the side of
the Plantagenets. But the policy, if policy it was, failed completely
in its object. John secured one friend at the expense of making many
enmities. The Lusignans were more influential than the Count of
Angoulême. They invoked the aid of their friends to avenge the
wrongs of Hugo; and by the spring of 1201 a great part of Poitou
was enlisted on their side.[2] John anticipated their declaration of
war by ordering his Seneschal to seize the Norman castles of the
Lusignans; but the fulfilment of the order was not easy. In
Normandy also the Lusignans had won supporters; a certain
number of the Norman barons came slowly or would not come at
all, to assist in the reduction of the castles.[3] And now Philip intervened, ostensibly as an impartial mediator, but with the secret
intention of fostering the rebellion. He extorted from John a
promise that no Poitevin should be disseised without a lawful trial
in the ducal court of Aquitaine; which meant that no rebel could
be punished except by the verdict of judges who were themselves
open to suspicion. John attempted to meet artifice with artifice.
He summoned the rebels to the ducal court. But he proposed to
substitute trial by battle for judgment of peers. He produced a
band of hired champions who appealed the Lusignans and their
friends of treason. But the defendants had no difficulty in proving
that they were only bound to do battle against knights of their
own rank.[4] They carried their grievances to the King of France

Poitevin Rebellion, 1201

by the account of Diceto, who says that the ambassadors were given to understand
that the Portuguese marriage was seriously meant (Diceto, ii., 170), and clearly
considers that John changed his mind at the last moment.
    [1] *Chronicon Bernardi Iterii* (ed. Duplès Agier), p. 67. T. D. Hardy, *Itinerary*.
    [2] *Foedera*, i., 81. *Rot. Chart.*, 103.
    [3] Stapleton, II., ccxxi., cclxxx.
    [4] The employment of hired champions was always illegal according to the strict
letter of the law. But in the course of the thirteenth century it became usual for

who in April, 1202, summoned John to appear at Paris, in his capacity as Duke of Aquitaine, and answer the charges which had been preferred against him.

Position of Philip and John

The moment was so favourable to Philip that he may now have formed the hope of expelling the Angevins root and branch. At the treaty of Le Goulet John had promised to break off his alliances with Otto and with Flanders, so far as these had been directed against France. It is improbable that he meant to keep the promise when it ceased to suit his convenience. In spite of their disputes over Richard's legacy he had maintained friendly relations with Otto, and had boasted to his English subjects of the advantages to be expected from the Imperial connection.[1] But the Count of Flanders and the minor members of the coalition, disgusted by his want of faith, had turned their thoughts to another enterprise, the Fourth Crusade, and Otto was still troubled by the opposition of Philip of Suabia. John stood alone, while Philip had recently extricated himself from his most serious embarrassment, a quarrel with the Papacy arising out of his irregular divorce from Ingeborg of Denmark. It is not surprising that the King of France showed an aggressive humour. When John denied his liability to personal suit and service at the court of France, Philip proceeded

The War of 1202

to assert his rights by force of arms.[2] An English chronicler asserts that before doing so he obtained from the French barons a formal verdict pronouncing John's fiefs forfeit for non-fulfilment of his service. Modern critics have improved upon the story by conjecturing that the Court of Peers was first summoned on this occasion, in order that the sentence might have a special sanction.[3] But, considering the fact that our French authorities omit any reference to a trial or sentence, it is more probable that John's failure to appear was taken as a sufficient ground for attacking him without further formalities ; and we have no trustworthy evidence as to the composition of the court by which John would

landholders to retain a professional champion. See the accounts of Bishop Swinfield (Camd. Soc., 1853), p. 125 : "In liberatione Thome de Brugg. *pugili* pro feodo suo de tribus terminis . . . xx s. ". Thomas was thus the recipient of an annual retaining fee. King John was only a little in advance of the public opinion of his day.

[1] *Rot. Pat.*, i., 18.   [2] So Rigord (Bouquet, xvii., p. 54).   Diceto, ii., 174.
[3] Coggeshall, 135, 136.   See Bémont in *Rev. Historique*, xxxii., pp. 33 ff.; Guilhiermoz in *Biblioth. de l'Ecole des Chartes*, lx., p. 45; Holtzmann in *Hist. Zeitschrift* (Sybel's), xcv., p. 29; and *infra*, p. 343.

have been tried had he appeared. At the end of April Philip
betrothed his infant daughter to Arthur of Brittany. Shortly
afterwards he received once more the homage of the Count, and
a treaty was concluded under which the whole of the Angevin
dominions except Normandy were recognised as Arthur's right.
"Concerning Normandy," the treaty ran, "the case shall stand
thus that the King of France shall keep for his own use what he
has already acquired and so much as may please him of what God
shall allow him to acquire hereafter."[1] The business of conquering
Normandy had already been taken in hand. Arthur was despatched to make head against Eleanor in Poitou.

This enterprise was the boy's ruin. He attacked the castle of Capture of
Mirebeau, in which the old Queen had shut herself to await Arthur
assistance from Normandy. But, when the outer works had been
already taken and the defenders of the keep were in despair, John
appeared upon the scene (Aug. 1, 1202). Eleanor's appeal for
help had reached him at Le Mans, and by forced marches he had
covered eighty miles in forty-eight hours. Surprised, outnumbered,
and penned within the walls of the castle, Arthur's followers had
no alternative but to surrender. The Count had with him only
250 knights, but among them were all the ringleaders of the
Poitevin rebellion. One stroke of fortune had given John the
upper hand in Aquitaine and had deprived Brittany and Anjou
of their ruler. But John did not know how to use success. He
released Hugh of Lusignan whom he should have detained; while
Arthur was kept in prison, although some of the knights who
fought on the royal side at Mirebeau had done so on the distinct
condition that the boy should be released. The King turned a
deaf ear to expostulations; in consequence he was deserted by
William des Roches the leader of Arthur's Angevin supporters,
who in a few months went over to the side of France.[2] Others,
who felt a less personal interest in the captives, were disgusted by
the King's brutality. Knights of good family were loaded with
fetters, and huddled "like calves" into rough country carts on
which they were sent to the sea-coast to be shipped to English
prisons. It was believed that twenty-two unfortunates, who had
no friends to pay their ransoms, were subsequently starved to death

[1] Round, *Calendar*, 475. Coggeshall, 137. Delisle, *Catalogue*, No. 726.
[2] *Histoire des ducs de Normandie* (ed. Michel), pp. 94, 95.

at Corfe.[1] Facts and rumours of this kind had something to do with the defections of Norman barons which began in the autumn of 1202, and suddenly turned what had been a victorious, into a defeated cause.

Norman Griev-ances

But the Normans had also their own grievances, both new and old. With Richard's death their hopes of victory over France had disappeared. They felt no confidence in John, and were weary of contributing to wars from which they reaped neither honour nor security. The fate of Eu was a warning to the towns that the King could not protect them. The burgesses of Eu had taken the King's part against the Lusignan Ralph of Exoudun, their immediate lord, but Philip came to Ralph's assistance and the loyal burgesses were expelled, and left to wander as homeless fugitives through Normandy. All classes had been plundered by the mercenaries who, in answer to the King's invitation, were streaming into Normandy to serve under his banner; and John either would not or dared not make examples of the worst offenders. It is little wonder that he was deserted even by those to whom he had given his full confidence. Guérin de Clapion, recently the seneschal of Normandy, was one of the first to join Philip. The Count of Alençon, after receiving John at Alençon with profuse assurances of his good faith, rode off the next day to the King of France.[2] Matters had come to such a pass that John trusted no one and travelled along byeways at unexpected hours for fear of treachery and ambush.

Murder of Arthur, 1203

The murder of Arthur of Brittany completed the ruin of his cause. The date, the place, and the circumstances of the crime are alike uncertain. As late as October, 1203, Philip Augustus remained doubtful whether Arthur was alive or dead.[3] The story which the English court disseminated was that the youth had fallen from a tower in attempting to escape; but the long concealment of his death is all but conclusive against the theory of an accident. We are told by a careful contemporary writer that John had given orders to blind the boy soon after his capture·

[1] G. le M., 12520 ff. Hoveden, iv., 169. Annals of Margam, s.a. 1202. Cf. the order respecting Hugo le Brun in Rot. Pat., i., 17.

[2] G. le M., 12619 ff.

[3] The Histoire des ducs, p. 95, expresses no opinion as to the manner of Arthur s death : "Li rois Jehans, quant il fu venus a Ruem, il mist Artu son neveu en prison en la tour, ù il moru". See Delisle, Catalogue, No. 783. Prof. Powicke, Loss of Normandy, pp. 462 et seqq., believes that the true story is that given in the Annals of Margam, which we reproduce above.

that the gaoler Hubert de Burgh had been moved to disobey the
order partly by the remonstrances of his knights, partly by a fear
that the King would repent and disown responsibility ; that some
time later the dead body of the captive was found in the Seine by
a fisherman and buried secretly at Rouen. The current story said
that John committed the murder with his own hand. It drove
the Bretons and Angevins into the arms of the French King and
supplied every vacillating traitor with a new motive or excuse.

Meanwhile Philip pressed the attack at every vulnerable point
of his enemy's long frontier but most of all on the Norman border.
The story that his Court condemned John for the murder of Arthur
is now generally rejected as a fable subsequently invented to justify
the invasion of England.[1] But the suspicions against John were
turned to good account. By the end of 1203 Rouen and the
surrounding country, Mortain, and the Cotentin, were the only
parts of Normandy on which John could count for revenue or
military assistance. Those of the English barons whom he had
persuaded to cross the Channel and take part in the war now
threw up his cause as lost, and demanded permission to go home.
Innocent III. who, if Wendover may be believed, afterwards averred
that the murder of Arthur was a lawful execution, endeavoured to
mediate and threatened Philip with ecclesiastical censures. But
the great vassals of France took the side of their suzerain against
the Pope, and Philip turned a deaf ear to the Pope's expostulations.
After one effort to relieve the garrison of Chateau Gaillard (Aug.,
1203) John ceased to offer any resistance. He remained as though
paralysed by his misfortunes in the neighbourhood of Rouen.
"Let be, let be," he is reported to have said. "One day I shall
win it all again." But his actions belied the confidence of his
words. Early in November he left Rouen, never to return, and
travelled to the sea-coast with the secrecy of a criminal escaping
from justice.[2] On December 6th he landed in England leaving his
Norman supporters to make what terms they could.

The French conquest was completed in 1204. Chateau Gaillard

*Philip
invades
Nor-
mandy,
1203*

---

[1] The controversy began with an article by M. Pardessus in the *Biblioth. de
l'Ecole des Chartes*, 2nd series, iv., 281, attacking the traditional story. The evidence in favour of the tradition is stated by Beugnot, *ibid.*, v., 1. The most noteworthy
of recent contributions to the controversy are those of M. Guilhiermoz (*supra*, p.
340); Miss Norgate, in *Trans. R. Hist. Soc.*, N.S., vol. xiv.; M. Lot, in *Fidèles
ou Vassaux* (Paris, 1904). Powicke, *Loss of Normandy*, pp. 453-81.

[2] *G. le M.*, 12920.

Final Re-
duction of
Normandy
fell on March 6th. Falaise, on which John had conferred a commune in the preceding year,[1] surrendered after a siege of seven days although reputed impregnable ; Caen and Bayeux followed the example. Philip announced that, by the flight of John, Normandy had escheated to the Crown of France ; whoever resisted further would be treated as a traitor. The defenders of every town and castle were intimidated by this threat ; they signed truces for a year, promising submission if not relieved by John within that time. The commandant of Rouen sent word to England that, if Rouen fell, there was no hope that any of the Normans would remain faithful. By the first of June Rouen, hitherto loyal, was in despair, and obtained a truce of thirty days. A last appeal to John produced a reply that the citizens must look to themselves for the King of England could not help them further. They accordingly capitulated on June 24th.[2]

Philip's
Gains in
Aquitaine
It remained to be seen whether Aquitaine would go the way of Normandy. Much of future history depended on the choice of masters which the inhabitants of the southern duchy had now to make. If the Plantagenets had lost, at this stage, every foothold on the western coast of France, England might have been spared the wars which were waged for the next three centuries with the object of recovering Normandy ; at the least these wars would have been much curtailed ; for no English general, before the reign of Henry V., was able to dispense for any length of time with an Aquitanian base of operations. It seemed at first that all the country south of the Loire would fall an easy prey to Philip. In Anjou, Maine, and Touraine few English families had taken root and the English supremacy had no important champions.[3] In Poitou the gallant resistance offered by John's seneschal Robert de Turneham and by Savaric of Mauléon produced insignificant results ; and the death of Queen Eleanor (April, 1204) deprived John of his last claim to Poitevin support. Except La Rochelle, Thouars, Niort, Chinon, and Loches, the whole country submitted to Philip in 1204 ; Chinon and Loches were reduced by the French in the next year.[4] But in Gascony the great communes of Bordeaux

---

[1] *Rot. Pat.*, i., 24. But, as Giry remarks, the grant of a commune was double-edged. It carried liability to military service (*Etablissements*, p. 46).

[2] Terms of the capitulation in Rigord, Bouquet, *Recueil*, xvii., 57.

[3] William des Roches was still seneschal of Anjou ; he came to terms with Philip in August, 1204 (Delisle, *Cat.*, No. 848).

[4] Viscount of Thouars recognised by Philip as his seneschal for Poitou (Delisle, *Cat.*, No. 850) in 1204.

and Bayonne held by England, both for the sake of their wine-trade and because the Angevins had always been more indulgent than the King of France was likely to prove. Their loyalty and that of the Poitevin towns received abundant encouragement in the shape of trading privileges and freedom from royal tolls; and John, notwithstanding the exhaustion of his treasury, contrived to supply his representative the Archbishop of Bordeaux with an enormous subsidy.[1] In consequence the whole of Gascony was saved, and enough of Poitou to make the recovery of that province appear a possibility.

The political effects of the greatest reverse which the English Crown had suffered since 1066 are written large upon the history of the next fifty years, and their importance can hardly be over-rated. On English social life the loss of Normandy had less influence than we might expect. Until the accession of the Angevins the tide of immigration had flowed from France to England, and the great baronial houses had preserved a keen interest in the politics of France. Now immigration had ceased—except for the occasional influx of court favourites and con-dottieri from Aquitaine or the Low Countries. Henry I. had begun to separate Norman from English estates by the division of inheritances between brothers; since his time the process had been voluntarily carried on by means of family settlements. It is true that John's defeat entailed for some Normans the loss of English, and for some Englishmen the loss of Norman, fiefs.[2] But in England the loss fell chiefly on the Crown; since those of the barons who were most affected obtained compensation in grants of royal demesnes. Trade suffered little; for Gascony remained in English hands, and the subjects of France were allowed to enter England with their wares, even during the continuance of hostilities, upon paying a duty of a tenth on their goods, a permission of which we know they availed themselves extensively.[3] The connection of English with French religious orders remained unaltered: and, if the University of Paris attracted fewer Englishmen than formerly, this is in part explained by the growing efficiency of Oxford and Cambridge. It is remarkable that French remained the language of the law-courts and of polite society. The beginnings, but only

[1] Coggeshall, 147, says 28,000 marks, but this is preposterous.
[2] The list of the Norman barons who held by John and incurred forfeiture is given in Powicke, *op. cit.*, p. 484.
[3] *Rot. Pat.*, i., 42. Stubbs, *Coventry*, ii., pp. xxxv. ff.

12

the beginnings, of a vernacular literature can be traced in England in the thirteenth century. So far there was little to stamp the English as insular, except the faintness of their interest in continental politics and the originality of their political ideas. And this originality may easily be overrated. The most audacious innovator in English politics of the thirteenth century was Simon de Montfort a Frenchman by birth and education.

CHAPTER XIV

THE STRUGGLE WITH THE PAPACY—BOUVINES

WHILE John was engaged in fighting for the possession of Normandy England enjoyed a season of comparative tranquillity.[1] The most serious danger which had confronted John at his accession was that of war with Scotland. William the Lion, like the English earls, had judged the moment a favourable one for reviving old pretensions. He demanded that the new King should fulfil the promise, which Henry II. had made to David, of surrendering Northumberland and Cumberland with their appurtenances. But the sense of advancing years and the lack of allies had soon induced the King of Scots to leave his claim in abeyance and to do homage for his English estates (Nov. 22, 1200). It does not appear that he concluded any league with Philip or attempted to profit by the continental war. In England public order was maintained by the Justiciar Geoffrey FitzPeter and by the Primate, who had cheerfully accepted the inferior office of Chancellor, and now worked harmoniously with his sometime subordinate. The King left them a free hand, only intervening now and then to bestow a sheriffdom or a grant of lands upon a foreign favourite. His personal confidants, the Poitevin Peter des Roches, the brothers John and Walter de Gray, the Normans Gerald d'Athée and Engelard de Cicogné, had not yet reached the high positions in which they afterwards became notorious. The Justiciar, though a man of harsh temper and narrow sympathies, enjoyed the respect of the baronage. The Earldom of Essex, which he had received in the right of his wife, put him on a footing of equality with the greatest houses; his connections were numerous and influential. He could answer, therefore, for

---

[1] Gervase, ii., 94: " Anglia tamen interim per Dei gratiam, agente archiepiscopo Cantuariensi Huberto et Gaufrido filio Petri, tranquilla pace gaudebat ".

the loyalty of the feudal classes as Hubert Walter answered for that of the Church.

Fiscal Griev- ances

Still it was impossible to ignore the fact that the government was for many reasons unpopular. The legal and administrative changes of Henry II. and of Hubert Walter left many loopholes for the abuse of authority by royal officials. No checks upon the sheriff could prevent extortion while he continued to farm a substantial portion of the royal revenue; and the Crown instead of checking malpractices, encouraged them by raising the amount of the firm demanded from the sheriff. The Crown moreover claimed exemption from the restraints which it imposed upon inferior landlords. In the last resort the tallages of the towns and of the royal demesnes were settled by a fiat of the Exchequer. Charters of privilege were liable to be revoked or over-ridden on the slightest pretext. The royal rights of wardship and marriage were shamelessly abused; while the rate of the relief which a mesne lord might demand from his military tenants was settled at 100s. on the knight's fee, the heir of an earl or baron was compelled to pay whatever the Exchequer chose to demand. The Church, finally, complained that the right of free and canonical election, which Henry II. had guaranteed, was practically withdrawn; and that the property of the clergy, both in land and in movables, was now taxed without regard to custom or the principles of the canon law.

Mediating position of FitzPeter

Confronted with such a state of feeling the Justiciar pursued a policy of concessions and conciliation. The King's need of money, rather than any deeper motives, may account for the readiness with which immunities and rights of jurisdiction were granted or confirmed to the great landowners. But it was with a political object that steps were taken to relieve the leading barons from some grievances of which they could legitimately complain. A number of the earls had never yet received the official insignia of their dignity or the privileges, such as the third penny of judicial profits, which were usually attached to it. Five of them received, within a short time of the King's coronation, the whole or a part of what they claimed. To soothe the clergy the government abandoned an important source of revenue. When a carucage was levied, in the year 1200, at the rate of 3s. on the ploughland, the Cistercians claimed exemption; through the mediation of Hubert

Walter they obtained the confirmation of a privilege which was warranted indeed by precedent but indefensible on grounds of equity. The other orders were less fortunate; and, when the King's half-brother Geoffrey of York forbade the payment of the carucage due from the monastic lands of his diocese, he was punished with the sequestration of his own estates. But the quarrel was not pushed to extremities; in the following year Geoffrey was allowed to make his peace on favourable terms.

Even more striking is the friendly attitude of the Justiciar towards the towns and the merchant-class. Encouraged by the example which Hubert Walter had set in the last reign, he showed the utmost readiness to confer rights of self-government upon the rising commercial communities of the south and midlands. Lincoln, Norwich, Nottingham, Northampton, Shrewsbury, Ipswich, Gloucester, Derby, all received, in the first five years of the reign, charters of which the essential feature was a permission to elect their own chief magistrates. We may attribute to the conservatism of the Justiciar the provisoes, to be found in several of these grants, by which the Crown is given a certain control over the election, the sheriff or the Chief Justiciar being sometimes empowered to choose between two candidates presented by the town, and sometimes to order a second election if the result of the first appeared unsatisfactory. Geoffrey FitzPeter was not inclined to advance as far as his predecessor in the path of decentralisation. But, save for this restraint, the town-moot is usually left to determine the constitution of the town ; where the government intervenes to create any office other than that of the chief magistrate the alleged object is to secure the citizen-body against oppression by their own representatives. It is on this ground that in 1200 Northampton is ordered to elect four coroners, and London in 1206 to elect a council of Twenty-four wise and legal men.[1]

The importance of these towns depended largely upon their foreign trade. The demand of the Flemish communes for English wool was steadily increasing; although the greater part of the supply was still furnished by the Cistercian, Gilbertine, and Premonstratensian houses, and by the descendants of the Flemings

FitzPeter and the Towns

Foreign Trade

---

[1] Grants of privilege to Lincoln, *Rot. Chart.*, p. 5 ; Norwich, *ibid.*, p. 20 ; Nottingham, *ibid.*, p. 39 ; Northampton, *ibid.*, p. 45 ; second charter to Lincoln, *ibid.*, p. 56 ; Shrewsbury, *ibid.*, p. 46 ; Ipswich, *ibid.*, p. 65 ; Gloucester, *ibid.*, p. 56 ; Derby, *ibid.*, p. 138 ; London, *Rot. Claus.*, p. 64.

whom Henry I. had established in South Wales, sheep-breeding promised to become a national industry. It benefited the towns not only by increasing the importance of their fairs and markets, but also by enabling the landowner to spend more freely on those manufactures of which the town-gilds, in virtue of their charters, enjoyed a local monopoly. The wine-trade with Aquitaine and the Rhineland was even more directly advantageous, since the foreign vintners usually took their payment in the form of manufactured goods. Under the Angevins wine, which had formerly been accounted a luxury, came to be regarded as a necessity of life ; the royal accounts of the period bear witness to an enormous consumption of the better vintages. Every year a wine fleet of thirty or forty vessels sailed to England from Poitou ; the Cologne trade was so important that the merchants of Cologne could negotiate for special privileges (1204). To advances of this kind the government responded in a friendly spirit ; even where there was no money to be made by a special bargain the Justiciar was careful to guarantee that the merchant who came in time of peace with due credentials should have the royal protection both by sea and land. Restrictions of an unnecessary kind still remained to hamper foreign trade. A merchant whose city or country had no general safe-conduct from the King of England could not with safety enter an English port until he had procured a special licence ; those who were most thoroughly protected by such documents might at any moment see their wares impounded, under the law of reprisals, because their fellow-countrymen had misused an English merchant. The Crown exercised the right of regulating prices by ordinance, and of prohibiting the exportation of food-stuffs when scarcity was apprehended. But in general the Justiciar recognised that the interests of the Crown and the merchant were identical; he fostered the prosperity of the chief commercial centres as the surest means of increasing the revenue and reconciling the nation to the government. It is a remarkable proof of his sagacity that he allowed the trade-relations of England and France to continue without interruption even after the English had been expelled from Normandy ; the tax of 2s. in the £ which he imposed upon French merchants was no higher than that paid by the men of Cologne for their special privileges.[1]

---

[1] The Cologne licence to trade, *Rot. Pat.*, i., p. 40. Their gild-hall in London, *Rot. Chart.*, 194. Licence to French merchants, *Rot. Pat.*, i., 42.

A policy so favourable to commerce explains the fact that a long time elapsed before the towns joined in active opposition to the Crown. But only a spark was needed to kindle the long-cherished resentment of the feudal classes. Though the King's first demand for a scutage, at the unprecedented rate of two marks on the knight's fee, was submissively granted in 1199, a call for military service in 1201 led to a formidable protest. The earls, having debated together, sent a unanimous message to John that they would not follow him to France unless he allowed them "the rights" which, as we have seen, they had been promised on an earlier occasion; the term apparently denotes the third penny and other customary prerogatives of their dignity; and we must suppose either that the concessions which had been already made to individual members of the order were deemed insufficient, or that those who had won their privileges stood out for the benefit of others who had not yet been gratified. A threat to seize their castles had the effect of reducing the earls to a more compliant spirit; they eventually compounded for their own service and that of their knights by the payment of fines and of a scutage at the increased rate. But they took their revenge in the two following years. An earnest appeal for help, which John addressed to his English subjects in May, 1202, produced very little result. The few barons who answered it seized an early opportunity of retiring from a campaign which they regarded as hopeless, and in which their own interests were slightly, if at all, involved. The defaulters admitted themselves to have been in the wrong; they paid in silence a fine of one-seventh of their movables, which the King imposed upon them in December, 1203, after he had definitely retired from Normandy; and the Great Council, early in the next year, made tardy amends by voting a scutage.[1] But no visible result was produced by these contributions, which were probably exhausted in the defence of Poitou and Gascony. A general impression arose that the King was a coward who would never fight, and that his wars were simply pretexts for extortion. Mistrust increased when John, in 1205, raised a false alarm of invasion, issued orders for the reorganisation of the fyrd, and called upon his tenants to render aid at the rate of one man

[1] Wendover, iii., 173-5. According to Swereford this scutage was at the rate of two marks (Norgate, *John Lackland*, p. 123). But Wendover gives the rate as two and a half marks.

at arms from every ten knights' fees.[1] The barons, deluded for the moment by the king's assertion that this force was required for the defence of the realm, acquiesced in the new burden. But on discovering the truth, that their quotas were to be used for a descent on France, they protested by the mouths of the Primate and the veteran Earl Marshal. The expedition, they said, was hopeless and they would not contribute to it. The King shed tears of rage and shame; he even made a feint of sailing without the barons; but on discovering, after a three days' cruise along the Channel, that no one followed him, he returned with ignominy. Public sympathy was on his side. The sailors of the fleet cursed the faint-heartedness and disloyalty of the barons. It might indeed be argued that the opposition had condemned the King upon slight evidence. Not content with abandoning the continental policy as inexpedient, they had blamed John for misfortunes which neither his father nor his brother could have well avoided. Misrule in Normandy, the feud with the Lusignans, and the murder of Arthur, had merely precipitated a struggle in which all the advantages of numbers, resources, and position were on the side of Philip Augustus. But at this juncture, when it was still possible to retrieve his character for ability, the King threw away whatever popularity he still retained by embarking on a conflict with the strongest Pope who had sat in Peter's chair since the death of Gregory VII.

Campaign in Poitou, 1206 Hubert Walter died a few weeks after he had helped to thwart the French expedition (July 13, 1205). The most popular and in some respects the greatest of the medieval statesmen who were rewarded with the Primacy, he had been to John, as Lanfranc to Rufus, a moderating and restraining influence, respected though disliked; and he had maintained intact the alliance with the Church which was the corner stone of Angevin power. On hearing of his death the King exclaimed, " Now for the first time I am King in England ". The first use which John made of his new liberty was to undertake a campaign in Poitou (1206), for which, by means of threats and promises, he brought together a considerable feudal force. He came too late to save Chinon and Loches; and the hope of winning a great victory was dashed to the ground by the bad faith of his Poitevin allies, who followed him obediently enough in a northward raid as far as Angers, but refused to fight when Philip brought the army

---

[1] *Foed.*, i., 92. The ordinance respecting the fyrd in Gervase, ii., p. 97.

of France to the borders of Poitou.[1] The campaign ended tamely
with a truce to last for two years on the basis of the *status quo*.
Yet the results were more considerable than we should gather from
the chroniclers. French influence in Poitou had received a blow
from which it did not recover in John's lifetime or for some years
after. The majority of the Poitevin barons, and all the important
towns, except Poitiers, declared for the English dynasty. But by
the time this result had been achieved the distracting quarrel with
Innocent III. had begun ; the hope of recovering Normandy, Brittany
and Anjou was destroyed as soon as it took shape.

It was John's intention to confer the Primacy upon the Bishop
of Norwich, John de Gray, whose lack of other qualifications was
outweighed in the King's judgment by the supreme virtue of complaisance. The bishops were willing enough, if the election had
lain with them, to accept the royal candidate. But by the canon
law this right belonged to the chapter of the Primate's cathedral,
to the monks, that is, of Christchurch, Canterbury. For a century
they had strenuously resisted the claim to assist in these elections
which the episcopate of the province, supported by the Crown had
not unreasonably put forward ; and they had obtained from the
Papacy a recognition of their own exclusive right. On the present
occasion the majority were willing to allow the attendance and co-
operation of the bishops. But some of the younger and more
hot-headed monks resolved for once to make a free election. They
met by night, elected Reginald the sub-prior of the Convent, and
despatched him to seek confirmation from the Pope, giving him
strict injunctions to say nothing of his elevation until he arrived at
Rome. The sub-prior however could not deny himself the luxury
of advertising his new dignity as he passed through Flanders, and
his tale soon reached the ears of John. Knowing the King with
whom they had to deal, the monks at once made haste to cover
their disobedience by submission, and repudiated Reginald. They
joined with the bishops in electing John de Gray (Dec. 11. 1205) ;[2]
and sent commissioners to Rome with a request that he should be
confirmed. The line which the King took and compelled them to

The Can-
terbury
Election
1206-7

---

[1] *Hist. des ducs*, p. 109. Petit-Dutaillis, *Louis VIII.*, p. 27.
[2] The Canterbury Chronicle (Gervase, ii., liv.) asserts that Reginald was elected
by the whole body of the monks and Gray by a mere section. But this authority
must be regarded with suspicion on such a question. A short and unsatisfactory
account of these proceedings from the Canterbury point of view in Gervase, ii., p. 98.

12*

follow was that of regarding Reginald's election as a tumultuary act of no validity.

The attitude of Innocent III. It was a natural view if Reginald was really elected in the manner described by our principal authority.[1] To Innocent however, who only knew that one Archbishop-elect had arrived with due credentials and had been followed by another claimant similarly equipped, the King's behaviour appeared irregular in the last degree. Further enquiries, while showing the weakness of the sub-prior's title, also inspired Innocent with a well-founded reluctance to accept De Gray, a political bishop of whom even John could only say that he deserved promotion because he knew the royal secrets. The Pope took the course which he considered would best protect the interests of the English Church. Concealing his intentions he induced the King to send him plenipotentiaries; a deputation of the Canterbury monks with power to make a new election in the presence of the Curia; representatives of the bishops and the Crown with power to confirm the election when made. John, who had spared no pains to bribe the Cardinals, thought that he could safely allow the new election. He expected that Reginald would be set aside and De Gray re-elected in due form. He gave strict injunctions to the monks that they should elect no one save De Gray; [2] and they are said to have made a promise in this sense. But Innocent refused to accept De Gray, and advised the monks to elect Stephen Langton, a distinguished Cardinal of English birth. At the Pope's persuasion they ignored their secret promise to the King, and accepted Langton; who, notwithstanding a protest from John's representatives, was at once invested with the pallium.

Election of Langton, Dec., 1206 Innocent, no less than John, had done violence to the canonical principle of free election. But the King, when he allowed the new election to take place at Rome, had committed an irreparable mistake. He had pitted his diplomacy against that of a past master in the art; he had been fairly defeated and would have done well to accept defeat with a good grace. Apart from the manner of his election, Stephen Langton was an unexceptionable

---

[1] The main authority for this and the following paragraphs is the Canterbury Chronicle (printed by Stubbs in Gervase, ii., liv. ff.) which embodies a number of letters connected with the quarrel.

[2] *Burton Annals*, *s.a.* 1211. Matt. Paris, *Chron. Maj.*, ii., 514. Wendover mentions no such promise. John sends letters of credit for large sums to Rome (*Rot. Pat.*, i., 65, 69).

choice.   Though he had spent the best years of his life abroad he
was a subject of the English Crown, and had always cherished an
affection for his native country.[1]   He owed his cardinalate to the
distinction which he had earned as a theologian in the schools of
Paris; and on the occasion of his promotion he had been compli-
mented by John as an honour to the English name.   Innocent had
chosen him as a man who would be personally acceptable to the
King.[2]   John however chose to resist, and weakened a bad case
by weak arguments.   He charged the monks with perjury, thus
confessing his underhand attempt to tamper with the freedom of
election.   Of Langton, he affirmed with gross effrontery, he knew
nothing except that the Cardinal had lived for a long time in the
realm of Philip, the worst enemy of England.[3]   Let the Pope
reflect, wrote John, how great were the revenues which Rome
derived from England ; for if this election were not cancelled the
golden stream would be diverted elsewhere.   The English bishops,
he added, were quite competent to settle all the litigation of the
English Church in their own courts; there was no reason why
they should buy justice from a foreign power.   This letter and the
further bribes which accompanied it failed completely in their purpose.   Innocent denied the necessity of the royal assent for an
election made at Rome, and exhorted John to acquiesce in " Our
good pleasure ".[4]

John's answer was to quarter mercenaries upon the Canterbury John takes
monks and to sequestrate their rich estates—measures which had violent
the effect of driving the majority into a self-inflicted exile.[5]   The measures
threat of an interdict was the natural consequence, but to John it
came as an unexpected shock.   He hesitated and, like Becket in a
different case, offered submission upon terms, " saving to ourselves
and our heirs our rights and dignity and liberties."   To this
transparent subterfuge the Pope replied, by the mouth of Simon

[1] See Langton's own letter in Gervase, ii., lxxxi.: " Ab annis enim teneris tam
tenere regnum nostrum amore dileximus naturali, quod per compassionem portavimus
casus regni prosperos et adversos ".
[2] Wendover, iii., 213.   Innocent, *Epp.*, ix., 206.   Pauli, i., 485.
[3] See Innocent, *Epp.*, x., 219.   Wendover, iii., 216.
[4] See Innocent's letter in Gervase, ii., lxxii.: " Ita secundum jus nostro studeas
honori deferre, ut gratiam Divinam et nostram merearis ".
[5] The Canterbury Chronicle (Gervase, ii., lxiii.) states that the expatriation
of the monks was voluntary, and that the older members remained behind.   But
Gervase, ii., 100, says that they were expelled ; but that a few " caeci et claudi " remained who also were expelled when the interdict began.

Langton, the Archbishop's brother, that only an unconditional sub-mission could be entertained.[1] Driven to the wall John defied the Pope to do his worst. He issued a proclamation announcing that the lands of any ecclesiastic who obeyed the impending interdict would be confiscated. Wendover asserts that the King descended to yet more violent menaces, pledging himself to exile all the clergy without distinction, to confiscate their lands, and to cut off the ears and noses of any Roman clerks whom he found in his dominions. None the less the interdict was imposed on March 23rd, 1208.

The Interdict, 1208-13

The sentence was one which had already been used with good effect to break the pride of Philip Augustus. It affected every class; it threw a gloom over the most solemn and important oc-casions of social life. It did not indeed deprive the dying of the last spiritual consolations, nor the living of the means of grace. But while an interdict was in force the dead were interred in un-consecrated ground and without the offices of the priest; the mass could only be celebrated in the churchyards and on Sunday morn-ing; weddings took place at the church-porch; baptisms in the churches, but with closed doors in the presence of the sponsors only.[2] Under ordinary circumstances the monastic and military orders enjoyed a partial exemption from these restrictions on the use of their churches. In the present case, however, the Pope de-creed that it should be inviolably observed without regard to any privilege; only a year later did he allow a partial relaxation in favour of conventual churches.[3] The interdict was as severe as it could be made. On his side the King acted with equal vigour. He shrank indeed from fulfilling the threat to exile all the clergy; an ordinance which he issued for that purpose was withdrawn in three or four days. But the sheriffs received orders to sequestrate the lands both of the religious and of the secular clergy, leaving to the victims a bare allowance for their daily food.[4] The sentence fell impartially on high and low, even on the bishops and on the great order of the Templars to whom the King was under many financial obligations. It was executed with superfluous zeal by the

---

[1] *Rot. Pat.*, i., 78. *Foedera*, i., 100.

[2] For the terms of this interdict see Innocent's letter in Gervase, ii., xcii.; see also the specimen form of interdict in Bouquet, *Recueil*, xvii., p. 51.

[3] The English Cistercians are taken to task for neglecting the interdict, Gervase, ii., xcvi. See the letter of Innocent forbidding any exceptions to be made, *Opera*, ed. Migne, ii., 1255. For the relaxation of 1209, W. Cov., ii., 201.

[4] *Rot. Claus.*, i., 109.

royal officers. They held the concubines of parish priests to ransom; they rabbled all ecclesiastics whom they encountered on the highways. The King publicly forbade, and privately connived at, these outrages. He announced that he would hang to the nearest oak [1] any one who harmed a clerk ; but there was a current story that, when a prisoner came before him charged with the murder of a priest, he ordered the man to be released, saying, " he has slain mine enemy : loose him and let him go ". Under this pressure many ecclesiastics gave way, obtaining the restoration of their property by a promise to disregard the interdict. Others were allowed, without submitting so far as this, to farm their own lands, at a heavy rate, from the Exchequer. But the bishops, with the exception of John de Gray and Peter des Roches, of whom the latter was now in possession of Winchester, fled the kingdom to find a refuge in Scotland, France, or Italy. Their temporalties remained in the King's hand so long as the interdict lasted, that is until the year 1213.

In spite of these outrages the laity remained passive in part and partly in active sympathy with the King.[2] Of anti-papal feeling, such as that which permeated all classes in the reign of John's successor, we find little or no trace at this period, although some sensation was caused by an itinerant preacher, one Alexander the Mason, who accused Innocent of unwarrantable interference in the secular affairs of the kingdom.[3] There was a general impression that Innocent had exceeded his authority, but no inclination to revive the arguments, striking at the very root of papal authority, which Gerard of York had formulated a hundred years before. The suspension of the usual services was felt as a loss ; but on the other hand the enormous sums which the spoliation of the churches brought into the Exchequer enabled John to dispense with aids and scutages. The monastic annals mournfully confess that his resistance received the general support of the nation.[4] But the

Attitude of the Laity

---

[1] *Rot. Claus.*, i., 111.

[2] Gervase, ii., 102, speaks of the barons as making the interdict a pretext for objecting to war with Scotland in 1209, and compelling the King to open negotiations with the Pope. But this, if true, is an isolated instance. We prefer to follow the evidence of the *Annales Monastici* for the general state of feeling.

[3] Wendover, iii., 230.

[4] *Annales Wigorn.*, *s.a.* 1209 : " Magna tribulatio fuit hoc anno et praeterito super omnes ecclesiasticas personas quia a cura Christianitatis omnes fere laici pedem reflectebant ; sed victualium plena fuit abundantia ".

Papacy had still a weapon in reserve. If the interdict proved un-availing it was possible to excommunicate the King and to release his subjects from their allegiance. John had many enemies who would be likely to avail themselves of so tempting an occasion: the King of Scots whose claim to the northern counties had never been abandoned; the Welsh princes, ever on the alert for an oppor-tunity of breaking through the iron cordon of the English marches; **Baronial Discon-tent** the discontented barons of England and Ireland. Some of the latter, it is said, had private injuries to avenge: John had intrigued with their wives or seduced their daughters, bringing the greatest houses of the land to open shame. The two stories which are commonly cited to prove this statement rest upon late authority,[1] and we know of at least one case in which a charge of this kind was falsely raised by the King's enemies; but there may be a substratum of truth in the general accusation which is brought against the King by several independent and contemporary writers,[2] and which re-ceives some colour from the long list of his bastard children. There is better reason for believing that the divorce of Isabel of Glou-cester, and the king's shameless refusal to restore the lands which he received with her, had alienated the numerous connections of the House of Gloucester. But the grand reason for defections was that the despotic power of Henry II. had passed into the hands of a man who was universally disliked and despised, who exacted the last farthing of his feudal rights to enrich unpopular favourites and pursue an unpopular war. All who were in debt to the Crown, all whose privileges had suffered by the new autocracy, conceived that they had a personal grievance against the King. **De Braose** William de Braose, the lord of Brecknock, may serve as an illustra-tion of the terms on which the King stood with the magnates. In high favour at the commencement of the reign, Braose had received a licence to augment his barony of Radnor by such con-quests as he could make at the expense of the Welsh princes; when to these were added the district of Limerick, which he in-herited from an uncle, he rose to a commanding position among the English barons. But the Crown demanded a relief of 5,000 marks for Limerick and this sum, though readily promised before De Braose obtained possession, he subsequently professed himself

[1] Norgate, *John Lackland*, pp. 289 ff.
[2] *e.g.*, *Chronique des ducs*, p. 105: "De belles femmes était trop convoiteux," etc.

unable to pay. After many excuses made and respites granted, the King distrained upon the lands of the defaulter both in Wales and Ireland.[1] In view of the grant which De Braose had received upon the Marches he cannot be said to have experienced exceptionally harsh treatment. His true quarrel, and that of his sympathisers, was with a system and not with the King. But the result of this and similar episodes was that the King, as a contemporary puts it, found himself face to face with as many enemies as he had barons.

Thus situated John would gladly have avoided excommunication, if a partial surrender would have served the purpose. He offered to accept Langton, but refused to give him the kiss of peace or treat him as a friend. He intimated his readiness to restore the temporalties of the bishops, and even to make some compensation for the profits received during the sequestration; but to complete restitution he would not pledge himself, and he demanded a personal indemnity.[2] Since these offers were rejected he decided to brave the sentence and to forestall, by precautionary measures, the dangers which it would entail. His first step was to demand hostages from the suspected barons. Many complied, surrendering their sons or grandsons, but the wife of De Braose told the King's messengers that children of hers should never be exposed to Arthur's fate. The King in great perturbation summoned her husband to appear and answer for his wife's contumacy. De Braose preferred the course of open rebellion. He harried the royal demesnes which lay in the Marches, attempted to recover by force the castles which had been distrained for his debt, and finally fled to Ireland, where he was cordially received and harboured not only by the disaffected lords of Meath and Ulster, but even by the loyal William Marshal. In England however De Braose found no open support. For the present the King contented himself with sending John de Gray in pursuit. The year 1209 was passed in securing the loyalty of England, Wales and Scotland. William the Lion, who had given offence by attacking Tweedmouth[3]

John's precautions

Scotland and Wales, 1209

---

[1] See the article by Mr. Round in the *Dict. Nat. Biog.*; and John's account of his relations with De Braose in *Foedera*, i., 107. Also *Rot. Chart.*, 66, 84. *Rot. Claus.*, i., 77.

[2] See the documents relating to the negotiation in Gervase, ii., c. ff. and cx.

[3] *Chron. Lanercost*, 4.

and harbouring certain of the exiled bishops, was terrified by the appearance of an English army on the border. For the sum of 15,000 marks he purchased a treaty of friendship and alliance which left Scotland, till his death (1214), in a position of dependence.[1] Advancing years, and the prospect of a disputed succession at his death, inclined the King of Scots to make large concessions in the interests of his young son Alexander. In return for help against the pretender Guthred, a descendant of Malcolm Canmore, John was permitted to arrange the marriage of Alexander, and to use Galloway as a recruiting ground for his expeditions in Ireland and elsewhere.[2] In Wales John intervened at this time to impose a peace upon the petty princes of the south and centre; Llewelyn ap Jorwerth, the aspiring prince of North Wales, was already bound to the King's cause by the marriage which he had contracted with John's illegitimate daughter Joanna. Hence, at the end of 1209, the King was able to show his subjects a spectacle of Welsh submissiveness such as they had not witnessed for a generation. In the month of October all the princes of the country appeared before him at Woodstock to do homage.[3] About the same time the oath of fealty was exacted from all English free men. When the decree of excommunication was at length promulgated (Nov., 1209) it found the King in a position as secure as oaths and hostages and treaties could give him.

Effects of the Excommunication, 1209-12

Still the sentence gave encouragement to his enemies and caused a panic among his supporters. The scruples of the latter were silenced by rough but effectual arguments. There was a certain clerk, Geoffrey of Norwich, who held the position of treasurer in the Exchequer. It came to John's ears that Geoffrey had expressed a doubt whether ecclesiastics could lawfully remain in the service of an excommunicated king. The unfortunate man was immediately thrown into a cell where he could neither sit nor stand; a leaden mitre of crushing weight was fastened on his head; and in this plight he was left to perish of starvation. With enemies, open or concealed, John found it more difficult to deal. It is possible that plans of invading Eng-

[1] The favourable nature of this treaty is an argument against the allegation of Gervase (ii., 102) that the barons used the Interdict as a pretext for remonstrating against war with Scotland. The treaty in *Foedera*, i., 103.

[2] W. Cov., ii., 206. *Rot. Claus.*, i., 131.

[3] " Quod anteactis temporibus fuerat inauditum " (Wendover, iii., 227).

land already floated before the mind of Philip Augustus, and that he was by this time in communication with the princes of Wales and the barons of Ireland.[1]   In any case the Papal sentence filled John with apprehensions as to possible risings in those countries. Wales and Ireland claimed his chief attention for the next two years.   His measures of precaution were well chosen and did much to restore the military prestige of England, which had been so rudely shaken in the Norman wars.   More fortunately situated than his predecessors, in that all his resources were now available for the settlement of the British Isles, John appears to have looked beyond the exigencies of the moment and to have formed plans for a lasting extension of the royal authority.   " All men bore witness," says an unprejudiced contemporary, " that never since the time of Arthur was there a king who was so greatly feared in England, in Wales, in Scotland, or in Ireland." [2]   In 1210 he intervened in Wales to prevent the principality of Powis from being absorbed in the dominions of Llewelyn ; in 1211 he invaded Gwynedd with the objects of fixing the English frontier and settling the position of Llewelyn in a manner more advantageous to England.   Twice in the latter year John marched almost to the foot of Snowdon ; on the first occasion the failure of supplies compelled him to retreat with dishonour, but on the second he was more successful.   Castles were built along the frontier ; a treaty was wrung from Llewelyn under which the prince rendered homage, promised an annual tribute and a war-indemnity, and renounced all claims on Powis.[3]   Before the conclusion of this treaty a semblance of good order was produced in Ireland by an expedition which the King conducted thither in the summer of 1210.   Before his arrival the government had been engaged in a series of interminable and hopeless struggles with the great feudatories.   After a war of six years' duration John de Courcy had been expelled from Ulster (1205), only to be succeeded by the equally turbulent Hugh de Lacy.[4]   Hugh's brother Walter de Lacy, the lord of Meath, had attempted to extend his feudal jurisdiction at the expense of the Crown and to lay violent hands

John's Activity

Ireland, 1210

---

[1] See Petit-Dutaillis, p. 28.   Delisle, *Catalogue*, No. 1416.
[2] *Hist. des ducs*, p. 109.
[3] *Tewkesbury Annals.   Brut y Tyw.*, 269.   Wendover, iii., 235.
[4] Sweetman, *Calendar*, 224, 263.   *Rot. Chart.*, 151.

upon the city of Limerick.[1]   William de Braose, though a declared
rebel for the past two years, was still at large and in possession of
the lordship of Limerick.   William Marshal, the lord of Leinster,
whom his biographer extols as a paragon of loyalty, had lately
been at war with Meiler FitzHenry, the royal Justiciar, and now,
after a reconciliation with the King, refused to abandon De Braose
on the plea that a vassal must support his lord even though that
lord chanced to be a rebel.[2]   Apart from these disturbances the
government was weak and inefficient.   In Meath and Leinster and
Limerick the King had no rights of any value save the patronage
of bishoprics and abbeys, jurisdiction in cases of freehold, and the
pleas of the crown.   In Ulster all rights of jurisdiction belonged to
Hugh de Lacy.[3]   There was no settled law, nor, outside the great
fiefs, any organised scheme of local administration ; the contributions of Ireland to the royal revenue were both scanty and infre-
John's   quent.   This state of things was somewhat improved by John's
Irish   vigorous measures.   The Lacys fled the country without venturing
Policy   to stand their trial, with the result that Ulster and Meath
escheated to the Crown.   Hugh de Lacy never succeeded in
regaining the King's favour; his brother subsequently recovered
Meath on paying a fine of 3,000 marks,[4] but, having received his
lesson, became a faithful subject for the future; he was one of the
few who did not desert John on the outbreak of civil war, and is
named, in 1216, as one of the executors of the King's testament.
At a Great Council of the Anglo-Irish baronage, held in Dublin,
native chieftains to the number of twenty appeared and rendered
homage ; and two administrative reforms of considerable importance were approved by the assembly.   On the advice of the lawyers
who had followed him from England the King decreed that for
the future the laws of England should hold good in Irish courts,
and he ordered that an official collection of these laws should be
deposited, for purposes of reference, in the Dublin Exchequer.   For
the better conduct of the administration new sheriffdoms were
instituted ; though in what numbers and for what districts we
are unable to say, owing to the loss of the official records.[5]   The
extant documents of the reign refer only to the three sheriffdoms

---

[1] Calendar, 315.   [2] G. le Mar., 14214 ff., 14304.
[3] Sweetman, Calendar, 147, 260, 381, 382.   [4] Rot. Pat., i., 151, 181.
[5] Calendar, 1458, 1602.   Wendover, iii.. 233.

of Dublin, Waterford and Cork; but it is probable that large parts
of Meath, Leinster, and Munster, were brought under shire-law in
consequence of John's reform.   Much remained to be done before
Ireland should enjoy even that moderate degree of peace and order
which obtained in England.   But this visit, the second and the
last which John paid to the island, is one of the bright spots in
the early history of the English settlement and, save for one terrible
crime, would materially enhance our estimate of his character.[1]
He could not resist the opportunity of taking a dastardly revenge
upon De Braose.   On learning of the King's arrival this delinquent
offered 40,000 marks for restitution to his estates and the royal
favour.   The offer was refused on the ground that Matilda de The De
Braose and her children were still at large; but when, a little Braoses
later, they fell into the king's hands he agreed to accept 50,000
marks, and named a term for payment.   The money could not
be raised within the time, and De Braose was again outlawed.
He made good his escape, but his wife and eldest son were less
fortunate.   " When the King returned to England he imprisoned
Matilda de Braose and her son William in the castle of Corfe;
they were given a sheaf of oats and a flitch of raw bacon; this
was all the meat they were allowed.   On the eleventh day the
mother was found dead between the knees of her son, sitting
upright except that she leaned back against her son like a dead
woman.   The son was dead in like manner, except that he was
leaning back against the wall; and his cheeks had been gnawed
by his mother in her anguish." [2]   This atrocious punishment produced in England an impression second only to that of Arthur's
fate, and gave the signal for organised conspiracy.

The fiscal exactions of the King were, however, the chief cause The
of disaffection.   The spoils of the Church, enormous as we know Burden of
them to have been,[3] failed to cover the expense of frequent expedi- Taxation
tions, of subsidies for the defence of Aquitaine, of the bribes and
presents which John scattered broadcast among his foreign allies.

---

[1] Even Gervase, in other respects hostile to John, admits that the Irish expedition was a success, ii., 106: " Hiberniam adquisivit, sed in omnibus aliis vanus erat
et inutilis ".
    [2] *Hist. des ducs*, p. 114.   See *Pat. Rolls*, ii., 134.   John made a grant for the
good of their souls shortly before his death.   His apology for his dealings with
them in *Foedera*, i., 108.
    [3] See the estimates in the *Red Book of the Exchequer*, p. 772, which amount to
over £79,000.

His scutages, levied at a higher rate than those of his father, brought home to every mesne tenant the ruinous profusion of his expenditure. No scutage had been taken between 1206 and 1209; but in 1209-10 scutage was levied at the rate of two marks on the fee; in 1210-11 it was levied twice, once for a Welsh expedition at the rate of two marks, and again for that of Scotland at the rate of twenty shillings.[1] The patience of the feudal classes was exhausted; a carucage or a general tax on movables would, under the circumstances, have been a perilous expedient. John therefore exhausted his ingenuity in wringing money from the clergy and the Jews. On his return from Ireland he convoked a representative assembly of the religious orders, military and monastic, and took from them, as a ransom for their estates, a sum which Roger of Wendover certainly exaggerates in stating at £100,000, but which was so heavy a burden that it caused a dispersion of some considerable convents.[2] From the Jews an enormous tallage was demanded; those who were dilatory in their payments suffered imprisonment, torture, and in some cases death. But these casual sources of revenue were insufficient. The King resolved to exact his feudal rights with greater strictness, and for this purpose ordered a new inquiry to be made in every shire respecting the liability of Crown tenants.[3] He also adopted the plan of farming the sheriff-doms to foreign miscreants who would not be deterred by any scruples from abusing the customary rights of the Crown for their own and the royal profit. Chance has preserved a judicial record of the misdoings of the two aliens, Gerald d'Athée and Engelard de Cicogné, who successively misgoverned Gloucestershire between the years 1208 and 1216. It appears that these ruffians were allowed to combine the powers of justiciar and sheriff, so that no complaint of their misdeeds could be preferred before any tribunal but their own.[4] The complaints which the men of York and Lincoln presented to the King in 1213 prevent us from supposing that Gloucestershire was singularly unfortunate. And in fact only the grossest and most far reaching maladministration can explain the sudden collapse of the King's cause.

[1] Norgate, *John Lackland*, pp. 101, 123. Hoveden, iv., 107. Wendover, iii., 17-35. Coggeshall, 101.
[2] *Waverley Annals.*
[3] Round, *Commune of London*, pp. 273, 274.
[4] Maitland, *Pleas of the Crown for the County of Gloucester*, pp. xiii. ff.

Disaster came with dramatic suddenness in the latter part of the year 1212. To himself and to ordinary observers the position of John in the preceding year seemed not merely safe but glorious; the temporary friendship of Scotland, the specious humility of the Welsh, the unfamiliar tranquillity of Ireland, gave colour to the boast of his supporters that he was lord and master throughout the British Isles. His hopes of recovering the French possessions revived with his success at home. The loyalty of the Gascons remained unshaken; a party among the Normans [1] had begun to regret the good old days when it had been possible to play off claimant against claimant and the Duke against the King. The European situation also seemed favourable. Otto, whom successes in Germany and an alliance with the Pope had rendered for a time indifferent to the friendship of England, was once more drifting among rocks and shallows. Through his imprudent haste to reclaim the imperial demesnes in Italy he too quarrelled with Innocent and, in 1211, fell under the ban of excommunication. In the young Frederic of Sicily, whom the Papacy had not yet learned to regard as Antichrist in human shape, Otto had now a formidable rival. There was no love lost between the Emperor and Philip; and an alliance with England seemed to Otto the natural means of resisting the league, which he foresaw, of France, the Papacy, and Sicily. Little by little the coalition, which Richard had planned, began to gather once more round his brother. Reginald of Boulogne whom Philip had dispossessed ; Ferrand of Flanders who had inherited from his predecessor the long standing claim on Aire, St. Omer, Artois and Péronne; the Duke of Limburg and the Counts of Louvain and Bar, always eager to fish in troubled waters ; Raymond of Toulouse, already hard pressed by the Albigensian Crusade, and despairing of success unless the Gascons were allowed to help him ; these and others came one by one to an understanding with the King of England.[2] The fortuitous union of three excommunicated princes fascinated the popular imagination, and gave colour to the story, which Matthew Paris embroiders with much circumstantial detail, of an embassy from John to the Emir of Morocco, promising that, if infidel help were rendered in the forthcoming war, the King would

Marginal notes: Collapse of the King's Party, 1212. The Coalition against France

---

[1] Coggeshall, 152. Luchaire, *H. G. de la France*, iii., i., p. 140.
[2] *Foedera*, i., 105, 106. Wendover, iii., 236. Coventry, ii., 203. *Rot. Chart.*, 186.

do homage to the Emir and would accept the faith of Islam.[1]   An
embassy there may have been; but the idea of renouncing Christianity, or even of destroying the Papacy, lay beyond the reach of John's
imagination.   Incidentally he expected that his alliances would
enable him to secure easy terms from Innocent; but he continued
to negotiate for a compromise throughout the year 1211, while the
plans of the coalition were taking shape.   An invasion of France
was his primary object; and in June, 1212, he ordered all the leading towns of England to furnish contingents of foot-soldiers for immediate service overseas.[2]   It was at this moment that the blow fell.

The Anglo-Welsh Conspiracy   Weary of delays and evasions Innocent began to think of re-
leasing the King's subjects from their allegiance.   Rumours of his
intention, and possibly a belief that it had already taken effect,
awakened the hopes of all malcontents.   Philip Augustus, well
aware of John's new alliances and their purpose, fanned the flame.
In May, 1212, a Welsh rebellion broke out which was probably
encouraged by French agents.[3]   All the princes of Wales made
common cause with Llewelyn ap Jorwerth; their design was
nothing less than to sweep the English out of the whole country;
in the north, centre, and south there were simultaneous attacks on
English colonies and castles.   The King postponed the invasion
of France and marched to deal with this unexpected outburst.
But at Nottingham, where he had halted to collect his levies
and to hang Welsh hostages, he received letters of warning both
from the King of Scots and from Joanna, the wife of Llewelyn.
They told him to beware of a general conspiracy among the English barons.   Details are not given in our authorities; but it may
be that letters inviting Philip or his son to come and take the
Crown had been already sent to France.   In any case John was
convinced of his danger.   He abandoned the Welsh expedition,
dismissed his English troops, sent for mercenaries to Flanders, and
began to demand from suspected barons their castles and their sons
as hostages.[4]   Eustace de Vesci and Robert FitzWalter, the two
ringleaders of the plot, confessed their guilt by flying the country.[5]

---

[1] Matthew Paris, *Gesta Abbatum*, i., 236-40.   *Chron. Maj.*, ii., 559-62, 566.
[2] *Rot. Claus.*, i., 130.
[3] See Llewelyn's letter to Philip in Delisle, *Catalogue*, No. 1416.   W. Cov., ii.
206, says that the Pope instigated Llewelyn; probably a mere guess
[4] *Rot. Pat.*, i., 94, 95.   Wendover, iii., 241.
[5] On their grievances see Norgate, *John Lackland*, pp. 289 ff.

The rest dissimulated so far that in the autumn we find them writing, at the King's instance, to protest against the Pope's approaching sentence of deposition. The King, justly suspicious of their sincerity, bethought him, now that it was too late, of enlisting the lower classes on his side by promises of better government. He did something to mitigate the severity of the forest administration; he put a stop to the unlawful tolls which the sheriffs and others were in the habit of levying on merchants and pilgrims; and in some cases commissioners were sent down to the shires to receive the complaints of the oppressed.[1] In spite of these overtures the people lent a ready ear to the predictions of a mad hermit, Peter of Pontefract, who announced that John had entered on the last year of his reign. The hermit was arrested and reserved for execution on the next anniversary of the King's coronation. But the apprehension of Peter merely increased the notoriety of his oracles;[2] it became the general impression that the King's cause was desperate.

Meanwhile Innocent approached the King of France with tentative suggestions that, if John continued obstinate, Philip should invade England and enforce the sentence of deposition.[3] It was not the intention of the Papacy that matters should come to this pass; since the union of France and England, even under the Most Christian House of Capet, could not fail to weaken the authority of Rome in both countries. Innocent desired to use Philip as a tool. But the King of France took the offer in good faith. Early in April, 1213, he held a Council of his barons at Soissons and, in their presence, arranged the terms on which Louis, his son and heir, should hold England and the Crown of France. April 21st was fixed as the date, Rouen as the place, for the gathering of the army of invasion, which there was every reason to expect would be a great one.[4] The project did not find John or his allies altogether unprepared. The Count of Flanders, who had openly broken with Philip at the Council of Soissons, might be expected to hinder the invasion by all the means in his power. The ships

Philip prepares to invade England, 1213

[1] W. Cov., ii., 207.   *Rot. Pat.*, i., 97.
[2] Coventry, ii., 208.   Wendover, iii., 240.
[3] Coventry, ii., 209.   Wendover, iii., 241, speaks as though Innocent gave a definite invitation to Philip; but this is probably erroneous.
[4] G. le Breton, *Gesta*, § 165.   Wendover, iii., 243.   *Foedera*, i., 104, for Philip's agreement with Louis.

of the English coast-towns gathered at Portsmouth, in readiness to repel the French, some days before Philip's intention was publicly announced at Soissons. The commanders took the first opportunity of destroying all the French ships which were to be found at Dieppe and in the mouth of the Seine; by April 21 the English fyrd was concentrated at Ipswich, Dover, and other likely landing-places. The King took up his head-quarters at Barham Down near Canterbury with an immense army of horse and foot, amply sufficient to repel any invader, if its loyalty were certain. But discontent was known to be rife; rightly or wrongly John anticipated that nearly all the baronage would desert him at the sight of Philip's army. He resolved to throw himself upon the mercy of Innocent, in order that every pretext for invasion and rebellion might be destroyed.

John submits, May, 1213 The terms of this submission, for which the Pope had long ago provided, were quickly arranged with the Papal nuncio, Pandulf, and published on May 13.[1] The King admitted Stephen Langton into his full favour and friendship, recalled the exiled monks and bishops, and promised compensation for their pecuniary losses; at the same time he gave an amnesty to all the inferior clergy.[2] These were moderate conditions, no worse indeed than might have been obtained in the first months of the struggle. Innocent, whose heart was set upon obtaining the assistance of John and the English for a new Crusade, had no wish to abuse his advantage; nor is he to be blamed for the famous transaction of May 15, when John made over his kingdom to the Holy See to be held as a fief for a rent of 1,000 marks. The idea was the King's,[3] and a perusal of the document containing his profession of homage will show that, beyond the tribute, he incurred no obligations more onerous than those which all prelates undertook by their oath of fidelity at the time of consecration. He purchased the fullest measure of protection by a sacrifice of dignity to which neither he nor the great mass of his subjects attached much importance. Some stigmatised the transaction as ignominious, but the most judicial chronicler of

---

[1] The outlines of the settlement were arranged between John and the Legate, at least as early as February, 1213. See the letters of Innocent in Bliss, *Papal Letters*, p. 37.

[2] Wendover, iii., 248. *Foedera*, i., 111.

[3] But it was no novelty to the statesmen of the age. Before John submitted, the sovereigns of the Two Sicilies, of Sweden, Denmark, Aragon, Poland, had already become Papal vassals.

the time calls it a prudent move;[1] for, he adds, there was hardly any other way in which John could escape from all his dangers. Even the hostile barons whose plans received an unexpected check did not venture either now or later to dispute the validity of the transaction.

The King's first thought, upon being relieved from the danger of domestic treason, was to meet the foreign peril. Hearing that the French were overrunning Flanders as a preliminary to the descent on England, he despatched a fleet, under the Earl of Salisbury, to attack the transports of his enemies at Damme, the port of Bruges. The English burned about 100 vessels and took 300 more, laden with every kind of supplies, a success which compelled Philip to raise the siege of Ghent and to withdraw the bulk of his army from Flanders. Immediately afterwards the Count of Flanders and the King of England commenced to treat with Otto for a joint incursion into France; while Philip's embarrassments were increased by a missive from the Pope prohibiting the invasion of a Papal fief. The King of France protested that he could not and would not abandon the costly enterprise on which he had entered at the Pope's suggestion. But there was small likelihood that Philip would take the aggressive now or for some time to come. *Philip receives a check*

In England there was a general hope that useless plans of foreign war would be abandoned, and that an era of domestic reforms would begin. This feeling was voiced by Stephen Langton who, in spite of the years which he had spent in France and Italy, grasped the political situation from the moment when he entered England. Pandulf had been content with vague assurances of better government; the Archbishop insisted that these should be made explicit before the King received absolution. The old Justiciar, Geoffrey FitzPeter, was in favour of taking practical steps to moderate the universal discontent. At the Council of St. Albans, in the month of August, an assembly primarily convened to assess the compensation due to the bishops,[2] he referred to the *John anxious to invade France*

---

[1] So W. Cov., ii., 210: " Prudenter sane sibi et suis providens, licet id multis ignominiosum videretur et enorme servitutis jugum ". Wendover, iii., 252, asserts that Innocent insisted on this surrender of the crown, but is probably mistaken. The terms of John's investiture in *Foedera*, i., 111.

[2] On the question of the representatives summoned to this council, if Wendover may be believed, from the demesne townships of the King, see *E. H. R.*, xx., p. 289.

Laws of Henry I. as the ideal which the government would keep in view; after the Council he began an Inquest of Sheriffs, and removed some of the worst delinquents from their offices. But the King was otherwise occupied. Immediately after his submission he invited the barons to join him in a descent upon Poitou. They refused to follow an excommunicated King; for John's absolution had not yet been pronounced. He renewed the demand when this excuse no longer existed; but the barons now pleaded their poverty or else, like Hugh of Lincoln in 1197, that they were not bound to foreign service. The King endeavoured to shame them by setting sail with none but his household servants for escort, but the manœuvre failed; and on reaching the Channel Islands he turned back. Still his purpose remained unshaken. The great plan had been formed of crushing Philip between two armies marching on Paris simultaneously from Flanders and Poitou; Otto was to lead the attack from the north-east; and in the west the Count of Toulouse had promised to co-operate with John. The latter now informed his allies that his expedition, though postponed owing to contrary winds, would be resumed in the following spring. His letters were accompanied by generous subsidies, and he spared no pains to make his military preparations perfect.[1]

New Breach with the Barons

Under any circumstances this obstinacy in pursuing a policy which they regarded as futile would have irritated the English baronage. But their resentment was sharpened by a fear that the mercenaries whom the King was collecting, ostensibly for the French war, would be used against themselves. The behaviour of John lent some plausibility to their suspicions. On returning from the Channel Islands he marched towards the north, with the avowed intention of taking vengeance on the barons of those parts for their default of service. He was prevented from fulfilling his threat by the Archbishop, who reminded him of the promise, made at the time of his absolution, that no man should be punished without a lawful trial. The King's first impulse was to disregard the warning; but Langton followed his march and threatened to renew the excommunication; whereupon John abandoned the expedition with a bad grace. The defaulters were legally in the wrong; but a sentence of proscription could never be obtained against them

[1] *Foedera*, i., 114. *Rot. Pat.*, i., 102, 103.

while Geoffrey FitzPeter presided in the highest court of justice.
The old Justiciar, although he fell in some respects below the
average standard of official honesty, might be trusted to uphold
the cause of the baronage against the Crown.   He suspected the
master through whose favour he had risen.   He feared that, if an
era of confiscation once began, his own ill-gotten wealth would make
him one of the earliest victims ; and, apart from more selfish considerations, he was inspired with the feeling which makes all self-
made men the stoutest champions of the class into which they
have won their way.[1]   Great therefore was the joy of the King
and the consternation of his opponents when the news was announced, on October 14th, of Geoffrey FitzPeter's death.   John bestowed on the Justiciar a characteristic valediction : " Let him go to
hell and bear my greetings to Hubert FitzWalter, whom I doubt
not he will find there ".   A more complaisant minister was found
without delay in the person of Des Roches.[2]

The barons were now driven to the wall.   Even from Rome Stephen
they had no prospect of assistance ; for a new legate, Nicholas of Langton
Tusculum, had lately arrived with a commission to break up all and the
Barons
factions and conspiracies which he might find in England.   With
the desire of Stephen Langton to safeguard the laity at the same
time as the clergy Innocent had no sympathy ; his agents, writing
under the influence of the King, stigmatised the Archbishop as a
firebrand and an enemy of royal prerogative.   The one hope for
the opposition lay in appealing through the Archbishop to the
people ; it might be that the head of the national Church, by
ancient custom regarded as the King's first counsellor and the
protector of the poor, would be able to arouse those whom the
head of the Church Catholic had ordered to remain subservient.
In the autumn of 1213 the Archbishop found himself recognised
as the leader of the barons.   He at once raised the struggle to a
higher plane by pressing them to accept as their programme the
charter of Henry I., a document in which the liberties of all classes
were equally secured.   A feudal rising was thus transformed into a

[1] See, for the personal relations of John and the Justiciar, the *Histoire des ducs*,
p. 115.
[2] Peter des Roches is described as prior of Loches in 1199 (*Rot. Chart.*, 10).
In January, 1200 he is described by John as *clericus noster* (*ibid.*, 34).   In 1205 he became bishop of Winchester.   Appointed Justiciar, February 1, 1214 (*Rot. Pat.*, 110) ;
an unpopular appointment, Coggeshall, 168.

national agitation, and claims of special privileges fell into the background behind broad principles of justice.[1]

Campaign of 1214— Bouvines The King was blind to the approaching crisis, or hoped that it would be averted by the success of his French enterprise. In January he sent to Flanders a considerable force, commanded by his half-brother William Longespée, Earl of Salisbury, whose instructions were to co-operate with Otto and Count Ferrand in attacking France from the north-east. In February, having committed his crown to the protection of the Holy See, John himself sailed for Poitou. Mercenaries formed the larger part of his army; unable to insist on feudal service, he left his opponents to shape their plans in his absence, comforting himself with the idea that a few victories would convert them or at least shame them into silence. During his first operations he continued to solicit the English for help by means of circular letters. The news which these bulletins contained was hopeful. Twenty-six castles surrendered within a month of his disembarkation. The Lusignans made peace on condition that Joanna, the King's daughter, should be given in marriage to the heir of Hugo de la Marche the younger; other noble families were bought over with gifts and pensions.[2] But the weeks wore on and Otto made no sign of commencing the campaign which was to give John his great opportunity. The Emperor loitered in the neighbourhood of Aachen, settling accounts with the unfriendly Bishop of Liège, and strengthening his connections in the Netherlands by a marriage with the daughter of the Duke of Brabant (May 19). Philip had ample time to visit the Loire and to make preparations for guarding the line of the river against John.[3] The duty of observing John was then committed to Louis, the heir of France, while Philip returned to the neighbourhood of Paris to observe the imperial forces; the design of paralysing France by vigorous operations in the west had proved a failure.

It would not be easy to distribute the blame of the fiasco between John and Otto. Each appears to have hoped that the other

---

[1] Two conferences of the barons are described in Wendover; one at St. Paul's, August 25, 1213; another at Edmundsbury before Christmas, 1214. The Charter of Henry I. is mentioned in connection with each. Ramsay suspects the first meeting as apocryphal (*A. E.*, p. 444).

[2] *Foedera*, i., 118. *Rot. Chart.*, i., 197, 208. *Rot. Pat.*, i., 111, 118.

[3] Philip was at Saumur in April. See Delisle, *Catalogue*. For the movements of Otto, see G. Langerfeldt, *Otto der Vierte* (Hanover, 1872); of John, Petit-Dutaillis, pp. 45-52.

would make the first move and would bear the chief burden of the
campaign ; each waited to hear of some great victory as a signal
for marching upon Paris. But John had the better excuse since
his new allies in Poitou, without whose help he was afraid to risk
decisive operations, refused to commit themselves beyond recall while
the Emperor's plans remained uncertain.   Owing to their objections John was prevented from pursuing an attack on Brittany
which had opened successfully with the capture of Ancenis.   He
laid siege to Roche au Moine, a castle not many miles to the west
of Angers which commanded the passage of the Loire and the
main road to Britanny ; but when Louis marched to the relief the
Poitevins refused to meet him in the field ; and John was compelled
to beat a retreat, leaving his tents and baggage in the hands of the
enemy (July 2).   Henceforward he stood on the defensive in
Poitou, waiting for some news of Otto.   But the news when it
came was calamitous.   At the bridge of Bouvines (July 27), the
Emperor and the rebellious French feudatories of the north were
completely routed after some hours of hard fighting.   Reginald of
Boulogne, William of Salisbury, Ferrand of Flanders fell into the
hands of Philip ; Otto and the Dukes of Limburg and Brabant
saved themselves by an ignominious flight.   The victory was the
more striking because Philip had fought the confederation single-
handed ; the assistance promised by Otto's rival, the young Frederick
II., had not appeared in time for the battle.   But Bouvines is less
important as a feat of arms than as a determining influence in the
history of three nations.   In France it set the seal upon the pre-
dominance of the Capets and ushered in a period of autocratic
centralisation.   In Germany it ensured the ruin of the Saxon
faction and the return of the Hohenstauffen to the imperial throne.
In England it removed the last fears of the opposition, and was the
prelude to half a century of civil wars and constitutional debates

CHAPTER XV

THE CHARTER AND THE STRUGGLE WITH THE FOREIGNER

Outbreak of the Barons' War, 1215

THE friendly mediation of Innocent III. did something, the exhaustion of France after her supreme effort of defence conduced still more, to give John the opportunity of retiring from the war upon comparatively favourable terms. By recognising the French conquests in Anjou, Brittany, and Poitou, he kept his title to Guienne and Gascony and obtained a truce until Easter, 1220. None the less he returned to England a disappointed and humiliated man, smarting under the consciousness that the failure was universally, and not altogether justly, ascribed to his incompetence. He was in no mood to adopt the conciliatory attitude which common prudence would have recommended. Again he demanded a scutage for the expenses of the war from those who had denied their liability to serve; and again the northern houses took the lead in a resistance which their bold example soon made universal.[1] In a meeting at Bury St. Edmunds, whither they had repaired under colour of a pilgrimage, the leaders of the opposrtion took an oath upon the relics of the saint that John should have no peace from them until he had confirmed the charter of Henry I.[2] At the Epiphany feast of 1215, when John was holding his court in London at the New Temple, they came before him in full armour to announce their ultimatum. He asked and obtained a truce

---

[1] On the question of foreign service see Norgate, *John Lackland*, p. 210. Round, *Feudal England*, p. 531, suggests a possible origin for the theory that foreign service was not compulsory. Innocent III. condemns the claim of the barons as contrary to law and custom, *Foedera*, i., 128. The question is dropped in Magna Carta: but the "Unknown Charter of Liberties," printed by Mr. Round (*E. H. R.*, viii., p. 288) represents the King as promising that he will not demand foreign service "nisi in Normanniam et Britanniam et hoc decenter". This may be a compromise suggested at some stage of the negotiations between King and barons.

[2] This is confirmed by the *Chronique des Ducs*, p. 145, which, like Wendover, emphasises the demand for the Charter of Henry I. For the Edmundsbury meeting, *supra*, p. 372.

until the following Easter, but the time of grace was wasted in
contradictory and futile schemes.   He allowed the Archbishop to
negotiate on his behalf, hoping that under cover of Langton's
popularity he might delude the opposition with illusory concessions.   He used every artifice to detach the lower orders and the
church from the cause of their superiors; promising the Church
the right of free election and despatching commissioners to state
his case in every shire-court.[1]   He exacted the oath of fealty and
homage from the whole body of freemen; and at the same time
sent abroad, to the Netherlands and elsewhere, for mercenaries,
only to countermand them in a week or two under the impression
that his ends would be better served by trickery than force.   But
with every class his promises, threats and intrigues were equally
unavailing.   The appeal to Henry's Charter had made the whole
nation at one with the baronial opposition.   On the King's side
there remained only a few barons and bishops, chiefly his kinsmen
or the creatures of his favour, whose retainers had by this time
thrown themselves into the party of the constitutionalists.   It was
in vain that Innocent issued letters denouncing the authors of
"factions and conspiracies".[2]   When Easter came the barons had
no difficulty in mustering a force computed as containing 2,000
knights besides innumerable men-at-arms and infantry.   They met
at Stamford, whence they marched towards London, the head-
quarters of the King.   At Brackley they halted to send forward
the schedule of their grievances and give the King a final opportunity of compromise.   But John was beside himself at the
audacity of the petitioners.   He told the messengers that they
might as well have demanded the kingdom in plain language; he
swore, with a superfluity of oaths, that he would never become the
slave of his own subjects.   Instead of wasting further time in
argument the barons acted.   They named Robert FitzWalter as
"Marshal of the Host of the Lord and Holy Church" and, under
his leadership, pursued their march on the capital, from which
John had now retreated into Wiltshire.   The King attempted to
restrain them by proposing that they should accept the arbitration
of the Pope, assisted by a committee of both parties.   But the
sympathies of Innocent had been too clearly manifested, and the
offer was refused with scorn.   On Sunday May 17th the baronial

[1] *Rot. Pat.*, i., 128, 129, 130. *Foedera*, i., 126.   [2] *Foedera*, i., 127.

army entered London; the gates were opened by the friends of the Charter while the majority of the citizens were at church; but the magistrates of London made no scruples about joining the opposition, and the city was from that time the head-quarters of the barons.   The secession of the capital from the King's cause gave the signal for a total suspension of government throughout the country.   The Exchequer and the Curia Regis ceased to hold their sessions; the authority of the sheriffs was set at nought; the collection of the revenue became impossible.   Finding that neither threats nor promises could destroy the solidarity of his opponents, John at length consented to accept whatever terms the Archbishop could procure for him.   The Great Charter was hurriedly prepared, on the basis of Articles[1] presented by the barons; and on June 17th, 1215, at Runnymede between Staines and Windsor, the King set his seal to this famous document in the presence of a great assemblage.[2]

The Charter, June, 1215   A French historian has remarked, not without justice, that Magna Carta would be less extolled if it had been faithfully observed by John and his successors.   Long after it was granted all evils, political, social, economic, were habitually explained as resulting from the violation of the Charter; and modern writers have not infrequently adopted such explanations without examining their truth.   In reality Magna Carta made few lasting innovations, and asserted no new liberties.   The framers appealed from the tyranny of John to the practice of his father and to the laws which Henry's Curia had respected.   They desired no alteration in the fabric of the executive or legislature; they threw upon individuals the blame for abuses which were the natural outcome of a system; they thought that a new age of gold would dawn if sheriffs and justices were honestly chosen as of old, and if those particular grievances were redressed which at the moment were fresh in the minds of the several orders composing their party.   It is no wonder that the party should have been thus misled, if we look for a moment at the names of the leaders in whom it trusted.   Of the lay barons there is not one who rose, either before or after the signing of the Charter, to the first rank among English statesmen;[3] while Stephen Langton, whose high intellectual gifts were coupled

[1] *Articuli Baronum* (*Statutes of the Realm*, i., 7, 8).
[2] McKechnie, *Magna Carta*, pp. 44 ff.
[3] See the list in Stubbs, *C. H.*, i., p. 580 (6th ed.).

with an earnest patriotism and practical sagacity, had entered English politics too recently to know how deep the evils of the existing system went.

With honesty of purpose the supporters of the Charter may fairly be credited, although there has been a disposition among recent writers to deny them even this faint praise.[1] Their party contained, as all parties must contain, some members who were actuated by private ambition or obsolete ideals; the rights of the lower classes receive much less attention and are less carefully defined than those of their superiors; and in one or two clauses of the Charter a reactionary spirit, a desire for the maintenance of invidious class-privileges, may be detected.[2] But it would be an unwarrantable inference that the ambition of one class alone produced the Charter. To those who have followed the course of the struggle which preceded the conference at Runnymede it will be clear that only the barons and the Londoners appeared in arms against the King; but it is also clear that the triumph of the opposition was due to the benevolent neutrality with which they were welcomed by the commons. The barons could not raise the fyrd against the King, because the technical right to do so was not in their hands; the English yeoman of the period, though gifted with an incurable propensity for private brawling, had little liking for warfare, and saw no reason why he should take the field for any cause whatever until the constituted authorities descended on him with a categorical imperative. The surprising fact in the situation is that John, in spite of numerous appeals, failed entirely to win such support from the commons as their ancestors had accorded to the worthless William Rufus. When Henry II. pruned the privileges of the barons he was not working altogether for the advantage of the Crown. By lowering to some extent the barriers between the privileged and the unprivileged he made it

The Charter and the Third Estate

[1] See in particular the remarks of M. Petit-Dutaillis, *Étude sur la vie et le règne de Louis VIII*. *Cf.* Mr. Jenks, *The Myth of Magna Carta* (in *The Independent Review* for March, 1904), and Miss Norgate, *John Lackland*, p. 235. Of contemporary authorities the most unfavourable to the barons are the *Histoire des ducs* and the Barnwell chronicle (the so-called Walter of Coventry).

[2] See especially §§ 15, 16, 60, with their curt concessions to mesne tenants; §§ 12, 13, 20, 35, 41, which contain all that was done for the towns and trade. As for the villein there is only one clause (§ 21) which is framed for his protection. It is pretty clear that the villein was not intended to participate in the rights of property and personal liberty which are guaranteed to free men by §§ 16, 28, 30, 39. See on this subject McKechnie, *Magna Carta*, pp. 113-6.

13

easier for these two great divisions of the people to realise the community of their interests. The time had passed when the most unscrupulous autocracy could seem preferable to a baronial ascendancy; nor was the new confidence of the commons in their natural leaders utterly misplaced. The magnate of the thirteenth century might be selfish; but he had realised the impossibility of founding his own fortunes upon reckless oppression of his inferiors, and he no longer hoped to exclude the public authority from sharing in the administration of his lands.

The Charter of Henry I. Magna Carta[1] is founded upon the Charter of Henry I., but a comparison of the two documents reveals some striking differences between them. In both the King's concessions to the Church and to the barons take precedence of all others and fill the largest space. But, whereas the older charter contains few promises which affect all classes of free men equally, that of John is justly famous for half a dozen promises of the most general kind. John guarantees that for the future all amercements shall be proportionate to the offence for which they are imposed; that no man shall be brought to trial on bare suspicion, without witnesses; that no penalty shall be inflicted on any free man except in consequence of a lawful trial, either by his peers or in some other form admitted by the law of the land; that justice shall not be sold nor delayed nor denied to any man. These guarantees are far more valuable than the bare promise to keep the peace and uphold the law of Edward which forms the epilogue of Henry's charter. It is noteworthy that they were demanded by the baronage, and in the precise terms in which they were conceded by John; they were not, therefore, a mere afterthought inserted to save the character of the opposition.

Concessions to the Church and Barons When we turn our attention from the general clauses of Magna Carta to those which affect special classes or interests, we are still as far as ever from obtaining the evidence to prove a class-conspiracy. The barons in their Articles may seem indifferent to the interests of the Church; and the only clause of importance to the Church which is to be found in Magna Carta was evidently added at the request of Stephen Langton. It is however probable that "the army of God and Holy Church" had omitted to discuss

---

[1] Best text (from the Lincoln copy) in *Statutes of the Realm*, vol. i., and *Foedera*, i., 129. Reissues in Blackstone's *Great Charter* (1759), Bémont, *Chartes des Libertés Anglaises* (1892). The best commentary is McKechnie's *Magna Carta* (2nd ed., 1914). In the *Chartulary of Chester Abbey* I. (1920), p. 102, Dr. Tait has edited the *Magna Carta* granted by Earl Ranulf of Chester to his barons in 1215 or 1216.

ecclesiastical grievances, not from any indifference to their settlement, but in the belief that the Archbishop needed no assistance.
On either hypothesis the moderation of the Archbishop and his
colleagues is remarkable. They ask nothing beyond a confirmation
of the Church's ancient liberties,[1] and of the right of free canonical
election which John had already conceded in a separate charter.
The barons made demands of a more extensive character; but the
majority of these turn out, upon examination, to be either more
definite statements of the concessions which Henry I. had made
respecting feudal aids and incidents, or else to represent unwritten
usages of great antiquity which John and Richard had overridden
without any equitable excuse. It is remarkable that the barons
made no attempt to abolish the royal right of wardship which
Henry I. had explicitly renounced; and that they petitioned the
King to restrain them from imposing on their tenants any taxes
but the three great aids which were recognised by feudal law all
over Europe.[2] The most reactionary of their demands is one
which relates to private jurisdictions; that the writ *Praecipe* be
not granted in such wise that any free man shall lose his court by
it. This demand, which was duly incorporated in the Charter,
struck at the root of the jurisdiction which Henry II. had claimed
over suits relating to all freehold land;[3] though included in later
and revised editions of the Charter it was not allowed to take
effect, and would have been merely mischievous if it had been
observed.[4] But we should not condemn the authors of the clause
without taking into consideration the fact that Henry II. had
exhausted the resources of chicanery to extend the power of his
Courts at the expense of private tribunals which had a lawful title
to their jurisdiction. A temporary reaction against the centralisation of justice was inevitable, and it was only natural that the
reaction should be occasionally unreasonable.

The articles which secure the liberties of the towns and trading
classes, of mesne tenants, and of villeins, are not numerous; and

---

[1] "Quod ecclesia Anglicana libera sit" (§ 1). See McKechnie, pp. 256 ff.

[2] In the *Articuli Baronum*, § 6, from which this rule passes into the Charter.
The rule was however struck out of the Charter, when it was reissued in 1217. See
McKechnie, p. 304.

[3] That this was the intention may be inferred from the way in which the clause
is paraphrased in the contemporary *Histoire des ducs*, p. 150: "Toutes hautes
justices vaurrent-il avoir en lor tierres".

[4] Other writs were substituted for that of *Praecipe*; notably the "writ of entry
sur disseisin". Pollock and Maitland, *Hist. of English Law*, ii., p. 65 (1st. ed.).

Conces-
sions
to the
Commons
the barons have been severely criticised for neglecting the special interests of inferior classes. Thus it has been pointed out that while they limited the power of the King to tax themselves and London, they did nothing to protect other towns against the King, or villeins against their lords, in the matter of taxation. The answer must be that interference between the villein and his lord, or between the King and his borough, would have been an innovation of a revolutionary kind. The special privilege which the Londoners exacted as the price of their support was one to which John might fairly have taken exception, if his position had left him free to criticise and bargain. Even in his isolation and friendlessness he was able to challenge and reject a proposal that all self-governing boroughs should be put on an equality with London.[1] The supporters of the Charter felt a reluctance to encroach on the admitted sphere of the prerogative; and they were accordingly content to ask for the towns a confirmation of existing liberties.

Consti-
tutional
Clauses
When we turn from the liberties of the subject to the executive and the national assembly, we find that here also the Charter is conservative. In 1213, the King had created a precedent for far-reaching changes in the constitution of the Great Council; he had ordered that four representatives from every shire should attend the Oxford meeting of November 15th. Presumably these delegates, vaguely described as *milites discreti*, were expected to act as spokesmen of the shire-courts. The precedent is ignored by the authors of the Charter; they endeavour to restore the ancient character of the Council as a mass-meeting of royal tenants great and small. The fourteenth clause provides that the *barones majores* shall be summoned individually, the *barones minores* by a general writ addressed to the sheriff of each shire. This makes the Council more narrowly feudal than John had contemplated in 1213; nor do the lesser barons appear to have made use of their privilege. That the constitutional party proposed to arrange for the representation of the lesser barons is a hypothesis supported by the greatest modern writer on the subject;[2] but it lacks confirmation. In other respects the

[1] This demand is made in the *Articuli Baronum*, § 32. The clause might be construed in the narrower sense, "all towns whose charters are modelled on those of London"; but London was regarded as the type of a self-governing borough and the phrase in the text probably expresses the intention of the petitioners.
[2] Stubbs, *C. H.*, i., p. 666 (6th ed.). The antiquity of the distinction between the personal and general summons appears from the case of Becket in 1164 (Council of Northampton, *Materials*, ii., 390; iii., 49-51; iv., 41).

fourteenth clause is too conservative. Taxation is the only subject explicitly reserved for the consideration of the Council; and by a remarkable want of foresight the Crown is left with an unrestricted control of customs-duties. A special clause, indeed, guarantees to merchants the right of entering and leaving the kingdom freely upon payment of the right and ancient customs; but these are not defined, nor did they engage the attention of the feudal party before the reign of Edward I. This is the most important, but it is far from being the only case in which the Charter betrays a want of foresight. Many particular abuses are prohibited by various clauses; but the number of the general safeguards which are provided is extremely small. The articles relating to the alien favourites are a case in point. The King is forced to banish certain individuals, whose names are given; but there is no precaution against future appointments of unworthy or unpopular ministers, unless it is to be found in the promise that the King will choose as sheriffs and justiciars none but those who know the law of the land and intend to observe it. The wording of this clause shows that the abuses of local administration were more deeply resented than the misconduct of the central executive. Yet the changes of local government which the Charter prescribes are insignificant; the most important being the new rule that pleas of the crown shall not be tried by any sheriff or coroner or bailiff of the King, but reserved for the hearing of the justices. We may treat this abstinence from innova- tion as another proof of respect for the Crown's prerogative; but it is difficult to avoid the conclusion that the barons had no wish to modify the existing system.

But while the ultimate settlement for which the Charter pro- *The Com- mittee of Twenty- five* vides is unduly conservative, the sanctions by which the settlement is secured are nothing short of revolutionary. With as much bold- ness as their successors in the following reign, but with less con- sideration for appearances and the dignity of the Crown, the barons of the Charter subjected John to a committee of Twenty-five, of whom all but one, the Mayor of London, were chosen from the ranks of the lay feudatories.[1] This committee is empowered to adjudicate upon all claims and complaints preferred against the Crown; a power the more dangerous because the men who wielded it were entirely members of the opposition. It is provided that in

[1] Matthew Paris, *Chron. Maj.*, ii., 604, 605. Blackstone, *Great Charter*, p. xx. The presence of the Mayor of London on the committee supports the contention of Professor Adams, *Origin of English Constitution*, App. III., that the commune of London was juridically regarded as a tenant-in-chief.

certain cases the committee shall consult with the Archbishop and his friends,[1] but no definite powers are conferred upon these assessors. The King's humiliation is completed by a promise that he will make his subjects swear obedience to the mandates of the Twenty-five, and by an admission that, if he fails to do what the Twenty-five demand, they have the right of taking arms against him. No term is assigned for the dissolution of this provisional government ; no check is imposed upon it ; and the members are empowered to fill such vacancies as may occur in their ranks by the simple process of co-optation. There was apparently an understanding that the Twenty-five would give the King a written assurance of their fealty, but they neglected to do this in spite of a protest from the Archbishop and the legate.[2]

John and the Twenty-five

All this lends considerable colour to the indictment which modern writers have drawn against the barons; and it must be admitted that a contemporary, not wholly favourable to John, brings the charge of arrogance against the Twenty-five. We are told for instance that, when John was confined by sickness to his chamber, they summoned him to come before them and would hear of no excuse ; if he could not walk, they said, he must be carried.[3] Yet there is no reason to believe that the Twenty-five abused their anomalous position to lay the foundations of a feudal oligarchy. The troubles which arose immediately after the conference of Runnymede were due in part to the King's impatience, and in part to the misconduct of the more lawless spirits among the baronage, who regarded the settlement as too favourable to the King and defied the authority of the Twenty-five. The northern barons refused to sign the Charter or to surrender the castles and demesnes which had passed into their clutches. Some of those who had signed did not behave much better. From many sides the King received intelligence of violence offered to his representatives, of raids upon his lands, of the destruction of his forests and his deer.[4] The general opinion was that the malcontents merely awaited the end of the harvest-season to begin a war for the annihilation of the royal power. Through the months of June

Turbulence of the Northern Barons

---

[1] See § 55; the reference is to unjust fines and amercements which are to be revised.
[2] *Rot. Pat.*, i., 181. [3] *Histoire des ducs*, p. 151.
[4] W. Cov., ii., 222. *Rot. Pat.*, i., 150.

and July the King observed a line of conduct to which no exception
could be taken. He dismissed a number of his mercenaries; he
ordered his castellans to cease from pillage and the exaction of
tenseries; he fulfilled the most unpalatable of the obligations which
the Charter had thrown upon him by ordering that in every shire
an oath of obedience to the Twenty-five should be taken, and
juries empanelled to inquire concerning the evil customs of the
sheriffs and their underlings.[1] The story that he retreated to the
Isle of Wight and brooded on his wrongs in solitude is a fable of
which his itinerary, compiled from documentary sources, supplies
the refutation.

But his slender stock of patience and good faith was soon
exhausted. In August the records reveal him borrowing from the
Templars, and spending the proceeds to recruit mercenaries in
Flanders, Hainault, and Angoulême. He approached the Count
of Britanny with an offer to restore the Honour of Richmond in
exchange for armed assistance.[2] He requested Innocent to annul
the Charter, supporting his request with the mendacious statement
that all his troubles and unpopularity arose from his submission
to the Holy See. The Pope required no second invitation. It
was not with the object of weakening a vassal-king that he had
ordered Stephen Langton to play the part of mediator; the Charter
had not been submitted for the approval of the Holy See, and its
nature was misunderstood at Rome. Above all, the existence of a
vigorous opposition to the English Crown was fatal to the most
cherished plans of Innocent. He intended that John should take
the leading part in a Crusade; and in furtherance of the Holy War
the Pope was prepared to go to any lengths. On August 24th he
annulled the Charter as derogatory to the Crown, as extorted by
force, as unjust and unlawful in its contents.[3] Later, when it became
apparent the barons would not yield without a struggle, Innocent
took the unprecedented step of preaching a Crusade on John's
behalf. Through the prelates of France and the adjoining lands
he offered remission of sins to any knight who would go to tne
rescue of a would-be crusader, precluded from fulfilling his vow by
the plots of factious subjects.[4]

[1] See John's letters in *Rot. Pat.*, i., 143. *Rot. Claus.*, i., 215, 217. *Rot. Pat.*, i.,
180. *Foedera*, i., 133.
[2] *Rot. Pat.*, i., 152, 153, 158, 160, 182. *Rot. Claus.*, i., 226.
[3] Potthast, No. 4990. *Foedera*, i., 135. [4] Bouquet, *Recueil*, xix., p. 601.

The uncompromising attitude of Innocent had the effect of weakening the baronial party. Their clerical supporters, after a brief period of hesitation, withdrew from the struggle. Stephen Langton, somewhat bolder than the rest, ignored the order of the Papal legate to excommunicate the King's opponents; but even Langton yielded when a sentence of suspension was issued against him. He left the kingdom for the ostensible purpose of attending the Fourth Lateran Council, but in reality with the hope of winning over Innocent. The appeal was useless; for Innocent confirmed the legate's sentence (Nov. 4);[1] and in future only a few audacious members of the hierarchy avowed their sympathy with the Charter. But the King's party lost rather than gained by the secession of opponents whose influence had been always on the side of moderation; and the laymen on the barons' side were merely exasperated by the unprecedented action of the Pope and legate. The arguments which Alexander the Mason had framed in the king's interests were now used for another purpose; it was the turn of the opposition to denounce the encroachments of the spiritual authority in secular affairs. But the time for a war of argument, or even for one of satire and invective, had gone by; both sides were mustering their forces. The recruiting agents of the King redoubled their activity; he committed sheriffdoms and castles to the charge of trusty aliens; he banished from his court, as secret traitors, most of the Englishmen who still professed his cause. The barons on their side ceased to give his officers even a nominal recognition, and, wherever their influence predominated, set up a provisional administration. Each of the leaders assumed in his own neighbourhood the style and the duties of a justiciar; the King's writ no longer ran in the north and eastern shires.[2] Already the more extreme talked of offering the crown to Louis of France. A present of siege engines which Philip sent them in the autumn was thankfully accepted as an earnest of more effectual help to come.[3]

Siege of Rochester, Oct., 1215

It would be hard to say which party ought to be considered as responsible for the outbreak of the war. But it was the opposition that, early in October, struck the first blow. John had chosen Kent as the rendezvous for his forces, in order to prevent the French from disembarking in the Cinque Ports; and the barons marched from

[1] Potthast, No. 5005.   [2] Coggeshall, 173, 174.   W. Cov., ii., 226.
[3] Coggeshall, 172.   *Rot. Pat.*, i., 155.

London to attack the King while his preparations were still incomplete. The advance was well-timed; the King retreated in
haste from Canterbury, where he had taken up his quarters, to
Dover. But the barons were misinformed by their scouts. They
heard that John was advancing on them in superior force, and
without waiting to test the intelligence fled from their flying adversary. On their return they left a garrison in Rochester to
observe the movements of the King; but in a few days the King's
courage returned, and he laid siege to Rochester. There had been
no time for the defenders to collect supplies; a force despatched to
their relief from London was easily repulsed by the besieging army;
and Rochester was soon starved into submission.[1] The King, who
had already begun to distribute the lands of the rebels among his
followers, wished to take this opportunity of striking terror by a
general massacre of prisoners. He was only deterred from the crime
by the earnest remonstrances of his mercenaries, to whom the prospect of fighting in a war where no quarter could be expected was
eminently distasteful.[2] The threat though unfulfilled struck home;
and the majority of the rebels, recognising that with John upon
the throne their safety would never be assured, joined in pressing
Louis to take up their cause and vindicate the claims which he derived from his marriage with Blanche of Castile.

The invitation was accepted without much delay. Soon after Louis
the fall of Rochester the first instalment of French aid arrived; joins the
and by January 7, 1216, the barons had been reinforced with 240 Barons
French knights and a corresponding number of arbalestiers, sergeants, and foot-soldiers.[3] But some months elapsed before the
Prince could make a public declaration of his acceptance. For his
own part Louis desired prompt action; but he was restrained by
the caution of Philip Augustus who, although anxious enough to
unite the thrones of France and England, knew from old experience
the dangers of an open conflict with Innocent III.[4] But by degrees
the subtle mind of Philip devised a plan for evading Papal censures.
There was no reason why the interests of Louis should be treated
as one with those of his father and of France; nor need a sentence

[1] *Histoire des ducs*, p. 157. The town of Rochester was taken by assault; but
the castle in which the baronial garrison took refuge was blockaded.
[2] Wendover, iii., 335.
[3] *Anon. de Béthune*, in Bouquet, xxiv., p. 770. Hoveden, iv., 189 *n.*
[4] See various remonstrances from Innocent, catalogued by Potthast, Nos. 5127 ff.

13*

of excommunication prove fatal to the Prince's cause in a country where such sentences had fallen into some discredit through frequent repetition. The Prince accordingly adopted for the occasion the attitude of a rebellious subject; and Philip in private lent the aid of his purse and influence to an enterprise which he disowned in every public utterance. At first the King affected indignation at the preparations of his son, even threatening to confiscate the lands of those allies whom Louis had secured by threats of his father's heaviest displeasure if they refused to join the expedition. Later the King assured the Papal envoy that it was impossible to prevent the Prince from vindicating a just claim by means of his private resources; France would stand neutral in the war and nothing more than neutrality could fairly be demanded.[1] But the month of April, 1216, had arrived before the preparations of Louis and the negotiations of his father with the legate were completed.

John's Operations, Dec., 1215-May, 1216

If the King of England had used the time of grace for a spirited attack on London it would have gone hardly with the rebels. Probably the reason why he preferred the less effective plan of ravaging at large and besieging scattered strongholds is to be found in the disaffection of the Cinque Ports, which made it impossible to equip a fleet of sufficient size to close the Thames. His strategy, though bad in principle, was vigorously pursued. He divided his forces into two divisions of which one, commanded by Savaric de Mauleon and other leaders of experience, was commissioned to ravage the home counties, while the second, led by the King in person, scoured the north and spread devastation through the lands of his opponents. The foreign mercenaries carried out the work with zest, and possibly with greater thoroughness than their master would have tolerated if he had been able to reward their services by more legitimate means. They made it their practice to seize the tenants of the King's opponents and to extort excessive ransoms by tortures of fiendish ingenuity; nor did they discriminate too nicely between friend and foe. By such behaviour they succeeded in spreading the terror of their master's name; at the news of his approach the villein fled from the plough, and the merchant took his goods for safety to cemeteries and consecrated places.[2] But the opposition gained more supporters than it lost; and terror merely increased the desperation of the leaders. On his return from

---

[1] Petit-Dutaillis, *Louis VIII.*, pp. 93 ff.   [2] Wendover, iii., 352.

MAP
to illustrate the
BARONS' WAR

English Miles
10 0 10 20 40   60

SCOTLAND

IRELAND

Dunbar
Haddington
Berwick
Roxburgh
Wark
Alnwick
Mitford
Morpeth
Durham
Darlington
Thirsk
York
Pontefract
Doncaster
Grimsby
Lincoln
Newark
Nottingham
Boston
Sleaford
 Slanger
Mountsorel
Rockingham
Worcester
Northampton
Bedford
Gloucester
Burford
Aylesbury
Cirencester
Oxford
Bristol
Marlborough
Wallingford
Windsor
Bath
Chippenham
Reading
Lambeth
Wells
Sherborne
Winchester
The Weald
Corfe

NORTH   SEA

IRISH SEA

WALES

Severn
Ouse
Trent
Avon

Kings Lynn
Norwich
Ely
Bury
Cambridge
Pleshey
Colchester
Coggeshall
Hertford
Tilty Abbey
Thames
Rochester
Canterbury
Tunbridge
Dover
Sandwich
Thanet
Romney

Explanation of Symbols
John's winter raid of 1215-16 upon the Northern Shires . . . .
Winter raid of Savaric de Mauléon John's lieutenant. 1215-16 . . . + + + + +
John's last march Aug. 26 – Oct. 19. 1216 . . . .

the north (1216) the King attempted London only to find it more stoutly held than ever. He was obliged to content himself with watching the capital from Reading or from Windsor; and his troops, their plunder already squandered, began to clamour for wages or, in default of wages, for discharge. Meanwhile French reinforcements continued to reach the barons, and the adventure of Louis assumed, with his father's connivance, the aspect of a national enterprise. The chief French feudatories learned that they could not safely ignore the appeals of the Prince to their generosity;[1] and the forces of Bar, Nevers, Brabant, Brittany, and St. Pol were well represented in the expedition which Louis collected at Calais. After many delays he set sail on May 20th, accompanied by a fleet of 800 ships, which carried, besides infantry, munitions and supplies, a total of 1,200 knights. The admiral was a noted privateer, Eustace the Monk, who had long been the terror of the narrow seas, practising the trade of pirate sometimes under the English flag, sometimes under that of France.[2]

The French Expedition, May, 1216

The fleet of John had been ordered to wait at Dover for the French. But the ships were dispersed by a violent tempest on the night of May 18th, and reassembled so slowly that Louis made the port of Stonor without encountering resistance. John, who had taken up his quarters at Canterbury, was only apprised of his rival's appearance when the French disembarkation was already effected; he resolved upon the advice of the Marshal to refrain from giving battle; and retreated by slow stages to Winchester which he reached upon the 28th. The French were therefore able to advance without delay on London. The castles of Canterbury and Rochester surrendered at their approach, and their entry into the capital was marked by the greatest rejoicing on the part of the citizens.[3] In the churchyard of St. Paul the mayor and a deputation of the citizens tendered their homage to the Prince, receiving in exchange a promise that he would respect their civic liberties. No one doubted that his success would be rapid and complete : the Earls of Warenne, Oxford, Aumâle, Arundel, and Salisbury considered that the time had come for abandoning the King and made their

[1] Petit-Dutaillis, p. 88.
[2] See F. Michel, *Eustache le Moine*, introd.; Meyer in *G. le Mar.*, iii., 242; and Petit-Dutaillis, p. 99.
[3] *Hist. des ducs*, 171 : " Li bourgois de la ville alerent encontre lui, qui grant joie orent de sa venue ".

peace with Louis; the young King of Scotland was quick to follow their example. A dwindling force of mercenaries, the Earls of Pembroke and Chester, and the legate Gualo formed the effective party of the King.

Last
Opera-
tions and
Death of
John,
June-Oct.,
1216 The first operations of Louis confirmed the general opinion of his prospects. Early in June he marched on Winchester which the King had now abandoned. The garrison of the royal castle fired the town to improve their prospects of resistance; but the result, as might have been expected, was to make the citizens, who had never loved the King, the allies of the foreigner. The royal castle capitulated on June 24th; after which date Windsor, Lincoln, and Dover were the only strongholds of importance left to the royalists in the east and south-east counties. It was in vain that John issued invitations to individual barons and to the Cinque Ports to repent of their disloyalty. His most lavish promises fell upon deaf ears and, although the Patent Rolls attest the fact that he still issued orders to the sheriffs of the eastern counties, his power was now limited to the south-west and the Welsh marches. But the invaders, in their reluctance to press forward leaving uncaptured castles in their rear, wasted precious months upon the sieges of Dover and of Windsor. Throughout July and August the King, who had taken Corfe for his head-quarters, was left at liberty to organise a new campaign. Some who had despaired of his success began to recover faith, and the disgrace of submission to the foreigner was slowly realised in those shires where French forces were most often to be seen. In Sussex an English freeholder of low condition, one William of Casingeham who was commonly known as Willekin of the Weald, raised a band of volunteers with which he carried on a successful warfare of ambushes and surprises; [1] while the heroic defence of the Justiciar, Hubert de Burgh, whom John had left in command of Dover, turned the current of Kentish feeling. It was with high hopes of a national reaction in his favour that the King marched, early in September, to the relief of Windsor and Lincoln. His heart failed him when he found that the besiegers of Windsor

---

[1] *Hist. des ducs*, p. 181: "Es Waus (*sic*) ot i siergant, qui par sa proece fu moult sires des Waudois; chil guerroia moult as gens Looys; apielés estoit Willekins de Kasingehem; mais li François l'apeloient Willekin des Waus, qui ne sorent noumer Kasingehem. Moult fu puis chil renommés en l'ost Looys." See Paris-Wendover in *Chron. Maj.*, ii., 655. His correct name William of Casingeham (*Pat. Rolls*, ii., 25, 56). After the treaty of Lambeth in the next reign he received a royal manor (*ibid.*, 101) and a pension of £20 (*Rot. Claus.*, i., 348).

would not yield ground without a battle ; but his northward march, drawing them off in pursuit, served his purpose as well as a victory. The blockade of Lincoln was raised at his approach ; and he made the city his head-quarters from whence to ravage and reduce the eastern counties. Meeting with no serious resistance he was uniformly successful in his raids ; the position which he occupied lay across the road by which alone the northern barons and the King of Scots could retire from London to their own possessions. It is not surprising to learn that the English supporters of Louis began to waver in their allegiance, or that the excommunications with which the legate bombarded them at length aroused their scruples. They had already discovered that the chief spoils of victory would fall to the countrymen of their elected king ; though Louis had confirmed the Charter, the Committee of Twenty-five were allowed no influence in the conduct of the campaign. Fear of John's incorrigible bad faith was the chief motive which held them to his rival. But this soon ceased to exist. On October 19th, after a short illness, caused as it is related by a surfeit of peaches and new cider, John breathed his last at Newark, bequeathing his body to the Cathedral Church of Worcester and his son to the protection of the Holy See.[1]

The character of John is written large upon the pages of his history. Bad faith, cruelty, a love of intrigue, an incapacity to read the present or foresee the future, a petulance which could brook no opposition, an ambition strong enough to make him reckless of consequences yet not sufficiently strong to outbalance his passions and his natural indolence, a bluntness of moral perceptions which astonished and disgusted the most indifferent of his subjects —all these are traits attributed to him by the unanimous testimony of contemporaries. But of his habits, his outward appearance, and his minor idiosyncrasies, they have little to say. He was under the middle height and in his latter years inclined to corpulence. He loved good cheer; he was accustomed to atone for eating meat on fast-days by a dole to a hundred paupers ; he took pains to provide himself on all his journeys with liberal supplies of the most costly

Character of John

---

[1] See John's letter of Oct. 15 (from Sleaford) to the Pope, Raynaldus, *Annales*, s.a. (ed. 1741) ; "Convocatis magnatibus nostris assistentibus, providimus regnum nostrum, quod est vestrum, necnon et haeredem nostrum protectioni vestrae et sanctae Romanae ecclesiae commendandum," etc. The will itself is printed by Thomas, *Survey of the Cathedral Church of Worcester* (London, 1836). App. p. 19.

wines. Unlike his father he delighted in personal display; jewels
and personal ornaments formed no inconsiderable item in his
treasures, and he spent large sums upon his dress. Of cultivated
tastes his letters show no trace, except that he was liberal in his
gifts to the choristers who sang in his chapel at great festivals.
His amours were numerous and prolific; he had by different
mistresses at least seven illegitimate children. The scandal of the
time describes his Poitevin queen as little better than himself, and
is corroborated by the fact that Isabelle was kept in strict confinement for a considerable portion of their married life. John delighted
in hunting, hawking, fishing and every form of sport; at the most
critical moments of his life he was never too busy to issue orders
respecting his hounds and falcons. There is a sirvente, composed
by the younger Bertrand de Born, which attributes his failure as
a King to his love of these amusements. Yet it would be unjust to
represent him as nothing but a trifler. In Poitou and in England,
even in Normandy when he commanded adequate resources, he
proved himself a soldier of ability, skilful in his strategy, and a past
master in the minor arts connected with military science. If his
energy had been less spasmodic, if he had possessed any of the gifts
of a leader of men, he might have proved himself not much inferior
in generalship to Richard Coeur de Lion. But as a statesman his
career was one of unvarying failure and humiliation, from the time
when he first landed in Ireland as his father's vicegerent to the
moment of his death. Beaten in war by Philip Augustus, in
diplomacy by Innocent, he crowned his career with a third and yet
more startling failure by hurling himself against an opposition
which, in spite of all defects of character and intellect, was still the
mouthpiece of the English nation. That he provoked, and perished
through, the first alliance of all classes in the kingdom must remain
his chief title to remembrance.

Corona-
tion of
Henry III
On October 28th, 1216, nine days after the death of his father,
the young King was crowned at Gloucester in the presence of four
bishops and a handful of barons and mercenary captains. It was a
perilous inheritance which thus devolved upon a boy of nine years
of age. The King's title depended for validity upon the swords of
foreign soldiers and the moral influence of a Pope who was still
an unknown quantity. With the death of Innocent (July, 1216)
the tiara had devolved upon the mild and cautious Honorius III.

who, however well disposed, could scarcely be expected to bring to the defence of his young ward that diplomatic craft of which Innocent had been a master. But, since they had no other ally, the royalists agreed to put their trust in Rome. They gave no formal title or commission to the legate Gualo ; but they allowed him to assume, as representing the suzerain of their young master, a leading place in the Council and such duties of a guardian as were consistent with his ecclesiastical profession. For the rougher work of the King's cause a lay regent was indispensable. All combined in pressing the Earl Marshal, octogenarian though he was, to accept the thankless office. He consented not without reluctance upon receiving a promise of co-operation from Ranulf, Earl of Chester, the only rival who could be seriously considered. A Council, held at Bristol (Nov. 12) under the presidency of the legate, confirmed the Marshal's appointment ; and he thenceforth carried the title of *Rector Regis et Regni.* The responsibility for the King's person he declined to undertake, as being incompatible with his military duties ; the care of the boy-king was entrusted to Peter des Roches, an unpopular but necessary appointment, since the bishop led the party of the alien favourites who controlled the army. The Marshal, however, kept in his own hands the entire control of the executive. Hubert de Burgh, the justiciar, was his subordinate; Gualo an unofficial colleague with no well defined position.[1]

No Regent could have been better fitted than the Marshal to win the confidence of moderate men. To the Crown he had been for twenty years a tower of strength. His influence had induced the Normans to acknowledge John as Richard's heir ; he had been the staunch supporter of John's cause in the wars of Normandy ; and although he had come into collision with the late King on more than one occasion his loyalty had never wavered. On the other hand he had endeavoured to mediate between John and the De Braoses ; he had taken the part of a peace-maker in the conferences which preceded the signing of the Charter ; and no rebel was likely to

---

[1] The appointment of De Burgh was made by John (*Rot. Pat.*, i., 110). De Burgh describes his own position after John's death in a document preserved by M. Paris, *Chron. Maj.*, vi., 64. Gualo is described in a legal record of 22 Hen. III. as "quasi tutor Dom. Regis et custos regni" (Bracton's *Notebook*, iii., 232). Mr. Turner thinks that he owed this position to an oral commission from John, supplemented by the King's will (*Trans. Roy. Hist. Soc.*, N.S., xviii., p. 283). Honorius is for some time inclined to ignore the Great Council and treat Gualo as solely responsible for his ward ; Pressutti, *Regesta*, i., iii., etc.

be deterred from repentance by the fear of finding in the Marshal a revengeful or unaccommodating spirit. The Earl wisely inaugurated the new epoch with a proclamation stating that King Henry desired a complete oblivion of all the feuds which had existed between his father and the barons; and with a reissue of the Charter, albeit in a mutilated form which showed the jealousy of his party for the prerogative.[1] From the new edition were omitted the clauses which recognised the Great Council's right to control taxation, together with others which were regarded as imposing undue restrictions on royal rights. But the significance of these omissions was diminished by a promise that they should be reconsidered when the young King came of age.

Growth of the Royal Party — The immediate result of this conciliatory measure was but small. Only four submissions are recorded in the first three months of the new reign. But the Regent showed both energy and skill in his efforts to conciliate the disaffected. He promised an amnesty and full restitution of lands to all who would submit. He appointed representatives in every part of the country to whom he gave full powers for receiving submissions, and used the influence of every proselyte to win over others who still hesitated. He promised the supporters of the young King that in the event of their capture by the French they should be promptly ransomed. He distributed lands and castles and other rewards to all whose fidelity required encouragement; and to the barons of Ireland he promised all the privileges and liberties of the Great Charter.[2] The legate, whom Honorius had commissioned to use his discretion for the advantage of the kingdom, utilised his powers to proclaim a crusade against the French and their supporters.[3] Soon, in spite of a few defections on the part of faint-hearted supporters who announced their purpose of going to the Holy Land, the royal party began to grow in numbers. The rebel barons were not at ease under their new master. They complained, not wholly with truth as it would seem, that he reserved all offices of trust and profit for his own country-men;[4] nor could they fail to be shaken by the ecclesiastical censures

---

[1] *Foedera*, i., 145. S. C., 340 ff.

[2] *Pat. Rolls*, ii., 4, 17, 21, 22, 24, 31, 55.

[3] Shirley, i., p. 527. *Pat. Rolls*, ii., 57 : " Cruce signentur ad eundum nobiscum in subsidio Dei et sanctae ecclesiae ".

[4] For castles committed by Louis to the care of English barons see the *Anonyme de Béthune*, p. 774. See also the remarks of Petit-Dutaillis, p. 118. Complaints of the barons in Wend., iv., 5, 10.

which the legate launched against them, and by the reprimands which Honorius III. addressed to each of them in person. Early in 1217 the French prince made the serious mistake of granting a truce till Easter and of returning to France for a period of two months. During his absence the injudicious behaviour of his lieutenant, Enguerrand de Couci, intensified the dissatisfaction of his English confederates; and although the visit to France enabled him to raise reinforcements and to find supplies for his ragged and almost starving mercenaries, it also cost him the support of between one and two hundred English barons who submitted in the interval.[1]

The prince returned on April 23. Three days later the truce expired and the royalists at once laid siege to the castle of Mount- sorel in Leicestershire.   The Prince despatched a considerable portion of his army from London with the object of raising the siege.   This was effected; on learning of the advance of the French force, which included 600 knights besides a large number of foot-soldiers, the Earl of Chester led off the royalists from Mountsorel to Nottingham, whence he could observe the march of the enemy at a safe distance.   The French, encouraged to foolhardi- ness by this facile success, pushed forward from Mountsorel to Lincoln where Nicolaa de la Haye, the widow of Gerard de Cam- ville, had so far succeeded in holding the castle against a baronial army.   But by their march on Lincoln the French were completely cut off from the Prince who still remained with his main force at London. The Regent, from his head-quarters at Oxford, perceived the blunder of the enemy and hastened to take the opportunity of defeating them in detail. On May 19th he collected at Newark the largest force that could be spared from the duty of guarding the royal castles. The numbers were smaller than those of the besiegers at Lincoln; there were only 406 knights with the Marshal; but the inferiority of his cavalry was to some extent compensated by his strength in crossbowmen of whom he had 317, skilled marksmen whose liberal pay attests the value which was set upon their aid.[2]

The Battle of Lincoln, May, 1217

[1] *Ann. Dunstaple* call Enguerrand " virum quidem nobilem sed non discretum ". See Petit-Dutaillis, p. 144.
[2] The numbers in the poem of *G. le Mar.* (ll. 16264-8). Wendover, iv., 18, says 400 knights and 250 crossbowmen. About the number of knights on the French side the poem and Wendover are substantially agreed; the one gives 611, the other 600. Wendover puts the French foot-soldiery at the absurd figure of 20,000. The poem gives 1,000, not counting English auxiliaries (Wend., iv., 15. *G. le Mar.*, ll. 16334, 17026).

With this force the Regent marched on Lincoln. He was assisted in his dispositions by the warlike Peter des Roches, a bishop of the old school and never so happy as when in the field; and by Falkes de Breauté the most audacious and experienced of John's mercenaries. But the French leaders, by their blunders, made the task of their enemies an easy one. The besiegers of Lincoln had collected within the walls to attack the castle which stood on the north-west of the city, adjoining the wall, and communicating by a postern with the open country. Instead of sallying forth to do battle in the open, where the weight of their superior numbers might have been used to good advantage, they decided to stand on the defensive behind the crumbling ramparts and crazy gates of Lincoln; a mistake so gross that we may well believe the account which makes their scouts completely over-estimate the strength of the English army. On perceiving the tactics of the French, the garrison of the castle opened the postern gate to their deliverers; and Falkes de Breauté entering the castle with the crossbowmen made a furious sally, while the remainder of the Marshal's force assailed the long line of the walls at various points. The city was entered without difficulty; and a furious combat between the mounted knights ensued, in streets so steep and narrow that the superior numbers of the French merely added to their confusion. The Count of Perche fell, mortally wounded by a pike-point which pierced his visor and penetrated through the eye to the brain. The Earls of Winchester and Hereford, with other knights and barons to the number of over three hundred, were taken prisoner. Two hundred knights or so escaped and made their way to London, though sorely harassed on the march by the country folk whom their previous depredations had exasperated. But the loss of life on either side was small; the royalists in derision called the fight the Fair of Lincoln.[1]

The Battle in the Straits of Dover, Aug., 1217
The loss of so many knights was a severe blow to Louis. He fortified himself in London, resolved if necessary to stand a siege until new reinforcements should arrive from France. The royalists

[1] Wend., iv., 19 ff., *G. le Mar.*, ll. 16130 ff., are the main authorities. The battle of Lincoln is discussed at some length in Oman, *Art of War in the Middle Ages*, pp. 408 ff.; in Meyer, *G. le Maréchal*, iii., pp. 227-40; and by Tout in *E. H. R.*, xviii., p. 240. The latter lays more stress than his predecessors upon the difficulties involved in the narrative of the French biographer; and gives weighty reasons for thinking that it offers duplicate versions of some incidents.

moved southward from Lincoln and advanced along the Thames from Oxford, their former head-quarters, to Chertsey where they lay for the greater part of June.[1] Hopes were entertained that the Londoners would purchase forgiveness for their rebellion by opening the gates to their native lord ; and Louis began, in despair, to treat for peace. The negotiations broke down on a single point; the prince insisted upon an amnesty for the English clergy of his party, but this the legate would not grant.[2] In August however a new defeat, this time at sea, dashed the last hopes of the prince and rendered it impossible that he should make a stand upon a point of honour.

Philip Augustus still refused to give his countenance to the English enterprise ; but his daughter-in-law, the masculine Blanche of Castile, was allowed to raise what troops she could with money secretly supplied from the royal treasury. According to the common story she obtained the money by dint of strong remonstrances, after her first request had been refused. " By the mother of God," she is reported as saying to King Philip, " I know what I will do. I have a fine boy by my lord and husband. I will offer him in pawn and well I know that I shall find some one to lend me money on that pledge." [3] From Philip and from her husband's vassals she obtained the means to raise a considerable force of ships and men. They sailed from Calais on August 17, under the command of the turncoat Eustace the Monk. There were with him ten large vessels of which four carried knights, and six were filled with men-at-arms. A flotilla of about seventy small craft carried supplies, arms, and munitions. To oppose him the Regent had only the navy of the Cinque Ports, consisting of between thirty and forty vessels great and small. But eighteen of these were large vessels ; and the command lay with Hubert de Burgh whose fame as a soldier, if not as an admiral, had been established by the long and successful defence of Dover Castle. The English sighted the enemy not far from the estuary of the Thames, and bore down upon them with the advantage of the weather-gage. The ship of Eustace the Monk was the first to be attacked. Five English vessels grappled it and prepared to board. The crew fought desperately but were blinded and bewildered by the shower of missiles and by the quicklime

---

[1] *Pat. Rolls*, ii., 68 ff.   [2] *Pat. Rolls*, ii., 69.   Petit-Dutaillis, p. 158.
[3] See the *Menestrel de Rheims*, §§ 301, 302 (ed. *Soc. de l'Hist. de France*).

which their assailants on the windward threw into the air. In a short while the deck was cleared and the English took possession. Eustace the Monk endeavoured to save himself from a traitor's death by taking to concealment in the hold; but he was detected and beheaded without formalities; a man who had served under him when he was in the English service acted as the executioner. Meanwhile the remainder of his large vessels saved themselves by their superior sailing powers, but a number of the small craft were sunk by ramming, or captured with their crews. The common sailors were thrown overboard, the knights reserved for ransom; and the pirates, as they were popularly styled, of the Cinque Ports returned triumphantly with the captured ships in tow.[1] The victory was announced through Kent by a messenger who carried the head of Eustace impaled upon a lance, and great was the rejoicing at the gruesome spectacle. The victory, though obtained without much difficulty and over a fleet which was far from representing the naval strength of France, had given the death blow to the hopes of Louis. It was now possible to blockade London both by land and sea, and the Regent prepared to do so. But the Prince declined to continue the useless struggle against overwhelming odds. He offered to accept the terms which he had formerly refused. They were granted, and peace was signed at Lambeth on September 11th, 1217.

Treaty of Kingston, Sept., 1217   It was a peace with the Roman Church as well as with the English Crown, and the terms which Louis obtained from the Regent were milder than those which the legate saw fit to impose. The Earl Marshal desired above all things to be rid of the French invaders; he knew too well the exhaustion of the royal treasury, the untrustworthiness of his principal supporters, and the disjointed condition of the government which he represented. He therefore granted an amnesty to all the English followers of Louis, guaranteed to London and the other rebel towns the full enjoyment of their former liberties, and paid the Prince 10,000 marks, which could be ill afforded, in order to leave him no excuse for delaying his departure.[2]

---

[1] The main authorities for the battle are the *Histoire des ducs*, pp. 200 ff., and Wendover, iv., 28. The accounts in other writers are usually meagre. The biographer of the Marshal (ll. 17294-17462) is better than the rest; but inaccurate as to the numbers engaged.

[2] Shirley, i., p. 7. *Hist. des ducs* (p. 204) says 17,000 marks. See *Pat. Rolls*, ii., 114, recording a loan of 6,000 marks, contracted for this purpose with merchants of St. Omer. Also *Rot. Claus.*, 360, 369. Terms of the treaty in *Foedera*, i., 148.

Gualo, on the contrary, insisted that the Prince should make a public profession of his penitence; the heir of France was forced to appear barefooted and half-naked at the conference in which he was re-admitted to fellowship with the offended Church.[1]   To the same influence it was due that the rebellious clergy were exempted from all the benefits of the amnesty.   After the conclusion of peace the legate sent his commissioners far and wide to collect the names of of the offenders; many were punished with deprivation of their benefices and suspension from their sacred functions; and although the majority were allowed to make their peace by journeying to Rome and obtaining absolution from the Pope, those who had been most prominent in opposition, as for example Simon Langton, the brother of the Archbishop, were sentenced to an indefinite period of exile.   Rightly or wrongly the legate incurred the suspicion of having taken bribes from both the guilty and the innocent; from those who should have been punished and from those who were threatened with an unjust condemnation.   Thus were sown the seeds of that hostility with which the national clergy, particularly those of humble rank, were to regard the Holy See and its preten-sions.   It was the lower clergy who suffered the most at Gualo's hands.   Their superiors had been more prompt to read and follow the signs of changing fortune.[2]

At the end of September the Prince left the kingdom with every mark of courtesy from the victorious party.   The deliverance from the foreigner was fitly celebrated at the end of the year by a re-confirmation of the Charter and the issue of a separate Charter of the Forest.   The Magna Carta of 1217[3] resembles that of the preceding year in its omissions, but contains new clauses which are significant of the pressure to which the Regency was exposed from powerful supporters.   The eyres of the justices of assize are now made annual instead of quarterly; the shire-courts are to be held but once a month, or less often still where such has been the

Second Reissue of the Charter, 1217

---

[1] *Chron. de Mailros*, 131.   *G. le M.*, ll. 17700 ff.

[2] For Simon Langton see Shirley, i., 532, and Pressutti, *Regesta*, i., pp. 228, 234. He was allowed, at his brother's request, to return in 1227 (*Pat. Rolls*, ii., 136; Auvray, *Reg. Gregoire IX.*, i., p. 43).   Gualo's character unfavourably handled in Wendover, iv., 33, who writes however with animus.   The English clergy re-sented the power which Honorius had conferred upon Gualo (Bouquet, xix., p. 623) of filling vacant sees and benefices.   The evidence of the Close and Patent Rolls, and of the letters in Shirley's collection, does not justify the strictures of modern writers.

[3] *Statutes of the Realm*, i., pp. 17-19.

previous custom; the sheriff's turn is to be made twice in the year, and the view of frankpledge taken at Michaelmas alone. Finally the right of the mesne tenant to alienate his land is limited in various ways, to protect his lord from the risk of losing dues and service. In fact the new Charter is remodelled in the interests of feudalism. The Charter of the Forest is however a document better adapted to secure the general good. It cancels all the afforestations which had been made at the expense of private persons since the accession of Henry II.; it abolishes the penalties of death and mutilation for offences committed against the forest-law; and it removes some of the more vexatious restraints which custom had imposed upon the owners of land lying within the forest-jurisdiction.[1]

The Resulting Settlement

Many though not all of the rights for which the barons had thrown down the gauntlet in 1215 were now secured. Nor must the measure of their success be estimated solely by the written concessions with which the return of peace was celebrated. The Regent had refused to recognise in formal terms the control of the Great Council over taxation; but in practice this control was not disputed, either during the regency or after Henry III. had asserted his right of misgoverning according to his private will and pleasure. The civil war had produced a wholesome dread of national resistance which was more valuable than any written guarantees. Unfortunately this dread was not tempered with good-will towards the men who had inspired it. The barons of the Charter found themselves in the new era as thoroughly mistrusted and shut out from power as were the Tories in the first two Hanoverian reigns. Some retired to their estates; others sought distraction in the Crusade of the year 1220;[2] alone of all the constitutionalists the Archbishop attained to influence and consideration under Henry III. Such is the common lot of revolutionaries unblessed with genius, when they survive the need which called them into being; and they are exceptionally fortunate if the historian after recounting their mistakes will concede to them the merit of a patriotic intention.

[1] *Statutes of the Realm,* i., pp. 20, 21.
[2] *Waverley Annals. Pat. Rolls,* ii., 185.

CHAPTER XVI

MINORITY AND MISRULE

THE storm of civil war was over, but the after-swell continued Death of
for some years to disturb the waters of society.   Those who the Earl
had been the best friends of the Crown in the hour of extremity May, 1219
became the worst of enemies when the occasions and excuses for
lawless aggrandisement were removed.   The last months of the
Marshal's life were employed in efforts to reclaim demesnes and
castles from those who had defended them against the foreigner.[1]
It was no easy task ; he found that the sheriffs were either unable
or unwilling to cope with the robbers ; and upon enquiry it seemed
wiser, in some cases, to postpone the vindication of royal rights.
But force was employed against one at least of the recalcitrant
soldiers of fortune; after a siege of eight days' duration Newark
castle was wrested from Robert Gaugi.[2]   A few months later a
General Eyre of the itinerant justices (Jan., 1219) dealt sharply with
petty oppressors, and gave the country a foretaste of the blessings
of justice.[3]   But, early in 1219, the great Marshal died leaving the
work of settlement to be completed by other hands.   His epitaph
was fitly pronounced by the father of his chief adversary.   "The
Marshal," said King Philip of France, "was the most loyal man that
I have ever known in any place where I have been."   The Marshal
had done for his young charge whatever could be done by strength
of character, by military prowess, and by a spirit of sage moderation ; and his very defects and limitations had been of service to
the royalist cause.   The narrow ground of legalism upon which he
took his stand had the merit of being intelligible, and of appealing
to all the conservative instincts of his countrymen.

[1] *Rot. Claus.*, i., 336. *Pat. Rolls*, ii., *passim.*
[2] Wend., iv., 35. *Pat. Rolls*, ii., 164.
[3] *Pat. Rolls*, 186, 206. *Ann. Dunstaple.*

With him expired the office of *Rector regis et regni* and the influence which he wielded was divided between three conflicting interests—that of the Papacy as represented by the legate, that of the foreign favourites and the military adventurers who found in the crafty Bishop of Winchester their most influential spokesman, and that of the native loyalists who looked for guidance to Hubert de Burgh, the Justiciar. As compared with these three personages the remaining members of the royal Council were mere cyphers. Which of the three would ultimately gain the upper hand was for a long time doubtful.

The
Legate
Pandulph
(1218-21)

The office of legate had been held until the end of 1218 by the Cardinal Gualo who, in spite of the extensive claims which he at first advanced, finally contented himself with lending the support of the spiritual arm to the Marshal's policy, and with exercising an absolute authority over the English Church. Although he was upbraided with venality we have no proof that he abused his trust; he seems to have resisted, on the whole, the suggestions of the lawless party [1] that he should take their side against the Marshal. His successor Pandulph, the same to whom King John's submission had been tendered, was not less devoted to the royal interests but testified his zeal in a manner which irritated both Church and laity. The Earl Marshal, when on his death-bed, committed the young king to the care of Pandulph, and may have intended that his office should devolve upon the legate. [2] This fact explains to some extent the attitude which the legate now assumed; but a little knowledge of English law would have taught him that the Marshal's private wishes were of no legal force. Pandulph however assumed that the chief place belonged to himself as of right. Towards the Justiciar and Peter des Roches he adopted the tone of a superior, dictating their movements and their measures, lecturing them when they ventured upon any step which he viewed with disapproval, and assuming an absolute control over the financial business of the Exchequer. [3] It was the less easy to resist him because

[1] *E.g.*, Falkes de Breauté (Shirley, i., 4). *Cf.* Shirley, i., p. 532.
[2] *G. le M.*, ll. 19000 ff. No doubt Pandulph regarded this transaction as a mere recognition of the rights pertaining to the Holy See. It took place in the presence of the barons, but there is no trace of a resolution in Pandulph's favour; a point which Mr. Turner (*Trans. Roy. Hist. Soc.*, N. S., xviii., p. 293) has overlooked. Honorius encouraged Pandulph to treat even the Earl Marshal as his inferior. Pressutti, i., p. 326. Shirley, i., p. 16.
[3] Shirley, i., pp. 28, 34, 36, 74, 76, 113, 167, etc. *Foedera*, i., 162.

the support of Rome was valuable in dealing with the swarms of actual or potential conspirators who surrounded the throne of the young King; nor could the Justiciar resent the financial meddlings of the legate at a time when the current expenses of administration could only be met by borrowing from Pandulph.[1] But Pandulph's withdrawal was hailed with universal relief; nor was it accounted the least of Langton's services to England that he prevailed upon the Pope to abstain from appointing a new legate.   It would have been well if English affairs had ceased to engage the attention of the Pope himself; but, when the struggle between the foreigners and the patriots reached a climax, the awkward, though well-meaning, interference of Honorius did much to aggravate the crisis.

For a year or two the Justiciar and Bishop Peter worked to-gether without an open rupture, the former maintaining that superi-ority to which his reputation as a patriot and soldier entitled him. When the King's sister was betrothed to the young Alexander II. of Scotland, the Justiciar received the hand of Alexander's sister, the princess Margaret, and through this alliance, unprecedented for an English subject, rose to the first rank of the baronage.   He wrestled manfully with the spirit of lawlessness in all the manifold forms which it assumed.   He prohibited tournaments; checked the wild feud of the Cinque Ports with their East Anglian rivals, the men of Yarmouth; sent out commissioners to do summary justice upon highway robbers and vagrants of ill-fame; and did not shrink from repressing the most august of feudal potentates.   Henry of Cornwall, who presumed on his descent to usurp the rights of an earl-palatine, lost his sheriffdom and his lease of the Stannaries; when he showed signs of resistance the fyrd of the western counties was called to meet the King at Exeter prepared for a campaign; and finally the Earl was fain to make submission.[2]   The Earl of Aumâle having refused to surrender the castles of Rockingham and Sauvey received a peremptory rebuke, which was enforced by the appearance, before Rockingham, of the King and the Justiciar at the head of an armed force.[3]   A more determined effort to defy the royal authority with regard to his other castles led in 1221 to the

Adminis-tration of De Burgh

[1] *Pat. Rolls*, ii., 283.
[2] *Ibid.*, 202, 241, 247, 248, 267.   These events took place in July-October, 1220.   Henry of Cornwall was a grandson of Henry I.
[3] *Ibid.*, 257, 238-40.   This in June, 1220.

capture, after a five days' siege, of Bytham, which the Earl had believed to be impregnable. Before the spectacle of such vigour the secret sympathisers of the Earl were cowed into silence; the Great Council, though filled with men who held lands and castles by no better title, voted for the expenses of this petty war a general scutage. The Earl was treated with great leniency, and the garrison of Bytham were dismissed without penalty or ransom. But the work of storming castles proceeded without hindrance: the mildness of the government was rightly interpreted as a proof of conscious strength. The severity of the Justiciar was reserved for offenders of a humbler sort. In 1222 a brawl between the citizens of London and the servants of Westminster Abbey assumed the proportions of a private war. The citizens took for their leader a wealthy alderman, by name Constantine FitzAthulf, who had been prominent among the supporters of Prince Louis.[1] At his suggestion the folk-moot resolved to raze the abbey level with the ground ; and the mob made a raid upon Westminster which, though not wholly successful, did considerable damage to the property of the convent. The insult to a foundation which lay under the special protection of the Crown was revenged by the summary trial and execution of Constantine FitzAthulf; while of his supporters some were imprisoned, others suffered the loss of hand or foot, and many fled the city. It was a sharp but a much needed lesson to the capital, and would have passed without comment if it had not contrasted so remarkably with the measure meted out to aristocratic disturbers of the peace.[2]

Intri-
gues of
Llewelyn

It was fortunate for the government that the most dangerous of these were slow in uniting. The lords of the Welsh Marches were the first to do so. A stranger and a natural enemy had undertaken, not without success, to compose the feuds which had hitherto divided them. This was Llewelyn son of Jorwerth who, during the barons' war, had achieved the feat, hitherto deemed impossible, of uniting beneath the lead of Gwynedd the smaller principalities of south and central Wales. Regarded by his countrymen as a patriot and deliverer, Llewelyn looked forward to the day

---

[1] See *Rot. Claus.*, 260. The wealth of FitzAthulf is shown by the later entries referring to his lands.
[2] M. Paris, *Chron. Maj.*, iii., 71, alleges that the followers of FitzAthulf raised the cry of "Mountjoy and King Louis"; but this may be mere scandal.

when he might openly repudiate the English suzerainty and perhaps expel the Marchers from their hard-won settlements. For the present however it was his policy to conduct himself as a vassal of the Crown ; in his alliances with the Earl of Chester, the Mortimers, and the Braoses, he professed no deeper object than that of limiting the encroachments of the central power upon March-privileges, and of taking from the younger William Marshal the influence which the Earl enjoyed as the representative of royal authority in Wales. In 1220 the Welsh Prince commenced a series of daring raids on Pembrokeshire, under the pretext of reclaiming lands which he asserted that the Marshal had fraudulently taken from him.[1] Covertly encouraged by the Marchers, and carefully avoiding an irreparable breach with the Regency, Llewelyn protracted the war for upwards of three years ; at length the castles of Carmarthen and Cardigan[2] were wrested from him by the Marshal (1222); and a year later he was reduced to order by a punitive expedition in which the King and the Justiciar co-operated, on the central Marches, with the forces of Pembroke advancing from the south.[3]

Small as had been the aid of the English malcontents to their ally, the danger of a combined Anglo-Welsh rebellion stirred the Justiciar to energetic action. He resolved to disarm his opponents by depriving them of the sheriffdoms and royal castles which they held ; as a preliminary to this step he obtained from Honorius a Bull declaring the young King of an age to govern for himself (April, 1223).[4] The significance of the Bull was patent to those who remembered that all grants and appointments made by the Regency were to terminate upon the King's majority. The Earls of Chester and Aumâle, than whom few had more to lose by a wholesale measure of resumption, seized the opportunity of the Welsh campaign to make an attempt upon the Tower of London in the absence of Justiciar and King. They failed through the unexpected resistance of the garrison, and were called before the King in Council to explain their conduct. But they appeared only to defy their judges and denounce the Justiciar as a traitor. A

The Resumption of Castles, 1223

---

[1] *Pat. Rolls*, ii., 254. Shirley, i., pp. 123, 141. *Foedera*, i., 164.

[2] Entrusted to him in 1218 (*Pat. Rolls*, ii., 143). Taken by the Marshal early in 1223 (*ib.*, pp. 352, 374).

[3] See the terms of L.'s submission in *Pat. Rolls*, ii., 411 ; safe-conduct for the troops of the E. Marshal, *ibid.*, 407. The war opened, July, 1223 ; peace concluded in September.

[4] Shirley, i., p. 430. But the legal powers of the King were limited by the Great Council, with the Pope's assent ; he might not make grants in perpetuity. See Powicke in *E. H. R.*, xxiii., pp. 221-223.

strange scene ensued. The Justiciar taxed the Bishop of Winchester with the responsibility for the conduct of the Earls. The bishop retorted that, if it cost him his last penny, he would turn the Justiciar out of office; and the confederates of the bishop, headed by the Earl of Chester, left the court without condescending to await their sentence.[1] The Christmas season saw both parties arrayed in arms for civil war, the royalists at Northampton, the rebels at Leicester. But the latter found themselves outnumbered and menaced by the Archbishop with excommunication. They gave way, and made their peace with the government by surrendering their spoil. The Earl of Chester lost the castles of Shrewsbury, Bridgnorth, Lancaster, the honour of Lancaster, the sheriffdoms of Shropshire, Lancashire, and Stafford.[2] Falkes de Bréauté, the captain of John's mercenaries who had been "more than a king" in the midlands, was similarly deprived of Oxford and Hertford castles, and of five sheriffdoms, Oxford, Bedford, Bucks, Cambridge and Huntingdon;[3] while his brother in arms, William of Cantelupe, lost the castle of Kenilworth and the sheriffdoms of Leicester and Warwick. For form's sake the Justiciar and his supporters also surrendered the castles of which they were in charge. But, since they excluded the Bishop of Winchester and all his partisans from the King's council, they gained infinitely more than they gave up.

Rebellion of Falkes de Breauté, 1224

It remained to be seen whether the promised surrenders would be made. Many of the malcontents found excuses to delay the fulfilment of their promises. Falkes de Bréauté, who felt his losses the more keenly because, without the grants which he had wrested from the Crown, he would relapse into his original insignificance,[4] ventured upon the bolder course of bidding defiance to the government. On being served with a writ to answer in the King's court for a disseisin, he told the summoner that if thirty pairs of writs were sent it was all one; he cared not for them. Writs in plenty were soon forthcoming to test his resolution. In the days of his power he had enriched himself at the expense of his neighbours,

---

[1] *Ann. Dunstaple.*   [2] See *Pat. Rolls*, ii., 417 ff.

[3] These appointments had been made by John, doubtless for military reasons. Mr. Turner (*Trans. Roy. Hist. Soc.*, N. S., xviii., p. 272) remarks: "In the early part of the thirteenth century the clerks of the Chancery evidently looked upon the custody of a castle as the chief work of a sheriff; for in the letters patent by which many sheriffs were appointed the King grants the custody of a castle 'together with' a county".

[4] For his origin see *Hist. des ducs*, p. 173. M. Paris, *Chron. Maj.*, iii., 88.

from the highest to the lowest, from the Earl Marshal to the petty freeholder and villein.[1]   At the Dunstable assizes, in the summer of 1224, he was found guilty of sixteen acts of disseisin.   The cases were tried in his absence; but the neighbouring castle of Bedford, which had been left him as a solatium for his losses, was in the hands of his brother and a garrison who boasted that they owed no allegiance to the King.[2]   William de Bréauté sallied forth and waylaid the Justiciars as they left Dunstable.   They were forewarned and forearmed, but one of their number was unfortunate enough to be taken; his captors carried him back to Bedford and put him in a dungeon to repent at leisure of his judgments.   It is probable that Falkes de Bréauté was guiltless of complicity in the outrage.   It came as a complete surprise to the Justiciar, who at the time was holding a Great Council (at Northampton) to arrange an expedition to Poitou; but the opportunity of crushing his most formidable adversary was too good to be neglected.   Falkes was summoned to appear before the King and answer for the conduct of his men. He failed to obey the first summons whereupon the Justiciar, without according him the usual time of grace, led all the available levies to the siege of Bedford Castle.   The garrison, when invited to surrender, returned a defiant answer and held out against an attack, conducted with all the resources of military science, from June 22 to August 14, only surrendering when the keep, to which they had finally retreated, was undermined and tottering to a fall. They had relied upon their master and his friends.   But the Earl of Chester and Peter des Roches, who were in secret sympathy with the besieged, were overawed by the Justiciar.   They obeyed his summons to attend the siege and, although they subsequently withdrew on the plea that they were no longer admitted to the royal Council, they did not venture to do more than protest their belief in the innocence of Falkes, who in the meantime lay concealed in Cheshire.[3]   The garrison, to the number of eighty, were hanged before the castle; but Falkes, in consideration of his former services and because his responsibility was doubtful, received a safe conduct to appear and plead his case.   He threw himself upon the mercy of the Crown and finally obtained permission to quit the

[1] *Cf.* Shirley, i., pp. 71, 105, 172.   [2] Wendover, iv., 95.
[3] *Ann. Dunstaple.* Shirley, i., pp. 224, 229, 233.   *Foedera*, i., 175.   Wendover, iv., 94 ff.   *Rot. Claus.*, 605 ff.

kingdom, leaving the whole of his property both land and movables, in the King's hand.   It was in vain that his friends prevailed upon Honorius to plead with the King on his behalf and theirs.   The Justiciar refused to modify his sentence against Falkes or to let the other malcontents resume their seats in the royal Council.   The disappointed mercenary repaired to Rome and laid his case before the Curia, with so much plausibility that the Pope was moved to renew his intercessions.   But an outburst of popular indignation confirmed the Justiciar in his attitude of resistance to the Holy See; and the death of Falkes (1226) prevented Honorius from pressing his request.[1]   With the fall of Bedford collapsed the party of feudal privilege.   Llewelyn, who had been bolder than his English associates in expressing sympathy for Falkes, continued for many years to be a thorn in the side of his brother-in-law and suzerain; and the movements of the barons were long watched with uneasiness by the court, every tournament being suspected as a pretext for the mustering of rebellion.   But the danger, if it existed, was averted by ceaseless vigilance; and the marriage of Eleanor, the King's sister, to William Marshal (1224) gave the most important of the baronial cliques a direct interest in the maintenance of royal authority.

Affairs of Gascony, 1216-25   It was in the continental possessions that the troubles of 1223-4 produced the most enduring and disastrous consequences.   The truce which John had concluded in 1214 ran out to its appointed term, and in 1220 was renewed for a period of four years.   But the time of grace did not enable the regency to put Aquitaine and Poitou in a posture of defence.   The difficulties to be overcome were such as disheartened the most loyal and energetic of lieutenants. Seneschal after seneschal threw up his thankless office in despair.[2] The feudatories were unmanageable and untrustworthy.   The communes, though genuinely attached to a suzerain who gave them easier terms than they could ever hope to obtain from France, were reluctant to incur expense for the English cause; they allowed their walls to fall into decay unless the King would come to the relief

[1] *Pat. Rolls*, ii., 461, 462, 478. *Foedera, u.s.* Shirley, i., pp. 313, 540, 543-5. Pauli, iii., 540-5.
[2] The list is as follows: 1217, the Archbishop of Bordeaux succeeds R. de Pontibus (*Pat. Rolls*, ii., 54); 1218, G. de Nevill replaces the Archbishop (*ibid.*, 152); 1220, Philip de Ulecote appointed at the request of G. de Nevill (*ibid.*, 249); 1221, Philip dies, and is succeeded by Hugh de Vivonia (*ibid.*, 275); Oct., 1221, Savaric de Mauleon appointed (*ibid.*, 304).

with a subsidy or a grant of tolls and customs.[1] They tolerated
no royal interference in their municipal affairs; but they expected
the King's Seneschal to fight their battles whenever they became
involved in quarrel with a neighbouring seigneur. Unable to impose taxation, and receiving from England only the most irregular
remittances, the Seneschal was usually penniless and invariably in
debt. Often he could only meet his current liabilities by negotiating
for a loan from Bordeaux or another commune; or by mortgaging
the customary dues of the Crown for many years in advance. In
the years 1219-20 the revenues accruing from Bordeaux were mortgaged to two several debtors of the Crown;[2] one Seneschal could
not leave La Rochelle till he had obtained from Hugh of Lusignan
a loan of 160 marks with which to pay his bill for board and lodging; another complains that for current expenses he had in hand only
the sum of £50.[3] A title thus defended might well be expected
to vanish at the first touch of an enemy; even though Philip
Augustus was stricken in years and weary of strife, it is surprising
that he forbore to use his advantage. The truth was that the King
of France had no mind to incur a second excommunication. The
guardianship of Honorius III. was not without material advantages
for England.

It was, however, impossible that Poitou should be saved. The La Marche
towns, from La Rochelle downwards, were linked by their commercial and An-
interests to the Touraine and other lands of French allegiance;[4] an goulême
English seneschal complains that the barons of the province respected
him "no more than a horse-boy".[5] The English government depended for the defence of Poitou upon the Lusignans; but their
fidelity was at the best of times precarious. The old Count of
La Marche had departed to join the crusade of Damietta, from
which he was fated never to return. His son Hugh played a double
game, corresponding on confidential terms with the English government, and meanwhile using every means in his power to molest the
Queen-mother Isabelle who had returned to administer her paternal
inheritance of Angoulême. Unable to defend herself by other
means the Queen, in the winter of 1219-20, married Hugh notwith-

[1] *Pat. Rolls*, ii., 242. *Foedera*, i., 173.
[2] *Pat. Rolls*, ii., 203, 243.   [3] Shirley, i., pp. 44, 55, 318.
[4] *Pat. Rolls*, ii., 232; *Foedera*, i., 192, showing that the money of Tours was
current in Poitou and Aquitaine.
[5] " Nec meamplius pretiunt quam si essem unum garciolum " (Shirley, i., p. 37).

14

standing that he was the son of the man whom she had cast off for John's sake, and was already betrothed to her own daughter.[1] This marriage, which she assured her son was contracted rather in his interest than in her own, soon multiplied the difficulties of the English party. The newly wedded pair demanded that Isabelle's dower, which in law reverted to the Crown upon her second marriage, should be left in their possession ; and would not surrender Joanna's marriage portion of Oleron and Saintes.[2] A war ensued, which was protracted long after the original pretexts on both sides had disappeared. In spite of frequent mediations on the part of Rome, there was little doubt that the rulers of La Marche and Angoulême would transfer their allegiance to France at the earliest opportunity.

Death of Philip Augustus, 1223

So the situation stood when the death of Philip Augustus filled France with mourning and awakened in England a passing hope that the waning fortunes of the Plantagenets might be restored in Aquitaine. Chimerical as it now seems, this hope was not surprising in those who remembered how much this King, the child of fate, had done by his personal influence and exploits to undermine the power of his rivals. In his private habits, bearing, and appearance, Philip Augustus was the reverse of a hero of romance : prematurely bald, red faced, a great eater and drinker ; inordinately given to luxury and loose-living, a fox-like politician who loved the base-born better than the noble, and rejoiced at every feud among his nobles ; prone to wrath, but easily soothed ; timid in spite of all his military experience—such is the unflattering portrait drawn by one of his subjects and admirers. Yet, the writer adds, and the praise comes more convincingly in the midst of so much criticism, the old King was sage in counsel, full of resource, a man of his word, a swift and upright judge ; though his hate was bitter no man could taunt him with the crime of John ; he never assassinated prisoners.[3] The son of a King who all but gained the honours of a saint, the grandfather of one to whom those honours were accorded by general acclamation, Philip presents a smirched and sordid aspect when his character is critically surveyed. But of all the Capet Kings there is none to whom the French monarchy and nation owed so great a debt. The expulsion of the English from the northern provinces,

[1] Boissonade, *Comites Engolismenses*, p. 23. Shirley, i., p. 114.
[2] Shirley, i., pp. 115, 133, 140, 224. *Foedera*, i., 161.
[3] *Chron. Turonense.*

the repulse of the German and Fleming from the eastern frontier,
the organisation of the royal demesne on a plan of which Henry II.
need not have been ashamed, are three feats which have sufficed to
give him a lasting reputation.

Much however remained to be accomplished before the King of Louis
France could call himself completely master of his realm.   In the attacks
north there were still the fiefs of Brittany, Flanders and Cham- Aquitaine,
pagne, friendly for the moment but powerful enough to shake the 1224
royal power to its base if they saw fit to act in concert; in the
south the Albigensians of Toulouse had still the means and the
spirit to resist the crusaders of the *Langue d'Oil*; and there were
many in Normandy, Maine and Anjou whose thoughts turned
regretfully to the days of Plantagenet supremacy.   Hubert de
Burgh, though conscious that English resources were wholly inadequate to a protracted war, thought it necessary to assert the
hereditary pretensions of his ward.   He invited Louis VIII. to surrender Anjou, Maine and Normandy; and summoned the inhabitants of those provinces to return to their natural allegiance.[1]   The
audacious challenge was taken more seriously than it was meant.
For the moment Louis returned an evasive answer.   He had still to
assure his position, and he was immersed in the preparations for an
Albigensian crusade.   But when the commencement of 1224 brought
with it a truce between the Papacy and Raymond of Toulouse, the
new King turned the crusade in the direction of Poitou.   He
entered the province at the time when the Justiciar's attention was
engrossed by the siege of Bedford.   The Count of La Marche had
been already won for France; less important barons only waited
for the King's approach to make their peace; Niort and St. Jean
d'Angely surrendered tamely; La Rochelle the natural metropolis
of Poitou, though stoutly defended by the Seneschal and a body of
militia from Bayonne, was starved into surrender in three weeks.
Rumour said that the rebellion of Falkes de Bréauté had been
timed to suit the plans of France; but there is good reason for
believing that it was an accidental coincidence which gave Louis the
opportunity of pursuing his conquests unopposed.[2]

His designs were not confined to Poitou.   His followers exhorted

[1] *Foedera*, i., 170.
[2] For the campaign of Poitou see Petit-Dutaillis, pp. 226 ff.   Falkes was imprisoned, after his banishment, by Louis.   Shirley, i., p. 242.

Further designs of Louis

him to leave the English no foothold on French soil, and their persuasions fell on willing ears. But he soon discovered that the Gascons had little love for France. A force which he sent across the Garonne received the submission of St. Emilion and La Reole, but found the men of Bordeaux resolutely hostile, and returned without risking an attack upon that city.[1] Neither Bordeaux nor any other Gascon commune was adequately fortified or garrisoned; and if Louis had advanced with his main army the odds were in his favour. But the summer was now far advanced; the remonstrances of Honorius could no longer be ignored; and Louis decided to suspend hostilities. No one doubted his intention to resume the war at the first opportunity; and rumours were afloat, which he did not scruple to encourage, to the effect that he had received from the English rebels an invitation to revive his claims upon the Crown.[2]

French policy of Hubert de Burgh

Much against his will the Justiciar was driven to warlike preparations. From the Great Council he obtained a fifteenth of rents and chattels for the expenses of recovering Poitou; in March, 1225, the King's brother Richard was despatched to Gascony to act as viceroy with the help of a council of veteran advisers;[3] alliances were formed with Raymond of Toulouse and Pierre Mauclerc of Brittany;[4] the pirates of Gascony and the Cinque Ports were unleashed upon the ships of France and Poitou. But an unexpected stroke of fortune made it superfluous to follow up these hostile demonstrations. Louis VIII., who had turned his attention once more to the Albigensian Crusade, was stricken, after capturing Avignon, with a fatal sickness at the moment when the final reduction of the heretics seemed assured. The Crown of France devolved upon Louis IX., a boy of twelve years of age; his mother, the heroic Blanche of Castile, found herself confronted by perils not unlike those which menaced the English Regency. She was compelled to lean for support upon a party of the baronage led by the half-brother of her husband, Philip Hurepel of Boulogne; but the arrogance of Philip intensified the dissatisfaction of another party of which Pierre Mauclerc and Thibault of Champagne were

[1] Shirley, i., pp. 236, 239. For the wider hopes of Louis see the epilogue to the *Philippeis* of Le Breton.
[2] Shirley, i., p. 241.
[3] *Pat. Rolls*, ii., 516, 527, 538, 560, 585.
[4] He belonged to the House of Dreux; obtained Brittany by his marriage with Alais, daughter of Constance by her third husband, Guy of Thouars.

the most important members. Both had quarrelled with Louis VIII.; both were inclined to take advantage of his son's minority; they readily entered on a correspondence with the King of England. De Burgh, by a judicious distribution of bribes and promises, blew up the flame of discontent in all the newly conquered provinces of France. He was so far successful that the Queen-regent, after purchasing the good will of Brittany and Champagne at their own price, showed every disposition to avoid the risks entailed by her husband's policy of annexation.

The Justiciar was not less fortunate in his dealings with domestic enemies. At the beginning of 1227 he proclaimed the King free from the restrictions which had been put on him in 1223; one object of the proclamation became apparent when it was followed by the dismissal of Peter des Roches from his position as the royal tutor. The bishop attempted to retaliate by fostering an agitation against his rival; and, to the perplexity of the nation, the King's brother, Richard of Cornwall, took the lead in taxing the Justiciar with treason and conspiracy.[1] But a timely bribe reduced the prince to silence; and the restless Poitevin left England to take part in the crusade of Frederick II. The Justiciar remained in sole possession of the royal ear. Fall of Peter des Roches

But the favour of Henry III. was more easily acquired than retained. His affection was reserved for those who flattered his vanity and ministered to his caprices. He had few ideas of policy; but to these he was obstinately wedded; and they were such as no honest minister could accept and no skill could render popular. In his own age Henry enjoyed the reputation of a pious fainéant, and he is placed by Dante in the region of purgatory reserved for simpletons and children. But he was cursed with an imagination which ran riot in day-dreams of the most fantastic order. He saw no reason why he should not by a few lucky strokes recover the lost provinces in France; he thought it possible that he might become the founder of a new imperial dynasty. By nature the most unpractical of men, he delighted to pit himself against the past masters of diplomacy; nor could repeated failures and disgraces convince him of his incapacity for war. Though easily managed by a favourite he was impervious to argument; though a coward when confronted by determined opposition, he was quick Schemes of Henry III.

---

[1] Wendover, iv., 139-141, with a good deal of obvious embroidery. Another object was, however, to raise money. The King now could, and did, sell confirmations of the grants of his predecessors (Norgate, *Minority*, pp. 265-267, and *supra*, p. 403).

to forget his fears and promises. No warnings could teach him
caution, no rebukes could impair his self-assurance. Naturally
susceptible to external impressions, he developed a love of splendour
which no considerations of prudence could restrain, and sought his
favourites by preference among the brilliant adventurers who flocked
to his court from Poitou and Provence. The best side of his
character was shown in his scrupulous observance of religious duties,
and in the gratitude which he always cherished towards the Papacy
for the protection accorded to him in his early years. But his
devotion and his gratitude found expression in a subservience to
Papal interests which contributed at least as much as his injudicious
foreign policy to alienate the affections of his subjects.

The King
plans a
French
War, 1229
It was not long before the difference in the views of the
Justiciar and his master led to an open quarrel. At the Christmas
feast of 1228 the King was visited by Norman envoys soliciting
assistance in rebellion. Under the influence of De Burgh he returned an indecisive answer; but in the following year he insisted
upon preparing for a great campaign. The measure of the King's
diplomacy is given by the terms which he demanded from the
French Regency as the price of his forbearance. He asked for the
restoration of Poitou, Anjou, Touraine and Brittany; and for so
much of Normandy as would give him a clear line of communications between the north coast and the Loire. The envoys were
instructed, in the event of these terms proving unacceptable, to
offer the hand of the King's sister to Louis IX., with the proviso
that Anjou and Maine should be settled on her and should return
to the King of England if she died without issue.[1] The Queen-
regent, who was then in the act of signing a peace with Raymond
of Toulouse under which she secured his friendship in the present
and the future reversion of his dominions for her third son, felt
herself at liberty to treat the English proposals with the contempt
which they deserved; and Henry proceeded to cast about him for
allies. He applied to Raymond of Toulouse, apparently unconscious
of the straits to which the Count was now reduced; and saw no
difficulty in the way of negotiating simultaneously with the Count
of Brittany and with Ferrand of Flanders, whose release from
captivity had been the death-blow to the most cherished ambitions

[1] Shirley, i., p. 350.

of Pierre Mauclerc.[1] The King's expedition was arranged for the Michaelmas of 1229 ; but at the appointed time when the troops had assembled at Portsmouth it was discovered that the ships collected for the passage were too few. The King flew into a passion, called the Justiciar a hoary traitor, accused him of taking bribes from France, rushed on him with a drawn sword, and was with difficulty restrained by the spectators. No doubt the Justiciar had welcomed the excuse for delaying an imprudent enterprise. But the charge of wilful neglect can be disproved. He had taken special steps to secure a larger fleet than was usually required for such expeditions ; and it was not for want of diligence that his arrangements failed.[2] Old soldier though he was he lacked the qualities of a successful quartermaster ; and at least one other occasion is recorded on which he ruined an expedition by similar mismanagement.

The invasion of France was necessarily postponed. But, in the spring of 1230, with the help of ships from Cologne, Flanders, and Friesland, a fleet upwards of 300 strong was assembled ;[3] and the army landed without mishap upon the coast of Brittany. The moment was not unfavourable ; for the barons of France were more concerned to fight with one another than with the English. The feudal host which Blanche had collected to guard the passage of the Loire, refused to serve beyond the legal term of forty days. Philip of Boulogne and his partisans left the camp to carry fire and sword through the territories of Champagne ; and the Queen-mother felt constrained to follow them in the hope of restoring peace. Throughout July and early in August[4] the English had only to fear such resistance as might be offered by the royalists of the western provinces. Little use was made of the opportunity. The Norman rebels renewed their invitation in more urgent terms ; but the Justiciar, anxious to limit the war which he had failed to prevent, insisted that the King should do nothing before he had paid a visit to Aquitaine. The army marched through Poitou

Henry invades Poitou, 1230

---

[1] *Foedera*, i., 194, 196. Pierre had hoped to obtain Flanders.
[2] *Pat. Rolls*, iii., 110. The Cinque Ports had covenanted to send double the ordinary number of ships.
[3] *Ibid.*, 370, 374.
[4] Blanche and Louis came to Poitou in mid-August. See their Itinerary in Bouquet, xxi., pref. Their peace with the rebels in Arbois de Jubainville, *Comtes, etc, de Champagne*, v., 2060.

without resistance, but also without winning support of any value. Hugh of Lusignan and the Viscount of Thouars had been lately confirmed in their French sympathies by new grants from the Queen-mother,[1] and their example decided the attitude of smaller men. After a short stay in Gascony the King returned to Brittany under a truce. His remaining funds were spent in a round of feasts and pageantries at Nantes; "in the manner of Englishmen" the soldiers drank "as deep as though every day were Christmas". At the end of September, having vainly importuned the Exchequer for supplies, Henry discovered that ill-health necessitated his re-

Later course of Breton War, 1230-4

turn.[2] He left the Earls of Chester and Pembroke with a small force to support the Count of Brittany. But Pierre Mauclerc was hampered by rebellion and desertion among his own subjects, to whom he was hateful both as an alien and as a tyrant.[3] In the summer of 1231 he was compelled to conclude a three years' truce with France. The truce ran for the agreed term, and was almost immediately followed by the conclusion of a lasting peace. When, in 1234, Pierre Mauclerc thought of resuming the war he was enthusiastically assisted with troops and money by the King of England.[4] But the Count was soon turned from his intention by a French invasion of Brittany. The young Louis marched through the length and breadth of Brittany; although he lost his baggage in an ambush, he reduced the Count's supporters to the last pitch of distress. Pierre Mauclerc resigned himself to the inevitable; his treaty of August, 1234, was for Brittany the beginning of a closer dependence on the Crown of France;[5] De Burgh's contempt for the Breton alliance was more than justified by the event.

Papal Encroach-ments, 1229-31

But before this collapse of his master's policy the Justiciar had fallen from power, overthrown by the combined influence of the Papacy and of the foreign favourites. It was an evil day for England when the fiery Gregory IX. succeeded to the placable Honorius (1227). The new Pope was over eighty years of age, but he had a youth's aversion from half-measures. He feared the designs of

[1] Shirley, i., p. 370.
[2] *Ibid.*, pp. 382, 385. In i., pp. 368-386, we have by far the best materials for the history of this campaign.
[3] For the desertions see *Layettes du Tresor*, ii., 2128-2139. Pierre had been excommunicated for flaying a priest alive (*Ann. Dunst., s.a.* 1229).
[4] Wendover, iv., 224; *Foedera*, i., 211, 212. Shirley, i., p. 441.
[5] So Wendover, iv., 316.

Frederick II.; he was determined at all costs, and on any pretext, to destroy the Emperor's power. Immediately on his accession Gregory excommunicated the Emperor for unnecessary delay in starting a Crusade; in 1229, when Frederick had brilliantly fulfilled his vow by securing the cession of Jerusalem, the Pope declared war upon him as the ally and confederate of infidels.[1] The churches of Europe were at once invited to aid the Holy See with subsidies. To England the Pope sent one of his own chaplains, Stephen of Anagni, who was commissioned to demand a tithe of clerical property. There was no little murmuring when the demand was presented to the Great Council. The right of taxing the English clergy had been claimed by the Papacy on one previous occasion only (1184); and Pope Lucius had then experienced from Henry II. and the barons a rebuff before which it had seemed advisable to yield. The barons were now, as ever, reluctant to admit that lay fiefs, whether held by the clergy or their own class, could be taxed for the benefit of the Universal Church. For their own part they declined to make any contribution. But the clergy they could not protect; for the King was a consenting party to Gregory's proposal. The tithe was in fact the bribe which Henry had offered to prevent the Pope from confirming an unsuitable Archbishop-elect in the see of Canterbury, left vacant by the death of Stephen Langton.[2] Stephen of Anagni was therefore allowed to collect the tax on the basis of a new and stricter valuation. But there was worse to come. The necessities of the Curia had suggested a new and nefarious trade in presentations. During the next year or two the bishops were repeatedly forbidden to institute to any vacant benefices until they had provided for long lists of Papal nominees, chiefly Italians, who had seldom the intention of taking up their residence in England. It was in vain for the bishops and the defrauded patrons to complain. The latter at length took the law into their own hands. They formed a secret society by means of which they organised attacks upon foreign clerks and the barns of " provided " absentees; two Papal couriers were attacked near Dover and one of them was killed. Threatening letters were sent to those bishops who had incurred the suspicion of abetting the aliens; the sheriffs found it impossible to protect alien property; and in some cases the rioters justified their outrages

Riots against Beneficed Aliens, 1231

---

[1] Potthast, 8430, 8431.   [2] Wendover, iv., 170, 185, 200.

14*

by producing letters which purported to be warrants under the royal seal.   One of the leaders, Robert Twenge, better known by the pseudonym of William Wither, was a knight of some position. Many of the superior clergy were thought to countenance the movement; and the Justiciar could not be induced to employ stern measures of repression.[1]   He may have connived at some of the outrages.   That he had done so, and that he was responsible for the forged warrants, was positively affirmed by his old rival Peter des Roches, who at this juncture returned to England, completely rehabilitated by the active part which he had taken in the Crusade and by the influence which he had acquired during a subsequent residence at Rome.[2]   These charges, if substantiated, were in Henry's estimation more than sufficient to call for the Justiciar's dismissal. But there was another charge as well.   The government was seriously embarrassed by the want of money.   The revenue scarcely met the usual and indispensable items of expenditure; the military operations which were rendered necessary by the contumacy of Llewelyn could not be prosecuted with effect for want of funds.   The true causes of the King's poverty are probably to be found in his own extravagance, and in the burden of the debt remaining over from the French campaign.   But the Bishop of Winchester taxed the Justiciar with dishonest or incompetent management of the finances; and the King caught at the suggestion that the treasury should be placed in other hands.   It was committed to the care of Peter des Rievaux, the nephew, or as scandal asserted, the son of the bishop; the new treasurer was immediately invested with the sheriffdoms of twenty-one shires, with the wardenships of innumerable castles, and with the office of chief escheator; and thus every grade in the financial administration, from the highest to the lowest, was filled with his dependents.[3]

Hubert de Burgh accused

Fall of Hubert de Burgh, July, 1232

Within a few weeks of this court revolution the Justiciar was dismissed, and required to give an account of all the sums which had passed through his hands since the death of the Earl Marshal. A long list of charges was raked together with the help of his private enemies.   Some were of a character so ridiculous as to suggest that even a prejudiced tribunal would find it no easy

---

[1] Wendover, iv., 228 ff., 245, 263.   *Annals of Burton* and *Dunstaple.*   *Pat. Rolls,* iii., 493.   *Chron. Maj.,* iii., 217.   Auvray, *Registres Greg. IX.,* i., 503.
[2] *Ann. Dunst.,* 126.   [3] *Pat. Rolls,* iii., 486-91.

matter to condemn the fallen favourite. It was alleged that he had seduced his wife before their marriage—a charge which on a later occasion was also brought against Montfort; and that having abstracted from the treasury a ring which made the wearer invincible he had sent it as a present to Llewelyn.[1] But against the graver charges De Burgh made but a lame defence. His complicity with the anti-Papal rioters seems to have been established; he declined to produce his official accounts on the plea that King John had guaranteed him a perpetual immunity from audits; and when this plea was waived aside he fled to sanctuary at St. Edmund's. By the King's order he was dragged forth and brought back to London with his feet tied beneath a horse's belly. But the Bishop of London insisted that he should be restored to sanctuary; the barons, even his old enemy the Earl of Chester, took his part from jealousy of the bishop; and the common people, with the exception of the Londoners who had never forgotten or forgiven the execution of Constantine FitzAthulf, showed their sympathy in no equivocal fashion. A common smith, when ordered to fetter the Justiciar, declared that he would never lay hands upon the man whose victory at Sandwich had restored England to the English.[2] De Burgh was indeed starved out of sanctuary and sentenced, as one who had confessed his guilt, to forfeit his chattels and the grants which he had received from the Crown. But his other lands were spared, four earls, of whom one was Richard of Cornwall, offered themselves as sureties for his good behaviour and he was allowed to live in honourable confinement at Devizes. It is worthy of notice that the King thought best to publish a statement of the charges upon which De Burgh had been disgraced, and an apology for his own conduct.[3]

But for the future Henry was resolved to rule through ministers and counsellors upon whose pliability he could count with confidence. Such men he expected to find among the foreign favourites; at the Christmas Council of 1232 nearly every post of consequence, whether in the household or in the administration, was conferred upon the Poitevins whom Peter des Roches had imported for that purpose. An Englishman was found, in the person of one Stephen Segrave, a knight of no character or consideration, to

The King's Favourites

---

[1] Wendover, iv., 245-8. *Chron. Maj.*, iii., 223.   [2] *Chron. Maj.*, iii., 227.
[3] *Foedera*, i., 207.   Gregory IX. asked for Hubert's release (Auvray, i., 588).

fill the office of Justiciar;[1] but that office was now shorn of its original powers, and no one minister was allowed a position of pre-eminence. The new system was intended to be autocratic; but in fact the rule of one minister gave place to that of the King's Secret Council. Independence, however much he might desire it, was impossible for Henry. Those whom he had designed to use as instruments became his masters, and did so with the less difficulty because their advancement created an irreparable breach between the King and barons.

Richard Marshal in Opposition, 1233-4

The latter were now led by Richard Marshal, the Regent's second son, who had succeeded to the earldom of Pembroke in 1231. The Earl made himself the spokesman of the general discontent, and in the name of the baronage demanded that the foreigners should be dismissed. The answer, delivered by the mouth of Peter des Roches, was to the effect that the King had need of foreigners to protect him from the treachery of his natural subjects; and it produced the more alarm because Henry, following in the footsteps of his father, was importing mercenaries to guard his person and the royal castles. The Earl Marshal withdrew from the court, and formed a league of which the members were pledged to fight even to the death against their common enemies.[2] The league was for defence alone; and the members were studiously loyal in their bearing towards the King, from whom they demanded nothing save the removal of the favourites. But a conference, which had been arranged to take place at London on 1st August, 1233, fell through because the Marshal received a warning from his sister, the Earl of Cornwall's wife, that there was a plot for his arrest. He fled to his lands on the Welsh border and prepared to resist attack. The King followed him, laid siege to Usk castle, and harried the lands not only of the Marshal but of all who were supposed to be his supporters. They offered to stand their trial if they might have the judgment of their peers; but on being told that they must submit to the judgment of the royal Justices, they no longer hesitated to resist. To give their cause a more popular complexion they sent an armed band to Devizes, and brought De Burgh in triumph to the Marshal's castle at Striguil.[3] Meanwhile the Marshal concluded an alliance with Llewelyn, and called upon

---

[1] Wendover, iv., 245, 263. [2] *Ibid.*, 265, 266. [3] Wykes, 42.

his Irish vassals to arm against the government.[1] The King led the feudal array, or as much of it as would answer the summons, to attack the Welsh lands of the Marshal, and filled the castle of the Marches with Poitevin and Breton routiers. But the royal garrisons were afraid to stir beyond the walls of the castles. The Marshal and Llewelyn were successful in several skirmishes; their combined forces captured and sacked the town of Shrewsbury; and the King found it advisable to evacuate the Marches. Even in England he was not safe from insult. The lands of his Justiciar were attacked and harried almost before his eyes by the sympathisers of the Marshal. Although the majority of the barons remained neutral they could not be trusted. In the spring of 1234 Henry gave way before the remonstrances of the bishops. He empowered them to make what terms they could with the Marshal, and he dismissed the Poitevins.

These concessions were made on April 9th. A week later the Earl Marshal was no more. He had crossed to Ireland with the object of rallying his supporters and making war upon the Irish loyalists. But the enterprise was too hard for him; about the 1st of April he was defeated and captured in the course of a battle, which he had been induced by treacherous advice to deliver against superior forces; and on the 16th he died from the effects of his wounds. There could be no better proof of the unpopularity into which the King had fallen than the fact that Church and people alike regarded the Marshal as a martyr, and those who had resisted him as murderers. Henry may be pardoned for the gratitude which he displayed towards his Irish supporters for their victory.[2] But he was compelled to disguise his true sentiments. The Primate, Edmund Rich, threatened him with excommunication unless he would dismiss the favourites who had been responsible for the war. He yielded to the threat, and sought to atone for the past by a persecution of Peter des Rievaulx and Stephen Segrave. They were brought to trial on charges connected with their official conduct; the former, though a clerk, was imprisoned in the Tower until he procured the intercession of the Primate; and the Justiciar only escaped a like sentence by the payment of a heavy composition. Peter des Roches was protected by his ecclesiastical dignity; but in

Edmund Rich remonstrates, 1234

---

[1] *Tewkesbury Annals*, 91.
[2] Sweetman, *Calendar*, 313 (Letter of thanks to Richard de Burgh).

1235 he left the country to help the Pope in the wars of Italy; although he was allowed to return in the following year and remained in England till his death (1238), he mixed no more in English politics. The King accepted Edmund Rich as his chief counsellor, and went through a formal reconciliation with the party of the Marshal. It seemed as though the policy of Hubert de Burgh would triumph in spite of his disgrace and the death of his lieutenant.[1]

The Provençals and Savoyards
But the King's repentance was of short duration. Stephen Segrave soon returned to favour; Richard Seward, who had been the boldest supporter of the Marshal, was banished on the pretext of a quarrel which he entertained against the Earl of Cornwall; Ralph Nevill, the Bishop of Chichester, who had received the Great Seal in the time of De Burgh (1226) and had managed to retain it through all the court revolutions of the last few years, was ordered in 1236 to surrender his office. He refused to do so, affirming that he could only be dismissed by the consent of the Great Council from which he had received his office.[2] But, two years later, he found it necessary to submit; and with his departure from the Chancery disappeared the most effectual check upon the royal extravagance, an evil which from year to year assumed more formidable dimensions. The marriage of Isabella the King's sister to Frederic II., which was celebrated in 1235, and the King's own marriage in the following year to Eleanor of Provence, were celebrated with a splendour which made heavy calls on the Exchequer, and brought no compensating advantages. They were expected by the King to improve his position for new attacks on France; but the Emperor himself was in no small need of assistance, and the Provençal connection saddled the King with the responsibility, which was more unwelcome to his subjects than to himself, of providing for the needy kinsmen of his wife. The Savoyards and Provençals rapidly became as unpopular and as influential as the Poitevins had been in the past. The most obnoxious were the four uncles of the Queen: William, Bishop Elect of Valence, Thomas, Peter, and Boniface of Savoy.[3] The career of William was a brief

---

[1] *Ann. Tewkesb.*, 92, 93. Sweetman, *Calendar*, 313, 314. Wendover, iv., 309 ff. *Chron. Maj.*, iii., 306, 309, 378, 439.

[2] *Chron. Maj.*, iii., 364. A curious statement, which does not represent the true state of the law.

[3] See Mugnier, *Les Savoyards en Angleterre* (Chambéry, 1890); who, however, produces little material which is not to be found in Matthew Paris.

one; he came to England in 1236 and died in 1239. Thomas of Savoy was known merely as an occasional visitor and recipient of royal grants until the death of his wife, the Countess Jeanne deprived him of all claims on Flanders; his residence in England commenced in the year 1244. But his brothers Peter and Boniface were, by that date, already established in the highest positions which it was in the King's power to bestow. The former was in 1241 created Earl of Richmond; the latter succeeded Edmund Rich in the see of Canterbury (1243). Boniface was, of the four, the least able but also the most honest. Elevated to a position for which his temperament appeared to be even more unsuitable than his training, he endeavoured to guide himself by the best obtainable advice, and in the exercise of his primatial functions showed an energy which, if it occasionally degenerated into violence, was at least inspired by creditable motives. He allied himself with the reforming party in the English church, and, in spite of frequent periods of absence from England, became an energetic champion of ecclesiastical liberties against both King and Pope.[1] The others, though endowed with qualities of no mean order, were essentially adventurers, who regarded England as a stepping stone to Papal favour or Italian principalities, and made it their first object to involve England in the conflicts of the Papacy and Empire. Their efforts were seconded by Pierre d'Aigueblanche, a Savoyard clerk who came to England in the train of William of Valence, attracted the King's favour, and rose to be Bishop of Hereford. To his advice contemporaries attributed some ingenious artifices by which the clergy were mulcted for the benefit of King and Pope; and the diplomatic missions connected with Henry's most questionable designs were entrusted to his charge.[2]

From the moment of the King's marriage the Queen's relatives Outcry and compatriots became the subject of complaints. Their removal against from the counsels of the King was demanded at the Christmas feast Foreigners of 1236, and again in the following year; upon their shoulders was cast the responsibility for all the evils which the lax administration of past years had fostered, and for the increasing deference which

[1] See, besides Matthew Paris, the references in *Mon. Francisc.*, i., 325. Wykes, 235.   *Ann. Dunst.*, 189.   *Burton Annals*, 405.
[2] *Ann. Tewkesb.*, 117, 179.   *Ann. Dunst.*, 199.   *Burton Annals*, 349; and Matthew Paris.

the King displayed towards the Pope's extravagant demands. There was some reason in the outcry. It was not to be expected that the aliens should pay attention to the domestic ills of England; or that they should counsel resistance to the Pope from whose favour they had so much to gain in their own country. But the prejudice against foreigners as such obscured the more important question of principle which was at stake. It was not enough that the King should consult his native subjects. A Stephen Segrave was a more pernicious counsellor than any Savoyard. The interests of the nation could only be secured by providing that the King should put himself in the hands of ministers acceptable to the baronage and nation. Amongst the barons and the superior clergy, on whom alone devolved the duty of guarding the national interests, there was no leader capable of recognising a

The National Party

truth which to us is obvious enough. The Archbishop, Edmund Rich, was a saint and a scholar, anxious to fulfil the political duties of his rank, and keenly alive to the abuses which were generated by the encroachments of the Curia, but incapable of suggesting practical remedies or of offering resistance to the united forces of the Crown and Rome. Richard of Cornwall, to whom the laity looked for guidance, was divided between his detestation of foreigners and his anxiety to protect the interests of the dynasty. By a curious irony of fate the one man who might have led the opposition laboured under the same suspicion as the Savoyards and Poitevins.

Early History of De Montfort

Simon de Montfort, Earl of Leicester, belonged to a French family; the estates to which he owed his title had come to his grandfather by marriage with an heiress of the Beaumont line about 1173, but had been forfeited after the loss of Normandy; and his father, the conqueror of the Albigensians, had lived on the worst of terms with John. The younger Simon, a second son and left without a maintenance upon his father's death, had obtained from Henry III. a pension in 1228, and two years later was admitted to his ancestral earldom. He became a counsellor of the King, and about 1236 began to be regarded as one of the alien mischief makers.[1] When, in 1238, he married the King's sister. Eleanor, there was a general outburst of indignation. Richard of Cornwall and his party protested that the match should never have

[1] Shirley, i., pp. 362, 401. *Pat. Rolls*, iii., 325. *Chron. Maj.*, iii., 369, 412.

been made without the consent of the Great Council; and when Richard allowed himself to be reconciled with his brother-in-law he was denounced by his former adherents as a turn-coat. The Earl of Leicester was therefore indirectly responsible for the collapse of the baronial opposition; no one dreamed that he would ever join it. Yet there was already considerable friction between himself and the King. In the year 1239 they quarrelled over a debt for Quarrels which the Earl vouched Henry as his surety, while the King denied with all liability.[1] The dispute came to such a point that the King passed from accusations of fraud to others of a yet more disgraceful character; he alleged that the Earl had seduced the Lady Eleanor before their marriage. The best answer to both charges is that the Earl demanded and was denied a trial. Only the remonstrances of Richard of Cornwall saved him from arbitrary arrest and imprisonment; he was ordered out of the presence, and left the country in high indignation. The quarrel appears to have been of a purely personal character, although some have conjectured that questions of high policy lay concealed beneath the ostensible issues, and that Simon was disgraced because he had supported the imperial as against the Papal interest in the royal councils.[2] The conjecture is indeed supported by the fact that Simon, in the course of a journey to Rome, undertaken to procure a dispensation for his marriage, had paid a visit to the Emperor. But the Earl was thought to be, as late as the year 1237, a pillar of the Papal cause.[3] He was the brother-in-law of Frederic, and no doubt solicited the Emperor's good offices with Henry III. Of any political alliance between the two most vigorous personalities of the thirteenth century there is no evidence. The Earl neither provoked nor avenged his disgrace by attacking the King's policy. After their rupture he made a crusading vow, which he had taken some years previously, the excuse for a temporary exile. In company with Richard of Cornwall and many other magnates he departed for the Holy Land in the summer of 1240. The Crusade, otherwise uneventful, gave him the opportunity of earning his first distinction as a statesman and soldier. The barons of the Kingdom of Jerusalem begged the Emperor to

[1] See the Earl's statement, printed in Bémont, p. 333. Also *Chron. Maj.*, iii., 566. The King ultimately admitted a part of the liability.
[2] Pauli, *Simon de Montfort*, p. 40 (Eng. tr.).
[3] Bliss, *Calendar*, i., 167. The Earl not to start on Crusade till he receives a special mandate from the Pope, as his counsel is necessary for the safety of England.

let them take the Earl for regent of the kingdom during the minority of the young Conrad. The petition led to no result; but it proves that the reputation of the Earl stood higher in the Holy Land than in his adopted country.[1]

The Legate Otho, 1237-41

While the political opposition was thus divided and brought to a halt, it fared no better with the clergy. Either because he felt the need of papal support or because he wished to show his reverence for the Holy See, the King had begged the Pope, in 1236, to send him a legate;[2] and the Cardinal Otho accordingly made his appearance in the following year. He met with a sumptuous reception from the court, and his personal bearing did something to allay the suspicions with which the events of recent years had taught the nation to regard all Roman envoys. But it needed very little to provoke hostile demonstrations. At a council of the clergy, held in London during November, 1237, the legate found it necessary to ask the King for a body-guard, and a visit which he paid to Oxford ended in a formidable riot. The legate's cook, who was also his cousin and possibly inflated with the pride of family, threw hot water in the face of an Irish scholar, who stood at the kitchen door begging for a meal and would not be denied. The wounded honour of the University was signally avenged. The scholars rang the great bell of the city and marched in full force to attack Oseney Abbey, in which the legate had his lodging. Otho, robed in full pontificals, fled to the steeple of the abbey church, while the scholars raged outside the gates. "Where is the usurer, the simoniac?" they cried, and his life was for some hours in considerable danger. Luckily the King, who was at Abingdon, heard of the riot in time to send the legate a sufficient guard, under the protection of which he escaped at nightfall from the neighbourhood of Oxford. The only victim of the scholars was the cook, whom a Welshman killed with an arrow aimed through an opening in the gates.[3] Opinions differed, we are told, as to the conduct of the scholars. But Grosseteste, the Bishop of Lincoln, took their part; and, when some of the ringleaders were thrown into the Tower, announced that he would excommunicate without exception all who made themselves parties to so gross a violation of the privilege

[1] Pauli, i., p. 637. [2] Bliss, *Calendar*, i., 157. Auvray, ii., 467.
[3] *Chron. Maj.*, iii., 482 ff. *Ann. Tewkesb.*, 107. *Ann. Dunst.*, 147. *Oseney Annals*, 85.

of clergy. The legate was eventually compelled to content himself with exacting masses for his cousin's soul, and a public penance from the members of the University. Otho's subsequent conduct did nothing to abate the animosity which this episode had roused against him. He demanded in his master's name extensive contributions from the bishops and religious houses. He assumed in the King's counsels the same degree of influence which Gualo and Pandulph had exercised during the minority; and Henry was weak enough to acknowledge that he had neither the right nor the desire to act in anything against the wishes of the Holy See. The last act of Otho, before he left the country, was to demand from the clergy a fifth part of their rents and movables. The monasteries, with few exceptions, submitted to this unprecedented burden. But the bishops mustered courage to excuse themselves upon the ground of poverty; and in at least one part of England the inferior clergy made a spirited protest. The rectors of Berkshire circulated a manifesto denying that the Roman Church had any claim to tribute from the sister churches; the Pope, they said, was the patron and protector, not the suzerain, of other ecclesiastical authorities; he should, like other bishops, maintain himself from his own revenues.[1] In spite of such arguments the legate obtained considerable sums by playing upon the hopes and fears of individuals among the bishops and the secular clergy. When he left England, at the commencement of 1241, it was said that he took with him more gold and silver than he left in the country, apart from the plate and jewels of the churches. Nor was he the only instrument of extortion. A certain Pietro Rosso went the round of the religious houses in 1240 demanding, in the Pope's name, a benevolence; the King answered the complaints of several priors and abbots by threatening to imprison them if they withstood the Holy See; and they were obliged to make what terms they could with Rosso. About the same time the Pope rewarded the loyalty of the Romans by granting them the next 300 English benefices which might happen to fall vacant. This usurpation filled the Primate with despair. He asked the King's leave to visit Rome that he might lay his remonstrances before the Pope in person; and, having received an evasive answer, finally set forth upon his own authority. He fell sick on the journey and went

Withdrawal and Death of Edmund Rich

[1] *Chron. Maj.*, iv., 39.

no further than Pontigny which had once, under somewhat different circumstances, afforded a refuge to St. Thomas. He died, in Nov. 1240, at Soisy and was buried at Pontigny. The vacant primacy was conferred by the King upon the Savoyard Boniface. But the place of Edmund Rich as the leader of the ecclesiastical opposition devolved upon his friend, the brilliant and lion-hearted Robert Grosseteste. The hand of this bishop can be traced in the protest of the Berkshire rectors ; and for thirteen years to come he was the most considerable opponent of royal and papal absolutism.

Grosseteste of Lincoln

Grosseteste [1] is one of the few English statesmen of this period who enjoyed a more than insular renown. He had become a bishop late in life (1235), and after he had abandoned all thoughts of such preferment. The highest office which he had hitherto enjoyed was that of an archdeacon ; and this he had resigned in the year 1232. But his reputation, both as a theologian and as a scientist, stood high. Roger Bacon, a severe and discriminating critic, says that Grosseteste alone of men was versed in all the sciences, and praises the independence of mind which he showed in turning aside from Aristotle to study the natural phenomena about which others were content to form their impressions from bad translations of the Aristotelian writings. Yet Grosseteste possessed a competent acquaintance not only with Aristotle but with the whole field of scholastic controversy ; and he was so far from despising the Greeks that he employed translators upon Latin versions of Greek books. It is to be regretted that the books which he selected for this honour, the "Testament of the Twelve Patriarchs" and the "Celestial Hierarchy" of the pseudo-Dionysius, are valueless except in so far as they form a link between the mystical imaginings of early Christianity and those of the medieval Church. [2] But in quieter times the example which he set might well have led to the realisation of Bacon's scheme for a school of English translators, who should bring the whole of classical literature within the reach of ordinary students. There were men in England who, either through a Greek descent or through long residence in countries of Greek speech, were qualified for such a task ; it only needed a generous

[1] See the collection *Roberti Grosseteste Epistolae* (R. S.), and F. S. Stevenson, *Robert Grosseteste* (1899).
[2] On the former work, Stevenson, p. 227. The "Celestial Hierarchy" had long been known to the West, through the translation by John Scot Erigena. See Taylor, *Classical Heritage of the Middle Ages*, pp. 82 ff., 367.

and judicious patron to command their services. But Grosseteste acquired the riches necessary for a patron when he was already old and immersed in practical affairs. His chief services to learning were rendered at an earlier date, when he was Master of the Oxford Schools and a lecturer to the Franciscan students.[1] The historian of the English Franciscans ascribes to Grosseteste's teaching the beginning of the intellectual life which made their Oxford convent the pride of the whole order and a nursery of professors. Only on his appointment to the See of Lincoln did Grosseteste show that the true bent of his genius lay towards action rather than reflection. He immediately undertook the reformation of his diocese, correcting the morals of the secular priests, degrading unworthy priors and abbots, checking laxity in the celebration of church-services, and prohibiting the use of sacred buildings for popular shows and entertainments. No obstacles were allowed to balk his zeal; the canons of his cathedral chapter, who had refused to recognise his right of visitation, were compelled to give way after almost ten years of constant lawsuits; and the abuse of provisions was confined within modest limits by a privilege which he obtained from Rome, to the effect that no foreigner should be intruded into benefices of his jurisdiction except by a special mandate of the Holy See. Though vigorous in dealing with offenders the Bishop showed no little tact in meeting and disarming opposition by a temperate statement of his own position. He never shrank from the strongest measures, if they were needed to secure the welfare of his diocese; but he preferred to gain his point by reason and persuasion. He had the art of making friends in every rank; the King respected and the Queen revered him; he gathered round him a band of devoted helpers and chose his recruits, with a wise discretion, from the mendicant orders who, at this time, still embodied the noblest aspirations of the medieval Church. The work which he did for a single diocese he would gladly have continued on a larger scale; and the universal admiration which he commanded by his dauntless courage and complete integrity gave him such a following among both the laity and the clergy, that under favourable circumstances he might have effected a moral revolution in the English Church. But the evils of royal and papal absolutism turned his energies into a channel for which they were unsuited.

[1] *Infra*, ch. xviii.

He became a politician and the recognised mouth-piece of the clergy whenever demands for money were to be evaded or refused. His political services to the nation were of considerable value. He served as a connecting link between the Church and the baronage ; he insisted on the necessity of uniting all classes in the defence of their common liberties ; and there were times, when he took political liberty for the theme of his discourses, or hinted a rebuke of the King's arbitrary conduct by expounding the distinction between monarchy and tyranny.[1] But he was born to direct rather than to oppose. He could not suggest a practical remedy for the mis-rule of which the whole country was complaining. He blamed the Pope rather than the King, and was not afraid of giving publicity to his opinion. At Lyons, in 1250, he presented the Pope and Cardinals with a memorandum in which he criticised with great freedom, not to say vehemence of language the cor-ruptions of the Curia ;[2] but he believed in common with the majority that the Pope was indispensable ; nor could his ingenu-ity suggest a practicable distinction between the lawful and the illegitimate uses of the power to bind and loose. The famous remonstrance, addressed to a representative of Innocent IV., by which Grosseteste is chiefly known to fame, is so outspoken that doubts have been cast upon its authenticity. As a critic of practical abuses the bishop rivals Wycliffe ; and indeed the founder of Lollardry is known to have utilised the arguments of his more orthodox precursor. But the letter to Master Innocent is still the work of one who is at a loss to find a logical basis for his moral indignation.[3] He can only urge that the power of the keys is given for the edification not for the destruction of the Church ; he cannot tell his readers who is to judge the limits of obedience in cases of dispute. From appealing to the Crown against the Pope he was precluded by his own theories of Church and State. The power of the Pope, he informed his recalcitrant canons, is derived from Christ, and that of the bishop from the Pope ; the commands of the Pope, he told the King, must be

[1] He wrote a treatise, De principatu regni et tyrannidis, which was studied by De Montfort (Mon. Francisc., i., 110).

[2] Brown's Fasciculus rerum fugiendarum et expetendarum (London, 1690), ii., 250-8, prints this memorandum.

[3] On the question of authenticity see Stevenson, p. 315, and A. G. Little in E. H. R., xv., p. 358. Both accept the letter as genuine. Cf. A. de Marsh, Epp. 325 ; and Chron. Maj., v., 389; vi., 229.

obeyed, and disobedience was even as the sin of idolatry and witchcraft. There is a passage in his letters which asserts that the magistrate who, even from the worthiest of motives, commits a trespass upon the sphere of spiritual power, is guilty of the sin of Uzzah and will be visited with Uzzah's punishment.[1] That Grosseteste should fail, when his hands were tied by theories of this kind, was only to be expected; nor can we desire that his ideal should have been completely realised. The language which he used respecting the relations of the lay and spiritual powers was more moderate than that of many medieval churchmen; for he admitted that each had its own sphere with which the other should not interfere. But he held that it lay with the Church to draw the boundary-line,[2] and in the government of his diocese repeatedly showed the old ecclesiastical instinct of encroachment. No man was stiffer in defence of clerical immunities, or complained more bitterly of the extent to which the jurisdiction of courts-Christian had been curtailed in recent times. He took an active part in the subterranean warfare waged by the canon lawyers against the royal jurisdiction. He brought trouble on himself by excommunicating sheriffs without the royal permission; and, in his zeal for the reform of manners, instituted an inquisitorial precedure under which juries of laymen were to be compelled to make presentments upon oath respecting the moral delinquencies of friends and neighbours. Only a royal prohibition prevented the bishop from carrying into effect this design, as mischievous in its consequences as it was laudable in purpose.[3] There was nothing of the tyrant in Grosseteste's nature; his pugnacity was tempered by a genial humour, his austerity by a robust common sense. A theocracy might have been tolerable when directed by a prelate who argued that laughter was one of the three things necessary to the welfare of the body; who prescribed a cup of wine for the melancholy of a fasting friar; who preached that holy poverty was a good thing, but to live by the labour of one's hands a better.[4] But his principles, in the hands of smaller men, would have subverted the existing order of society. When we reflect that it was Grosseteste who deduced the power of princes from the power of the Church and drew the corollary that princes

---

[1] *Epp.*, 340 ff.
[2] *Ibid.*, 90; and the *Articuli* from his pen in *Burton Annals*, 422 ff.
[3] *Chron. Maj.*, iv., 579; v., 109.   [4] *Mon. Francisc.*, i., 69.

should on no account withstand the Church, we may be grateful that the work of political reformation passed to other hands than his.

The State of Europe, 1241-4   So England drifted leaderless, the prey of adventurers, the despair of patriots, and at the mercy of an incapable sovereign's lightest whim. In Europe and the East great events were taking place. Italy was convulsed by the throes of civil war. Excommunicated and deposed by the indomitable Gregory, Frederic had turned to bay resolved, since he was allowed no other choice, to be indeed what his adversaries called him, "the hammer of the Church". Before his onslaught the main pillars of the Roman supremacy showed signs of tottering. Elias, the General of the Franciscan order, joined his party; Louis of France defended him against the accusations of the Pope; the imperial forces pressed forward upon Rome; the Guelf standard went down before the Ghibelline wherever Frederic passed. Russia, Poland, Hungary, and Germany itself, were menaced by the advance guard of the Mongol power which, even after the death of Genghis Khan, still dominated Asia from the Yellow Sea to the Caspian and Euphrates. Syria and the Levant were already threatened by the Kharismian hordes whom the successor of Genghis, able to defeat but not subdue them, was driving to the west. Indifferent to these great events, except so far as they favoured his ambitions, Henry III. planned to seize the opportunity of the general confusion and alarm for renewing his attack on France.

Rebellion in Poitou, 1241   The old tempter Hugo de la Marche and the Queen-mother Isabelle were chiefly responsible for this resolve. The reality of French supremacy had at last come home to Poitou with the appearance of the French King's brother, Alphonse, as Count and suzerain (1241). Hugo would have submitted to fulfil the duties of a vassal, but his wife's imperious temper goaded him into revolt. "Out of my sight!" she said to her husband when they returned from visiting the Count and Countess at Poitiers; "Am I a waiting-maid that I should stand before them while they sit at ease?" She left him and went away to nurse her offended dignity at Angoulême; when Hugo followed her with his excuses he found the gates of the castle barred against him. To appease the termagant he sent for the barons of Poitou, and found them also eager for revolt. Already, they told their host, the meanest lackey

of the French King could do his will in Champagne and in Burgundy ; the barons of those parts were but as slaves who dare not
move a finger till their master gives permission. A league was
formed ; the help of the Gascon towns and seigneurs was invoked,
and willingly accorded. The rule of France, said the Gascons,
would be their ruin and destruction; at present the land was
their own and they did whatever they thought good ; even at
Bordeaux and Bayonne no one cared in the least for the orders
of the King of England ; but under the King of France matters
would be different indeed.[1]   Thus supported the Count of La
Marche defied his lord at the Christmas court of 1241, set fire
to his lodgings, and rode away to invoke the aid of England,
of Toulouse and of Navarre. With Henry at least he had no Henry
difficulty. On February 2nd, 1242, the King announced to the Prepares
Great Council his intention of taking an army to Aquitaine and War
a French
asked for a subsidy. It was refused in accordance with an understanding which the barons had previously made among themselves ;
they said that the plan was formed without consulting them and
might be executed without their help, although they would have
gladly given personal service if it had been asked in proper form.[2]
The debate was stormy ; in the end the opposition drew up and
presented to the King a list of all the taxes which had been paid
since the beginning of the reign ; not a long list, when measured
by modern standards of taxation,[3] but a convincing proof of waste
and luxury to an age which was convinced that the King both
could and should " live of his own ". All that Henry obtained was
a number of presents from individuals; with these, and with such
loans as his credit would allow, he equipped an exiguous army for
the conquest of Poitou.

He landed in Gascony on May 19th, accompanied by his brother The
Richard and some 300 English knights. With such a force it was Battle
of Taille-
impossible to cross the Charente ; for the King and the whole army bourg,
of France were already at Chinon in readiness to meet attack. July 20th
1242
A month was consumed by Henry in diplomatic correspondence
of which the apparent object was to cast the responsibility for
the war upon his adversary. But, apart from the disaffected

---

[1] *Bibl. de l'Ecole des Chartes*, 2nd Series, iv., 513. Boissonade, pp. 43, 44.
[2] *Chron. Maj.*, iv., 181 ff.
[3] See a list compiled by Stubbs, *C. H.*, ii., p. 60.

Poitevins, no allies made their appearance in the English camp. Although Raymond of Toulouse, irritated to madness by the rigours of the Languedocian Inquisition, raised the standard of rebellion in the south, the King of France declined to meet this danger by dividing his main army, and continued a methodical campaign against the castles of the Poitevins. When the last had fallen Louis made his appearance on the Charente. The bridge of Taillebourg had been left unguarded by the English; they put their trust in Geoffroi de Rançon, the lord of Taillebourg, whose stronghold on the north bank of the river commanded the approaches to the bridge. But Geoffroi proved himself a traitor double-dyed. The English King, hastening up from Saintes, with all his available forces, to prevent the passage of the French, arrived too late to hold the bridge; and, as the result of an engagement in the meadows south of the river, found himself surrounded and cut off from Saintes. He would have been captured if Richard of Cornwall had not prevailed on the French King and barons to forgo the doubtful advantage of making a royal prisoner. Under cover of a truce Henry was enabled to fall back on Saintes; but the pursuit was soon commenced and vigorously pressed home. The French only halted at Blaye on the Dordogne; nor did Henry consider himself secure until he reached the friendly walls of Bordeaux.[1] The Count of La Marche made haste to forsake a hopeless cause; his example was followed by the rebels of lesser note; and Louis in a short time was master of all Poitou. He might have entered Gascony itself with considerable prospect of destroying the English power there, if his scruples had not come to the relief of his opponent. The rebellion of Toulouse collapsed immediately after the victory of Taillebourg; and Raymond, by the Treaty of Paris (1243), was compelled to promise every assistance in the persecution of the heretical subjects in whose interests he had taken arms.[2] This last defection brought the English King to reason. He concluded (April, 1243) a five years' truce with France, and only prolonged his stay in Gascony because he shrank from facing the anger

[1] The main authorities are: the letter of Henry to the Emperor in Shirley, ii., p. 24. *Foedera*, i., 244 ff. *Chron. Maj.*, iv., 192-217; and of the French writers De Nangis, *Vie de Saint Louis*, and Joinville. See also the Itinerary of Louis in Bouquet, xxi, pref. For the rebellion in Toulouse see *Hist. Gen. Languedoc*, viii., 1087-94.
[2] *Hist. Gen. Languedoc*, viii., 1097-1110.

and derision of his subjects.[1]   The war for the recovery of the
Angevin inheritance was at an end ; and the King of France could
now devote his whole attention to the problem of fusing the
conquered provinces with the older possessions of his house.   Poitou
gave no further trouble ; the last links between the aristocracies of
France and England were severed when Louis proclaimed that those
who held lands both in France and England must make their choice
between their French and English fiefs, and when Henry retaliated
by confiscating, without the offer of an option, all the English fiefs
which were still held by Frenchmen.[2]

Late in 1243 the King returned to England, having dissipated
in idle revelry at Bordeaux not only his small stock of money, but
also whatever popularity he had once possessed in Aquitaine.   The
Gascons were now able to judge him from personal acquaintance ;
the evils which had formerly been ascribed to seneschals were now
laid upon their master.   Loyalty to England waned even in the
towns, since the ability of England to defend them from the French
was now discredited ; and the nobles presumed upon the weakness
which they had seen with their own eyes.   Faction fights in the
towns, robberies, private wars, and forcible seizures of castles make
up the sum of Gascon history for the next ten years.

In England during the same period there was outward peace, The Dis-
but an under-current of disaffection which came to the surface every content of
little while in different forms and on different pretexts.   London London, 1243-53
then as always was a storm-centre, in which the feelings that moved
slowly through the rustic minds of the provinces flamed out occasionally with electric violence and unexpectedness.   It was indeed
an intolerable anomaly that the citizens of the most important
community in the kingdom, men of wealth and intelligence, proud
of their city and jealous of their independence, should be legally
as much at the mercy of the Exchequer as the villeins of the
smallest manor on the royal demesne.   Each new tallage was resented as an extortion ; and there were bitter complaints when the
King compelled the citizens to close their shops during the annual
fair which he had granted to the monks of Westminster (1250).[3]
A royal counsellor was sent to negotiate with the city magistrates
upon this subject.   The Mayor received him in the presence of the

[1] *Foedera*, i., 251.   *Chron. Maj.*, iv., 229.
[2] *Ibid.*, iv., 288.   [3] *Ibid.*, v., 127, 333.

folk-moot; and when the envoy asked for a private audience, the answer was given by shouts of dissent from the assembly. The citizens cried out that this dispute which touched them all should be settled by the voice of all.[1] The King attempted to disarm their suspicions by a public apology when he took the cross in the year 1250. He summoned all of twelve years old and upwards to come before him in the Hall of Westminster and asked their pardon for any infringements of their privileges of which he had been guilty. They gave the pardon, but sullenly enough, suspecting that it would be followed by new demands for money. Three years later, when the King was once more at Westminster, the Londoners quarrelled with his foreign servants at a quintain-match, and trounced them roundly. These episodes were of more than local significance. The part which the Londoners had played in the struggle for the Charter made them the acknowledged advocates of liberty. Their quarrels with the Crown are carefully noted by the chroniclers; the last manifesto of Grosseteste against the Curia is addressed both to the barons and to the citizens of London.

Innocent IV. (1241-54)   In the country at large the exactions of the Papacy continued for a time to divert attention from the King; who even mitigated in some degree his growing unpopularity by a timid and intermittent opposition to the new demands. Many hopes of reform had been founded upon the election of Sinibald Fiesco, Innocent IV., as Celestine's successor in 1243, but it is not clear why this should have been the case. The new Pope was a man of marked ability, eminent for his learning in the canon law; but grasping, crafty, as unscrupulous in his policy as Gregory IX., and, unlike Gregory, devoid of personal integrity or religious zeal. In 1243 he sent a confidential agent, Master Martin by name, to suspend all the bishops of England from the right of collating to benefices until a long list of Papal nominees, including some of Innocent's own kinsmen, should have due provision made for them. Immediately afterwards the Pope acceded to a request from David of North Wales, the successor of Llewelyn, that he might be accepted as the immediate vassal of the Holy See. Lastly the envoy Martin convened the clergy and required a subsidy. These accumulated encroachments stung Henry to resistance. He wrote to Innocent protesting against the misuse of provisions. He also forbade the clergy to impoverish

[1] *Chron. Maj. et Vicecom.*, 14-16.

their temporalties by making contributions to the Pope.   But neither step was more than partially successful.   The nuncio made a merit of relinquishing his claim to benefices of small value ; the religious houses, more afraid of Rome than of the Crown, paid by stealth the subsidy which had been ostensibly refused.   In 1245 the The barons took the defence of the Church into their own hands.   To the General Council of this year, convoked by Innocent at Lyons, they submitted a long list of *Gravamina*, threatening that, if these were not redressed, the tribute promised by King John should cease. They watched the seaports for Papal couriers and destroyed all the briefs that could be intercepted.   Finally they sent one of their number, Fulk FitzWarin, to warn the nuncio that if he prolonged his stay in England he would be hewn in pieces.   Master Martin took the warning ; and with him departed many aliens who valued their lives more highly than their benefices.   But their flight made little difference to the situation.   The Pope turned a deaf ear to the *Gravamina* ; he amused the English proctors with vague promises which were immediately made null and void by a new clause of *non obstante* in his grants of benefices.   The clergy bowed to the inevitable.   When the King attempted, in 1246, to prevent them from paying a new Papal tallage even Grosseteste protested that their duty to the Holy See took precedence of all other obligations.[1]   Henry withdrew his prohibition ; and his resistance to Rome, though continued for a little time, grew fainter by degrees.   He too believed in the absolute prerogative of Rome, and it was scarcely worth his while to defend those who were afraid to be defended. Possibly he soothed his injured pride with the quaint reflection of an English canonist of the period, that " albeit in this world the Pope can turn all things topsy-turvy, his judgment will be the more terrible hereafter ".

Fear had something to do with the submissiveness of Henry. But it also gave him pecuniary advantages.   He was occasionally allowed to share in the spoils of the Curia, which he could the less afford to despise because from year to year his necessities became more desperate and the Great Council more reluctant to relieve them.   Already in 1236 he had been driven to make money by repudiating his own charters as invalid without papal confirmation. His creditors were now so clamorous that he could hardly show his

The Council of Lyons, 1245

The Great Council and the King, 1244

[1] *Dunstaple Annals,* 169.   *Chron. Maj.,* iv., 527, 554.   Grosseteste, *Epp.,* 340.

face in public for fear of their reproaches. The opposition were resolved to use his needs as a lever for obtaining the redress of grievances; and each demand for money was met by a demand for the appointment of ministers of native birth and acceptable to the country. In 1244 a committee was appointed to fix the conditions of a grant. It was a mixed body of the King's critics and supporters, the chief place among the latter being taken by Richard of Cornwall, and by the Earl of Leicester who on returning from his Crusade had gone through a formal reconciliation with the King. But the royalists were outvoted; the committee reported that for the future the Justiciar, Chancellor, Treasurer, and certain of the judges ought to be elected by the Great Council; that four of the King's ordinary counsellors should be representatives of the same body; and that these four should have the power of summoning the Great Council whenever they thought fit. The King postponed his answer and used the Earl of Leicester's mediation with the clerical estate, hoping that the prelates, if not the barons, would make a grant without conditions.[1] But Grosseteste warned his brethren against separating from the common cause. "It is written," he said, "that if we be divided we shall all straightway perish;" and the King was answered in the negative.[2] A second session, later in the year, found the King and opposition as far as ever from a basis of agreement. But, since his necessities were urgent and intolerable, the Council relented so far as to allow a scutage for the marriage of his eldest daughter.

The King's half-brothers

But no warnings could restrain either the King's extravagance or his predilection for alien counsellors. In 1247 there was a new invasion of the court by foreigners. The death of Isabelle of Angoulême (1246) and the increasing weight of French supremacy drove the children of her second marriage to seek their fortunes in the realm of their half-brother.[3] They came to England with followers as insatiable as themselves. The young and illiterate Athelmar, after being unsuccessfully proposed as a candidate for the abbacy of Abingdon and the bishopric of Durham, was at length forced on the reluctant electors to the bishopric of Winchester (1251); William of Valence received the hand of a wealthy heiress, and was subsequently created Earl of Pembroke

[1] Bémont, S. de Montfort, p. 18.
[2] Chron. Maj., iv., 362-6.   [3] Boissonade, p. 50.

(1250). Their sister Alicia was married to the young Earl Warenne; a third brother was equipped at the King's expense for a crusade; and a fourth received the custody of the barony of Hastings. The Poitevins were even more unpopular than the Savoyards. William of Valence and his brothers claimed to stand above the law ; they abused the Crown's prerogative of purveyance more scandalously than the King himself.[1] They fostered in England the absolutist theories which in France they had so bitterly resented, and the King was encouraged by their flattery to take a higher line with the Great Council. To a new request, in the year 1248, that he would dismiss the aliens and accept elected ministers, he answered with a sharp retort: " Servants do not judge their master," he said ; " vassals do not judge their prince or bind him by conditions. Much rather should they put themselves at his disposal and be submissive to his will." [2] Such answers led to no subsidies; but the exchequer was supplied by other and more desperate expedients. The King sold his plate and jewels ; he also sold new grants of privileges to all who would buy them, derogating in some cases by a *non obstante* clause from previous grants by which he had made a similar profit in the past. He demanded New Year gifts from the Londoners; and from individual magnates a contribution to the expense of a French war which he had not the slightest intention of declaring. He ceased to pay his servants and officials, with the result that they paid themselves by highway robbery or by taking secret bribes.[3] When such offenders were detected the law was allowed, for very shame, to take its course with those of the first class ; but corruption, even amongst the judges, was condoned for a pecuniary consideration.[4] The judges were too useful an instrument of extortion to be lightly punished. The forest-courts in particular were a great and increasing source of revenue; at a hint from the King they had begun to discover and punish all kinds of encroachments on the forests of the Crown; and men of gentle birth were not infrequently reduced to beggary for the coursing of a single hare.[5] Even his religious emotions were turned to profit by the King. The example of Louis IX. fired him, in 1250, to take the cross and confess himself a miserable sinner with every circumstance of pomp and ceremony. The hearts

Henry in straits for Money

Talks of a Crusade (1250-2)

[1] *Chron. Maj.*, v., 316, 343, 370.   [2] *Ibid.*, v., 5.   [3] *Ibid.*, v., 56.
[4] See the case of Henry de Bath, *ibid.*, v., 213, 223, 240.   [5] *Ibid.*, v., 136.

of the multitude were melted; barons and prelates made haste to imitate their sovereign's example; there was much talk of an English expedition which should put the Empire to shame, and prove that Louis was not the only saint among the Kings of Christendom.[1] There the matter rested. The King of France fought and failed in Egypt with no further help from Henry than a truce, granted with hesitation and reluctance, for the term of the Crusade. But in 1252 the King of England laid before the clergy a demand, supported by the Pope, that they should give him towards the purposes of the Crusade a tithe of their rents and movables for the next three years. The French Church, he said, had done as much for the same purpose; would they be behind-hand? They hesitated about their answer; although they knew the hollowness of the alleged pretext they did not see how King and Pope together were to be resisted. Once more Grosseteste urged his brethren to resist. The experience of recent years had killed his former reverence for the Papacy; at Lyons he had characterised the Curia as the fountain-head of every evil in the Church. That the French had paid was only, he argued, another reason for refusal; "twice makes a custom". But if there must be payment, the clergy ought to demand in return a confirmation of the Charters, and a promise that the grant should be really applied to the Crusade. The compromise thus suggested was proposed to the King, and proved equivalent to a refusal; for he swore great oaths "that never, while breath was in his body, would he submit to be a slave".[2]

Death of Grosse-teste, 1253   Grosseteste's career was almost ended. He was old and worn, weary of strife, and hopeless of success; but in this very year he published an appeal to the nation for help against the evil of provisions; and, a little later, on being required to admit a nephew of the Pope, who was eminently unfitted for preferment, to a canonry at Lincoln he addressed to the Pope's secretary a spirited letter of refusal and expostulation, saying that a request which ran counter to the injunctions of Christ and the Apostles could not be obeyed even though it emanated from the Holy See. Once before Grosseteste had made a similar refusal and had then been punished with suspension. Innocent would now have been glad to use severer measures, but desisted on a warning from the cardinals that they could not

---

[1] *Chron. Maj.*, v., 100, etc.   [2] *Ibid.*, v., 325-332.

safely attack a prelate who for piety and learning had neither equal
nor superior in the West.[1] The bishop was unmolested, and passed
quietly away in the autumn of 1253. His last words were a
prophecy that only the sword could deliver the Church from her
Egyptian bondage.

Perhaps he did not speak entirely at random. The hopes of those who placed their faith in the Empire had vanished with the death of Frederick II. (1250). The power of the Hohenstauffen was broken; in Germany all was anarchy; in Italy the gallant Conrad IV. was not long to maintain a sinking cause. The time could be foreseen when the Pope would no longer be restrained by the necessity of defending the temporal possessions; the future hopes of the national churches must depend on national resistance. But Grosseteste had some reason for believing that the English Church was at length to produce a Maccabeus. There had been a friendship of the closest kind between himself and the Earl of Leicester. They had exchanged their secret thoughts concerning the evils of the time; in common they had deplored the subversion of law by arbitrary power; and the Earl had promised that his party, if such a party could be formed, should fight the battle of the English Church.[2] What reforms they had in mind, to what lengths and by what paths they were ready to venture in the pursuit of their ideal, we cannot say. But, in the last years of Grosseteste's life, the slender ties which bound the Earl to the King's person were snapped and broken by the King's own fault; and the Earl was left at liberty to criticise the political as freely as the ecclesiastical situation.

Breach between Montfort and the King

In the year 1248 the English power in Gascony had fallen to the lowest ebb; the towns were defiant of all authority, the nobles in secret league with France or with Navarre; and disorder reigned supreme. At the urgent request of King and Council the Earl of Leicester undertook the restoration of order; but upon the condition that he should have for seven years a free hand to deal with rebels and complete control of the Gascon revenues.[3] His mission had been crowned with great success. The greater nobles were

Montfort in Gascony, 1248-52

---

[1] *Chron. Maj.*, v., 226, 389; vi., 229. *Mon. Francisc.*, i., 325.
[2] See especially the letters of Adam de Marsh in *Mon. Francisc.*, i., 107, 110, 111, 225.   This collection proves a close connection between De Montfort and the leaders of the English Franciscans.
[3] See the agreement in Bémont, p. 264; and the Earl's statement, *ibid.*, p. 341.

15

judiciously conciliated; those of less consequence if they persisted in their robberies, were punished with fines, imprisonment, and the confiscation of their castles. In the towns the Earl imposed a truce upon contending factions, and prevented the majority from establishing a tyranny. When audacious party-leaders ventured, as at Bordeaux, to pursue their feuds with arms and violence, he forced them to an unconditional surrender, kept them in his own hands as prisoners or hostages, and excluded their followers from any share in the administration of the commune. He secured his object; the King's authority was again respected, the poor were freed from their oppressors. But the Earl had made many foes. He was charged with perjury, with inflicting arbitrary punishments upon guiltless persons, with discovering royal rights where they had never existed in the past.[1] Complaints of this kind, and veiled threats of

Advice of Adam de Marsh

rebellion from those who held themselves aggrieved, came to the King's ears and were supported by the envy of the alien ministers. The King, who at first had been more than satisfied, began to doubt the honesty of his lieutenant; and even the Earl's friends expressed some misgivings whether righteous zeal had not carried him beyond the bounds of justice. "It should be your part to guide him," writes one faithful adviser to the Countess, "if through want of reflection, and with the best of motives, he has been less careful than he ought in observing contracts and agreements."[2] This was the Franciscan scholar, Adam de Marsh, who had followed Grosseteste as lecturer to the Oxford convent of the order. Few private men were better situated to observe and direct the shifting currents of opinion in high places. He was the chosen counsellor of Archbishop Boniface, to whom he told home truths such as that well-meaning but hot-headed prelate would never have endured from other lips; and Adam's correspondence proves that his views on public questions were solicited and carefully weighed by the Queen, by Richard of Cornwall, and by other influential persons. The King disliked him as a firebrand; for the honest Franciscan had once preached to the Court in most uncourtly terms respecting the evils of the times.[3] Adam could still move those who moved the King; and all his efforts were directed towards defending the man whom,

[1] Bémont, pp. 22 ff., and the documents given on pp. 279, 286, 301, 304, 311. Shirley, ii., pp. 51, 72, 74, 86, 90. *Chron. Maj.*, v., 103, 104.
[2] *Mon. Francisc.*, i., 298.   [3] *Ibid.*, i., 275, 290, 325, 335.

in common with Grosseteste, he regarded as the future saviour of
the Church. But in the end the Gascons and the alien counsellors
secured their point. Bewildered by the torrent of accusations,
alarmed for the safety of Gascony, and irritated by the Earl's demands for men and money, the King resolved to hold a formal
trial (1252).[1]

The indignity of such treatment was keenly resented by the   Montfort
Earl, who had come to England fresh from a series of victories over on his
                                                   Trial,
rebel seigneurs ; and it was aggravated by the obvious inclination of 1252
the court to treat him as guilty till the contrary was proved.
Chance has preserved a number of the complaints which were, at
the King's invitation, submitted by the towns, the clergy, and the
baronage of Gascony ; and in one or two cases we have the answers
of the Earl.[2] These documents produce the impression that he
had enforced his master's dues with rigour, that he had made
excessive demands of military service, and that in doing justice
upon rebels he had been, though equitable in the main, too contemptuous of ordinary forms. He had in fact proceeded on the
not unnatural view that Gascony as he found it was a rebellious
country, and that military law was good enough for open disturbers of the peace ; in some cases his bailiffs and his provosts
had committed grave excesses. But commissioners, who were sent
in 1252 to investigate all charges on the spot, reported strongly
in his favour.[3] The King reluctantly acquitted him, but with
characteristic meanness refused to pay the sums which the Earl had
spent on Gascony from his own purse ; to traitors, as Henry put it,
there was no obligation. The Earl told him he lied in using the
word traitor, and would have cause to rue the word if he were not
a King. After more recrimination in this vein they parted, and
the Earl returned to Gascony to complete his term of seven years.[4]
He found his enemies in arms and convinced that they would have
the King's support; but, raising what troops he could with the help
of friends and kinsmen, he took the field and routed the largest
force which had ever been put into the field against him. Meanwhile, however, the King had proclaimed a truce and announced his

---

[1] Shirley, ii., pp. 68, 70, 81. *Chron. Maj.*, v., 276. Bémont, pp. 267, 339.
[2] Printed in the appendices to Bémont's valuable book.
[3] Bémont, pp. 37 ff. Pauli, i., p. 684. *Mon. Francisc.*, i., 127. *Chron. Maj.*, v.,
277. Specimens of favourable evidence in *Mon. Francisc.*, i., 124. Shirley, ii., p. 58.
[4] *Chron. Maj.*, v., 290. *Mon. Francisc.*, i., 128, 129.

intention of either visiting Gascony in person or sending thither his eldest son, the Lord Edward. In the midst of his campaign the Earl received a command to lay down his arms and surrender his command. It was in vain that he protested, appealing to the terms

Montfort Super- seded

on which he had been appointed.[1] The utmost which he could obtain was the repayment of his expenses and an additional sum of 7,000 marks. He left Gascony in high indignation and retired to France, which he found in great confusion owing to the King's absence and the death of the Queen-mother Blanche. The barons of France paid him the highest compliment in their power by offering to make him their seneschal and regent. But he was unwilling to cut himself adrift from England. In 1253 when Henry came tc Gascony, and realised at length the true state of affairs, he pressed the Earl to return and give assistance in meeting difficulties which were too great for any other man. Simon reluctantly obeyed this appeal to his allegiance ; he returned and for a short while remained with the royal army.[2] But it was no longer possible that he should work with the King. Contempt on the one side, suspicion on the other, formed insuperable barriers between them. At the beginning of 1254 the Earl returned to England leaving the King behind in Gascony.

[1] Bémont, pp. 322, 343.
[2] *Ibid.*, p. 338. *Chron. Maj.*, v., 366, 383, 396.

CHAPTER XVII

THE PROVISIONS OF OXFORD

THE King remained in Gascony for the greater part of the year 1254. In his absence the Queen and Richard of Cornwall undertook the thankless duty of negotiating yet another subsidy. There was some danger that Alfonso X. of Castile would enter Gascony, to assert the shadowy claims which he based upon his descent from Eleanor, the daughter of Henry II. and wife of Alfonso IX.; and of this argument the Regents made the utmost. The magnates however returned no liberal response to the appeal. They promised to contribute from their own resources for the defence of Gascony; but they utterly refused to speak for their inferiors.[1]   It was necessary therefore to summon representatives of the lower clergy and the third estate to attend a second meeting of the Council (April 26). The clerical estate was presumably represented on one or other of the various systems which were in use for the provincial synods of Canterbury and York; it may have been the archdeacons of each diocese who were summoned; or the bishops may have nominated representatives; and finally the inferior clergy may have been allowed to elect their own spokesmen. All these plans had been tried in the case of convocations;[2] but the writs of summons to the clergy for this year are not extant. Respecting the third estate we are better informed. Two knights were to be elected in each shire-court by the suitors. Four had been summoned to the assemblies of 1213 and 1225; but the reduction in the number of representatives is without significance. It is more important to notice the changed terms of the summons. In 1213 the knights were summoned to discuss the affairs of the realm, in 1225 to present the grievances of their constituents. Now, however, they are convoked for the sole purpose of relieving the

Discontent in the Great Council

---

[1] Shirley, ii., p. 101.   [2] *Select Charters*, 453 ff.

King's poverty.[1] The representative principle, although at length admitted by the Crown, was still suspected as a dangerous innovation ; and the Regents desired to leave the elected members of the Council no excuse for an active share in the debates. The precaution failed to secure its object. Though reduced to silence the third estate showed an independent spirit. They listened sympathetically while the Earl of Leicester exposed in a long speech the hollowness of the pretexts which were alleged to justify a subsidy ; and they finally dispersed without voting an aid.[2] It was, therefore, to a Great Council of the old sort that the King applied for help on his return (1255). But now it was the turn of the magnates to be obdurate. They renewed the familiar demand that they should be allowed to elect the chief royal ministers, and, upon receiving an evasive answer, declined to unloose their purse-strings. The pretext of an impending war with Castile could no longer be urged ; for the King had but lately arranged a match between his heir, the Lord Edward, and Eleanor the half-sister of Alfonso (1254).

Marriage of Edward, 1254

This marriage is the first event which brings the prince into a prominent position. According to French custom, Henry III. gave to his son, at the time of the marriage, an extensive appanage, which in fact comprised all the outlying possessions of the Crown. Henceforward Edward is Lord of Gascony and the Channel Isles, of the Earldom of Chester and the royal demesnes in Wales, and of all Ireland. Within his possessions he holds the rank of a viceroy, and in all but name he is a dependent sovereign. It was a position which afforded an excellent apprenticeship to an heir-apparent, and Edward rose to his new responsibilities. But such an appanage was, in the embarrassed state of the finances, over-liberal ; and in other respects the King went far beyond the dictates of prudence in his anxiety to secure the match. One of the inducements which he offered to Alfonso was a pledge, happily unfulfilled, to join Castile in an African Crusade. Such preposterous engagements can only be explained by the desire of a firmer footing in the circle of the continental powers. This ambition soon committed Henry

The Crown of Sicily, 1254

III. to a wilder scheme than that of the Crusade. Since the death of Frederic II. the chief object of the Papacy had been to expel the Hohenstauffen from Sicily and Naples by bringing in a rival candidate. The difficulty was to find a prince who would undertake

[1] See the writs in S. C., 287, 376.   [2] Chron. Maj., v., 440.

the whole expenses of the enterprise. Richard of Cornwall, twice
approached by Innocent IV., twice declined the empty honour; at
first on the plea that he could not supplant his nephew Henry; and
again, on Henry's death (1253), with a frank confession that he
thought the conquest an impossibility.[1] Less cautious than his
brother, Henry III. accepted Sicily on behalf of Edmund Crouch-
back, his second son, pledging himself to find an army and to provide for the war the sum of £90,000 (1254).[2] It was an insane
contract. In England the opposition had assumed so threatening
an aspect that John de Gray, a member of the royal Council,
resigned rather than face the day of reckoning which he foresaw.
But to the King's mind politics were a question of personal feuds and
friendships. He feared no opposition except from those with whom
he had quarrelled upon private grounds. A number of the great
barons, in particular the Earls of Gloucester, Warenne, Lincoln
and Devon were indebted to him for signal marks of favour. On
these he thought that he could count; and with their help he anticipated no difficulty in over-riding the opposition. In October, The
1255, he published his acceptance of Sicily[3] and asked the Great Barons
Council for assistance, while the Papal nuncio Rustand demanded the Sicil-
from the clergy a contribution for the same purpose. Both applica- ian enter
tions were refused; the barons and the clergy alike protested that prise
they were in no way bound to further an enterprise to which they
had never given their consent. For the next two years the Sicilian
crown was the main topic of discussion. Afraid to incur a Papal
censure, equally afraid to press his demands upon the barons, the
King drifted aimlessly from side to side. In 1257 he agreed that
a commission, of which his opponent the Earl of Leicester and his
friend Peter of Savoy were the leading members, should be appointed
with full authority to extricate him from his bargain with the
Pope.[4] But in the end the King's ambition proved stronger than
his fears. He determined at all costs to persevere; he believed
that the help of Rome would enable him to wring the necessary
funds from the English clergy; and he built great hopes upon the
result of the Imperial election of 1257.[5] The intrigues of the Papal

---

[1] *Chron. Maj.*, v., 347, 448, 457.
[2] *Ibid.*, 457, 470. *Foedera*, i., 308-318. *Cf.* Shirley, ii., p. 115.
[3] *Calendarium Rot. Pat.*, p. 27 (Rec. Com.). *Chron. Maj.*, v., 513, 520.
[4] *Foedera*, i., 359. See *Cal. Rot. Pat.*, p. 29, for the amicable relations of the
King and Simon at this date.
[5] Shirley, ii., p. 114.

party, assisted by a lavish expenditure of English gold, induced three of the electors to confer their votes upon the Earl of Cornwall. The others, four in number, were won by the like considerations to the side of Alfonso X. The two elections took place almost simultaneously; while the claim of the Castilian was technically the stronger, the event proved that neither he nor his rival commanded the allegiance of the German nation. Their rivalry was but another disturbing influence in the long Interregnum which undermined the foundations of the medieval Empire; what fragments of imperial authority survived were to be finally vested in the hands of a native German, Rudolf the founder of the Hapsburg line. But, for the present, Richard's star appeared to be in the ascendant. A coronation of unexampled splendour, in the church of Charles the Great at Aachen, was followed by some victories and the accession of a few cities and magnates to his cause. The Emperor-elect entered on the year 1258 with the most sanguine anticipations for the future.[1]

Richard of Cornwall Emperor, 1257

But events in England could not wait for the issue of the German civil wars. New troubles in Wales showed more convincingly than ever, the contrast between the ambitions and the resources of the King; for Gwynedd, after some years of apathy and weakness, had come into the hands of a second Llewelyn, eager to continue the patriotic policy of his namesake and to make the Welsh a nation. Patriotism of a kind had always existed amongst Welshmen. Even when the tribes were most submissive to the Angevin they felt a pride in their traditions. A current proverb boasted that in the day of doom no other race or language should answer for "wild Wales". But the country, as described by Gerald de Barri about 1189, was a congeries of petty states, formed in one generation to be disintegrated in the next. Their patriotism was only shown by the tenacity with which, in the midst of civil wars, they defied the English Marchers. Prince strove with prince and family with family; it was rarely that men of condition disgraced their birth by dying in their beds. The Welshman of the twelfth century showed no trace of political capacity. For good or evil the slave of his impulses, he prayed with the passion of a fanatic and fought with the fury of a madman. The most genial of com-

Wales and Welsh disturbances, 1254-7

The Welsh character

[1] *Foedera*, i., 353, 356. For the German situation see Redlich, *Rudolf von Habsburg* (Innsbruck, 1903).

panions, oriental in his ideas of hospitality, and honourable according to his code, he was still unfitted by temper and education for a settled life. Though dependent upon foreign trade for the commonest necessities, he cherished a profound contempt for manual arts and industry. By preference he remained a herdsman; in his heart of hearts he was a nomad. He lived with his family in solitude, upon the edge of a forest or a mountain-slope. His house was little better than a hut, flimsily constructed of timber, mud and wattle, and needing to be renewed from year to year. Seventy years had produced little change in the habits and disposition of the nation. But the genius of Llewelyn I. of Gwynedd, the same Llewelyn who had joined with the barons of the Charter in attacking John, I. (1194- had produced among the leading princes a semblance of harmony. 1240) They had accepted him as their superior; and while he lived the affairs of Wales were ordered from time to time by Councils in which he presided.[1] Llewelyn used his power wisely, and gave his countrymen an influence among English parties such as they had never before possessed. The lesson of unity which he had inculcated was enforced by the humiliations which the Welsh princes suffered when his death allowed them to resume their feuds (1240). Divided between two claimants Gwynedd fell into insignificance. Henry III. seized all the outlying territories of the principality, both in the south and in the east. He compelled the grandsons of Llewelyn I. to recognise his annexations, leaving them nothing but Anglesey and the Snowdon country (1247); and he revived the old policy of using Powis as a check on Gwynedd.[2] These encroachments, which threatened not merely Gwynedd but the whole Welsh race with subjection to the new English colonies, revived the desire for a Llewelyn leader. When Llewelyn II., the second grandson of his namesake, II. secured the whole of Gwynedd by a successful war against his brothers (1254), he found himself at the head of a patriotic party extending far beyond his private territories.

It was at this moment that the Welsh demesnes passed into the hands of the Lord Edward. They comprised all that had been wrested from Gwynedd; in particular the Four Cantreds of Pervedd-wlad on the north coast, and the lands lying between the Dovey and Carmarthen Bay. That discords should break out between Edward and Llewelyn was only to be expected. An excuse for

[1] *Brut y Tyw.*, 291, 327.   [2] *Foedera*, i., 267. *Ann. Wigorn.*, 438.

15*

representing his cause as that of the Welsh nation was afforded to the latter by the policy which Edward's delegates pursued. They aimed, both in the Four Cantreds and in the south-west, at introducing the English machinery of shire and hundred ; and Geoffrey Langley, the bailiff of the south, took the unprecedented step of levying a poll-tax.[1] In the north the prospect of living under English law was enough to produce rebellion ; in the south, where national feeling did not run so high, some of the natives would have welcomed English law, but were infuriated by taxation. From both quarters Llewelyn received appeals for help ; his willing response made the revolt a general war of liberation (1256). His successes were swift and startling. A raid of a week's duration made him the master of the Four Cantreds ; in the south he was able to set up a vassal prince ; early in the following year Gruffydd of Powis, the one chieftain who still upheld the English cause, fled into England before Llewelyn's army ; and a destructive raid carried fire and sword through the marcher lordships of the southern coast.[2] These successes produced effects which reached far beyond Wales. In Scotland the English faction, which had for some time ruled in the name of the young Alexander III., was overthrown by the Earl of Menteith, whose first act in his capacity of minister was to conclude a treaty with Llewelyn for mutual defence against the English.[3] In England the opposition, incensed at defeats which they regarded as a national disgrace, demanded vigorous measures and inveighed against the supineness of the King. An abortive campaign,[4] in which Henry and his son marched to the frontier of Gwynedd only to return without offering battle (1257), put the finishing touch to the royal humiliations and drove the Great Council to take vigorous action.

The session which opened on April 28, 1258, was more than usually stormy. The opposition threw the blame for all extravagance and failures on the aliens. William of Valence, whose earldom of Pembroke had suffered heavily from the Welsh war, retorted with insinuations that the opposition were in league with the Welsh rebels ; and, descending to particulars, attacked the

[1] *Ann. Dunstaple*, 200. *Tewkesbury*, 158. *Brut y Tyw. Chron. Maj.*, v., 613.
[2] See Professor Tout's article " Llewelyn ap Gruffudd," in *D. N. B.*, vol. xxxiv., and the authorities there cited.
[3] *Foedera*, i., 370.
[4] *Chron. Maj. et Vicecom.*, 29. *Chron. Majora*, v., 639, 645, 648.

Earl of Leicester as a traitor. Montfort turned upon his accuser with a fierce reply; and for the moment it seemed that the two Earls would come to blows.

It was no favourable moment for opening the business of Sicily. The course of the debate the King had been assailed with sarcasms on the score of his inglorious Welsh campaign; nothing was less likely than a grant for wider enterprises. But he feared the Pope more than the barons; and Alexander IV. had lately intimated that further delays in the commencement of the Sicilian war would be punished with excommunication. The Council was therefore asked for a subsidy. Shire-representatives had been summoned to attend and ratify the grant, in order that the opposition might not repeat the dilatory excuses of four years ago. But the barons were immovable. They resolved that the excesses of the royal administration called for special treatment, and announced that the question of satisfying the Pope's demands could only be considered upon definite conditions. These were, that the King should dismiss the aliens; that he should sanction the appointment of a committee of reform, chosen in equal numbers from his own supporters and the opposition; that he should give this body the complete control of the Exchequer and full power to reform the kingdom. These terms were presented by the entire body of the knights and magnates, who came for the purpose to the audience-chamber. They appeared in their full armour, although they were scrupulous to leave their swords outside the room. The King was filled with alarm. " Am I your prisoner ? " he asked submissively ; and, being reassured on this head, promised whatever was demanded. The committee, of twelve members from the King's party and twelve from that of the barons, was appointed with instructions to present a report before the Great Council on June 11th.[1]

During the period of suspense the Earls of Gloucester, Hereford, Leicester and Pembroke formed a league for the purpose of mutual defence; while the clergy prepared in a different manner to assert their solidarity and common grievances. A synod, over which the Primate Boniface presided, met at Merton on June 6th and drew up a lengthy series of *Gravamina*, which are chiefly interesting as a proof that reaction and reform had united to resist the King. The

The Baronial Ultimatum, April, 1258

Provisions of Oxford, 1258

---

[1] *Tewkesbury Annals*, 163. *Lords' Report*, i., 460. *Foedera*, i., 370, 371. *Chron. Maj.*, v., 689.

complaints of the clergy related almost entirely to the jurisdiction of their courts and the privileges of their order.[1] In many respects, it was alleged, the Crown judges had infringed the settlement of Henry II. They disregarded the right of sanctuary; they declined to punish excommunicates; they claimed for themselves all cases of contract and a monopoly of the power to amerce; they imprisoned clerks upon a bare suspicion; they summoned prelates to show cause for sentences of a spiritual character. Whatever part the clergy may have taken in the subsequent debates at Oxford, these complaints and others of a similar kind were entirely disregarded by the barons. The proceedings of the Great Council opened with the presentation of Articles of complaint[2] some of which displayed as much animus against the Church as against the Crown; and the Provisions, which were drawn up on the basis of the Articles, were entirely political in character.

The Provisions of Oxford are, even more obviously than the Great Charter, the work of a feudal party. But they show that in forty years the baronage had learnt one lesson of importance. The Charter contains no organic changes of the constitution; the Provisions contain little else but changes of this character. It had at length been realised that the evils of the time were due to the system as much as to the personnel of the executive. The new government, which the Provisions adumbrate, is an attempt to destroy the personal absolutism of Henry II. and to vest the royal prerogative in the hands of men who are qualified to speak for the nation.

But the means adopted are less defensible than the object for which they are devised. In effect the Provisions substitute for an autocracy an oligarchy. They vest all power in the hands of men who are chosen by one section of the community alone, and are left entirely irresponsible. If we exclude from consideration the arrangements of a temporary character, we find the supreme power vested in a Council and a Parliament. The former is composed of fifteen members chosen from both sides. It is in complete control of the ordinary administration. The King's ministers are responsible to it; the King himself is bound by an oath to do nothing of importance without consulting it.[3] The so-called Parliament is a

[1] *Burton Annals*, 410 ff.
[2] These and the Provisions are printed in *S. C.*, 382 ff.   [3] *Foedera*, i., 377.

body of even smaller size, containing twelve barons elected by the whole order, who are to meet the Fifteen thrice a year and to discharge the ordinary functions of the Great Council, in order that the baronage at large may be spared the expense and trouble of attendance. It will be noticed that representatives of the shires find no place either in the executive or in the deliberative body; nor is any machinery created by which the commons may exercise a control upon their nominal representatives. A certain regard to popular grievances is apparent in the clauses which provide for the choice of good sheriffs and bailiffs and escheators. But the baronage had no intention of sharing power and the spoils of office with the third estate. It is a significant fact that Montfort, the most public-spirited of their leaders, disliked the new Constitution and was with difficulty persuaded to endorse it.[1]

Yet for some time the majority made a popular use of their position. The members of the Great Council, while still at Oxford, took an oath that they would allow their tenants the same rights which the King allowed to themselves. They resolved that a copy of Magna Carta, written in the English language, should be sent to every shire-court, read publicly at the first opportunity, and preserved in the archives of the court for future reference. There was a general feeling of relief when the Poitevins, who had taken flight from Oxford, were pursued and compelled by promises and threats to leave the kingdom. These alone of the royal party had repudiated the Provisions; the fact that Henry and his eldest son swore, albeit with manifest reluctance, to observe the terms of the settlement was taken as a guarantee that abuses would disappear and all go smoothly for the future.[2]

The Provisional Government, 1258-9

These anticipations were disappointed. The barons, indeed, were induced by De Montfort to consult the citizens of London as to the measures of reform which would be most acceptable to the third estate.[3] Justices in eyre were sent out to hear complaints against the royal officials, and committees of four knights were empanelled in each shire to prepare the indictments of oppressive

---

[1] *Chron. Lanercost*, 67. A Minorite source, and well informed.

[2] Until the end of 1258 Henry seems to have co-operated loyally with the Council, issuing no writs without their approval (*Calendarium Rot. Pat.*, p. 30).

[3] *Chron. Maj. et Vicecom.*, 38. *Chron. Maj.*, v., 704. *Cf.*, *Cal. Rot. Pat.*, p. 30.

sheriffs.[1] But amongst the baronial representatives in the Council of Fifteen there were some who had resolved that no reforms should affect their own relations with their tenants. The Earl of Gloucester was the chief of these self-seekers. He refused to let the law take its course with the officials of his vast estates; and the Parliament of Feb.-March, 1259, witnessed a violent altercation on the subject between himself and the Earl of Leicester. The latter, unable to convince his fellow-counsellor, threatened to break off all connection with the government, and actually left the country to take up his residence in France. With great difficulty the remainder of the party induced Richard de Clare to yield his point; and the promise of the barons to their tenants was renewed in a special proclamation.[2]

Attitude of the Lord Edward

De Montfort resumed his place in the government; but until the end of the year he was engaged in negotiating with Louis IX. the final settlement of the quarrel respecting the Angevin inheritance; for the Council of Fifteen had wisely resolved that peace with France, at whatever price, should be their first step in foreign policy. In his absence from England the Earl came to an agreement with the Lord Edward, which is not the least surprising incident in a period of unexpected enmities and friendships. Edward, whose sympathies were never democratic, had hitherto been distinguished by his contempt for the classes of which the Earl was already the acknowledged leader. None of the aliens were more lawless, none abused the right of purveyance more gratuitously, than the heir-apparent. The conduct of the Prince and his household in their frequent progresses was a scandal. The new constitution imposed a check upon him; and for this he bore its authors no good will.[3] But youth though he was the Lord Edward could disguise his feelings. He had decided, it would seem, to save the Crown by his own independent action. He professed detachment from his father's cause;[4] and, making capital of his exclusion from the oligarchy, came forward as the protector of the commons. They became his dupes; and their mistake was shared for a time by Montfort, whose native honesty inclined him to believe in the

---

[1] *Foedera*, i., 375. Shirley, ii., pp. 130, 141. *Flores Hist.*, ii., 427.
[2] *Foedera*, i., 381. *Chron. Maj.*, v., 744.
[3] *Chron. Maj.*, v., 593. *Burton Annals*, 445.
[4] The relations of the two were strained both in 1258 and 1259. See the *Annals of Winchester, Tewkesbury, Dunstaple.*

honesty of others. Had the Earl been guided by a personal ambition the Prince was the last person whose alliance he would have
courted. The heir-apparent could not fail to take the lead on any
side which he embraced. But for one who merely desired to make
the baronage fulfil their promises an agreement with Edward was
obviously expedient.

Edward played his part with a due regard to effect. In October, The Pro-
1259, the King held his court at Westminster to celebrate the feast visions
of the Confessor, the abbey's patron-saint, and the court was minster,
thronged with knights and barons. A deputation of "the 1259
bachelors of England" came to the Prince and told him that, whereas the King had fulfilled his promises to the barons, the latter had
done nothing of what they promised for the common weal. The
bachelors threatened that, unless this omission were repaired, the
commonalty would resort to other means of redress. The bachelors
evidently claimed to speak for the whole body of free men. It is
possible that we may see in them the knights of the shire whom we
have more than once encountered. But there is no direct evidence
to prove that knights of the shire had been summoned to the
Michaelmas session of the Parliament, and it may be that the
members of the deputation were self-appointed, or even acting at
Edward's instigation.[1] In any case they expressed the general
feeling, and were strongly supported by the Prince, who announced
that he would stand for the rights of the commons to the death if
needful, and at once invited the Council of Fifteen to satisfy the
petition of the bachelors.[2] The Earl of Gloucester and his friends
decided that it was better to give way with a good grace. They
accordingly prepared a list of supplementary reforms, which were
proclaimed in the Great Hall at Westminster before the King and
a great gathering of the common people. These Provisions of
Westminster,[3] less sweeping in their character than those of Oxford,
still mark an epoch in the history of English feudalism. Their
most important terms related to the rights of private lords over
military tenants. One clause, exempting from suit and service at a

---

[1] So Professor Tout argues in *E. H. R.*, xvii., p. 89. But the " bachelors " may be
the knights who had been empanelled to present the grievances of their shires ;
vide supra.
[2] *Burton Annals*, 471.
[3] Printed in *S. C.*, 401 ff., in the Latin form. On the differences between the
French and Latin versions see *S. C. H.*, ii., 84. Both given in the *Burton Annals*.

feudal court all tenants who were not made expressly liable by the terms of their enfeoffment, abolished the doctrine, which had come in with the Conqueror, that the landlord enjoyed over his tenant a jurisdiction as of course. Another forbade private lords to entertain appeals from the courts of their tenants, enacting that all appeals should in future go before the royal courts. Thus at one stroke the courts of lords were robbed of half their suitors and of all their most lucrative business. Henceforth it was scarcely worth the while of an ordinary baron to hold a court for his free tenants; and by the end of the century the manor-court, still useful for enforcing the labour-services of villeins, was the only feudal tribunal which remained in active operation throughout the kingdom.[1]

Treaty of Paris, 1259

These timely, though reluctant, concessions enabled the provisional government to exist for some months further. The most valuable measure of the Fifteen was the Treaty of Paris which they concluded at the end of the year. Under this settlement Henry III. renounced all claims on Normandy, Anjou, Maine, Touraine and Poitou, but kept Gascony with parts of the dioceses of Limoges, Cahors and Perigord, on condition of doing homage as a peer of France for all that he thus retained or received.[2] To mitigate their sovereign's humiliation the English envoys insisted on pecuniary compensation for the claims which he renounced. Louis agreed to pay such a sum as would maintain 500 knights for two years in the service of God and Holy Church or for the profit of the realm of England. It was thus suggested that the indemnity might be employed for the conquest of Sicily from Manfred; and the King in writing to the Curia represented the treaty as a substantial advance towards the fulfilment of their bargain.[3] But such instalments of the indemnity as were actually paid went towards a project very different from that which Louis had anticipated.

Plans of Henry III.

Henry in fact designed to use the gold of France against his English subjects. The more circuitous methods which his son was using to undermine the baronial position he mistrusted and probably failed to comprehend. For his own part he preferred to take his stand upon the theory of an irresponsible and inalienable pre-

[1] Maitland, *Select Pleas in Manorial Courts*, Introd.
[2] *Layettes du Trésor*, iii., 4416, 4554, for the text of the Treaty. A good commentary by Gavrilovitch, *Étude sur le traité de Paris* (Paris, 1899).
[3] Shirley, ii., p. 147.

rogative; confident that if he did so the more conservative among the barons, and all who hated De Montfort, would rally to his side. That his son should negotiate with the arch-enemy was only explicable, in his eyes, on the hypothesis that both were scheming for his deposition. In this idea he was encouraged by the Earl of Gloucester, the first of the baronial party to desert the common cause. It may have been a scruple of feudal honour which produced the Earl's apostasy; but the favour which he obtained was abused for the purpose of his private quarrels. Not content with sharpening the King's resentment against De Montfort he also encouraged Henry to treat the Prince as a secret traitor; and thus by the action of one man both parties in the state were split asunder. In 1260 the King shut himself within the walls of London, called the citizens to arms, and began to fortify the Tower. He would see neither his son nor any of the barons who were still loyal to the Provisions.[1]

It was not long before Edward succeeded in establishing his innocence and returned to favour. But he gained his forgiveness at the expense of a breach with De Montfort, which left the royalists and constitutionalists irrevocably estranged. The Earl insisted upon being heard in his own defence, and was successful in rebutting the former charge of treason. But the facts which he admitted were sufficient to prove that his conception of royalty was fundamentally opposed to that of the conservative majority. It appears from the articles of accusation and defence [2] that, in the beginning of the year 1260 the King, who had gone to Paris with the object of ratifying the new treaty, forbade the Council of Fifteen to hold any parliament till he returned. But, since the Provisions ordained that Candlemas (Feb. 2nd) should be one of the three fixed dates for the holding of Parliament, Leicester and his adherents came as usual to the meeting place. Induced by the Justiciar to wait three weeks for the King's return, they refused at the end of that term to allow a second adjournment. The Parliament accordingly sat and transacted important business. It accepted the resignation of Peter of Savoy, one of the few royalists upon the Council, and ratified the appointment of a substitute, who was co-opted by the Council.[3]

De Montfort heads the Opposition

[1] *Tewkesbury Annals*, 169. *Chron. Maj. et Vicecom.*, 44. Gervase, ii., 210, *Ann. Dunst.*, 214.
[2] Printed by Bémont, pp. 343 ff. Probably the charge was raised in the July Parliament of 1260. *Chron. Maj. et Vicecom.*
[3] Bémont, p. 351.

If Parliament could deliberate, if ministers and counsellors could be chosen in defiance of the King's command, then the monarchy had become a merely ornamental office ; and the Earl's action can only be defended on the supposition that he suspected Henry of deliberately absenting himself in order that the provisional government might be brought to a standstill.

Henry Repudiates the Provisions Such suspicions, if they had existed, were speedily justified by the King's actions. Early in 1261 he applied to Rome for absolution from his oath to the Provisions. His request was readily granted ;[1] for the Pope was offended at the expulsion of Athelmar the Poitevin bishop of Winchester, and at the strongly worded protests on the subject of provided aliens which the Fifteen had already presented to him. Armed with his dispensation the King at once threw off the mask. None were against him, so he informed the Roman court, except a few malicious schemers whom he trusted shortly to outwit.[2] He began to enlist foreign mercenaries, an example which the Earl was not slow to imitate; at the Easter court at Winchester (April 24th), the King deposed the ministers appointed at Oxford and chose others in their place ; and on August 16th he published a proclamation asserting that the power of choosing officials and ministers was inherent in the royal dignity.[3] It was a bold step and met with general resistance. The barons prevented the royal Justices, on various pretexts, from holding their assizes. In some places the shire-courts refused to assemble for the Eyre ; in others the new sheriffs were treated with contempt, and the commons persisted in acknowledging the Guardians of the Peace whom the barons nominated in lieu of sheriffs. There were, for the moment, two executives with conflicting titles to legitimacy.[4] Both appealed to the commonalty. The Council summoned three knights from every shire to meet them at St. Albans; the King issued a counter-summons to a parliament at Windsor.[5] But the Council, in spite of popular sympathy, were afraid of proceeding to extremities. The Earl of Gloucester, who had not yet made his defection public, prevailed on the majority to accept a compromise with the King. In spite of Leicester's remonstrances it was agreed that arbitrators should be chosen, in equal numbers from both

---

[1] See the Pope's letter of April 13th, 1261, in *Foedera*, i., 405.
[2] Bémont, p. 191.   [3] Wykes, 129. *Foedera*, i., 408. Shirley, ii., p. 192.
[4] *Flores Hist.*, ii., 468-73.   [5] *S. C.*, 405.

sides, to revise the Provisions of Oxford.[1]   Immediately afterwards
Gloucester announced himself a royalist.   The barons had been
duped; but they were weary of the struggle, and held by their
agreement with the King.   Only De Montfort refused to make this
tame submission; he announced his intention of going on Crusade
and left the country for a time.[2]   The arbitrators began their
work, and at the outset admitted the King's right to nominate all
sheriffs.   But they did not move rapidly enough to satisfy the
King, who on May 2nd, 1262, published an ordinance revoking the
Provisions.   It was in vain that the leaderless Council offered to
renounce the more obnoxious articles, if the rest might be allowed
to stand.   The King had taken their measure; he was not afraid
of force while the great Earl remained in voluntary exile.[3]

But he could not exclude Montfort permanently from the king- Montfort
dom, since the prosecution of the Earl had failed.   And Montfort resorts to
only awaited a favourable moment to return.   He thought that it 1263
had come when in July, 1262, death removed his rival Richard de
Clare.   In the autumn of the year, when the King was absent
from the country on a visit to Louis IX., Montfort appeared at a
Parliament, held by the Justiciar and sounded the dispositions of
the barons.   It is said that he read before them letters from the
Pope which announced that the Holy See had condemned the Provisions in consequence of a misapprehension, and now, being better
informed of their true nature, desired that they should hold.[4]   If
the story be true we cannot acquit Montfort of the charge of
forgery; but a fraud so unskilful can hardly be laid to his charge
on the evidence of a single annalist.   Whatever passed at this
Parliament, it left the barons hesitating.   Not until the following
spring did they invite the Earl to return and take their lead.   He
came with alacrity, and found himself at the head of a following in
which the King of the Romans and the young Earl of Gloucester,
the most influential of the magnates, were included.   In a Parliament, which they held at Oxford without the knowledge of the
King, the confederates resolved to treat as public enemies all the
opponents of the Provisions.   Immediately afterwards the Earl of
Leicester led a considerable army through the south and central

[1] *Foedera*, i., 411. Gervase, ii., 213.   [2] *Oseney Annals*, 128.
[3] Bémont, p. 195. *Foedera*, i., 419.   Wykes, 130, 131.
[4] Gervase, ii., 214. *Foedera*, i., 422.

Marches to attack those who came under the terms of the Oxford resolution.   At Hereford he arrested the Savoyard bishop, Pierre d'Aigueblanche, on the steps of the cathedral altar and threw him into prison ; Gloucester, Worcester, Shrewsbury, Bridgnorth were then occupied in rapid succession and cleared of their royalist garrisons.   On his march the Earl harried the lands of the King's friends and gave those of the aliens to his own supporters.[1]   The King, the Queen, and the Lord Edward took refuge in the Tower, where they remained as helpless spectators of the Earl's campaign.

London was in a ferment of rebellion although the more cautious and substantial of the citizens were royalist at heart.   In the last few years the control of the city had passed from the hands of the rich families into those of a democratic Mayor, who submitted every question to the folk-moot and paid no attention to the wishes of the aldermen.   The commons of the city had ceased to look for guidance to their natural superiors.   They had formed clubs and associations which were controlled by elected leaders and, while existing nominally for the conservation of the peace, were in fact a cause of continual disorders.[2]   The royal family dared not trust themselves to the loyalty of this mob, and Henry attempted to send his wife away to Windsor.   Her barge, however, was pursued ; she was pelted with stones and mud and curses, and at length sought a refuge with the Bishop of London since she could neither leave the city nor regain the Tower.   Late in June the approach of the barons was announced.   The King of the Romans, who had been driven back to his brother's side by the outbreak of hostilities, went forth to meet the Earl and make a truce.[3]   It was useless ; the baronial army marched down the Thames to Reading ; then southeast by way of Guildford to the Cinque Ports, where they were amongst friends and could prevent the landing of foreign mercenaries.   Even those who cared little for the cause of the Provisions thought it prudent to feign sympathy, and in some cases joined the rebel army.

Henry Proposes Arbitration
The proximity of a hostile and triumphant force dissipated the King's small stock of resolution.   On July 21st he accepted the terms which the barons offered him ; consenting to place all castles

[1] *Dunstaple Annals*, 221, 222.   Bliss, *Calendar*, 411.   Rishanger, pp. 11 ff. (R. S.). Gervase, ii., 221.
[2] *Chron. Maj. et Vicecom.*, 54, etc.   Wykes, 138.   [3] Shirley, ii., pp. 247, 248.

in their hands, to banish all the aliens who still remained or had returned, and to observe the Provisions without alteration. These terms were ratified in a parliament of September 9th.[1] But already by that time the reaction had begun. The Earl's supporters murmured that his treatment of the royalists had been illegal, that he had dealt too severely with the King, that he was an alien no less than the Poitevins and Savoyards.[2] Upon these doubts and scruples the Lord Edward played with a master hand. He alone had endeavoured to organise resistance in the summer campaign ; he had openly expressed his aversion from the peace, and was at no pains to observe it. He appealed to the pride, the loyalty, the cupidity of the opposition lords; among those of the Welsh and northern marches he soon made many converts. The feudal nucleus of the Earl's party dissolved with dramatic rapidity; and in London itself the royalists began to gather courage. Though Montfort was encamped at Southwark a party of the citizens formed, and all but carried through, a plot for betraying London to the King. By the end of the year the King was able in his turn to impose conditions ; the Earl's party were obliged to agree that all questions in dispute, whether touching the Provisions or other matters, should be referred to the arbitration of Louis IX. The Earl's promise was unconditional; yet it is clear from the sequel that he made mental reservations. He may have been over-confident as to the result of the award ; he may have argued that the bad faith with which the royalists had interpreted the agreement of the summer absolved him from the necessity of treating them more scrupulously. But the construction which he put upon his promise is one of the few obliquities that can be detected in his long career.[3]

The decision of Louis IX., the famous Mise of Amiens, was pronounced on January 24th, 1264, before the King of England and a great assembly of his partisans ; the Montfortians sent proctors with full powers, preferring for their own part to remain in England that, if it came to blows, they might not be taken unprepared. The terms of the award cannot have surprised those who had any knowledge of the French King's character ; the story that his true

The Mise of Amiens, 1264

[1] *Chron. Maj. et Vicecom.*, 55 ff. *Ann. Dunst.*, 223, 224.
[2] *Ann. Dunst.*, 221, 222. *Tewkesbury Ann.*, 180. Gervase, ii., 226.
[3] Bémont, p. 205. Halliwell's note to the *Chron. de Bellis*, p. 121. *Foedera*, i., 434. Shirley, ii., p. 251.

inclinations were over-ruled by the influence of his wife and her sister, the Queen of England,[1] may be dismissed as idle gossip. In deciding against the constitutionalists on the two essential matters in dispute, in cancelling the Provisions and asserting Henry's right to employ aliens, or any other persons whom he pleased, as counsellors and ministers, Louis merely followed the line which was prescribed by his own convictions and by the pronouncements of two successive Popes.[2] Before these terms were known in England the Earl had already mustered his forces to attack Roger Mortimer who, on the Welsh marches, was molesting the adherents of the Provisions. When the news arrived Henry de Montfort was despatched to the west, with orders to cross the Severn and co-operate with Llewelyn, whose adhesion had been secured in the preceding year; a second force, under the younger Simon, went northward to prevent the royalists of Yorkshire and Northumberland from bringing their forces to the assistance of the King.[3]

Montfort Rejects the Mise

For his breach of faith with Henry the Earl did not condescend to apologise. But in the eyes of the commons it was more than pardonable. Some argued that the oath to uphold the Provisions must override all other obligations. Others asserted that the Mise of Amiens was obtained by fraud or bribery, and therefore binding upon no man; or, more ingeniously, that it was inconsistent with itself since Louis, while cancelling the Provisions, had recognised the validity of Magna Carta, of which the Provisions were but a logical corollary. Such reasoning was little suited to the prejudices of the feudal classes. Those barons who remained on Simon's side were either enthusiastic youths, such as Gilbert of Gloucester, or men who felt that they were irrevocably committed.[4] The publication of the Mise was followed by desertions which filled the Earl of Leicester with a passionate resentment. " I have been in many lands," he said to his confidential friends, " and nowhere have I found men so faithless as in England ; but, though all forsake me I and my four sons will stand for the just cause." It soon appeared that the Montforts would not stand alone. All the chief cities of the kingdom rallied to his side,

---

[1] *Tewkesbury Annals*, 176.   [2] Text of the Mise in *S. C.*, 406.
[3] *Chron. de Bellis*, 17 ff. Gervase, ii., 232. Shirley, ii., p. 253.
[4] *Worcester Annals*, 450, give a list; " duces erant strenui sed maxima pars juvenum " (*Waverley Ann.*, 356).

notwithstanding that the municipal patriciates were royalist. Following the example of London the poorer citizens everywhere set aside their old magistrates and improvised new governments, of which the members were devoted to the cause of the Provisions.[1] The Franciscans and the party of ecclesiastical reform accepted Montfort as their champion, the Hercules who should destroy the hydra-headed corruption of the Church. The Oxford students were for the most part his admirers; a body of them joined the younger Simon at Northampton and formed a separate corps fighting under their own banner.[2]

The recruits were numerous, but they were not trained soldiers; nor, on the Earl's side, were there any skilled generals save himself. Hence the campaign opened with disasters for his cause, although the return of the King and Edward was imprudently delayed for several weeks. Henry de Montfort moved slowly in the Marches. He did not attack Gloucester until Edward had appeared to put heart into the garrison; and, when on the point of capturing the castle, he accorded a truce under cover of which the Prince escaped to join his father at Oxford.[3] The Earl, who was undoubtedly the greatest soldier then in England, delayed offensive operations with the double object of securing London and of making a last effort for a compromise. In London he was successful; the commons organised a militia which they placed at the disposal of Montfort's lieutenant, Hugh Despenser. But the King refused to accept the moderate proposal that he should employ no aliens in his service, and otherwise be free to govern as he pleased.[4] While the Earl negotiated, the royalists were called to arms; at the beginning of April they moved from Oxford to Northampton, obtained access to the city through the treachery of the prior of St. Andrews, and made prisoners of the younger Simon and his army. The Earl, who had marched out from London to relieve his son, was met at St. Albans by the news of this disaster. He at once fell back upon the capital, leaving the North and Midlands at the disposal of the King. His disappointed followers and the baser sort among the Londoners found consolation in an attack upon the Jewry. The helpless inmates were offered their choice between baptism and

---

[1] *Chron. Maj. et Vicecom.*, 55 ff. *Chron. de Bellis*, 22.
[2] Hemingburgh, i., 311.
[3] *Chron. de Bellis*, 20, 21. *Rob. of Gloucester*, 11,234. *Dunstaple Ann.*, 228.
[4] Pauli, *S. de Montfort*, p. 141 (E. T.).

death; the houses of the martyr and the proselyte were indiscriminately pillaged. It is an episode which reflects discredit on the Earl, even though we reject the statement that he stooped to be a partner in the spoil.[1] But, in common with many of his followers and with his famous father, he entertained against the Jews the same intolerant rancour which the first crusaders displayed in their relations with the infidel.

Southward March of the King
When Simon resumed his campaign it was against Rochester that his army was directed; for this stronghold intercepted his communications with the Cinque Ports, and formed the chief obstacle to his ascendancy in south-east England. He encountered an obstinate defence; but siege-engines were brought up from London, and the garrison were driven from the city into the castle, from the outer works of the castle to the keep. Another two days would have reduced them to surrender; but the news arrived that the royal army, reinforced by all the barons of the North country, was marching upon London. The Earl broke up the siege of Rochester to visit the capital and assure himself that the commons could hold their own against the treachery of secret royalists. But the King's army avoided London. It came by forced marches through the north part of the Sussex Weald to Tunbridge; took the castle, which was held by the men of Earl Gilbert; and then proceeded to the Cinque Ports, where Henry hoped that he would be able to secure a fleet.[2]

The Battle of Lewes, May 14th, 1264
The "barons" of the Cinque Ports were not, however, to be conciliated. They embarked on their ships, and remained at sea so long as the King was in the neighbourhood. He was at a loss to know what his next step should be; and precious days were wasted while the Earl, at London, mustered all his available forces to give chase. A large force of the city militia, whose only experience of service had been gained in harrying the royalist estates near London, added to the numbers without increasing the efficiency of his host; and it was certainly with an inferior force that he pursued the King.[3]

---

[1] This charge in the Royalist Wykes, 141. The best accounts are in the *Chron. de Bellis*, 24, 25, and *Ann. Dunstaple*, 230; but both repeat vulgar calumnies against the Jews.

[2] *Chron. de Bellis*, 25. *Worcester Ann.*, 450. *Dunstaple*, 231. Gervase, ii., 236. Wykes, 147.

[3] *Chron. de Bellis*, 27, says 15,000 Londoners; but says that the whole army was smaller than Henry's (p. 32). *Dunstaple Annals*, 232, say the royalists were four to one. *Worcester Annals*, 451, that they were 60,000 against 40,000. None of these figures can be trusted.

Henry retreated southward to Lewes, which he reached on May 12th, closely followed by the Earl; on that night the rebel army lay at Fletching, a village some nine miles distant from the King's position. The following day was consumed in negotiations. The Earl protested that he fought, not against the King, but against the evil counsellors; the King replied that those who attacked the counsellors attacked himself. Three bishops of the Earl's party, those of London, Chichester and Worcester, then essayed to act as mediators. They offered that, if the King would conform the provisions, the Earl would pay the sum of £30,000 in compensation for the damage inflicted upon royalist property; it is possible that they offered a bribe for the help of Richard of Cornwall.[1] A contemporary satire, the earliest in the English language, gives us to understand that the Emperor-elect was not unwilling.

> The Kyn of Alemaigne bi mi leauté
> Thritti thousent pound askede he
> For to make the pees in the countré.

These proposals were not accepted, and on the night of May 13th the Earl prepared for battle. He determined the order in which the troops should advance, and spent sleepless hours in prayer; while the Bishop of Worcester gave absolution to the soldiers, and exhorted them to face death cheerfully for the sake of the true cause. All sewed white crosses on their breasts and backs, both as a distinguishing badge and also in token that they were crusaders. They left their camp before dawn and marched towards Lewes, not by the straight road, but along the crest of a wooded down from which they would be invisible to the royalist outposts. About six in the morning the army reached a point at which the heights sloped gently down towards the town of Lewes and the Cluniac priory, outside the walls, in which the King was lodged. Here the Earl halted to make his final dispositions. The baggage and the standard of the host were left upon the heights and in the charge of a small guard. The Earl kept for himself the command of the reserves; he committed that of the right wing to his sons Guy and Henry, that of the centre to Gilbert de Clare; the Londoners, who are said to have numbered 15,000, were posted on the left. When all was ready the Earl addressed his troops: " We shall fight this

---

[1] *Chron. de Bellis*, 29, 30. Wykes, 148. Gervase, ii., 236. Kingsford, *Song of Lewes*, p. 71.

day," he said, "for the weal of England, and to keep our faith. Let us beseech the Lord of all, that, if it be His pleasure, He will give us strength and help." The soldiers prostrated themselves, extending their arms in the form of a cross and crying: "Lord, give us victory for the honour of Thy Name".[1] By this time the royalists had taken the alarm, and were mustering in haste to meet the attack. They moved out towards the enemy in three divisions, of which that commanded by Prince Edward faced the Londoners, and marched somewhat in advance of the centre and the left wing, commanded by Richard of Cornwall, and the King. The two armies met at the charge and, although the rebels had the advantage of the slope, the first encounter was unfavourable to them. Edward and his knights, having broken the line of the Londoners, hunted them to a distance of four miles from the field, and, in returning, captured the baggage and the standard of the Earl. But in the meantime the Earl had concentrated his attack upon the division led by the King of the Romans. It broke at length; that of Henry was left to bear the whole weight of the battle, and in turn gave way. The royal charger fell, hamstrung by the Earl of Gloucester; and the King was only rescued with the greatest difficulty. He took refuge in the priory outside the walls, while the barons hunted the fugitives into Lewes, and stormed a neighbouring windmill in which the King of the Romans had taken refuge.[2] Edward regained the field only to find that all was lost. He retired to Lewes castle, and desired to attempt a sally against the troops which were coming up to storm the priory. But the position was hopeless; the royalist barons insisted on a peace; and that night the Mise of Lewes was concluded between the King and Earl, by the mediation of certain Dominicans and Franciscans.[3]

---

[1] John of Oxenede in Halliwell, *Chron. de Bellis*, 129. Rishanger, *Continuatio* 26 (R. S.), and Hemingburgh, i., 314 ff., agree as to the battle-order. Other accounts of the battle in the *Chron. of Lanercost*, 74, *Chron. de Bellis*, 30 ff., *Chron. Mailros*, 193-5, Wykes, 149, *Waverley Annals*, 357, of which the first two supply picturesque details, but not a clear account of the tactics. Halliwell, in his notes to the *Chron. de Bellis*, 136, collects from MS. sources various estimates of the slaughter, ranging from 5,000 downwards.

[2] The Kyng of Alemaigne wende do ful wel
He saisede the mulne for a castel ;
With hare sharpe swerdes he grounde the stel,
He wende that the sailes were mangonel
To helpe Wyndesore.

[3] Rishanger, p. 28 (R. S.). Hemingburgh, i., 318. Pauli, i., p. 772.

CHAPTER XVIII

THE RULE AND FALL OF MONTFORT

THE Mise of Lewes, known to us only through epitomes,[1] intentions of the Earl and the secret hopes of his opponents. The beaten party negotiated better than they fought. They seemed to give up everything which was demanded; but in reality they laid a trap from which the Earl was only to escape with considerable damage to his reputation.

Montfort's demands were moderate and almost conservative. The reforms on which he insisted were expressed or implied in the Provisions of 1258. He stipulated that the King's Council should be selected by a board of arbitrators, and exclusively composed of Englishmen; that the King's expenses should be regulated by the Council until his debts were discharged; that the Council should guide the King in the appointment of ministers and the execution of justice; that the Charters should be inviolably observed. All other questions than these the Earl consented to leave in the hands of the arbitrators. The duties of the latter were therefore of the first importance. But the Earl allowed the board to be so constituted that it could scarcely fail to support the Crown against the popular party. Two alternative schemes were proposed in the Mise. According to the first the duty of arbitration was vested in a committee composed of the Archbishop of Rouen, the Bishop of London, Hugh the Despenser and Pierre le Chambellan, the chief minister of Louis IX. If these four were equally divided on any question the casting vote of the legate, Guy Foulquois, was to be invited. Should this committee fail to consult the legate in such cases, their proceedings were to be altogether null

The Mise of Lewes *(margin note)*

[1] Bémont, p. 222, gives an official abstract which agrees with that of the *Chron. de Bellis*, 37. See also *Chron. Maj. et Vicecom.*, 63.

and void; and their work was to devolve upon a committee of five French nobles, chosen with the approval of Louis IX.[1]

The appointment of Guy Foulquois as a referee doomed the Mise to failure. The royalists knew, and Simon apparently did not, that the instructions which Urban IV. had transmitted to his legate were marked by a strong dislike to the party of the Provisions.[2] A few weeks later, having received fuller information on this head, the Earl forbade Foulquois to enter England.[3] Consequently the legate could not act as referee; the original committee of arbitration became useless. Some attempts were made to form the alternative committee of French nobles; and we possess a letter from Henry III. in which he urges the Earl to arrange with Louis IX. a preliminary conference for this purpose.[4] The King knew that such a committee would be favourable to his party. The Earl on the other hand, had never supposed that French arbitrators would be needed; he had pinned his hopes upon the first committee which contained two of his partisans and, in the person of the Archbishop of Rouen, a neutral with whom he had a friendship of some standing. Montfort escaped from his difficulty by insisting that the original scheme should be modified. A new board was constituted, of two French and two English members with the Archbishop of Rouen, as a fifth to give a casting vote where the opinions of the four were equally divided.[5] But even so the Earl was dissatisfied. He did not rely upon the new board as he had relied upon the old; probably he foresaw that the influence of Louis and the Pope would prevent the French commissioners from judging with impartiality. Hence the indefinite postponement of the arbitration; the royal party pressed for it, but the Earl on one plea or another refused to gratify them. Meanwhile he took the law into his own hands, and framed another scheme of settlement which, although possessing many merits, was in no sense warranted by the agreement made at Lewes. For the second time Montfort found himself constrained, in the interest of his cause, to repay duplicity in kind. His misfortune was that his opponents, in the war of recriminations which naturally ensued, got possession of the public ear and were able, while advertising his evasions, to conceal their own.

The new settlement was promulgated in a Parliament which

[1] Shirley, ii., p. 258. Wykes, 152.   [2] Bliss, *Calendar*, 396.
[3] Wykes, 155.   [4] Shirley, ii., p. 262.   [5] Pauli, *S. de Montfort*, p. 165 (E. T.).

met on June 22nd. The name of Parliament, which was now coming The
into common use did not, as yet, connote a representative assembly. *Forma Regiminis*
A Parliament was but a meeting of the Great or Common Council 1264
under a new name. In this case, however, representatives, four in
number, were called from every shire;[1] an intimation that the Earl
would not carry his defence of the Provisions to the point of restoring their exclusive scheme of government. The summons to
the knights of the shire intimates that they will be allowed to
discuss the affairs of the King and kingdom; and it is highly
probable that Montfort counted on the third estate to give him
a majority in the debates. The barons and prelates of both parties
had been summoned to attend;[2] and in a full gathering of magnates
the advantage of numbers would be with the King. Of the debates
we have no record beyond an official statement that the new scheme
was approved by all the prelates and barons and "the whole community of the realm". The scheme is entitled "A Form for the
Government of the King and Kingdom".[3] It provides for the
appointment of a committee of three persons upon whom shall rest
the responsibility of nominating the royal Council. These three,
who may for convenience be called Electors, are expressly made
responsible to the "community of the prelates and barons," that
is, to the Great Council; and may be superseded, if their conduct
gives dissatisfaction, by others whom the King shall nominate with
the consent of the same body. The ordinary Councillors are to be
nine in number. Without their consent the King shall not do
anything; but they may act in the King's name when he is absent,
provided that two-thirds of them are in agreement; or, if they
disagree, the question at issue may be settled by the three Electors.
The King is to choose the Justiciar, Treasurer, Chancellor, and
other ministers; but his choice requires the approval of the Council.
Should any Councillor be guilty of misconduct the King may, with
the consent and counsel of the Electors, make a new appointment.
All the Electors and Councillors shall be native Englishmen.

This constitution was promulgated, according to the preamble, Effect of
with the consent of the King and the Lord Edward; but, as both the Settle-
were in effect the prisoners of the Earl, we cannot lay stress upon ment
their acquiescence. The preamble also states that the constitution
is a temporary expedient, to hold good until the terms of the Mise

[1] *S. C.*, 400.   [2] Shirley, ii., p. 256.   [3] Printed in *S. C.*, 401.

arranged at Lewes should be completely fulfilled; but the care with
which the details of the provisional executive are contrived
suggests that it was not meant to be provisional; and it would
seem that Montfort soon abandoned the idea of allowing the Mise
to be literally fulfilled. The Parliament showed by its choice of
Electors that it was strongly Montfortian in sympathies; not only
was the Earl appointed, but he obtained as colleagues the Bishop
of Chichester and the Earl of Gloucester, the one a devoted
partisan of Montfort, the other too young and inexperienced, so
far as could be seen, to prove a serious rival. Provided that future
Parliaments showed the same spirit, the Earl remained indisputably
supreme. Writs and proclamations were issued in the King's name
and attested by the council for which the Form of Government
provided; but we know that the Earl consulted the wishes neither
of Henry nor of his nominal colleagues. Whether from interested
motives or from a conviction that he alone could steer the kingdom
through the difficulties of the moment, the fact remains that he
made himself an autocrat.

But we cannot fairly judge this constitution from the manner
in which it was administered during Montfort's brief period of
supremacy. From his victory at Lewes to his death at Evesham
the entire country was in a state of siege. In quieter times, and
with opportunities for independent criticism of the executive, the
new scheme might have worked smoothly. It has the great
merit of simplicity; it provides the means of making some minister
of the Crown responsible for every act of the Crown; it establishes
a moderate compromise between the claims of King and Parliament
to nominate the executive. In some respects the Earl anticipated
the principles of the Cabinet system, and it is unfortunate that his
downfall left his system of government discredited. As a constructive statesman he failed chiefly because he was in advance of his
contemporaries and lacked the patience to convert them by degrees.

The Op-
position
It must be admitted that many of his enemies were utterly
irreconcilable. A certain number of the barons who had escaped
from Lewes fortified themselves in Pevensey Castle, and all efforts
to dislodge them proved unsuccessful. Many of the northern
families, headed by John of Balliol, had refused to attend the
June Parliament and were covertly negotiating for the help of
Scotland in a revolt against the new dictatorship. One chronicler

affirms that every castle in the country had become a nest of robbers, and that every magnate stood for his own hand.[1] This statement, so far as it applied to the north and the Welsh marches, is perfectly correct. Apart from all domestic disturbances there was hourly danger of invasion. The Earl Warenne, William of Valence, and Hugh Bigod had joined the Queen in France, and were raising mercenaries for the King's assistance. The Earl made vigorous preparations to meet force with force. While negotiating with France to procure the expulsion of the exiles, he called out the fyrds of all the seaboard shires, commanding the Guardians of the Peace whom he had appointed to let neither the harvest nor any other consideration prevent them from maintaining a proper guard at all the ports and landing places. "It is better," he wrote, "to secure our personal safety at some cost than to lose goods and life and all at the hands of those who are thirsting for your blood."[2] The feudal levies were called out in like manner, but responded to the summons with less enthusiasm, many of the barons alleging that they were kept at home by the fear of private enemies. By raising a loan, and by inducing the clergy to grant a tithe, the Earl secured the means of keeping an efficient fleet at sea. The greater part of the ships were furnished by his faithful adherents of the Cinque Ports, whose zeal was stimulated by a general permission to detain all foreign ships which they might discover leaving or entering an English port. They did their work with the thoroughness of experienced pirates, making little distinction between Englishmen and foreigners; they threw their prisoners overboard, and appropriated ships and cargoes. Soon they had cleared the seas; the price of wine and all imported commodities rose by leaps and bounds; and bitter complaints poured in upon the government from every side. But so great was the fear of invasion that the Earl openly justified their conduct. "Why," he is reported to have asked complainants, "why could not Englishmen subsist on the produce of their own country without recourse to strangers?"[3] The argument has often done duty since the time of Montfort; but in this case the appeal to national pride was far from satisfying the commercial classes.

[1] Shirley, ii., pp. 260, 270. *Chron. de Bellis*, 41. *Opus Chronicorum* (R. S.).
[2] Shirley, ii., p. 271, a mutilated copy; more completely in *Chron. Maj. et Vicecom.*, 67, and *Foedera*, i., 444.
[3] *Chron. Maj. et Vicecom.*, 73. Wykes, 158. *Cf.* Bémont, p. 139.

Gloucester deserts Montfort
The danger of invasion passed away when the Queen's mercenaries discovered that for the present they could expect no pay save promises. But the malcontents in England were supported by powerful allies. The cardinal-legate, incensed by the Earl's refusal to admit him, employed himself at Boulogne in issuing sentences of excommunication against all the chief supporters of the government.[1] He produced for the moment little effect upon the bishops or those whom he condemned ; but he became a dangerous enemy on his election to the Papal chair, which took place early in the following year (Feb. 5th, 1265). And before this event the Earl of Gloucester, the second person in the government, had come forward to denounce his leader. Earl Gilbert first showed signs of discontent in the latter part of the year 1264. After a campaign in which Montfort had humbled the Mortimers and other rebel Marchers to such a degree that they purchased peace by undertaking to leave the country for a year, Gilbert took them under his protection and instigated them to remain in the Marches in defiance of their promises. For this he was called to account in the February parliament of 1265. He replied by a fierce attack upon Montfort, whom he accused of appropriating to himself and to his sons all confiscated lands, all wardships, marriages, castles, ransoms, and in fine all the revenues of the Crown. There was a certain truth in these complaints. The Earl, no doubt, in keeping the finances under his personal control, had acted as the head of the government and in the interests of the Crown ; but his extensive grants to his three sons could not be justified on grounds of policy. The younger Montforts were arrogant and lawless ; nor were they the most suitable agents whom their father could have found. Their recorded actions expose them to the charge of incapacity ; and Henry the eldest of them, who had been put in charge of Dover Castle and the Cinque Ports, abused his position, it is said, to plunder the wool-merchants of the kingdom. Such blots upon the administration deserved a more disinterested criticism than they received from Gloucester. His chief complaint was that he had been kept out of his just share in the spoil ; and it was on a purely personal quarrel that he finally raised his banner against Montfort. The latter forbade a tournament which had been arranged by his own sons; Earl Gilbert who had intended to hold

[1] *Foedera*, i., 447. Wykes, 155. *Chron. de Bellis*, 38, 39.

the lists against the Montforts, and had spent large sums upon his preparations, took offence at this assumption of authority, although it had been for years the practice of the executive to prohibit these encounters, which were invariably the cause of bloodshed and frequently a mask for treasonable preparations.   On the appointed day (April 19th), hearing that Gilbert intended to defy the proclamation, Earl Simon marched to Dunstable with a strong force of the London militia to support him.   There was no difficulty in preventing the tournament ; for the Earl of Gloucester had been forewarned and abstained from appearing.   But soon the news arrived that he was mustering his vassals at Gloucester, and on his Welsh estates behind the barrier of the Severn.[1]

This quarrel apparently had the effect of blinding contemporaries to the importance of the Parliament in which it first broke out.   Only a single writer of the time notices that a new class of members, the representatives of cities and boroughs, now for the first time made their appearance ; but the official writs leave no room for questioning the truth of his account.   The significance of the innovation may be variously interpreted.   We have seen that the towns, during the struggle for the Charter, asked to be released from the burden of arbitrary tallage ; it was only a step from the claim of 1215 to the claim of representation.   Taxation, however, was not the object of the Parliament of 1265.   It was convened that it might witness the solemn confirmation of the recent settlement, and the release of the Lord Edward from his confinement as a hostage.[2] We may rather suppose that the Earl applied to all chartered boroughs the principle of continental jurisprudence, which Magna Carta had recognised in the case of London, that a commune is a feudal lordship vested in a multitude instead of a single person. This supposition is confirmed when we observe that the towns, on this occasion, received their summons, like other tenants-in-chief, directly from the Crown and not, as in 1295, through the sheriffs of their shires.   But there was also a more practical reason for summoning the burgesses.   This Parliament was a packed assembly.   Only those barons who were favourable to the revolution received a summons ; whereas of the heads of religious houses, who

The Parliament of 1265

---

[1] For the causes of the quarrel see Wykes, 53.   *Chron. de Bello*, 377 (ed. Bémont). *Chron. Maj. et Vicecom.*, 73.   *Chron. de Bellis*, 42.   Rishanger (ed. Riley), 32.   Hemingburgh, i., 319.
[2] *S. C.*, 416.   *Foedera*, i., 453, 454.   *Chron. Maj. et Vicecom.*, 71.

were generally in sympathy with Montfort, a larger number were
called than on any previous occasion. It was only natural that
the towns should be invited to assist in demonstrating to the world
the strength of the Earl's party ; the more natural, because the
writs were issued at a time when the open breach with Gloucester
was already imminent. The question arises, whether the towns
were to be represented in all future Parliaments ; but on this point
we have no evidence. Some stress has been laid on the fact that
representatives of the lower clergy were summoned to attend a
second Parliament of this same year ; it has been argued that representatives of the shires and towns were probably summoned also.
This may be the case, but it is also probable that the clergy were
summoned because, unlike the laity, they had not been under arms
for fyrd-service or the Welsh expedition, and were therefore expected to grant the government an aid. It is a better argument
that Montfort would scarcely have ventured to take from the
boroughs a privilege which he had once accorded ; for representation can hardly have been regarded by the towns as other than a
privilege, when it was their only guarantee against arbitrary imposts
and had not yet come to entail taxation at a heavier rate.

Outbreak of War, April, 1265

The withdrawal of Earl Gilbert to the west meant war ; and
Leicester did not hesitate to accept the challenge. Taking the
King and Prince with him he advanced on Gloucester. They
entered the city without encountering resistance, for Gilbert had
retired beyond the Severn. He shrank from offering battle single
handed, and made delusive offers of peace which Leicester unsus-
pectingly accepted. It was agreed that all disputes should be
referred to arbitration ; the dictator endeavoured to quiet the
agitation of the country by a formal announcement that there had
never been any breach of friendship between himself and Gloucester.
From Gloucester the Montfortian army advanced on Hereford, and
here Simon took up his quarters that he might deal at leisure with
the disaffected Marchers.[1]

His position was, however, more precarious than he had suspected ; and in moving to the west of the Severn he had committed
an error of which his enemies took full advantage. On May 10th a
force of 120 knights and foot-soldiers, commanded by the Earl Warenne and William of Valence, landed in Pembroke. Their coming

[1] *Waverley Annals*, 358 ff. *Foedera*, i., 455.

fanned the sparks of rebellion in the southern Marches, and raised
new doubts of the Earl of Gloucester's good faith.   On May 28th
Prince Edward, riding with his guards in the open country outside Edward
Hereford, made good his escape by a stratagem and was received escapes
by Roger Mortimer at Wigmore Castle.   The Prince and his host
were immediately joined by the Earl of Gloucester.   Edward
pledged his word that, if his father were restored, the alien counsellors should be removed, and the evil customs done away; the
promise removed the last scruples of Earl Gilbert, and he at once
raised the royal banner.   The shires of Chester, Salop, Worcester,
and Hereford declared for the prince; his partisans broke down
the bridges at Shrewsbury, Bridgnorth and Worcester; Gloucester
castle was surrendered by Montfort's garrison on June 29th; and the
whole line of the Severn was thus barred against him.[1]

We are not told why Montfort had neglected to pursue the Montfort
Prince.   Probably the escape, occurring in the Earl's absence from behind the
Hereford, only became known to him when Edward had passed out May-July,
of reach.   On June 22nd Montfort was still at Hereford.   There is [1265]
an extant treaty of that date between himself and Prince Llewelyn,
in which the latter receives extensive grants of lands and castles as
the price of his assistance.   Even with this support the Earl despaired of forcing a way across the Severn, and preferred to attempt
the Bristol Channel.   Marching down the Wye, and capturing
Monmouth castle on the way, he established himself at Newport to
await the ships which he had summoned from Bristol.   But the
plan had been anticipated by the royalists; and their fleet sank his
transports under his very eyes in Newport harbour.[2]   No course
remained but to try the passage of the Severn.   The Earl returned
to Hereford, while the royalists occupied the country in his rear.
Their numbers were superior to his own, and the retreat was only
effected with great difficulty; the capture of Brecon by Prince
Edward, and of Monmouth by Gloucester, precluded the idea of
regaining the east by any route save those across the Severn.   For
some days the Earl lay at Hereford, watching for an opportunity;
the main force of the royalists, commanded by the Prince, took up

[1] *Foedera*, 155.   Shirley, ii., p. 283.   *Chron. Maj. et Vicecom.*, 73.   Wykes, 163.
Rishanger, 33, 34.
[2] *Foedera*, i., 457, for the Welsh treaty.   Hemingburgh, i., 321.   *Chron. de
Bellis*, 43.   Wykes says that Simon's transports were not allowed to enter Newport
harbour, but repulsed from the entrance.

their position at Worcester. Either through fear of Montfort's generalship, or from a well-founded conviction that delay would weaken his position, they made no effort to assume the offensive

The Rout of Kenilworth, Aug. 1st

The Earl's hopes rested on his son, the younger Simon, whom he had left behind him to prosecute the siege of Pevensey. In response to an urgent summons the youth drew off from Pevensey to London, and made his preparations for marching to the west. The Londoners, who were still enthusiastic for the good cause,

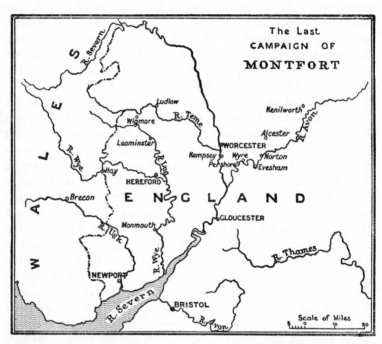

supplied him with a force of infantry; but in other places through which he passed there was more division of opinion. Winchester refused him admission and only yielded at length to the threat of force. Oxford and Northampton were more friendly; but, although the midlands showed as yet no inclination to follow the Welsh Marches in the path of a royalist reaction, they preferred to remain neutral in the war. On August 1st the army which the younger Simon had collected came to Kenilworth. Thirty miles from the royalist head-quarters, they thought themselves secure

against a surprise, and decided to sleep in the town rather than in
the castle ; in order, says one authority, that they might all bathe
the more easily in the morning, for they thought that a bath
would be a good preparation for a battle.[1] The knights lodged
themselves in the priory ; the common soldiers were quartered in
the dwelling houses of the town. But their slumbers were rudely
disturbed. The Prince had a spy in the town, a woman named
Margot who had disguised herself as a man ; and the news which
she sent him was turned to good account. He made a forced
march from Worcester in the darkness, and attacked the enemy
at dawn on the next morning while they were still in their beds.
Simon, with a few knights, escaped to the castle ; but fifteen of the
twenty bannerets who had followed him were taken. His infantry
and men-at-arms had no time to arm themselves or indeed to dress.
Many were slain in the act of flying with their clothes under their
arms ; the rest dispersed to their own homes.[2]

It was a bold idea to attack the relieving force before it could The Earl
join hands with the Earl. But Edward's march to Kenilworth left reaches
the passage of the Severn undefended ; and Leicester, who was Evesham,
duly informed of his son's approach, had not failed to keep a watch Aug. 3rd
upon the movements of the Prince. On August 2nd, the day after
the fight at Kenilworth, the Earl's army crossed the river at Kempsey
in boats, four miles below the town of Worcester, without encountering opposition ; and Edward, returning on the 3rd to Worcester, learned that his enemy was already on the way to Kenilworth.
That night the Earl encamped at Evesham, a town enclosed on
three sides by the river Avon. He had avoided the direct road to
Kenilworth, doubtless with the object of joining his son before
giving battle to the royalists. But he showed less than his usual
judgment in the choice of a camping-ground. At Evesham there
was but one bridge across the river. This exit was barred at dawn
by a force acting under the Prince's lieutenant, Roger Mortimer ;[3]
simultaneously two other corps, commanded the one by Edward in
person, the other by the Earl of Gloucester, appeared on the north

---

[1] *Chron. de Mailros*, 198 f.
[2] Hemingburgh, i., 322. *Chron. de Mailros.*
[3] " Rogerus de Mortimer a tergo veniebat," Hemingburgh, i., 323 ; " ab occi-
dente et a tergo," *ib.*, 324. The writer speaks from the point of view of the Earl
who faced Edward's force coming from the north. The position of the Earl of
Gloucester is doubtful ; but he and Edward attacked different flanks of the Earl's
army.

and north-west. They were at first supposed to be the army of the younger Simon; for the Prince had given orders to display the banners taken in the fight of Kenilworth. When the artifice was detected it was no longer possible to escape. The Earl, out-numbered and out-manœuvred, recognised that the end was come; the lesson which he gave the royalists at Lewes had been turned to good account. "By St. James," he said, "they come on bravely; but it was from me they learned this order. Let us commend our souls to God, for our bodies are theirs."[1] The less

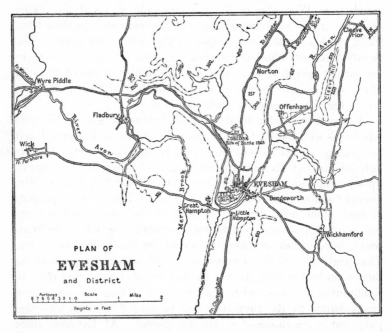

PLAN OF

EVESHAM

and District

experienced Henry de Montfort bade his father not to despair. The Earl turned on him with a last word of reproach. "I do not despair," he said; "but it is thy presumption and the pride of thy brothers which have brought me to this pass. Now however, as I believe, I shall die for God and the just cause."[2]

A contest between forces so unequal could only have one issue. The Montfortians however resolved to sell their lives as dearly as

[1] Rishanger, p. 37 (ed. Riley). *Chron. de Mailros,* 207.
[2] Hemingburgh, i., 324.

they might. Headed by the Earl they marched out along the up-hill road which leads from Evesham to Wyre, and made a desperate attempt to break through the royalist lines. About a mile from Evesham they were brought to a stand-still, and the enemy closed in upon them. The 5,000 Welshmen whom the Earl had borrowed from Llewelyn turned to flight, leaving their general with a handful of knights and a few English foot-soldiers. The Earl besought his friends to fly and save themselves for better days. But they refused, and fought in a ring round him until they were slain or dropped exhausted with the loss of blood. Henry de Montfort, who struck the first blow in the fight, was also the first to fall. The Earl survived most of his companions; his horse was killed, but he extricated himself and stood "like a tower," warding off attack with great sweeps of his two-handed sword. At last he fell, stabbed in the back, and was instantly despatched. His fate was all but shared by the miserable King, who had accompanied his gaoler to the battlefield. A knight, who failed to recognise the royal armour, struck Henry on the shoulder, and would have slain him had he not cried out, " I am Henry of Windsor, I am your King ; for God's love, strike me not; I am too old to fight ". Prince Edward came to the rescue and sent his father from the field in the care of a guard of knights, returning for his own part to complete the butchery. But after Simon's death the battle was virtually over. It had begun at nine in the morning and had lasted only three hours; but a thunderstorm arose while it was still in progress, and men noticed as a prodigy that there was almost total darkness when the great Earl succumbed. With him there lay dead on the field 180 knights, 220 squires, and about 2,000 infantry—the forlorn hope of the democracy. Guy de Montfort was found on the field covered with wounds but still alive. He and his brother Simon, the latter still safe behind the walls of Kenilworth, were the sole survivors of note ; but their lives were prolonged only to bring dishonour on their name and cause.[1]

The body of the great Earl suffered all the indignities which malice could suggest, and his head was sent as a gift to the wife of Roger Mortimer. The Prince, however, permitted the Franciscans of Evesham to give the mutilated trunk a Christian burial. To

---

[1] Hemingburgh, i., 324, 325. *Chron. de Mailros.* *Chron. de Lanercost.* *Chron. de Bellis*, 46. Rishanger (ed. Riley), p. 36.

the friars, who had always repaid his patronage with their sympathy, he seemed a martyr; by the vulgar, in spite of prohibitions from the Pope and King, the Good Earl was worshipped as a saint for many years; it was currently believed that his corpse worked miracles. Such tardy honours move us to ask why popular support had not been forthcoming in his last campaign. But the truth is, that he had been the especial friend of those who were powerless to help their friends. It is his chief glory to have inspired the hope that he could end or mend the secular miseries and oppressions of the lower orders. Trust of this kind does not come unmerited. The people are no bad judges of sincerity. It is the enthusiast who inspires them with enthusiasm; whatever else he may be, their man of destiny is at least a man of faith. Faith and the love of justice are qualities which the Earl possessed in no ordinary degree. He saw how, in the long chain of cause and effect, the frivolity and vices of the court brought misery on common men; the knowledge consumed him with a generous indignation; and he believed that he could right the wrong. Because he believed he was believed. We smile at the simplicity of the believers. We no longer hope that any individual, however heroic, will make all things new. We know that Montfort deceived himself and others. But if men had never promised more than it was possible they should perform, society would be the poorer; for the achieved reform is the child of the unachieved ideal.

So it was in Montfort's case. The victor of Evesham accomplished far more than his defeated rival; possibly more than the Earl could have done with a free hand and longer time for his experiments. Montfort was, for a strong man, marvellously versatile. He was great alike in war and peace. He established order in a land where order had been unknown for the best part of a hundred years; his management of Gascony stamps him as a prince among administrators. The schemes of constitutional reform which he devised for England are startling in their boldness, their simplicity, their consonance with the subsequent course of political development. And in each case he had to conquer the country which he afterwards reorganised. But he failed in Gascony because there were no foundations upon which to build, and in England through not using the foundations which existed. Impatience, the natural vice of an idealist, was his undoing; confident that his object was a just one, he took what seemed to be the shortest way of reaching it. He trampled upon vested interests and the letter of the law ; he broke with all traditions, he did violence to all forms.   Hated by the King and barons, he was viewed by the middle-class conservative with a wondering suspicion.   He fought for the Commons, but not as they would have had him fight.   Edward, no doubt, was a man of smaller mould, who in Montfort's place would never have established Montfort's reputation.   As Prince and King the younger man showed the craft of an attorney ; he was seldom generous and often less than just ; he fell so far short of his rival's sympathy for popular aspirations that he treated nations like the live-stock of a farm or the villeins of a manor ; he meted out reforms ungraciously, inadequately, and always at a price.   He succeeded because he knew his own limitations and the prejudices of his world ; he pursued his ends by well-worn roads ; and came nearer to attainment than the Earl, because he was content with less.   So far the comparison may be in favour of Edward as a politician, of Montfort as a man. But if we look to Edward's objects then at once it is plain that, without Montfort's ideas, he never would have won the name of greatness.   Edward is praised as the creator of a new legislature, but he did his utmost to make Parliament a mere machine for voting taxes.   His own ideal was that of his father, although more skilfully developed.   The ideal with which he is popularly connected was conceived by his opponent.   The Prince, in 1265, fought against it with the sword ; the King, from his accession to 1295, was systematically working to dissolve it by illusory concessions.

After Evesham the royalists had little more to do, save to appropriate the fruits of victory.   The news of the battle filled the Londoners with consternation.   They sent immediately to depre- cate the anger of the King and thought themselves fortunate to escape with the loss of their charter and a fine of 20,000 marks. Some murmuring was heard among the lower citizens when they realised that the right of appointing their own chief magistrate was gone; and a number left the city in fear that they might be pro- scribed.   But the old liberties, even that of the mayoralty, were restored before the end of the reign ; most of the exiles returned in a year or two ; the number of those who remained under the ban was less than sixty in the year 1269.   The resistance of the

Margin notes: Edward and Montfort

The Towns make Terms

16*

Cinque Ports lasted a little longer. The citizens went on board ship with their wives and families, took to the sea, burned Portsmouth, and began to prey upon the traffic of the Channel. But early in 1266 Prince Edward marched against the Ports, offering them the choice of peace or war. They accepted peace and received an amnesty on far more favourable terms than London.

All that the rebel barons could hope was to make a stand until reasonable terms of peace were granted. The first thought of the royalists was for vengeance. On September 21st, a proclamation disinheriting all followers of the earl was issued, with the consent of a Great Council which had been convoked at Winchester to discuss the settlement. The younger Simon, who had appeared under a safe conduct to plead the cause of his friends before the Council, returned to Kenilworth. Subsequently he fled to the Isle of Axholme where he prepared to maintain himself by force. Others imitated his example, and the government began to reconsider the judgment passed at Winchester. The legate Ottoboni, whose original mission had been to preach a crusade and to extirpate the family of Montfort,[1] offered his services as a mediator ; Clement IV., hitherto the most bitter enemy of the constitutionalists, wrote to the King in an unexpected strain of magnanimity, enjoining him to show forgiveness ;[2] and Edward, in fact though not in name the master of the realm,[3] relented so far as to negotiate with Simon. At Christmas the latter agreed to accept the arbitration of the legate, the King of the Romans, and Philip Basset, on the understanding that their judgment should not extend to life or limb or perpetual imprisonment. He received a promise of pardon if he would induce the garrison of Kenilworth to submit. He tried to do so, but without avail ; the defenders alleged that they had received their trust from the Countess Eleanor, and could surrender it into no other hand ; since Eleanor had retired to the continent, her son remained in captivity. He escaped however from his prison in the following year, and fled to France. The garrison of Kenilworth held out until the autumn. So weak was the government that the reduction of this one stronghold proved to be impossible. The whole country was in a state of confusion and unrest ; the commons

---

[1] Bliss, *Calendar*, 419, 427, 437. The letters of Ottoboni to Clement, printed by Miss Graham in *E. H. R.*, xv., pp. 90 ff., are valuable for the events of this time.
[2] Potthast, 19382.   [3] Shirley, ii., p. 189.

hardly concealed their regret for the great Earl; bands of rebels and outlaws roamed the highroads or lurked in the forests. The King found it advisable to prohibit foreign merchants from journeying inland, on the ground that he could not guarantee their safety. A band of the Disinherited took up their quarters in the Isle of Ely and pillaged the surrounding shires; the Earl of Derby in the midlands, and Adam de Gurdon in Hampshire, waged war on the Crown with their own unaided resources. To external observers it seemed that the monarchy was hardly less in danger than it had been during Montfort's term of power.[1]

For five months (June 25th-Dec. 13th) the best army which Edward could put into the field attacked Kenilworth with every device known to military engineers. But machines and mines failed to effect a breach, and the garrison maintained a stout resistance; every morning the great gates of the castle were thrown open in defiance, and almost every day there was a sortie. In the autumn Ottoboni again induced the Prince to offer terms. These were framed by a board of twelve arbitrators, and embodied in the so-called Ban of Kenilworth (Oct. 31st, 1266).[2] It was soon agreed to restore the Disinherited upon payment of a fine; but those who had profited by the confiscations endeavoured to prevent the King from acceding, or at least to reserve for him the power of fixing the fine at an impossible amount; and it was only after vigorous remonstrances from Gloucester that the maximum of the fines was fixed at seven years' rental for the worst offenders, while the rest escaped with five, or two, or one, according to the nature of their guilt. Even with this modification the sentence was a hard one. The garrison of Kenilworth refused to accept it until their provisions were exhausted. The defenders of Ely maintained themselves even longer, and finally obtained better terms through the powerful assistance of the Earl of Gloucester. The Earl had experienced a severe disillusionment; for the promises of reform which he had received when he forsook De Montfort appeared to be totally forgotten by the Prince; and the Ban of Kenilworth had reaffirmed with no uncertain sound the theory of an absolute prerogative. Early in 1267 the Earl sent to Henry demanding that the aliens should be expelled and the Provisions of Oxford re-enacted; and, receiving no

The Ban of Kenilworth

Gloucester's Rebellion, 1267

---

[1] Bliss, *Calendar*, 420, Clement to Ottoboni. Shirley, ii., pp. 300 ff. Wykes, 188.
[2] *E. H. R.*, xv., p. 109. *S. C.*, 407 (extracts).

satisfactory answer, seized London while the Prince and King were engaged with the siege of Ely. The Disinherited flocked to the capital, which remained in the hands of their protector for two months. Only after the fall of Ely was he induced to make his peace; and it was made on condition of pardon for his friends. Probably he also stipulated for a measure of reform in the government. For the close of the year was marked by legislation of the kind which he had previously demanded. The Statute of Marlborough (Nov., 1267) does not restore the government prescribed by the Provisions; but it confirms the most useful among the supplementary Provisions of 1259. The government was to remain in the hands of a single person; but it was henceforth to be government in the interest of the nation.[1]

Wales,
and the
Crusade
of 1270

The last embers of rebellion were now extinguished. It only remained to settle the long outstanding account with the Prince of North Wales. Here, as in other cases, the mediation of the Legate was successfully employed. Llewelyn did not presume upon the temporary weakness of his enemy. He was prepared to acknowledge the English overlordship, and to pay handsomely for the privilege of retaining the Four Cantreds. His offer was accepted, and a peace was signed. Considering that the Prince had never been chastised for the outbreak of 1257, such terms were humiliating enough to England. But the treasury was exhausted; the allegiance of the barons, from Gilbert of Gloucester downwards, was uncertain; Henry, worn out with age and strife, asked nothing better than to end his days in peace; Edward the future conqueror of Wales, was absorbed for the moment in the plan of a Crusade. It may have been remorse for his part in the civil war; more probably it was nothing more than the example of Louis IX. which fired him with this ambition. Clement IV. endeavoured to turn Edward from his purpose, but the Prince would not be deterred. He obtained a liberal aid in money from Louis and started in 1270 to follow the French King. His adventures in Tunis and at Acre are of little importance in the history of England or of the Crusades. The enterprise was belated; for the doom of the Latin principalities had been sealed when Richard turned his back upon Jerusalem.[2] But it was not inappropriate that the wave of

---

[1] *Foedera*, i., 472. *Statutes of the Realm*, i., 19.
[2] For Edward's Crusade see Riant in *Archives de l'Orient Latin*, i., pp. 617-630.

reaction which had swept away De Montfort's work should spend its last remaining force in Palestine. Those who had done their best to destroy the ideal of the future could hardly do less than offer their services to the ideal of the past; nor could a better means have been devised for opening the Prince's eyes to the hollowness of the principles which had governed his father's life and his own boyhood.

When the Prince departed the reign of Henry III. had still Deaths of three years to run, but they are notable for little except their 1270-2 death-roll. Louis IX., whose arbitration had been the occasion of so many evils, succumbed to a fever in his camp at Carthage, when on the point of attacking the infidels of Tunis (Aug., 1270). Philip III., his son and heir, at once abandoned the campaign; and early in 1271 started on his homeward journey by way of Italy, taking with him amongst others the young Henry of Almaine, who had sailed with Edward but abandoned the crusade in consequence of the death of Louis. At Viterbo, where Philip had halted to interview the cardinals then engaged in electing a successor to Clement IV., Henry was assassinated by the brothers Guy and Simon de Montfort. They came upon the Prince in church as he was listening to a sermon; he fled to the high altar, but they pursued, and stabbed him through and through, answering his cries for mercy with the taunt that he should have such mercy as their father and brothers had received (March 13th, 1271). The news broke the heart of Richard of Cornwall; he died early in the following year, a prematurely aged and soured man, whose last fifteen years of life had been one long humiliation. Derided in Germany, and in his native land detested as a traitor, he was less fortunate than his elder brother in whom none but flatterers had ever professed to see the promise of a great career. The insignificance of Henry III. shielded his declining years from hatred and almost from scorn; and if his ambitions had been not less soaring than those of Richard, they had stamped themselves less deeply on his heart. Always sickly, and overstrained by the vicissitudes of the last few years, he aged and grew feeble after the departure of Prince Edward; on November 16th, 1272, he breathed his last at Westminster. His death-bed was disturbed by a riot among the Londoners, the lower orders contending with the rich for the privilege of electing a new mayor. " We, we are the commune of the city," roared the populace till the lattices of the sick-room rattled with the din. This war-cry of the democracy, against which Henry had fought so long and to all appearance so successfully, was perhaps the last sound audible to his dying ears; a dramatic and unanswerable protest against the absolutism of which he was the feeble but triumphant representative.

CHAPTER XIX

ENGLAND IN MONTFORT'S DAY

WE have now passed in review the political events which con- Position tributed to the remodelling of Anglo-Saxon England. of the
It remains to glance at the more salient features of the society in Estate
which, for over two hundred years, Teutonic and Latin influences
had been contending for the mastery.   There are long periods when
a nation, like clay in the hands of the potter, passively accepts the
form and impress of ideas which come from without; at other times
the national intellect is awake and alert, political issues are instantly
appreciated, and the masses take a side, so strongly, perhaps, that
the boldest of men can only hope to lead them by following their
bent.   Crises of this kind were rare in medieval England.   A
popular poet thought that the Barons' War of 1215 was caused by
the mob's desire to rule.

> Ordinem praeposterum Anglia sancivit,
> Nam praeesse capiti corpus concupivit
> Regem suum regere populus quaesivit.[1]

Yet we have seen that the inspiration of this rising came from
the heads of the feudal party.   In the somewhat similar upheaval
of 1264 and 1265 the lower orders played a more important part;
the feelings of the towns, the universities, the mendicant friars and
the lower clergy were strongly expressed, and not in words alone.
We cannot say that the nation overthrew the royal and feudal
parties, or dictated the policy of De Montfort.   But this much is
clear, that, of the two political experiments which we have just
described, the first failed because the promoters were indifferent
to popular ideas; while the second broke down, after a brief trial,
because it gave the nation more than the nation felt justified in
taking from the King;   because it alarmed the privileged classes

[1] *Chron. de Lanercost,* p. 15.

without winning the confidence of their inferiors. The rôle played
by the nation was therefore an important though a passive one;
and passivity was in this case due, not so much to indifference as to
the equilibrium of opposing forces, which we must briefly indicate
and characterise.

Decay of French language and manners

The England of Henry III. was more English than that of
Henry II.; for, between the death of the one and the accession of
the other, both the march of political events and the internal development of the nation had tended to increase the insularity of
governors and governed. The first Plantagenet was a foreigner,
who laboriously adapted himself to English ideas and institutions.
His grandson was, with all his foreign tastes, an Englishman, who
did not cross the Channel till the age of manhood and chiefly lived
in England. As with the dynasty so with the aristocracy. Under
Henry II. many baronial houses, which were deeply rooted in England before he came to the throne, still regarded France as their
mother-country. It was their practice then to put their sons to
school in a French monastery or private family, that the boys might
learn to speak their native tongue without provincialisms. In a
single generation this colonial habit of mind completely disappeared.
Not that the baronage became completely national in ceasing to be
French. In some respects they were as foreign as the Poitevins and
Savoyards whom they branded with the name of "aliens born"
(*alienigenae*). France was still the glass of chivalry and fashion;
French remained the language of polite conversation, of familiar
correspondence, of courtly and romantic literature. Even in the
fourteenth century the pious founder of an Oxford College, who
sought to make his scholars gentlemen, forbade the use of English
at the common table. Under Henry III. a conversational knowledge
of French was less an accomplishment than a necessity. Latin was
indispensable for legal documents; it was preferred to French as
the language of formal and official letters. But it was in French
that the pleadings of the law-courts and the debates of the Great
Council were conducted. French-speaking judges drew fine-spun
corollaries from the laws of Athelstan and Edgar; French-speaking
orators defended the good customs of the Confessor against the
encroachments of the royal prerogative. It is a unique event when
the King addresses his subjects in their native tongue. No ordinary
occasion would have warranted so gross a breach of the conven-

tions. At the same time this Anglo-French is a tongue which
sounds as strangely in the ears of Frenchmen as in those of any
English hind. Philippe de Reimes remarks of his charming English heroine :—

> Un peu parroit à son langage
> Que ne fu pas née à Pontoise;

and the criticism is all the more significant because it is passed on
a lady who was otherwise a model of polite accomplishments. In
their language, as in their manners and ideas, the English upper
classes were passing through a stage of transition. They were
nowhere completely at home.

All the more powerful then was the influence of the uncouth *Growth of*
but vigorous speech, racy of the soil and saturated with familiar *English*
Language
associations, in which the lower orders conversed among themselves.
English was fast becoming the most natural and appropriate
vehicle of English thought. From the beginning of the thirteenth
century we can trace the development of a new literature which,
however deeply influenced by the style and the matter of foreign
works, is rarely content with slavish imitation. The pioneer of the
movement, and its most characteristic figure, is Layamon, the mass-
priest of Ernley-upon-Severn. About the year 1205 he composed
a patriotic chronicle, the *Brut*, in honour of the ancient heroes " who
had held Britain from the time of the Great Flood ". The title of
the work is borrowed from an Anglo-Norman source, the *Brut* of
Wace ; and hence also Layamon drew the greater portion of his
facts and legends. But the inspiration of his verse, despite the
frequent use of rhyme, is derived from old English literature ; and,
even when he approaches most nearly to translation, there is a
national flavour in his work which is certainly not derived from
Wace. Layamon is not afraid at times to trust his own imagination. For rhetorical outbursts of triumph or defiance, for the
suggestion by words of a scene of mystery and gloom, he needs no
model. He has fancy, thought, and feeling ; he commands a style
which can express with some distinction all that he imagines, thinks,
and feels. Equally remarkable with the *Brut* is the work of Orm,
a Mercian canon of the Augustinian order, who translated, in un-
rhymed verse, the lessons prescribed by the church's calendar ; adding
his own comments for the benefit of simple folk (*c.* 1215). Ten
thousand lines of his work survive, perhaps an eighth part of the

whole ; a marvellous quarry for the modern philologist, and in their own day no mean instrument of education. Another devotional work, the *Ancren Riwle,* comes to us from an anonymous author who wrote for the nuns of Tarrant Keynes in Dorset. Apparently a paraphrase of a French treatise, it is nevertheless original in form ; the first attempt to write continuous English prose since the cessation of the Peterborough Chronicle. Such writers mark no epoch in the development of thought ; but they teach the art of expressing common thoughts in daily language. They are, in England, the precursors and the teachers of the secular poets. Of these a number arose in the second half of the thirteenth century. Like Layamon, who showed them the way, they are usually translators working for a humble audience. Robert of Brunne confesses as much with a frank naiveté :—

> For lewed men I undyrtoke
> In Englysh tonge to make this boke ;
> For many beyn of such manere
> That talys and rymys will blithely here
> In gamys and festys at the ale.

National Themes in Literature

In this unassuming spirit the minstrels of the fair and ale-house took in hand the tales of Troy and Alexander, of Julius Caesar, of Charlemagne, and of many another hero celebrated in the French romances. But soon, like Layamon, they became in their own despite original. The village audience demanded the heroic figures of English myth and history. The stories of Arthur, and Tristan, and the Holy Graal, were reclaimed as a national heritage from the courtly romancers who had invented or discovered them. Folk-lore supplied material for the lays of King Horn and Havelock the Dane; and the history of the near past was marvellously transformed to magnify the prowess of Richard Coeur de Lion. In Thomas of Ercildoun the poets discovered a Teutonic Merlin ; Alfred "the Truth-teller, the Darling of the Angles," became under their touch a second Solomon: and thus, through foreign metres and foreign forms of poetry, the traditions, the proverbial philosophy, the aspirations, of the native English gained literary recognition. Daily the breach with French models becomes wider. Apart from rhyme, and the idea of the poetic contest of two singers, the poem of the *Owl and Nightingale* is an entirely English product; and in such a lyric as the Cuckoo-song, "Sumer is ycumen in," the secular commonplaces of literature are suddenly restated

with the freshness and the force of genius. This literary development is for the historian a fact of paramount importance. It reveals
a more genial side of that patriotism which we have seen plundering
the barns of Roman clerks, and making war upon Poitevin princes
of the blood. The English hatred of the foreigner was no longer
that of the boorish serf for his moral and intellectual superior ; it
was that which arises between natural equals, when one of them
abuses an inherited position of command.

National pride is near akin to national self-satisfaction ; the Conserva-
bad side of the new patriotism was a blind attachment to es- tive fee·
tablished institutions ; and many time-honoured abuses of Henry's Towns
government might have escaped criticism if they had not been
fortuitously associated in the popular mind with foreign favourites.
The radical doctrines of the fourteenth century would have found
few adherents in the thirteenth. It is true that the constitution of
the chartered borough was usually democratic. Ipswich, under the
charter which John conceded soon after his accession (1200-1), was
governed by a mass meeting of all the citizens, to whom were responsible the bailiffs and the twelve portmen elected by the common
voice ; and such was the general type to which town-governments
conformed.[1] It is in fact the type which we have already seen in
London, a city which every English borough aspired to imitate.
But all that we know of the inner history of the towns, from London downwards, suggests that the citizen-body were far from
emulating the activity of a Greek *ecclesia*. Sooner or later a ring
of wealthy families acquired a virtual monopoly of office. The
indignation of conservative chroniclers is loudly expressed when the
London folk-moot ventures to make a free election of a mayor ; still
more loudly when the mayor refuses to be guided by the aldermen,
takes the folk-moot into partnership, and is guided in all matters
by their " Yea, yea " and " Nay, nay ". It may be that the growth
of oligarchy was facilitated by the share which the merchant-gild
sometimes acquired in the administration ;[2] but, whatever the
cause, the fact cannot be disputed that in most English towns a
few influential persons were using or abusing the magistracies for
their private ends. The resentment thus provoked led, during the
critical years of Henry's reign, to a number of municipal revolutions. But the ordinary burgess had no desire to be saddled with

[1] *E. H. R.*, v., p. 640. [2] *Ibid.*, xv., p. 156.

the routine of administrative business. He became a democrat to resist oppression; when he had turned the evil-doers out of office he looked about him for a new set of rulers. Such being the temper of the urban population, we must not expect to find democrats among the peasants and mesne tenants of the country side. These men objected to taxation, unless it was approved by representatives whom they could trust. With the daily politics of the kingdom they had no more desire to meddle than with those of their own shire-courts. All they desired was the conservation of their ancient rights.

Feudal Privileges   In one respect it must be owned that this conservatism was highly radical. Against feudal privilege there was a never ending struggle. To judge merely from royal charters we should say that rights of private jurisdiction were as important and as frequently granted now as they had ever been. The charters of John to the Hospitallers and of Henry III. to Westminster Abbey seem ample enough to satisfy the most grasping of feudal aristocrats; the owners of great liberties such as Glamorgan, Ely, Chester, and Durham, laboured hard and successfully to maintain their privileges. On the other hand we find incidental admissions that in some cases the rights which are claimed by landlords have only a nominal existence. A charter of Henry III. to the abbess of Rumsey mentions that this foundation, which possessed the right of free gallows, had hanged no thieves for almost fifty years, so that the gallows had fallen into decay and the nuns themselves were doubtful if they might lawfully revive their privilege. In another case we are told of an abbot's bailiffs who, having caught a thief, knew not how to deal with him; for never within their memory had the court of their master tried a case of theft. Such incidents show that, whether through indifference or timidity, the privileged landlord sometimes allowed his rights to lapse by long desuetude. Often he allowed the royal justices to try his thieves and breakers of the peace on condition that he received the whole or a portion of the fine. Often he shrank from provoking a conflict with his tenants in which the sympathies of the Crown were certain to be on their side. The manor-court, indeed, remained a powerful and active institution. The landlord could not do without it; for the manor-court enforced his right to labour-services. The community accepted it as a convenient means of settling petty quarrels, and punishing the smaller offenders against public order. There was little danger that the peasantry, disunited and apathetic even in times of famine and oppression, would combine to defy seigniorial jurisdiction. It was otherwise with freeholders, more especially with those who held in burgage or by military tenure. Henry II. had made it impossible for lords to deprive such tenants of their holdings without a judgment in a public court. They were sufficiently protected against arbitrary usurpation; but they chafed against the liability to suit and service at a private court. It was becoming necessary for the landlord, in admitting new tenants, to protect his rights of jurisdiction by strictly worded stipulations. The concessions which were wrung from the baronage in the Provisions of 1259 show that the struggle has turned in favour of the tenant; for by these Provisions the private courts lose their most valuable rights of civil jurisdiction.

Such legislation did not help the citizens of private boroughs. But the burgess, individually insignificant, acquired audacity through his membership of a community. The knight-tenant gained his end by litigation; the burgess not infrequently resorted to the arguments of sticks and stones. In the Chronicle of Jocelyn de Brakelond we see the embarrassments of a religious house which has been only too successful in promoting the development of a small borough. The men of Bury St. Edmunds are like a hornet's nest at the gates of the great abbey. Once they were villeins; now they resent the slightest traces of their former servitude. On the whole they are leniently treated. The government of their town is divided between the moot, to which all the burgesses are convoked by note of horn, and bailiffs who may be nominated by the abbot and convent but are more often elected in the moot; the monks rarely interfere except when complaints are raised against the bailiffs for default of justice. But there are still manorial dues, hen-silver, hearth-money, and so forth, which the abbey is both too poor and too proud to surrender. Therefore the monks are branded with the name of tyrants; and they are fortunate when the time of collection passes without tumult. A shivering cellarer walks down the main street of the town; it is discovered that he has come to demand the dues; the hue is raised, the crones pour out from the cottages to beat him with their distaffs; he is glad to make good an inglorious escape.[1] Wise landlords, such as

Bury St. Edmunds

---

[1] A recently discovered document describes an attempt to form a commune at Bury in 1264. See *E. H. R.*, xxiv., p. 313.

Abbot Samson, did their best to escape the recurrence of these stormy rent days. By means of new charters and favourable compositions the boroughs which stood in the position of Bury moved rapidly towards independence.[1]

The Cry for Equal Law

That all free men should be subject to the King's law alone, and that this law should be applied without respect of persons was the great hope of the middle classes. It is clearly stated in the *Song of Lewes*, a rhyming Latin poem which was written, about 1265, to vindicate the character and policy of Montfort. According to the author, who was perhaps a friar, two causes are chiefly responsible for the evils of the time. First, the king has alien counsellors who break the law and sell justice ; secondly, the king believes himself to be above the law. Since this is so it is the duty of the barons to expel the aliens, and to bring the king back to a true sense of his position. The King is God's steward who holds his power on condition of using it well, that is according to the law. No one but God is above the law :

> Dicitur vulgariter: ut rex vult lex vadit.
> Veritas vult aliter, nam lex stat rex cadit.

Such is the chain of reasoning which made converts to the boldest political experiment of the middle ages, the popular dictatorship of Simon de Montfort. It is reasoning most characteristic of the thirteenth century, which was essentially an age of legal reform and of great lawyers, producing in Castile an Alphonso X., in Sicily a Frederic II., in Rome an Innocent IV. In fact the doctrine of the supremacy of law may have been learned by the panegyrist of De Montfort from the pages of Bracton, the greatest of our early lawwriters and a justice of the Curia Regis. Bracton has a professional admiration for the majesty of law ; and while admitting that in a strictly legal sense the King can do no wrong, he repeatedly emphasises the moral obligation of the King to keep the law. Those are wrong, he says in one famous passage, who maintain that the prince's pleasure has the force of law. Laws are rules enacted in a lawful way, that is with the consent and counsel of the magnates. A King who rules according to justice and the law is God's Vicar upon earth ; but he becomes a minister of the devil if he turns aside to do injustice, and God will punish him though man cannot.[2]

---

[1] *Joc. de Brakelond*, pp. 53, 54, 57, 73.
[2] Bracton, *De Legibus*, i., 269; ii., 173 ; v., 402.

This general reverence for law, this pride of the lawyer in his own profession, explain the otherwise perplexing phenomenon that no misrule could check the Courts of Common Law in their steady process of development. Business flowed in upon the central tribunals ; the eyres for gaol delivery and taking the assizes of freehold became more frequent ; new remedies were devised, and the old were made more perfect; the royal justices encroached, with general approbation, upon the feudal courts and the courts-Christian, questioning every right for which the lords of the former could not show the explicit warrant of a royal charter, and taking from the latter, in spite of noisy protests, not only the jurisdiction which they had usurped, but also many of the cases which Henry II. had left to them. In the hands of judges such as Martin Pateshull and theorists such as Bracton the common law, so long a disorderly heap of precedents and customs, became a scientific system, without ceasing to be practical and national. The King's courts refused, indeed, to borrow more than could be helped from the civil or the canon law ; they attached greater importance to ill-comprehended tags from the code of Alfred than to the most lucid definitions and the most logical deductions of the Digest or the Decretals. But, when we reflect upon the consequences which must have followed if they had adopted Roman theories of sovereignty, or had applied to villeinage the Roman law of slavery, when we remember that respect for the canon law would have entailed the surrender to the courts-Christian of almost every case of contract, we may on the whole be grateful to Pateshull and Bracton for their insularity. It certainly contributed to make the King's justice popular. On one famous occasion, when the bishops demanded that the common law of marriage should be brought into conformity with that of the Church, the Great Council took the side of the royal judges; and the pithy dictum *Nolumus leges Angliae mutari* though uttered with reference to this special controversy, expresses correctly the national attitude towards the common law.

Yet it was the law-courts and their judges that gave occasion to the bitterest complaints against the government. The judges were suspected of venality, and not without reason ; unless we suppose that the Chief Justiciar who was condemned, in 1251, for taking bribes fell below the ordinary level of his class. Even if incorruptible they were inclined to favour the Crown at the expense of equity. It was noticed that, when the King had been disappointed of a subsidy, fines at once became heavier, and forfeitures more frequent; nor was there much hope of obtaining a conviction against an official who had stretched a point of law in the royal interest. Especially unpopular was the whole procedure in criminal cases. The grand jury was at best an imperfect instrument of justice. Acting on their private knowledge of the facts, the jurors can hardly have failed to oscillate between the two extremes of accusing on the strength of the vaguest rumours, and keeping silence when there was the slightest room for doubt. Their interests ran counter to their instincts of fair play, since the law of *murdrum* was still applied with rigour and, in the case of other offences besides homicide, a failure to produce the delinquent might be taken as a proof that the neighbouring townships were liable to a fine for not maintaining a sufficient watch and ward. If the jurors made reckless presentments there was little hope for the innocent accused. Formerly the ordeal had given him a prospect of escape; but the ordeal, in obedience to a canon of the Lateran Council, was abolished in 1219. The petty jury, which supp'ied a more effectual check upon the vagaries of grand jurors, was only beginning to appear as a special privilege allowed in special cases. It is not therefore wonderful that eyres for hearing criminal cases created general consternation in the wilder parts of England, where few could boast of a character above reproach. On one particular occasion the men of Cornwall took to the moors and forests, with their cattle and all their belongings, when the approach of the Justices Itinerant was signified; and from time to time we hear a demand that the Great Eyre shall not be held more often than once in seven years. Perhaps the shires would have been better advised if they had thrown a part of the blame upon the police system. Judges dealt hardly with the malefactor because he was so rarely apprehended. The Guardians of the Peace were dependent upon unpaid auxiliaries; on the watchmen whom all towns and townships were obliged to provide for night duty in the summer months; and on the reluctant service of the able-bodied freeman when the Hue and Cry was raised. Nothing was easier for an expert criminal than to slip through the meshes of this system; but the idea of radical reform occurred to neither King nor country. The

Assize of Arms was repeatedly reissued ; and in 1253 the King vainly
attempted to sharpen the zeal of sheriffs and Guardians of the Peace
by proclaiming that he would hold them personally responsible for all
undetected robberies.   The desirability of employing a paid force to
guard the highways, and break up the robber gangs by which they
were infested, can hardly have failed to strike the King and Council.
Hubert de Burgh had made occasional use of such a force to repress
exceptional outbreaks of crime in certain shires; Edward I. subsequently revived this method by his commissions of Trail-baston.
But the extravagance of Henry III. left him without the funds for
the most necessary expenses.   We may be surprised that the shortcomings of his government were not made good by voluntary
associations ; there would have been nothing contrary to the prejudices of the age in a *Treuga Dei* directed against the enemies of
property.   But England was in that perilous stage of political development which is reached when the central power has grown
jealous of all private combinations made for public purposes,
though it is not yet strong enough to make them superfluous ; and
when men are sufficiently civilised to feel that life and property
should be protected by the magistrate, but not civilised enough to
realise that police work must, at all costs and all hazards, be
efficiently performed.

In spheres with which the Crown had no desire to meddle the Borough
instincts of association and co-operation found free play ; seldom, Privileges
if ever, has society been more prolific of corporations framed to
further the purposes of religion, of charitable relief, of education,
of trade and commerce, than it was in the twelfth and thirteenth
centuries ; and nowhere is the progress of medieval society more
clearly to be traced than in the history of these corporations.
Under the Norman Kings the ambition of the trader had hardly
reached beyond the project of uniting with his fellows for the
purchase of privileges and monopolies.   Under the Plantagenets
he aims at nothing less than securing for his class the government
of the town in which they live; it may be disputed whether the
charters which John and Henry III. granted to so many boroughs
were actually purchased by the merchant-gilds, and whether the
new governments were often administered by these older associations ; what evidence we have on the subject goes to prove that
the sovereign power in the chartered borough of this period was

ostensibly vested in the general body of the burgesses. But there can be no doubt that the individuals who urged the towns to seek self-government, and who appropriated to themselves the more important magistracies after a charter had been granted, were of the same class and standing as those who a century before had haggled for the freedom of a gild. For this reason the policy of a borough was normally as selfish as that of any gild. The prosperity of Oxford trade was regarded as an injury to Abingdon; the Cinque Ports never missed an opportunity of a piratical attack upon the merchant-vessels of London or the East Anglian towns. But it was something gained that the corporations between which these feuds were prosecuted should have grown sufficiently large to give their members an opportunity of pursuing a common good which was not always identical with the immediate interest of the individual.

Religious Orders

If we turn from the towns to associations over which the Church held sway, the growth of wider interests and of an increased capacity for common action is still more obvious. A monastic order, despite the subordination of the houses to a common rule, was essentially a federation, in which each house normally pursued the course prescribed by its own welfare, and was regarded as in the healthiest state when most exclusively concerned with the spiritual health of its own inmates. The Knight-orders which arose, in the course of the Crusades, for the succour of pilgrims and the defence of the Sepulchre, the Mendicant Orders which early in the thirteenth century began another Holy War against heresy and unbelief, against misery and disease, were inspired with the sense of duties incumbent on the whole of Christendom, in comparison with which the individual and even the corporation should regard their welfare as matters of no moment.

Of Knights

These new orders originated outside England; and those of the military type, the Templars and the Hospitallers, though richly endowed with English lands, never succeeded in winning the general esteem. They were useful in their capacity as bankers; enormous treasures, private and public, were deposited for safe-keeping in the New Temple at London; and the Knights fulfilled their trust with conspicuous integrity. No monastic treasury was safe against the King's demands for a forced loan; but the Masters of the Temple showed greater courage in defending the treasures of their clients.

When Hubert de Burgh was disgraced, the King demanded of the Templars the chattels of the fallen minister; but they refused to surrender anything without a mandate from De Burgh. But those who made use of the Templars for financial purposes carped at their privileges, and questioned their devotion to a cause which was rapidly ceasing to be fashionable. Many crusades were preached in England, and multitudes took the cross, in the century which followed the great enterprise of Coeur de Lion. But it was well understood that a release from the crusader's vow could and would be purchased on easy terms by the majority of those who took it. The peril from the infidel had decreased; the hope of converting him, though cherished in some quarters, excited no general enthusiasm; increased knowledge of the Latin principalities had produced a contempt for their ruling classes; the perversion of the Fourth Crusade to the service of Venetian greed cast a doubt upon the sincerity of all who subsequently pleaded for the succour of Jerusalem. Despite the censures of the Church, the Emperor Frederic II. was in accord with the common sense of his age when he endeavoured to establish a lasting peace between Christendom and Islam. Even the invitation of Louis IX., whose purity of motive could not be called in question, produced little response in England, except from a few great nobles, discontented with the condition of their native country or influenced by the example of their ancestors.

But the aims of the Mendicant Orders found a ready and gener- Of Friars ous appreciation among all classes of the English laity. The handfuls of Dominican and Franciscan friars who in 1221 and 1224 came to England, bare-footed and destitute of the commonest necessities, set on foot a movement which even their buoyant faith can scarcely have anticipated.[1] The Franciscans found in England a particularly congenial soil. In almost every town which was visited by their pioneers there presently arose a Franciscan priory and chapel, planted in the poorest quarter and among the classes whom the secular clergy, in despair or disgust, had left to work out their own salvation. The first houses of the order were built of mud and timber, surrounded by narrow gardens in which the brethren grew herbs and vegetables to season their meagre diet of sour ale and porridge; the first chapels were so small that a carpenter

[1] For the Dominicans, Trivet, p. 209. For the Franciscans, Eccleston in the edition of Mr. A. G. Little (Paris, 1909) and the same critic's *Thomas of Eccleston* (Soc. Franciscan Studies, 1907).

could sometimes build one in a day.   But gifts and legacies flowed
in upon the order and could not be rejected ; soon the communities
relaxed the primitive strictness of their rule so far as to accept
endowments which were vested in trustees ; stately churches and
spacious priories arose, to the scandal of the more ascetic brothers ;
though poor in comparison with the monastic orders, and always
dependent in great measure upon the alms which they collected
from door to door, the Mendicants acquired a fixed status and a
vested interest in the existing order of society.   In 1256, within a
generation of their first coming, the English branch of the Franciscan order comprised six wardenries, containing forty-nine foundations, and Scotland was erected to the rank of a separate province.[1]
Matthew Paris asserts that the Order degenerated rapidly under
the influence of a prosperity which the Founder had dreaded and
forbidden ; and the change in their condition caused them many
searchings of heart.   The superiors sought by various expedients
to maintain, in part, the tradition of poverty.   One of their earliest
Generals forbade them to involve themselves, however indirectly,
in litigation respecting property.   The third of the English Provincials, Brother Haymo (1239-40), invariably wore a tattered
frock and, when presiding at a provincial chapter, would sit like a
beggar cross-legged on the ground.   Such protests proved unavailing ; but the Order none the less maintained a hold on popular
respect and performed a great work in England.   The Friars
Minor never forgot their original mission to the poor, to whom
they ministered not only with spiritual consolations, but also with
that medical skill for which they were universally renowned.   As
popular preachers the Mendicants took upon themselves a duty which
was altogether neglected by the parochial clergy.   As confessors
and almoners they came into touch with every class ; the advice
of eminent Franciscans and Dominicans was solicited by prelates
struggling to reform a diocese or chapter, and by lay magnates
upon whose consciences the evils of the time lay heavily.   In all
the civil wars and controversies of this century the mediation of
the Mendicants was frequently invoked ; and their influence was
less usefully, but not less strikingly, displayed whenever the Papacy,
whose servants they had always been in a special sense, desired to
state a case before the masses.   It is not wonderful, nor can it be

---

[1] For the chronology see Mr. Little's article in *E. H. R.*, vi., pp. 742 ff.

accounted a reproach against them, that in the latter years of Henry III. they abandoned their former neutrality to declare in favour of political reform. None were better situated than the Friars to realise the evils which the King's misrule had bred in Church and State; none were more alive to the needless suffering which lax government and dishonest officials inflicted on the poorest of the poor. Their knowledge of men gave them faith in human nature; and they could view with equanimity the audacious experiment of De Montfort in appealing against the Crown and feudalism to the general body of the nation.

The Franciscan Order was recruited, as St. Francis had pre-scribed, from the educated classes; and at an early date the superiors, disregarding the prohibitions of their founder, resolved to emulate the Dominicans in forming connections with the Universities, and in redeeming the higher studies of these centres from the reproach of heterodoxy. One of the earliest of the English convents was planted at Oxford; here Agnellus the first of the English provincials (1224-35) founded a lectureship which he persuaded Grosseteste, then Master of the Schools, to undertake.[1] The original purpose of the Franciscan lectures was to train future preachers, "in the art of public speaking and in subtle moralities". Grosseteste, not yet a bishop but already famous as a commentator, philosopher, and scientist, was unlikely to accept this narrow view of his functions. Some at least of his lectures on the experimental sciences, so highly praised by Roger Bacon, were probably delivered to Franciscan novices. Grosseteste and his learned successor, Adam de Marsh, gave the Oxford convent a European reputation[2]; it became the nursery of teachers for foreign houses of the Order. Soon there were thirty Franciscan lectureships in different parts of England, and provision was made for a regular succession of teachers at the Universities (1251).[3] It is more than accident that Duns Scotus, Roger Bacon, and William of Ockham, the three greatest of Franciscan teachers, were all of English birth, and all pupils of the Oxford school. *(margin: Mendicant Teachers)*

The Universities, which had been thus successfully invaded, were already well frequented. The centralisation of learning was not yet complete. The tribe of wandering teachers still existed; some of the monastic and capitular schools, such as those of *(margin: The Universities)*

[1] Eccleston, p. 37.
[2] On the academic attainments of Grosseteste, see the essay by Ludwig Baur in the centenary volume of *Roger Bacon Essays* (Oxford, 1909).
[3] *Ibid.*, p. 38. For the date Little, *u.s.*

Lincoln and St. Albans, attracted from time to time a professor of repute, and enjoyed under his charge a brief period of prosperity. It was even possible for discontented students, or an ambitious prelate, to found a new *studium* and purchase corporate privileges. Salisbury, Northampton, Stamford, Lincoln, Reading, even the remote and rustic Exeter, seemed at one time or another likely to rival the glories of the older universities; any considerable monastery, any cathedral town, could afford a nucleus of students, since Councils of the Church made strenuous and repeated efforts to enforce a higher education both for the religious and for the parochial clergy. Chance however decided that English learning should have two centres and no more. In spite of dispersions and other adversities Oxford, established as a *studium generale* in the reign of Henry II., and Cambridge, which begins to be mentioned in the reign of John, held their own against all rivals. Until the feud of Angevin and Capet became acute, the schools of Paris offered superior attractions to the English scholar; as late as the year 1220, when the University of Paris was organised in four nations, the English gave their name to one of these. But in 1167 the English scholars were expelled from Paris by a royal mandate; Henry II. retaliated with an ordinance forbidding clerks to go abroad for purposes of study; and in consequence we find that the Oxford schools at once leap into prominence. A few years later Gerald de Barri visited Oxford to give public readings from his book on the Topography of Ireland. He remarks that he chose Oxford for the purpose, " because more clerks were to be found there, and they more clerkly " than in other towns ; and incidentally he informs us that these clerks were organised in faculties and taught by licensed doctors. Oxford and Cambridge soon acquired a European reputation; a Frisian and a Hungarian scholar, both studying in Oxford, appear among the recipients of gifts from Richard I.; early in the reign of Henry III. a paternal government intervened to fix the price of lodgings, in Oxford and in Cambridge, " on account of the multitude of scholars who flow together from these parts and those beyond the sea for study ".[1] It may be the case, as commonly supposed, that Cambridge only became a university in 1209, owing to a temporary dispersion of the Oxford

[1] Shirley, i., p. 398.

schools. But the ordinance which we have cited shows that, already
in 1231, the two great universities ranked on an equal footing.

Both took, from the first, a lively interest in politics. The Political
scholars of Cambridge sided with Louis and the barons against Influence
John ; those of Oxford distinguished themselves in the next reign versities
by their hostility to foreign influence and their sympathy with Montfort. As the thirteenth century advances we hear more of Oxford
than of Cambridge in political controversies ; but this may be due
to accidents of situation. Oxford was a town of military and political importance, the meeting-place of Councils, a stage on several
intersecting high-roads. The news of an Oxford riot spread at once
to every corner of the kingdom ; if civil war arose, the students were
near the scene of operations and could easily slip away to join a
rebel army. But these casual ebullitions do not represent the true
nature of the influence which the universities exercised on politics.
It does not follow that they were most important when they were
most noisy. We should lay more stress upon the fact that the
science of politics came within the scope of their curriculum, and
was expounded by English teachers to an audience chiefly recruited
from the middle class of English society. The foreign element
among the scholars was prominent and picturesque ; but it was the
Englishmen who fixed the tone of thought. This fact is obscured
by the panegyrics which are most usually quoted. It is for example
a palpable exaggeration when Boniface of Savoy, with true Italian
politeness, assures his Oxford hosts that their schools are as cosmopolitan as those of Paris.[1] Oxford and Cambridge never found it
necessary to create a separate organisation for their foreign scholars.

In their opposition to Papal interference the universities had Their
the warmest approval of their ecclesiastical superiors. The satirical Specu-
poems in which anonymous scholars attacked the Curia seem to Thought
have circulated without incurring censure. It was otherwise when
the spirit of revolt invaded the region of the sciences. The universities were intended for the education of the clergy ; their
original curriculum was theological ; they were subject to episcopal
visitations. None the less the scholars turned with relief from
theology to studies of a more secular character ; or, if they remained
theologians, displayed an unwelcome aptitude for heterodox speculations. These tendencies were more easily reprimanded than

[1] *Chron. Maj.*, v., 433.

repressed. At Oxford a Master of the Schools or Chancellor, elected by the licensed teachers, acted as the bishop's delegate in relation to the university. It was his business to maintain intellectual no less than moral discipline. But he found a more congenial task in defending the privileges of his order against the town authorities; and each individual master of arts remained *de facto* free to study and disseminate the opinions which met his fancy. Nor was the scholar more restricted. The prescribed curriculum for graduation was severe; and he was bound to place himself under the tuition of a master. But he chose his own master and his own time of graduation. He studied or rioted as his inclinations prompted; and in his studies, no less than in his rioting, he showed a Bohemian contempt for the authorities. If he contemplated entering major orders he would no doubt read theology. But if he was ambitious he would prefer the civil and the canon law; if he was consumed with intellectual curiosity he would betake himself to philosophy. Whether he gave the preference to Justinian or to Aristotle, he ran considerable risk of imbibing a spirit hostile to the Church.

Philo-
sophic
Heresies

For the popular heresies of the twelfth century England had proved an uncongenial soil. She produced no Albigeois or Patarins; she offered no welcome to the missionaries of schism. Heretics were so rare in England that a law of heresy had never taken shape. Those who appeared were illiterate foreigners, waifs and strays who were not in the least likely to corrupt the seats of learning. In 1166, some Flemish weavers of doubtful orthodoxy were whipped and branded by order of a Great Council which sat at Oxford: but they were not connected with the nascent university. Still less had scholars to do with the citizen of Amiens who was burned at London in 1210, or with the leader of the Pastoureaux whom a mob of Shoreham rustics tore in pieces when he attempted to convert them. But there was an overpowering fascination, for independent minds, in the more subtle forms of unbelief which Aristotle, especially as interpreted by Avicenna and Averroes, tended to produce. English knowledge of the physical and metaphysical works, from which heresy was principally deduced, goes back at least to the year 1180 when Alexander Neckam, afterwards abbot of Cirencester, lectured on them at Paris. But he was in advance of his age. Thirty years elapsed before the Aristotelian books became notorious by their condemnation at a legatine council in Paris (1210); Edmund Rich, the future Archbishop, confined himself in his Oxford lectures to the comparatively innocuous logic of the Organon;[1] nor did the Aristotelian fever take hold of Oxford until, in 1230, Michael Scott returned from Toledo, bringing with him partial translations of the Metaphysics and the scientific treatises. So bad were these first renderings, made through the Arabic and doubly infected with error, that Grosseteste refused to make use of them, although he lectured on the subjects which they covered.[2] Better work was done by the German Hermann who completed, about 1240, a translation of the Nicomachean Ethics, also from the Arabic; and some tincture of the doctrines of the Politics, from whatever source it may have been derived, was current in the Oxford schools by the year 1265. To these writings, which it was comparatively easy to reconcile with the dogmas of revealed religion, it would appear that the Franciscans and other orthodox teachers sought to direct the attention of their pupils. The result however was unexpected. Greek ideas on the subject of justice, the natural constitution of society, and the duty of the governor to the governed, were no less inconsistent with the principles of medieval politics than were the postulates of Greek physical philosophy with the Book of Genesis and the central mysteries of Catholicism. Dogmatic conservatism was purchased at the price of political ferment, and the Oxford scholars became in their own way as revolutionary as the London rabble.

Another mode of coping with the scepticism of the learned classes was suggested by Grosseteste and more fully adumbrated by his disciple Roger Bacon. Confident that true science could never be repugnant to the teaching of the Church, they proposed to neutralise the ill effects of Aristotelian science by studying it more accurately and then superseding it. This is the project to which Bacon devoted his more important writings, the *Opus Majus*, *Opus Minus*, and *Opus Tertium*, in which he brought together, for the information of Clement IV., the result of long enquiries in many fields of study. "Much have I laboured," he told his patron, "both in the sciences and in languages for forty years since first I

The Sciences. Roger Bacon

---

[1] Rashdall, ii., p. 754 (quoting from Bacon's *Compendium Studii Theologiae*).
[2] Bacon, *Compendium Studii*, ed. Brewer, 469. Stevenson, *Robert Grosseteste*, chap. ii. There is authority for the statement that Grosseteste translated the Nicomachean Ethics, but his version is not extant. Jourdain, *Récherches Critiques*, p. 60.

17

learned my alphabet. Except for two years of the forty I have
been always studying." Early in life he found good reasons for
taking no authority as final; for twenty years before he began to
write he had pursued untrodden paths. He had spent more than
£2,000 on books, experiments, tables, instruments; in purchasing
the friendship of the wise or in training the necessary assistants.
He passed much of his working life in Paris. Here he graduated
as a doctor in 1245; here in 1277 he was cast into an imprisonment which lasted fifteen years. But it was in Oxford that he
conceived the idea of his enquiries; to Oxford he looked back
with affection, as the one place in Western Europe where the
mathematical sciences were competently taught; and he speaks
of Grosseteste as the teacher who excelled all others in his range
of useful knowledge.

Bacon follows Grosseteste in proposing, as a remedy for intellectual anarchy, the organised and co-operative pursuit of knowledge in all its various branches.[1] But the hints of the master are
developed by the pupil. Bacon explains at length the curriculum
of the ideal Academy. It must study Greek and Hebrew; it must
educate translators; it must furnish the scientist with a resumé of
all the results attained by the thinkers of antiquity. Further it
must test, correct, and enlarge the theories of the ancients by
experimental investigations on the widest scale. It should regard
the sciences, the physical equally with the moral, as avenues to a
right understanding of revealed religion, and as instruments with
which the Church may refute the scoffer, convince the doubting,
and convert the heathen. In science Bacon finds the best protection of religion; and science, he is convinced, is capable of infinite
expansion. But to fill men with the desire of scientific truth is the
grand difficulty. Truth, he complains, must battle with many
counter-influences; with the authority of all teachers from Aristotle
down to Alexander Hales, Bacon's fellow-countryman and fellow-
Minorite; with the extravagant rewards attached to legal studies;
with the perverse humours of the clergy. The latter, he finds, have
no desire for truth. " Wherever clerks are met together, as happens
at Paris and at Oxford, they scandalise the whole world with their
feuds, their contentions, and their vices."

Clement IV. did not live to reward the long patience of the

<hr>
[1] On Grosseteste's *Compendium Scientiarum* see Stevenson, p. 49.

persecuted scholar; and in 1277 Bacon was convicted of heresy by a General Chapter of his Order, to whom attacks on Alexander Hales seemed little short of blasphemy. The sentence inflicted was one of close confinement; only in 1292 was Bacon released from prison; and by that time age and disappointment had destroyed his genius. It was a heavy punishment for one whose chief fault lay in criticising with more justice than discretion the shortcomings of his rivals. But the heaviest was his failure to discredit the *a priori* reasoning of the scholastics whom he detested. His work lies outside the main lines of medieval thought, although it is in a sense the legitimate completion of enquiries opened by his Oxford predecessors. But it is not the least noteworthy feature of this remarkable age that, in the interval between two civil wars, in the crisis of the absorbing conflict between Papacy and Empire, when the minds of men, in England and outside it, were engrossed with practical questions of law and politics and religious education, there should have arisen a scientific genius to whom the common thoughts and anxieties of his contemporaries were a vain distraction, who worked and suffered for an ideal which, after the lapse of 300 years, was at length to be rediscovered and to subjugate all thinking men. History would be less than just if it ignored a man who failed to move his generation because he stood above it.[1]

We have seen how men were thinking and how thought was The Artistic Movement being made. It only remains to cast a glance upon the lives which men too busy for much thought were leading, and upon the external appearance of the world in which they moved. Let us first remark that the growth of law and form and regularity was not confined to the political and speculative sides of social life. As the twelfth century is characterised, from every point of view, by a riotous exuberance and a fertility of invention, so the thirteenth has for its distinctive trait the impulse to elaborate and organise the legacy inherited from the past. The tumultuous revel becomes an ordered pageant; the disconnected lays of minstrels are welded into a romance; acts of forbearance or of courtesy, which had been the fruit of generous impulse, are prescribed and defined by the code of chivalry; the rude ceremonies with which the youth of noble birth had been initiated into the brotherhood of arms are now disguised in a solemn ritual, and dignified with an allegorical interpretation. Nowhere is the change more apparent than in the

---

[1] The results of recent research concerning Bacon's life and work are summed up in the centenary volume *Roger Bacon*, edited by A. G. Little (Oxford, 1914).

architecture of the age. Round the bare shell-keep or rectangular tower, in which the barons of the eleventh and twelfth centuries had housed themselves like birds of prey, there sprang up walled enceintes, containing all the multifarious buildings necessary to a fortress which is at the same time a palace; and the increased complexity of these strongholds is not more remarkable than the artistic skill with which a certain beauty of form is imparted to the most utilitarian of structures. Even where the older architects had deliberately aimed at beauty they are now surpassed. In the churches built during Stephen's reign and the early years of Henry II. the massive Norman style gradually assumes a lighter and more graceful aspect; the span of the arches is increased, the bulk of the supporting pillars is diminished; a richer ornamentation is applied, a sense of proportion becomes more conspicuous. The culminatior. of the Norman style is reached about the middle of the twelfth century in the churches of Iffley, Malmesbury, and St. Cross's, Winchester. Immediately afterwards, under the influence of French architects, begins the era of the Early English style, artistically more elaborate, and mechanically more perfect, than that which it supersedes. A soaring grace, an elegance which is inherent in the structural plan, give the rank of masterpieces even to such early experiments as the Trinity Chapel of Canterbury Cathedral (1175), and the choir erected by St. Hugh at Lincoln (1190-1200). The succeeding generation produced the austere and faultless symmetry of Salisbury Cathedral (1220-58), and the mellower glories of Wells (1230-9), and Westminster (1245), in which sculptured reliefs, stained glass, mosaics, and frescoes appear to spring from the main design as naturally as blossoms from the tree. Something of the old exuberance and passion for variety survives in these and the other great churches of the time; a reminder of the free scope which was allowed, within certain limits, to the ingenuity of every master-craftsman who worked upon the building. The central idea of the architect is illustrated and amplified by the fancies of innumerable assistants: but the beauties of the parts are never allowed to obscure the general effect. The technical skill, the artistic taste, which these churches of the thirteenth century reveal, is marvellous. And yet—the fact must be emphasised—they do not represent the birth of a new art. Their architects continue and complete a development which runs back far into the past; and the same must be said of those who made the century famous in the minor arts. It was an age of perfecting, not an age of new beginnings. As for the higher arts of painting, music, sculpture, something was added to the rude efforts of an earlier school; but there was no attempt, except perhaps in sculpture, to reach a higher plane of conception and design.

The difference between medieval and modern civilisation is partly to be found in the difference between the great achievements of the two; between our music and their architecture; between their theology and our science; between their skill in forming societies, and ours in recognising and protecting the rights of the individuals who make up those societies. But there is another difference. The dominant ideas of that age were less completely woven into life than those of ours. Vast tracts of medieval society remained barbarous and uncouth, even when judged by medieval standards. Reason and unreason, ugliness and beauty, dwelt peacefully in the nearest neighbourhood. The traditions of feudal loyalty might return at any moment upon the mind of the coldest statesman. The rationalist who called one mystery in question accepted all the rest. A refined and almost morbid sympathy for physical suffering was compatible with callous brutality to criminals and enemies. Beneath the stately cathedral were clustered sordid huts and booths; and nothing short of pestilence or a royal visit could induce the wealthy citizen to cleanse the reeking kennel which lay half a dozen paces from his door. To this familiarity with the incongruous we may perhaps attribute the surprising fitfulness with which the medieval Englishman pursued reform of any kind. He hardly dreamed of a government which should always work efficiently and smoothly; as easily would he have conceived a stage of material development in which pestilences and famines would not be regularly recurrent.

The wonder is that, when such a temperament was almost universal, we find no little energy and method infused into the affairs of daily life. Trade was often brisk within the crumbling walls of the medieval town; and not only brisk but diversified and highly organised. In any important centre we find as many as twelve or fifteen crafts connected with each of the staple industries. At Norwich, cloth and leather-goods were the chief articles of manufacture. The city records mention, in connection with the woollen trade, the wool-mongers, weavers, fullers, shearers, dyers, wool-

(marginal notes:) Incongruities of Medieval Thought

Trade

merchants, drapers, mercers, blanket-makers; while the raw or finished leather was handled by skinners, tanners, leather-dressers, leather-brokers, curriers, harness-makers, glovers, shoemakers, tawers, cobblers, purse-makers, girdlers and cordwainers. In the working of metals, in the production and distribution of comestibles, we find an equally elaborate division of labour. Besides the common market there were in Norwich at least thirty special markets or quarters, each devoted exclusively to some one trade or craft.[1] In such a hive of commerce great interests were concentrated, and a great volume of business was transacted; the outward appearance of the community bore witness to strenuous and varied industry. The lower part of almost every house was an open booth with wares displayed for sale before a bargaining and cautious stream of purchasers. In workshops behind the booths the craftsmen toiled long hours to replenish the depleted stock. Heavy carts, hauled with infinite pains through miry roads, brought in at every gate the produce of upland manors, to be sold or stored against the winter in the master's town-house. From port to port, and along all navigable rivers, clumsy ships and barges plied incessantly. The great highways, maintained in passable order by the grumbling freemen of the shires through which they ran, saw a continual going and coming of merchants and packmen. Thousands resorted to the great country fairs held annually at Stourbridge, Yarmouth, Boston, Winchester, St. Ives and many another town. The stalls of the sellers covered many acres; here the rural proprietor could buy almost everything that was needed to supplement the produce of his own estate; wine from Gascony or the Rhineland or Lorraine, fine cloths from Italy or Flanders, salt-fish and tar from Norway or the Baltic, skins from Ireland, pepper, spices, silks and precious stuffs from the far East. Each shire looked to the nearest ports for foreign produce; in each shire one or more fairs served as the centres of distribution.

The Foreign Merchants   The foreign trade of England was only nascent. Raw wool, unwrought lead and tin and jet, cattle, fish, and salted meat were the chief exports; and the value of the wine which came in probably exceeded, in this as in the following century, that of all other imports put together. Still the foreign merchant was a frequent visitor to England, as the safe-conducts on the Patent Rolls bear

[1] See W. Rye, *Short Calendar of the Deeds relating to Norwich, passim.*

witness.   As wool-buyers several leading firms of Florentines had regular relations with all the principal religious houses.   Cahorsin and Italian usurers competed eagerly with Jews and Templars in the London money market,[1] and successfully evaded all the efforts of the law-courts to expel them.   The London Hanse of Cologne, which already in the reign of Henry II. had obtained a royal charter,[2] had now grown greater by admitting the merchants of Lubeck and the Teutonic league : their Steelyard, by the Thames, was a thriving and well fortified establishment ; smaller factories of the same kind were to be found at Lynn and Boston.   Even with distant Norway there were regular relations; Henry III. did not disdain to make a commercial treaty and maintain an amicable correspondence with King Haco.[3]   Foreigners assisted to develope the long neglected industry of weaving.   When, in 1271, a commercial dispute arose between Flanders and King Henry, and the order went forth for the banishment of Flemings, it was thought advisable to exempt those who had bought houses and settled in England for the purpose of working wool; to these the King announced that he would guarantee the rights of native Englishmen.[4]

Weaving and the dependent trades of dyeing, shearing, fulling, were the most highly organised which England could then show ; and even these had not passed beyond the stage of domestic industry subject to gild-law.   Shipping came next in order of importance ; the Cinque Ports, though not yet organised as a federation, were highly privileged because of the fleet which they could produce for the service of the Crown; the East Anglian coast-towns, London, Southampton, Poole, Dartmouth, Bristol and Chester could also boast of a considerable sea-faring population.   For the Crusade of Richard I. the Cinque Ports produced thirty-three ships ;[5] their ordinary contingent was twenty-five [6] in the reign of Henry II., but in that of his grandson it was raised to fifty-seven.[7]   The fleet which was raised for the French expedition of 1230 contained about 290 ships, of which the greater part came from English ports.[8]   The quality of the seamanship was good; the victory of Hubert de Burgh in the straits of Dover seems to have been won

(margin note: Industrial Development)

---

[1] *Chron. Maj.*, iii., 328; iv., 8; v. 241.   [2] *Rot. Chart.*, 194.
[3] *Pat. Rolls*, ii., 384.   Shirley, ii., *passim.*
[4] *Chron. Maj. et Vicecom.*, 138.   [5] *Pipe Roll*, 2 Rich. I.
[6] Map, *De Nugis*, v., § 6.   [7] Jeakes, p. 25.   [8] *Pat. Rolls*, ii., 370.

by the aid of skilled manœuvring, and in 1270 the English squadron of the Crusading fleet suffered comparatively little from a storm which wrought havoc among the remainder. But English ships were small. The regulation crew which the Cinque Ports furnished for an impressed vessel comprised a captain, twenty sailors, and a cabin boy, about one-fifth of the complement which the best Venetian vessels of the time required. A ship so manned would carry no more than eighty passengers, and forty horses. Though English vessels were to be found as far afield as Marseilles and Acre, they were chiefly used for coast-work; England had not yet become the general carrier of Europe.

For the rest, iron-mines were worked in the Sussex Weald and the North Riding;[1] lead and silver at Carlisle; the lead-mines of the Mendips and Derbyshire were already a source of profit in the reign of Richard I.;[2] the tin of the Cornwall stannaries had an extensive sale, though the discovery of German tin, in 1241, took away the monopoly which the English had hitherto enjoyed in respect of this metal.[3] The salt pans of Worcestershire and Cheshire and the maritime counties were probably not less flourishing than they had been in 1086; and, towards the end of the century, the sea-coal of Newcastle began to be extensively employed for fuel in England and abroad.[4]

Com-
mercial
Law
There were thus the beginnings of industrial development, which did not fail to affect both social life and law. It is a remarkable fact that, when a confirmation of their charter was granted to the Londoners in 1268, the king found it necessary to limit the judicial privileges of the city. Henceforth the citizens were not to have the benefit of pleading in their own courts, when the *Lex Mercatoria* demanded that a suit should be decided elsewhere.[5] This law, relating to cases of commercial contract, was formulated in no royal ordinance before the time of Edward I.; it was the unwritten custom of the mercantile community. But it was recognised by the public courts; and was defined by the merchants themselves in the courts of Pie Powder, which gave a summary decision on all disputes arising in the great annual fairs. Similarly the *Laws of Oleron*, a code of maritime law popularly ascribed to Eleanor of

---

[1] *North Riding Records, n.s.*, ii., 42, 229. [2] Monasticon, ii., 289.
[3] *Chron. Maj.*, iv., 151. [4] *Rot. Parl.*, i., 405, 433.
[5] *Chron. Maj. et Vicecom.*, 103.

Aquitaine or Richard I., regulated the relations of captains with their sailors and employers, the law of wreck and pilotage, and cognate matters.

Still England at large remained an agricultural community, Manorial in which the majority of men knew little of any law but that Economy administered in the courts of hundred, shire, and manor. Each manor was, or aimed at being, self-provided with the chief necessities of life.[1] The regularity with which manor-courts claimed to apply the Assize of Ale may be taken as a proof that this, the staple beverage of the lower classes, was produced by village brewers. Bread and cheese and bacon were commodities which all but the poorest could provide from their own holdings ; the smallest cottier had a plot of ground for growing herbs and fruit, the parsley, leeks, and kale, the chervil and shallots, the cherries and apples, with which Piers Plowman diversified a frugal diet. Butcher's meat was the mark of a wealthy table ; the sucking-pigs and fowls which formed the villein's festal fare came from his own sty and poultry-yard. Salt-fish, of which all classes consumed an enormous quantity in Lent and on fast-days, was almost the only article of common food which must be bought in the open market. For dress and household purposes all but the wealthiest made use of homespun cloth and linen, which were woven upon hand-looms by the women of the family. In most manors there might be found the indispensable craftsmen, a smith, a mason, a carpenter, a tailor, who in many cases received a holding as the price of their professional service to the lord. The accounts of great households prove that wealthy men did not depend entirely upon manorial supplies. When they visited their London houses, or went upon a progress, they bought large quantities of provisions. For luxuries, such as sugar, wine, and spices, they incurred heavy bills ; and we find them sending to distant fairs and boroughs for the materials of costly dresses. But the staple articles of food were raised on the estate, and sent to London or wherever the master might be residing for the moment. A prudent manager, even if of episcopal or baronial rank, removed from manor to manor at intervals of a few weeks, remaining in each place till his household had consumed the contents of the barn and store-rooms. The canons of St. Paul's,

---

[1] See Cunningham's introduction to *Walter of Henley* (ed. Lamond) and the *Reules Seynt Roberd* printed in the same volume.

when in residence, drew their commons daily from the brewery and bakehouse of the chapter; the corn and malt required for these establishments were supplied by the chapter-lands, which acquitted in this manner a substantial proportion of their rents.

The Manor-House

The life of the landholder can be reconstructed without much difficulty. Under the rule of Henry II. the most lawless of the class found it no longer possible to live the life of bandits. In spite of occasional civil wars the upper classes now adopted a mode of life which implied their confidence in the king's power to maintain the peace. Those who possessed a castle seldom cared to live in it; the Norman keep was still a common feature of the landscape; but it was more often than not allowed to remain without a garrison, or even to fall into decay. The manor-house, though it might assume the dimensions of a palace, could rarely be regarded as a fortress. It was frequently provided with a moat and palisade; royal licences to crenellate were not uncommonly asked and granted. But such defences only served as a protection against sturdy robbers, or the nocturnal attacks to which a private feud might expose the proprietor at any moment. The hall was usually the one part of the manor-house for which stone was employed. Not only the outhouses and offices, but even the private apartments were built of timber. In domestic architecture there was a surprising degree of uniformity. The manor-house of the twelfth century is substantially the same in ground plan as that of the thirteenth; the only difference between the great house and the small is in the size of the apartments. The house stood on one side of a court which was more or less enclosed with stables, barns, and sheds. The ground-floor was called the cellar and reserved for purposes of storage. An external staircase led to the first-floor, and was usually the sole means of communication with the ground, although in rare cases we find an internal staircase reserved for the private use of the owner's family. The greater part of the first-floor formed the hall or principal living-room which, if of any size, was divided into three aisles by pillars of stone or timber. An open fireplace stood in the centre of the hall; the smoke escaped by a lantern in the roof, which was of open timber work and covered with wooden shingles, tiles, or thatch, or lead, according to the means and fancy of the owner. Near the main entrance of the hall were smaller doors communicating with the buttery and kitchen. At the upper end was the dais, reserved for the family and their principal guests ; behind the dais was the door leading to the solar or private rooms.   The floor of the hall was strown in summer with green rushes, in winter with fresh hay.   The tables were mere slabs of timber, which were laid on trestles at the dinner hour and afterwards removed.   At night the domestics slept promiscuously on benches in the hall ; and here too they passed the spare hours of their day.   The solar had originally been a single room ; but in the thirteenth century it was broken up by wooden partitions ; a number of separate bed-chambers were grouped round a with-drawing-room, in which the family congregated after dark, or when the weather made out-door occupations impossible.   The walls of these private rooms were sometimes plastered and adorned with paintings.   In the residences of Henry III. we commonly find that the walls are of a green colour picked out with stars of gold ; while mural paintings are occasionally mentioned.   In the Saxon and Norman periods there seems to have been a preference for tapestry ; but hangings were out of fashion in the thirteenth century.   The windows were small and rarely, if ever, glazed. They were as a rule furnished with shutters or lattices of wood, which could be closed in cold weather ; but the inmates of the medieval house were compelled to make their choice between light and warmth.   Even in wealthy establishments the stock of silver plate was small and the furniture scanty.   Men and women lived too much in public and in the open air to be greatly concerned about the comfort of their homes ; to judge from the accounts of Bishop Swinfield they spent more upon minstrels, jugglers, musicians, and other forms of entertainment than upon the commonest household comforts.   Evenings were short in that age ; the current proverb, giving the hours of a healthy day, names five for rising, nine for dinner, five for supper, nine for bed ; and in-deed there was little temptation to remain out of bed when darkness came.[1]

[1] *Domestic Architecture in England from the Conquest to the Thirteenth Century*, by T. Hudson Turner (Oxford, 1851).   The chief evidence is to be found in Neckam, "*De nominibus Utensilium*" (Cotton MS., Titus D. xx.) ; the Pipe, Patent, and Close Rolls ; the leases given in the *Domesday of St. Paul's* (Camden Society). Halls and houses of the twelfth and thirteenth century exist at Oakham (co. Rutland), Appleton (co. Berks), Lincoln, Charney Basset (co. Berks), Aydon, (co. Northumberland), etc.   Illustrations in Hudson Turner, *u.s.*, and *Social England*, vol. i.

The
Villein

No Langland appeared in this century to give a picture of the voiceless and laborious peasant-class upon whose labours the sustenance of the whole community depended. But the more fragmentary evidence of manorial and legal documents leads to the conclusion that circumstances had raised the villein to a higher level of comfort and security, despite the efforts of lawyers and landlords to depress him. To the state the villein was now a person of importance; the introduction of taxes upon movables made it possible for the Crown to deal directly with him; villeins were made liable to the fifteenth of 1225, the fortieth of 1232, and the thirtieth of 1237.[1] The Assize of Arms, originally applied to free men only, was in 1252 enforced upon the villeins also.[2] It followed, as a natural consequence, that the royal judges showed an inclination to give the villein all the rights of a free man which did not conflict with those of his lord. They allowed him to make and enforce a contract, although in the lord's interest they decided that against a villein no contract was enforceable. Villeins who had purchased freehold property could protect it against third persons by the Assize of Novel Disseisin. A distinction was drawn between the native bondsman and the free man who had agreed to take up a holding upon villein tenure; and it was held that the latter class were not *adscripti glebae ;* if they threw up their holdings they would not be compelled to return. Nor was it an easy matter to procure a writ for the recovery of a man who was a villein in status as in tenure. The justices took the verdict of a jury in such cases, and made it a fixed rule that the defendant should have the benefit of any doubt. The manorial extents of the period show that the number of villein tenants reputed to be of free descent increased in numbers. These at all events the lord was bound to treat with some degree of equity. But we have no reason to suppose that the born bondsman was treated much more hardly than the free man who held in villeinage. Usually the one was subject to some personal imposts, tallage and the like, from which the other was free; but to this rule there were exceptions. The free man was subject like the *nativus* to the frankpledge system, whether this was administered by the sheriff or by the lord. The general rule was that no free man could be compelled to serve as the lord's reeve; but, as this was an office to which emoluments and privileges were attached,

---

[1] *S. C.,* 360, 366.   [2] *Ibid.,* 371.

free men may have been willing in some instances to serve. So far
as rents, whether in money or in labour-service, were concerned,
both classes stood on the same footing; both were protected by immemorial custom against an arbitrary increase even of those payments which, like tallage, were liable to be modified at the pleasure
of the lord. Nothing is more difficult than to decide whether the
customary services weighed heavily upon the ordinary villein. They
differed greatly in different districts, and even on contiguous manors;
and, while in each manor there was a rough attempt to make the
services proportionate to the size of the holding, the class of the
cottiers (who were, in many cases, the descendants of landless slaves,
but in others skilled artisans who required a retaining fee) might
be assessed in a much higher or in a much lower ratio than the
superior classes. But if we confine ourselves to the typical villein,
the hind who holds a virgate of about thirty acre-strips and finds
the fourth part of a team for the ploughs which the whole village
use in common, some approximate statistics may be given. The
principal obligations of the virgater were plough-work and other
kinds of agricultural labour. On two Peterborough manors, under
Henry I., we find that 156 and 138 days of such labour are demanded
annually from the virgate; on two St. Paul's manors, in 1222, the
days are, in the one case 108, in the other 172. On the manors of
Ramsay Abbey, in the thirteenth century, we find a rather higher
average; in one case 178 days, in a second 259, in a third 229.
The lowest of these figures may seem excessive, but we must re-
collect that feast-days, on which by the canon law no work could
be done, reduced the burden of labour service by about one-sixth;[1]
that the family which tilled a virgate usually sent into the common
fields three or four pairs of hands, only one of which was required
for the lord's service at any season save that of harvest; and that
the day's work, the *operatio*, was fixed at such an amount that it
could usually be performed by noon. The amount of service was
less a grievance than the way in which it was exacted. Many of
the *operationes* could be demanded whenever the lord pleased, and
at the shortest notice; the villein is described by Bracton as a man
who does not know at night what his lord may require of him in
the morning. And, to crown all, there was a large number of petty

---

[1] *Walter of Henley*, p. 8, calculates that about eight weeks' work in the year
will be lost through feast-days or similar causes.

dues, in kind or money, which were collected at the most various seasons, and were resented far more than their mere amount would warrant. It was these which did most to produce the Villeins' Rising of 1380. As yet there was no thought of rebellion, and little tendency towards change. The manor-court, attended by all the tenants, had not yet broken up into three separate tribunals of the leet, the court-baron, and the court-customary; nor do the contemporary writers who deal with the subject of estate management suggest any radical reforms. There was a tendency to let small parcels of the demesne at money-rents, but the division of the manor into demesne and tenants' land was accepted as if it had been the result of a natural law. The three-field system, the intermingled acre-strips, the common-ploughing remained unaltered; and while they remained it was impossible that the productive power of the soil should be materially increased, or the lot of the peasant materially improved. Of escape from his class the villein had little hope. Manumission, if it came at all, was delayed till he had become aged and infirm; flight, though not unheard of, entailed the loss of chattels and a life-long exile; for removal meant exile and the next shire seemed a foreign land. Only the surplus sons and daughters of the villein household could buy the lord's permission to emigrate and make for themselves a new career. It is not wonderful that men who were doomed to this stationary and hopeless life looked apathetically on the greatest of political revolutions. The fall of a king or a dictator could not help them; nothing short of a return to the first days of feudalism was likely to alter their position for the worse. Of all the contrasts which strike us in medieval life, none is so acute as that between the intellectual ferment in the upper classes and the oriental passivity of their inferiors.

APPENDICES

I.—THE EARLS OF THE NORMAN PERIOD

THE Earldom of Shrewsbury appears to have been almost as highly privileged as that of Chester. Earl Roger received from the Conqueror all the demesnes of the Crown lying within the shire, the city of Shrewsbury, " et totum comitatum " (D. B. fo. 254). The word *comitatus* seems here to mean " earldom " ; for the word *scira* occurs in the same sentence. Earl Roger then received all the rights of an earl in Shropshire. There were eight tenants-in-chief besides himself in the shire, and over their fiefs he would exercise no jurisdiction. But we learn from a charter of Earl Roger to St. Evroul, (Orderic, vol. ii. p. 414) that he appointed the sheriff of Shropshire ; the shire-court therefore was his court. We may infer that the first inclination of the Conqueror was to regard the sheriff merely as a bailiff of the royal demesne. Having granted away the demesne-lands in Shropshire he saw no reason for retaining the appointment of the sheriff. It may be that Earl Roger enjoyed the same palatine powers in Sussex as in Shropshire ; such at least is the opinion of Mr. Round (*Mandeville*, p. 322), and the passage which he cites from the *Dialogus de Scaccario* makes the hypothesis very probable. The title " *Counte Palais* " is given to Roger in the curious romance called the Legend of Fulk FitzWarin, which is printed in the Rolls edition of Coggeshall (p. 278). In its present form the romance is a late compilation, but it appears to be based on older materials.

If we ask what " *totus comitatus,*" the whole rights of an earl, included, we have to be guided by the evidence of two law-books belonging to the reign of Henry I. (1) The *Institutio Cnuti* (Textus Roffensis, p. 45) says that the Earl is entitled to the third penny, to the vills which pertain to his earldom ; and should also have *dupliciter* (whatever that may mean) the customs of all free men. As Mr. Round has pointed out (*Feudal England*, p. 114), there is a reference in Domesday to certain *mansiones* as pertaining to the earldom in Somerset. The same author has collected (*Mandeville*, p. 287) the evidence relating to the third penny. It appears that, at the time of the Domesday Survey, the third penny of the revenue of boroughs might or might not be found in the hands of the Earl. The Earl has it in six cases, but in other cases it has been granted to some one else. The third penny of the shire was, at the time of Domesday, only conferred upon the Earls of Danish shires ; and it is noteworthy that the passage of the *Institutio Cnuti* cited above affirms that before the Conquest the rights which it mentions only belonged to the earls of the Danelaw. The third penny of the pleas of the shire appears to be of Frankish origin, and it would be interesting to know why it is found in the Danelaw earlier than elsewhere. Possibly the custom was introduced after the West Saxon conquest to remunerate the earl for the trouble of dealing with rebellion. Matilda's charter of 1141 to Geoffrey de Mandeville speaks of the third penny of the pleas of the shire as if it were the right of every earl, "*sicut comes debet habere*" ; no doubt this idea had gained ground through the rivalry of the earls among themselves. Each claimed all the privileges that belonged to any other member of the order. But Mr. Round has shown (*Mandeville*, p. 293) that Henry II. resisted the claim, and granted the third penny of the shire, if at all, only as a mark of grace and favour. When the office ceased to be important, owing to the restoration of settled conditions and the growth of general loyalty to the new dynasty, it was natural that the Crown should resist any and every claim of privilege which the earls advanced. There appears, however, to be a trace of the doctrine that the Earl should have the third penny, as of right, in the *Dialogus de Scaccario*, ii. § 17. Mr. Round takes the passage differently, but we venture to differ from his rendering.

(2) The *Leges Henrici Primi* contain two passages which relate to the Earl's jurisdiction, c. 20 § 2, and c. 19. The first of these says that earls, archbishops, bishops, and other functionaries (*aliae potestates*) have not only soc and sac, but also tol and theam and infangthief over the lands which belong to their office ; while over their other lands they have only sac and soc in common causes and those belonging to manor-courts. It is difficult to disregard the testimony of a writer who was familiar with the practice of the King's court and a strong admirer of royal justice. Nor need we do so ; for the evidence of the *Leges Henrici* agrees with the conclusions which we should naturally draw from the case of Shropshire under Roger of Montgomery. We have seen that he received, along with the royal demesnes in his shire, the complete control of the shire-court. We may infer from the passage in the *Leges* that this arrangement was regarded as a natural one and advantageous to the Crown.

There is no warrant from official documents for the title Earl Palatine, at this early period, except as regards William Fitzosbern (*Chart. S. Trin. Roth.*, p. 455). Odo of Bayeux is styled Consul Palatinus by Orderic Vitalis (*e.g.* iv. 22). Speaking of Odo's position under the Conqueror, Orderic says, "Palatinus Cantiae comes erat et plures sub se comites virosque potentes habetat"; but this looks as though Orderic confused the powers which Odo possessed as Earl of Kent with those which he possessed as Chief Justiciar. *Comes Palatinus* in its original sense would be a fair translation for the title of Justiciar. It appears to be used in this sense both in Normandy and England. See Delisle in *Bibl. de l'École des Chartes*, 2nd series, v. 267. Odo is merely described as "Comes Cantiae" in a record of the Pennenden suit (Wilkins, i. p. 323), and in a royal charter printed in the Monasticon (i. 302). Nor is the title *Comes Palatinus* given to the Bishop of Durham in the Conqueror's charter of 1069-75 (Symeon, *H. E. D.* iii. 20). This charter merely confirms all the laws and customs of St. Cuthbert, as established by earlier kings, and it appears to be the sole title of the bishop to all the rights of jurisdiction which he exercised in this period. The earliest official document in which we have found the title is a charter of Richard II., confirming to the Bishop of Durham all the possessions of his see "simul cum dominio et libertatibus comitis palatini" (Monasticon, i. 240). Probably the Bishop of Durham, in the Norman period, was on no better footing than the Archbishop of York, who received in 1101-8 the complete and exclusive jurisdiction over the lands and tenants of his see (Raine, *Historians of York*, iii. p. 22).

We may, in fact, argue with some confidence; first that there was originally no sharp line of distinction drawn between the three earldoms which are commonly called palatine, and those of less importance; secondly that there were no important attributes by which the earls in general were distinguished from all other barons. Odo of Champagne in Holderness, and the Marcher Robert in Rhyddlan, only lacked the formal insignia of office to be on an equal footing with most earls. The rights of each Earl seem to have been settled by special agreement. It was a fairly common practice, in the early Norman period, to give the Earl the right of nominating, or of acting as, his own sheriff. Thus Robert Mowbray has his dependant Morel for sheriff in Northumberland (Monasticon, i. 241). Robert of Gloucester had his own sheriff for the shire-court of Cardiff (*Cartul. Glouc.*, ii. pp. 135, 139). If in addition the Earl acquired the right of acting as Justiciar in his own shire, and there were no powerful landowners to act as checks upon him in the exercise of this power, he would be to all intents and purposes an Earl Palatine.   The practice of appointing such Justiciars commenced before the death of Rufus (see the charter of "W. rex Angliae" in Monasticon, i. 143) and was fairly common during the first half of the twelfth century.   The policy of the Crown was to keep the office distinct from that of the Earl.   Thus, at the commencement of Stephen's reign, we find Milo of Gloucester acting as Justiciar in that shire, while the earldom is in the hands of Robert (*Gesta Stephani*, p. 16; Round, *Mandeville*, p. 11).   But the ambition of every Earl was to become a Justiciar; and, sometimes, as in the case of Geoffrey de Mandeville, this aspiration was realised by Earls of secondary importance.

II.—LOCAL JUSTICE UNDER THE NORMAN KINGS

IT has generally been supposed that the Norman Conquest led quickly to the decline of the local, communal courts of the shire and hundred, which lost much of their jurisdiction to the royal courts on the one side and the private courts on the other. This view was supported by reference to the writ of Henry I, issued between 1109 and 1111 (S.C., p. 122), ordering that the shire and hundred courts should meet as they had done in the time of Edward the Confessor, *et non aliter*. This was taken as an attempt to revive courts which were falling out of use. But this was a misinterpretation of the ordinance, the purpose of which was to prohibit the sheriff from summoning these courts more frequently than had been customary before the Conquest. Henry I reserved the right, however, to summon them at any time for his own requirements. His ordinance, therefore, points to the increased activity of the local courts, not to their decline. Moreover, it was ineffective to prevent more frequent sessions. Whereas the shire court had met only twice a year and the hundred court once a month, by the end of the twelfth century the former was meeting every month, or in the northern counties every six weeks, the latter was meeting every two or three weeks. The encroachments of royal and private jurisdiction cannot, therefore, have been so serious as has been thought.

The effect of private jurisdiction on the communal courts has been much exaggerated. There is no evidence that the feudal courts ever monopolised jurisdiction over land actions. Henry I's writ itself lays down the rule that actions concerning freehold in which the parties claim to hold the land in dispute of different lords shall be heard in the county court. There is no indication that this rule was new and it would apply not only to a great many boundary disputes, but to many others, since one man might hold of many lords and in different ways, and on his death problems affecting the different lords would be likely to arise, *e.g.* over land held for term of life, or by the courtesy of England. The competence of the manorial courts in criminal matters was normally limited to cases of assault and battery. According to *Leges Henrici Primi*, 20, 2, only the greater magnates and prelates normally enjoyed *infangentheof* as well.

William the Conqueror does not appear to have set up a new judicial system in England. While consolidating the royal power in the greater part of the country, he left the border regions under the rule of earls, whose authority in judicial matters was at first almost unlimited. Elsewhere he allowed the authority of the earl in the shire to lapse, relying on the sheriff and, probably, the bishop to preside over the shire court. In certain districts he may have appointed a justiciar with authority over a number of county courts. Æthelwig, Abbot of Evesham, seems to have held such a position in the region under Mercian law, the western midlands (*v.* Darlington, " Æthelwig, Abbot of Evesham," *E.H.R.*, 1933). More often, the Conqueror sent commissioners to deal with specific cases as they arose, but created no permanent judicial offices. The confiscation of many English estates and the settlement of the Normans gave rise to many disputes about land. The Domesday inquiry brought many of these to light. The normal method of securing a just settlement was the appointment of an *ad hoc* commission, which might include neighbouring sheriffs as well as barons of the Curia Regis. One or more shire courts were summoned before the commissioners, and the dispute was generally determined by the testimony of the suitors. References to royal justices in the counties may relate only to these commissioners. It is unsafe to assume that there was any system of resident shire justiciars under the Conqueror, or of itinerant justices with the general commission *ad omnia placita*. Thus the reference in the *Miracula Sancti Eadmundi* (§ 42) to *quibusdam regis primoribus, qui dictante justitia in eadem villa regia tenebant placita*, cannot be taken to establish the holding of a general eyre in this period (between 1075 and 1079). The danger of assuming that such references must be to itinerant justices or to resident, local justiciars has been pointed out by Darlington in the article quoted above. The belief that a general eyre was held in 1096, since royal justices were present in Devon and Cornwall in that year *ad investiganda regalia placita*, has been shown to rest on a fourteenth-century account of what was really only an *ad hoc* commission (*v.* Finberg, " The Early History of Werrington," *E.H.R.*, 1944). Similarly, the justice mentioned in the writ quoted on p. 520 from *Monasticon*, i. p. 143, is just as likely to have been a special commissioner as a resident justiciar.

That resident local justiciars were to be found in the counties before 1102 has also been inferred from the record of a dispute over wreck between Aldwin, Abbot of Ramsey, and Ralph de Belphago, Sheriff of Norfolk, and Ralph Passeleue, " ejusdem provinciæ justiciarius " (*Cart. Mon. de Ram.*, I, p. 149). But since Ralph de Belphago was still alive in 1130 (*v. Pipe Roll*, 31 Henry I, pp. 11, 95) and Ralph Passeleue had only recently died (*ibid.*, p. 90) it seems clear that this record refers to Aldwin's second abbacy, 1107–1113, not to his first, 1091–1102. There is not enough evidence, then, to warrant the conclusion that the system of county justiciars had been introduced before the time of Henry I, but it was established before the middle of his reign. The *Leges Henrici Primi* contain many references to a royal justice whose activities are clearly local, and later the justiciar is included among those addressed in royal writs to the counties. It seems possible that as the bishop ceased to play an important part in the county court, the justiciar took his place by the side of the sheriff. In one county, Lincoln, the bishop actually became justiciar, the office being held by Robert Bloett, 1094–1123, and Alexander of Lincoln (probably only until 1139), and being restored by Stephen to Robert Chesney (1148–1166). (*Registrum Antiquissimum*, ed. Foster, I, no. 103). Meanwhile Earl William de Roumara seems to have held the justiciarship (*v.* Stenton, *First Century of English Feudalism*, p. 225). The local justiciar was probably mainly concerned with the pleas of the Crown and saw to it that the sheriff did not appropriate the profits in those matters which were outside his *ferm* and payable direct to the royal fisc. The view that the sheriff himself might lawfully hold pleas of the Crown until Magna Carta cl. 24 forbade the practice is untenable. A charter of Stephen (according to a late *inspeximus*) grants to the nuns of Barking the hundred of Becontree ' salvis tantum placitis corone mee que per justitiam meam debent placitari ' (*Cal. Charter Rolls*, v. 282). Similar grants by John before 1215 also show that crown pleas were reserved to be tried before royal justices, now the justices in eyre instead of the local justiciar. (*v. Pipe Roll* 9 John, p. 70 : grant of the wapentake of Langeberge to Peter de Brus, on condition that he replies before the itinerant justices for pleas of the Crown, and before the sheriff for the pleas which belong to the sheriff ; *cf. Rot. Chartarum*, i, p. 200, grant to Godfrey Spigornall, 1214).

By the time of Stephen the work of the local justiciar was being supervised by the itinerant justices, though the Barking charter suggests that he still had authority to try pleas of the Crown. This is confirmed by Matilda's grant to Geoffrey de Mandeville of the hereditary justiciarship of Essex 'de placitis et forisfactis que pertinuerint ad Coronam meam ', with the promise that no other justices shall be sent into the county, except that sometimes one of his peers may be sent, ' qui audiat cum illo quod placita mea juste tractentur,' (Round, *Geoffrey de Mandeville*, p. 92.) The eyre system seems also to have been developing by the middle of Henry

I's reign. Orderic Vitalis (iii, p. 126) says that Ralph Basset held a session at Huntingdon in 1116, all the men of the shire being assembled before him, ' ut mos est in Anglia '. It was Ralph Basset who held the famous *gemot* at Hundehoge in 1124 (S.C. p. 115) and he was certainly acting as an itinerant justice before 1130 (v. *Pipe Roll* 31 Henry I, pp. 9, 19, 31, 49, 101, 145). The Pipe Roll of that year reveals the fact that more than one judicial visitation had occured, in addition to forest eyres. Under Surrey, for example, there are references to ' vetera placita ' before Ralph Basset, as well as to his forest pleas, then to pleas before Geoffrey de Clinton, and finally, under *nova placita*, to forest pleas before Walchelinus Visus Lupi (pp. 49–50). In Lincolnshire, Ralph Basset (pp. 110, 114), Clinton (p. 112), and William de Albini and Richard Basset (pp.114–120) had all held pleas. Other counties had had at least two visitations. It is probable, therefore, that the system of regular eyres *ad omnia placita* and forest eyres was in operation throughout the second half of the reign, if not earlier.

III.—THE HEREWARD LEGEND

THE principal sources are (1) the Latin romance *De Gestis Herewardi* which is printed by Michel in his *Chroniques Anglo-Normandes,* vol. ii., and in the Rolls edition of Gaimar; (2) the pseudo-Ingulph (1300-1370), which is printed by Fulman; (3) the *Annales Burgo-Spaldenses* ("John of Peterborough"), ed. Sparke, *Scriptores,* a fourteenth-century compilation; (4) the *Historia Eliensis,* Bk. II., edited by Stewart for the Anglia Christiana society, a local chronicle written between 1174 and 1189; (5) Gaimar's *L'estoire des Engles;* (6) the *Liber de Hyda* (ed. Edwards, R. S.), written at Lewes before 1136.

Of these authorities Gaimar is the most trustworthy. He wrote between 1135 and 1147; he shows a special familiarity with the events of North and Eastern England during the Conqueror's reign, and his account of Hereward cannot be traced to any extant source. The *Gesta* profess to be based in part upon an old English poem about Hereward; but the author says that of this he had only been able to discover a few leaves, which were mildewed and otherwise defaced. The poem was written, according to its title, by Leofric the chaplain of Hereward. But since the author of the *Gesta* tells us that the fragments at his disposal related to the early adventures of Hereward, and these as reported in the *Gesta* are purely fabulous, it is probable that the poem, whether contemporary with Hereward or not, was a mere romance. Leofric the Deacon is in fact described in the *Gesta* as a romancer who wrote for edification. But the author of the *Gesta* also mentions information derived from two of Hereward's followers, Siward and Leofric the Black, and from monks who had seen and conversed with Hereward. If these statements are veracious, then the older parts of the *Gesta* must belong to the twelfth century and probably to the first half of it; Liebermann fixes the date of composition about 1150. There is mention of popular ballads about Hereward in the pseudo-Ingulph. This authority speaks of the innumerable dangers and conflicts of Hereward, " prout adhuc in triviis canuntur " (p. 68). The resemblances and differences in the six accounts

(525)

of Hereward which we have enumerated are best explained by the
supposition that all drew upon a ballad-cycle, which was constantly
undergoing modification in the hands of minstrels.   There is no reason
for maintaining that all these ballads were conscious works of fiction ;
Leofric the Deacon is not a typical ballad-maker ; and if we eliminate
from the legend the fables about the early wanderings of Hereward,
which occur only in the *Gesta* and are derived from Leofric alone,
there remains a story which is at least not improbable.   The *Historia
Eliensis* gives many details respecting the siege of Ely which are not
to be found in the other sources ; but it is only natural that an Ely
writer should be especially well informed about this incident.   The
great mistake of the *Historia Eliensis* is in describing *two* sieges of Ely ;
a mistake which is explained by the author's remark that he has put
together his account "ex pluribus historiis" (Bk. II. § 107).   Evidently he wrote long after the event, and the *Gesta* appear to have
been among the sources which he used ; but some of the stories for
which the *Historia* is alone responsible have all the marks of verisimili-
tude.   All the authorities concur in outline as to Hereward's doings
in the Bruneswald.   The great difficulty however is that Gaimar gives
an account of Hereward's end which is absolutely at variance with the
Gesta.   These say that Hereward died in peace while Gaimar gives the
version with which Kingsley has made us familiar.   The natural course
would be to prefer the story of Gaimar ; but it is hard to suppose that
a Croyland writer was mistaken about the death of a man who was
buried in the church at Croyland.

   The historical basis of the Hereward legend has been discussed by
Freeman in an appendix to the third volume of the *Norman Conquest ;*
and by Mr. Round in *Feudal England*, pp. 159 ff.   Both lay stress upon
the inconsistencies and demonstrable errors of the traditional account.
It seems however as important to insist that we are dealing with a
genuinely popular tradition, in which there is much truth intermixed
with fable ; and that the historical Hereward must have possessed
great qualities to become in popular eyes the champion of the English
national cause (see Liebermann, *Ueber Ostenglische Geschichtsquellen,*
§§ 21 ff.).

IV.—NORMANDY BEFORE THE CONQUEST

O F English works on this subject the most important are : Pollock and Maitland's *History of English Law*, Bk. I. c. ii. ; the articles of Professor Haskins in the *English Historical Review* (xxii. pp. 636 ff.), and *American Historical Review* (xiv. pp. 453 ff.) ; and Professor Powicke's *Loss of Normandy* (pp. 48 ff.). Brunner's *Entstehung der Schwurgerichte* (1872), and Valin's *Duc de Normandie* (1910), and Bochmer's *Kirche und Staat* (1899) are also important. The earliest Norman law-book is the first part of the *Très Ancien Coutumier*, which was compiled about 1200. For the eleventh century we must chiefly rely upon the sparse evidence of chronicles and charters.[1] These authorities throw some light upon the character of Norman feudalism. Tenants-in-chief held their lands by military service ; they were liable to pay reliefs, upon succession to their fiefs, and also the three feudal aids ; over female heirs and minors the duke exercised the rights of marriage and wardship. The fief is sometimes called a *beneficium ;* this term points to the Frankish origin of Norman feudalism ; so does the title of count which begins to occur in the early eleventh century. The barons had feudal jurisdiction over their vassals, and often received grants of the whole or part of the ducal justice over their other tenants ; and the lands of churches were exempted from the jurisdiction of the public courts by charters which are closely modelled upon those of the Frankish kings. All this goes to prove that the Normans appropriated the social institutions. of the people among whom they settled ; and we may fairly ascribe to a Norman source those institutions of Anglo-Norman England which, like the jury of inquest, have their parallels in Frankish history. There are however facts which forbid us to suppose that the Conqueror and his successors made a systematic attempt to reproduce in England the main features of Norman society. Their policy was eclectic. They did not introduce into England the *Treuga Dei*, although this institution, introduced into Normandy during the minority of William the Bastard, was recognised and encouraged, by the great Duke and his successors, until it finally became part and parcel with the common law of Normandy (Council of Lillebonne, 1180, Orderic, vol. ii. p. 316 and note ; Council of 1095, *ib.* iii. 470 ; Inquest at Rouen, 1205, ap. Duchesne, *Script. Normann.*, p. 1060). On French soil the dukes gladly adopted the French expedient : in England they preferred to use such native institutions as the shire-court. It is in dealing with the English Church that the Conqueror shows himself most faithful to the model of his Norman policy. In Normandy he had only allowed clerical synods

[1] Professor C. H. Haskins has, however, published an official account of some Norman customs, which was drawn up in 1091 [*E. H. R.*, xxiii., p. 502].

to meet at his advice or suggestion, and frequently acted as their president (*Will. Pict.*, p. 194). His court claimed the right of deposing spiritual dignitaries, and he denied the claim of Rome to revise his judgments in such cases (*Ord. Vitalis*, 481 B., ed. Duchesne). For a long time he disregarded the interdict which the Papacy laid on Normandy in consequence of his marriage with Matilda. We need not look further afield than Normandy for the origin of the "customs" enumerated by Eadmer. Again we have some reason for believing that the still more famous "customs," which Henry II. embodied in the Assize of Clarendon, were not unknown to early Norman law. William of Poitiers observes that the Conqueror's practice was to punish clerks guilty of abominable offences, with whom the church courts had dealt too lightly. But it is probable that the ducal court had renounced this practice before the end of the Conqueror's life. The Council of Lillebonne, in 1080 (Orderic, ii. 318), lays down the law as to criminous clerks with considerable independence (see App. vii.), and even ventures to assert that, where disputes arise between the spiritual and secular courts respecting the boundaries of their jurisdictions, the bishop's decision should be final. The decrees of this Council deserve more attention than they have received. Issued with the sanction of the Conqueror they form a valuable commentary on the ordinance separating the spiritual and secular courts. By comparing their spirit with that of the passage cited above from William of Poitou, we learn how rapidly the Norman Church passed from an Erastian attitude to the ideas of Hildebrand.

In the twelfth century, and particularly under Henry II., the government of Normandy was often in advance of that of England; some of that sovereign's most famous measures were first introduced in the duchy. In the eleventh century the case was different. Norman law and institutions were then at least as primitive as those of Anglo-Saxon England. An anecdote in the *Vita Herluini* (*Opera. Lanfranci*, i. 262, ed. Giles) suggests that, even under Robert the Devil, the Norman barons might indulge in private war until they were expressly commanded by the duke to accept the arbitration of his court. The favourite method of proof in Norman courts was the ordeal of battle, which was invested with usages and ceremonies dating from pre-Christian times. In this, as in many other respects, "veterum ritu Danorum adhuc universi vivebant" (*Vita Herluini*, p. 263). Norman law was in many essential particulars vague and unsettled. The first family of Tancred de Hauteville migrated to Italy for fear of being involved in those disputes which commonly arose when an inheritance had to be divided between heirs (*Gaudfridus Malaterra*, ap. Bouquet, xi. p. 139). That the rule of division between the sons of a dead man still prevailed is a sufficient reply to those who hold that the Norman Dukes had already, before 1066, succeeded in shaping Norman feudalism to their will (see the charter of Herluin to Bec, in *Opera Lanfranci*, i. 350). Primogeniture developed on English soil ; and Brittany, the first French province into which it was introduced, owed the innovation to Count Geoffrey, the son of Henry II. (Stapleton, *Norman Exchequer Rolls*, I. lvi., lxxii ; Brunner, *Erbfolgesystem*, p. 31).

A constitution can hardly be said to have existed. The duke was accustomed to consult with the *maiores* or *principes* of the duchy on weighty questions of policy. His relations with this *Curia* are well illustrated by the debate at Lillebonne, on the eve of the expedition of 1066. The great men are asked to give assistance ; they refuse collectively ; but the duke's confidant argues with individuals and terrifies them until a majority decide to grant the duke's request. Dudo (ed. Duchesne) mentions cases in which the *Curia* is consulted, *e.g.* pp. 85, 86, 93. The *Curia* was also the highest law-court in the duchy ; and there is some reason for thinking that, even before 1066, there may have been a regular staff of justices attached to it. The chief officials of the duchy were household officers—the chamberlain, the seneschal, the butler and the constable. The English Exchequer system cannot be traced as yet to a Norman origin. But the fiscal organisation of the duchy was more highly developed than that of contemporary France. The duke derived a large money revenue from his demesnes and other sources. The most important of his agents in local administration were the *vicomtes* whose duties resemble those of the English sheriff in being partly domanial and partly of a public character. But the bailiwick of the *vicomte* seems to have been an artificial administrative area ; it does not necessarily coincide with one of the old Frankish *pagi*.

V.—CUMBERLAND AND SCOTLAND, 1092-1154

THE ancient connection of Cumberland with Northumbria is attested by the enigmatical charter of Gospatric which has lately been edited by Mr. Ragg and Mr. Wilson (*Ancestor*, Oct., 1903 ; *Scottish Hist. Review*, No. 1). From at least the date 1083-4 Carlisle formed a part of the diocese of Durham (Monasticon, i. 239-240) ; and Rufus after the conquest of 1092 ordered that this arrangement should be continued. Carlisle was placed under a sheriff (Monasticon, i. 241) and colonised with "churlish folk" whom the King sent thither from the south (*A. S. C.*). In the reign of Henry I. Carlisle became reunited for a time to the other lands which had been included in the old province of Cumbria. Ralph Meschin, who held Carlisle for some years prior to 1120, was also the lord of Kendal, Ewecross and Copeland, *i.e.* of the three baronies which lay between Cumberland and the Honour of Lancaster ; he also held the Honour of Lancaster for some little time after 1102 and before 1123 (when we find the Honour in the hands of Stephen). All these lands Ralph resigned into the King's hands in return for the Earldom of Chester at a date which falls between 1120 and 1123 (Tait, *Medieval Manchester*, pp. 162-4). The year is probably 1122, when we find that Henry I. visited Carlisle (Symeon, *Hist. Reg.*, *s.a.*). In the Pipe Roll of Henry I. we find that Stephen is in possession of the Honour of Lancaster ; the lands to the north of this are divided into the shires of Cumberland and Westmoreland. The old unity of Cumbria was thus destroyed once more. A charter granted by David I. of Scotland, in the early years of his reign, to Robert Bruce proves that the Scots now regarded the boundary as definitely established. Robert Bruce receives Annandale "et totam terram usque a divisa Dunegal de Straint usque ad divisam Randulfi Meschin" ; to be held with all those customary rights which Ralph ever possessed in Carlisle and his land of Cumberland (Lawrie, pp. 48, 49). David thus creates a new march-fief to keep watch upon Carlisle ; a measure which would have been impolitic if he had hopes of recovering the English Cumbria.

David obtained a part of what he desired by his treaty of 1136 with Stephen. The terms of the treaty are given by John of Hexham, p. 287. Stephen gave to Henry, the son of David, the Earldom of Northampton, the Honour of Huntingdon, *Carlisle*, and Doncaster (so also *Rich. of Hexham*, pp. 145, 146.) Carlisle no doubt carried with it the shire of Cumberland. But a few years later we find David laying claim to the whole Honour of Lancaster, actually disposing of Lancastrian lands at Bispham and Kirkham to the north of the Ribble, and asserting his lordship over Westmoreland (Lawrie, pp. 105, 106). The charters in which these pretensions are asserted cannot be dated with precision. The earliest of the two relating to the Honour of Lancaster was granted before September, 1141 (Tait, *op. cit.* 167). It is probable that David had taken advantage of Stephen's defeat and capture, earlier in the year, to lay violent hands upon Westmoreland and the Honour of Lancaster; if indeed Westmoreland had not been included in the grant of 1136. From this point onwards the printed charters of David I. contain no reference to Lancaster. On the other hand Ranulf of Chester appears, before May, 1147, in possession of the land between the Ribble and Mersey; so that, if Stephen ever held the southern part of the Honour, he soon relaxed his hold. In May, 1149, David released his claims on the Honour to Earl Ranulf in order to win over the Earl to the Angevin party (John of Hexham, Hen. Hunting.). Respecting Cumberland and Westmoreland the charters are similarly silent. We learn however from the chronicles that, in 1149, Henry of Anjou confirmed David in the possession of the three northern shires (Diceto, i. 376; Newburgh, Bk. I. c. 22; R. de Monte, p. 192; Hoveden).

It should be mentioned that the Honour of Lancaster was granted to Ranulf of Chester both by Stephen and by Henry of Anjou. The dates of the grants are disputed. See Mr. Round's article in *E. H. R.*, x. p. 87, and Tait, *Medieval Manchester*, p. 171. But since the grants were probably posterior to the Earl's occupation of the Honour, and in any case would be of little value unless enforced by his own resources, the question need not concern us here. All we can say with certainty is that he held the southern part of the Honour by May, 1147.

VI.—THE BULL LAUDABILITER

THE earliest mention of Adrian's grant of Ireland occurs in the *Metalogicus* (iv. 42). John of Salisbury, writing at latest in 1160 and a witness of unimpeachable honesty, says that he went to Adrian IV. to solicit this favour. Adrian complied; he granted Ireland to Henry II. to hold by hereditary right, and sent the King an emerald ring in token of investiture. After this positive statement of fact the main interest of the controversy, which centres round *Laudabiliter*, evaporates. But the following points in reference to this celebrated document are worthy of mention. (1) The text of *Laudabiliter* is given by Giraldus in the *Expugnatio Hibernica* (Opera, v. 316); also by Diceto (i. 300). The latter authority is above the suspicion of fraud; but he may have got the document from the *Expugnatio*. Giraldus says that the original of *Laudabiliter* was preserved in the treasury at Winchester. He also quotes a privilege, purporting to have been granted by Alexander III. in 1172, which mentions and confirms the grant of Adrian. But there is good reason for believing this privilege to be a forgery.

(2) *Laudabiliter* is mentioned in a letter from John XXII. to Edward II. The text is given both in Wilkins' *Concilia* and in Theiner's *Vetera Monumenta* (p. 201). There is a difference between the two texts; that in Wilkins admits the existence of the Bull; that in Theiner's collection speaks of the letters "quas praedictus Adrianus . . . eidem Henrico regi de terra Hiberniae *concessise dicitur*". The reading in Wilkins is "*concessit*". But presumably Theiner's text, which does not vouch for the existence of the Bull, is the more correct.

(3) The *Liber Niger Scaccarii* contains three letters of Alexander III. which relate to the conquest of Ireland and are admittedly genuine; they are reprinted in the new *Foedera* (i. p. 45). These are sufficient, independently of *Laudabiliter*, to prove that Rome approved the conquest of Ireland. They are of the date September 10, 1172.

(4) Whether we accept or reject the Bull *Laudabiliter*, our ideas as to the conquest of Ireland will remain unaltered. Adrian IV. approved of the undertaking; it was postponed until a much later date; and,

so far as we can see from our authorities, it was completed before any partisan of Henry thought of basing the King's title to Ireland upon the permission of Adrian.

There is a considerable literature dealing with the authenticity of *Laudabiliter*. We may refer in particular to Miss Norgate's article in *E. H. R.*, viii. pp. 18-52; to that of Mr. Round in the *Commune of London*, p. 272; and to that of Scheffer Boichorst in the *Mittheilungen des Instituts für Oesterreich. Geschichtsforschung*, 1893, iv. 101-122.

VII.—THE PUNISHMENT OF CRIMINOUS CLERKS

HENRY II's claim that cl. 3 of the *Constitutions of Clarendon* was a statement of the practice of the time of Henry I seems to have been justified. It was not seriously contested by Becket and his supporters. The punishment of degraded clerks by the secular courts has been shown by Génestal, in his detailed study of the *Privilegium Fori*, to have been allowed in France and Normandy. The practice was recognised by the canonists, including Gratian himself and the contemporaries of Becket. There is, unfortunately, very little evidence about the practice in Norman England. In cases of treason, clerks, even bishops, were tried in the Curia Regis. But this was a different matter. Treason was considered to be a special case, and the rule stated in cl. 3 obviously was not applied to it. One small piece of contemporary evidence, however, suggests that the Anglo-Norman Church did not disapprove of capital punishment being inflicted on a degraded clerk. The Abbot of Abingdon obtained from Henry I a writ authorising him to hang a thief who was a priest. (*Hist. Mon. Abingdon*, ii. p. 90.) It must be presumed that the abbot would not have sought permission to exercise his liberty of *infangentheof* in this way unless the clerk had already been degraded.

Under Stephen the situation changed. In his charter of 1136 Stephen had granted the Church jurisdiction over all ecclesiastical persons and property (S.C. p. 143). While he himself did not keep his promise, but attempted to try at least one clerk for an offence other than treason (*v.* Pollock and Maitland, i, p. 452), it is probable that the secular courts often failed to take any further action against degraded clerks. At the same time, or at least in the early years of Henry II, the Church courts were preventing secular punishment by refraining from sentencing the culprits to degradation. Becket was determined to maintain the Church courts' monopolisation of the punishment. It is possible that he was not at first aware how strongly the custom of Henry I's day supported Henry II's claim, although he is likely to have known that this claim accorded with continental practice. In a letter to the Pope in 1163 he wrote of the attacks of the secular power on the (English) clergy, ' qui ab hac jurisdictione hucusque *speciali* privilegio fuerunt exempti ' (*Materials*, V, pp. 48–9). But once the customs of Henry I's reign had been recognised it was useless for him to argue from practice, and he had to fall back on canon law, although this was generally taken to support Henry's claim. Gratian's Decretum II, xi, Q.1, cc. 26, 30, 47 seem clearly to approve the secular punishment of degraded clerks. Nor could Becket produce any text of canon law prohibiting this practice which had hitherto been at least tolerated by the Church, except by raising an entirely new issue and applying to the punishment of criminous clerks a maxim which had not till now been applied to their case : *non iudicat Deus bis in idipsum.* No objection seems previously to have been raised to clerks being punished in two ways. Becket himself had had one clerk degraded and exiled ; in another case he had decreed degradation and imprisonment ; and in a third, degradation and branding (*Materials*, iii, pp. 267, 265, 46). Henry's legal experts could quote Decretum II, xi, Q.i, c. 18, ' curiae tradatur et recipiat quod inique gessit ' in support of the legality of the double punishment. Becket asserted that this meant only that the degraded clerk could be tried in a secular court for any future crime. But while Gratian was, of course, using the phrase *curiae tradatur* in a sense other than the original, his meaning was almost certainly that the secular courts should sentence the clerk for the same crime as that for which he had just been degraded. This is the procedure indicated in a more general way in cc. 26, 30, 47, and this was the sense in which Gratian was interpreted by other canonists at this time (*v.* Génestal, ii, ch. II). Thus Becket's argument was a novel one, and was inconsistent with his own practice, unless he relied on drawing a distinction between a *twofold* punishment inflicted in the Church court, and a *second* sentence in a separate court. It seems clear, at any rate, that what he objected to was not the two kinds of punishment, but the participation of the secular court and the sentence of death or mutilation which seemed to him sacriligious in the case of one who until recently had discharged the priestly functions (*v. Materials*, iii, 269). His view was not eventually accepted. Although Alexander III upheld it after Becket's death, forbidding delivery to the secular court in his Decretal *at si clerici* (*v.* Génestal, ii, p. 21), later Popes, notably Innocent III, required clerks guilty of certain crimes (or even of all) to be degraded and delivered to the lay court for further punishment. But in England there is little evidence of this double punishment. The Church courts in the thirteenth century punished clerks *either* by degradation *or* by imprisonment. No further punishment was inflicted by the secular power except in the case of clerks who had fled from justice. Such clerks were outlawed if they did not return to stand their trial, since they had not claimed and established their right to benefit of clergy. If they did

18

536 APPENDICES

return and stand their trial, their chattels were confiscated, because flight
was regarded as an offence in itself. If a layman fled, but later returned
and was acquitted, his chattels similarly were confiscated on account of
his original flight. This practice was extended to clerks who had not
fled, their chattels being seized and kept by the King if they failed to purge
themselves in the Church court. (v. Cheney, *The Punishment of Felonous
Clerks*, E.H.R., 1936.) To this extent, but only to this, was there double
punishment of criminous clerks in England. But while Becket's view of
double punishment triumphed, the canonical rule against trial in a lay
court was not so well maintained. In the thirteenth century clerks were
required to plead in the lay court and a jury gave a verdict on their guilt
or innocence. Then, if they were found guilty, they pleaded their
benefit of clergy and so secured a second trial and chance of acquittal
in the Church court.

Becket's objection to the Constitutions of Clarendon cl. 3 was contrary
to practice, to earlier canon law and to the views of contemporary canonists. The new argument by which he sought to avert the punishment of
degraded clerks was hardly consistent with his own practice. It was not
ultimately accepted by the Popes, except Alexander III, and the additional punishment by the secular court was expressly laid down in certain
cases, though it was seldom inflicted in England. Here Becket's martyrdom secured the victory of a novel and unconvincing theory, but failed
to secure complete observance of the canons forbidding trial in a lay court.

VIII.—THE PROVISIONS OF OXFORD AND OF WESTMINSTER

THE documents printed in Stubbs's Charters to illustrate the work of the Parliaments of 1258 and 1259 are incomplete and may give a false impression of the aims and methods of the baronial party at this time. The fullest contemporary collection of documents is that in the *Annals of Burton* (Annales Monastici, i.), but even this needs to be supplemented from other sources, comparison with which shows that different versions of some of the most important documents existed. (For a summary of these *v.* Jacob, *Studies in the Period of Baronial Reform and Rebellion*, ch. iii.) It has been shown that the *Provisions of Oxford* were not a piece of legislation, but a rather haphazard collection of memoranda, comprising the resolutions of the Parliament of June, 1258. These resolutions related first, to immediate administrative action, *e.g.* the appointment of a justiciar, and of new sheriffs, the election of the Council of Fifteen, and the investigation by four knights in each county into unjust and fraudulent acts already committed by the local officials ; second, to modifications in administrative practice to be put into operation forthwith, but perhaps only experimentally ; and third, to matters to be reformed by the Council, which was thus supplied with agenda for its future deliberations. A second version of these provisions is known only from an abstract printed by Sayles and Richardson (*Bulletin of the John Rylands Library*, 1933). This is clearly based on a slightly later collection of these memoranda and reveals some significant modifications of the original decisions, emphasising the authority of the Council, and including two more clauses of the *Petition of the Barons* (clauses 10, 22). This petition had been presented at the June Parliament, having been drawn up in the interval since the appointment of the Council of Twenty-four in May, probably by the twelve members representing the barons. It asked for legislation on a number of points of feudal law, administration and judicial procedure. This legislation, which would have benefitted the barons themselves to a large extent, but not exclusively, was not for the most part enacted until October, 1259, when many of the points raised were dealt with in the *Provisions of Westminster*. In the meantime the Council, composed of the Fifteen elected at Oxford together with the royal justices and other official members, such as the principal chancery and exchequer officials and probably the justiciar, drew up further schemes of reform, which was now to extend to maladministration by the officials of the barons and to problems connected with suit to private courts. The first draft of these reforms is that given in the *Providentia baronum Anglie*, drafted before the end of October, 1258, but not yet officially published. In February a second version, *Nova Provisio magnatum Anglie*, was drawn up, and in March the barons promised to observe the same rules in relation to their tenants and neighbours as were to be laid down for the royal officials (*Foedera*, i, p. 381). But publication of this legislation was still delayed until the autumn of 1259, perhaps because it was intended to produce a more comprehensive enactment then. The *Provisions of Westminster* were made public in October and included this draft legislation in addition to the articles based on the *Petition of the Barons*. But in addition to the legislative section (printed S.C. p. 390 from the *Close Roll*), the Provisions included a number of important administrative clauses (v. *Burton Annals* pp. 471–9, and Jacob, p. 370). These called for immediate action and so were omitted from the legislative section which was handed to the justices now sent out to continue the enforcement of the reforms in local administration. It was provided that the itinerant justices themselves should be accompanied by baronial nominees, and that members of the Council were to accompany the King to France, while the justiciar and four barons were to act as an executive Council in England during his absence. The effect of this administrative section of the *Provisions of Westminster* would be to strengthen the Council and especially the baronial element in it.

Thus the discussion and drafting of the reforms occupied a considerable period and it is clear that while there were many matters on which it was agreed that legislation was desirable there was no cut and dried plan of administrative and judicial reform ready in the spring of 1258. The barons were able to produce their *Petition* within a few weeks, but the additional reforms were probably largely the work of the justices and perhaps owed something to the information acquired by Hugh Bigod as he heard *querelæ* in the counties, or that brought by the four knights. The abuses with which they dealt were certainly not enough to have provoked open opposition to Henry III's government. But the scope of the reforms was wide and shows that the barons were not attempting to exploit Henry's difficulties merely for the benefit of their own class. No doubt the prime motive of the opposition was dislike of further taxation. Whenever Henry had asked for a grant the occasion had been taken to secure the confirmation of Magna Carta or to press for the appointment of a justiciar, chancellor and treasurer acceptable to the barons, or even of a baronial executive council. Many of the demands of 1258 were, therefore, only to be expected. But there were new considerations as well and the King, threatened with excommunication, was more completely at the mercy of his subjects, who had learnt from experience the need to ensure the fulfilment of his undertakings. Henry had respected the barons' right to consent to taxation, but this right was nugatory so long as the King was free to pursue his own foreign policy and enter into foreign commitments entailing very heavy expenditure. Accordingly, the first objective of the opposition in 1258 was to secure control of foreign policy and to extricate Henry from his various continental entanglements as cheaply as possible. The second was to improve the financial administration at home, and so reduce the sums which would have to be provided by taxation. This taxation was not to be granted until the desired reforms had been assured. For this reason, and to avoid the danger of the renewal of Henry's foreign adventures, the council was to remain under baronial influence for a considerable period. The reference to the period of twelve years in the clause dealing with the custody of castles in the *Provisions of Oxford* suggests that the barons meant to maintain their position as long as there was any danger of Henry's reasserting his control of foreign policy—probably, indeed, for the remainder of his reign. They did not deliberately draw up a new 'constitution' nor was their scheme for reconstituting the government published. Probably they relied on their conception of their duty as the King's 'natural counsellors' to justify their setting up a continuous council, and believed that precedent justified their demand to consent to the choice of the justiciar, chancellor and treasurer. The requirement that these officers should answer to the council at the end of their year's term of office was a more obvious novelty. Yet the scheme at first depended upon the King's co-operation. What was intended was not a purely baronial government but a coalition or 'national' government, acting in the general interest. It was only later that the council was seen to be acting as an executive independent of the King. The 'national' government would, it was hoped, show how the kingdom should be governed. It would amend those things which were seen to need amendment.

It is not necessary, therefore, to attribute the reforms touching local and private justice solely to pressure from the middle classes. The royal justices may have been largely responsible for them ; the *Providentia baronum Anglie* reveal the fact that they were not drawn up without some opposition and discussion within the Council. The belief that knights of the shire attended the Easter Parliament of 1258 has been shown to rest on evidence which in fact relates to the appearance of the four knights at Michaelmas to report on their investigation of local grievances (*v.* Cam., E.H.R., 1931). The significance of the protest of the ' bachelors ' in 1259 should not be exaggerated : it is clear that the *Provisions of Westminster* were not drawn up as a result of it. It was, however, necessary to consider the interests of the middle classes. It was part of the baronial plan to prevent the local officials' appropiating profits of justice or other perquisites which should have gone to the exchequer. The punishment and prevention of such defalcations depended on the co-operation of the local knights and gentry, and to secure this it was necessary to punish and prevent injustice and extortion as well. Even John had grasped this when he wrote to the men of Yorkshire and Lincolnshire in 1213 : " Frequentes querelas a pluribus audivimus quod vicecomites nostri et servientes eorum et alii ballivi nostri plura a vobis extorserunt que ad commodum nostrum non devenerunt, et vos male tractaverunt, unde non modicum movemur " (*Rot. Lit. Pat.*, i, p. 97). Moreover, in 1254 the barons had refused to make a grant unless representatives of the shires were also consulted. They could hardly now undertake to raise an aid without consulting them and without redressing their grievances, as they expected the King to redress their own. But the barons did not deny their responsibility for the just administration of their franchises, and these considerations of expediency were reinforced by the desire to provide good government, or at least to show up the deficiences of Henry III's administration.

BIBLIOGRAPHY

PLAN OF THE BIBLIOGRAPHY

Note.—To enable the reader to take in recent works at a glance the additions to the bibliography made for the 11th edition are given as appendices to their respective sections.

References are made to monographs in the footnotes; to include the full list in the Bibliography has been thought inadvisable. The bibliography contains (a) Sources, (b) Books of general reference for the period. The sources are arranged as follows :—
  (1) Documents, Records, Collections of Chronicles.
  (2) Narrative Sources (Chronicles, Annals, Biographies, etc.).
  (3) Treatises, Correspondence, etc.
Modern books of reference are grouped thus :—
  (1) Political, Constitutional, and Legal.
  (2) Economic.
  (3) Social, Literary, etc.
  (4) Military History.
  (5) Biographical.

(a) SOURCES

(1) DOCUMENTS, RECORDS, CALENDARS, COLLECTIONS OF CHRONICLES

Ancient Laws and Institutes of Wales. *Record Commission.* 2 vols. 1841.

Annales Monastici [-1432], ed. H. R. Luard. *Rolls Series.* 5 vols. 1864-9. Invaluable for the thirteenth century.

Auvray, L. Les Registres de Gregoire IX. Paris, 1896, etc. In progress.

Bémont, C. Chartes des libertés anglaises, 1100-1305. Paris, 1892. The best text of the charters. A good introduction.

Berger, E. Les Registres d'Innocent IV. [1253-4]. Paris. In progress.

Bigelow, M. M. Placita Anglo-Normannica. [1066-1199.] Boston, 1879.

Boldon Buke, ed. W. Greenwell. *Surtees Society.* Durham, 1852. A twelfth century survey of the lands of the see of Durham.

Bouquet, Martin. Recueil des Historiens des Gaules et de la France. 24 vols. Paris, 1738-1904.

Bourel de la Roncière, de Loye, et Coulon. Les Registres d'Alexandre IV. [1254-61], Paris. In progress.

Bullaire du Pape Calixte II. [1119-1124], ed. U. Robert. Paris, 1891.

Calendar of the Charter Rolls. Vol. i. [1226-1257]. *Rolls Series.* 1903.

Calendar of Entries in the Papal Registers, relating to Great Britain and Ireland, ed. W. H. Bliss. Papal Letters, vol. i. [1198-1304]. *Rolls Series.* 1893.

Calendar of Documents preserved in France illustrative of the History of Great Britain and Ireland [918-1206], ed. J. H. Round. *Rolls Series.* 1899.

Calendar of Documents relating to Ireland [1171-1307], ed. H. S. Sweetman. *Rolls Series.* Vol. i. 1875.

Calendarium Rotulorum Patentium [3 John-23 Ed. IV.]. *Record Commission.* 1802. Still useful for the latter years of Henry III.

Cartularium Monasterii de Rameseia, ed. W. H. Hart and P. A. Lyons. *Rolls Series.* 3 vols. 1884-93.

Cartularium S. Petri Gloucestriae, ed. W. H. Hart. 3 vols. *Rolls Series.* 1863-7.

Cartulary of St. Frideswide at Oxford, ed S. R. Wigram. *Oxford Historical Society*. 2 vols. 1895-6.

Chronicles of the Reigns of Stephen, Henry II., and Richard I., ed. R. Howlett. *Rolls Series*. 4 vols. 1884-9. Contain valuable introductions.

Chronicles of the Reigns of Edward I. and Edward II., ed. W. Stubbs. *Rolls Series*. 2 vols. 1882-3.

Chronicon Monasterii de Abingdon, ed. J. Stevenson. *Rolls Series*. 2 vols. 1858.

Collectanea, ed. C. R. Fletcher and Montagu Burrows. *Oxford Historical Society*. Vol. i. 1885. Contains a collection of sources for the early history of the University.

Davis. H. W. C., *Regesta Willelmi Conquestoris et Willelmi Rufi*. Oxford, 1913.

Delisle, L. Catalogue des Actes de Philippe Auguste. Paris, 1856.

Domesday Book, ed. Farley and Ellis. *Record Commission*. 4 vols. 1783-1816. Vol. iii. contains introduction and indices by Ellis. Vol. iv., the Inquisitio Geldi of 1084 ; the Exon Domesday ; the Inquisitio Eliensis ; the Liber Winton ; the Boldon Book.

Domesday of St. Paul's, ed. W. H. Hale. *Camden Society*. 1858. Surveys of manors and early leases.

Duchesne, A. Historiae Normannorum Scriptores Antiqui. Paris, 1619.

Dugdale, W. Monasticon Anglicanum. 6 vols. in 8. (Re-edited by Caley, Ellis and Bandinel.) 1817-30. A vast collection badly edited.

Foedera, Conventiones, etc. Vol. i. Part i. [1069-1271]. *Record Commission*. 1816. A revised and augmented edition of Rymer's work. See, for supplementary documents, C. P. Cooper's Report on Rymer's Foedera [*Record Commission*. 3 vols. n.d.].

Gloucestershire. Inquisitiones Post Mortem. Henry III.-Edward I., ed. S. Madge. London, 1904-5.

Guirand, M. J. Les Registres d'Urbain IV. [1261-4]. Paris. In progress.

Historians of the Church of York, ed. J. Raine. *Rolls Series*. 3 vols. 1879-94.

Jaffé, P. Regesta Pontificum [-1198]. 2nd ed., rev. W. Wattenbach. 2 vols. Leipsic, 1885-8.

Jordan, E. Les Registres de Clement IV. [1265-8]. Paris. In progress.

Landboc of Winchelcumba, ed. D. Royce. Vol. i. [798-1332]. Exeter, 1892.

Lawrie, Sir A. Early Scottish Charters. 1904.

Liber Eliensis, ed. D. J. Stewart. London, 1848.

Liber Niger of Peterborough, ed. T. Stapleton, in *Chronicon Petroburgense, Camden Society*, 1849. A survey of estates temp. Henry I.

Liebermann, F. Die Gesetze der Angelsachsen. 2 vols. Halle, 1898, etc. The best text, elucidated by exhaustive glossaries.

Liebermann, F. Ungedruckte Anglo-Normannische Geschichtsquellen. Strassburg, 1879.

Michel, F. Chroniques Anglo-Normandes. 3 vols. Rouen, 1836-40.

Migne, J. P. Patrologiae Cursus Completus. *Series Latina*. 221 vols. in 222. Paris, 1844-64.

Monumenta Franciscana, ed. J. S. Brewer and R. Howlett. *Rolls Series*. 2 vols. London, 1858-62.

Monumenta Historica Britannica, ed. H. Petrie. London, 1848.

Morris, R. Specimens of Early English [1150-1300]. Oxford, 1882.

Munimenta Gildhallae Londoniensis, ed. H. T. Riley. *Rolls Series*. 3 vols. in 4. 1859-62.

Pertz, G. H. Monumenta Germaniae Historica Scriptores. 30 vols. Hanover, 1826-96.

Pipe Roll Society Publications. London, 1884, etc. Pipe Rolls from 1158, with an introductory volume by Hubert Hall, etc. In progress.

Pipe Rolls—31 Hen. I.-2, 3, 4 Hen. II., 1 Rich. I., 3 John, ed. J. Hunter. *Record Commission*. 2 vols. 1833-44.

Political Songs from the Reign of John to that of Edward II., ed. T. Wright. *Camden Society*. London, 1839.

Potthast, August. Regesta Pontificum [1198-1304]. 2 vols. Berlin, 1874-5.

Pressutti, P. Regesta Honorii III. 2 vols. Roma, 1888.

Records of the Borough of Leicester, ed. M. Bateson. Vol. i. Cambridge, 1899.

BIBLIOGRAPHY

543

Recueil des Historiens des Croisades. Paris, 1841, etc. Comprises a valuable series of *Historiens Orientaux.*
Red Book of the Exchequer, ed. Hubert Hall. *Rolls Series.* 3 vols. 1896. Many documents of the twelfth and thirteenth centuries.
Reports from the Lords' Committee on the Dignity of a Peer. 5 vols. London, 1820-9. Appendices containing many documents which relate to the Great Council.
Rôles gascons [1242-55], ed. F. Michel and C. Bémont. *Documents Inedits.* 3 vols. Paris 1885-99. Official documents connected with English rule in Gascony.
Rotuli Chartarum [1199-1216], ed. T. D. Hardy. *Record Commission.* 1837.
Rotuli Litterarum Clausarum [1204-27], ed. T. D. Hardy. *Record Commission.* 1835.
Rotuli Litterarum Patentium [1201-16], ed. T. D. Hardy. *Record Commission.* 1835. The editor gives a valuable itinerary of King John.
Rotuli Normanniae [1200 5], ed. T. D. Hardy. *Record Commission.* 1835.
Rolls, Close [1227-]. *Rolls Series.* In progress.
Rolls, Patent [1216-]. *Rolls Series.* In progress.
Round, J. H. Ancient Charters [1095-1200]. *Pipe Roll Society.* London, 1888.
Satirical Poets of the Twelfth Century, ed. T. Wright. *Rolls Series.* 2 vols. 1872.
Schmid, Reinhold. Die Gesetze der Angel-Sachsen. Leipsic, 1858. A valuable glossary and notes.
Select Cases from the Coroners' Rolls [1265-1413], ed. C. Gross. *Selden Society.* London, 1896.
Select Charters [-1307], ed. W. Stubbs. Oxford, 1895.
Select Pleas in Manorial Courts, ed F. W. Maitland. *Selden Society.* Vol. i. London, 1889. Contains a valuable introduction on seigniorial courts.
Select Pleas of the Crown, ed. F. W. Maitland. *Selden Society.* London, 1888.
Select Pleas of the Crown for the County of Gloucester, 1221, ed. F. W. Maitland. London, 1884.
Select Pleas of the Forests [10 John-8 Ed. III.], ed. G. J. Turner. *Selden Society.* London, 1900. A valuable introduction.
Select Pleas from the Rolls of the Exchequer of the Jews, ed. J. M. Rigg. *Selden Society.* London, 1902.
Stapleton, T. Magni Rotuli Scaccarii Normanniae. 2 vols. London, 1840-4. Valuable for English rule in Normandy. See the comments and deductions of Leopold Delisle in the *Bibliothèque de l'École des Chartes.* 2nd series, vol. v.; 3rd series, vols. i. and iii.
Statutes of the Realm [1235-1703]. *Record Commission.* Vol. i. 1810.
Swinfield, Richard de, Household Expenses of [1-89-90], ed. J. Webb. *Camden Society.* 2 vols. 1854-5.
Teulet, A. Layettes du Trèsor des Chartes. 4 vols. Paris, 1863-1902.
Textus Roffensis, ed. T. Hearne. Oxford, 1720.
Theiner, Augustin. Vetera Monumenta Hibernorum et Scotorum historiam illustrautia [1216-54]. Rome, 1864. Ecclesiastical documents from the Vatican.
Three Rolls of the King's Court (1194-5), ed. F. W. Maitland. *Pipe Roll Society.* London, 1891.
Wharton, Henry. Anglia Sacra. 2 vols. London, 1691. Contains lives of bishops, etc., not printed elsewhere.
Wilkins, David. Concilia Magnae Britanniae et Hiberniae. 4 vols. London, 1737.

APPENDIX

Anderson, A. O. Scottish Annals from English Chroniclers. London, 1908.
Ballard, A. British Borough Charters, 1042-1216. Cambridge, 1913.
Ballard, A. and Tait, J. British Borough Charters, 1216-1307. Cambridge, 1923.
Bateson, M. Borough Customs. 2 vols. *Selden Society.* 1904-6.
Curia Regis Rolls, vols. i-viii. Public Record Office, London, 1922-37.
Delisle, L. Receuil des Actes de Henri II. 3 vols. Paris, 1909-29. The introduction to vol. I. contains the best account of the Anglo-Norman Chancery in the twelfth century.

18*

Douglas, D. C. Feudal Documents from the Abbey of Bury St. Edmund. *British Academy Records.* Vol. viii. Oxford, 1932.

Douglas, D. C. The Domesday Monachorum of Christ Church, Canterbury. *Royal Historical Society.* London, 1944.

Farrer, W. Lancashire Pipe Rolls and Early Charters. Liverpool, 1902.

Farrer, W. Early Yorkshire Charters. 3 vols. Edinburgh, 1914-16. A valuable collection of charters anterior to the thirteenth century, arranged under the fiefs which are taken alphabetically up to and including the fee of Mortemer. Index to vols. i-iii. Clay, C.T. and E.M., 1942.

Farrer, W. and Clay, C. T. Early Yorkshire Charters. Vols. iv., v. The Honour of Richmond. Edinburgh, 1935, 1936. Vol. vi. The Paynel Fee, 1939.

Fees, the Book of, commonly called Testa de Nevill. 3 vols. Stationery Office, 1921-31. This edition displaces the Testa de Nevill published by the Record Commission in 1807.

Foster, C. W. and Major, K. Registrum Antiquissimum of Lincoln Cathedral. 5 vols. *Lincs Record Society.* Lincoln and London, 1932-40.

Foster, C. W. and Langley, T. The Lincolnshire Domesday and the Lindsey Survey. *Lincs Record Society.* Lincoln and London, 1924.

Fowler, G.H. and Jenkins, J. G. Early Buckinghamshire Charters. *Buckinghamshire Archæological Society.* Bedford, 1940.

Fry, E. A. Calendar of Feet of Fines relating to the county of Wiltshire, 1195-1272. *Wiltshire Archæological Society.* 1930.

Gibbs, M. Early Charters of St. Paul's. *Royal Historical Society. Camden Third Series.* London, 1939.

Goodman, A. W. Chartulary of Winchester Cathedral. Winchester, 1927. Edited in English.

Gross, C. Select Coroners Rolls, 1265-1413. *Selden Society.* 1896.

Hall, H. Select Cases Concerning the Law Merchant. 2 vols. *Selden Society.* 1908-29.

Harding, N. D. Bristol Charters, 1155-1373. *Bristol Record Society.* 1930.

Holtzmann, Walther. Papsturkunden in England. 2 vols. Berlin, 1930-1936. Contains the record of all the papal letters to England prior to 1198 that the author could find in England. Much useful material relating to the monasteries.

Hughes, Crump and Johnson. Dialogus de Scaccario. Oxford, 1902. The authoritative edition.

Hughes, M. W. and Jenkins, J. G. Calendar of the Feet of Fines for the County of Buckingham, 7 Richard 1 to 44 Henry III. *Buckinghamshire Archæological Society.* Bedford, 1942.

Jenkinson, H., and Formoy, B. E. R. Select Cases in the Exchequer of Pleas. *Selden Society.* 1931.

Leadam, I. S. and Baldwin, J. F. Select Cases Before the King's Council, 1243-1482. *Selden Society.* 1918.

Lees, B. A. Records of the Templars in England in the Twelfth Century. *British Academy Records.* Vol. ix. Oxford, 1935. A complete text of the great Inquest of 1185, together with a useful collection of illustrative charters and documents. A long introduction includes a detailed account of the early history of the Templars in England. An invaluable work for students of social, economic and ecclesiastical history.

Lunt, W. E. The Valuation of Norwich, 1254. London, 1926.

Maitland, F. W. and Baildon, W. P. The Court Baron. *Selden Society.* 1891.

Pantin, W. A. General and Provincial Chapters of the English Black Monks. 3 vols. *Camden Society.* London, 1931-7.

Parker, J. Feet of Fines for the County of York, 1246-72. *Yorks Archæological Society.* 1932.

Pipe Roll Society. Old Series. 38 vols. 1884-1925.
  The Pipe Rolls of 5 to 34 Henry II. 30 vols. 1884-1925.
  Ancient Charters prior to 1200. ed. J. H. Round. 1888.

Rolls of the King's Court, Richard I. 2 vols. 1891-1900.
Feet of Fines, Henry II. and Richard I. 4 vols. 1894-1900.
Rotuli de Dominabus. 1913.
Pipe Roll Society. New Series. 1925, etc.
  The Pipe Rolls of Richard I. and John. In progress. (9 John. 1944).
  The Pipe Roll of 14 Henry III. 1927.
  The Chancellor's Roll of 8 Richard I. 1930.
  Memoranda Roll, 14 Henry III. 1933.
  The Itinerary of Richard I. 1935.
  Cartæ Antiquæ Rolls, 1-10. 1939.
  Memoranda Roll, 1 John. 1943.
Public Record Office, Calendars, Rolls, etc. In general reference should be made to the bibliographies of the Cambridge Mediæval History, vols. v. and vi. and to P.R.O. " Lists and Indexes " and " List Q ".
Richardson, H. G. and Sayles, G. D. Select Cases of Procedure without Writ under Henry III. *Selden Society.* London, 1941.
Robertson, A. J. Laws of the Kings of England from Edmund to Henry I. Cambridge, 1925.
Salter, H. E. Feet of Fines for Oxfordshire, 1195-1291. *Oxford Record Society.* 1930.
Savage, H. E. Magnum Registrum Album of Lichfield Cathedral. *William Salt Archæological Society.* 1926.
Stenton D. M. Earliest Lincolnshire Assize Rolls, 1202-9. *Lincoln Record Society.* 1925. Connects Glanvill with the procedure revealed in the earliest Assize Rolls.
Stenton, D. M. Earliest Northamptonshire Assize Rolls, 1202-3. *Northants Record Society.* 1930. Useful for the study of the personnel responsible for the administration of law.
Stenton, D. M. The Chancellor's Roll of 8 Richard I. *Pipe Roll Society.* London, 1930.
Stenton, D. M. Rolls of the Justices in Eyre for Lincolnshire, 1218-19, and Worcestershire, 1221. *Selden Society.* London, 1934.
Stenton, D. M. Rolls of the Justices in Eyre for Yorkshire, 1218-1219. *Selden Society.* London, 1937.
Stenton, D. M. Rolls of the Justices in Eyre for Gloucestershire, Warwickshire and Staffordshire, 1221-1222. *Selden Society.* London, 1940.
Stent n, F. M. Documents Illustrative of the Social and Economic History of the D nelaw. *British Academy Records.* Vol. v. Oxford, 1920.
Stenton, F. M. Transcripts of Charters relating to Gilbertine Houses. *Lincoln Record Society,* 1922.
Stenton, F. M. Facsimiles of Charters from Northamptonshire. *Northants Record Society.* 1930.
Stewart-Brown, R. The Calendar of County Court, etc., Rolls of Chester, 1259-97. *Chetham Society.* Manchester, 1926.
Stokes, E. and Wellstood, F. C. Warwickshire Feet of Fines. *Dugdale Society* 1932.
Tait, J. Domesday Survey of Cheshire. *Chetham Society.* Manchester, 1916.
Tait, J. Chartulary of Chester Abbey. 2 vols. *Chetham Society.* Manchester, 1920-23.
Taylor, A. J. Records of the Barony and Honour of the Rape of Lewes. *Sussex Record Society.* Lewes, 1940.
Thomas, A. H. Early Mayor's Court Rolls of London. Cambridge, 1924.
Turner, G. J. Feet of Fines for the County of Huntingdon. Cambridge, 1913.
Turner, G. J. and Salter, H. E. Register of St. Augustine's Abbey, Canterbury, commonly called The Black Book. 2 vols. Oxford, 1915-25.
West, J. R. The Cartulary of St. Benet of Holme, 1020-1210. Vols. ii. and iii. *Norfolk Record Society.* 1932.

(2) NARRATIVE SOURCES
(CHRONICLES, ANNALS, BIOGRAPHIES)

Ambroise. L'estoire de la guerre sainte [1190-2], ed. G. Paris. *Documents Inédits.* Paris, 1897. Contemporary Account of Richard's Crusade.

Amiens, Guy of. De Bello Hastingensi Carmen, ed. Petrie. *Monumenta Historica* 1848.

Anglo-Saxon Chronicle, ed. B. Thorpe. *Rolls Series.* 2 vols. 1861. Also ed. Plummer, Two of the Saxon Chronicles Parallel (Parker and Laud MSS.). 2 vols. Oxford, 1892-9.

Annales Cambriae (-1288), ed. J. W. ab Ithel. *Rolls Series.* 1860.

Annales Prioratus de Dunstaplia (-1297), ed. H. R. Luard. *Annales Monastici,* vol. iii. *Rolls Series.* 1886. Contemporary and valuable from 1210.

Annales de Margan (1066-1232), ed. H. R. Luard. *Annales Monastici,* vol. i. A South Wales Chronicle. Valuable for thirteenth century.

Annales de Burton (1004-1263), ed. H. R. Luard. *Annales Monastici,* vol. i. A storehouse of thirteenth century documents.

Annales de Oseneia (1016-1347), ed. H. R. Luard. *Annales Monastici,* vol. iv. Contemporary from 1233 ; but meagre.

Annales de Theokesberia (1066-1263), ed. H. R. Luard. *Annales Monastici,* vol. i. Specially useful for reign of Henry III.

Annales de Waverleia (-1291), ed. H. R. Luard. *Annales Monastici,* vol. ii. From 1219 a contemporary record.

Annales de Wigornia (-1377), ed. H. R. Luard. *Annales Monastici,* vol. iv. Useful for thirteenth century.

Annales S. Edmundi (-1212), ed. Liebermann. *Ungedruckte Geschichtsquellen.* Strassburg, 1879. A contemporary authority for the reign of John.

Annales S. Pauli Lundonienses (1604-1274), ed. Pertz. SS. xxviii. Valuable from 1260.

Annales Londonienses (1194-1330), ed Stubbs. *Chronicles of Edward I.,* etc., vol. i. *Rolls Series.* 1882. Based on the preceding. Useful from 1260.

Annales Stanleienses et Furnesienses (1202-71), ed. R. Howlett. *Chronicles of the Reign of Stephen,* etc. *Rolls Series.* 1885. Useful for reign of John, and again after 1241. Royalist.

Annals of the Kingdom of Ireland. By the Four Masters. Ed. J. O'Donovan, 7 vols. Dublin, 1848-51. A seventeenth century compilation, but based on older sources.

Anonyme de Béthune. In Bouquet, *Recueil,* vol xxiv. Valuable for the English campaign of Louis VIII.

Benedictus Abbas. Gesta Regis Henrici Secundi [1169-92], ed. W. Stubbs. *Rolls Series.* 2 vols. 1867. Contemporary, and perhaps of official origin ; incorrectly ascribed to Benedict, Abbot of Peterborough. A mine of documents and exact information.

Bohâdin. Ed. *Recueil des Hist. des Croisades, Hist. Orientaux,* vol. iii. Paris, 1884. The friend and biographer of Saladin.

Breton, G. le (Guillelm. Armoricus). Gesta Philippi and Philippeis. In Bouquet, *Recueil,* xvii. Valuable for Philip Augustus.

Brevis Relatio de Origine Willelmi, ed J. A. Giles. *Scriptores Rer. Gest. Willelmi Conquestoris.* London, 1845. Written temp. Henry I. ; useful for the period of the Conquest.

Brut y Tywysogion [681-1282], ed. J. W. ab Ithel. *Rolls Series.* 1866. A Welsh vernacular source (with translation). Meagre, inaccurate as to dates, but often useful.

Canterbury, Gervase of (+ *circ.* 1210), The Historical Works of, ed. W. Stubbs. *Rolls Series.* 2 vols. 1879-80. Include Chronica (1100-1199), which are of occasional value ; and Gesta Regum (-1210), which are useful for the last ten years which they cover. The Gesta are continued, partly with excerpts from a Dover Chronicle, to 1328 by another hand.

Chronicon Majorum, Vicecomitum, etc., ed. T. Stapleton in the *Liber de Antiquis Legibus. Camden Society.* 1846. The work of Arnold FitzThedmar, a

German, and an alderman of London, under Henry III. A valuable source ; strongly hostile to the Montfortians.

Chronicon de Bello [1258-65], ed. Bémont *Simon de Montfort*, pp. 373-80.

Chronicon de Lanercost [1201-1346], ed J. Stevenson. *Bannatyen Club.* Edinburgh, 1839.

Chronicon de Mailros [-1275], ed. J. Stevenson. *Bannatyne Club.* Edinburgh, 1835. Both these chronicles are valuable for the period of De montfort. They have much material in common, apparently from a Minorite source.

Coggeshall, Ralph of, Chronicon Anglicanum [1066-1223], ed. J. Stevenson. *Roll Series.* 1875. Becomes valuable after 1187.

Caventry, Walter de. Memoriale (-1225), ed. W. Stubbs. *Rolls Series.* 2 vols. 1872-3. Best for the years 1201-25, when it incorporates Barnwell annals.

Dermot, Song of, ed. G. H. Orpen. Oxford, 1892. Written about 1225 ; based on the testimony of eye-witnesses. Contains a rhymed Domesday of the first settlement of the English in Ireland.

Devizes, Richard of. De Rebus Gestis Ricardi Primi [1189-92], ed. J. Stevenson. *English Historical Society.* London, 1838. Also edited by Howlett, *Chronicles of Stephen*, etc. *Rolls Series.* 1886.

Diceto, Ralph of. Opera Historica, ed. W. Stubbs. *Rolls Series.* 2 vols. 1876. The Imagines Historiarum in vol. ii. are invaluable for the years 1188-1202.

Durham, Simeon of. Opera, Omnia, ed. T. Arnold. *Rolls Series.* 2 vols. 1882-5. Useful for Northern history in the Anglo-Norman period.

Eadmer. Historia Novorum [960-1122], and Vita Anselmi, ed. M. Rule. *Rolls Series.* 1884. The friend and confidant of Anselm. An honest and valuable writer.

Ernoul. Chroniques [1183-1228]. French chronicle of the Kingdom of Jerusalem, ed. Mas Latrie in *Societé de l'Histoire de France*, 1872.

Fantosme, Jordan. Chronique de la Guerre entre les Anglais et les Écossais [1173-4], ed. R. Howlett. *Chronicles of Stephen*, etc., vol. iii. An eye-witness, and the best authority.

Gaimar, Geoffrey, L'estorie des Engles [495-1100], ed. T. D. Hardy and C. Martin. *Rolls Series.* 2 vols. 1888-9. A compilation of Stephen's reign. Occasionally useful.

Gesta Herwardi, ed. T. D. Hardy and C. Martin in Gaimar, vol. i., *u.s.* A twelfth century Latin romance, containing some curious traditions and fictions.

Gesta Stephani [1135-47], ed. R. C. Sewell. *English Historical Society.* London, 1846. Also Ed. Howlett. *Chronicles of Stephen*, etc., vol. ii. A valuable contemporary narrative, by a clerk of Henry of Blois.

Giraldus Cambrensis. Opera, ed. J. S. Brewer, J. F. Dimock, G. F. Warner. *Rolls Series.* 1861-91. Containing *inter alia* the Conquest and Topography of Ireland, the Itinerarium Cambrense, and the Description of Wales. Giraldus, who died about 1220, is a vivid but prejudiced and inaccurate writer

Guillaume le Maréchal [+ 1219], Histoire de, ed. Paul Meyer. *Societé de l'Histoir de France.* 3 vols. 1891, etc. Useful after 1199.

Hemingburgh, Walter of. Chronicon [1048-1346], ed. H. C. Hamilton. *English Historical Society.* 2 vols. London, 1848-9. Valuable for Simon de Montfort though this part was not written before 1297.

Hexham, John of. Historia [1130-54], ed. T. Arnold in Simeon of Durham, vol. ii. *Rolls Series.* 1885 Not strictly contemporary, but useful for Northern history.

Hexham, Richard of. Historia de Gestis Regis Stephani [1135-9], ed. R. Howlett, *Chronicles of Stephen*, etc., vol. iii. *Rolls Series.* 1886. Contemporary and valuable for Northern history.

Histoire des ducs de Normandie et des rois d'Angleterre [-1220], ed. F. Michel. *Societé de l'Histoire de France.* Paris, 1840. Valuable for the war between the barons and John.

Hoveden, Roger of. Chronica [-1201], ed. W. Stubbs. *Rolls Series.* 4 vols. 1868-71. Valueless before 1169 ; thence to 1192 based on Benedictus Abbas, *q.v.* ; after 1192 a primary authority.

Huntingdon, Henry of. Historia Anglorum (-1154), ed. T. Arnold. *Rolls Series.* 1879. Useful after 1100.

Ibn al Athir in *Rec. des Hist. des Croisades, Hist. Orientaux,* vol. ii. A history of the Mohammedan world [-1231]. Written about 1259.

Ingulf. Historia Croylandensis, ed. W. Fulman, *Scriptores.* Oxford, 1684. A famous forgery of the fourteenth century. Some curious Croyland legends.

Itinerarium Peregrinorum et Gesta Regis Ricardi [1187-9], ed. W. Stubbs. *Rolls Series.* 1864. Mainly a translation of Ambroise, *q.v.*

Joceline de Brakelond. Chronica [1173-1203], ed. J. G. Rokewode. *Camden Society.* 1840. An Edmundsbury chronicle. Valuable for social history.

Joinville. Vie de Saint Louis, ed. L. Delisle. Paris.

Jumièges, William of. Historiae Normannorum Libri Octo [851-1137], ed. Duchesne. *Hist. Norm. Scriptores.* Paris, 1619. Valuable. Book VIII. is by a Continuator who commences at 1087.

Liber Eliensis, ed. D. J. Stewart. London, 1848.

Magna Vita S. Hugonis Ep. Lincolniensis, ed. J. F. Dimock. *Rolls Series.* 1864.

Malmesbury, William of. De Gestis Regum [449-1127], Historia Novella [1125-42], ed. T. D. Hardy. *English Historical Society.* 1840. Also ed. W. Stubbs. *Rolls Series.* 2 vols. 1887-9. Valuable for last three Norman reigns; but the work of a time-server.

Malmesbury, William of. De Gestis Pontificum, ed. N. E. S. Hamilton. *Rolls Series.* 1870. Of some biographical value.

Malmesbury, William of. Vita Wulstani, ed. H. Wharton. *Anglia Sacra,* vol. ii.

Materials for the History of Thomas Becket, ed. J. C. Robertson. *Rolls Series.* 7 vols. 1875-85. Vols. i.-iv. contain the biographies of William the Monk, Benedict of Peterborough, John of Salisbury, Alan of Tewkesbury, Edward Grim, William FitzStephen, Herbert of Bosham, etc.

Monmouth, Geoffrey of, [+ 1154]. Historia Britonum, ed. J. A. Giles. London, 1844. First writer to popularise the Arthur legend.

Newburgh, William of. Historia Rerum Anglicarum, ed. H. C. Hamilton. *English Historical Society.* 2 vols. 1856. Also ed. R. Howlett in *Chronicles of Stephen,* etc., vols. i. and ii. *Rolls Series.* 1884-5. Valuable from 1154 to 1198, as an acute critic of events and persons.

Norwich, St. William of, Life and Miracles of, ed. A. Jessopp and M. R. James. Cambridge, 1896. Useful for the history of Jewish persecutions.

Oxenede, John of, ed. H. Ellis. *Rolls Series.* 1859. Annals from St. Benet Holme; written 1290-1300. Interesting for the years 1264-5.

Paris, Matthew. Chronica Majora [-1259], ed. H. R. Luard. *Rolls Series.* 7 vols. 1872-83. Copies Wendover to 1235. Thenceforward our chief authority, though often prejudiced and imaginative. Anti-papal and anti-royalist.

Paris, Matthew. Historia Anglorum, ed. F. Madden. *Rolls Series.* 3 vols. 1866-9. Mainly an abridgment from the larger work.

Paris, Matthew. Vita Sancti Stephani Cantuariensis, ed. Liebermann. *Ungedruckte Anglo-Norm. Geschichtsquellen,* pp. 323 ff. Strassburg, 1879.

Poitiers, William of. Gesta Willelmi [1035-67], ed. A. Duchesne. *Hist. Norm. Scriptores.* Paris, 1619. The work of a royal chaplain. Violently anti-English.

Radulfus Niger. Chronicon succinctum [-1206]; Chronicon ab initio Mundi ad a. 1199, ed. R. Anstruther. London, 1851. A violent critic of Henry II.

Rievaux, Ailred de. Relatio de Standardo, ed. R. Howlett. *Chronicles of Stephen,* etc., vol. iii. Describes the Battle of the Standard.

Rigord, Gesta Philippi Augusti [1179-1208], ed. H. F. Delaborde. *Societé dé l'Histoire de France.* Paris, 1882.

Rishanger, William. Chronica [1259-1306], ed. H. T. Riley. *Rolls Series.* 1865. Useful for the Barons' War.

Rishanger, William. Chronicon de Duobus Bellis [1263-7], ed. J. O. Halliwell. *Camden Society.* 1840. Also ed. H. T. Riley in Walsingham's Ypodigma Neustriae. *Rolls Series.* 1866. Doubtful whether really by the same author as the Chronica.

Suger. Historia Ludovici VII., ed. A. Molinier. Paris, 1887.
Taxster or Tayster, John de. Chronica Abbreviata [-1265], ed. B. Thorpe in Florence of Worcester. *English Historical Society*. 1849. Contemporary and useful for years 1258-65.
Torigni, or Monte, Robert de. Chronica [-1186], ed. R. Howlett in *Chronicles of Stephen*, etc., vol. iv. *Rolls Series*. 1889. Valuable for years 1153-70; but misleading on English affairs.
Vitalis, Orderic. Historia Ecclesiastica [-1141], ed. A. le Prévost. *Societé de l'Histoire de France*. 5 vols. Paris, 1838-55. Valuable, especially for twelfth century; but confused in arrangement and highly discursive.
Wace. Le Roman de Rou [-1106], ed. H. Andresen. 2 vols. Heilbronn, 1877-9. Written after 1150; drawn chiefly from extant sources, and has been over-rated.
Wendover, Roger of. Flores Historiarum [-1235], ed. H. O. Coxe. *English Historical Society*. 4 vols. 1841-4. Original after 1188, and from 1200 the best of the general chronicles, but often inaccurate in details.
Worcester, Florence of. Chronicon ex Chronicis [-1117]; Continuator i. [-1141]; Continuator ii. (Taxster). [-1265], ed. B. Thorpe. *English Historical Society*. 2 vols. 1848-9. Based on Marianus Scotus and the English Chronicle. The first two continuations are valuable. The first well edited by J. H. Weaver as *John of Worcester* (Oxford, 1908). See also Taxster.
Wykes, Chronicon [1066-1289], ed. H. R. Luard. *Annales Monastici*, vol. iv. *Rolls Series*. 1869. Valuable from 1262; a royalist source.

APPENDIX

Butler, H. E. ed. and trans. The Autobiography of Giraldus Cambrensis, with an introduction by C. H. Williams. London, 1937.
Chronicle of Melrose. A complete facsimile in collotype of the Cottonian MS. Faustina, B. IX, with an introduction by A. O. and M. O. Anderson, and an index by W. C. Dickinson. London, 1936. Since the Bannatyne Club edition of the Chronicle by J. Stevenson is not a reliable one this facsimile is very valuable, particularly as it is well indexed.
Damascus Chronicle of the Crusades, the, extracted and translated from the Chronicle of Ibn al-Qalānisī by H. A. R. Gibb. London, 1932.
Gesta Francorum, the anonymous, ed. B. A. Lees. Oxford, 1924.
Jumièges, William of, Gesta Normannorum Ducum, ed. J. Marx. Rouen, 1914.
Monmouth, Geoffrey of. Historia Regum Brittaniae, ed. A. Griscom. London, 1929.
Salisbury, John of. Historia Pontificalis, ed. R. L. Poole. Oxford, 1927.

(3) TREATISES, CORRESPONDENCE, ETC,

Anselmi Opera, ed. Migne. *P.L.*, vols. clviii., clix. Paris, 1853-4. Contain a valuable collection of letters.
Bacon, Roger. Opera quaedam Inedita, ed. J. S. Brewer. *Rolls Series*. 1859.
Bacon, Roger. Opus Majus, ed. J. Bridges. 2 vols. Oxford, 1897. Text faulty, but now partially corrected in a supplementary volume.
Bernardi Sancti Opera, ed. Mabillon. Paris, 1690.
Blois, Peter of. Opera Omnia, ed. Migne. *P. L.*, vol. ccvii. Contains a collection of letters, useful for reign of Henry II.
Bracton, Henry de (+ 1268). De Legibus Angliae, ed. Travers Twiss. *Rolls Series* 6 vols. 1878-83. The greatest law-book of the period.
Bracton, Henry de. Notebook, ed. F. W. Maitland. 3 vols. London, 1887. Excerpts from the plea-rolls. A valuable introduction.
Bracton and Azo, ed. F. W. Maitland. *Selden Society*. London, 1895. Excerpts to show the relation of Bracton's work to Azo's. Illustrates the influence of Roman upon English law.
[Dialogus.] De Necessariis Observantiis Scaccarii Dialogus. By Richard, son of Nigel. Ed. A. Hughes, C. G. Crump, C. Johnson. Oxford, 1902.

Epistolae Cantuarienses [1187-99], ed. W. Stubbs. *Chronicles and Memorials of Richard I.*, vol. ii. *Rolls Series.* 1865.
Foliot, Gilbert. Epistolae, ed. Migne. *P. L.*, vol. cxc. Paris, 1854. Useful for reign of Stephen and the Becket controversy.
[Glanvill.] Tractatus de Legibus, ed. 1604. Probably the work of Hubert Walter. Valuable though less authoritative than Bracton.
Grosseteste, Robert. Epistolae, ed. H. R. Luard. *Rolls Series.* 1861. Valuable for the reign of Henry III.; mainly ecclesiastical.
Henley, Walter of. Husbandry, ed. Miss E. Lamond, with introduction by W. Cunningham. *Royal Historical Society.* London, 1890. Useful for manorial economy in thirteenth century. Contains also *Les Reules Seynt Robert.*
Ivo of Chartres. Epistolae, ed. 1610. Useful for investitures controversy.
Lanfranc. Opera Omnia, ed. J. A. Giles. 2 vols. Oxford, 1844. Contain the life by Milo Crispin, and correspondence.
Libelli de Lite Imperatorum, etc., vol. iii. *Mon. Hist. Germ.*, 4° series. Tracts of the reign of Henry I. criticising Papal claims; probably by Gerard of York.
Losinga, Herbert de. Epistolae, ed. R. Anstruther. Brussels, 1846.
Losinga, Herbert de, Life, Letters and Sermons of. Translated (with notes) by E. M. Goulburn and Henry Symonds. London, 1878. Valuable for the history of scholarship.
Map, Walter. De Nugis Curialium, ed. T. Wright. *Camden Society.* 1850. Valuable for social history and personal anecdotes (twelfth century).
Map, Walter, the Latin Poems commonly attributed to, ed. T. Wright. *Camden Society.* 1841. Illustrates the growth of feeling against the Papacy and the regular orders.
Nigellus Precentor (Nigel Wireker). Speculum Stultorum, ed. T. Wright in Anglo-Latin Satirical Poets. Vol. i. *Rolls Series.* 1872.
Ottoboni, Letters of [1258-65], ed. Miss R. Graham. *E.H.R.*, xv., pp. 87-120.
Salisbury, John of. Opera Omnia, ed. J. A. Giles. 5 vols. Oxford, 1848. The Letters illustrate the origin of the Becket controversy. The Polycraticus and Metalogicus are valuable for the history of thought and manners. The Polycraticus has been critically edited by C. C. I. Webb. 2 vols. (Oxford, 1909.)
Shirley, W. W. Royal and other Historical Letters [1216-71]. *Rolls Series.* 2 vols. 1862-6. Valuable, especially for Gascon affairs.
Vacarii, Magistri. Summa de Matrimonio, ed. F. W. Maitland. 1898.

APPENDIX

Arnulf of Lisieux. Letters. ed. Barlow, F. *Royal Historical Society. Camden Third Series.* London, 1939.
Bracton, De Legibus et Consuetudinibus Angliae, ed. G. E. Woodbine. 4 vols. New Haven, etc. 1922-42.
Bracton and Azo. Select passages from the works of, ed. F. W. Maitland. *Selden Society*, 1895.
Edwards, J. G. Calendar of Ancient Correspondence concerning Wales. Cardiff, 1935.
Glanvill, De Legibus et Consuetudenibus Regni Angliae, ed. G. E. Woodbine. New Haven, etc. 1932.
Littere Wallie. Ed. Edwards, J. G. Cardiff, 1940.
Map, Walter. De Nugis Curialium, ed. M. R. James. Oxford, 1914. The best edition. First and badly edited by T. Wright. *Camden Society.* 1850.
Salisbury, John of. Metalogicon, ed. C. C. I. Webb. Oxford, 1929.

(b) GENERAL WORKS OF REFERENCE

(1) POLITICAL, CONSTITUTIONAL, AND LEGAL

Adams, G. B. Origin of the English Constitution. London, 1912.
Archer, T. A. Crusade of Richard I. London, 1888. Extracts from sources (translated) with useful appendices.

Blaauw, W. The Barons' War. 2nd ed. Cambridge, 1871.
Böhmer. Kirch und Staat in England und in der Normandie [1066-1154]. Leipzig, 1899.
Borderie, A. de la. Histoire de Bretagne. 3 vols. Rennes, 1896-1900.
Brunner. Die Enstehung des Schwurgerichte. Berlin, 1871.
Cartellieri, A. Philipp II. August. Leipsic, 1899, etc. In progress. Usefulf for diplomatic history.
Dictionary of National Biography, ed. Leslie Stephen and Sidney Lee. 63 vols. London, 1885-1900. Usually gives full references to authorities and good bibliographies.
Digby, K. S. An introduction to the History of the Law of Real Property. Oxford, 1897. Contains a useful selection of passages from Glanvill and Bracton.
Dowell, S. A History of Taxation in England. 4 vols. London, 1888.
Freeman, E. A. History of the Norman Conquest. 6 vols. Oxford, 1867-9.
Freeman, E. A. The reign of William Rufus. 2 vols. Oxford, 1882.
Gneist, Rudolph. Englische Verfassungsgeschichte. Translated by P. A. Ashworth. 2 vols. London, 1886.
Green, J. R. History of the English People. 4 vols. London, 1895-6.
Gross, Charles. The Gild Merchant. 2 vols. Oxford, 1890. Valuable for early municipal history.
Hall, Hubert. Antiquities and Curiosities of the Exchequer. London, 1891.
Hall, Hubert. History of the Custons-revenue of England. 2 vols. 1885.
Histoire de France, ed. E. Lavisse. Tome ii., Part 2. *Les Premiers Capétiens* (987-1137). Par Achille Luchaire. Tome iii, Part 1. *Louis VII., Philippe Auguste, Louis VIII.* Par Achille Luchaire. Tome iii., Part 2. *Les derniers Capétiens directs* (1226-1327). Par C. V. Langlois. Paris, 1901-2.
Histoire Genérale de Languedoc, ed. Vic et Vaisset. Toulouse, 1872-89. 14 vols.
Hook, W. F. Lives of the Archbishops of Canterbury. 12 vols. London, 1860-76.
Hume Brown, P. History of Scotland. Vol. i. Cambridge, 1899.
Hurter, Friedrich. Geschichte Papst Innocenz III. 4 vols. Hamburg, 1834-42. Valuable for the relations of the Papacy with the English Crown.
Lang, A. A History of Scotland. Vol. i. Edinburgh, 1900.
Lappenberg, J. M. Geschichte von England. 2 vols. Hamburg, 1834-37. (Translated by B. Thorpe. 2 vols. London, 1845.)
Liebermann. Ueber Pseudo-Cnut's Constitutiones de Foresta. Halle, 1894. A valuable introduction on the history of the forest laws, etc.
Liebermann, F. Ueber Ostenglische Geschichtsquellen, etc. Hanover, 1892.
Lloyd, J. E. A History of Wales from the Earliest times to the Edwardian Conquest. 2 vols. 3rd ed. London, 1939.
McKechnie, W. S. Magna Carta, a Commentary. 2nd ed. Glasgow, 1914.
Maddox, T. Firma Burgi. London, 1726.
Madox, T. History of the Exchequer. London, 1711. Valuable for the many citations from unpublished Exchequer records.
Maitland, F. W. Domesday Book and Beyond. Cambridge, 1897.
Maitland, F. W. Roman Canon Law in the Church of England. London, 1898. Valuable for Papal relations, Constitutions of Clarendon, etc.
Maitland, F. W. Township and Borough. Cambridge, 1898. Discusses the legal status of early boroughs.
Makower. Constitutional History of the Church of England. London, 1895 (English translation). Chiefly concerned with church law.
Manwood, J. A Treatise and Discourse of the Laws of the Forest. London, 1598.
Morris, W. A. The Frankpledge System. New York, etc., 1910.
Norgate, Kate. England under the Angevin Kings [1100-1206]. 2 vols. London, 1887. Special attention is paid to continental policy.
Norgate, K. The Minority of Henry III. London, 1912.
Orpen, G. H. Ireland under the Normans. 2 vols. Oxford, 1911.
Palgrave, Francis. History of Normandy and England [-1101]. 4 vols. London, 1851-64. Learned and suggestive, but often fanciful and uncritical.

552 BIBLIOGRAPHY

Pauli. Geschichte von England. Vol. i. [1154-1272]. Hamburg, 1853. Still the best narrative history of the reign of Henry III.
Pearson, C. H. England during the Early and Middle ages. Vol. ii. London, 1867. The best English political history of the reign of Henry III.
Pike, L. O. A History of Crime in England. 2 vols. London, 1873-6.
Pike, L. O. A Constitutional History of the House of Lords. London, 1894.
Pirenne, Henri. Histoire de Belgique. Vol. i. Bruxelles, 1900.
Pollock, F., and Maitland, F. W. The History of English Law (-1272). 2 vols. Cambridge, 1895. 2nd edition, 1898. As a study of Legal doctrines supersedes all earlier works.
Pollock, F. The Land-laws. London, 1896. A useful sketch.
Poole, R. L. The Exchequer in the Twelfth Century. Oxford, 1912.
Powicke, F. M. The Loss of Normandy. Manchester, 1913.
Ramsay, Sir J. H. The Foundations of England [-1154]. 2 vols. London, 1898. A useful chronological narrative with full references.
Ramsay, Sir J. H. The Angevin Empire [1154-1216]. London, 1903. Useful for purposes of reference.
Rhys, J., and Jones, D. B. The Welsh People. London, 1900. Essays by various hands ; interesting, though often uncritical.
Richey, A. G. A Short History of the Irish People. Dublin, 1887.
Röhricht, R. Geschichte des Königsreichs Jerusalem, 1898. Valuable for the third Crusade.
Round, J. H. Feudal England [1066-98]. London, 1895. Invaluable for the study of Domesday, history of knight service, etc.
Round, J. H. Geoffrey de Mandeville. London, 1892. The most important monograph on the reign of Stephen.
Round, J. H. The Commune of London. Westminster, 1899. Essays chiefly on the Angevin period. Maintains the Norman origin of the Commune of London. Valuable.
Stephens, W. R. W. The English Church from the Norman Conquest to the Accession of Edward I. London, 1901.
Stephens, J. F. A. History of the Criminal Law of England. 3 vols. London, 1883.
Stubbs, William. Lectures on Early English History. London, 1906.
Stubbs, William. Lectures on Medieval and Modern History. Oxford, 1886.
Stubbs, William. Select Charters. Ninth edition, revised by H. W. C. Davis. Oxford, 1913.
Stubbs, William. The Constitutional History of England [-1485]. 3 vols. Oxford, 1895-7. The best work on the subject, though his conclusions on the Norman period have been to some extent modified by later research. A French translation of the first two volumes, with valuable notes and appendixes by Charles Petit-Dutaillis, has now been published (Paris, 1907-13).
Stubbs, William. The Early Plantagenets [1135-1327]. London, 1876.
Varenbergh, E. Histoire des relations diplomatiques entre le comté de Flandre et l'Angleterre au moyen âge. Brussels, 1874.
Victoria History of the Counties of England. In progress. The Domesday articles by J. H. Round are valuable.
Vinogradoff, P. Villeinage in England. Oxford, 1892. A comparison of the law with the working usage of the villein system.
Vinogradoff, P. English Society in the Eleventh Century. Oxford, 1908.
Wissowa, Felix. Politische Beziehungen zwichen England und Deutschland bis zum untergang der Staufer. Breslau, 1889.

APPENDIX

Adams, G. B. Council and Courts in Anglo-Norman England. New Haven, 1926.
Baldwin, J. F. The King's Council. Oxford, 1913.
Barraclough, G. Papal Provisions. Oxford, 1935.
Bolland, W. C. The General Eyre. Cambridge, 1922.

Boussard, J., Le comté d'Anjou sous Henri Plantegenêt et ses fils. Paris, 1938.
Brooke, Z. N. The English Church and the Papacy from the Conquest to the Reign of John. Cambridge, 1935. Valuable both for the relations of Church and State and for an approach to the study of Canon Law in England.
Cam, H. Liberties and Communities in Medieval England. Cambridge, 1944.
Cam, H. M. Studies in the Hundred Rolls. *Oxford Studies.* Vol. vi. Oxford, 1921.
Cam, H. M. The Hundred and the Hundred Rolls. London, 1930.
Cambridge Mediæval History, the. Vols. v. and vi. 8 vols. Cambridge, 1924-36.
Chartrou, J. L'Anjou de 1109 à 1151. Paris, 1928.
Cheney, C. R. Episcopal Visitation of the Monasteries in the Thirteenth Century. Manchester, 1931.
Cheney, C. R. English Synodalia of the Thirteenth Century. Oxford, 1941.
Churchill, I. Canterbury Administration. 2 vols. London, 1933. An authoritative work on English archiepiscopal administration.
Chew, H. M. The English Ecclesiastical Tenants-in-Chief and Knight Service. Oxford, 1932.
Clarke, M. V. Medieval Representation and Consent. London, 1936.
Cockayne, G. E. Complete Peerage. 8 vols. Exeter, 1887-98. A new and enlarged edition (ed. V. Gibbs) is in progress. London,1910, etc.
Coulton, G. G. Five Centuries of Religion. Cambridge.
Curtis, E. History of Mediæval Ireland. London, 1938.
Curtis, E. History of Ireland. London, 1936.
Darby, H. C., ed. An Historical Geography of England Before 1800. Cambridge, 1936.
Deansley, M. History of the Mediæval Church, 500-1500 London, 1925.
Denholm-Young, N. Seignorial Administration in England. Oxford, 1937.
Dueball, M. Die Suprematstreit zwichen den Erzdiözesen Canterbury und York, 1070-1126. Jena, 1929.
Ehrlich, L. Proceedings against the Crown, 1216-1377. *Oxford Studies.* Vol. vi. Oxford, 1921.
Farrer, W. Outline Itinerary of Henry I. Oxford, 1920.
Farrer, W. Honours and Knights' Fees. 3 vols. London and Manchester, 1923-5. Identifies the component parts and traces the descent of the tenants from the eleventh to the fourteenth century of the following Honours. Vol. i., Bidun, Choques, Visdelou, Wahull, Curcy, Peverel of Nottingham. Vol. ii. Chester, Huntingdon. Vol. iii., Arundel, Eudes the Sewer, Warenne.
Flower, C. T. Introduction to the Curia Regis Rolls. *Selden Society.* London, 1944.
Foreville, R. L'Église et la Royauté en Angleterre sous Henri II. Plantagenet. Bloud & Gay, 1943.
Génestal, R. Histoire du droit public normand. Caen, 1928.
Génestal, R. Le privilegium fori en France. 2 vols. Paris, 1921, 1924.
Gibbs, M. and Lang, J. Bishops and Reform, 1215-72. Oxford, 1934.
Goebel, J. Felony and Misdemeanour. Vol. i. New York, 1937.
Haskins, C.H. Norman Institutions. *Harvard Hist. Studies.* Cambridge, Mass., 1918. The Authoritative work on this subject.
Holdsworth, W. S. History of English Law. Vols. i-iii., 3rd ed. London, 1922-3.
Hutton, E. The Franciscans in England, 1224-1538. London, 1926.
Jacob, E. F. Studies in the Period of Baronial Reform and Rebellion. *Oxford Studies.* Oxford, 1925.
Jarrett, Dom B. The English Dominicans. London, 1921.
Jolliffe, J. E. A. The Constitutional History of Medieval England. London, 1937.
Kimball, E. G. Serjeanty Tenure in Medieval England. New Haven, 1936.
Knowles, D. The Monastic Order in England. Cambridge, 1940.
Knowles, D. The Religious Houses of Medieval England. London, 1940.
Knowles, D. M. The Religious Orders in England. Cambridge, 1948.
Landon, L. The Itinerary of Richard I. *Pipe Roll Society.* London, 1935.

Lemarignier, J. F. Étude sur les privilèges d'exemption et de juridiction ecclés-
iastique des abbayes normandes. Paris, 1937.
Le Patourel, J. H. The Medieval Administration of the Channel Islands. Oxford,
1937.
Little, A. G. Studies in English Franciscan History. London, 1917.
Lunt, W. E. Papal Revenues in the Middle Ages. 2 vols. New York, 1934.
Lunt, W. E. Financial Relations of the Papacy with England. Cambridge, Mass.,
1939.
Lyte, Sir H. Maxwell. Historical Notes on the Great Seal. Stationery Office, 1926.
The definitive work on the operations of the English Chancery.
Malden, H. E., ed. Magna Carta Commemoration Essays. London, 1917.
Mayer, Ernest. Geschworenengericht und Inquisitionsprozess. Munich, 1916.
Mitchell, S. K. Studies in Taxation under John and Henry III. New Haven, 1914.
Moorman, J. R. H. Church Life in England in the Thirteenth Century. Cam-
bridge, 1945.
Morris, W. A. The Early English County Court. Berkeley, Cal., 1926.
Morris, W. A. The Mediæval English Sheriff. Manchester, etc., 1927.
Murray, K. M. E. The Constitutional History of the Cinque Ports. Manchester,
1935.
Painter, S. Studies in the History of the English Feudal Barony. Baltimore, 1943.
Petit Dutaillis, Ch. Le déshèritement de Jean sans terre. Paris, 1925.
Petit Dutaillis, Ch. La Monarchie Féodale en France et en Angleterre, Xe-XIIIe
siècle. Paris, 1933.
Petit Dutaillis, Ch. and Lefebvre, G. Studies and Notes Supplementary to Stubbs
Constitutional History. Translated by W. E. Rhodes and T. Waugh. 3 vols.
Manchester, 1923-9.
Poole, A. L. Obligations of Society in the Twelfth and Thirteenth Centuries.
Oxford, 1946.
Powicke, F. M. Handbook of British Chronology. *Royal Historical Society*.
London, 1939.
" Revisions," Historical. Brief articles presenting the up-to-date view on historical
questions in which, owing to research work and changing opinions, confusion
might arise, are printed regularly in *History* (the journal of the Historical
Association).
Roth, C. A History of the Jews in England. Oxford, 1941.
Sayles, G. O. The Medieval Foundations of England. London, 1948.
Stenton, F. M. The First Century of English Feudalism, 1066-1166. Oxford,
1932. A most important contribution to the study of English feudalism.
Stenton, F. M. Anglo-Saxon England. Oxford, 1943.
Stephenson, C. Medieval Feudalism. New York, 1942.
Stewart-Brown, R. The serjeants of the Peace in Medieval England and Wales.
Manchester, 1936.
Tout, T. F. Chapters in the Administrative History of England. 6 vols. Man-
chester, 1920-33. Invaluable for the history of the Royal Household, the
Chancery and the Exchequer, 1066-1399.
Treharne, R. F. The Baronial Plan of Reform. Vol. i. Manchester, 1932. A
detailed study of the years 1158-64.
Turner, G. J. The Minority of Henry III. *Transactions of the Royal Historical
Society*. New series, vol. xviii. and 3rd series, vol. i. London, 1904-7.
Weske, D. B. Convocation of the Clergy. London, 1937.
Zimmermann, H. Die papstliche Legation in der ersten Hälfte des 13 Jahrhunderts.
Paderborn, 1913.

(2) ECONOMIC

Ashley, W. J. An Introduction to English Economic History and Theory. 2 vols.
London, 1888-93.
Beazley. The Dawn of Modern Geography. London, 1901.
Birch, W. de Gray. Domesday Book. London, 1887.

BIBLIOGRAPHY 555

Cunningham, W. Alien Immigrants to England. London, 1897.
Cunningham, W. The Growth of English Industry and Commerce. Vol. i. Cambridge, 1896.
Goldschmidt, S. Geschichte der Juden in England. Vol. i. Berlin, 1886. Unfinished. Covers eleventh and twelfth centuries.
Jacobs, Joseph. The Jews of Angevin England [-1206]. London, 1893. A large collection of translated excerpts with valuable appendices.
Seebohm, F. The English Village Community. London, 1890.
Tovey, D'Blossiers. Anglia Judaica. Oxford, 1873.
Vinogradoff, P. The Growth of the Manor. London, 1905. A synthetic account. Valuable.

APPENDIX

Ballard, A. The English Borough in the Twelfth Century. Cambridge, 1915.
Boissonade, P. Life and Labour in Mediæval Europe. Trans. by Eileen Power. London, 1927.
Cambridge Economic History. Vol. i. Cambridge, 1941.
Darby, H. C. The Medieval Fenland. Cambridge, 1940.
Douglas, D. C. The Social Structure of Mediæval East Anglia. *Oxford Studies.* Vol. ix. Oxford, 1927.
Gras, N. S. B. The Early English Customs System. *Harvard Econ. Series.* Cambridge, Mass., 1918. The authoritative work.
Homans, G. C. English Villagers of the Thirteenth Century. Cambridge, Mass., 1942.
Jolliffe, J. E. A. Pre-Feudal England : the Jutes. Oxford, 1933. Works back from thirteenth century manorial records.
Lipson, E. Economic History of England. Vol. i., 7th ed. London, 1937.
Lobel, D. M. The Borough of Bury St. Edmunds. Oxford, 1935.
Page, F. M. The Estates of Crowland Abbey. Cambridge, 1934.
Page, W. London : its origin and early development. London, 1923.
Pirenne, H. Economic and Social History of Mediæval Europe. Trans. by I. E. Clegg. London, 1936.
Salzman, L. F. English Industry in the Middle Ages. New ed. Oxford, 1923.
Salzman, L. F. English Trade in the Middle Ages. Oxford, 1931.
Smith, R. A. L. Canterbury Cathedral Priory. Cambridge, 1943.
Stenton, F. M. Manorial Structure of the Northern Danelaw. *Oxford Studies.* Vol. ii. Oxford, 1910.
Stephenson, C. Borough and Town. Cambridge, Mass, 1933.
Tait, J. The Medieval English Borough. Manchester, 1936.
Trenholme, N. M. English Monastic Boroughs. Univ. of Missouri Studies, ii. No. 3. 1927.

(3) SOCIAL, LITERARY, ART, MANNERS

Bloxham, M. H. The Principles of Gothic Ecclesiastical Architecture. 2 vols. London, 1882.
Chambers, E. K. The Mediæval Stage. 2 vols. Oxford, 1903.
Clark, A. The Colleges of Oxford. London, 1891.
Fergusson, James. A History of Architecture in all Countries. Vol. ii. London, 1893.
Gierke, O. Political Theories of the Middle Ages. Translated with an introduction by F. W. Maitland. Cambridge, 1900.
Jourdain, A. and C. Récherches Critiques sur l'age et l'origine des traductions latines d'Aristote. Paris, 1843.
Jusserand, J. J. Histoire Littéraire du Peuple anglais des Origines à la Renaissance. Paris, 1894.
Mullinger, J. B. History of the University of Cambridge, 1873.
Planché, J. R. Cyclopædia of Costumes. 2 vols. London, 1876-9.

Poole, R. L.   Illustrations of the History of Medieval Thought.   London, 1884.
Rashdall, Hastings.   The Universities of the Middle Ages.   2 vols. in 3.   Oxford, 1895.   The introductory chapters are particularly valuable.
Ruprich, Robert V.   L'Architecture normande en Normandie et en Angleterre. 2 vols.   Paris, 1884-9.
Social England, ed. H. D. Traill and J. S. Mann.   Illustrated edition.   Vol. i. London, 1901.
Strutt, Joseph.   Sports and Pastimes of the People of England, ed. W. Hone. London, 1830.
Strutt, Joseph.   A Complete View of the Manners, etc., of the Inhabitants of England.   London, 1774-6.
Ten Brink, Bernhard.   Geschichte der Englischen Litteratur.   Vol. i.   Strassburg, 1877.
Turner, T. H.   Some Account of Domestic Architecture in England.   Oxford, 1851.

APPENDIX

Borenius, T. and Tristram, E. W.   English Mediæval Painting.   London, 1928. A well illustrated survey of the whole subject.
Carlyle, R. W. and A. J.   A History of Mediæval Political Theory in the West. 6 vols.   Edinburgh and London, 1903-36.
Clapham, R. W.   English Romanesque Architecture after the Norman Conquest. Oxford, 1934.
Coulton, G. G.   Social Life in Britain.   Cambridge, 1919.
Coulton, G. G.   The Mediæval Village.   Cambridge, 1925.
Coulton, G. G.   Life in the Middle Ages.   Cambridge, 1928.
Davis, H. W. C., ed.   Mediæval England.   Oxford, 1923.
Gardner, A.   Mediæval English Sculpture.   Cambridge, 1935.
Haskins, C. H.   Studies in the History of Mediæval Science.   Cambridge, Mass., 1924.
Haskins, C. H.   The Renaissance of the Twelfth Century.   Cambridge, Mass., 1927.   Deals with the Latin side of the movement.
Haskins, C. H.   Studies in Mediæval Culture.   Oxford, 1929.
Kendon, F. S. H.   Mural Paintings in English Churches during the Middle Ages. London, 1923.
Millar, E. G.   English Illuminated Manuscripts, 10th to 13th Century.   Paris and Brussels, 1926.
Oakeshott, W.   Artists of the Winchester Bible.   London, 1945.
Prestage, E., ed.   Chivalry.   By members of King's College, London.   London, 1928.
Rashdall, H.   The Universities of Europe in the Middle Ages.   A new and revised edition by F. M. Powicke and A. B. Emden.   Oxford, 1936.
Russell, J. C.   Dictionary of Writers of thirteenth-century England.   London, 1936.
Thomson, S. H.   The Writings of Robert Grosseteste.   Cambridge, 1940.
Tristram, E. W.   English Medieval Wall-painting.   Oxford, 1944.
Wagner, A. R.   Historic Heraldry.   Oxford, 1939.

(4) MILITARY HISTORY

Clark, G. T.   Medieval Military Architecture of England.   2 vols.   London, 1884.
Delpech, Henri.   La tactique au treizième siècle.   2 vols.   Paris, 1886.
Grose, Francis.   Military Antiquities.   London, 1801-12.
Oman, C. W. C.   History of the Art of War.   2nd edition.   Vol. i.   London, 1924.

(5) BIOGRAPHICAL

Bémont.   S. de Montfort.   Paris, 1884.
Berger, E.   Blanche de Castile.   Paris, 1895.
Bloch, H.   Forschungen zur Politik Heinrichs VI.   Berlin, 1892.

Church, R. W. St. Anselm. London, 1870.
Dictionary of National Biography, ed. L. Stephen and S. Lee. 63 vols. London, 1885-1900.
Dixon, W. H. Fasti Eboracenses. Vol. i. London, 1863.
Eyton. Itinerary of Henry II. London, 1878.
Freeman, E. A. William the Conqueror. London, 1894.
Froude, J. A. Short Studies on Great Subjects, vols. ii. and iv. London, 1883.
    (Becket, Hugh of Lincoln).
Graham, Miss Rose. St. Gilbert of Sempringham. London, 1901.
Green, Mrs. J. R. Henry II. London, 1888.
Hardy, T. D. Itinerary of King John, in *Rot. Lit. Patentium, q.v.*
Hasse, F. R. Anselm von Canterbury. 2 vols. Leipsic, 1843-52.
Hook, W. F. Lives of the Archbishops of Canterbury. 12 vols. London, 1860-76.
Hurter, F. Geschichte Papst Innocenz III. 4 vols. Hamburg, 1834-42.
Hutton, W. H. Philip Augustus. London, 1896.
Needler, G. H. Richard Cœur de Lion in Literature.
Norgate, Kate. John Lackland. London, 1902.
Pauli. Simon de Montfort. Translated by C. M. Goodwin. London, 1876.
Petit-Dutaillis, Charles. Etude sur la vie et le régne de Louis VIII. [1187-1227].
    Paris, 1894.
Poole, S. L. Saladin. London, etc., 1898.
Prothero, G. W. Simon de Montfort. London, 1877.
Rössler, Oskar. Kaiserin Mathilde. Berlin, 1897.
Round, J. H. Geoffrey de Mandeville. London, 1892.
Rigg, J. M. St. Anselm of Canterbury. London, 1896.
Rule, Martin. Life and Times of St. Anselm. London, 1883.
Stenton, F. M. William the Conqueror. New York and London, 1908.
Stevenson, F. S. Robert Grosseteste. London, 1898.
Thurston, Herbert. Life of St. Hugh of Lincoln. London, 1898.
Tillemont. Saint Louis, ed. de Gaulle. Paris, 1847-51.
Wallon, H. Saint Louis et sons temps. Paris, 1885.

APPENDIX

Bémont, C. Simon de Montfort. Revised ed. translated by E. F. Jacob. Oxford, 1930.
Clayton, J. St. Anselm : A Critical Biography. Milwaukee, 1933.
David, C. W. Robert Curthose, Duke of Normandy. Cambridge, Mass., 1920.
Denholm-Young, N. Richard of Cornwall. Oxford, 1947.
Hutton, W. H. Thomas Becket. Revised ed. Cambridge, 1926.
Jarman, T. L. William Marshal. Oxford, 1930.
MacDonald, A. J. Lanfranc. Oxford, 1926.
Morey, A. Bartholomew of Exeter. Cambridge, 1937.
Newbolt, M. R. Edmund Rich, Archbishop and Saint. London, 1928.
Norgate, K. Richard the Lion Heart. London, 1924.
Painter, S. William Marshal. Baltimore (Johns Hopkins Univ.), 1933.
Powicke, F. M. Stephen Langton. Oxford, 1928. [Prof. Powicke also contributes a note on recent work upon Stephen Langton. *E.R.H.*, 1933.]
Powicke, F. M. King Henry the Third and the Lord Edward. 2 vols. Oxford, 1947.
Salzman, L. F. Henry II. London, 1918.
Voss, Lena. Heinrich von Blois, Bischof von Winchester, 1129-71. Berlin, 1932.
Webb, C. I. John of Salisbury. London, 1932.
    Note.—Lists of important Articles in Historical Journals may be found in the Annual Bulletins of Historical Literature, published by the *Historical Association* and in the Bibliographies of the Cambridge Mediæval History.

I.

THE HOUSE OF NORMANDY

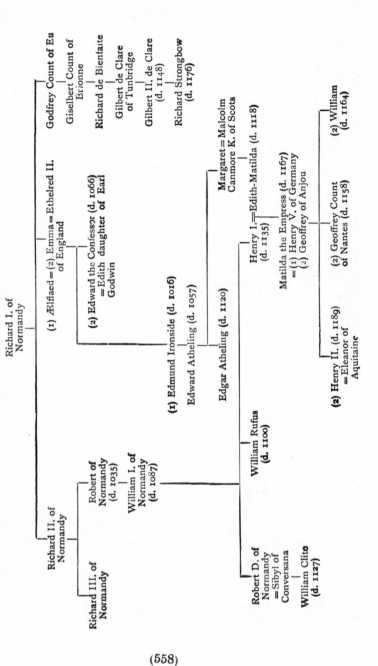

THE HOUSE OF ANJOU

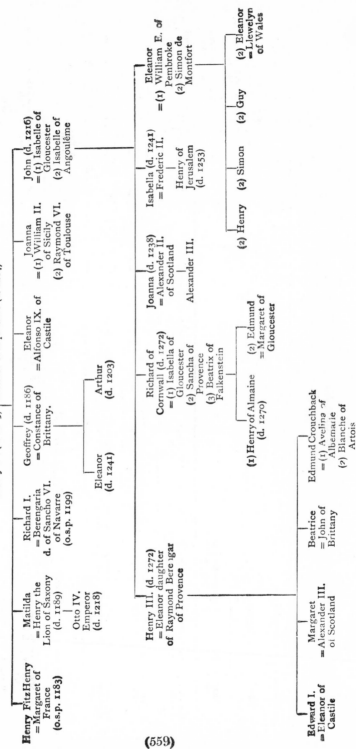

III.

THE OLD ENGLISH DESCENTS

(1) Aelfaed = Aethelred II. = (2) Emma of Normandy
979-1016

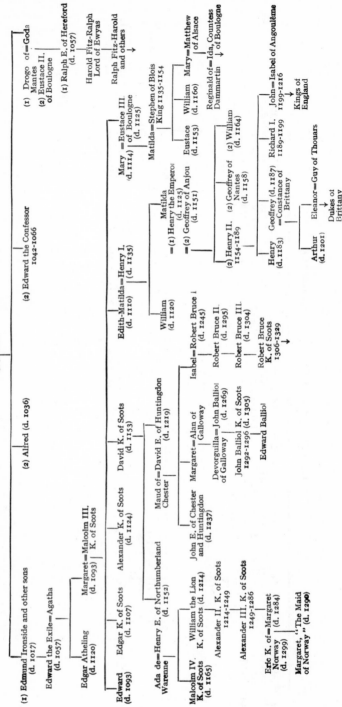

INDEX

to Canterbury, 90 ; repents of his repentance, 92 ; his compact with Anselm, *ibid.* ; his policy during the Papal schism, 93 ; again attacks Normandy (1094), 93 ; first quarrel with Anselm, 94 ; brings Anselm to trial at Rockingham, 96 ; with unsatisfactory results, 97 ; acknowledges Urban, 98 ; attitude towards Rome, 99 ; deals with the conspiracy of Robert Mowbray, 106 ; Welsh campaign (1095), 107 ; punishes rebels, *ibid.* ; receives Normandy in pawn, 108 ; final quarrel with Anselm, 109 ; relations with Edgar of Scotland, 111 ; Welsh expeditions of, 112, 113 ; continental policy of his later years, 115 ; war in Maine, 116 ; receives the Duchy of Aquitaine in pawn, *ibid.* ; death of, 118 ; designs on Ireland, 228.

William II. of Sicily, 296.

William IX., Duke of Aquitaine, Count of Poitou, 72, 115, 116.

William the Lion, King of Scotland, joins the princes in 1173, 250 ; raids England, *ibid.* ; captured at Alnwick, 251 ; becomes the vassal of Henry II., 252 ; is released from vassalage by Richard, 288, 289 ; offers to buy Northumberland, 322 ; demands northern shires from John, 347 ; later relations with John, 359, 366.

William Atheling, son of Henry I., his betrothal, 148 ; interferes with the rights of the See of Bath, 135 ; his marriage, 149 ; his death, 150.

William, eldest son of Henry II., 201 ; death, 202.

William Fitzosbern. See Fitzosbern.

William of Poitiers. See Poitiers, William of.

Winchester, submits to the Conqueror, 7 ; seat of Exchequer, 43, 118, 141, 268 ; trade of, 142 ; Church council at (1139), attacks Stephen, 163 ; Matilda acknowledged at, 170 ; siege of Wolvesey Castle, 172 ; Richard's second coronation takes place at, 322 ; taken by Louis of France, 388 ; anti-Montfortian, 474.

Winchester, Henry of. See Henry of Winchester.

Windsor Castle, holds out for John, 388.

"Wither, William," 416.

Wolvesey Castle, besieged, 172.

Woodstock, Great Council at, 211 ; Welsh chiefs at, 360.

Worcester, Bishop of, supports De Montfort, 463.

Worcester, Wulfstan of. See Wulfstan.

Worcester, city of, burned, 166 ; army of the Lord Edward at, 474.

Worms, Concordat of, 132.

Wulf, son of Harold, 62.

Wulfnoth, son of Godwin, 62, 70.

Wulfstan, Bishop of Worcester, submits to William I., 9 ; supports Norman rule, 14 ; loyalty in 1075, 34 ; not highly educated, 47 ; attacks the slave-trade, *ibid.* ; supports Rufus against Odo of Bayeux, 75 ; his housekeeping, 183.

Würzburg, diet of (1165), 218.

YARMOUTH, feud with Cinque Ports, 401.

Yom-Tob, the Rabbi, 293.

York, Archbishops of. See Thomas of Bayeux, Gerard, Thurstan, Henry Murdac, William FitzHerbert, Geoffrey Plantagenet.

York, submits to William I. (1068), 18 ; Castle of, attacked and relieved, 19 ; taken by the Danes, 20 ; recovered by William I., 21 ; massacre of Jews at, 293.

York, See of, highly privileged, 135.

Yorkshire, complaints of, 364.

Yprès, William of, 158, 168, 170, 171.

PRINTED IN GREAT BRITAIN AT THE UNIVERSITY PRESS, ABERDEEN